Managing Enterprise Projects

Using Microsoft Project Server 2010

Gary L. Chefetz
Dale A. Howard
Treb Gatte
Tony Zink

Managing Enterprise Projects
Using Microsoft Project Server 2010

Copyright © 2011 Chefetz LLC dba MSProjectExperts

Publisher:	Chefetz LLC
Authors:	Gary L. Chefetz, Dale A. Howard, Treb Gatte, Tony Zink
Copy Editor:	Rodney L. Walker
Cover Design:	Emily Baker
Cover Photo:	Peter Hurley

ISBN: 978-1-934240-11-3

LCCN: 2010942261

Published and distributed by Chefetz LLC dba MSProjectExperts, 90 John Street, Suite 404, New York, NY 10038. (646) 736-1688 http://www.msprojectexperts.com

We provide the information contained in this book on an "as is" basis, without warranty. Although we make every effort to ensure the accuracy of information provided herein, neither the authors nor the publisher shall have any liability to any person or entity with respect to any loss or damage caused or allegedly caused directly or indirectly by the information contained in this work.

MSProjectExperts publishes a complete series of role-based training/reference manuals for Microsoft's Enterprise Project Management software including Microsoft Project and Microsoft Project Server. Use our books for self-study or for classroom learning delivered by professional trainers and corporate training programs. To learn more about our books and courseware series for Administrators, Implementers, Project Managers, Portfolio Managers, Resource Managers, Executives, Team Members, and Developers, or to obtain instructor companion products and materials, contact MSProjectExperts by phone (646) 736-1688 or by email info@msprojectexperts.com.

Contents

Contents

Contents

vi

Contents

Contents

Contents

Contents

About the Authors

Gary Chefetz is the founder and President of MSProjectExperts, which exists to support businesses and organizations that choose the Microsoft enterprise project management platform. Gary has worked with Microsoft Project since 1995 and has supported Microsoft Project users since the introduction of Project Central in early 2000. Gary continues to receive the prestigious Microsoft Project Most Valuable Professional (MVP) award for his contributions to the Project community and possesses the Microsoft Certified IT Professional (MCITP) and the Microsoft Certified Trainer (MCT) certifications. As a long-time MVP, he works closely with the Microsoft Project product team and support organizations. Gary is dedicated to supporting Microsoft Project Server implementations through his business efforts with clients and through his contributions in TechNet forums. Contact Gary Chefetz online in one of the Microsoft Project forums on TechNet or e-mail him at:

gary.chefetz@msprojectexperts.com

Dale Howard is an enterprise project management trainer/consultant and is Vice President of Educational Services of MSProjectExperts. Dale possesses the Certified Technical Trainer (CTT) and Microsoft Certified Technology Specialist (MCTS) certification for Microsoft EPM, and has more than 15 years of experience training and consulting in productivity software. He has worked with Microsoft Project since 1997 and volunteers many hours each week answering user questions in the various Microsoft Project communities. Dale continues to receive the prestigious Most Valuable Professional (MVP) yearly award for Microsoft Project since 2004 for his expertise with the software and for his contributions to the user communities. Dale is married to Mickey and lives in Dunedin Florida. Contact Dale online in one of the Microsoft Project forums on TechNet or e-mail him at:

dale.howard@msprojectexperts.com

Treb Gatte is a seasoned business expert with significant experience with the Project Server tool as well as with process and project management. Treb has over 20 years of experience in project management, business process development, and software development management. Treb was the Microsoft Program Manager responsible for Setup, Upgrade and Business Intelligence features for the Microsoft Project Server 2010 release. He also has experience as the former Project Manager for a large national bank's Project Server implementation. Treb holds a BS in Management from Louisiana State University and an MBA from Wake Forest University. Contact Treb at:

treb.gatte@msprojectexperts.com

Download the Sample Files

Instructions to set up your Project Server instance along with the sample files you use to complete the Hands On Exercises can be found by pointing your browser to the following URL:

http://www.msprojectexperts.com/managing2010

Introduction

Thank you for choosing *Managing Enterprise Projects Using Microsoft Project Server 2010*, an unprecedented learning guide and reference for project managers who use the Microsoft EPM platform. Our goal for this book is to provide a combination of training and reference manual; a vital learning tool to help you build on your knowledge of the stand-alone tool by mastering the Microsoft enterprise project management environment. Follow our best practices to success and heed our warnings to avoid the pitfalls.

We take a systematic approach to the topical ordering in this book, beginning with a Project Server 2010 overview in Module 01 and a primer for using the interface in Module 02. Module 03 teaches you how to use Project Server 2010 workflows to create project proposals. In Modules 04-07, you learn to use Project Professional 2010 to define, plan, baseline, and publish an enterprise project and manage deliverables. Modules 08-09 take you through the project updating process from team member progress reporting in Project Web App and in Outlook, through your acceptance of the updates into the enterprise project plan. Module 10 wraps up with analyzing project variance. In Modules 11-14, you learn how to set up personal options, how to use the features in the Project Workspace, and how to create Status Reports. In Module 16, you learn how to use Project Web App to view enterprise project information and in Module 17, you learn how to use the exciting new Business Intelligence features provided by Microsoft SharePoint Enterprise edition, including working with pivot tables in Microsoft Excel to connect to the reporting database and OLAP cubes to create visually stunning reports.

Throughout each module, you get a generous amount of Notes, Warnings, and Best Practices. Notes call your attention to important additional information about a subject. Warnings help you avoid the most common problems experienced by others and Best Practices provide tips for using the tool based on our field experience.

With this book, we believe that you can become more effective at using Microsoft Enterprise Project Management tools. If you have questions about the book or are interested in our professional services, please contact us at our office. If you have questions about Microsoft Project or Project Server, contact us through the Microsoft TechNet forums.

Gary L. Chefetz

Dale A. Howard

Treb Gatte

Module 01

Introducing Microsoft Project Server

Learning Objectives

After completing this module, you will be able to:

- Understand the PMI definition of a project

- Understand Project Server's enterprise project management terminology

- Describe the project communications life cycle used in Project Server

- Be familiar with Project Server team collaboration tools

- Understand how Microsoft SharePoint Server (MSS) provides functionality in Project Server

- Understand the Project Server databases

- Acquire an overview understanding of OLAP and Business Intelligence (BI) tools

- Be familiar with the Enterprise Global file and the Enterprise Resource Pool

- Understand custom enterprise fields and Lookup Tables

- Understand how tracking methods impact progress reporting

Inside Module 01

What Is Microsoft Project Server?

Microsoft Project Server 2010 is an enterprise project management (EPM) automation system. Microsoft designed Project Server to support business and industry-specific project management and tracking requirements. Project Server 2010 is an out-of-the-box project and assignment tracking system, as well as a platform for business-specific configuration and customization. Using Project Server 2010, your organization can manage dozens, hundreds, or thousands of projects, along with dozens, hundreds, or thousands of resources.

Project Server 2010 is Microsoft's fifth-generation, server-based project management solution. The previous generations of Microsoft's EPM tool included Project Central, along with Project Server 2002, 2003, and 2007. The combination of Microsoft Project Professional 2010 and Project Server 2010 provides a powerful enterprise portfolio management system that is rich in features but fraught with complexity and challenges. Our goal is to help you maximize the feature benefits and minimize the frustrations.

Understanding Project Management Theory

According to *A Guide to the Project Management Body of Knowledge* (PMBOK Guide, 4th Edition) from the Project Management Institute (PMI), a project is "a temporary endeavor undertaken to create a unique produce, service, or result." According to this definition, a project is:

- **Temporary** – Every project has a definite beginning and end.

- **Unique** – Every project is something your organization has not done before, or has not done in this manner.

Because Microsoft Project 2010 is a project management tool, you use the software most effectively in the context of the normal project management process. Therefore, it is important to become acquainted with each of the phases of the project management process and with the activities that take place during each phase. According to the Project Management Institute, the project management process consists of five phases including Definition, Planning, Execution, Control, and Closure.

Understanding Enterprise Project Management Terminology

In the world of enterprise project management, you hear the terms program and portfolio. For the purposes of this book, a **program** is "a collection of related projects" and a **portfolio** is "a collection of programs and/or projects within a business unit or across an entire enterprise". Many companies have their own interpretation of these terms, reflecting their approach to project management. Sometimes the sheer size of the organization drives these definitions.

The concept of a portfolio is flexible, depending on the size of the deployment. A smaller organization may have a single portfolio of projects, whereas a larger business may conceive of an enterprise portfolio made up of numerous departmental or line-of-business portfolios, each containing its own set of programs and projects. However your organization conceives programs and portfolios, you can model them in Project Server 2010.

Understanding Project Server Terminology

Two terms that you must understand in the context of the Project Server 2010 environment are **enterprise project** and **enterprise resource**. Very specific criteria determine whether a project is an enterprise or non-enterprise project, and whether a resource is an enterprise or local resource. In addition, you must also understand how to **check in** and **check out** a project. Finally, it is helpful to understand two other terms, **portfolio analysis** and **portfolio analyses**.

Enterprise Project

An **enterprise project** is any project stored in the Project Server database using one of the following methods:

- You create the project using the Project Professional 2010 client while connected to Project Server 2010 and save the project in the Project Server database.

- You import the project to the enterprise using the *Import Project Wizard* in Project Professional 2010.

- You create a proposed project using the demand management process from the *Project Center* page in Project Web App.

The system stores all enterprise projects in the Project Server database. Any project not stored in the Project Server database, such as a project saved as an .MPP file, is termed a **non-enterprise project** or a **local project**.

Enterprise Resource

An **enterprise resource** is any resource stored in the Enterprise Resource Pool in the Project Server database using one of the following methods:

- The Project Server administrator creates the resource in the Enterprise Resource Pool using the Project Professional 2010 client while connected to Project Server 2010.

- The Project Server administrator imports the resource into the Enterprise Resource Pool using the Import Resources Wizard in Project Professional 2010.

- The Project Server administrator creates the resource using Project Web App.

If a resource exists in an enterprise project but does not exist in the Enterprise Resource Pool, then this resource is termed a **non-enterprise resource** or **local resource**. This means that the resource is local to the project only.

Check In and Check Out

The terms **check in** and **check out** apply to enterprise objects such as projects, resources, calendars, fields, lookup tables, and even to the Enterprise Global file. As a project manager, when you open an enterprise project for editing, the system checks out the project to you exclusively. While you have the project open, no other user can edit your project. When you close the enterprise project, the system checks in the project so that other users can edit the project, if they have the permission to do so.

Portfolio Analysis

The term **portfolio analysis** refers to an analysis of a group of projects for the purposes of selecting projects for execution by best matching the strategic objectives of the organization and fitting resource and cost constraints within the parameters set by management consensus. This term differs dramatically from Microsoft's previous definition in Project Server 2007.

Portfolio Analyses

When you encounter the term **portfolio analyses** in Project Server 2010, it refers to the collection of individual analysis studies performed by various users in the system to determine the viability of proposed project investments in the system.

Using Enterprise Resource Management Tools

A centralized **Enterprise Resource Pool** is vital to the advanced resource management functionality in Project Server 2010. The Enterprise Resource Pool contains resources and resource attributes that drive functionality, such as matching people to tasks using skills or based on department or location. The system models these resource attributes using custom enterprise fields that contain a lookup table. These custom fields might describe practice groups, location, department, or other company-specific information that project and resource managers use to intelligently assign resources to task assignments, and that management can use to drive reporting and analysis. After defining custom fields for your organization, your Project Server administrator assigns values for these fields to each resource in the Enterprise Resource Pool.

As a project manager, after you complete the task planning process in Project Professional 2010, you begin the resource planning process by building your project team using resources from the Enterprise Resource Pool. Initial resource planning activities include assembling the project team and making specific task assignments. By using manual staffing tools such as the **Build Team dialog** and the **Assign Resources dialog**, Project Server 2010 allows you to locate resources by both skill and availability, even if you are using a large Enterprise Resource Pool. This simplifies the project staffing process not only by leveraging the custom attributes in the pool, but also by providing instant access to availability data enhanced with graphical representations.

In addition to manual staffing tools, Project Server 2010 offers an automated staffing tool called the **Resource Substitution Wizard**. This wizard rapidly analyzes the resources in the Enterprise Resource Pool to identify skills and availability for staffing a single project or a group of projects. You can save the subsequent staffing results as a recommendation for input into manual team building or directly update the results into the working plan.

Understanding Enterprise Global Concepts

There are two global entities always present in any Project Server 2010 environment: the Enterprise Resource Pool and the Enterprise Global file (sometimes referred to as the Enterprise Global template). The Enterprise Resource Pool contains all information pertaining to enterprise resources. The Enterprise Global file contains all of your company's custom enterprise objects, such as enterprise views, tables, filters, groups, reports, etc. The system dynamically distributes these custom features to all project managers each time they connect to Project Server 2010 through Project Professional 2010. Every time you launch Project Professional 2010 and connect to Project Server, the following events occur:

1. The system opens the Global.mpt file into memory. This file contains all of the default objects that ship with Microsoft Project 2010, including views, tables, filters, groups, etc. This file also contains custom objects you created for your own personal use.

2. The system opens the Enterprise Global file into memory. Remember that this file contains all of your organization's custom enterprise objects, such as enterprise views, tables, filters, and groups.

3. The system combines these two global files into a single global entity used during the current session. In this combined global entity, you have access to all of the default and custom objects in the Global.mpt file, and all of your organization's custom enterprise objects in the Enterprise Global file.

You can view all of the objects in the combined global entity using the *Organizer* dialog in Microsoft Project 2010. To access the *Organizer* dialog, complete the following steps:

1. Click the *File* tab and then click the *Info* tab in the *Backstage* menu. The system displays the *Information* page in the *Backstage*, as shown in Figure 1 - 1.

Figure 1 - 1: Information page in the Backstage

2. In the *Organize Global Template* section at the bottom of the *Information* page, click the *Manage Global Template* pick list button and select the *Organizer* item on the list. The system displays the *Organizer* dialog shown in Figure 1 - 2.

The *Organizer* dialog includes nine tabs, one for each type of object available in the combined global entity. These tabs allow you to see all of the views, tables, filters, and groups in the combined global entity, along with other objects such as toolbars, calendars, modules (used with macros in VBA), and maps (used with the *Import/Export Wizard*). The

Fields tab shows only local fields included in the active project. Notice in the *Organizer* dialog shown in Figure 1 - 2 that the list shown on the left side of the *Views* page shows the views available in the combined global entity, indicated by the *Global (+ non-cached Enterprise)* selection on the *Views available in* pick list. Notice that the list on the left side contains five custom enterprise views, indicated by the *_msPE* prefix in each view name, plus one personal custom view, indicated by the *_DAH* prefix in the view name.

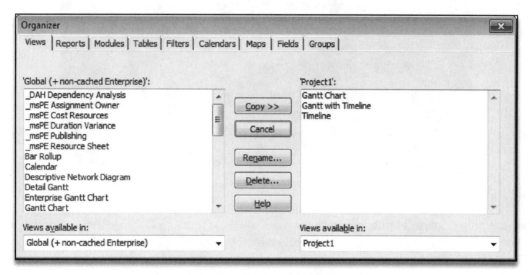

Figure 1 - 2: Organizer dialog

Click the *Cancel* button to close the *Organizer* dialog. Click the *File* tab to exit the *Backstage* and return to your project.

Understanding the Communications Life Cycle

A key piece of the core functionality in Project Server 2010 provides a cyclical assignment and update process between project managers and team members. This cycle is the heart of Project Server's work and resource management system. Work assignments flow from the plan to resources performing the work, and resources report progress data back to the plan. This project communication cycle flows through the following steps:

1. The project manager saves the project plan in the Project Server database, as shown in Figure 1 - 3. This action saves the project in the **Draft** database only. At this point, neither team members nor executives can see the project anywhere in Project Web App.

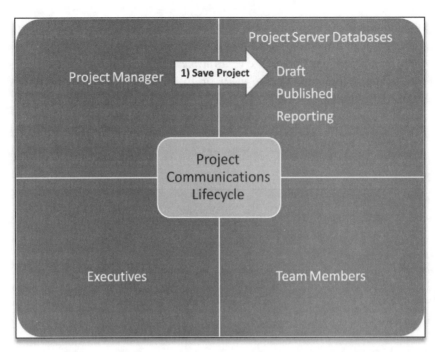

Figure 1 - 3: Save the project in Project Server Draft database

2. When the project manager publishes a project, as shown in Figure 1 - 4, the system writes the project data to the *Published* and *Reporting* databases. If enabled by the Project Server administrator, the system sends an e-mail message to each project team member to notify them of their new task assignments. Using an embedded link in the e-mail message, they can quickly click to view their task assignments in the project through Project Web App or through Outlook. Publishing makes project data visible in the *Project Center* and *Project Detail* views, and the system includes the project data in the next cube build.

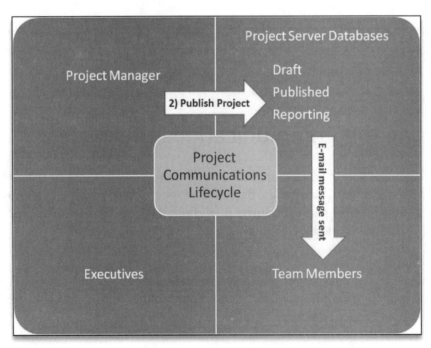

Figure 1 - 4: Publish the project with e-mail sent to team members

3. At the end of each reporting period, team members enter their actual progress on the project and send the task updates to the project manager via the Project Web App interface, as shown in Figure 1 - 5. Actual progress includes completion percentages and/or hours worked on each task, based on the organization's reporting method. The updates are visible to the project manager, but the system does not apply the updates to the plan until the project manager accepts the updates in the next step, or unless the project manager uses automation rules.

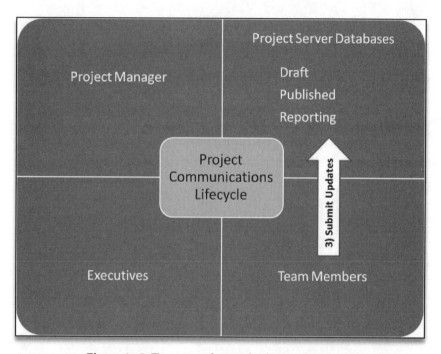

Figure 1 - 5: Team members submit actual progress

4. The project manager receives and reviews each set of task updates from project team members as shown in Figure 1 - 6. The project manager can individually accept or reject each task update, or the project manager can process them in batches using automation rules.

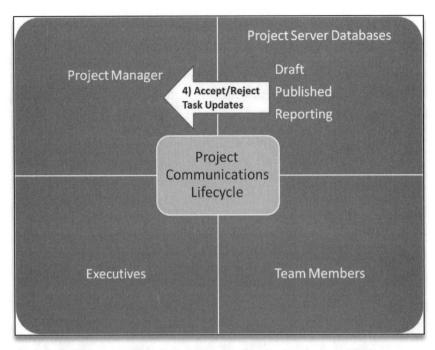

Figure 1 - 6: Project manager reviews and processes updates

5. After accepting or rejecting each task update, the project manager saves the latest schedule changes in the *Draft* database, as shown in Figure 1 - 7.

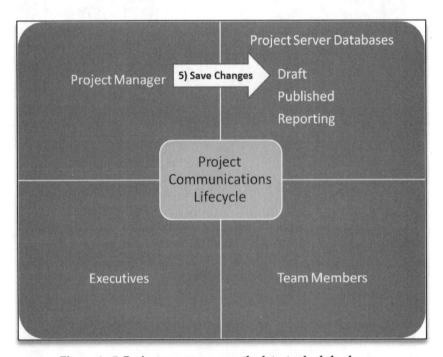

Figure 1 - 7: Project manager saves the latest schedule changes

6. After saving the project, the project manager publishes the latest project schedule changes to the *Published* and *Reporting* databases, as shown in Figure 1 - 8. This makes the schedule changes visible in the *Project Center* page, the *Timesheet* and *Tasks* pages for team members, along with the *Reporting* database and the OLAP cubes.

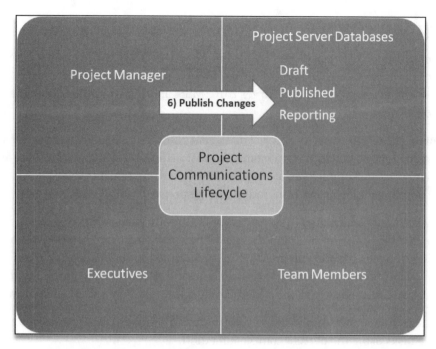

Figure 1 - 8: Project manager publishes the latest schedule changes

At any time throughout the life of the project, executives within the organization can view the organization's entire portfolio of projects, as shown in Figure 1 - 9. Project Server 2010 provides numerous view entry points, including the *Project Center* and *Resource Center* pages in Project Web App, which are gateways to detailed project and resource information.

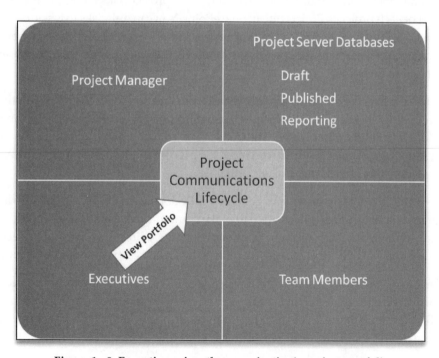

Figure 1 - 9: Executives view the organization's project portfolio

Understanding SharePoint Collaboration Tools

Beyond the core communication between project managers and project team members, Project Server 2010 provides additional features for project team collaboration. Some of these features are native to Project Server, whereas others leverage integration with Microsoft SharePoint Server 2010 (MSS) and Microsoft Windows SharePoint Foundation. These features include:

- **Status Reports** – Status Reports allow project managers, resource managers, and executives to establish single or periodic status reports to which team members must respond. Team members may also create their own unrequested reports and submit them at any time. The status report feature can save a manager time, as it automatically compiles a team report from individual responses.

- **Automated Alerts and Reminders** – Project Server 2010 features an automated reminder system that generates e-mail notices for a variety of situations, including reminding team members of upcoming and overdue task work, and of status reports that are due. In addition to reminders, alerts provide instant notification when certain events occur, such as a new task assignment. All users have the ability to set their own alerts and reminders, and managers have the added ability to set reminders for their resources.

- **Exchange Integration** – This feature allows users to display Project Web App tasks on the Outlook task list and status the tasks using the percent complete method.

- **Task Reassignment** – The system supports a team lead structure where functional leaders participate in the work distribution and management process. If the project manager enables task reassignment for team members in a project, team members can transfer work to each other, subject to the project manager's approval.

- **Ad hoc Reporting** – You can quickly print information from data grids in Project Web App, selecting and ordering fields and formatting the results. You can also export grid data and analysis cube data to Microsoft Excel for additional manipulation and reporting.

- **Risks** – Team members can identify, prioritize, and track project risks using the Project Server list feature created as part of each project's Project Site in SharePoint. You can link risks to tasks, or to issues, documents, and other risks. The links create indicators that appear in the *Project Center* views, where the system flags a project with an icon indicating it contains risks. Similarly, the system flags tasks in *Project* views when they have risks linked to them.

- **Issues** – Team members log and track project issues from creation to resolution using the Project Server list feature created as part of each project's Project Site in SharePoint. As with risks, you can link issues to tasks, or to risks, documents, and other issues. The links create indicators that appear in the *Project Center* views, where the system flags a project with an icon indicating it contains issues. Similarly, the system flags tasks in *Project* views when they have issues linked to them.

- **Documents** – Project Web App provides a general public document library available to all system users. The public document library is an excellent place to make common process documentation available as part of a standardized environment. Each project has its own document library within the Project Site in SharePoint, into which users can load documents and link them to tasks, issues, risks and other documents in the system.

- **Deliverables** – Project managers can define deliverables linked to tasks that other project managers can consume in their projects, thereby creating a new way of cross-linking projects. With the addition of Microsoft SharePoint Server (MSS) to the server farm, managers can apply SharePoint workflows to the deliverables. Workflows are new in the 2010 version of MSS.

- **Project Proposals** – System users can create and submit project proposals for consideration and approval. This feature enables the enterprise to build a demand-management system for new projects in the enterprise. You can tailor the approval process to meet your organization's workflow.

- **Resource Plans** – Used in conjunction with project proposals and enterprise projects, resource plans provide a means to estimate and measure future resource loads.

- **Timesheets** – Timesheets provide enterprise users with fully functional time reporting capabilities that can collect time at any reporting level. Most importantly, the timesheet feature includes the ability to create a full audit trail, allowing system implementers to create regulatory-compliant solutions. You can use timesheet data to drive task progress or maintain this data without using it to drive task updates. You can also use the *Tasks* page to collect task progress as in previous versions of Project Server.

Understanding Project Server Databases

The database structure in Project Server 2010 is the same as it was in the 2007 version of the software. Project Server uses four distinct databases to represent and manage project data. This arrangement provides data management granularity through a well-defined data flow. Each database serves a specific purpose. Because Microsoft now provides a distinct database for reporting purposes and a much more functional Advanced Programming Interface (API) called the Project Services Interface (PSI), it provides documentation for the *Reporting* database only. Microsoft recommends that consumers never directly use the other three databases for reporting or building additional system functionality, and doing so can disqualify Microsoft supportability. The four databases used by Project Server 2010 are as follows:

- **Draft** – When a project manager saves a Microsoft Project 2010 project file to Project Server for the first time, the system saves it to the *Draft* database. This project it is not yet visible to users through Project Web App. The copy of the plan in the *Draft* database is always the working version. When a project manager modifies a project plan, the system saves the changes only to the *Draft* database.

- **Published** – When a project manager publishes a project, the system writes the information to the *Published* database. Once published, users can see the project in Project Web App.

- **Reporting** – When a project manager publishes a project, the system also writes the information to the *Reporting* database. Your Project Server administrator can generate custom SQL reports using the project data in the *Reporting* database.

- **Archive** – Project managers cannot see the data in the *Archive* database. Instead, the Project Server administrator uses the *Archive* database to backup project plans and other server objects.. If necessary, the Project Server administrator can also restore a project from the *Archive* database in an emergency situation, such as when the project becomes corrupted.

In addition to the four databases used by Project Server 2010, the system also includes two Windows SharePoint Services databases:

- **WSS Configuration** – Required for SharePoint Server and Project Server 2010, this database defines the WSS farm.

- **WSS Content** – Required for Project Server 2010, this database contains the SharePoint content data for the Project Server instance, including documents, risks, issues, deliverables and other content that users create or upload to the SharePoint sites created for each project published in the Project Server system.

Understanding Custom Fields

Your Project Server administrator must mold the raw functionality provided in Project Server 2010 to match your organization's specific requirements for categorizing and reporting on projects, resources, and tasks. Although the default information in the system provides useful tracking and statistical data, the Project Server can accomplish a more meaningful presentation by seeding the database with custom attributes. These custom attributes exist in Project Server 2010 as custom fields and lookup tables.

Custom enterprise fields can contain formulas to display calculated information, and can display graphical indicators instead of numeric data. Custom enterprise fields can also contain a lookup table to present the user with a pick list of allowable values.

Using custom enterprise fields, your Project Server administrator can create *Project Web App* views to display meaningful project information. For example, in the *Project Center* view shown in Figure 1 - 10, the Project Server administrator created three custom enterprise project fields called *% Work Variance*, *% Cost Variance*, and *% Duration Variance*. Each of these fields displays a green, yellow, or red stoplight indicator to show the severity work, cost, or duration variance. The Project Server administrator also created two other enterprise project fields called *Risk* and *Region*, and applied grouping by risk and then by region. Using this special dashboard-like view, project stakeholders and executives can easily determine the variance for each project across the portfolio of projects.

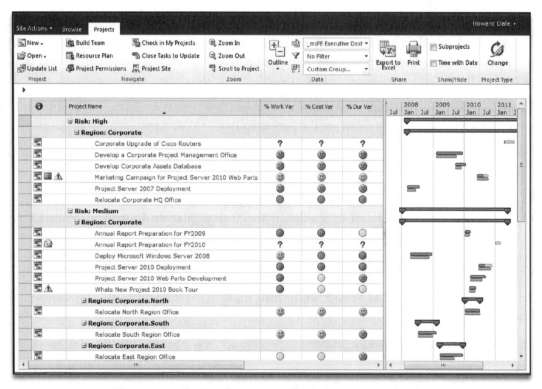

**Figure 1 - 10: Project Center view displays custom enterprise
Project fields with graphical indicators and grouping**

Project Server 2010 includes six types of custom enterprise fields at the Task, Resource, and Project level. The system allows an **unlimited** amount of each of the following field types:

- Enterprise **Cost**
- Enterprise **Date**
- Enterprise **Duration**
- Enterprise **Flag**
- Enterprise **Number**
- Enterprise **Text**

When creating a custom field of any type, the Project Server administrator has the option to make the field a free entry field that allows a single line of text or multiple lines of text, to create a formula in the field, to display graphical indicators in the field, or to use a lookup table of acceptable values in the field.

Understanding Tracking Methods

The default method of tracking progress chosen by your organization has a significant impact on both project team members and project managers, and how they interact with Project Web App. Specifically, the tracking method selected determines the appearance of the *Tasks* page and the *Detailed Assignments* page in Project Web App, and determines what type of data team members must report on either of these two pages. Beyond this, the tracking method selected also affects each project manager as it affects the type of data the project manager must approve in the *Approval Center* page in Project Web App.

After selecting the default tracking method for your organization, the Project Server administrator must also choose whether to "lock down" the selected method. With the tracking method locked down, project managers and team members **must** use this method for tracking progress in every enterprise project. Project Server 2010 offers four methods for tracking task progress:

- **Percent of Work Complete** allows team members to enter % Work Complete and a Remaining Work estimate on each task assignment.
- **Actual Work Done and Work Remaining** allows team members to enter the cumulative amount of Actual Work value and to adjust the Remaining Work estimate on each task assignment.
- **Hours of Work Done per Period** allows resources to enter the hours of Actual Work completed for the current period and to adjust the Remaining Work estimate on each task assignment.
- **Free Form** tracking allows the user to enter progress using any of the three previous methods.

 Percent of Work Complete is the system default method for tracking progress unless your organization selects another method.

In addition to selecting the default method of tracking progress in Project Server 2010, the Project Server administrator must also define what constitutes a "current task" in the system. This definition determines which tasks team members see by default on their *Tasks* page in Project Web App. By default, the system defines a "current task" as any task that meets one of the following criteria:

- An unstarted task scheduled in the past.

- A task that is in-progress but is not yet completed.

- A rejected task that the team member has not resubmitted.

- A task completed in the last two reporting periods (10 days) prior to the current week.

- A task scheduled to start in the next two reporting periods (10 days) after the current week.

The Project Server administrator has the option to leave the default setting for "current tasks" at 2 reporting periods (10 days), or to increase or decrease the number of reporting periods as needed by your organization.

Understanding Business Intelligence

Business Intelligence (BI) is a set of processes, tools, and techniques for gathering, organizing, and analyzing large volumes of complex data in an effort to develop an accurate understanding of business dynamics, and you use it to improve strategic and tactical business decision-making. In other words, the purpose of BI is to capture large amounts of data, make some sense out of it, and use it to make sound business decisions. The ultimate goal is to develop the ability to spot problems and trends, and to make informed decisions to mitigate risks, improve efficiencies, and identify opportunities.

Organizations spend time and money implementing Project Server 2010 to capture work data, make sense out of it, and use it to make decisions such as:

- Spotting problems and trends - Is the project running late or over budget?

- Mitigating risks - What can we do to avoid missing our launch deadline?

- Improving efficiencies - Who is the best-qualified person to perform the work?

- Identifying opportunities - What if we design the database and the user interface at the same time?

A well-designed BI system should do the following:

- Extract large amounts of complex data from one or more sources, such as CRM, supply chain management, ERP, and EPM systems

- Centralize, organize, and standardize information in repositories such as data warehouses or data marts

- Provide analytical tools through multiple delivery methods that allow business and technical specialists to run queries against the data and to perform analyses to uncover patterns and diagnose problems

- Present the right information, at the right time, in the right format in order to make the right decisions and take the right actions to achieve the right performance

Project Server helps to do these things already. It aggregates different types of complex work data from different locations into a central set of databases and OLAP cubes, or BI Data Store, such as those shown in Figure 1 - 11.

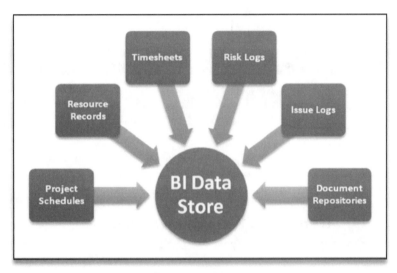

Figure 1 - 11: Aggregating Project Server Data into the BI Data Store

Project Server 2010, when used in conjunction with Microsoft SharePoint Server 2010, also provides a set of rich analytical tools to build reports and visuals for analysis of that data, such as the following:

- Project Center Reports

- Project Detail Reports

- Project Professional Reports

- Microsoft Visio Diagrams

- Microsoft Excel Tabular and Pivot-Style Reports

- Key Performance Indicators

- Balanced Scorecards

- Interactive Dashboards

As a project manager, you have access to all of these types of *Business Intelligence* reports. In addition, you have access to the *Business Intelligence Center* page in Project Web App. Using the *Business Intelligence Center* page, you can not only view all types of reports, you also have permission to create your own reports. For example, Figure 1 - 12 shows a custom Excel report containing an Excel PivotTable and PivotChart, opened in the *Business Intelligence Center* page. This custom Excel report shows the total amount of work for all IT projects, broken down by project type and by year. Every time a manager or executive opens this report, the system refreshes the data to show the latest information about all IT projects.

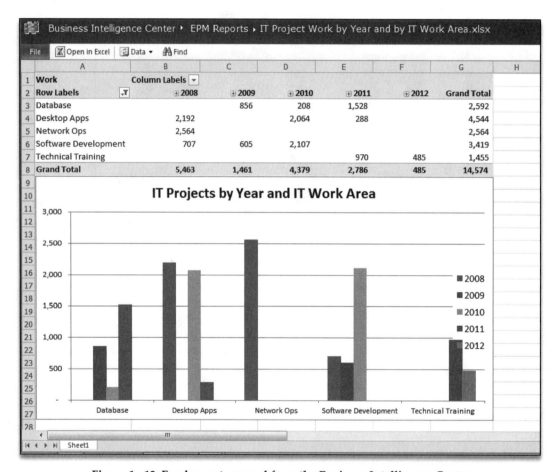

Figure 1 - 12: Excel report, opened from the Business Intelligence Center

In Module 17, *Working with Business Intelligence*, I provide an in-depth presentation of all the features available in the *Business Intelligence Center* page in Project Web App.

Module 02

Preparing to Use Project Server

Learning Objectives

After completing this module, you will be able to:

- Understand and use the Project Web App user interface
- Log in to Project Web App from the workstation of another user
- Become familiar with Project Server ribbon navigation
- Use the new grid objects in Project Web App pages
- Understand and use the Project Professional 2010 user interface
- Become familiar with the Ribbon and the Backstage in Project Professional 2010
- Import a customized Ribbon into Project Professional 2010
- Create a Project Server login account in Project Professional 2010

Inside Module 02

Using the Project Web App User Interface

When you log in to Project Web App with a valid user account, the system presents the *Home* page. Figure 2 - 1 shows the *Home* page for a user named George Stewart who has Project Manager permissions in the system. Notice that the *Home* page of Project Web App consists of two parts: a *Quick Launch* menu on the left and a main content area in the middle.

 All of the screenshots included in this book show Project Web App for a user who is a member of only the Project Managers group. If you are a member of any group with higher permissions, such as the Portfolio Managers or Administrators groups, the system displays more features in Project Web App.

If you are already familiar with SharePoint websites, you probably recognize the Project Web App user interface as a standard SharePoint site layout. Project Server 2010 fully embeds the entire Project Web App interface into Share-Point. All of the Project Web App pages function just like any other SharePoint site.

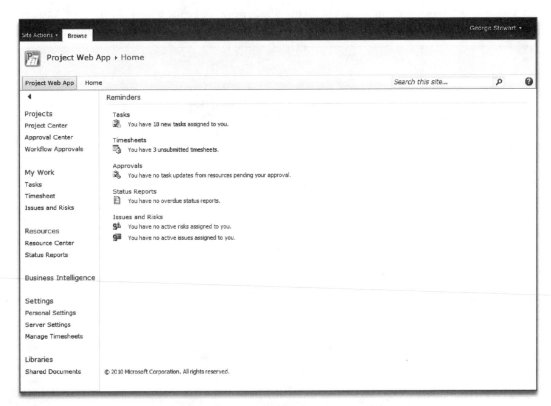

Figure 2 - 1: Project Web App Home page for a project manager

The *Quick Launch* menu contains links to all areas of Project Web App that you can reach based on your security permissions. The main content area contains *Reminders* about your action items including tasks, timesheets, approvals, status reports, and issues and risks. Across the top of the page, Project Server 2010 offers you a number of additional options and selections as well.

Starting at the upper left of the screen and working across, you first see the *Site Actions* menu, a SharePoint artifact that provides standard SharePoint options as shown in Figure 2 - 2. These include:

1. The *Edit Page* selection allows you to put the page into edit mode to introduce additional web parts or change the page layout. Editing the page from this menu selection affects all users by the changes.

2. The *New Document Library* selection allows you to create a new document library to attach to the PWA site.

3. You can access the full range of available content types that you can create by selecting the *More Options* menu item, which includes new sites and document libraries.

4. The *View All Site Content* selection allows you to see the entire site's content in one page.

5. The *Edit in SharePoint Designer* selection allows you to edit the site using SharePoint Designer. Note that you cannot edit the PWA site using SharePoint Designer; however you can edit subordinate sites and Project sites using SharePoint Designer.

6. Finally, the *Site Settings* selection takes you to the *Site Settings* page for Project Web App. As a project manager, this page allows you only a small amount of administration capabilities for your Project Server 2010 instance.

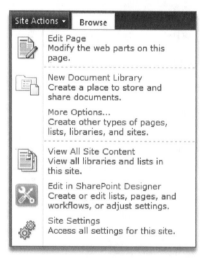

Figure 2 - 2: Site Actions Menu

7. Project Web App inherits the *Browse* tab from SharePoint, and it is visible throughout the site. In PWA, this contains title information only, and serves no functional purpose in the PWA user interface other than to provide you with a quick way to access the *Home* page in Project Web App from any page in the system.

To return to the *Home* page from any other page in Project Web App, click the *Browse* tab and then click the *Home* tab or the *Project Web App* tab.

In the far upper-right corner of the page shown in Figure 2 - 3, notice that your name appears with a *Personal Menu* shown in Figure 2 - 4. This menu contains selections that allow you to change your personal settings, personalize the page, sign out, or sign in as a different user.

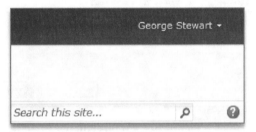

Figure 2 - 3: Personal Menu

Figure 2 - 4: Personal Menu
with personal settings options

Immediately below the personal menu is a search tool you can use to search for specific information in the Project Web App site. To use this tool, enter your search terms in the *Search* field and then click the *Search* button (it looks like a magnifying glass).

To the right of the search tool, click the *Help* icon 🔵 to see context-sensitive help displayed in a floating window.

Logging into Project Web App from another Workstation

Project Server 2010 allows you to log in to Project Web App from another user's workstation while the user is logged on to your corporate network with his/her own network user ID. To log in to Project Web App from another user's workstation, click the *Personal Menu* and then click the *Sign in as Different User* item on the menu, as shown previously in Figure 2 - 4.

The system displays the standard Windows network logon dialog shown in Figure 2 - 5. In the *Windows Security* dialog, begin by clicking *Use another account* option. Enter your domain and user ID in the *User name* field, enter your network password in the *Password* field, and then click the *OK* button. The system automatically logs you in to Project Web App using your network user credentials, and displays your name in the upper right hand corner of the screen.

Figure 2 - 5: Connect dialog

Using the Quick Launch Menu

The Project Web App user interface offers a *Quick Launch* menu on the left side of every primary page. This menu lists your viewable selections based on your role in the project management environment. In Figure 2 - 6 shown below, the *Quick Launch* menu contains menu options for a user with Project Manager permissions. Notice that the options available on the *Quick Launch* menu include:

- The *Projects* section contains three links. Click the *Project Center* link to navigate to the *Project Center* page where you can view your project portfolio. Click the *Approval Center* link to view and navigate to the *Approval Center* page, where you approve task updates (task progress) from your team members. Click the *Workflow Approvals* link to navigate to the *Project Server Workflow Tasks* page where you approve or reject steps in the workflow for new proposed projects. If you click the *Projects* section header, the system navigates to the *Project Center* page.

- The *My Work* section contains three links. Click the *Tasks* link to navigate to the *Tasks* page to view and update tasks assigned to you. Click the *Timesheet* link to navigate to the *Timesheet* page where you can view and update your timesheet for the current reporting period. Click the *Issues and Risks* link to navigate to the *Issues and Risks* page where you can view issues and risks assigned to you in all of your projects. If you click the *My Work* section header, the system navigates to the *Tasks* page.

- The *Resources* section contains two links. Click the *Resource Center* link to navigate to the *Resource Center* page where you can view resource availability and assignment information. Click the *Status Reports* link to navigate to the *Status Reports* page where you can create or respond to a *Status Report* request. If you click the *Resources* section header, the system navigates to the *Resource Center* page.

**Figure 2 - 6: Quick
Launch Menu**

- Click the *Business Intelligence* link to access the *Business Intelligence Center* page where you can view all types of *Business Intelligence* reports and perform project data analysis.

- The *Settings* section contains three links. Click the *Personal Settings* link to navigate to the *Personal Settings* page where you can set up e-mail subscriptions for alerts and reminders, set up alerts and reminders for your resources, manage your own queued jobs, manage your delegates, or act as a delegate. Click the *Server Settings* link to navigate to the *Server Settings* page and configure the options available to you as a project manager. Click the *Manage Timesheets* link to view a list of all of your past, current, and future timesheets. If you click the *Settings* section header, the system navigates to the *Personal Settings* page.

> **Warning:** The default permissions for the Project Managers group **do not** allow project managers to manage delegates or to serve as a delegate. If this functionality is beneficial for the project managers in your organiztion, your Project Server adminstrator must enable all of the *Delegate* permissions in the Project Managers group. For the purposes of writing this book, I have enabled every *Delegate* permission for project managers so that you can see this powerful functionality.

- The *Libraries* section contains only one link. Click the *Shared Documents* link to navigate to the *Shared Documents* page where you can view or share public documents with everyone using the Project Server system. Click the *Libraries* section heading to navigate to the *All Site Content* page where you can see all available public content.

A new feature in the *Quick Launch* menu for Project Server 2010 allows you to collapse the menu to give you more room to display the rest of the page. This feature is particularly handy when you view pages that contain a data grid object, such as the *Tasks* or *Timesheet* pages. Click the *Collapse* icon, the small left-pointing triangle image shown in Figure 2 - 7, to completely collapse the *Quick Launch* menu. When you collapse the *Quick Launch* menu, the system displays the *Expand* icon, which reverses the direction of the triangle image. Click the *Expand* icon to expand the *Quick Launch* menu.

**Figure 2 - 7: Collapse
the Quick Launch menu**

Using the Ribbon Menus

Every Project Web App page that contains a data grid includes a *Ribbon* with one or more ribbon tabs at the top of the page. When you click a *Ribbon* tab, Project Server 2010 displays one or more buttons on the *Ribbon*, depending on your Project Server permissions. For example, Figure 2 - 8 shows the *Project Center* page for a user with project manager permissions. Notice the *Projects* ribbon at the top of the page, along with the *Projects* tab at the top of the *Projects* ribbon.

Figure 2 - 8: Project Center page

Notice that the *Project Center* ribbon has one context-sensitive tab, the *Projects* tab. Some pages contain only the *Browse* tab when the software handles their functionality within the page itself. The *Projects* ribbon contains menu selections in seven sections: *Project, Navigate, Zoom, Data, Share, Show/Hide* and *Project Type*. If you used prior versions of Project Server, you can see right away that Project Web App has a much richer set of available functionality than ever before. For example, Project Web App now supports project editing in the browser, a new feature in Project Server 2010. Notice that the *Project* section contains an *Update List* button. This button allows you to synchronize data between projects and SharePoint lists, which is another new feature for 2010. Notice also that the *Navigate* section includes a *Project Site* button which allows you to navigate to the Project Site for a selected project. **Project Site** is the new terminology for what Microsoft called a **Project Workspace** in Project Server 2007.

Some pages contain more than one context-sensitive tab, such as the *Project Details* page. This page contains three such tabs, including the *Project, Task,* and *Options* tabs, grouped together under the *Schedule Tools* section, as shown in Figure 2 - 9. You navigate to the *Project Detail* page by clicking on the name of a project in the *Project Center* page. The *Project Details* page contains both a *Project* and a *Task* tab because you must access both project-level and task-level functions to fully leverage the features on this page. Notice the convenient *Status* bar notification just below the *Task* ribbon.

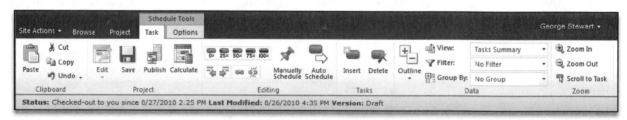

Figure 2 - 9: Project Details page with the Task ribbon selected

In the *Task* ribbon shown in Figure 2 - 9, notice the *Clipboard* section on the far left and the *Editing* and *Tasks* sections in the center. These three sections contain the new web-based project editing tools available in Project Server 2010 using familiar functionality similar to what you find in Project Professional 2010. This exciting new capability supports much stronger project management collaboration, allowing numerous users to participate in project schedule development, or even to manage simple projects from end-to-end, including project tracking, without using Project Professional 2010.

The project editing tools in Project Web App are a small subset of the editing tools you find in Project Professional 2010, and are limited in their functionality. For example, you cannot specify a *Units* value when assigning resources to tasks; the system uses the 100% units value automatically. When setting dependencies between tasks, the system limits you to only the Finish-To-Start (FS) dependency, and you cannot add Lag time or Lead time. Despite these limitations, this new capability represents a giant advance in Project Web App usability.

If you click the *Project* tab, the system displays the *Project* ribbon shown in Figure 2 - 10. This ribbon provides redundant *Edit* and *Save* buttons and provides the only way to close and check in a project after editing on the web via the *Close* button in the *Project* section. The *Navigate* section includes the new *Project Permissions* button that allows you to set project-level permissions specific to your selected project. Note in Figure 2 - 10 that the system grays out the *Edit* button because I have the project open for editing.

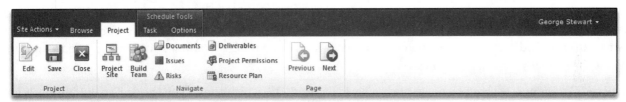

Figure 2 - 10: Project Details page with the Project ribbon selected

Note that the *Project* tab in the *Project Details* page differs significantly from the *Project* tab you see in the *Project Center* page. This is because the operations available on the *Project* tab in the *Project Center* page apply to all projects in the data grid, while the operations available on the *Project* tab in the *Project Details* page apply to only the project open for editing.

Click the *Options* tab and the system displays the *Options* ribbon shown in Figure 2 - 11. Notice that the *Link To* section contains buttons that allow you to create links from tasks to documents, issues and risks contained in the *Project Site* for the selected project. You can even create any one of these objects and link them all in one operation. The *Options* ribbon also provides quick access to the *Close Tasks to Updates* feature, a feature also available from the *Project Center* page as well.

Figure 2 - 11: Project Details page with the Options ribbon selected

Applying and Working with Views

Project Web App pages that contain data grids include a *Data* section in their default ribbon. You use the tools in the *Data* section of the ribbon to apply various views and to control those views by restricting data outline levels, applying filter conditions and grouping the data in the view. Figure 2 - 12 shows the *Data* section of the *Resource* ribbon on the *Resource Center* page.

**Figure 2 - 12: Data Section
of the Resource Ribbon**

The *View* selector allows you to select any view that you can access on the page that you are viewing. Although Project Server ships with a number of out-of-the-box views, for the most part you work with customized versions of the views or an entirely different set of views created specifically for your organization. You should familiarize yourself with the views that your organization uses.

Notice the *Outline* pick list button shown previously in Figure 2 - 12, which allows you to select all outline levels in the data grid or restrict the view by outline level up to 9 levels. When you apply outline restrictions to a view in the Resource Center, it acts upon the grouping structure in the view. When you apply outline restrictions to a *Project Detail* view, it acts upon the project structure itself. Selecting *Outline Level 1* from the pick list, for example, restricts the view to display only the most top level data lines. Similarly, if you select *Outline Level 3* from the pick list, the system displays only the first three levels of data and collapses the rest of the data below it.

The *Filter* selector provides two options: *No Filter* and *Custom Filter*. You use the *No Filter* option to clear a custom filter once you have applied it. To filter a view, from the *Data* section of the ribbon, select the *Custom Filter* item from the *Filter* pick list. The system displays the *Custom Filter* dialog shown in Figure 2 - 13.

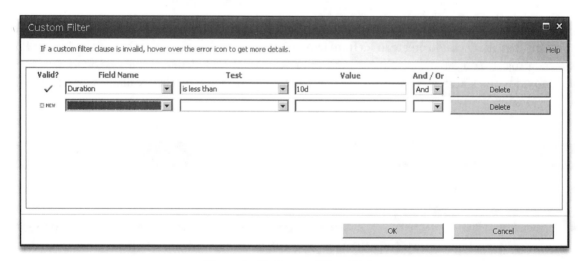

Figure 2 - 13: Custom Filter Dialog

The *Custom Filter* dialog allows you to build a filter by creating test conditions for the fields available in the view. In order to filter on a field in Project Web App, it must be included in the view. You use the *Field Name* selector to choose the field for your first filter condition. Use the *Test* selector to apply an available test condition from the list as shown in Figure 2 - 14.

Figure 2 - 14: Test Conditions

In the *Value* field, you must then enter a valid value for your test. When you test against a *Text* field, you enter a *Text* value, when you test against a *Date* field, you must enter a valid *Date* format and you must enter numeric data for fields containing numeric values.

The *Group By* selector is the last tool in the *Data* section of the ribbon shown previously in Figure 2 - 12. Like the *Field* selector in the *Custom Filter* dialog, the *Group By* selector displays only fields that are available in the view. You cannot group your fields using data fields not included in the view. When you apply a group by value, the system redisplays the view grouped by the unique values it finds in the field. Logically, not all data fields are good candidates for grouping. For instance, grouping by *Resource Name* in a *Resource Center* view would not make sense as most resource names are unique unto themselves. On the rare occasions that names are repeated in the resource pool, the most you can gain from this grouping is to understand how many times the repetition occurs in your resource pool. Grouping by *Resource Type*, however, is a very useful exercise because it organizes your resources in a logical presentation.

Manipulating the Data Grid

Some Project Web App pages contain a data grid that displays task, resource, or assignment data. Some data grids, such as the *Project Center* page, have a vertical split bar separating the grid into two sections, while other pages contain a single grid only. For example, notice that the *Project Center* page, shown previously in Figure 2 - 8, consists of two sections: the project list on the left side of the split bar, and the Gantt chart on the right side. To work with the data in the grid most effectively, it is important to know how to take the following actions:

- **Moving the Split Bar** - You move the split bar in the grid by floating your mouse pointer anywhere over the split bar itself. When the mouse pointer changes from a single arrow to a double-headed arrow, as shown in Figure 2 - 15, click and hold the mouse button to "grab" the split bar and then drag it to the new position on the screen.

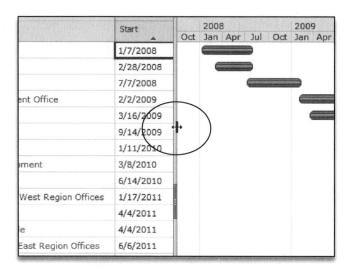

Figure 2 - 15: Move the Split Bar

- **Changing Column Widths** - To change the width of any column in the grid, float the mouse pointer anywhere on the right edge of the column in the header row. The mouse pointer changes from a single arrow to a double-headed arrow, as shown in Figure 2 - 16. Click and hold to "grab" the right edge of the column, and drag the edge of the column to the desired width.

Figure 2 - 16: Widen the Project Name Column

To widen any column to "best fit" the data in the column, you can use the Microsoft Excel trick by double-clicking the gridline on the right edge of the column header.

- **Moving Columns** - To move any column in the grid, click and hold the column header of the column you want to move. Drag the column into its new position in the grid and then drop it. Notice in Figure 2 - 17 that I am dragging the *% Complete* column to a new position to the left of the *Start* column. Notice how the column floats over the other columns in a transparent format as I move it across the other columns.

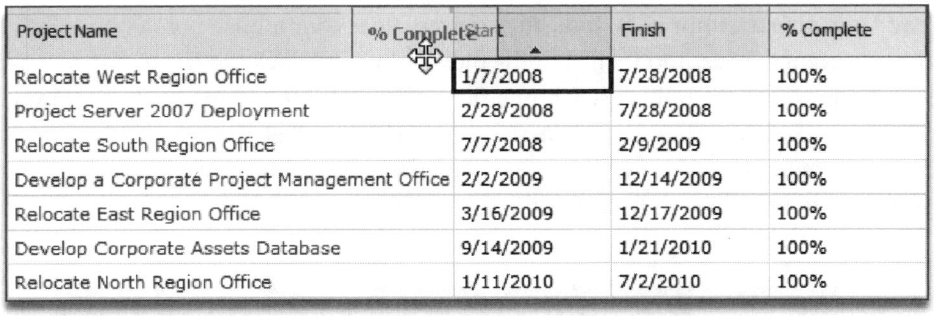

Project Name
% Complete
Start
Finish
% Complete
Relocate West Region Office
1/7/2008
7/28/2008
100%
Project Server 2007 Deployment
2/28/2008
7/28/2008
100%
Relocate South Region Office
7/7/2008
2/9/2009
100%
Develop a Corporate Project Management Office
2/2/2009
12/14/2009
100%
Relocate East Region Office
3/16/2009
12/17/2009
100%
Develop Corporate Assets Database
9/14/2009
1/21/2010
100%
Relocate North Region Office
1/11/2010
7/2/2010
100%

Figure 2 - 17: Drag the % Complete column to the left of the Start column

- **Sorting Columns** - To sort the data in the grid, float your mouse pointer over the column header of the column upon which you want to sort, and then click the pick list button. The system displays the pick list shown in Figure 2 - 18 for the *Start* column. Click either the *Sort Ascending* or *Sort Descending* item on the pick list to apply the type of sorting you want. Remember that you can apply sorting to only one column in a data grid.

Project Name
Start
Finish
2010
Jan Apr
CBT Implementation for the Corporate HQ Office
1/16/2012
CBT Implementation for the North and East Regi
6/6/2011
CBT Implementation for the South and West Reg
1/17/2011
Informis HR Software Upgrade
4/4/2011
Knowledge Management Systems Enhancements
9/6/2011
Microsoft Office 2010 Corporate Upgrade
4/4/2011
Open Houston Southern Subregional Office
9/10/2012
Relocate Corporate HQ Office
4/2/2012
Project Server 2010 Deployment
6/14/2010
Project Server 2010 Web Parts Development
3/8/2010
Develop a Corporate Project Management Office
2/2/2009
Develop Corporate Assets Database
9/14/2009
Project Server 2007 Deployment
2/28/2008
Relocate East Region Office
3/16/2009
Relocate North Region Office
1/11/2010
Relocate South Region Office
7/7/2008
Relocate West Region Office
1/7/2008
Hide Column
Configure Columns...
Sort Ascending
Sort Descending
Clear Filter
1/7/2008
2/28/2008
7/7/2008
2/2/2009
3/16/2009
9/14/2009
1/11/2010
3/8/2010
6/14/2010
1/17/2011
4/4/2011
6/6/2011

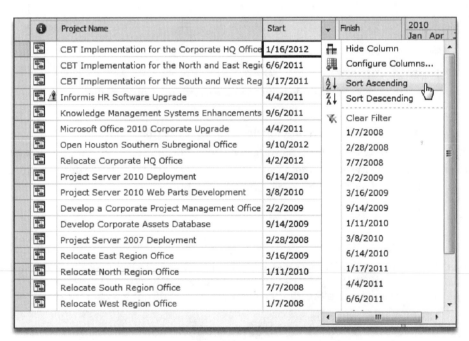

Figure 2 - 18: Apply Ascending sorting on the data in the Start column

- **AutoFilter** - To auto filter the data in any column, float your mouse pointer over the column header of the column whose data you want to filter, and then click the pick list button. Select any value on the list of column values, such as the list of dates in the *Start* column shown previously in Figure 2 - 18. To remove the auto filter, click the pick list again and select the *Clear Filter* item on the pick list.

- **Hiding and Unhiding a Column**: To hide any column, float your mouse pointer over the column header of the column you want to hide, and then click the pick list button. Click the *Hide Column* item in the pick list to hide the selected column. To unhide a column, float your mouse pointer over any column header, click the pick list button, and click the *Configure Columns* item on the pick list. The system displays the *Configure Columns* dialog shown in Figure 2 - 19. In the *Configure Columns* dialog, select the option checkbox of the column(s) you want to unhide and then click the *OK* button.

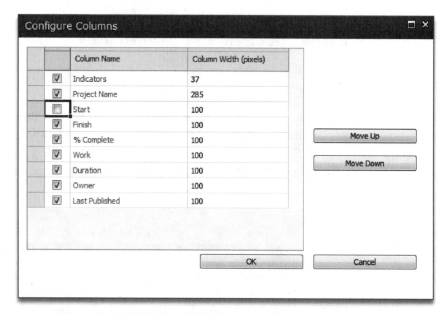

Figure 2 - 19: Unhide column in the Configure Columns dialog

Notice in the *Configure Column* dialog shown previously in Figure 2 - 19 that Project Server 2010 also allows you to set column widths and the column display order, as well as hiding and unhiding column. To change the width of any column, enter the width in pixels in the *Column Width* field. To change the display order of columns, select any column and use the *Move Up* and *Move Down* buttons. Click the *OK* button when finished.

Project Server 2010 automatically saves any changes you make to the layout of a grid (such as column order, column width, etc.) in your user profile. The layout of the grid reappears the next time you return to the page. These changes affect the current user only and do not affect other users.

Printing the Data Grid

Project Server 2010 allows you to print a report from a data grid or export the data grid information to Microsoft Excel. To print a data grid, click the *Print* option in the *Share* section of the ribbon on a page containing a data grid, such as on the *Project Center* page. The system opens the *Print Grid* window in its own Internet Explorer window, and then displays the *Print* dialog in front of the window, and with the default printer selected, as shown in Figure 2 - 20.

The *Print Grid* window is a duplicate of the grid in the parent window. Notice in Figure 2 - 20 that the *Print Grid* window shows the *Project Center* page, for example. In this window, you can rearrange and resize the columns, but you cannot hide or unhide columns. Before you can change the data in the *Print Grid* window, however, you must close the *Print* dialog. After you change the arrangement of the data in the data grid, use the **Ctrl + P** keyboard shortcut to display the *Print* dialog again.

Click the *Print* button in the *Print* dialog to print the data grid. If you print the data grid that includes a Gantt chart, such as the *Project Center* page, the system prints both the data grid and the Gantt chart. The ability to print the Gantt chart in Project Web App is a new feature in Project Server 2010. In prior versions of Project Server, you could apply additional formatting to the grid prior to printing; this feature is no longer available in the 2010 version.

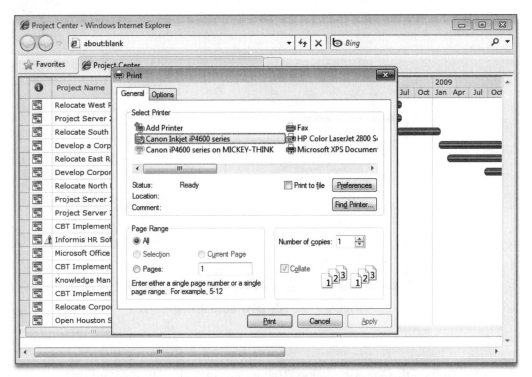

Figure 2 - 20: Print Grid window with the Print dialog displayed

 Warning: If you attempt to print a data grid that exceeds 100 lines of information in the grid, Project Server 2010 does not allow you to print the data grid. Instead, the system forces you to export the data grid to Microsoft Excel. From Excel, you can then print the data grid.

Exporting the Data Grid to Excel

Warning: The default security settings for your Internet Explorer may prevent you from exporting a data grid to Microsoft Excel. If this is the case, add the URL of the Project Web App home page to the *Trusted Site* section of the *Internet Options* dialog in your Internet Explorer, and then set the *Security Level* setting for the *Trusted Sites* zone to *Low*.

In addition to printing the data grid, you can also export the data grid to a Microsoft Excel workbook by clicking the *Export to Excel* button from the *Share* section of the ribbon on a page containing a data grid. When you select this option, the system displays the *File Download* dialog shown in Figure 2 - 21.

Figure 2 - 21: File Download dialog

Click the *Open* button in the *File Download* dialog. The system may display the confirmation dialog shown in Figure 2 - 22. If so, click the *Yes* button in the confirmation dialog to continue the process of exporting the data grid to a Microsoft Excel workbook.

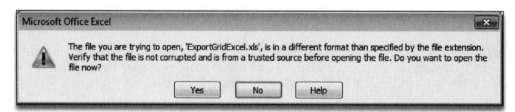

Figure 2 - 22: Confirmation dialog when exporting data to Excel

The system opens Microsoft Excel and exports the grid into a blank workbook, as shown in Figure 2 - 23.

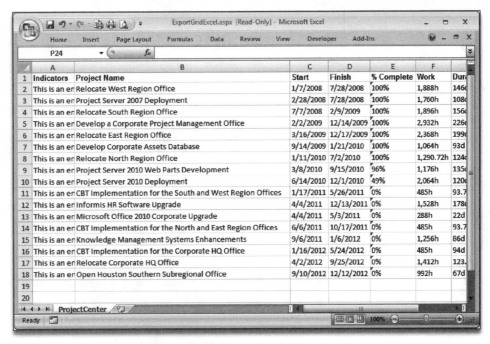

Figure 2 - 23: Tasks Exported to Excel

Warning: When you export grid data to Microsoft Excel, the exporting process exports the data in **every column**, including hidden columns. Keep in mind that in Microsoft Excel, it is very simple to delete a column or to hide a column.

Warning: All of the Hands On Exercises in this book assume that you installed and are using the Project Server 2010 instance included with the download files that accompany this book. Module 00, *Setting Up the Learning Environment*, documents the process for downloading the sample files and setting up the Project Server 2010 instance. If you do not install the Project Server 2010 instance included with this book, keep in mind that the Hands On Exercises may not correspond with the features in your own organization's Project Server 2010 instance.

Hands On Exercise

Exercise 2-1

Explore the features of the Project Web App user interface.

1. Log in to Project Web App sample Project Server 2010 instance.

The exercises in this book are based on sample files that you can download and install into your own Project Server instance. The URL for the download is located on page xv in the front of the book. The download also includes instructions for configuring your system.

2. Click the *Resource Center* link in *Resources* section of the *Quick Launch* menu.

3. Click the *Browse* tab in the upper left corner of the *Resource Center* page.

4. Click the *Home* link at the top of the *Quick Launch* menu to return to the *Home* page of Project Web App.

5. Click the *Project Center* link in the *Projects* section of the *Quick Launch* menu.

6. Collapse the *Quick Launch* menu by clicking the *Collapse* icon at the top of the menu. The *Collapse* icon is the small left-pointing triangle in the upper left corner of the *Quick Launch* menu.

7. Examine the buttons in each section of the *Projects* ribbon.

8. Drag the split bar to the right side of the *Duration* column.

9. Widen the *Indicators* column to a width that shows the indicators for every project.

10. Drag the *Duration* column and drop it in between the *Start* and *Finish* columns.

11. Float your mouse pointer over the *Project Name* column header, click the pick list button, and then select the *Sort Ascending* item on the menu.

12. Float your mouse pointer over the *Start* column header, click the pick list button, and then select the *Sort Ascending* item on the menu.

13. Float your mouse pointer over the *% Complete* column, click the pick list button, and then select the *Hide Column* item on the menu.

14. Float your mouse pointer over the Project Name column header, click the pick list button, and then select the *Configure Columns* item on the menu.

15. In the *Configure Columns* dialog, select the checkbox to the left of the *% Complete* row, and then click the *OK* button. Notice how the system unhides the *% Complete* column.

16. Click the *Export to Excel* button from the *Share* section of the *Projects* ribbon.

17. If the system displays a *File Download* dialog, click the *Open* button in the dialog.

18. If you see a *Microsoft Office Excel* warning dialog concerning file formats, click the *Yes* button in the warning dialog.

19. Examine the data in the Excel workbook, and then close Microsoft Excel without saving the file.

20. Expand the *Quick Launch* menu by clicking the *Expand* icon in the upper left corner of the *Project Center* page. The *Expand* icon is the small right-pointing triangle.

Using the Project Professional 2010 User Interface

To the experienced user, the most striking new feature of Microsoft Project 2010 is the user interface, which conforms to the standard of other applications in the Microsoft Office 2010 suite, such as Word, Excel, or PowerPoint. Previous users of Microsoft Office 2007 should find this user interface familiar as well. Figure 2 - 24 displays the Microsoft Project 2010 user interface after starting the application.

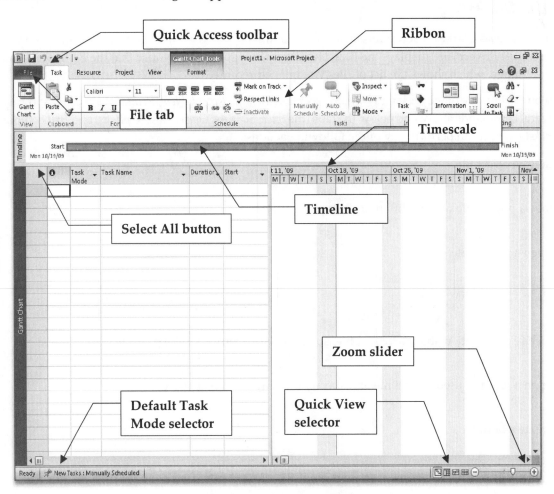

**Figure 2 - 24: Features of the Microsoft
Project 2010 User Interface**

You use these user interface features as follows:

- Use the *Ribbon* to access commands found on menus in previous versions of Microsoft Project.

- Use the *File* tab to access all file-related commands, such as open, save, print, etc.

- Use the *Quick Access Toolbar* to display frequently used commands such as open, undo, save, etc.

- Use the *Timeline* to view the current progress of the project in any task view, such as the *Gantt Chart* view or the *Tracking Gantt* view.

- Right-click on the *Select All* button to apply a different table in the current view.

- Use the *Timescale* to determine the current level of zoom applied to the active project.

- Use the *Zoom slider* to quickly zoom to pre-set levels of zoom in the *Gantt Chart* view.

- Use the *Quick View* selector to apply four of the most commonly used views.

- Use the *Default Task Mode* selector to determine the default *Task Mode* for new tasks in the project.

Using the Backstage

Click the *File* tab to access the most commonly used file commands, such as *Open, Save,* and *Print*. When you click the *File* tab, Microsoft Project 2010 displays the *Backstage* shown in Figure 2 - 25. Notice that the *Backstage* defaults to the *Recent Projects* page, which shows the list of files you opened recently.

The menu on the left side of the *Backstage* contains six tabs (the *Info, Recent, New, Print, Save & Send,* and *Help* tabs), as well as several commands above and below the tabs (the *Save, Save As, Open, Close, Options,* and *Exit* commands). Using the *Backstage,* you can perform any of the following actions:

- Save a project file.

- Save a project file using a different file type.

- Open a project file.

- Close a project file.

- Specify information about a project file, such as the properties for the project.

- Open a recently used project file and specify the number of recently used files.

- Create a new project file.

- Print a project file.

- Share a project file with others.

- Access Microsoft Project 2010 Help topics.

- Specify options settings for the active project, for all new projects, and for the application.

- Exit Microsoft Project 2010.

 You may also see an *Add-ins* command item below the *Options* item in the *Backstage* menu if your system has an add-in that Microsoft Project 2010 recognizes, such as a Bluetooth device.

While in the *Backstage*, if you decide not to perform any action, click the *File* tab again to exit the *Backstage* and return to the Project Professional 2010 main screen.

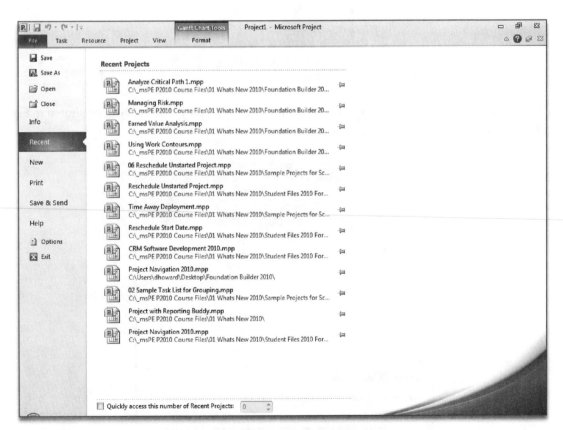

Figure 2 - 25: Microsoft Project 2010 Backstage

Using the Ribbon

Perhaps the most noticeable new feature in Project Professional 2010 is the *Ribbon,* which replaces the familiar system of menus found in all previous versions of Microsoft Project. These familiar menus included *File, Edit, View, Insert, Format,* etc. Replacing these menus are a series of ribbon tabs that display the *Task* ribbon, the *Resource* ribbon, the *Project* ribbon, the *View* ribbon, and the *Format* ribbon for the current view.

Microsoft Project 2010 displays the *Task* ribbon by default on application startup. The *Task* ribbon contains all of the buttons and commands you need for task planning. Figure 2 - 26 shows the *Task* ribbon.

Figure 2 - 26: Task ribbon

The system organizes the buttons and commands on the *Task* ribbon into eight sections, which include the *View, Clipboard, Font, Schedule, Tasks, Insert, Properties,* and *Editing* sections. The *Font* section also includes the *Font Dialog Launcher* icon, shown in Figure 2 - 27.

**Figure 2 - 27: Font Dialog
Launcher icon**

When you click the *Font Dialog Launcher* icon, Microsoft Project 2010 displays the *Font* dialog shown in Figure 2 - 28. This dialog is the same *Font* dialog used previously in Microsoft Office Project 2007.

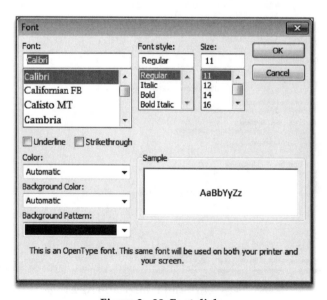

Figure 2 - 28: Font dialog

Use the first four ribbons in Project Professional 2010 as follows:

- Use the *Task* ribbon for all aspects of task planning

- Use the *Resource* ribbon to manage the resources in your project.

- Use the *Project* ribbon to specify high-level information about your project, such as saving a baseline, or to generate reports for your project.

- Use the *View* ribbon to apply task and resource views in your project, and to apply tables, filters, and groups in the view you select. You can also use the *View* ribbon to zoom the *Timescale* and to run macros.

You can only use the *Format* ribbon with the current view applied in the active project. Before you click the *Format* tab, select a view to format (such as the *Gantt Chart* view), and then click the *Format* tab. Microsoft Project 2010 displays the *Format* ribbon for the current view, and allows you to customize that view. Figure 2 - 29 shows the *Format* ribbon for the *Gantt Chart* view. Notice in Figure 2 - 29 that the software indicates I am editing the *Gantt Chart* view by the *Gantt Chart Tools* header above the *Format* tab. Remember that the *Format* ribbon shows the appropriate formatting options for **only** the current view. This means that the buttons and commands on the *Format* ribbon vary widely depending on the formatting options available for the current view.

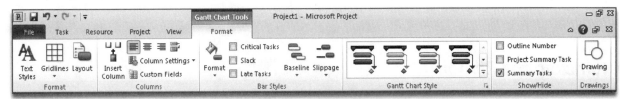

Figure 2 - 29: Format ribbon for the Gantt Chart view

 ## Hands On Exercise

Exercise 2-2

Explore the *Ribbon* and the *Backstage* in Microsoft Project 2010.

1. Launch Microsoft Project 2010, if necessary.

2. Click the *File* tab and then click the *Open* item in the *Backstage* menu.

3. Navigate to the folder containing the course sample files and then open the **Project Navigation 2010.mpp** sample file.

4. Click the *Task, Resource, Project, View,* and *Format* tabs individually and study the buttons available on each ribbon.

5. Click the *File* tab again to display the *Backstage*.

6. In the *Information* page of the *Backstage,* click the *Project Information* pick list (upper right corner of the page) and choose the *Advanced Properties* item on the list.

7. Enter your name in the *Author* field and then click the *OK* button.

8. Click *Recent, New, Print, Save & Send,* and *Help* tabs in the *Backstage* and study the options available on each page.

9. Click the *Save* button to save the project.

10. Click the *File* tab and then click the *Close* button to close the sample file.

Collapsing the Ribbon

Microsoft Project 2010 allows you to expand and collapse the *Ribbon* by double-clicking the ribbon tab currently selected. When you collapse the *Ribbon,* you can see more tasks in the active project.

> You can also collapse the ribbon by right-clicking on any ribbon tab and selecting the *Minimize the Ribbon* item on the shortcut menu.

Customizing the Ribbon

You can customize the *Ribbon* by adding ribbon tabs, ribbon groups, and ribbon buttons. To begin the process of customizing the *Ribbon,* complete the following steps:

1. Click the *File* tab.

2. In the *Backstage,* click the *Options* item.

3. In the *Project Options* dialog, click the *Customize Ribbon* section in the left side of the dialog.

> The fastest way to access the *Customize Ribbon* section of the *Project Options* dialog is to right-click on any ribbon tab and then click the *Customize the Ribbon* item on the shortcut menu.

The system displays the *Project Options* dialog with the *Customize Ribbon* section displayed, as shown in Figure 2 - 30. Notice in the figure that the *Customize Ribbon* section of the *Project Options* dialog contains two sections:

- Use the *Choose Commands From* section to locate the commands you want to add to the *Ribbon.*

- Use the *Customize the Ribbon* section to display the ribbon(s) you want to customize.

Click the *Choose Commands From* pick list to choose the type of commands you want to add to the *Ribbon.* The pick list offers you the following choices: *Popular Commands* (the default setting), *Commands Not in the Ribbon, All Commands, Macros, File Tab, All Tabs, Main Tabs, Tool Tabs,* and *Custom Tabs and Groups.* Select your option on the *Choose Commands From* pick list.

Click the *Customize the Ribbon* pick list and choose which ribbon tabs to display in the dialog. You have three choices: *Main Tabs* (the default setting), *Tool Tabs* (used for formatting views), and *All Tabs* (offers both the *Main Tabs* and the *Tool Tabs*). Select your option on the *Customize the Ribbon* pick list.

After you select your options on the *Choose Commands From* pick list and the *Customize the Ribbon* pick list, you are ready to customize the *Ribbon*. The software offers you multiple choices for customizing the *Ribbon*:

- Show or hide a ribbon tab.

- Create a new ribbon tab.

- Create a ribbon group in a new or existing ribbon tab.

- Add or remove buttons on a default or custom ribbon tab.

- Rename a ribbon tab, a ribbon group, or a button.

- Move buttons, ribbon groups, and ribbon tabs on the *Ribbon*.

- Reset the *Ribbon* to its default settings.

- Import or export the customized *Ribbon* and *Quick Access Toolbar* settings to a file.

Figure 2 - 30: Project Options dialog, Customize Ribbon section

Importing Custom Ribbon Settings

Microsoft Project 2010 allows you to import the *Ribbon* customization settings from a file so that you can import ribbon customizations created by another user. To import a customized *Ribbon*, click the *Import/Export* pick list button and select the *Import Customization File* item on the pick list. The system displays the *File Open* dialog shown in Figure 2 - 31. In the *File Open* dialog, navigate to the location of the customization file and select it, and then click the *Open* button.

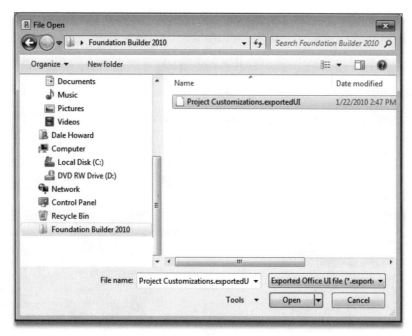

Figure 2 - 31: File Open dialog

The system displays the confirmation dialog shown in Figure 2 - 32. In the confirmation dialog, click the *Yes* button to import the customized *Ribbon* and *Quick Access Toolbar* settings, and replace your current *Ribbon* and *Quick Access Toolbar*. Click the *OK* button to close the *Project Options* dialog and view your new customized *Ribbon* and *Quick Access Toolbar*.

**Figure 2 - 32: Warning dialog when importing
a customized Ribbon**

Using the Quick Access Toolbar

Perhaps the least noticeable new feature in Project Professional 2010 is the *Quick Access Toolbar*. By default, the *Quick Access Toolbar* appears **above** the *Ribbon*, in the upper left corner of the application window, as shown in Figure 2 - 33. Notice that the *Quick Access Toolbar* contains only a few buttons, including the *Save, Undo*, and *Redo* buttons.

Figure 2 - 33: Quick Access Toolbar above the Ribbon

You use the *Quick Access Toolbar* to provide quick access to the buttons you use most often. For example, many users like to add the *Open* and *Print* buttons to the *Quick Access Toolbar*. Microsoft Project 2010 allows you to customize the *Quick Access Toolbar* in two ways:

- Move the *Quick Access Toolbar* below the *Ribbon*.

- Add or remove buttons on the *Quick Access Toolbar*.

To move the *Quick Access Toolbar* below the *Ribbon*, right-click anywhere on the *Quick Access Toolbar* and then select the *Show Quick Access Toolbar Below the Ribbon* item on the shortcut menu. To customize the *Quick Access Toolbar*, right-click anywhere on the *Quick Access Toolbar* and select the *Customize Quick Access Toolbar* item on the shortcut menu. The system displays the *Project Options* dialog with the *Quick Access Toolbar* tab selected. You customize the *Quick Access Toolbar* in exactly the same manner as you customize the *Ribbon*. Because of this, I do not repeat these steps again. Refer back to the *Customizing the Ribbon* section of this module for help, if necessary.

Hands On Exercise

Exercise 2-3

Import *Ribbon* and *Quick Access Toolbar* customization settings from a file.

1. In Project Professional 2010, right-click anywhere on the *Ribbon* and select the *Customize the Ribbon* item on the shortcut menu.

2. In the *Project Options* dialog, click the *Import/Export* pick list button and select the *Import customization file* item on the list.

3. In the *File Open* dialog, navigate to the folder where you unzipped your sample files for class.

4. Select the **Project Server 2010 Ribbon tab.exportedUI** file and then click the *Open* button.

5. When prompted in the confirmation dialog, click the *Yes* button to replace all existing customizations.

6. Click the *OK* button to close the *Project Options* dialog.

7. Right-click anywhere on the *Quick Access Toolbar* (in the upper left corner of the Microsoft Project 2010 application window) and select the *Show Quick Access Toolbar Below the Ribbon* item on the shortcut menu.

Creating a Login Account in Project Professional 2010

Before you can use Project Professional 2010 in your organization's Project Server environment, you must create a login account so that you can log in to Project Server 2010. You have two options available to you for creating a Project Server login account. You can do this by launching the *Microsoft Project Server 2010 Accounts* tool under the *Office Tools* folder in the *Office* folder in your *Start* menu, or you can launch Project Professional 2010 and complete the following steps:

1. Click the *File* tab and select the *Info* tab on the left hand navigation menu, and then click the *Manage Accounts* button in the *Project Server Accounts* section of the *Information* page shown in Figure 2 - 34.

Figure 2 - 34: Project 2010 Information Page

2. After you click the *Manage Accounts* button, the system displays the *Project Server Accounts* dialog shown in Figure 2 - 35.

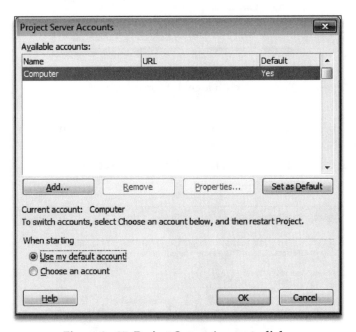

Figure 2 - 35: Project Server Accounts dialog

3. Click the *Add* button and the system displays the *Account Properties* dialog shown in Figure 2 - 36.

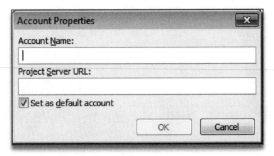

Figure 2 - 36: Account Properties dialog

4. Enter a friendly name for your new account in the *Account Name* field and enter a valid URL in the *Project Server URL* field. You must enter the URL with the **http:// or https://** prefix. Select the *Set as default account* option. Figure 2 - 37 shows the completed *Account Properties* dialog for the new account that connects to my organization's production Project Server 2010 instance.

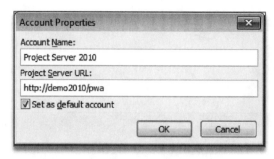

**Figure 2 - 37: Account Properties dialog
with login information**

5. Click the *OK* button. If you enter a URL using the http:// protocol rather than the secure https:// protocol, the system displays the warning dialog shown in Figure 2 - 38. Ignore the warning unless your server requires a secure URL. Click the *Yes* button to continue if you see this warning.

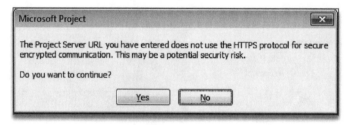

Figure 2 - 38: Security warning dialog

6. The system redisplays the *Project Server Accounts* dialog with your new account, as shown in Figure 2 - 39.

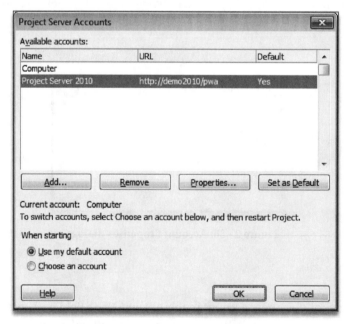

**Figure 2 - 39: Project Server Accounts dialog
with new account information entered**

7. In the *Project Server Accounts* dialog, select the *Choose an account* option. This is particularly important if you connect to multiple Project Server instances and if you want to completely control the connection state.

 MsProjectExperts recommends that you always select the *Choose an account* option. This provides better control for users who connect to multiple instances and allows for better control of off-line feature use.

8. Using steps #3-7, create an additional Project Server login account for each instance of your Project Server 2010 system, such as for test or training Project Server instances.

9. Click the *OK* button to close the *Project Server Accounts* dialog.

Logging into Project Server from Project Professional 2010

After you create your Project Server login account profiles in Project Professional 2010, exit and then re-launch the software. This is a necessary step because creating your login accounts does not connect you to a Project Server instance. The system displays the *Login* dialog shown in Figure 2 - 40. Because you selected the *Choose an account* option in the *Project Server Accounts* dialog, the system allows you to select the Project Server instance for connection. Had you not chosen this option, the system automatically connects to the instance you set as default.

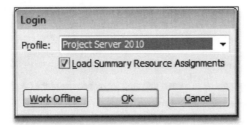

Figure 2 - 40: Login dialog

The *Login* dialog pre-selects the account you set as the default account in the *Project Server Accounts* dialog. If you wish to connect using a different login account, click the *Profile* pick list and select a different account, such as the Project Server 2010 Training account shown in Figure 2 - 41.

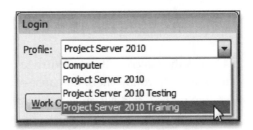

Figure 2 - 41: Select a different Profile

You can select the *Computer* profile to use Project Professional 2010 without connecting to a Project Server instance. This causes the software to function in "desktop only" mode and disables all enterprise features.

 The *Load Summary Resource Assignments* option determines how Project Professional 2010 displays resource assignment information when you open an enterprise project and apply the *Resource Usage* view. If you select this option, the *Resource Usage* view displays resource assignments for the current project **plus** a single line for each additional project in which the resource is assigned to tasks. If you deselect this option, the *Resource Usage* view displays resource assignments only for the current project.

Click the *OK* button to connect to your desired Project Server instance. If the system cannot connect to the selected Project Server instance, it displays the *Could not connect to Server* dialog shown in Figure 2 - 42.

Figure 2 - 42: Could not connect to Server warning

If you see the dialog shown in Figure 2 - 42, click the *Cancel* button to return to the *Login* dialog and then click the *Cancel* button in the *Login* dialog. At this point, you must troubleshoot the cause of the login problem, which is likely one of the four possible reasons previously shown in the *Could not connect to Server* warning dialog.

Hands On Exercise

Exercise 2-4

Create a login account in Project Professional 2010 for a Project Server 2010 instance.

1. Click the *File* tab and select the *Info* tab on the left hand navigation menu.

2. Click the *Manage Accounts* button in the *Project Server Accounts* section of the *Information* page.

3. In the *Project Server Accounts* dialog, click the *Add* button.

4. In the *Account Properties* dialog, enter the name *Project Server 2010 Sample* in the *Account Name* field.

5. In the *Account Properties* dialog, enter the URL for your Project Server instance in the *Project Server URL* field.

If you do not intend to use the Project Server 2010 instance included with the sample files for this book, enter a URL for one of your own organization's Project Server instances in the *Account Properties* dialog.

6. Click the *OK* button to close the *Account Properties* dialog.

7. If you see a warning dialog about using the HTTPS protocol, click the *Yes* button to continue.

8. In the *Project Server Accounts* dialog, select the *Choose an account* option.

9. Click the *OK* button to close the *Project Server Accounts* dialog.

10. Exit Project Professional 2010 and then relaunch the application.

11. In the *Login* dialog, click the *OK* button to connect to the *Project Server 2010 Sample* instance.

12. Exit Project Professional 2010 again.

Module 03

Creating New Proposed Projects

Learning Objectives

After completing this module, you will be able to:

- Understand lifecycle management
- Understand phases and stages in a workflow
- Create a new project proposal
- Add a resource plan to a proposal
- Build a team for a resource plan

Inside Module 03

Understanding Lifecycle Management

One of the most exciting new capabilities Project Server 2010 provides is a sophisticated demand, decision-making and lifecycle management system. This system allows your organization to capture project requests and work through a manual or automated procedure to collect information about proposed projects and ultimately use Project Server 2010's new Portfolio decision-making tools to select the organization's portfolio of projects and then manage each project through an appropriate governance lifecycle.

Project Server 2010 provides a complete cradle-to-grave lifecycle management capability by combining a built-in proposal creation process with the decision-making tools that were formerly included with Microsoft Office Portfolio Server 2007, and the ability to govern the end-to-end process using a workflow that moves projects through a series of user-defined *Stages*. You can define lifecycles (workflows) to control all types of governance or process lifecycles.

The sample workflow that ships with Project Server 2010 uses the predefined enterprise custom fields with the names that start with the word *sample*. The system also contains pre-defined *Phases*, *Stages*, and *Project Detail Pages (PDPs)* used to construct an example of an end-to-end lifecycle. Microsoft provides this sample to help you understand how lifecycle management works, so I use this as my example for this module as well.

The highest form of automated governance you can achieve using Project Server 2010 is to apply workflows to your project types specifically customized for each type of project you allow into the system. With a workflow, you can automate business logic, interact with external data systems, and create multiple branching decision trees–all of this limited only by your development capabilities. Even when you use only simple linear workflows, you can establish powerful governance control of your organization's project lifecycle(s). To get up and running quickly with workflows in Project Server 2010, you can customize the sample workflow to some extent, you can explore third-party solutions that provide graphical interfaces for building sophisticated workflows, or you can use Microsoft's Dynamic Workflow starter solution.

Understanding Demand Management

Project Server 2010 provides you with the tools for very basic demand management without using workflows by providing the ability to display multiple *Project Detail Pages* in the project drilldown window in Project Web App. Those of you who have worked with earlier versions of Project Server will be astounded with the changes Microsoft made to this window, which now has the ability to display multiple project information pages as well as provide an interface to edit the project itself. I teach you about editing projects in Project Web App in Module 16, *Working with the Project Center and Project Views*. The most basic form of demand management you can perform uses this window to display *Project Detail Pages* that expose required fields for a specific *Project Type*. When a user creates an instance of that *Project Type*, the system compels the user to fill in the required fields before completing the initial save. When you add workflows to this equation, your company can build extremely complex demand and lifecycle management scenarios.

Understanding Decision Management

Project Server provides decision support tools integrated from previous versions of Portfolio Server. To force projects through a selection process that includes a portfolio analysis step, you must govern your projects using a workflow. Of course, you can use the portfolio analysis capabilities without a workflow, without limiting your analysis ability, which is largely a function of the metadata you capture and create for use in your analyses. Some organizations choose to implement Project Server strictly for portfolio analysis and not for project management.

Introducing Project Types

Project Types are an important innovation in the Project Server 2010 metadata architecture. They give you the ability to establish, as the feature name suggests, project types. The important thing to know about *Project Types* is that you use them to connect workflows with *Enterprise Project Templates* and *Project Site Templates.* This is a very big advance in Project Server's capabilities. Previous versions of Project Server were limited to using only one template for all *Project Workspaces* (Project Server 2007). The system now supports multiple *Project Site* (Project Server 2010) templates connected through *Project Types,* which also gives you the ability to specify a unique base project template for each project type.

A *Project Type* consists of a *Project Template,* a set of *Project Detail Pages,* an optional *Workflow* and a *Project Site* template. You can associate a *Project Type* with one or more departments in Project Server. Figure 3 - 1 shows an illustration of the collection of objects contained in the definition of a *Project Type.*

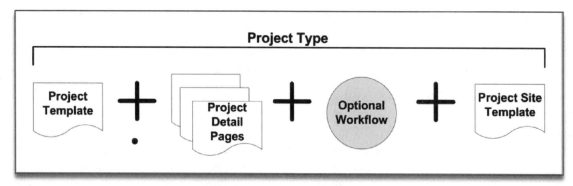

Figure 3 - 1: Project Type Representation

 When an *Enterprise Project Type* does not have an associated workflow, an Administrator must specifiy the PDPs that display for the EPT. When an *Enterprise Project Type* does have a workflow, the display of PDPs is controlled by the workflow.

- A **Project Template** is a pre-built schedule model that ideally contains a well-structured schedule with generic resources assigned to tasks as well as duration and effort information that the author estimated in the template. To the degree that the template can eliminate manual schedule building, the more valuable it is to the managers who use them. When your Project Server administrator does not specify a specific project template for a *Project Type,* the system uses a blank project template.

- **Project Detail Pages** are web-part based web pages that your Project Server administrator creates to display and collect project related information. *Project Detail Pages* appear in the Project drilldown window in Project Server Web App. Sometimes a workflow controls the display of PDPs while *Project Types* that are not associated with a workflow allow users to select through the pages manually without the system governing the order of their access. *Project Detail Pages* can contain Project Server 2010 enterprise custom fields and other web parts that display information, or interact with data such as an Excel Services workbook. These can also contain InfoPath forms integrated programmatically.

- **Workflows** are code-based solutions that can control the entire lifecycle flow of projects in Project Server 2010, from proposal through project closure. Workflows can contain very sophisticated business logic such as processing a project request through an automated criteria-based selection or rejection process. Complex workflows can contain multi-branching process logic and can interact with external data sources. Microsoft Project Server 2010 contains one sample workflow that you can use with the *Sample Proposal* that ships with the system. The sample workflow interacts with the portfolio analysis and selection tool in Project Server 2010, forcing project approval through that process. The system requires a workflow to accomplish this.

- **Project Site Templates** are what Project Server uses to create project sites for new projects (formerly named *Project Workspaces* in previous editions). Your Project Server administrator can build new project site templates to meet the specific requirements of your project types, rather than living with the one-size-fits-all model used in previous Project Server versions. If your Project Server administrator does not specify a *Project Site* template for a *Project Type*, the system uses the default *Project Site* template.

Understanding Phases and Stages

To support lifecycle management through workflow, Microsoft Project Server 2010 provides standard lifecycle elements *Phases* and *Stages*. *Phases* are a collection containing at least one *Stage* that contains at least one *Project Detail Page*. While *Phases* primarily serve as containers or groupings, *Stages* contain a number of properties and constituents that support a governance flow.

Figure 3 - 2 shows the *Workflow Stages* page which displays the *Phases* and *Stages* Microsoft ships to support the sample workflow. You cannot access this page unless you have administrator rights in the system.

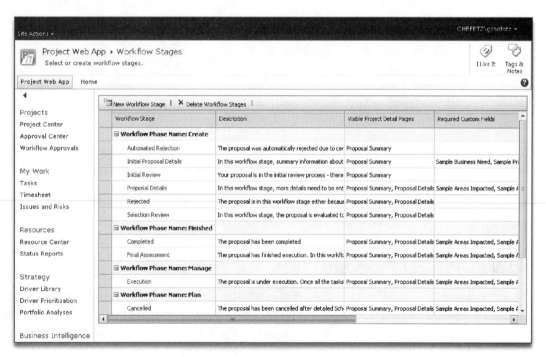

Figure 3 - 2: Workflow Stages page

Notice in the figure that the sample *Stages* are grouped by their respective *Phase*. Notice also that the *Create* workflow phase contains six stages: Automated Rejection, Initial Proposal Details, Initial Review, Proposal Details, Rejected and

Selection Review. Each of these *Stages* represents a step in the sample workflow and contains at least one PDP. Your Project Server administrator can define *Project Detail Pages* in a variety of ways to include required fields as well as to apply automated progress control in and out of stages using workflow.

Understanding Project Detail Pages

The base element of the Phase/Stage construct is the *Project Detail Page* or PDP. A PDP is a special kind of web part page that displays in the project drilldown window. While *Stages* can contain more than one PDP, they must contain at least one PDP and often contain multiple PDPs that may show up in multiple stages. In fact, it is common that the system always displays a page that shows the current state of the workflow in every stage, it is also common for the schedule page to display within numerous stages.

From the Project Web App *Quick Launch* menu, select the *Project Center* link from the *Project* section. The system displays the *Project Center* shown in Figure 3 - 3.

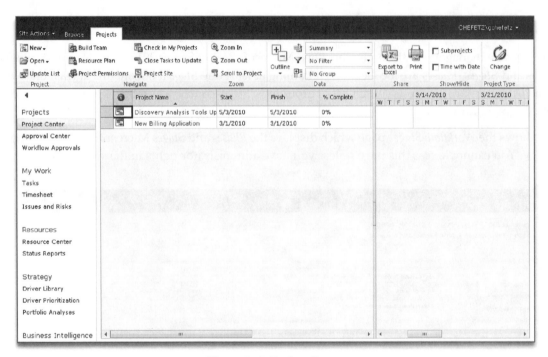

Figure 3 - 3: Project Center

Creating a New Project Proposal

The proposal construct and implementation in Project Server 2010 is radically different than Project Server 2007, as you might imagine with the all the new functionality and supporting elements that I just described. For 2007, proposals were a distinct entity and contained functionality unique to the proposal feature. In 2010, this separate construct is gone in favor of workflow.

Definition of a Proposal in Project Server 2010

Simply put, a proposal is a normal Project Server project record defined as a proposal by its state in a workflow. Unlike its predecessor, Project Server 2010 makes this a soft construct rather than a hard construct. In the 2007 model, you converted a proposal into a full-fledged project, in the 2010 model; you release it into production using a select or reject process.

Initiating a Proposal

For this example, I use the *Sample Proposal* project type that installs with Project Server 2010. To invoke the sample workflow you click on the *New* menu in the upper left corner of the *Projects* ribbon and select the *Sample Proposal* item from the pick list shown in Figure 3 - 4.

Figure 3 - 4: New menu

When you click on the selection, the system starts a new instance of the *Sample Proposal* workflow and displays the first *Project Detail Page* shown in Figure 3 - 5.

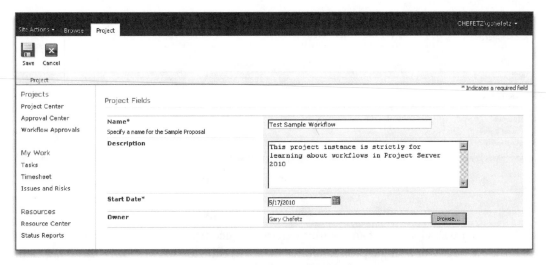

Figure 3 - 5: Sample Proposal Initiation page

Notice that this page contains only three fields accepting user entry, *Name, Description* and *Start Date*. Notice also, the asterisks at the end of the *Name* field and *Start Date* field, which indicate that these are required fields. You cannot save your entries on this page until you provide information in these fields. After you complete your entries, click the *Save* button in the *Project* section of the *Project* ribbon. Note that after clicking the button, the system displays a series of messages in upper right hand corner of the screen to indicate that it is working on your request. The first message you see is *Processing* followed by *Creating Sample Proposal* as shown in Figure 3 - 6.

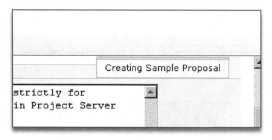

Figure 3 - 6: Processing messages

When the processing completes, the system displays the *Workflow Status* page shown in Figure 3 - 7. This is the second *Project Detail Page* that the system displays in the sample workflow process.

Figure 3 - 7: Workflow Status page

Keep in mind that you are still looking at and working in the project drilldown window in Project Web App, which now displays multiple pages for a single project. Notice that above the top left section of the *Quick Launch* you now see an additional navigation section for the project that you are in the process of creating, in my case "Test Sample Workflow," and that the project displays as selected in the menu. Every stage in a workflow has a *Workflow Status* page. The *Workflow Status* page always displays by default when you first enter a stage. Below the project name selection is another link, *Proposal Summary*. This link corresponds with the one shown in the table in the middle of the page in the *Available Pages in this Workflow Stage* section. All *Project Detail Pages* that are available for the current stage are accessible from either the left hand navigation or the *Workflow Status* page. When you click the link in one of the sections, the system displays the selected *Project Detail Page*. Figure 3 - 8 shows the *Proposal Summary*.

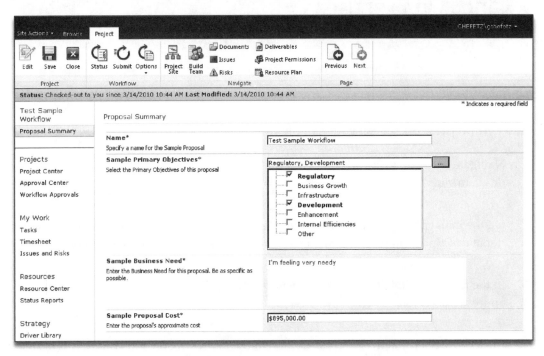

Figure 3 - 8: Proposal Summary page

Enter your own clever choices and remarks in these fields, including a value in the *Sample Proposal Cost* field that is below one million dollars. It is very important that you **do not enter a value over a million dollars** if you wish to completely work through the sample workflow, as crossing this cost threshold will cause your project to be automatically rejected. I selected the *Regulatory* item from the *Sample Primary Objective* area. Notice the options available in the *Project* and *Workflow* sections of the *Project* ribbon. At this point, you can save your information and submit it later, or you can save and then click the *Submit* button. To proceed to the next workflow stage, click the *Submit* button. The system displays the *Message from webpage* dialog shown in Figure 3 - 9.

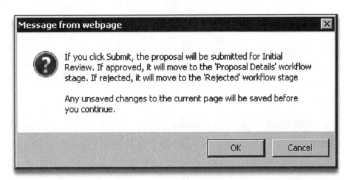

Figure 3 - 9: Message from Webpage dialog

Click the *OK* button to continue. The system accepts your input and moves the workflow to an approval checkpoint where an authorized approver must approve the initial request before it moves to the next stage in the workflow.

Hands On Exercise

Exercise 3-1

Create a new project proposal using the sample workflow.

1. Navigate to the *Project Center* and click the *New* pick list and select *Sample Proposal* from the drop down menu.

2. On the initial page enter a name for your new proposed project in the *Name* field, enter an optional description in the *Description* field and select a future start date for your new project.

3. In the *Region* section of the *Proposal Summary* page, click on the ellipsis button ⬛ and choose the appropriate region.

4. Click the *Save* button in the *Project* section of the *Project* ribbon and wait for the system to create your new proposal. Notice that the system reports progress in the upper right hand corner of the display area in a yellow rectangle. Progress indicators include *Processing, Creating Sample Proposal,* and *Save completed successfully.* Depending on the speed of your system, not all of these may have time to display on the screen.

5. When the system displays the *Workflow Status* page, select the *Proposal Summary* item from either the *Quick Launch* menu or the data grid in the center of the page.

6. On the *Proposal Summary* page, click on the ellipsis button ⬛ in the *Sample Primary Objectives* section and select values accordingly, then enter a sentence or two in the *Sample Business Need* field. Enter a cost by using numbers only in the *Sample Proposal Cost* field, but do not enter a value that exceeds $1,000,000.00 unless you want to test the automatic rejection feature. Note: If you enter a value exceeding one million dollars, you cannot complete the entire series of exercises in this module.

7. Click the *Save* button from the *Project* section of the *Project* ribbon.

8. After the system completes the save action, click the *Submit* button from the *Workflow* section of the *Project* ribbon.

9. When the system prompts, click the *OK* button in the *Message from webpage* dialog. Wait until the system completes processing and redisplays the *Workflow Status* page.

Approving a New Project Proposal

To both view and approve the request, select the *Workflow Approvals* link from the *Project* section of the *Quick Launch* menu. The system displays the *Project Server Workflow Tasks My Tasks* page, which contains the *Workflow Approvals* page, shown in Figure 3 - 10.

Figure 3 - 10: Workflow Approvals page

Notice the *Approval required for project: 'Test Sample Workflow'* item that appears on the list. Note also that this is a standard SharePoint task list. Float your mouse pointer over the item to reveal the checkbox next to the item and select the checkbox. The page display changes to reveal the *Workflow Approvals* page shown in Figure 3 - 11.

 The approval step in this case does not authorize the project for execution, it simply authorizes the project to move to the next stage in the workflow.

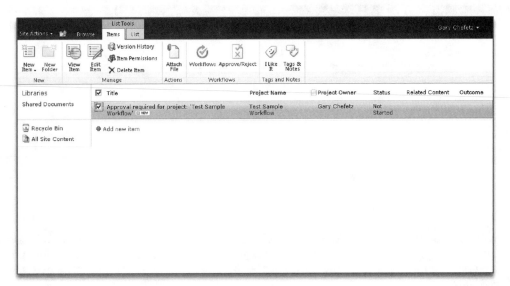

Figure 3 - 11: Workflow Approvals page with item selected

After you select the item, the *List Tools* ribbon appears. Select the *Edit Item* button from the *Manage* section of the ribbon. The system opens the item for editing in the dialog shown in Figure 3 - 12.

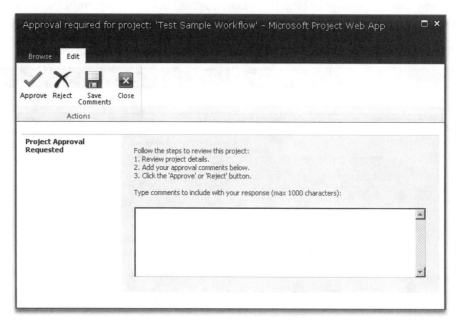

Figure 3 - 12: Edit Approval Item

The *Sample Workflow* requires that one person with approval rights approve the request. The system also supports *Majority* and *Consensus* approval types. Notice that you can approve, reject, or simply add and save comments before closing the item. In this case, you want to select the *Approve* button from the *Actions* section of the ribbon to approve the request and move it forward in the workflow. The system redisplays the *Workflow Approvals* page, which now shows that you have approved the request and can move to the next workflow stage after the *Initial Request* stage as shown in Figure 3 - 13.

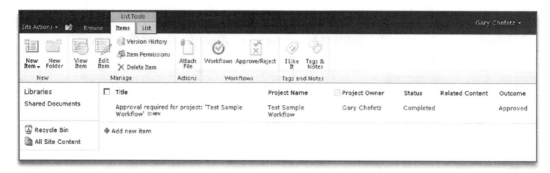

Figure 3 - 13: Workflow request approved

Warning: To proceed with the workflow, your account must be a member of the *Portfolio Managers* security group, and the *Administrators* security group, or you must log on using an account that is a member of both groups. This may or may not be the case for all workflows, as this is determined in the workflow.

Hands On Exercise

Exercise 3-2

Approve your new proposal for further development. Note that your account must be a member of the *Portfolio Managers* security group in order to perform this exercise. If your current account is not a member of the *Portfolio Managers* security group, log on to Project Web App with an account in this group.

1. Select the *Workflow Approvals* link from the *Projects* section of the *Quick Launch* menu

2. Locate the approval record for the proposal you created, float your mouse pointer over the time to reveal the checkbox next to the item and select it.

3. In the *Manage* section of the *List Tools* ribbon, click the *Edit Item* button.

4. In the resulting dialog window, enter comments in the *Comments* field and click the *Approve* button from the *Actions* section of the *Edit* ribbon. The system returns to the *Workflow Approvals* page.

Completing the Sample Workflow Proposal Details Stage

Once approved, the project proposal advances to the *Proposal Details* stage, which displays five *Project Detail Pages* in addition to the *Workflow Status* page as shown in Figure 3 - 14. Notice the series of pages listed in the left-hand navigation as well as the grid in the *Available Pages in this Workflow Stage* section of the page. Notice the status of each page in the grid display. Before you can advance to the next workflow stage, you must complete the pages marked as incomplete. After completing the required information for all of the PDPs shown in the *Proposal Details* stage, the workflow moves the project into the *Select* phase, where the workflow waits for selection using the portfolio analysis tools where your new project must be committed to the portfolio before you can move on to the *Planning* phase.

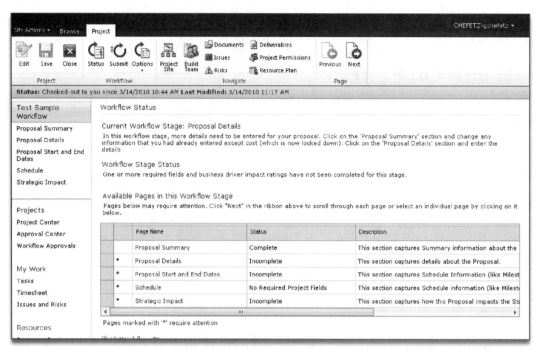

Figure 3 - 14: Project Details Workflow Stage

Behind the scenes, the workflow has already processed some custom business logic included in the automated rejection stage. The stages of the workflow that you advanced through are as shown in Figure 3 - 15.

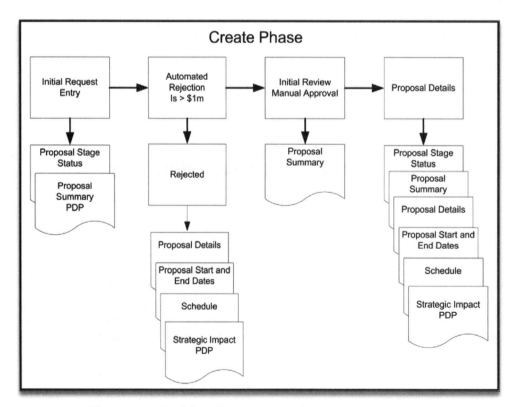

Figure 3 - 15: Workflow Stages for Sample Proposal Create Phase

Behind the scenes, the system created a project file, in this case the default blank project file because the sample does not specify an enterprise project template. It also created a *Project Site* using the custom enterprise template specified for the workflow; in this case, it used the default *Project Site* template because the sample does not specify a custom *Project Site* template.

Your sample workflow is now in the *Proposal Details* stage, a point at which numerous PDPs are exposed, many of which require your attention. You must provide required information before the system will allow you to submit your proposal to the next stage of the workflow unless either the automated or manual initial selection process already rejected your proposal or someone manually rejected it. When you select your started proposal from the *Project Center*, your started proposal should open to the *Workflow Status Page*. Notice that there are three pages marked as incomplete and one that has no required fields. Select the *Proposal Details* link from either the left hand navigation or the grid in the middle of the page. The system displays the *Sample Proposal Details* page shown in Figure 3 - 16.

You can save your information at any time during a workflow and return to the proposal later to complete it. Depending on the design of the workflow, your project may be governed by it from initiation through project closure.

Figure 3 - 16: Sample Proposal Details page

To continue your tour of the sample workflow, add entries to the page and use the *Save* button on the *Project* ribbon to save your entries on each page. The next page that requires attention is the *Proposal Start and Finish Dates* page shown in Figure 3 - 17.

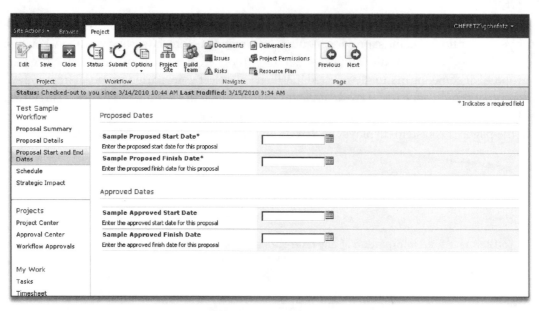

Figure 3 - 17: Proposal Start and Finish Dates page

Provide information in the required fields marked with an asterisk and click the *Save* button to save your entries. Click on the *Schedule* page link and the system displays the *Schedule* page shown in Figure 3 - 18.

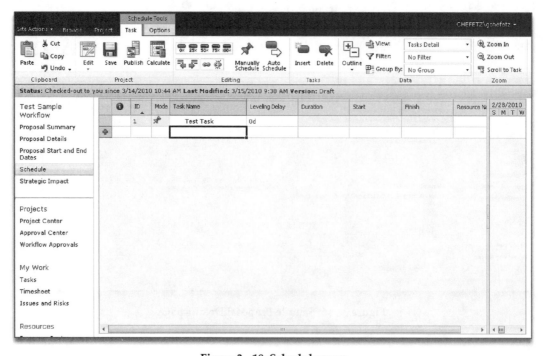

Figure 3 - 18: Schedule page

The *Schedule* page exposes the project schedule for editing. Notice in Figure 3 - 18 that I entered a "Test Task" name to create a single task in the new schedule. At this point in the workflow, there is no requirement for the project to have a developed schedule and there are no required entries for this page. If the sample workflow had an enterprise project template attached, the template schedule would display now. When you click on the *Strategic Impact* link on the left hand menu, the system opens the *Strategic Impact* page shown in Figure 3 - 19.

Figure 3 - 19: Strategic Impact page

The *Project Strategic Impact* web part displays the appropriate business drivers based on the department to which the *Project Type* and Business Drivers belong. You must provide information in the page to analyze your portfolio using strategic alignment analysis. The sample workflow includes this page because its creator designed it to use the portfolio analysis capability to select projects for execution.

Warning: Because the system does not include any predefined business drivers, your Project Server administrator must create business drivers before you can submit your new proposal into the selection process.

At this point, your first sample workflow should be completely through the *Proposal Details* stage and *Create* phase as shown previously in Figure 3 - 15. If you have not completed all the *Project Detail Pages* in the *Proposal Details* stage, do so at this time.

msProjectExperts recommends that before you submit your proposal, that you build a resource plan for the project in order to use Resource Constraint analysis during Portfolio Anaysis. Portfolio Managers can use resource loading from a Resource Plan or from the project plan. Because this project does not have a fully developed schedule, a Resource Plan is necessary to support Resource Constraint analysis.

The Hands On Exercises in this section do not include Resource Constraint analysis, so it is not necessary to build a resource plan at this time. I show you how to build a resource plan later in this module.

Hands On Exercise

Exercise 3-3

Complete the Sample Workflow Proposal Details Stage.

1. Return to the proposal you started in Exercise 3-1 by navigating to the *Project Center* page. Apply the *Summary* view, if necessary, and locate and select your new proposal in the grid. The system displays the *Workflow Status* page for your proposal.

2. Select the *Proposal Details* item from the *Quick Launch* menu or from the *Available Pages in this Workflow Stage* data grid in the center of the page to open the *Proposal Details* page.

3. Make any selection you like in both the *Sample Areas Impacted* and *Sample Compliance Proposal* fields by using the selection tools.

4. Enter some text in both the *Sample Assumptions* and *Sample Goals* text fields and click the *Save* button in the *Project* section of the *Project* ribbon. Wait for the save action to complete.

5. Select the *Proposal Start and End Dates* item from the *Quick Launch* menu to open the *Proposal Start and End Dates* page.

6. Select future start and end dates in both the *Sample Proposed Start Date* and *Sample Proposed Finish Date* fields using the date pickers. Leave the *Approved Dates* section blank and click the *Save* button in the *Project* section of the *Project* ribbon. Wait for the save action to complete.

7. You can ignore the *Schedule* link for now; this page displays the project schedule, which you have not built yet. If the workflow were associated with a schedule template, you would see it on this page.

8. Select the *Strategic Impact* item from the *Quick Launch* menu and rate your proposal against the available business drivers. When you complete your selections, click the *Save* button in the *Project* section of the *Project* ribbon. Wait for the save action to complete.

9. Click the *Submit* button in the *Workflow* section of the *Project* ribbon and click the *OK* button in the subsequent *Message from webpage* dialog to move your proposal to the *Selection Review* stage.

Moving a Proposal through Portfolio Selection

The next phase in the process is the *Select* phase. The *Select* phase has only two stages: *Selected* or *Not Selected*. In order for the proposal to move forward, a portfolio manager must select and commit it through a Portfolio Analysis commit action.

Creating a Driver Prioritization

The point of the steps in this section and the next is to show you how the sample workflow works and is not intended to teach you about using the Portfolio Analyses feature in 2010. Complete the steps demonstrated in this section and included in the Hands On Exercises to move your proposal to the next phase in the workflow:

1. You first need to create a driver prioritization using the business drivers your Project Server administrator provided. Click the *Driver Prioritization* selection in the *Strategy* section of the *Quick Launch* menu. The system displays the *Driver Prioritization* page shown in Figure 3 - 20.

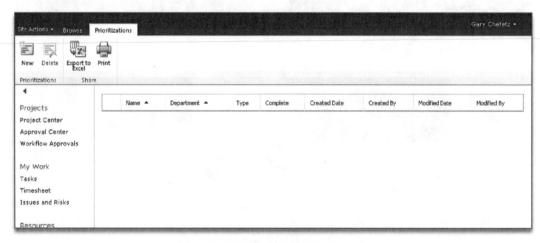

Figure 3 - 20: Driver Prioritization page

2. Click the *New* button in the *Prioritizations* section of the *Prioritizations* ribbon. The system displays the *New Driver Prioritization* page shown in Figure 3 - 21.

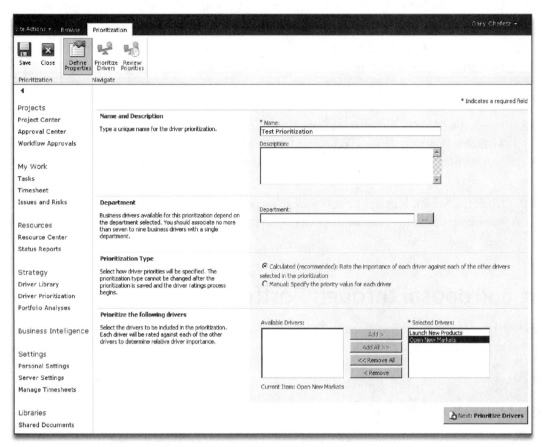

Figure 3 - 21: New Driver Prioritization page

3. Enter a name for your new prioritization, leave the *Department* selections blank, and add all of your drivers to the *Select Drivers* list in the *Prioritize the following drivers* section; then click the *Next: Prioritize Drivers* button to advance to the next page. The system displays the *Prioritize Drivers* page shown in Figure 3 - 22.

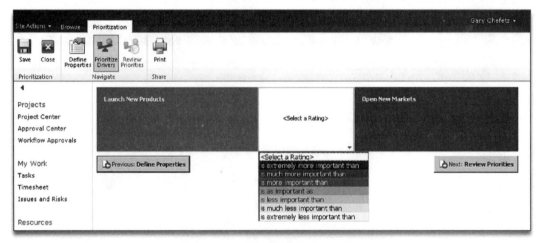

Figure 3 - 22: Prioritize Drivers Page

4. Use the *Select a Rating* pick list to prioritize your drivers. Depending on how many drivers you defined, you may need to work through more than one pair-wise comparison. Click the *Next: Review Priorities* button when you complete your entries. The system displays the *Review Priorities* page shown in Figure 3 - 23.

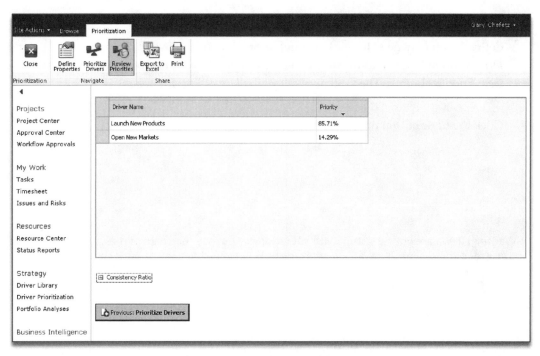

Figure 3 - 23: Review Priorities page

5. Click the *Close* button on the *Prioritization* ribbon.

Hands On Exercise

Exercise 3-4

Create a Business Driver Prioritization.

1. Click the *Driver Prioritization* link in the *Strategy* section of the *Quick Launch* menu. The system displays the *Driver Prioritization* page.

2. Click the *New* button on the *Prioritizations* ribbon. The system displays the *New Business Driver Prioritization* page.

3. In the *Name and Description* section, enter a name in the *Name* field and a description in the *Description* field for your new prioritization.

4. In the *Department* section leave the *Department* field blank. In the *Prioritization Type* section, leave the *Calculated* option selected

5. In the *Prioritize the following drivers* section add all of your drivers to the *Selected Drivers* field by clicking the *Add All* button; then click the *Next: Prioritize Drivers* button to advance to the next page. The system displays the *Compare Drivers* page.

6. Use the *Select a Rating* pick list to prioritize your drivers. Depending on how many drivers you defined, you may need to work through more than one pair-wise comparison. Click the *Next Driver* button to move to the next driver. Once you have prioritized all drivers, click the *Next: Review Priorities* button. The system displays the *Driver Priorities* page.

7. Click the *Close* button on the *Prioritization* ribbon.

Warning: If you are not consistent with your ratings, you may see an error message that warns of a low consistency ratio, meaning that you contradicted yourself when making your comparisons.

Creating a Portfolio Analysis

1. From the *Quick Launch* menu, select *Portfolio Analyses* from the *Strategy* section. The system opens the *Portfolio Analyses* page shown in Figure 3 - 24

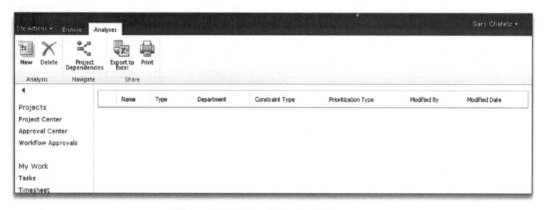

Figure 3 - 24: Portfolio Analyses page

2. Click the *New* button in the *Analysis* section of the *Analyses* ribbon. The system displays the *New Portfolio Analysis* page shown in Figure 3 - 25.

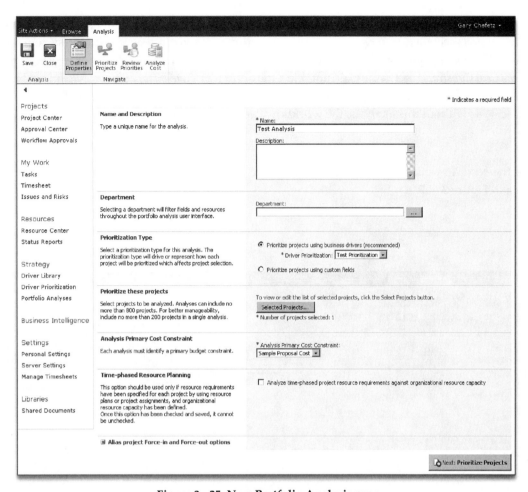

Figure 3 - 25: New Portfolio Analysis page

3.   Give your new analysis a name, leave the *Department* field blank, and in the *Prioritization Type* section select the *Prioritize projects using business drivers* option. Click the *Selected Projects* button and the system displays the *Select Projects* dialog shown in Figure 3 - 26.

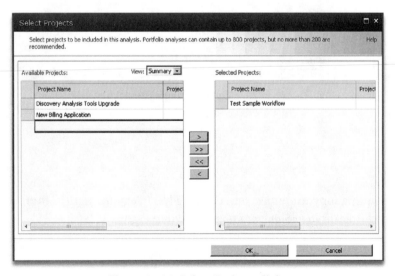

Figure 3 - 26: Select Projects dialog

4. As I did in the example in the figure, select your new proposal and use the arrow button to move it to the *Selected Projects* section on the right. Click the *OK* button when you are done, and the system returns you to the *New Portfolio Analysis* page shown previously in Figure 3 - 25. Leave the default selection in the *Analysis Primary Cost Constraint* section, and do not select the option for *Time-phased Resource Planning*. Note that this is for demonstration purposes only and that not selecting this option will ultimately stall this new project in the workflow, as without this analysis, the workflow cannot proceed.

5. Click the *Next: Prioritize Projects* button to continue. The system displays the *Driver Strategic Impact* page shown in Figure 3 - 27.

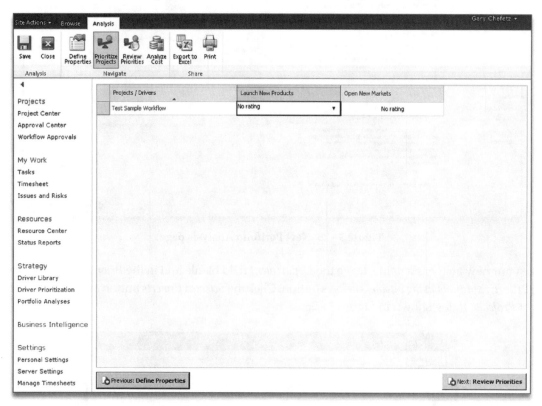

Figure 3 - 27: Driver Strategic Impact page

6. Select at least one rating for your project and click the *Next: Review Priorities* button to continue. The system displays the *Project Prioritization Summary* page shown in Figure 3 - 28.

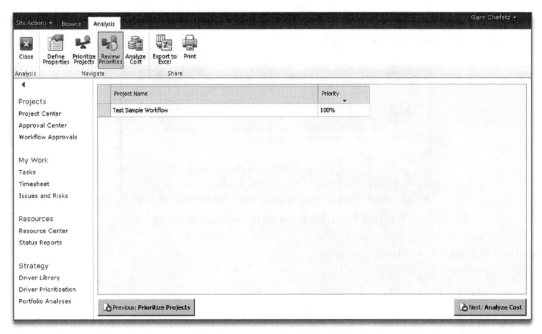

Figure 3 - 28: Project Prioritization Summary page

7. Click the *Next: Analyze Cost* button to continue. The system advances to the *Cost Constraint Analysis* page shown in Figure 3 - 29.

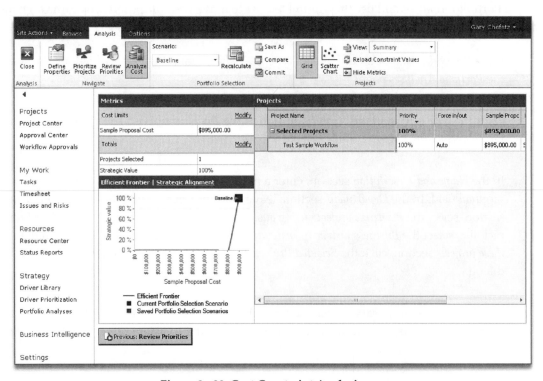

Figure 3 - 29: Cost Constraint Analysis page

8. In the *Portfolio Selection* section of the *Analysis* ribbon, click the *Commit* button. The system displays the *Message from webpage* warning shown in Figure 3 - 30.

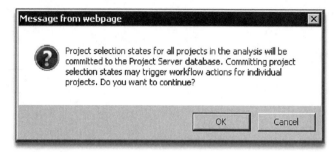

Figure 3 - 30: Message from webpage warning

9. Click the *OK* button to continue.

Hands On Exercise

Exercise 3-5

Create a Portfolio Analysis and use the commit feature to move your proposed project through the *Selection Review* phase.

1. From the *Quick Launch* menu, select *Portfolio Analyses* from the *Strategy* section. The system opens the *Portfolio Analyses* page.

2. Click the *New* button in the *Analysis* section of the *Analyses* ribbon. The system displays the *New Portfolio Analysis* page.

3. In the *Name and Description* section, enter a name in the *Name* field and a description in the *Description* field. In the *Department* section, leave the *Department* field blank. In the *Prioritization Type* section, select the *Prioritize projects using business drivers* option and from the *Driver Prioritization* pick list, select the *Business Driver Prioritization* that you created in Exercise 3-4. In the *Prioritize these projects* section, click the *Selected Projects* button and the system displays the *Select Projects* dialog.

4. Select your new proposal and use the arrow button to move it to the *Selected Projects* section on the right. Click the *OK* button when you are done, and the system returns to the *New Portfolio Analysis* page.

5. In the *Analysis Primary Cost Constraint* section, select the *Sample Proposal Cost* item from the drop-down menu. Do not select the option in the *Time-phased Resource Planning* section.

6. Click the *Next: Prioritize Projects* button to continue. The system displays the *Project Strategic Impact* page.

7. Select at least one rating for your project and click the *Next: Review Priorities* button to continue. The system displays the *Project Priorities* page.

8. Click the *Next: Analyze Cost* button to continue. The system advances to the *Cost Constraint Analysis* page.

9. In the *Portfolio Selection* section of the *Analysis* ribbon, click the *Commit* button. The system displays a *Message from webpage* warning.

10. Click the *OK* button to continue.

Editing an Existing Proposal

As you can see, you use the project drilldown pages to edit your project at every stage of the workflow. Both the workflow and specific settings in the *Project Details* page determine what fields you can edit in the various stages of the workflow. Because these vary with each workflow, the experience you will have with workflows in your environment are not predictable. Rather, you must learn each workflow individually. To edit your project simply select it from the *Project Center* and select *Edit* from the *Project* section of the *Project ribbon*.

Because the sample workflow contains code that hooks into portfolio analysis, you cannot move to the next stage of the workflow until your project is committed through the portfolio analysis commit process. Return to the *Project Center* and select your new proposal project in the grid. You should now see that the project has advanced to the *Resource Planning* stage, as shown for my new project proposal in Figure 3 - 31. At this point in the process, the project manager actually assigns resources to the tasks in the project moving away from using a *Resource Plan*.

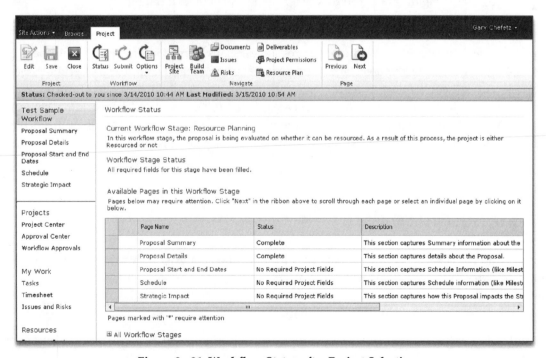

Figure 3 - 31: Workflow Status after Project Selection

The *Resource Planning* stage requires a portfolio manager to perform a resource analysis using the portfolio analysis tools as well, and the manager must commit the project through this process to move it into the *Scheduling* stage. The rest of the workflow progresses through execution and project closure following the diagram shown in Figure 3 - 32.

In the previous example, I did not perform a *Resource Constraint* analysis because the system would have to contain a significant number of projects to exercise the tool in a meaningful way. Normally, you build a resource plan to prepare the project for resource constraint analysis. I show you how to do this in the balance of this module.

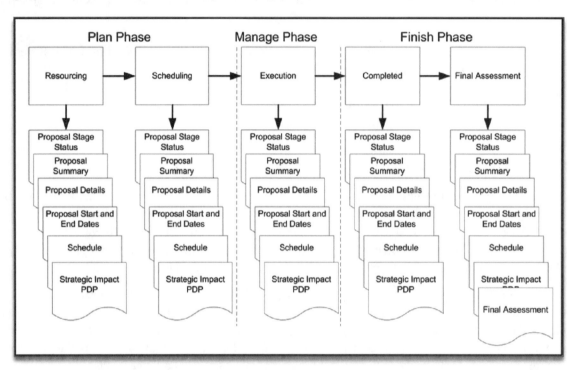

Figure 3 - 32: Workflow Stages for Sample Proposal continued

As you can see in the diagram, the *Project Detail Pages* that the workflow uses remain constant until the final stage, which introduces a *Final Assessment* page, which captures some lessons learned information. Before the plan can move from the *Scheduling* stage to the *Execution* stage, the system requires a manual approval after the project manager submits the project from the *Scheduling* stage. The project manager cannot submit the project from the *Execution* stage to the *Completed* stage until all of the tasks in the project are marked 100% complete. The workflow logic immediately rejects any attempt that the project manager makes to submit the project to this stage while there are incomplete tasks in the plan. Once the project manager marks all tasks complete, the project is eligible for submission to the *Finish* phase.

Creating a Resource Plan

In many if not most Project Server configurations used for Portfolio Analysis, early resource planning relies on *Resource Plans*. A *Resource Plan* is a way to "reserve" a resource for specific periods without assigning the resource to tasks. In the *Sample Workflow* example, building a project team and assigning individual resources to tasks happens during the *Resource Planning* stage that occurs after portfolio selection.

In a typical workflow, after you create a new proposal, and before portfolio selection, you need to commit resources to the proposal to show demand. To create a *Resource Plan* for a proposal, navigate to the *Project Center* page in Project

Web App. Select your proposal by clicking the row header to the left of its name and then click the *Resource Plan* button from the *Navigate* section of the *Project* ribbon. Project Server 2010 displays the *Resource Plan* page for the selected proposal shown in Figure 3 - 33.

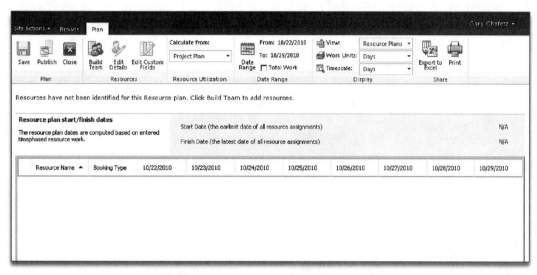

Figure 3 - 33: Resource Plan page for a proposal

Building a Team on a Resource Plan

Notice that the message immediately below the ribbon in Figure 3 - 33, states "Resources have not been identified for this Resource Plan. Click Build Team to add resources." The first step in creating a *Resource Plan* is to add resources to the *Resource Plan*. Click the *Build Team* button from the *Resources* section of the *Plan* ribbon. The system displays the *Build Resource Plan Team* page shown in Figure 3 - 34.

Figure 3 - 34: Build Resource Plan Team page

From the list of resources shown on the *Build Resource Plan Team* page, you must select the resources to serve on your project team. Begin by selecting the option checkbox to the left of each resource who may be a potential team member. You can select any type of resource using this page. Use the *View* pick list in the *Data* section of the *Team* ribbon to change views and select from various subsets of your resource pool. Most organizations are likely to use *Generic* resources to represent resource loading. I cover resources extensively in Module 06, *Resource and Assignment Planning*.

Generic resources are a special type of work resource that you use to represent resources by role or capability type. You use these to show generic demand for resources.

MSProjectExperts recommends that you design your process to always use generic resources for early-phase resource demand modeling rather than actual resources. This allows you to easily differentiate between actual loading and proposed resource loading.

If you elect to use actual resources from your resource pool, Project Server 2010 offers you two ways to determine whether each resource is available to serve on your proposed team by using the *Resource Assignments* and *Resource Availability* buttons in the *Navigate* section of the *Team* ribbon. You can use these after selecting one or more resources. Because the expectation is that you are using *Generic* resources exclusively at this point in the process, I do not cover these in this module. I describe these tools in detail in Module 15, *Working in the Resource Center*.

Adding Resources to the Team on a Resource Plan

To add generic resources to your plan, select the option checkboxes to the left of each resource name and then click the *Add* button. The system shows the list of selected resources in the upper right corner of the *Build Resource Plan Team* page shown in Figure 3 - 35.

	Resource Name	Type	Generic	Cost Center	Timesheet Manage	Default Assignme				Resource Name
☐	Software Deve	Work	Yes				Add >		☐	Accountant
☐	Software Deve	Work	Yes				< Remove		☐	DBA
☐	Stephanie Stra	Work	No		Stephanie Strasburg	Stephanie Strasbu			☐	HR staff
☐	Stephen Sand	Work	No		Stephen Sanderlin	Stephen Sanderlin			☐	IT Executive
☐	Steve Garcia	Work	No		Steve Garcia	Steve Garcia			☐	Marketing and Sales
☐	Sue Burnett	Work	No		Sue Burnett	Sue Burnett			☐	Network Admin
☐	Susan Manche	Work	No		Susan Manche	Susan Manche			☐	Network Operations
☐	Susan Tartagli	Work	No		Susan Tartaglia	Susan Tartaglia			☐	Operations staff
☐	Technical Educ	Work	Yes						☐	Project Manager
☐	Technical Train	Work	Yes						☐	Quality Assurance T
☐	Teresa Didrikse	Work	No		Teresa Didriksen	Teresa Didriksen			☐	Software Developer
☐	Terry Madison	Work	No		Terry Madison	Terry Madison				
☐	Terry Uland	Work	No		Terry Uland	Terry Uland				
☐	Tim Clark	Work	No		Tim Clark	Tim Clark				

Figure 3 - 35: Build Resource Plan Team page with generic resources selected

Click the *Save and Close* button from the *Team* section of the *Team* ribbon to add the selected resources to the team for the proposal. Project Server 2010 redisplays the *Resource Plan* page with the new team members, as shown in Figure 3 - 36.

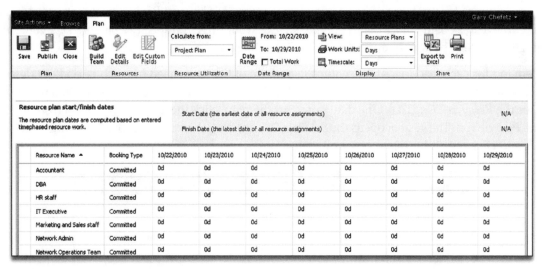

Figure 3 - 36: Resource Plan page with generic team members

Modeling Resource Demand in a Resource Plan

After you add resources to the proposal, you must designate the *Booking Type* for each resource and then "reserve" each resource for the periods for which you need them. Project Server 2010 offers two potential *Booking Type* values for a resource in a *Resource Plan*. Use the **Proposed** booking type to indicate a tentative resource booking when you are not certain that you will use the resource in the *Resource Plan*. Leave the default **Committed** booking type selected to indicate a firm resource commitment to the *Resource Plan*.

To set the *Booking Type* for a resource, select the name of a resource and then click the *Edit Custom Fields* button. Project Server 2010 displays the *Edit Custom Fields* page shown in Figure 3 - 37.

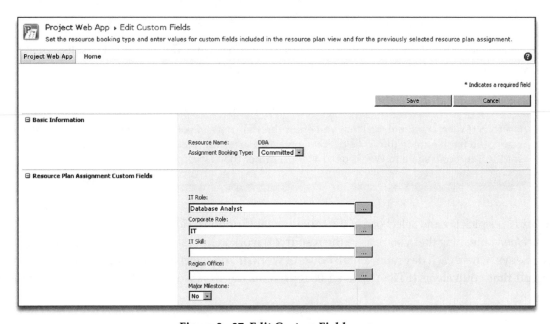

Figure 3 - 37: Edit Custom Fields page

To change the *Booking Type* field value from *committed* to *proposed*, click the *Booking Type* pick list and select the *Proposed* value. In addition to changing the *Booking Type* field value, the system also allows you to set custom resource field values at the assignment level for the selected resource's assignments in the proposal. Notice in Figure 3 - 37 that I can specify assignment-level values for the *IT Role, Corporate Role, IT Skill,* and *Region Office* custom fields. Notice also that assignment-level task field values display on the page as well. After you specify a *Booking Type* value and custom field values, click the *Save* button to return to the *Resource Plan* page.

To model demand for each resource's time, enter the amount of time you need for each period. By default, Project Server 2010 displays the current date as the first available date in a *Resource Plan*, so you must manually specify the date range for the *Resource Plan*. To set the date range for the plan, click the *Date Range* button from the *Date Range* section of the *Plan* ribbon. The system opens the *Set Date Range* dialog shown in Figure 3 - 38. Enter dates in the *From* and *To* fields and click the *Ok* button to save your selections.

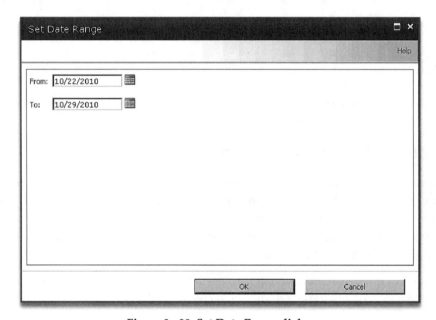

Figure 3 - 38: Set Date Range dialog

Click the *Timescale* pick list to set the timescale for resource planning. Typically, you want to select weeks or months, but for very long- duration projects, you also have the option of selecting quarters or years.

 MSProjectExperts recommends that you enter the start date of your proposal in the *From* field and the estimated finish date in the *To* field. For simplicity's sake, MSProjectExperts also recommends that you set the *Timescale* value to *Weeks* or to *Months* rather than *Days*.

Click the *Work Units* pick list and select one of the three available options: *Hours, Days,* or *Full-time equivalent*. The default value is *Hours*, meaning that you reserve the resource's work in hours. Select the *Days* option if you wish to reserve work in days, where each day represents 8 hours of work. If you select the *Full-time equivalent* option, you enter the work in full-time equivalents (FTE's), where 1.00 represents full-time work and .50 represents half-time work, for example.

Using the *Full-time equivalent* option is an easy way to reserve full or part-time work for the resources in your resource plan and then to allow the system to calculate the necessary number of hours.

When you select the *Full-time equivalent* option, Project Server 2010 determines the number of hours of work in each time period based on how your Project Server administrator configured your system. The system allows the Project Server administrator to define an FTE as either a specific number of hours per day (such as 8 hours/day), or according to the number of hours each day shown on each resource's calendar in the *Enterprise Resource Pool*.

If you enter work values or FTEs you can display the total work reserved for each resource by selecting the *Show total work* option from the *Date Range* section of the *Plan* ribbon. When you finish selecting your resource plan options, click the *Save* button in the *Plan* section of the *Plan* ribbon.

Because my proposal runs from early October 2010 through late March 2011, I entered 10/22/2010 in the *From* field, entered 3/25/2011 in the *To* field, and selected *Months* from the *Timescale* pick list. The system redisplays the *Resource Plan* page as shown in Figure 3 - 39. Figure 3 - 40 shows the same information, but with the *Show total work* option selected.

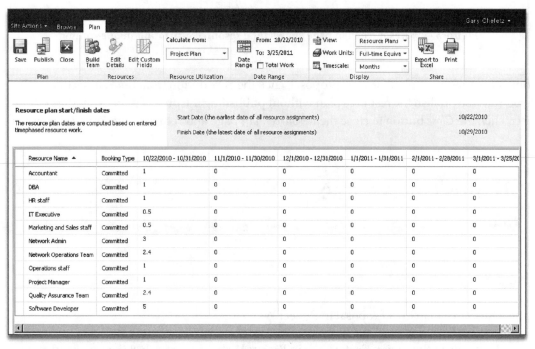

Figure 3 - 39: Resource Plan page shows monthly periods

For each resource on the team, enter time in one or more periods to "reserve" the resource during each period. The information you enter shows your "forecast" of anticipated resource utilization over the life of the proposed project, even though you did not assign the resources to tasks.

Figure 3 - 39 shows the FTE totals that I started entering into the monthly grid. Notice that my anticipated utilization of each resource varies by resource and that these can vary by period as well, even though I did not add values beyond the first month, my intention is to create contoured resource demand across many months.

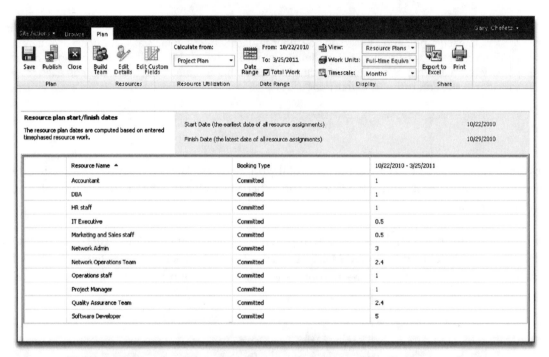

Figure 3 - 40: Resource Plan page shows total resource utilization in one column

When you finish your resource plan for your proposal, click the *Save* button from the *Plan* section of the *Plan* ribbon. Notice that you can also publish the resource plan without publishing the project plan. After the system finishes saving the project, click the *Close* button to close the *Resource Plan* page and return to the *Project Center* page.

Hands On Exercise

Exercise 3-6

Create a Resource Plan on a Proposal in Project Web App.

1. Navigate to the *Project Center* page in Project Web App and select the row header for the proposal you created earlier in this module.

2. In the *Navigate* section of the *Projects* ribbon, click the *Resource Plan* button. Project Web App displays the *Resource Plan* page for the selected proposal.

3. In the *Resources* section of the *Plan* ribbon, click the *Build Team* button. The system displays the *Build Resource Plan Team* page.

4. Add some generic resources to your plan by selecting the option checkboxes to the left of each generic resource name and then click the *Add* button. The system shows the list of selected generic resources in the upper right corner of the *Build Resource Plan Team* page.

5. In the *Team* section of the *Team* ribbon, click the *Save & Close* button to add the selected resources to the team for the proposal. Project Web App redisplays the *Resource Plan* page with the new team members.

6. Select a resource on the *Resource Plan* page. In the *Resources* section of the *Plan* ribbon, click the *Edit Custom Fields* button. Project Web App displays the *Edit Custom Fields* page. Notice that you can set the Assignment Booking Type for a resource in the *Basic Information* section of the page. You can also add other custom field values in the *Resource Plan Assignment Custom Fields* section of the page. Click the *Cancel* button to exit without making changes.

7. In the *Date Range* section of the *Plan* ribbon, click the *Date Range* button. The system opens the *Set Date Range* dialog. Enter dates in the *From* and *To* fields that span several months and click the *OK* button to save your selections.

8. In the *Display* section of the *Plan* ribbon, click the *Work Units* pick list and select the *Full-time Equivalent* item from the pick list.

9. Enter FTE values for at least one column in the monthly grid.

10. In the *Date Range* section of the *Plan* ribbon, select the *Total Work* option to display the FTE totals for your new resource plan.

11. In the *Plan* section of the *Plan* ribbon, click the *Save* button, then click the *Close* button to close your new resource plan

Importing Resources from a Resource Plan

Typically, you apply a resource plan in order to enable the resource constraint analysis in a portfolio analysis. Now that you have moved your proposal through the selection process and built a resource plan, it is time to get your plan detailed with task assignments. Resources in a resource plan are not eligible for assignments in Project unless you copy them from your resource plan into your project. To do this I must open my project from the *Project Center* and then use the *Build Team* tool to accomplish this. Select the row header for your project and click the *Build Team* button from the *Navigate* section of the *Projects* ribbon. The system displays the *Build Team* page shown in Figure 3 - 41.

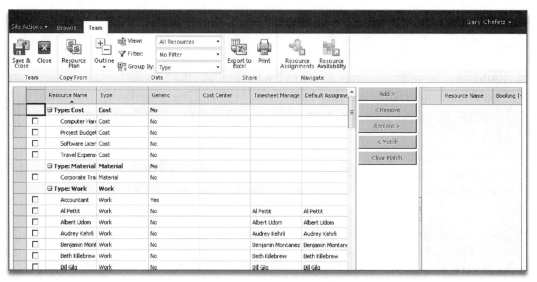

Figure 3 - 41: Build Team for a Project

This is essentially the same tool that you used to build your team for your *Resource Plan*. Notice that the *Team* ribbon now contains a *Copy From* section with a button labeled *Resource Plan* that allows you to copy the resources in your resource plan into your project. To copy the resource into your project, click the *Resource Plan* button and the system redisplays with the resources selected in the *Selected Resources* section on the right as shown in Figure 3 - 42.

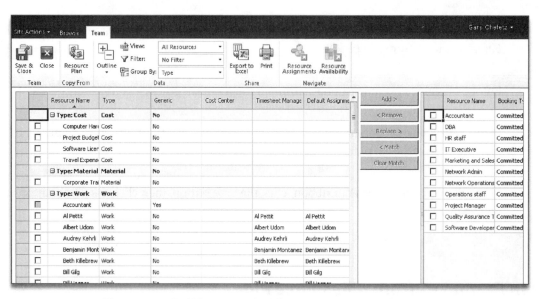

Figure 3 - 42: Build Team tool with Resources Copied from Plan

Now that you copied your resources from the *Resource Plan* you use the *Build Team* tool the same way you did in the previous example. You can add or remove resources at this point and use the *Match* tool to replace your generic resources with human workers. Click the *Save and Close* button when you complete your resource selections. The system returns to your resource plan page.

From the *Build Team* page, you can also determine the availability for one or more selected resources by clicking the *Resource Assignments* button or the *Resource Availability* button. Refer to Module 15 for complete information on how to use these two features.

Using a Resource Plan during Project Execution

As you can see, resource plans are very powerful for modeling resource demand during the proposal process allowing you to create a rich resource model at a high level with very little effort, and a more complex and contoured model with a moderate amount of effort. Resource plans are also very useful during project execution, particularly for projects with long durations or projects where detailed planning is possible for only a near-term horizon. On the *Resource Plan* page shown previously in Figure 3 - 40, notice in the *Resource Utilization* section of the *Plan* ribbon the *Calculate From* pick list shown in focus in Figure 3 - 43.

**Figure 3 - 43: Calculate
From pick list**

As you execute a project that you cannot fully detail, you can use a combination of resources assigned to specific tasks in your project plan and resource loading represented in your resource plan. You do this by selecting the *Project Plan until* item on the pick list and the system displays the *Set Date* dialog shown in Figure 3 - 44.

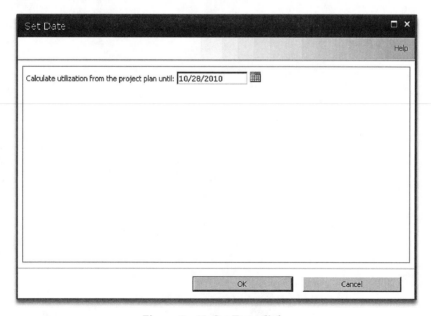

Figure 3 - 44: Set Date dialog

Selecting a date in the dialog tells the system to use the resources assigned to tasks in the project plan to determine utilization until the specified date; and thereafter, use the values in the resource plan allowing you to combine detailed bottom-up planning with high-level top-down planning to support this scenario.

The web-based resource tools you learned about in this module are also useful for organizations where project managers by policy may not select resources for their own teams. In this case, resource managers or other designated staff members use the same tools to apply resources to resource plans and directly to projects. You learn more about the advanced team building tools available to you within Project Professional in Module 06.

Proposals Summary

Supported by workflows and project type objects, the proposal feature in Project Sever 2010 is very rich and flexible. So flexible, in fact, that I cannot predict what you have in your environment. As long as you keep in mind that working through a workflow in Project Server is a matter of moving from stage to stage, you should find using the tool with your own configuration an easy experience.

Module 04

Creating Enterprise Projects

Learning Objectives

After completing this module, you will be able to:

- Create a new enterprise project using Project Professional 2010
- Define a new enterprise project using a 6-step method
- Save an enterprise project in the Project Server database
- Understand the Local Cache
- Open and close enterprise projects
- Work with a project in Offline mode
- Import a project into the enterprise

Inside Module 04

Creating an Enterprise Project Using Project Professional 2010

As I indicated previously in Module 03, you can create a new enterprise project as a proposed project from the *Project Center* page in Project Web App using the demand management process. You can also create a new enterprise project in Project Professional 2010 using either of the following methods:

- You import the project into the Project Server database using the *Import Project Wizard* in the Project Professional 2010 client while connected to Project Server 2010.

- You create the project in the Project Professional 2010 client while connected to Project Server 2010 and you save the project in the Project Server database.

Warning: Do not open an .mpp project file, click the *File* tab and click the *Save As* item in the Backstage, and then save the project in the Project Server database. Saving a .mpp local project file directly into the Project Server database **bypasses** all of your organization's standards for setting project, resource, task, and calendar information in the project.

I discuss both of these methods for creating an enterprise project as separate topics in this module.

Importing a Local Project into Project Server 2010

If you have existing non-enterprise projects saved outside the Project Server system, you must bring them into the Project Server 2010 database by importing them. To import an existing project, complete the following steps:

1. Click the *Project Server* tab to display the *Project Server* custom ribbon.

2. Close any projects currently open in Project Professional 2010 and make sure you have **no projects open**.

3. In the *Admin Tasks* section of the *Project Server* ribbon, click the *Import Project to Enterprise* button. The system displays the *Open* dialog shown in Figure 4 - 1.

4. In the *Open* dialog, navigate to the folder containing the non-enterprise project you want to import.

An alternate way to initiate the import process is to open the local project first, and then click the *Import Project to Enterprise* button in the *Admin* Tasks section of the *Project Server* ribbon.

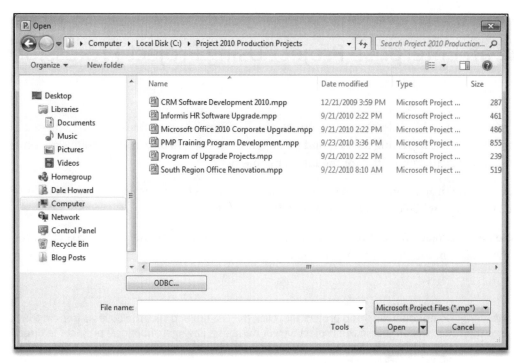

Figure 4 - 1: Open dialog

5. Select the project and then click the *Open* button. Project Server 2010 opens the project in Project Professional 2010 and then displays the *Import Project Wizard* sidepane, as shown in Figure 4 - 2. The *Import Project Wizard* assists you with the process of importing non-enterprise projects into the enterprise environment.

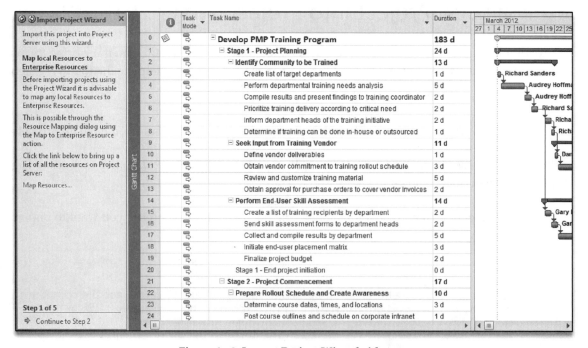

Figure 4 - 2: Import Project Wizard sidepane

6. If your project contains resources, click the *Map Resources* link in the sidepane. The system displays the *Map Project Resources onto Enterprise Resources* dialog shown in Figure 4 - 3.

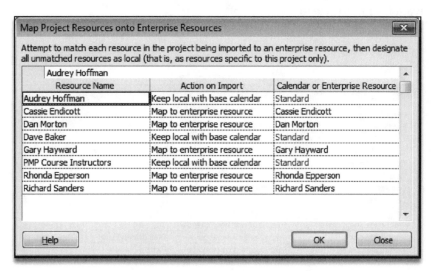

**Figure 4 - 3: Map Project Resources
onto Enterprise Resources dialog**

Use the *Map Project Resources onto Enterprise Resources* dialog to match local resources in the project with enterprise resources in your organization's Enterprise Resource Pool. The default behavior of this dialog is as follows:

- If you named the local resource with exactly the same name as the enterprise resource, the system maps the local resource onto the enterprise resource automatically. For example, notice in Figure 4 - 3 that the name of the local resource named Cassie Endicott matches the name exactly with the enterprise resource named Cassie Endicott.

- If the name of the local resource does not match the name of any enterprise resource, then the system leaves the local resource unmatched. Notice in Figure 4 - 3 shown previously that the local resources named Audrey Hoffman, Dave Baker, and PMP Course Instructors do not map to any enterprise resources in the Enterprise Resource Pool.

7. To map a resource, click the *Action on Import* pick list and select the *Map to enterprise resource* item on the list.

8. Click the *Calendar or Enterprise Resource* pick list and select the name of the enterprise resource in the Enterprise Resource Pool.

You must repeat this process individually for every local resource in the project that does not match a corresponding enterprise resource in the Enterprise Resource Pool. The exception to this rule, however, concerns resources that you want to leave as local resources intentionally. For example, you can leave resources as local resources if they are contractors or consultants who are not in your Enterprise Resource Pool, or they are generic resources such as the PMP Course Instructors resource shown previously in Figure 4 - 3.

Notice in Figure 4 - 4 that I mapped the local resource named Audrey Hoffman to the enterprise resource named Audrey Kehrli, and I mapped the local resource named Dave Baker to the enterprise resource named David Baker. Notice also that I left the PMP Course Instructors generic resource unmapped, since this resource is a contractor that is not part of our organization's Enterprise Resource Pool.

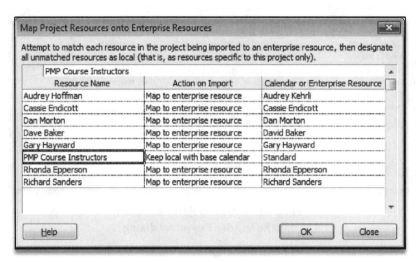

**Figure 4 - 4: Match resources in the Map Project
Resources onto Enterprise Resources dialog**

9. When you finish mapping local resources with enterprise resources, click the *OK* button in the *Map Project Resources onto Enterprise Resources* dialog. The system returns to the *Import Project Wizard* sidepane.

10. Click the *Continue to Step 2* link in the sidepane. If you are not a Project Server administrator, the system may display the warning dialog shown in Figure 4 - 5. The message in this dialog refers to any resources you left as local resources in the project. Furthermore, the message in this dialog means what it implies: because you are not a Project Server administrator, you do not have permission to add the local resources to the Enterprise Resource Pool.

Figure 4 - 5: Warning message about new resources

11. If you see the warning dialog, click the *OK* button. Project Server 2010 displays the *Confirm Resources* page of the *Import Project Wizard* sidepane as shown in Figure 4 - 6. This page lists the number of local resources remaining in the project, along with the number of resource errors. The system might trigger a resource error if the Windows User Account information for a resource no longer matches the same information on the network.

If you see resource errors on the *Confirm Resources* page, cancel the process of importing the local project and contact your Project Server administrator immediately for assistance. Only someone who is a Project Server administrator can correct resource errors.

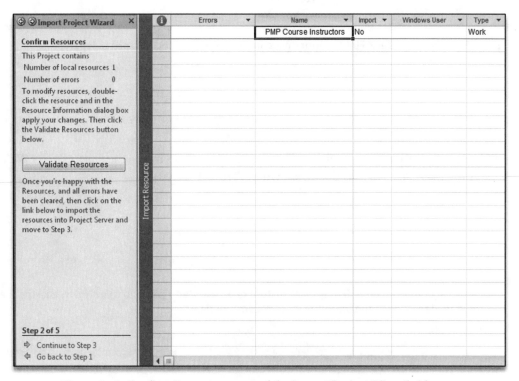

Figure 4 - 6: Confirm Resources page of the Import Project Wizard sidepane

12. Click the *Continue to Step 3* link in the sidepane. Project Server 2010 displays the *Task Field Mapper* page in the *Import Project Wizard* sidepane shown in Figure 4 - 7. Use the *Task Field Mapper* page to match any local custom task fields in your project with enterprise custom task fields in your Project Server 2010 system.

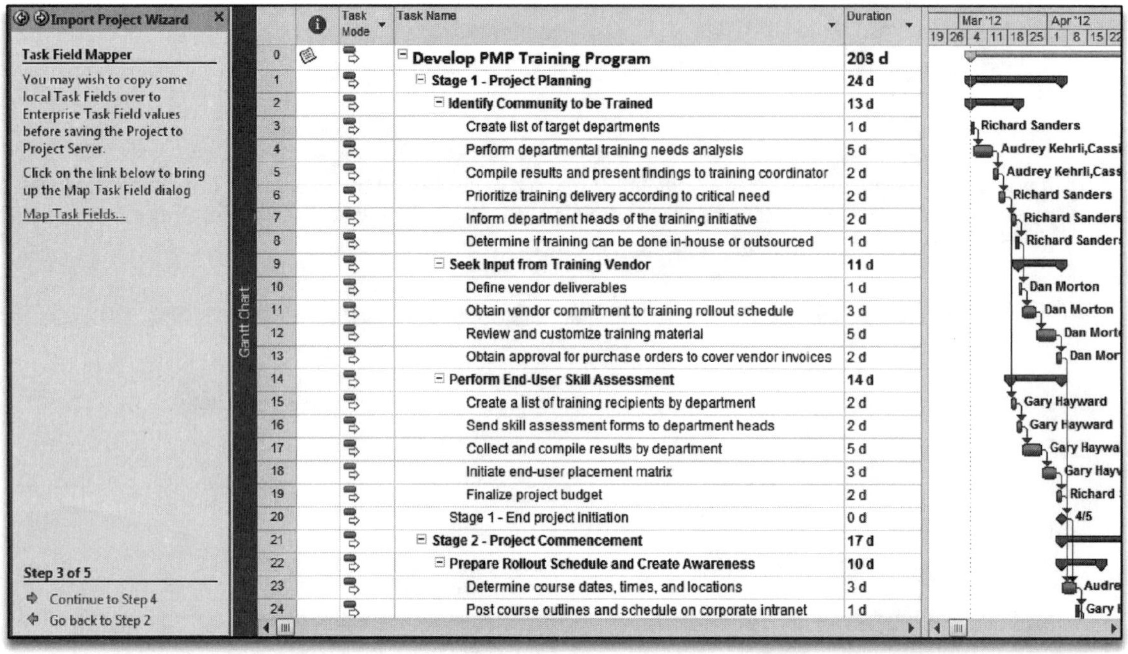

Figure 4 - 7: Task Field Mapper page in the Import Project Wizard sidepane

If your project contains any local custom task fields, click the *Map Task Fields* link in the *Import Project Wizard* sidepane. The system displays the *Map Custom Fields* dialog shown in Figure 4 - 8.

If your project does not contain any local custom task fields, you can skip this step by clicking the *Continue to Step 4* link in the *Import Project Wizard* sidepane.

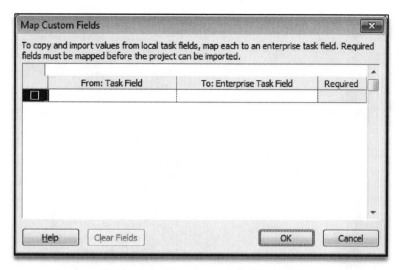

Figure 4 - 8: Map Custom Fields dialog

In the *Map Custom Fields* dialog, click the *From* pick list and select a local custom task field. Click the *To* pick list and select the corresponding enterprise custom task field. For example, notice in Figure 4 - 9 that the *Is Key Milestone* local custom field maps to the *Major Milestone* enterprise custom field. Repeat this process for every local custom task field and then click the *OK* button when finished.

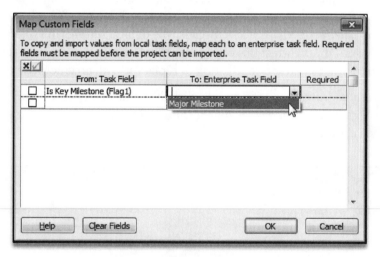

Figure 4 - 9: Map Custom Fields dialog; map the Is Key Milestone field to the Major Milestone field

The system returns control to the *Task Field Mapper* page in the *Import Project Wizard* sidepane. Click the *Continue to Step 4* link in the sidepane. The system displays the *Confirm Tasks* page in the *Import Project Wizard* sidepane shown in Figure 4 - 10.

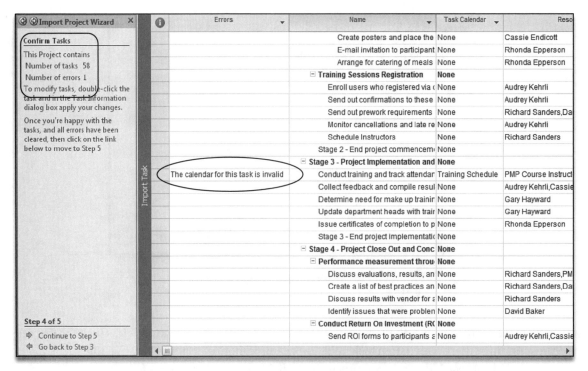

Figure 4 - 10: Confirm Tasks page in the Import Project Wizard sidepane

If you see task errors on the *Confirm Tasks* page, you must correct the errors before the system allows you to continue. The *Errors* column tells you the nature of the each task error and identifies the tasks triggering the errors. Notice in Figure 4 - 10 that the system found one task error caused by a local task calendar (the *Training Schedule* calendar) applied to the *Conduct training and track attendance* task. Because the default settings in Project Server 2010 do not allow the use of local base calendars, I must correct this error before I can continue to the next step. To correct this error, I must either remove the local task calendar from the task or replace it with an enterprise calendar.

As part of your error correction process, you can double-click the name of any task containing an error and examine information about the task in the *Task Information* dialog shown in Figure 4 - 11. Correct any task errors in the *Task Information* dialog and then click the *OK* button.

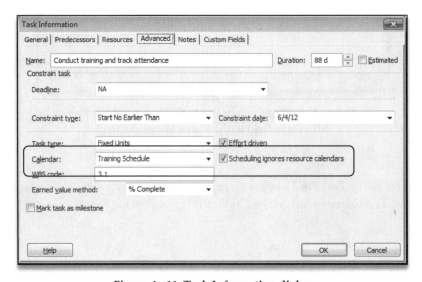

Figure 4 - 11: Task Information dialog

After you correct the task problems, the system redisplays the *Confirm Tasks* page in the *Import Project Wizard* sidepane, but without errors listed in the *Errors* column. Click the *Continue to Step 5* link in the sidepane. Project Server 2010 displays the *Save Project to Project Server* page in the *Import Project Wizard* sidepane shown in Figure 4 - 12.

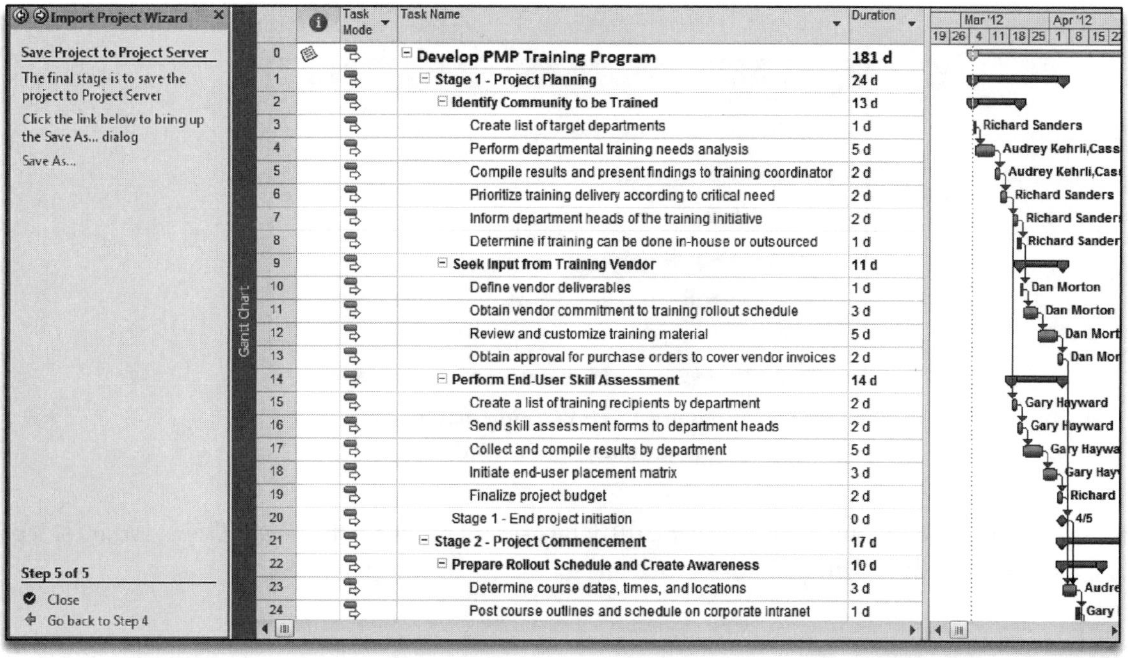

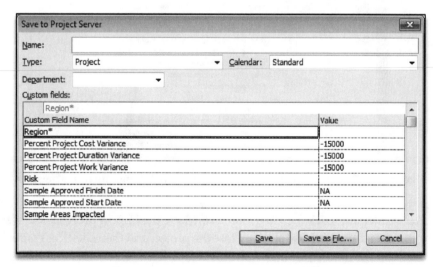

Figure 4 - 12: Save Project to Project Server page in the Import Project Wizard sidepane

Click the *Save As* link in the sidepane. The system displays the *Save to Project Server* dialog shown in Figure 4 - 13. In the *Save to Project Server* dialog, enter a name for the project in the *Name* field according to your enterprise naming conventions for enterprise projects. You may optionally click the *Calendar* pick list and select an enterprise calendar to serve as the *Project* calendar for the project, if necessary. Enter or select values for required and optional enterprise fields. Click the *Save* button in the *Save to Project Server* dialog. Before the system saves the project, it displays the warning dialog regarding enterprise calendars shown in Figure 4 - 14.

Figure 4 - 13: Save to Project Server dialog

If you do not select an enterprise calendar on the *Calendar* pick list in the *Save to Project Server* dialog, the system displays the warning dialog shown in Figure 4 - 14. Click the *Yes* button in the warning dialog to continue the project import process. The system replaces you local *Standard* calendar with the enterprise *Standard* calendar, which may result in the schedule change indicated in the dialog.

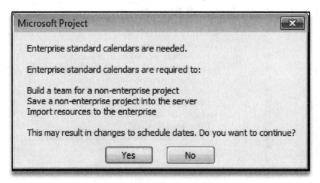

**Figure 4 - 14: Warning dialog
about Enterprise calendars**

The system saves the project in the Project Server 2010 database and refreshes the *Import Project Wizard* sidepane with a *Congratulations* section, as shown in Figure 4 - 15.

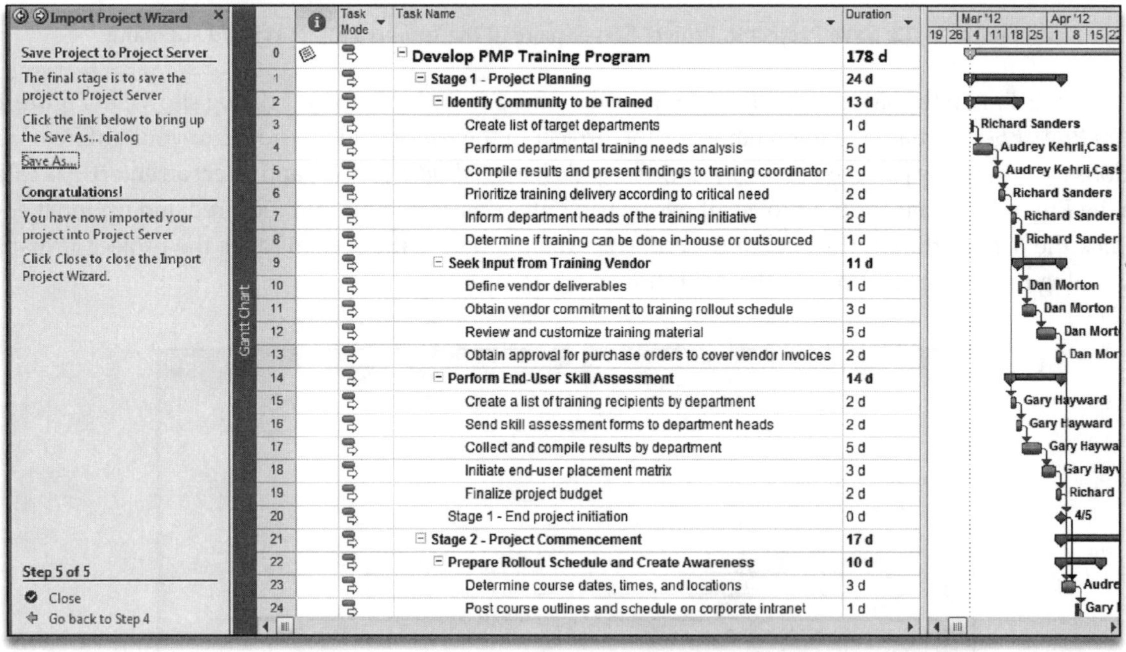

Figure 4 - 15: Save Project to Project Server page with congratulations message

In the *Import Project Wizard* sidepane, click the *Close* link to conclude the import process. The system closes the sidepane but leaves the project open for additional action. Close the project and then click the *Yes* button when prompted to check in the project.

Hands On Exercise

Exercise 4-1

Import a local project into the Project Server database using the *Import Project Wizard*.

1. Close any open projects

2. Click the *Project Server* tab to display the *Project Server* ribbon.

3. Click the *Import Project to Enterprise* button in the *Admin Tasks* section of the *Project Server* ribbon.

4. In the *Open* dialog, navigate to the folder containing your student files and open the **Existing Production Project 2010.mpp** sample file.

5. In the *Import Project Wizard* sidepane, click the *Map Resources* link.

6. In the *Map Project Resources onto Enterprise Resources* dialog, map the local resource named *MJ Ray* with the enterprise resource named *Marilyn Ray*.

7. Leave the *msPE Contractor* resource a local resource and then click the *OK* button.

8. In the *Import Project Wizard* sidepane, click the *Continue to Step 2* link.

9. When prompted with a warning message about local resources, click the *OK* button.

10. In the *Confirm Resources* page of the *Import Project Wizard* sidepane, click the *Continue to Step 3* link.

11. In the *Task Field Mapper* page of the *Import Project Wizard* sidepane, click the *Continue to Step 4* link.

12. In the *Confirm Tasks* page of the *Import Project Wizard* sidepane, widen the *Name* column and the *Task Calendar* column.

13. Click the *Task Calendar* pick list for the *Implement P3* task and select the *None* item on the pick list.

14. Click the *Continue to Step 5* link in the *Import Project Wizard* sidepane.

15. In the *Save to Project Server* page of the *Import Project Wizard* sidepane, click the *Save As* link.

16. In the *Save to Project Server* dialog, enter the following project name in the *Name* field:

    Your First Name Your Last Name New Imported Project

17. Select the *West* value for the *Region* field and select the *Low* value for the *Risk* field.

18. Click the *Save* button to save the enterprise project.

19. If you see a warning dialog about local base calendars, click the *Yes* button.

20. Click the *Close* link in the sidepane to close the *Import Project Wizard* sidepane.

21. Close and check in your newly imported enterprise project.

Creating a New Project from an Enterprise Template

To create a project under the first condition, you may begin either with a blank project or with an enterprise template. To create a new project using a template, click the *File* tab and then click the *New* item in the *Backstage* menu. The system displays the *Available Templates* page in the Backstage, as shown in Figure 4 - 16. Notice that the *Available Templates* page allows you to create a project a number of different ways, including the following:

- From a blank project

- From a template you used recently

- From a template stored in your system *Templates* folder

- From a Project Server enterprise template

- From an existing project

- From an Excel workbook

- From a SharePoint task list

- From templates found in Office Online

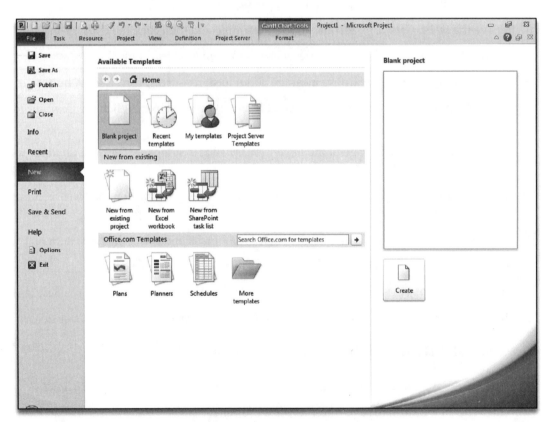

Figure 4 - 16: Available Templates page in the Backstage

To create a new project from a Project Server enterprise template, click the *Project Server Templates* icon in the first section of the *Available Templates* page. The system displays the *Templates* dialog with the *Project Server Templates* tab selected, as shown in Figure 4 - 17. The *Project Server Templates* page of the dialog contains all of your organization's enterprise templates. Notice in Figure 4 - 17 that our organization currently offers seven enterprise project templates.

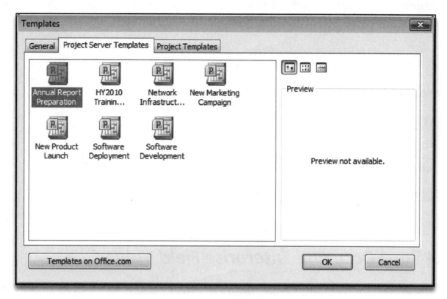

Figure 4 - 17: Templates dialog

Notice also in Figure 4 - 17 that our organization currently offers seven enterprise project templates in our Project Server 2010 system. Select any enterprise template in the *Templates* dialog and then click the *OK* button. The system creates a new project based on the template you select.

Hands On Exercise

Exercise 4-2

Create a new project from an enterprise template.

1. Launch Project Professional 2010 and log in to Project Server.

2. Click the *File* tab and then click the *New* item in the *Backstage* menu.

3. Click the *Project Server Templates* icon in the first section of the *Available Templates* page in the Backstage.

4. On the *Project Server Templates* tab of the *Templates* dialog, select the **HY2010 Training Template** icon and then click the *OK* button.

5. Leave this project open and do not save it yet as you must use it through Hands On Exercise 4-8 (at which point you save the project).

Defining an Enterprise Project

After you create a new enterprise project, either from scratch or from a template, you are ready to define the project in Project Professional 2010 using the six-step method recommended by MSProjectExperts. The six-step method includes the following steps:

1. Set the project *Start* date and enterprise field values.

2. Enter the project properties.

3. Display the Project Summary Task (aka Row 0 or Task 0).

4. Set the working schedule for the project using a calendar.

5. Set project options unique to this project.

6. Save the project using your organization's naming convention.

I discuss each of these steps individually.

Set the Project Start Date and Enterprise Field Values

When you define a new project in Microsoft Project 2010, you must set the *Start* date of the project. When you set a project's *Start* date, you allow the software to calculate an estimated *Finish* date based on the information you enter during the task, resource, and assignment planning process. To enter the *Start* date for a new project, complete the following steps:

1. Click the *Definition* tab to display the *Definition* ribbon.

2. Click the *Set Project Start Date* button in the *Start Date* section of the *Definition* ribbon. The system displays the *Project Information* dialog shown in Figure 4 - 18.

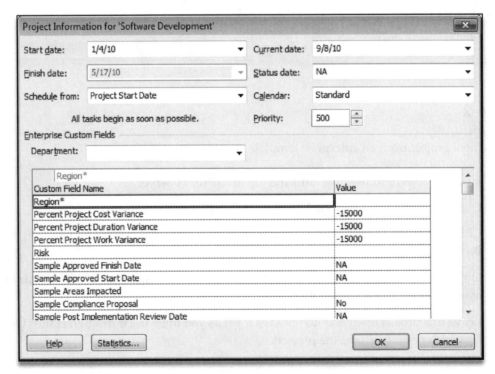

Figure 4 - 18: Project Information dialog

You can also display the *Project Information* dialog by clicking the *Project Information* button in the *Properties* section of the *Project* ribbon.

3. Enter or select your desired project *Start* date in the *Start date* field.

4. Click the *Department* pick list and select one or more departments for the project, as needed, as shown in Figure 4 - 19.

The *Department* field is new to Project Server 2010. If configured by your Project Server administrator, your organization can use the *Department* field to display department-specific custom fields in the *Project Information* dialog. Notice in Figure 4 - 19 that our organization includes seven departments, including the Accounting, Human Resources, IT, Legal, Marketing and Sales, Operations, and Publishing departments. In addition to the seven departments, our Project Server administrator also made the *Department* field a multi-value (MV) field, which allows users to select one or more departments in the field as needed. In Figure 4 - 19, notice that I selected the *IT* department.

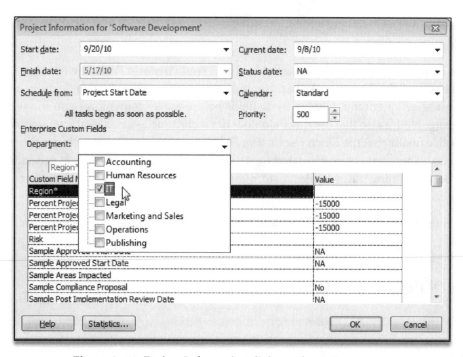

Figure 4 - 19: Project Information dialog, select a Department

If you select a value in the *Department* field, the system may refresh the *Enterprise Custom Fields* section of the *Project Information* dialog to include any department-specific custom fields. After selecting the *IT* item in the *Department* field, notice in Figure 4 - 20 that the *Enterprise Custom Fields* section of the dialog now contains one additional field, the *IT Work Area* field.

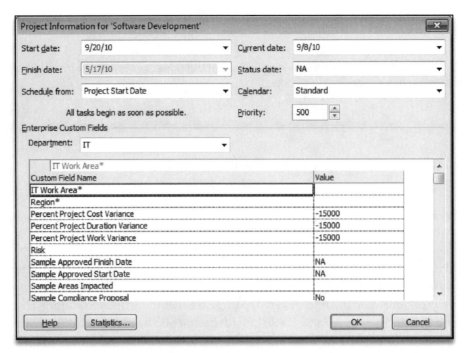

**Figure 4 - 20: Project Information dialog includes one additional
field in the Enterprise Custom Fields section of the dialog**

5. Enter values in any required or optional enterprise custom field values in the *Enterprise Custom Fields* section of the dialog.

Notice in Figure 4 - 20 that two custom enterprise fields, the *IT Work Area* and *Region* fields, show an asterisk character (*) after the name of the field. The asterisk character indicates that these two custom fields are required fields. This means that you must select or enter a value in these fields before the system allows you to save the project in the Project Server database. Notice also that the *Risk* field does not include an asterisk character, indicating that this field is non-required. Notice finally that the *Enterprise Custom Fields* section of the dialog includes three fields that show a current value of -15000. These fields are calculated fields, each containing a formula that generates the number you see. If your Project Server administrator creates custom enterprise project fields containing a formula, you cannot enter or select a value in these fields.

6. After you enter a *Start* date and specify values in the enterprise custom fields, click the *OK* button.

Hands On Exercise

Exercise 4-3

You are the project manager of the Training Advisor Rollout project. The purpose of this project is to implement a new enterprise Learning Management System (LMS) that allows employees to create and manage their own professional development program by taking in-house and external training classes.

1. Click the *Definition* tab to display the *Definition* ribbon.

2. Click the *Set Project Start Date* button in the *Start Date* section of the *Definition* ribbon.

3. In the *Project Information* dialog, enter or select the following information:

Field Name	Value to Enter/Select
Start date	Monday of the current week
Department	Human Resources and IT departments
HR Work Area	Employee Training
IT Work Area	Desktop Apps
Region	Select any region
Risk	Low

4. Click the *OK* button.

Enter the Project Properties

Although you may be in the habit of skipping the file properties settings when creating a new Word document or Excel spreadsheet, you should set the properties for each new project you create in Project Professional 2010. This causes the software to display your properties information automatically in various places throughout the project such as in the headers and footers of printed views and reports. To set the properties information for a new project, complete the following steps:

1. Click the *Project Properties* button in the *Properties* section of the *Definition* ribbon. The system displays the *Properties* dialog for the new project, as shown in Figure 4 - 21.

Figure 4 - 21: Properties dialog

You can also display the *Properties* dialog by clicking the *File* tab to display the Backstage. Click the *Info* tab in the *Backstage* menu to display the *Information* page for the current project. In the upper right corner of the *Information* page, click the *Project Information* pick list and select the *Advanced Properties* item.

2. Click the *Summary* tab, if necessary, and then enter values in each of the fields.

3. Click the *OK* button when finished.

Table 4 - 1 provides descriptions and recommendations for the use of project *Property* fields in a Project Server 2010 environment.

Field Name	Description and Recommendations
Title	Displays as the task name in the Project Summary Task (Row 0), as the task name for subprojects inserted in a master project, and in the headers or footers of printed views and reports.
Subject	Not used with Project Server 2010.
Author	Enter the name of the person who manages the project. The system optionally displays the *Author* field in the headers or footers of printed views and reports.
Manager	Enter your name, or the name of the customer, or the name of your functional manager. The system optionally displays the *Manager* field in the headers or footers of printed views and reports.
Company	Enter the customer's company name, or the name of your own company. The system optionally displays the *Company* field in the headers or footers of printed views and reports.
Category	Not used with Project Server 2010.
Keywords	Not used with Project Server 2010.
Comments	The system displays the *Comments* information in the *Notes* field of the Project Summary Task (Row 0).
Hyperlink base	Not used with Project Server 2010.
Template	The system displays the name of the template you used to create the project file.
Save preview picture	Not used with Project Server 2010.

Table 4 - 1: Project Properties fields

Hands On Exercise

Exercise 4-4

Enter the properties information for your Training Advisor Rollout project.

1. Click the *Project Properties* button in the *Properties* section of the *Definition* ribbon.

2. Click the *Summary* tab, if necessary.

3. Enter the following values in the properties fields:

Field Name	Value to Enter
Title	Training Advisor Rollout
Author	Your name
Manager	Name of your functional manager
Company	Name of your organization
Comments	Implement the Training Advisor software to allow employees to plan and direct their own continuing education program.

4. Click the *OK* button when finished.

Display the Project Summary Task

The Project Summary Task, also known as Row 0 or Task 0, is the highest-level summary task in your project. The Project Summary Task summarizes or "rolls up" all task values in the entire project. For example, the value in the *Duration* column for the Project Summary Task represents the duration of the entire project, while the values in the *Work* and the *Cost* columns represent the total work and total cost for the entire project. By default, Microsoft Project 2010

does not display the Project Summary Task automatically in any new blank project, so you must display it manually. To display the Project Summary Task in a project, complete the following steps:

1. Select the *Display Project Summary Task* checkbox option in the *Project Summary Task* section of the *Definition* ribbon. The system displays the Project Summary Task (Row 0) at the top of the current project, as shown in Figure 4 - 22.

		Task Mode ▾	Task Name ▾	Duration ▾
0			⊟ **TimeAway 2010 Development**	**99.75 d**
1			⊟ **Scope**	**3.5 d**
2			Determine project scope	4 h
3			Secure project sponsorship	1 d
4			Define preliminary resources	1 d
5			Secure core resources	1 d
6			Scope complete	0 d

Figure 4 - 22: Project Summary Task (Row 0)

2. Widen the *Task Name* column, if necessary, to "best fit" the task name of the Project Summary Task.

3. If you widen the *Task Name* column, drag the split bar to the right side of the *Duration* column, as needed.

> You can also display the Project Summary Task by applying the *Gantt Chart* view and then clicking the *Format* tab to display the *Format* ribbon with the *Gantt Chart Tools* applied. In the *Show/Hide* section of the *Format* ribbon, select the *Project Summary Task* option.

When you display the Project Summary Task, Microsoft Project 2010 uses the text you enter in the *Title* field of the *Properties* dialog as the task name of the Project Summary Task. The system also uses the text you enter in the *Comments* field of the *Properties* dialog as the body of the note for the Project Summary Task.

Hands On Exercise

Exercise 4-5

Display the Project Summary Task in an enterprise project.

1. Select the *Display Project Summary Task* checkbox option in the *Project Summary Task* section of the *Definition* ribbon.

2. Widen the *Task Name* column, if necessary, to "best fit" the task name of the Project Summary Task.

3. Drag the split bar to the right edge of the *Duration* column, as needed.

Notice that the system uses the *Title* information from the *Properties* dialog as the task name of the Project Summary Task.

4. Float your mouse pointer over the note indicator in the *Indicators* column for the Project Summary Task.

Notice that the system uses the *Comments* information from the *Properties* dialog as the text of the note for the Project Summary Task.

Set the Project Working Schedule

Setting the project working schedule is an optional step, and is only required if your project schedule does not follow the schedule specified on the enterprise *Standard* calendar. To determine which alternate calendar you may need to select, complete the following steps:

1. Click the *Change Working Time* button in the *Set Working Schedule* section of the *Definition* ribbon. Microsoft Project 2010 displays the *Change Working Time* dialog shown in Figure 4 - 23. Notice that the enterprise *Standard* calendar contains no company holidays, indicated by the blank data grid in the *Exceptions* section in the bottom half of the dialog.

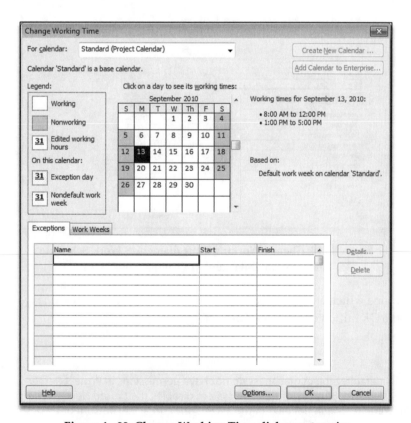

Figure 4 - 23: Change Working Time dialog; enterprise
Standard calendar contains no company holidays

You can also display the *Change Working Time* dialog by clicking the *Change Working Time* button in the *Properties* section of the *Project* ribbon.

2. Click the *For calendar* pick list at the top of the *Change Working Time* dialog and select any calendar other than the enterprise *Standard* calendar. For example, Figure 4 - 24 shows the *US Work Schedule* enterprise calendar, which contains the company's holidays for offices in the United States.

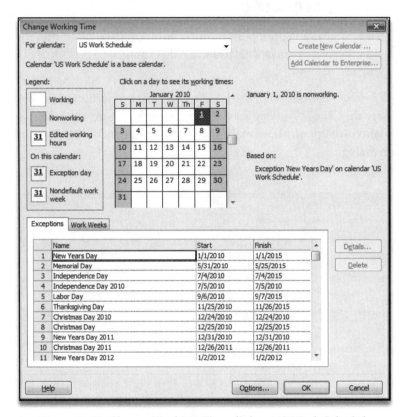

**Figure 4 - 24: Change Working Time dialog; US Work Schedule
enterprise calendar contains company holidays**

3. After you determine which enterprise calendar you want to use, close the *Change Working Time* dialog by clicking either the *OK* button or the *Cancel* button.

Warning: By default, project managers **do not** have permissions in Project Server 2010 to create or edit enterprise calendars. Because of this, the system disables the *Create New Calendar* button and does not allow you to create or edit holidays in the *Exceptions* grid at the bottom of the *Change Working Time* dialog.

Setting the Project Calendar

In Microsoft Project 2010, the system allows you to specify two calendars for your project. When you select the *Project* calendar, the system uses this calendar to schedule all tasks in your project. Think of the *Project* calendar as the master schedule of the project. The system also allows you to specify the *Non-Working Time* calendar for the project. The system uses the *Non-Working Time* calendar for only one purpose: to display nonworking time as gray shaded vertical bands on the Gantt chart. If you select any calendar other than the enterprise *Standard* calendar as the *Project* calendar, you should select the same calendar as the *Non-Working Time* calendar as well.

If you need to specify a calendar other than the enterprise *Standard* calendar as the *Project* calendar, complete the following steps:

1. Click the *Set Project Calendar* button in the *Set Working Schedule* section of the *Definition* ribbon. The system displays the *Project Information* dialog shown previously in Figure 4 - 18.

2. In the *Project Information* dialog, click the *Calendar* pick list and select any calendar, as shown in Figure 4 - 25. Notice that I am selecting the same *US Work Schedule* enterprise calendar previously shown in Figure 4 - 24.

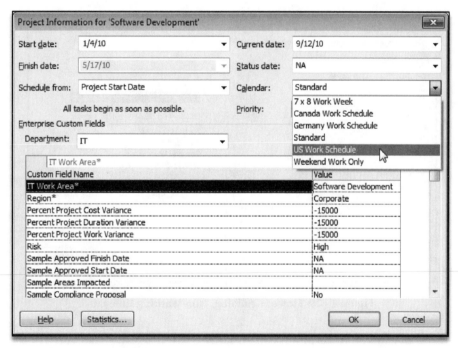

Figure 4 - 25: Project Information dialog; set the Project calendar

3. Click the *OK* button.

In the preceding steps, I set the *US Work Schedule* calendar as the *Project c*alendar, which designates it as the master calendar for scheduling all tasks in the project. This means that Microsoft Project 2010 automatically schedules all tasks according to the working schedule shown on this calendar. If a task occurs on a US company holiday, the system automatically reschedules the task to the next working day.

Setting the Non-Working Time Calendar

After setting the *Project* calendar for the project, you must also set the *Non-Working Time* calendar as well. Remember that this calendar displays the nonworking time from the *Project* calendar in the Gantt chart, and shows this nonworking time as gray shaded bands. To set the *Non-Working Time* calendar, complete the following steps:

1. Click the *Set Nonworking Time Calendar* button in the *Set Working Schedule* section of the *Definition* ribbon. Microsoft Project 2010 displays the *Timescale* dialog with the *Non-working time* tab selected.

 You can also display the *Timescale* dialog by double-clicking anywhere in the *Timescale* bar and then selecting the *Non-working time* tab. The fastest way to do this, however, is to zoom the Gantt chart to Weeks Over Days and then double-click anywhere in a gray shaded vertical band.

2. In the *Timescale* dialog, click the *Calendar* pick list and select the same calendar you specified previously as the *Project* calendar. For example, notice in Figure 4 - 26 that I am selecting the *US Work Schedule* enterprise calendar. Notice also that Microsoft Project 2010 designates this calendar as the *Project* calendar for the project.

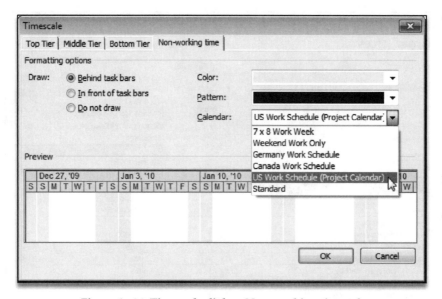

Figure 4 - 26: Timescale dialog, Non-working time tab

3. Click the *OK* button.

 Warning: You must complete **both sets of steps** to set an alternate working schedule for your project. If you set the *Project* calendar but fail to select the *Non-Working Time* calendar, Microsoft Project 2010 schedules each task correctly; but you cannot confirm this schedule because you cannot see the holidays as gray shaded bands on the Gantt chart.

Hands On Exercise

Exercise 4-6

Set the working schedule of the Training Advisor Rollout project using an enterprise calendar that contains company holidays.

1. Click the *Change Working Time* button in the *Set Working Schedule* section of the *Definition* ribbon.

2. Examine the working schedule shown for the enterprise *Standard* calendar.

Notice that the enterprise *Standard* calendar contains no company holidays.

3. Click the *For calendar* pick list and select the *US Work Schedule* calendar.

Notice that the *US Work Schedule* enterprise calendar **does** contain company holidays.

4. Click the *OK* button to close the *Change Working Time* dialog.

5. Click the *Set Project Schedule* button in the *Set Working Schedule* section of the *Definition* ribbon.

6. In the *Project Information* dialog, click the *Calendar* pick list and select the *US Work Schedule* enterprise calendar.

7. Click the *OK* button to close the *Project Information* dialog.

8. Click the *Set Nonworking Time Calendar* button in the *Set Working Schedule* section of the *Definition* ribbon.

9. In the *Timescale* dialog, click the *Calendar* pick list and select the *US Work Schedule* enterprise calendar.

Notice on the *Calendar* pick list that the system designates the *US Work Schedule* calendar s the *Project* calendar for this enterprise project.

10. Click the *OK* button to close the *Timescale* dialog.

Set Options Unique to the Project

You need to specify two types of options for your new enterprise project. I discuss each of these types of options individually:

- Set the *Task Mode* option.

- Set options in the *Project Options* dialog.

Setting the Task Mode Option

One of the major changes to Microsoft Project 2010 is the *Task Mode* setting that allows you to specify tasks as either *Auto Scheduled* or *Manually Scheduled*. *Auto Scheduled* tasks were the default type of tasks in all previous versions of the software. *Manually Scheduled* tasks are a new feature in Microsoft Project 2010. You can use this new feature for tasks that you know you need to include in the project, but for which you may not have enough information to properly schedule, and you can use these for top-down planning exercises. Other potential purposes for this feature include more relaxed scheduling approaches that are preferable when modeling schedules for sprints in the SCRUM methodology.

The default *Task Mode* setting in Microsoft Project 2010 is the *Manually Scheduled* option, which specifies all new tasks as *Manually Scheduled* tasks. Every time you launch the software, you see this default *Task Mode* setting as a ScreenTip on the *Status* bar in the lower left corner of the application window, as shown in Figure 4 - 27.

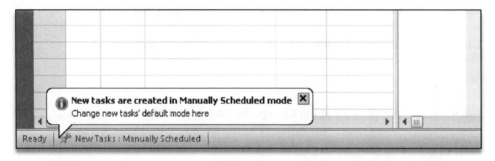

Figure 4 - 27: Task Mode option set to Manually Scheduled for all new tasks

To change the *Task Mode* setting and specify that all tasks must be *Auto Scheduled* in your new project, use either of the following methods:

- Click the *New Tasks* button on the *Status* bar and select the *Auto Scheduled* option.

- In the *Tasks* section of the *Task* ribbon, click the *Task Mode* pick list button and choose the *Auto Schedule* item on the pick list, as shown in Figure 4 - 28.

After selecting this option, when you create new tasks in your new project, Microsoft Project 2010 creates them as *Auto Scheduled* tasks. If you want to specify the default *Task Mode* setting for all new blank projects, you must specify this setting in the *Project Options* dialog. I discuss this setting in the next section of this module.

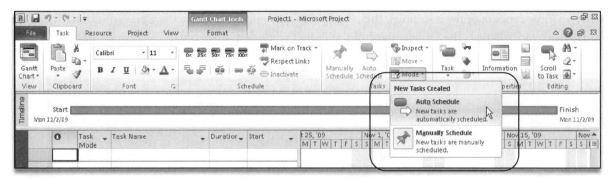

Figure 4 - 28: Task Mode pick list

 If you create a new enterprise project from a template, and the template author set the *Task Mode* option to *Auto Schedule*, then you do not need to specify a *Task Mode* option unless you want to change the option back to *Manually Schedule*.

Setting Options in the Project Options Dialog

After you specify the *Task Mode* setting for your new project, you are ready to specify options in the *Project Options* dialog. Microsoft Project 2010 allows you to specify three types of options settings in the *Project Options* dialog as follows:

- Application options that control how the software looks and works.

- Options specific to any project currently open.

- Options for all new projects created from a blank project.

 For the purpose of brevity, I discuss only the new options in Microsoft Project 2010, along with those options whose default settings I recommend you change in the *Project Options* dialog. For a thorough explanation of every option in the *Project Options* dialog, please consider purchasing a companion volume to this book, which is our *Ultimate Study Guide: Foundations Microsoft Project 2010* book.

To specify all three types of options settings, click the *Set Project Options* button in the *Options* section of the *Definition* ribbon. The software displays the *General* page of the *Project Options* dialog shown in Figure 4 - 29.

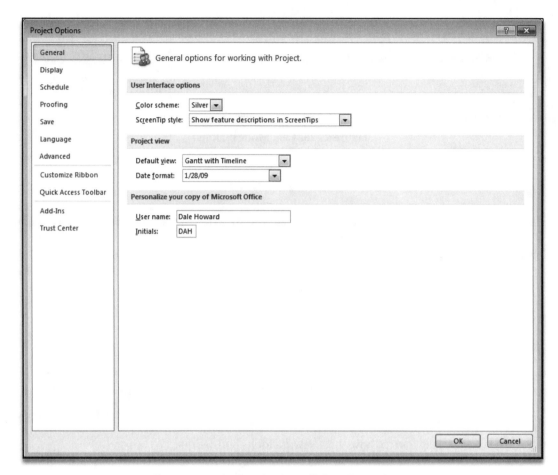

Figure 4 - 29: Project Options dialog, General page

Notice in Figure 4 - 29 that the *Project Options* dialog includes tabs for the following eleven pages of options: *General, Display, Schedule, Proofing, Save, Language, Advanced, Customize Ribbon, Quick Access Toolbar, Add-Ins,* and *Trust Center*. With the exception of the *Customize Ribbon* and *Quick Access Toolbar* pages, which I discussed previously in Module 02, I discuss all of the other pages in detail below.

You can also display the *Project Options* dialog by clicking the *File* tab and then clicking the *Options* item in the *Backstage* menu.

The *General* page of the *Project Options* dialog, shown previously in Figure 4 - 29, contains application options only. Remember that these options control how the software looks, works, and displays every project you open. The *User Interface options* section of the *General* page includes two new options for Microsoft Project 2010, the *Color Scheme* and *ScreenTip Style* options.

Use the *Color Scheme* option to control the color scheme that the system applies to all display elements in the Microsoft Project 2010 application window. These elements include the *Title* bar, Quick Access Toolbar, Ribbon, column headers and row headers, *Timescale* bar, vertical and horizontal scroll bars, *View* bar (displayed along the left side of every view), and *Status* bar. Click the *Color Scheme* pick list and choose the *Blue, Silver,* or *Black* item. The *Silver* item is the default setting for the *Color Scheme* option.

When you float your mouse pointer over an object in the Microsoft Project 2010 application window, the software displays a ScreenTip to give you more information about that object. For example, the system displays ScreenTips for objects in the Gantt chart, such as *Gantt* bars or link lines, column headers for the columns shown in the current table, and buttons on the active ribbon. Figure 4 - 30 shows the ScreenTip for the *Project Information* button in the *Properties* section of the *Project* ribbon.

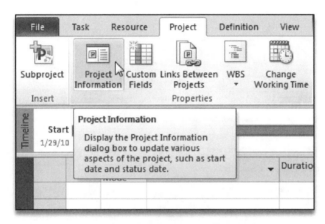

**Figure 4 - 30: ScreenTip for the
Project Information button**

When you click the *ScreenTip Style* pick list in the *Project Options* dialog, the software offers you three settings. Leave the default *Show Feature Descriptions in ScreenTips* setting selected to show the most information possible in every ScreenTip, as shown for the *Project Information* button in Figure 4 - 30. Choose the *Don't Show Feature Descriptions in ScreenTips* setting to display only a minimum amount of information in the ScreenTip. Choose the *Don't Show Screen-Tips* setting to disable the display of ScreenTips. When you choose the last setting, you **do not** see a ScreenTip for any object when you float your mouse pointer over it in the Microsoft Project 2010 application window.

Table 4 - 2 shows the non-default options settings recommended by MSProjectExperts on the *General* page of the *Project Options* dialog.

Option	Setting
Date format	1/28/09
User name	Your name
Initials	Your initials

Table 4 - 2: Recommended options on the General page

Click the *Display* tab in the *Project Options* dialog to view the options on the *Display* page shown in Figure 4 - 31. As indicated at the top of the *Display* page, use the options on this page to control how Microsoft Project 2010 displays project data on the screen.

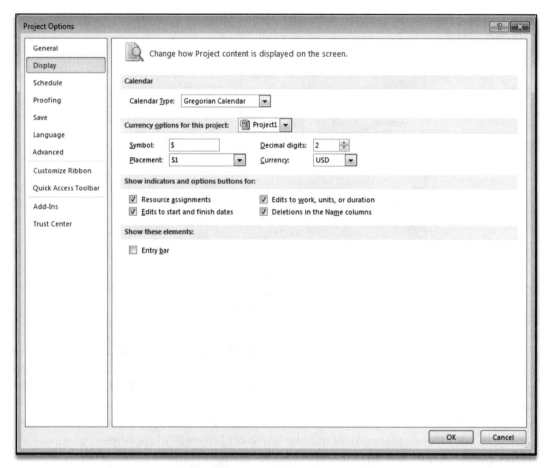

Figure 4 - 31: Project Options dialog, Display page

A new feature in Microsoft Project 2010 allows you to specify option settings for any project currently open, regardless of whether that project is the active project or not. You see this new feature on the *Display* page in the *Currency options for this project* section. Click the *Currency options for this project* pick list to view a list of projects currently open, and then select one of the open projects. By default, the pick list pre-selects the active project, but you can choose any other open project and then specify the *Currency options for this project* setting for that project. This new functionality means that you can specify a unique set of options settings for each open project without the nuisance of continually selecting a new active project and opening and closing the *Project Options* dialog for each project.

Warning: You cannot change the information in any of the fields in the *Currency options for this project* section of the dialog if the Project Server administrator locked the currency settings on your organization's Project Server 2010 instance.

Click the *Schedule* tab in the *Project Options* dialog to view the options on the *Schedule* page shown in the Figure 4 - 32. As indicated at the top of the *Schedule* page, you use the options on this page to control scheduling, calendars, and calculations in Microsoft Project 2010. Notice in Figure 4 - 32 that the *Schedule* page includes sections in which you may specify the following types of options: *Calendar, Schedule, Scheduling,* and *Schedule Alerts,* along with two sections for *Calculation* options.

Notice in Figure 4 - 32 that four of the six sections include the new ability to select any open project from a pick list. The pick lists on the *Schedule* page, however, differ slightly from the pick list shown on the *Display* page. For example, if you click the *Calendar options for this project* pick list, the list includes all projects currently open, plus an *All New Projects* item as well. If you select the *All New Projects* item, the system allows you to specify an options setting for all future projects created from a new blank project.

There are new options on the *Schedule* page in Microsoft Project 2010 in the *Scheduling options for this project* section and the *Schedule Alerts Options* section. In the *Scheduling options for this project* section, new options include the *New tasks created* option, the *Update Manually Scheduled tasks when editing links* option, and the *Keep task on nearest working day when changing to Automatically Scheduled mode* option.

The *New tasks created* option affects the default *Task Mode* setting for new tasks you add to your project. When you click the *New tasks created* pick list, the system offers you two ways to set the task mode for new tasks, *Manually Scheduled* and *Auto Scheduled*. On the *Auto scheduled tasks scheduled on* pick list, you can select the *Project Start Date* or *Current Date* options. The system creates *Auto Scheduled* tasks with dates in the *Start* and *Finish* fields and with a default duration value of *1 day* in the *Duration* field; the system creates all *Manually Scheduled* tasks with no values in the *Duration, Start,* and *Finish* fields.

Although not entirely obvious, you can use the *New Tasks Created* pick list to set the default *Task Mode* option to *Auto Scheduled* for **every new blank project** you create. To do this, click the *Scheduling options for this project* pick list and select the *All New Projects* item. Then click the *New tasks created* pick list and select the *Auto Scheduled* item. Click the *Auto scheduled tasks scheduled on* pick list and select either the *Project Start Date* or the *Current Date* option. When you click the *OK* button, Microsoft Project 2010 sets the default *Task Mode* option to *Auto Scheduled* for every new blank project you create from this point forward.

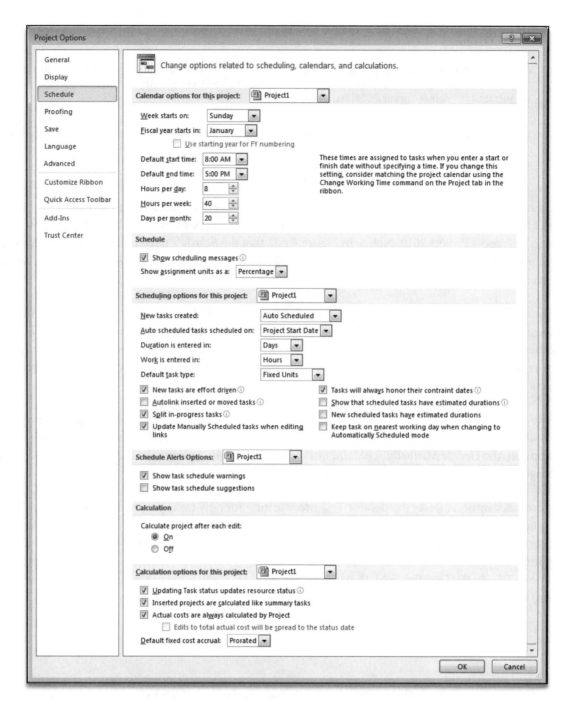

Figure 4 - 32: Project Options dialog, Schedule page

Warning: Depending on the settings specified in your Project Server 2010 system by your Project Server administrator, you may not be able to change the *New Tasks Created* option for all new projects.

Another new option in the *Scheduling Options* section is the *Update manually scheduled tasks when editing links* option, which works as you might expect. When you select this option and you link two *Manually Scheduled* tasks with a task dependency, the system reschedules the successor task automatically. If you deselect this option, and you link two *Manually Scheduled* tasks with a task dependency, the system **does not** reschedule the successor task but leaves it at its original start date instead.

The final change in the *Scheduling Options* section is the *Keep task on the nearest working day when changing to Automatically Scheduled mode* option. You can see how this option affects a task when you convert it from *Manually Scheduled* to *Auto Scheduled* in the example I show you in Figure 4 - 33. Notice that I have two *Manually Scheduled* tasks, Task A and Task B. In this example, I manually scheduled Task A to start on Monday and Task B to start on Wednesday.

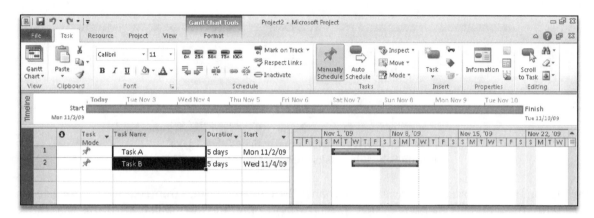

Figure 4 - 33: Two Manually Scheduled tasks

Figure 4 - 34 shows the result of the operation when I change the *Task Mode* setting to *Auto Schedule* for both Task A and Task B with the *Keep task on the nearest working day when changing to Automatically Scheduled mode* option **deselected** (the default setting). Notice that Microsoft Project 2010 schedules Task A and Task B to start on Monday, in spite of the fact that I indicated I want Task B to start on Wednesday.

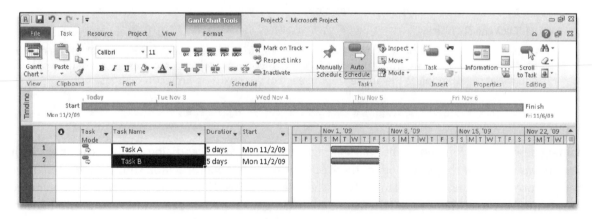

**Figure 4 - 34: Convert Manually Scheduled Tasks
to Auto Scheduled tasks with the Option DESELECTED**

Figure 4 - 35 shows the result of changing the *Task Mode* setting to *Auto Schedule* for these two tasks after **selecting** the *Keep task on the nearest working day when changing to Automatically Scheduled mode* option. Notice in Figure 4 - 35 that there is an indicator showing to the left of each task in the *Indicators* column. This indicator represents a Start No Earlier Than (SNET) constraint placed by Microsoft Project 2010 on each task to enforce my start dates. This means that Task A continues to start on Monday and Task B continues to start on Wednesday, as I specified when I created these two tasks as *Manually Scheduled* tasks.

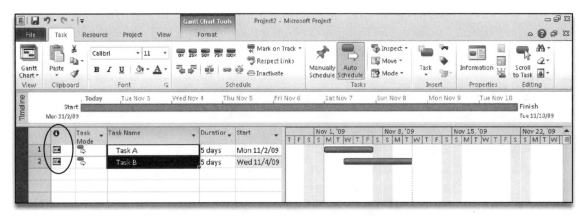

**Figure 4 - 35: Convert Manually Scheduled Tasks
to Auto Scheduled tasks with the Option SELECTED**

Two other options in the *Scheduling Options* section change their default settings from selected to deselected in Microsoft Project 2010. These options are the *New tasks are effort driven* option and the *Autolink inserted or moved tasks* option. In Microsoft Project 2007, the system selected these two options by default.

If the majority of tasks in your projects are *Effort Driven* tasks, MSProjectExperts recommends that you do the following early in your use of Microsoft Project 2010:

1. Create a new blank project.

2. Click the *Scheduling options for this project* pick list and choose the *All New Projects* item.

3. Select the *New tasks are effort driven* option.

4. Click the *OK* button.

Completing the preceding steps sets the default value for all tasks to *Effort Driven* in all of the new blank projects you create from this point forward. If you use project templates to create new projects, you should also complete the above steps in each of your existing project templates.

The remaining new options you find on the *Schedule* page of the *Project Options* dialog are the two options in the *Schedule Alerts Options* section of the page. Both of these options control the information shown in the *Task Information* pane when you use the *Task Inspector* tool to analyze schedule problems. The *Task Inspector* pane, which started as the *Task Drivers* feature in Project 2007, shows the factors controlling the start date of any task, along with Warnings and Suggestions for correcting task schedule problems. By default, the system selects the *Show task schedule warnings* option and **deselects** the *Show task schedule suggestions* option. To take maximum advantage of the new *Schedule Alerts* feature, I recommend you select **both of these options** for the current project and for all new projects. I discuss the *Task Inspector* tool in detail in Module 05, Project Task Planning.

Table 4 - 3 shows the non-default options settings recommended by MSProjectExperts on the *Schedule* page of the *Project Options* dialog. Furthermore, MSProjectExperts recommends you set these options for all open projects and for all new projects as well.

Option	Setting
New tasks created	Auto Scheduled
New tasks are effort driven	Selected
Show that scheduled tasks have estimated durations	Deselected
New scheduled tasks have estimated durations	Deselected
Show task schedule suggestions	Selected

**Table 4 - 3: Recommended options on the
Schedule page for all current and future project**

Click the *Save* tab in the *Project Options* dialog to view the options on the *Save* page shown in Figure 4 - 36. As indicated at the top of the *Save* page, use the options on this page to determine options for saving a project in Microsoft Project 2010.

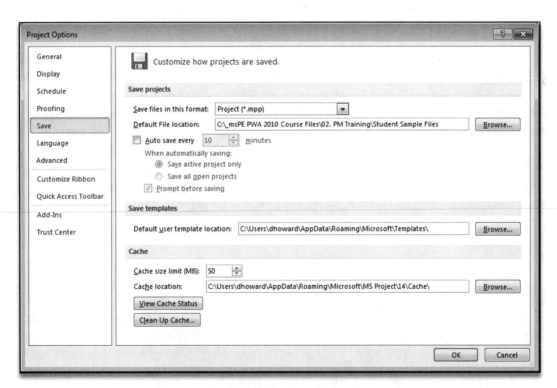

Figure 4 - 36: Project Options dialog, Save page

The only new options on the *Save* page are those found in the *Cache* section at the bottom of the page. You use the options in the *Cache* section to set the Cache location, view the Cache status, or clean up the Cache. I discuss how to work with the Cache later in this module.

Warning: If you like to perform a "what if" analysis in your project, and you select the *Auto save every ___ minutes* option, be sure to leave the *Prompt before saving* option **selected**. Otherwise, you risk the possibility of ovewriting your production project with the "what if" changes, with no recourse to use the *Undo* button since the save action clears the *Undo* cache.

Click the *Advanced* tab in the *Project Options* dialog to view the options on the *Advanced* page shown in Figure 4 - 37. As indicated at the top of the *Advanced* page, use the options on this page to specify advanced settings for Microsoft Project 2010.

Notice in Figure 4 - 37 that the *Advanced* page includes sections where you specify the following types of options: *General, Project Web App, Planning Wizard, General options for this project, Edit, Display, Display options for this project, Cross project linking, Earned Value,* and *Calculation*. The *Project Web App* section is available **only** in the Professional version of Microsoft Project 2010. If you have the Standard version of the software, you do not see the *Project Web App* section.

Microsoft Project 2010 includes two new options on the *Advanced* page: the *Show add-in user interface errors* option in the *General* section, and the *Automatically add new views, tables, filters, and groups to the global* option in the *Display* section. The first option displays errors originating from Project Add-ins in the project client interface. When you select the *Automatically add new views, tables, filters, and groups to the global* option (the default), the software automatically adds new views, tables, filters, and groups, to your Global.mpt file when you create them, making them available to all current and future projects. If you want to create custom views, tables, filters, and groups on a per-project basis, or if you want to manually control the content available in the Global.mpt file using the *Organizer* dialog, you should **deselect** the *Automatically add new views, tables, filters, and groups to the global* option.

Although not a new option, the *Show Project Summary Task* option offers a new setting state. To display the Project Summary Task in all new blank projects, click the *Display options for this project* pick list and choose the *All New Projects* item, and then select the *Show Project Summary Task* option. In prior versions of Microsoft Project, the system required you to select this option for each project individually.

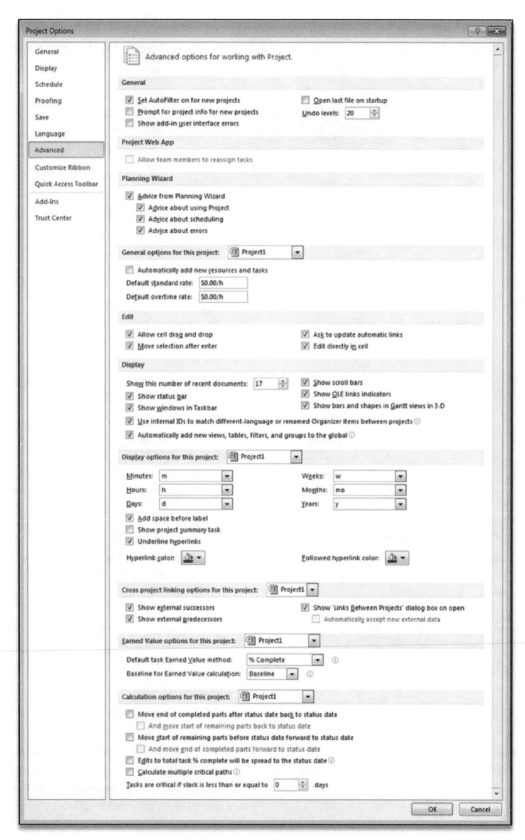

Figure 4 - 37: Project Options dialog, Advanced page

Table 4 - 4 shows the non-default options settings recommended by MSProjectExperts on the *Advanced* page of the *Project Options* dialog. Furthermore, MSProjectExperts recommends you set these options for all open projects and for all new projects as well.

Option	Setting
Automatically add new resources and tasks	Deselected
Minutes	m
Hours	h
Days	d
Weeks	w
Months	mo
Years	y
Show project summary task	Selected

Table 4 - 4: Recommended options on the
Advanced page for all current and future project

Click the *Trust Center* tab in the *Project Options* dialog to view the options on the *Trust Center* page shown in Figure 4 - 38. As indicated at the top of the *Trust Center* page, use the options on this page to provide security for your project and for your computer. The *Trust Center* page in the *Project Options* dialog provides three sections of security-related information:

- Protecting your privacy

- Security & more

- Microsoft Office Project Trust Center

The *Protecting your privacy* section includes three links, the *Show the Microsoft Office Project privacy statement*, the *Office.com privacy statement*, and the *Customer Experience Improvement Program* links. I do not discuss these options, as they are self-explanatory. The *Security & more* section includes the *Microsoft Trustworthy Computing* link that displays the *Microsoft Trustworthy Computing* website. Again, I do not discuss this option, as it self-explanatory.

Figure 4 - 38: Project Options dialog, Trust Center page

In the *Microsoft Office Project Trust Center* section, click the *Trust Center Settings* button to specify a range of security settings. For the sake of brevity, I discuss only two of these sections for security settings: the *Macro Settings* and *Legacy Formats* sections.

The system displays the *Macro Settings* page of the *Trust Center* dialog shown in Figure 4 - 39. Use the *Macro Settings* page to set your level of macro security. By default, Microsoft Project 2010 selects the *Disable all macros with notification* option, which prevents you from running macros in the application. The software notifies you in a warning dialog about this limitation when you attempt to run a macro. To avoid the security warnings, select the *Disable all macros without notification* option. To specify a lower level of macro security, select either the *Disable all macros except digitally signed macros* option or the *Enable all macros* option. Notice in the dialog shown in Figure 4 - 39 that Microsoft does not recommend selecting the *Enable all macros* option.

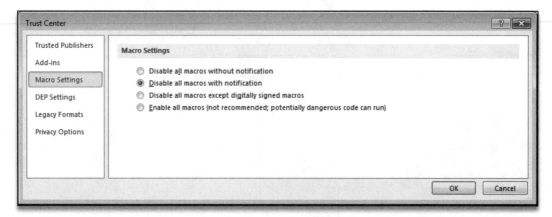

Figure 4 - 39: Trust Center dialog, Macro Settings page

Click the *Legacy Formats* tab to display the *Legacy Formats* page in the *Trust Center* dialog shown in Figure 4 - 40. The options on the *Legacy Formats* page control how Microsoft Project 2010 works with non-default and legacy file formats. Legacy formats controlled by this setting include:

- Microsoft Project Database files

- Microsoft Excel .xls workbook files

- Microsoft Access databases

- Project Exchange Format .mpx files

- Text .txt files

- Comma Delimited .csv files

The default *Do not open/save file with legacy or non-default file formats in Project* option prevents you from opening or closing files that are non-default or legacy format. If you need to work with non-default or legacy files, select either the *Prompt when loading files with legacy or non-default file format* option or the *Allow loading files with legacy or non-default file formats* option in the dialog.

Figure 4 - 40: Trust Center dialog, Legacy Formats page

Warning: If you do not change the default option setting in the *Legacy Formats* page of the *Trust Center* dialog, the system prevents you from either importing or exporting with a legacy or non-default file format such as the Microsoft Excel workbook format.

After selecting your options in the *Trust Center* dialog, click the *OK* button to close the dialog. Click the *OK* button to close the *Project Options* dialog as well. Table 4 - 5 shows the options settings recommended by MSProjectExperts on the *Trust Center* page of the *Project Options* dialog.

Option	Setting
Macro Settings	Disable all macros without notification
Legacy Formats	Allow loading files with legacy or non-default file formats

Table 4 - 5: Recommended options for the Trust Center page

Hands On Exercise

Exercise 4-7

In your new enterprise project, specify the settings recommended by MSProjectExperts in the *Project Options* dialog.

1. Click the *Set Project Options* button in the *Options* section of the *Definition* ribbon.

2. On the *General* page of the *Project Options* dialog, click the *Date format* pick list and select the *1/28/09* setting.

3. On the *Schedule* page, set the following options **for the active project** in the *Scheduling options for this project* section:

New tasks created	Auto Scheduled
New tasks are effort driven	Selected
Show that scheduled tasks have estimated durations	Deselected
New scheduled tasks have estimated durations	Deselected

4. On the *Schedule* page, click the *Scheduling options for this project* pick list, select the *All New Projects* item, and then set the following options **for all new projects**:

New tasks are effort driven	Selected
Show that scheduled tasks have estimated durations	Deselected
New scheduled tasks have estimated durations	Deselected

5. On the *Schedule* page, select the *Show task schedule suggestions* option **for the active project** in the *Schedule Alerts Options* section.

6. On the *Schedule* page, click the *Schedule Alerts Options* pick list, select the *All New Projects* item, and then select the *Show task schedule suggestions* option again **for all new projects**.

7. On the *Advanced* page, deselect the *Automatically add new resources and tasks* option **for the active project** in the *General options for this project* section.

8. On the *Advanced* page, click the *General options for this project* pick list, select the *All New Projects* item, and then deselect the *Automatically add new resources and tasks* option **for all new projects**.

9. On the *Advanced* page, set the following options **for the active project** in the *Display options for this project* section:

Minutes	m
Hours	h
Days	d
Weeks	w
Months	mo
Years	y
Show Project Summary Task	Selected

10. On the *Advanced* page, click the *Display options for this project* pick list, select the *All New Projects* item, and then specify **the same settings** from the previous step **for all new projects**.

11. On the *Trust Center* page, click the *Trust Center Settings* button.

12. On the *Macro Settings* page of the *Trust Center* dialog, select the *Disable all macros except digitally signed macros* option.

13. On the *Legacy Formats* page of the *Trust Center* dialog, select the *Allow loading files with legacy or non-default file formats* option.

14. Click the *OK* button to close the *Trust Center* dialog.

15. Click the *OK* button to close the *Project Options* dialog as well.

Save the Project

The final step in the 6-step definition process is to save your project according to your organization's naming convention for enterprise projects. To save the project, complete the following steps:

1. Click the *Save* button in the *Save* section of the *Definition* ribbon. The system displays the *Save to Project Server* dialog shown in Figure 4 - 41.

You can also display the *Save to Project Server* dialog by clicking the *Save* button on the Quick Access Toolbar, or by clicking the *File* tab and then clicking the *Save* or *Save As* items in the *Backstage* menu.

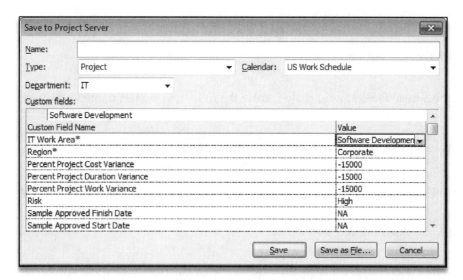

Figure 4 - 41: Save to Project Server dialog

2. In the *Name* field, enter a name that meets your organization's standards for naming an enterprise project.

Warning: When entering the name of your enterprise project, use only alphanumeric characters, spaces, and the underscore (_) character. **Do not** use any other special characters, such as ampersands (&), pound signs (#), dashes (-), or commas.

3. Click the *Save* button in the *Save to Project Server* dialog.

Notice in Figure 4 - 26 that the *Save to Project Server* dialog contains a *Calendar* pick list and a *Custom Fields* section, as seen previously in the *Project Information* dialog. This dialog gives you one last chance to change any of these values before saving your project.

Hands On Exercise

Exercise 4-8

Save your new project as an enterprise project using a naming convention.

1. Click the *Save* button in the *Save* section of the *Definition* ribbon.

2. In the *Save to Project Server* dialog, enter the following project name in the *Name* field:

    Your First Name Your Last Name Implement Training Advisor Software

3. In the *Custom Field Name* section of the dialog, change the value for the *Risk* field to *Medium*.

4. Click the *Save* button.

5. Observe the progress of your save operation on the *Status* bar at the bottom of your Project Professional 2010 application window.

Understanding the Local Cache

When you save a new enterprise project to the Project Server database, the Project Server 2010 system saves a complete copy of your project file on your hard drive in a location known as the **Local Project Cache**, and then "spools" the project information to the Project Server database. As you revise the project and save the changes, the system again saves a complete copy of your project in the Cache, but "spools" only the changes to the Project Server database. When you open a project, the system opens the copy in your Cache and then synchronizes this local copy with the enterprise project saved in the Project Server database. Because the Cache works in the background, it makes the process of opening and saving enterprise projects much faster, even over a Wide Area Network (WAN) connection.

When you save a project in the Project Server database, you can see the status of the Cache's "spooling" operation on the *Status* bar at the bottom of your Project Professional 2010 application window. When the system completes the "spooling" operation, it displays a *Save completed successfully* message in the application *Status* bar.

Adjusting Local Cache Settings

To view and adjust the default settings for the Cache, click the *Set Project Options* button in the *Options* section of the *Definition* ribbon. In the *Project Options* dialog, click the *Save* tab. Project Server 2010 displays the default settings for the Cache in the *Cache* section of the *Save* page in the *Project Options* dialog, as shown in Figure 4 - 42.

You can also access the *Save* page of the *Project Options* dialog by clicking the *File* tab and then clicking the *Options* item in the *Backstage* menu. In the *Project Options* dialog, click the *Save* tab.

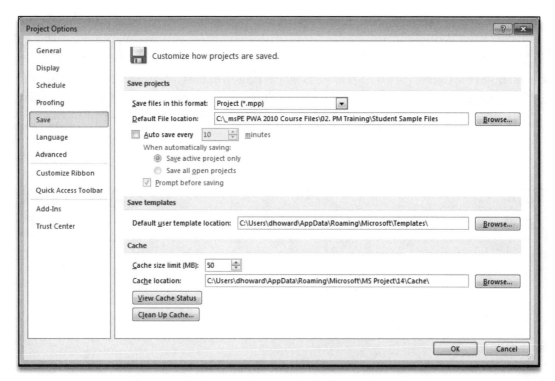

Figure 4 - 42: Cache settings in the Project Options dialog

The options in the *Cache* section of the *Project Options* dialog allow you to change two settings for the Cache: its size limit and its location. To adjust the size limit of the Cache, enter a new value in megabytes in the *Cache size limit (MB)* field. To change the location of the Cache, click the *Browse* button to the right of the *Cache location* field and select a new file location. Click the *OK* button when finished.

By default, Project Server 2010 stores the Cache data in the following folder:
C:\Users\YourUserID\AppData\Roaming\Microsoft\MS Project\14\Cache

Warning: If your job requires you to travel, and you need to take enterprise projects with you while traveling, **do not** specify a *Cache location* value that is outside your laptop's hard drive, such as on a network share. Project Server 2010 uses the Cache for offline projects, which allows you to check out and modify enterprise projects while away from your corporate network.

Viewing Local Cache Contents

To view the contents of the Cache, click the *Set Project Options* button in the *Options* section of the *Definition* ribbon. In the *Project Options* dialog, click the *Save* tab. In the *Cache* section of the *Save* page in the *Project Options* dialog, click the *View Cache Status* button. The system displays the *Active Cache Status* dialog shown in Figure 4 - 43.

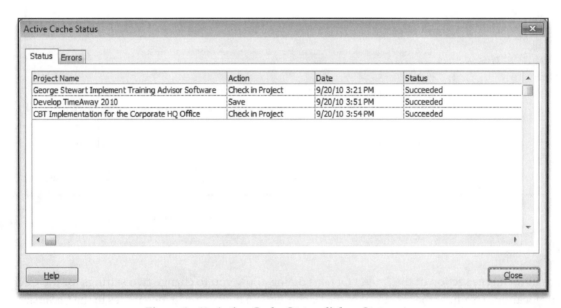

Figure 4 - 43: Active Cache Status dialog, Status page

The *Active Cache Status* dialog contains two pages: the *Status* and *Errors* pages. The *Status* page shows the status of recent Cache activities, such as saving or publishing a project. Notice in Figure 4 - 43 that I successfully saved one enterprise project and checked in two other projects. Click the *Errors* tab to see errors that occurred during a save or publish operation. The system displays the *Errors* page shown in Figure 4 - 44. Notice that I see no errors on the *Errors* page in the *Active Cache Status* dialog.

Figure 4 - 44: Active Cache Status dialog, Errors page

If you see errors of any kind on the *Errors* page in the *Active Cache Status* dialog, contact your Project Server administrator immediately for help.

When finished, click the *Close* button in the *Active Cache Status* dialog and then click either the *OK* or *Cancel* button to close the *Project Options* dialog as well.

Cleaning Up the Local Cache

At some point, you may wish to clean up the Cache to remove projects with which you no longer work, such as completed or cancelled projects, or to remove a project "stuck" in a checked-out state. To remove projects from the Cache, click the *Cleanup Cache* button in the *Plan and Publish* section of the *Project Server* ribbon. Project Server 2010 displays the *Clean Up Cache* dialog shown in Figure 4 - 45.

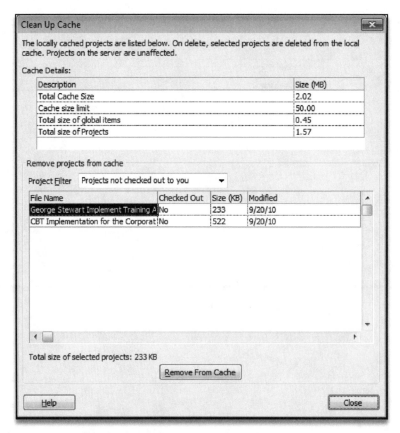

**Figure 4 - 45: Clean Up Cache dialog with the
Projects not checked out to you filter applied**

You can also access the *Clean Up Cache* dialog by clicking the *File* tab and then clicking the *Options* item in the *Backstage* menu. In the *Project Options* dialog, click the *Save* tab and then click the *Clean Up Cache* button in the *Cache* section of the dialog.

The *Clean Up Cache* dialog displays statistics about the Cache in the *Cache Details* section at the top of the dialog. Using the *Project Filter* pick list, you can apply two filtering options: *Projects not checked out to you* and *Projects checked out to you*. The system applies the *Projects not checked out to you* filter by default. Notice in Figure 4 - 45 that the system lists two projects not checked out to me currently.

Figure 4 - 46 shows the *Clean Up Cache* dialog after applying the *Projects checked out to you* filter on the *Project Filter* pick list. Notice that the *Clean Up Cache* dialog shows no projects currently checked out to me.

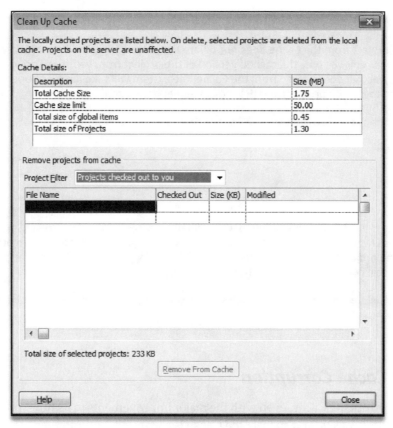

**Figure 4 - 46: Clean Up Cache dialog with the
Projects checked out to you filter applied**

To remove a project from the Cache, select the project in the *Remove projects from cache* list and then click the *Remove From Cache* button. If you select a project not checked out to you, the system simply removes the project from the Cache. If you attempt to delete a project checked out to you currently, the system displays the warning dialog shown in Figure 4 - 47.

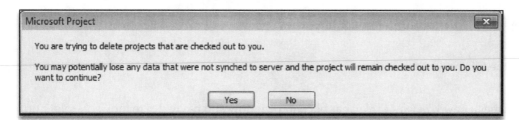

Figure 4 - 47: Warning dialog before deleting checked out project

If you are absolutely certain that the project is "stuck" in a checked-out state, and not checked out because the project is in *Offline* mode, then click the *Yes* button to delete the project from the cache. Click the *Close* button to close the *Clean Up Cache* dialog.

Deleting a project from the Cache **does not** delete the project from the Project Server database; instead, the operation removes only the cached version of the project from your hard drive. The next time you open a project that you deleted from the Cache, the system will take longer to open the project because it must load the entire project from the Project Server database.

Warning: If your Project Server administrator deletes a project from the Project Server database, and you are the Owner or Manager of the project, the system does not delete the project from your Cache. Because the project continues to appear in the *Open* dialog, you should delete the project from your Cache to avoid confusion and frustration.

Resolving Local Cache Corruption

Project Server 2010 can corrupt the Cache, even with the major improvements to its functionality. If you see unusual behavior in your enterprise projects, and suspect the Cache is corrupted, you can then safely delete the Cache files using the following steps:

1. Close Project Professional 2010.

2. Click the Start ➤ All Programs ➤ Accessories ➤ Run in your Windows application.

3. In the *Run* dialog, enter the following command:

    %appdata%\Microsoft\MS Project\14\Cache

4. Click the *OK* button.

Windows launches a new *Windows Explorer* application window and navigates to the *Cache* folder on your PC's hard drive.

5. Delete all of the folders and files in the *Cache* folder.

The next time you attempt to open projects in the Project Server database, you must use the *Retrieve the list of all projects from Project Server* option in the *Open* dialog.

Hands On Exercise

Exercise 4-9

Explore the features of the Local Project Cache.

1. Return to your new enterprise project, if necessary.

2. Click the *Set Project Options* button in the *Options* section of the *Definition* ribbon.

3. In the *Project Options* dialog, click the *Save* tab.

4. Examine the default settings in the *Cache* section of the dialog.

5. Click the *View Cache Status* button to display the *Active Cache Status* dialog.

6. Examine the information shown on the *Status* page and the *Errors* page of the dialog.

7. Click the *Close* button to close the *Active Cache Status* dialog.

8. Click the *Clean Up Cache* button to display the *Clean Up Cache* dialog

9. Study the information shown in the *Clean Up Cache* dialog with the *Projects not checked out to you* filter applied.

10. Click the *Project Filter* pick list and choose the *Projects checked out to you* item on the list.

11. Study the information shown in the *Clean Up Cache* dialog with the *Projects checked out to you* filter applied.

12. Click the *Close* button to close the *Clean Up Cache* dialog.

13. Click the *Cancel* button to close the *Project Options* dialog.

14. Save and close your enterprise project, and then check in the project when prompted.

Opening and Closing Projects

To open any project, click the *Open* button on the Quick Access Toolbar. Project Professional 2010 displays the *Open* dialog enterprise projects selected, as shown in Figure 4 - 48. In the *Open* dialog, you see only the projects that you have permission to access. By default, the system displays those projects currently in your Cache, along with the *Retrieve the list of all projects from Project Server* item at the top of the list. Notice that the *Open* dialog shown in Figure 4 - 48 shows only three projects, which are the only projects currently in the Cache.

> You can also display the *Open* dialog in Project Professional 2010 by clicking the *File* tab and then clicking the *Open* item in the *Backstage* menu.

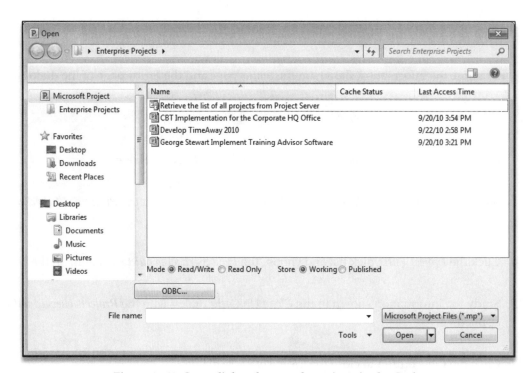

Figure 4 - 48: Open dialog shows only projects in the Cache

To display a list of all enterprise projects you have permission to access, double-click the *Retrieve the list of all projects from Project Server* item in the dialog. Based on your security permissions, the *Open* dialog refreshes with a list of all available projects in the Project Server database, as shown in Figure 4 - 49. Notice that the *Open* dialog now shows a number of additional projects that I have permission to access.

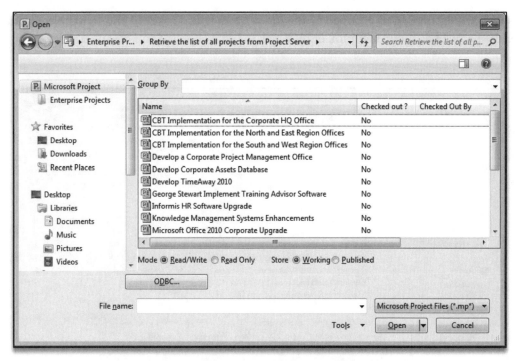

**Figure 4 - 49: Open dialog shows all projects available
to me in the Project Server 2010 database**

When viewing the list of available projects in the Project Server database, the *Open* dialog includes a *Group By* pick list above the list of projects. This pick list allows you to apply grouping to the projects listed in the dialog by any custom enterprise project field that contains a lookup table. If you want to group the projects listed, click the *Group By* pick list and select a custom enterprise field from the list, as shown in Figure 4 - 50.

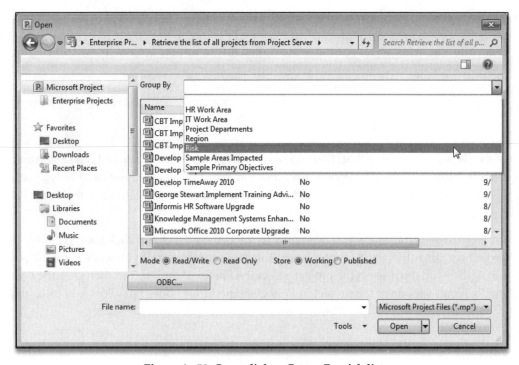

Figure 4 - 50: Open dialog, Group By pick list

Figure 4 - 51 shows the list of projects grouped by the *Risk* custom field. This field allows a project manager to determine whether the project has a low, medium, or high risk for date slippage and cost overruns.

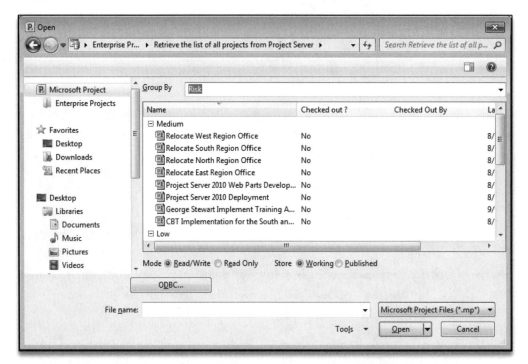

Figure 4 - 51: Open dialog, projects grouped by the Risk field

Warning: An odd behavior of the *Open* dialog is that the system sorts the project list in **Descending** order after you select an item on the *Group By* pick list. To sort the project list in Ascending order, you must click once on the *Name* column header.

At the bottom of the *Open* dialog, notice that there are two *Mode* options (*Read/Write* and *Read Only*) and two *Store* options (*Working* and *Published*). To open an enterprise project in *Read/Write* mode, you need only to select the project and click the *Open* button. To open a project in *Read Only* mode, select the project, select the *Read Only* option, and then click the *Open* button.

To open a project from the *Working* store, you need only to select the project and click the *Open* button. The *Working* version of the project contains all of the current information about the project. If you wish to see the published information for a project, then you must select the project, select the *Published* option, and then click the *Open* button. The system opens the *Published* version of the project in *Read Only* mode, and does not allow you to save changes to the project.

The *Working* version and *Published* version of a project may differ because you have edited an enterprise project and saved the changes, but have not yet published the changes to the Project Server database. Remember that only the *Published* version of the project is visible in the *Project Center* page in Project Web App.

If you attempt to open an enterprise project for which you only have permission to open in *Read Only* mode, Project Professional 2010 displays the warning dialog shown in Figure 4 - 52. Click the *Yes* button to open the project in *Read Only* mode.

Figure 4 - 52: Warning dialog when opening project with Read Only permissions

Deleting or Renaming a Project

Project Professional 2010 offers two additional features in the *Open* dialog when you have the list of all enterprise projects displayed. When you right-click on the name of any enterprise project, the system displays the shortcut menu shown in Figure 4 - 53.

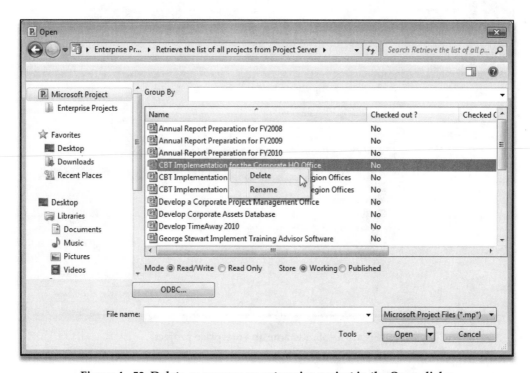

Figure 4 - 53: Delete or rename an enterprise project in the Open dialog

To delete an enterprise project, right-click on the name of the project and then select the *Delete* item on the shortcut menu. The system displays the confirmation dialog shown in Figure 4 - 54. Click the *Yes* button in the dialog to complete the deletion process. When the system deletes your project, it will delete the project in both the *Draft* and *Published* databases, and will delete the Project Site associated with the project as well.

Figure 4 - 54: Confirmation dialog to delete an enterprise project

 Warning: There is no *Undo* button to undo the deletion of an enterprise project. If you delete a project accidentally, contact your Project Server administrator immediately. Your administrator may be able to restore the project from the *Archive* database, if a backup of the project exists.

To rename an enterprise project, right-click on the name of the project and then select the *Rename* item on the shortcut menu. The system highlights the name of the project in renaming mode as shown in Figure 4 - 55.

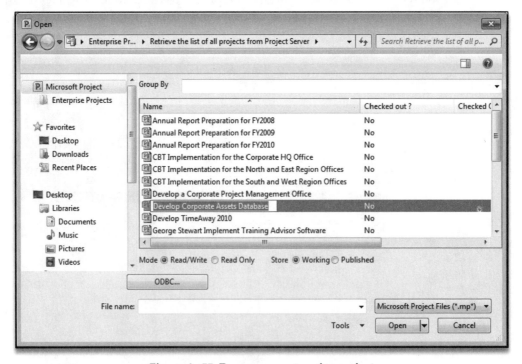

Figure 4 - 55: Rename an enterprise project

Edit the name of the project and press the **Enter** key on your computer keyboard. Project Professional 2010 displays the confirmation dialog shown in Figure 4 - 56.

Figure 4 - 56: Confirmation dialog for renaming a project

Click the *OK* button to close the confirmation dialog. To see the new name of the project, click the *Cancel* button to close the *Open* dialog. Click the *Open* button on the Quick Access Toolbar and then double-click the *Retrieve the list of all projects from Project Server* item in the *Open* dialog. Project Professional 2010 displays the new name of the enterprise project, as shown in Figure 4 - 57.

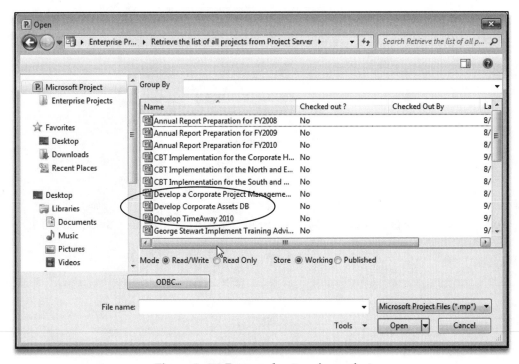

Figure 4 - 57: Renamed enterprise project

Warning: Using this process to rename a project only changes the project name in the *Draft* database. If the renamed project is a published project, you must open the project and publish it to change the project name in the *Published* database.

Opening a Non-Enterprise Project

Beyond opening enterprise projects, the *Open* dialog also allows you to open non-enterprise projects (local projects) stored outside the Project Server database in other file formats. For example, click the *My Documents* icon in the folder list on the left side of the dialog to open projects stored as .mpp files in the *My Documents* folder. You can also click the *ODBC* button to open projects stored in an *ODBC* database, such as an SQL Server database that is not part of the Project Server 2010 database system.

Closing an Enterprise Project

When you open an enterprise project in *Read/Write* mode, the system checks out the project to you. This allows you to edit the project exclusively, and limits all other users to opening the project in *Read Only* mode. To close an enterprise project properly, click the *Close* button on your Quick Access Toolbar. When you close the project, the system prompts you to check in the project with the confirmation dialog shown in Figure 4 - 58. Click the *Yes* button to check in the project.

**Figure 4 - 58: Check in
enterprise project dialog**

 You can also close a project by clicking the *File* tab and then clicking the *Close* item in the *Backstage* menu.

 Warning: Do not close an enterprise project by clicking either the *Close Window* button (**X**) or the *Close* button (big **X**) in the upper right corner of the Project Professional 2010 application window. Using either of these buttons to close your enterprise project is the primary cause of projects getting "stuck" in a checked-out state in the Cache.

To close an enterprise project, MSProjectExperts recommends that you click the *File* tab and then click the *Close* item in the *Backstage* menu. To exit the application, click the *File* tab and then click the *Exit* item in the *Backstage* menu. Make this a habit to avoid the possibility of an enterprise project becoming "stuck" in a checked-out state.

Hands On Exercise

Exercise 4-10

Experiment with features in the *Open* dialog in Project Professional 2010.

1. Click the *File* tab and then click the *Open* item in the *Backstage* menu.

2. Examine the list of projects in the Cache shown in the *Open* dialog.

3. Double-click the *Retrieve the list of all projects from Project Server* item at the top of the project list.

4. Examine the list of projects you can access in the Project Server database.

5. Click the *Group By* pick list and select the *Region* field from the list.

6. Notice how the *Open* dialog groups the projects by regions.

7. Click the *Name* column header to sort the projects by region in Ascending order.

8. Click the *Group By* pick list again and select the blank item at the top of the list to remove grouping in the *Open* dialog.

9. Right-click on the *Your Name Implement Training Advisor Software* project and select the *Rename* item on the shortcut menu.

10. Change the name of the project to *Your Name Deploy Training Advisor Software* and press the **Enter** key on your keyboard.

11. Click the *OK* button in the resulting confirmation dialog stating *The rename job was successfully submitted to server*.

12. Click the *Cancel* button to close the *Open* dialog.

13. Click the *File* tab and then click the *Open* item in the *Backstage* menu.

14. Double-click the *Retrieve the list of all projects from Project Server* item at the top of the project list.

15. Notice the new name of the project you renamed.

16. Select the *Your Name Deploy Training Advisor Software* project and click the *Open* button.

Working with Offline Projects

Project Professional 2010 and Project Server 2010 allow you to work on projects in *Offline* mode in situations where you must travel away from your company network. If you are a traveling project manager and need to take a project with you on the road, complete the following steps to save a project in *Offline* mode:

1. Before you disconnect from the corporate network, launch Project Professional 2010 and log in to Project Server.

2. Open the enterprise project you wish to make an *Offline* project.

3. Click the *Close* button on your Quick Access Toolbar. The system displays a confirmation dialog shown previously in Figure 4 - 58.

4. In the confirmation dialog, click the *No* button to close the project but leave it in a checked-out state.

5. Click the *File* tab and then click the *Exit* item in the *Backstage* menu to exit Project Professional 2010.

The first set of steps loads the latest version of the enterprise project into your Cache as an *Offline* project, but leaves the project checked out so that no one can modify it while you are working with it in *Offline* mode. While you are away from your corporate network, you can work with the *Offline* project by completing the following steps:

1. Launch Project Professional 2010. The system displays the *Login* dialog shown in Figure 4 - 59.

Figure 4 - 59: Login dialog

2. In the *Login* dialog, click the *Profile* pick list and select the Project Server login account for your production Project Server 2010 instance (**do not** select the *Computer* account from the *Profile* pick list).

3. Click the *Work Offline* button.

Project Professional 2010 launches in *Offline* mode without connecting to your Project Server system. The *Status* bar at the bottom of the application indicates that the software is in *Offline* mode, as shown in Figure 4 - 60.

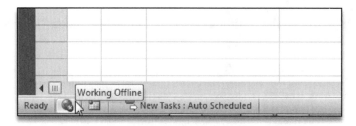

**Figure 4 - 60: Project Professional 2010
launched in Offline mode**

4. Click the *Open* button on your Quick Access Toolbar.

The system displays the *Open* dialog with a list of projects saved in the Cache, as shown in Figure 4 - 61. Notice that the *Cache Status* column in the dialog indicates that the *Develop TimeAway 2010* project is currently checked out.

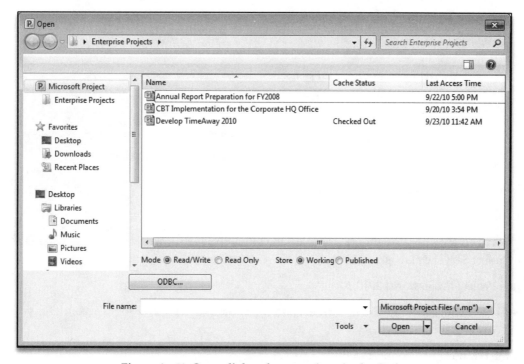

Figure 4 - 61: Open dialog shows projects in the Cache

5.   In the *Open* dialog, select your *Offline* project and click the *Open* button.

While working with a project in *Offline* mode, you can perform many activities that you can do while working online, such as adding and editing tasks, setting task dependencies, etc. However, you cannot perform any activity in the project that requires a login connection to Project Server, such as using the *Build Team* dialog.

6.   Edit your project as needed and then click the *Save* button on your Quick Access Toolbar to save the *Offline* project in the Cache.

When you save your project while working in *Offline* mode, the system displays the message *Project Offline. Cannot synchronize data to server* in the right end of the *Status* bar at the bottom of the Project Professional 2010 application window.

7.   Click the *Close* button on the Quick Access Toolbar to close the *Offline* project.

8. When the dialog prompts you to check in your project, click the *No* button once again. If your project contains resources assigned to tasks, and you revised the task schedule in any way, the system displays the informational dialog shown in Figure 4 - 62.

Figure 4 - 62: Information dialog about resource schedule changes

9. Click the *OK* button to close the informational dialog.

10. Click the *File* tab and then click the *Exit* item in the *Backstage* menu to exit Project Professional 2010.

When you return to your corporate network, complete the following steps to save the changes you made to the *Offline* project to the Project Server database:

1. Launch Project Professional 2010.

2. In the *Login* dialog, click the *Profile* pick list and select the Project Server login account for your production Project Server 2010 instance.

3. Click the *OK* button to connect to Project Server.

4. Click the *Open* button on your Quick Access Toolbar.

5. In the *Open* dialog, select your *Offline* project and click the *Open* button.

6. Click the *Save* button on the Quick Access Toolbar to synchronize your changes to the *Offline* project with the Project Server database.

Hands On Exercise

Exercise 4-11

Save an enterprise project in *Offline* mode, edit the project, and then synchronize the changes with the Project Server database.

1. Click the *Open* button on the Quick Access Toolbar and open your class project, if necessary.

2. Click the *Close* button on the Quick Access Toolbar to close the *Offline* project.

3. In the dialog, click the *No* button when prompted to check in the project.

4. Click the *File* tab and then click the *Exit* item in the *Backstage* menu to exit Project Professional 2010.

5. Launch Project Professional 2010 again.

6. In the *Login* dialog, leave the *Profile* value set to the Project Server instance used for this training course, and then click the *Work Offline* button.

7. Open your class project, now saved in *Offline* mode.

8. Change the *Duration* value to *4d* for task ID #2, the *Determine Hardware Specifications* task.

9. Click the *Save* button on the Quick Access Toolbar to save the changes to the *Offline* project.

10. Click the *Close* button on the Quick Access Toolbar to close the project and click the *No* button when prompted to check in the project.

11. If prompted in an informational dialog about resource changes, click the *OK* button to close the dialog.

12. Click the *File* tab and then click the *Exit* item in the *Backstage* menu to exit Project Professional 2010.

13. Launch Project Professional 2010 again.

14. In the *Login* dialog, leave the *Profile* value set to the Project Server instance used for this training course, and then click the *OK* button.

15. Click the *Open* button on the Quick Access Toolbar and open your class project again.

16. Click the *Save* button on the Quick Access Toolbar to save the changes to your class project.

Notice that you have now saved your project in *Online* mode and it reflects the change you made to the *Duration* value of task ID #2 while in *Offline* mode.

17. Click the *Close* button on the Quick Access Toolbar to close the project and click the *Yes* button when prompted to check in the project.

Module 05

Task Planning

Learning Objectives

After completing this module, you will be able to:

- Understand the task planning process
- Understand change highlighting
- Use Manually Scheduled tasks and Auto Scheduled tasks
- Use basic task planning skills to create a project schedule
- Set task dependencies, constraints, and deadline dates
- Document the task list with appropriate task notes
- Use cell background formatting to display tasks of interest
- Estimate task Durations
- Enter a Fixed Cost on a task

Inside Module 05

Understanding the Task Planning Process

After you define your project, the planning process begins. The first step in the planning process is task planning. If you do not create your project from a template, then you must manually complete a series of steps in Project Professional 2010 to complete the task planning process.

When you create a task list manually, you must thoughtfully analyze the activities required to complete the project. Depending on the size of your project, this may mean lots of typing! You can use either a "top down" or "bottom up" approach to create the initial task list. The "top down" approach begins by listing the major phases of the project, as well as the project deliverables under each phase. Under each deliverable you list the activities necessary to produce the deliverable. To help you with the process of "top down" planning, Project Professional 2010 includes a new feature that allows you to insert "top down" summary tasks. I discuss this new feature later in this module.

The "bottom up" approach works in the opposite direction. Using this approach, you list all of the activities in the project and then organize the activities into phase and deliverable summary sections. You can be effective in creating the task list for the project using either approach. Your organization may adhere to pre-defined project lifecycle standards, which obligate you to use a structured framework. Whenever you create a new project manually, it is a good idea to follow this methodology:

1. Create the task list.

2. Create summary tasks to generate the project's Work Breakdown Structure (WBS).

3. Create project milestones.

4. Set task dependencies and document unusual task dependencies with a task note.

5. Set task constraints and deadline dates, and document all task constraints with a task note.

6. Set task calendars for any task with an alternate working schedule and document the task calendars with a task note.

7. Estimate task effort or durations according to your preferred or required methodologies.

8. Enter known fixed costs.

In successive topical sections in this module, I discuss each of the steps in the preceding task planning methodology.

Auto-Wrapping Task Names

During the task planning process, you see the new *Auto-Wrap Task Names* feature in Project Professional 2010 when you enter a task name that exceeds the width of the *Task Name* column. This feature increases the row height automatically and wraps the text inside the cell. In all previous versions of the tool, the only way to auto-wrap task names was to manually increase the height of the task row until the task name wrapped completely within the cell. In Project Professional 2010, the software auto-wraps task names in cells when one of several events occurs:

- You manually type a task name that exceeds the width of the *Task Name* column and then press the **Enter** key to complete the data entry. The software automatically increases the row height for that task to wrap the task name within the cell.

- You paste a task name that exceeds the width of the *Task Name* column. The software automatically increases the row height for that task to wrap the task name within the cell.

- You manually decrease the width of the *Task Name* column. The software automatically increases the row height for **every** task with a name exceeding the width of the *Task Name* column.

- You manually increase the width of the *Task Name* column. The software automatically decreases the row height for that task and un-wraps the text.

Warning: Project Professional 2010 **does not** decrease the row height of wrapped tasks automatically when you widen the *Task Name* column to "best fit" the longest task name. This means you must manually decrease the row height of every task row that includes a task name formerly wrapped using the new *Auto-Wrap Task Names* feature.

Understanding Change Highlighting

Whenever you make a change anywhere in a Project Professional 2010 schedule, the software uses change highlighting to graphically show you all tasks impacted by the change. This behavior begins the moment you enter the first task in the project and continues until you complete the project. For example, if you change the schedule of any task with successors, the software applies the light blue cell background color in the *Duration*, *Start*, and/or *Finish* columns for every impacted task. Figure 5 - 1 shows a project before I make revisions to the schedule. Figure 5 - 2 shows the same project after I change the duration of the Test task from 2 days to 4 days. Notice how Project Professional 2010 changes the cell formatting color for the *Duration* and *Finish* columns of the Test task, and changes the cell formatting color to the *Start* and/or *Finish* columns of each impacted task and summary task, including the Project Summary Task.

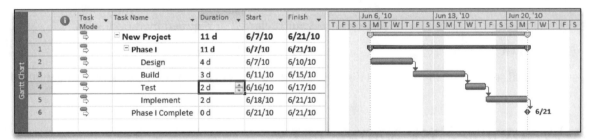

Figure 5 - 1: Project before schedule changes

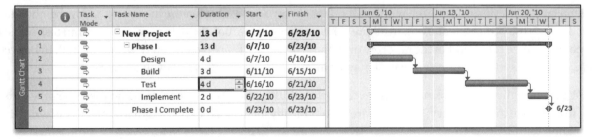

Figure 5 - 2: Project after making schedule changes

To change the cell background color used to indicate changed tasks, click the *Format* tab to display the *Format* ribbon. In the *Format* section of the *Format* ribbon, click the *Text Styles* button. In the *Text Styles* dialog, click the *Item to Change* pick list and select the *Changed Tasks* item on the list. Select a different color in the *Background Color* pick list and click the *OK* button.

Understanding Manually Scheduled vs. Auto Scheduled Tasks

By now you must be more than a little curious about how you actually use what is probably the most important change to Project Professional 2010 in many years, *Manually Scheduled* tasks. You may also be wondering why Microsoft chose to introduce manual scheduling, and if you are a dynamic scheduling purist, you might even be close to convulsions when you think about how uncontrollable a schedule can be using this feature.

One of Microsoft's goals in introducing *Manually Scheduled* tasks is to lower the barrier for entry-level users accustomed to managing their projects in Excel so that they can start to learn how to use a scheduling tool. The thinking is that this at least gets them into the correct environment. When a user sets a task to *Manually Scheduled* mode, entering task data into a project does not cause task dates to change unless the user specifies them. Users who are untrained in the behaviors of the Microsoft Project scheduling engine are typically put off by the scheduling engine's insistence on remaining in control of dates in all prior versions of Microsoft Project.

The new *Manually Scheduled* tasks feature also addresses another previously unmet Microsoft Project user need by providing a way to represent tasks where scheduling information is unavailable, such as during early phase planning. Additionally, this feature helps Microsoft Project work better with real-world scenarios, such as scheduling projects where agile methodologies are in use.

Manually Scheduled tasks do not require duration, start date, or finish date data, thereby providing complete flexibility. As you learned previously in Module 04, among your first steps in specifying options settings for a new project is to set the *Task Mode* setting to either the *Manually Scheduled* or *Auto Scheduled* option. Unless specified by your Project Server administrator, Project Professional 2010 sets the default *Task Mode* option to *Manually Scheduled* for all tasks in every new project. As you create your task list, the software sets each new task to the *Task Mode* setting you specified in your first task entry or to the *Task Mode* setting your Project Server administer specified as the default value in Project Server 2010.

Using Basic Task Planning Skills

You should possess a variety of basic task skills to use Project Professional 2010 effectively. I discuss each of these basic task planning skills in the following topical sections.

Entering and Editing Tasks

Entering *Auto Scheduled* tasks and *Manually Scheduled* tasks in Project Professional 2010 is very similar to entering data in a Microsoft Excel spreadsheet. To enter a new task, complete the following steps:

1. Select a blank cell in the *Task Name* column of the task sheet.

2. Type the task name.

3.   Press the **Enter** key or **Down-Arrow** key on your computer keyboard.

To edit the name of an existing task, select the task and then use any of the following methods:

- Double-click the task and edit the name in the *Task Information* dialog.

- Retype the task name.

- Press the **F2** function key on your computer keyboard and edit the task name.

- Select the name of the task and then click anywhere in the cell to enable in-cell editing.

Entering Manually Scheduled Tasks

During the task planning process, you can designate any task as either a *Manually Scheduled* task or an *Auto Scheduled* task. To specify the *Task Mode* setting for any task, complete the following steps:

1.   Click the *Task* tab to display the *Task* ribbon.

2.   Select the task(s) whose *Task Mode* setting you want to change.

3.   Click the *Manually Schedule* button or the *Auto Schedule* button on the *Task* ribbon.

To specify the *Task Mode* setting for an individual task, you can also select a cell in the *Task Mode* column for the task, click the pick list in the *Task Mode* cell, and choose either *Manually Scheduled* or *Auto Scheduled* from the list.

Figure 5 - 3 shows a project in which I included four *Auto Scheduled* tasks (Design, Build, Test, and Implement) and two *Manually Scheduled* tasks (Rebuild and Retest). Notice the following about this project:

- Project Professional 2010 displays a unique indicator to the left of each task in the *Indicators* column to identify the *Task Mode* setting for each task.

- Every *Auto Scheduled* task includes a duration value in the *Duration* column, along with date values in the *Start* and *Finish* columns.

- The Rebuild and Retest tasks have no values in the *Duration*, *Start*, or *Finish* columns.

- The *Gantt Chart* view does not include Gantt bars for these two *Manually Scheduled* tasks.

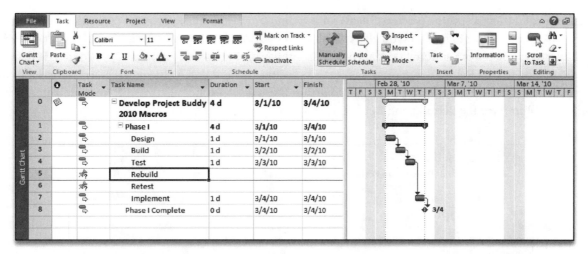

Figure 5 - 3: New project includes both Manually Scheduled and Auto Scheduled tasks

When you specify any task as a *Manually Scheduled* task, Project Professional 2010 allows you to specify values in the *Duration*, *Start*, and *Finish* columns in a number of ways, including:

- Specify no duration, start, or finish values until you have an estimated duration, start, or finish date.

- Enter text information in the *Duration* column about an approximate duration, and enter text information in the *Start* and *Finish* columns about approximate start and finish dates.

- Enter an estimated duration (such as *5 days*) in the *Duration* column, and/or an estimated date (such as *03/18/2012*) in the *Start* and *Finish* columns.

> In addition to typing text to enter an approximate duration, start date, or finish date, you can enter other textual information, such as *TBD* or *Decision by 11/01/10*.

In Figure 5 - 3 shown previously, you can see an example of two *Manually Scheduled* tasks with no duration, start, or finish date information. When you create a new *Manually Scheduled* task, Project Professional 2010 leaves the *Duration*, *Start*, and *Finish* columns blank. In Figure 5 - 4, you see an example of two *Manually Scheduled* tasks with approximate duration values (entered as "About 1w" and "About 2d") and approximate start dates (entered as "Late May" and "Early June").

4			Test	1 d	3/3/10	3/3/10
5			Rebuild	*About 1w*	*Late May*	
6			Retest	*About 2d*	*Early June*	
7			Implement	1 d	3/4/10	3/4/10

Figure 5 - 4: Approximate Duration and Start values for *Manually Scheduled* tasks

If you enter a valid duration value (such as *5 days*) for a *Manually Scheduled* task, Project Professional 2010 displays a "highlighted" Gantt bar for the task. If you also enter a valid date value (such as *12/21/2012*) in the *Start* or *Finish* columns, the software displays a silhouetted teal-colored Gantt bar for the task. In Figure 5 - 5, notice that I entered a valid duration value for the Rebuild and Retest tasks, and specified a valid date value in the *Start* column for only the Retest task. Notice the two different types of Gantt bars for these tasks. Notice also the different indicators shown in the *Indicators* column for the Rebuild and Retest tasks.

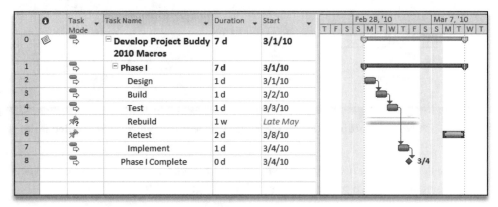

Figure 5 - 5: Manually Scheduled tasks with Duration
and Start date values specified

Moving Tasks

During the task planning process, you may create the task list with tasks in the wrong order. To move a task, complete the following steps:

1. Click the task ID number (row header) on the far left end of the task and then release the mouse button.

2. Click and hold the task ID number to "grab" the task.

3. Move the mouse pointer up or down on the screen to move the task.

As you move the mouse pointer, you see a gray I-beam bar to indicate that you are moving the task, as shown in Figure 5 - 6.

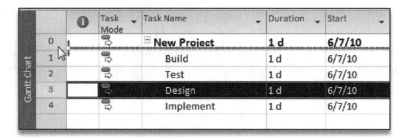

Figure 5 - 6: Moving a task

4. Drag the task until you position the gray I-beam indicator where you want to place the task.

5. Release the mouse button to complete the move and "drop" the task in its new location.

You can move a single task, or you can move a group of tasks using this technique. When you move a summary task, all of its subtasks move with it.

164

Warning: Using cut and paste, or copy and paste, instead of using the proper move technique described above can lead to data corruption for enterprise projects stored in the Project Server database. When you cut and paste entire rows, you duplicate key data that can cause corruption in the database.

Hands On Exercise

Exercise 5-1

Add new tasks and move tasks in your enterprise project.

1. Reopen the enterprise project you created in Exercise 4-2 (your Deploy Training Advisor Software project), if necessary.

2. Select the first blank cell in the *Task Name* column below task ID #15, the *PROJECT COMPLETE* task.

3. On the left end of the *Status* bar at the bottom of your Project Professional 2010 application window, click the *Default Task Mode* selector and select the *Manually Scheduled* option on the pick list.

4. Add a new task named *Build P3* and press the **Enter** key on your computer keyboard.

5. Add another new task named *Test P3* and press the **Enter** key again.

6. Drag the split bar to the right side of the *Finish* column.

Notice that the two new *Manually Scheduled* tasks do not have a value in the *Duration*, *Start*, or *Finish* columns.

7. For task ID #16, the *Build P3* task, enter *3d* in the *Duration* column and then press the **Enter** key.

8. For task ID #17, the *Test P3* task, enter *Next Week* in the *Start* column and then press the **Enter** key.

Notice how Project Professional 2010 draws a light blue shaded Gantt bar for the *Build P3* task. Notice also that the software allows you to enter a non-date value in the *Start* column for the *Test P3* task.

9. Drag the split bar back to the right side of the *Duration* column.

10. Select the row headers (the ID numbers) for the two new tasks and then release the mouse button.

11. Click and hold the mouse button on either task ID #16 or #17 and then drag the selected task immediately below task ID #13, the *Design P3* task.

12. Click the *Default Task Mode* selector in the left end of the *Status* bar and select the *Auto Scheduled* option on the pick list.

13. Click the *Save* button on the Quick Access Toolbar to save the changes to your enterprise project.

Inserting Tasks

While entering a task list, you may discover that you omitted one or more tasks. To insert new tasks in your project plan, select any cell in the row where you want to insert the new task and then use one of the following methods:

- On the *Task* ribbon, click the *Task* button in the *Insert* section of the ribbon.

- Press the **Insert** key on your computer keyboard.

- Right-click in the row and then select the *Insert Task* item on the shortcut menu.

Project Professional 2010 adds a new blank task row automatically above the selected task. If you add the new task using the **Insert** key on your keyboard, the system simply adds a new blank task. If you use the *Task* button on the *Task* ribbon or the *Insert Task* item on the shortcut menu, the system adds a new task named *<New Task>* with a default duration of 1 day. After using any of these three methods, you must still enter the name of the new task.

To add multiple new tasks simultaneously, select as many rows as the number of new tasks you would like to add, and use one of the preceding methods. For example, in Figure 5 - 7 I want to add two new tasks before the Implement task, so I select the Implement task and the following blank task as the location of the two new tasks.

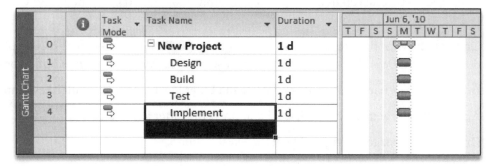

Figure 5 - 7: Preparing to insert two new tasks after the Test task

When I click the *Task* button on the *Task* ribbon, the software inserts two new tasks named *<New Task>* with a *Duration* value of *1 day*, as shown in Figure 5 - 8.

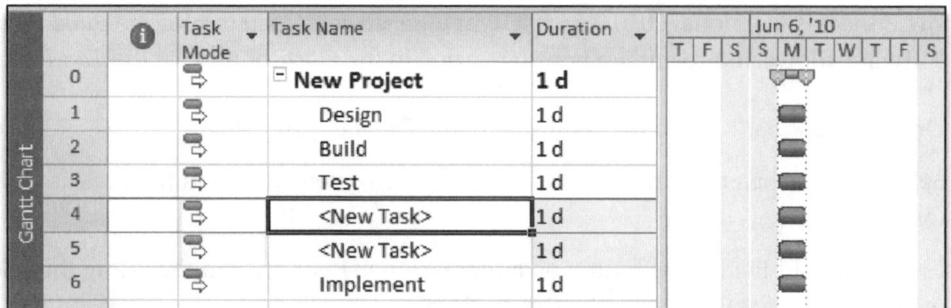

Figure 5 - 8: Two new tasks inserted before the Implement task

Deleting Tasks

While entering a task list, you may find that you no longer need one or more tasks in the project plan. To delete a task, complete the following steps, select the ID number of the task you want to delete and use one of the following methods:

- Press the **Delete** key on your computer keyboard.

- Right-click in the selected row and then select the *Delete Task* item on the shortcut menu.

If you select any cell in the *Task Name* column (rather than selecting the task ID number) and then press the **Delete** key on your computer keyboard, the software displays a *Smart Tag* to the left of the cell. When you float your mouse pointer over the *Smart Tag*, the system displays a pick list. Click the *Smart Tag* pick list and then select whether to clear the contents of only the *Task Name* cell or to delete the entire task. Figure 5 - 9 shows the *Smart Tag* for deleting a task after selecting only the name of the task, rather than the task ID number.

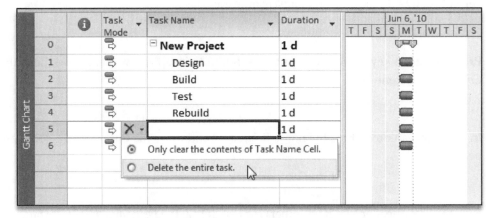

Figure 5 - 9: Smart Tag displayed after deleting a task

 When you select a cell in the *Resource Name* column in any resource view and press the **Delete** key, the software also displays a *Smart Tag* to the left of the cell. The choices are similar to those offered while deleting a cell in any task view.

Hands On Exercise

Exercise 5-2

Team members proposed adding a new task called Rebuild P2 in the Phase II section of the project. They also propose deleting the Determine Hardware Specifications task since they believe you do not need it in this project. Therefore, insert the new proposed task and delete the unnecessary task in your enterprise project.

1. Return to your Deploy Training Advisor Software project, if necessary.

2. Click the *Default Task Mode* selector in the left end of the *Status* bar and select the *Auto Scheduled* option on the pick list, if not already selected.

3. Select task ID #12, the *Phase II Complete* milestone task.

4. Press the **Insert** key on your computer keyboard to insert a new blank row above the *Phase II Complete* milestone task.

5. In the new blank row, type the name *Rebuild P2* and press the **Enter** key on your computer keyboard.

6. Select the row header (the ID number) for task ID #2, the *Determine Hardware Specifications* task, and then press the **Delete** key on your computer keyboard.

7. Click the *Save* button on the Quick Access Toolbar to save the changes to your enterprise project.

Creating the Work Breakdown Structure (WBS)

The Work Breakdown Structure (WBS) divides the project tasks into meaningful and logical components. The WBS consists of summary tasks representing major aspects of the project, such as phase and deliverable sections, along with subtasks in each summary section. Figure 5 - 10 shows a simple generic Work Breakdown Structure comprised of phase and deliverable sections, with four subtasks in each deliverable section.

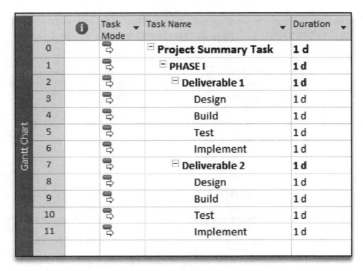

Figure 5 - 10: Work Breakdown Structure

To create a Work Breakdown Structure in a project, you must create a series of summary tasks and subtasks. The purpose of summary tasks is to summarize or "roll up" the data contained in the subtasks. Project Professional 2010 offers you several ways to create summary tasks and subtasks. As with all previous versions of the software, you can create summary tasks and subtasks by completing the following steps:

1. Type the names of a summary task and its subtasks.

2. Select the tasks that you want to make subtasks of the summary task.

3. Click the *Indent* button in the *Schedule* section of the *Task* ribbon.

In the project shown in Figure 5 - 11, I select from the Design task through the Implement task to prepare to make them subtasks of the PHASE I summary task.

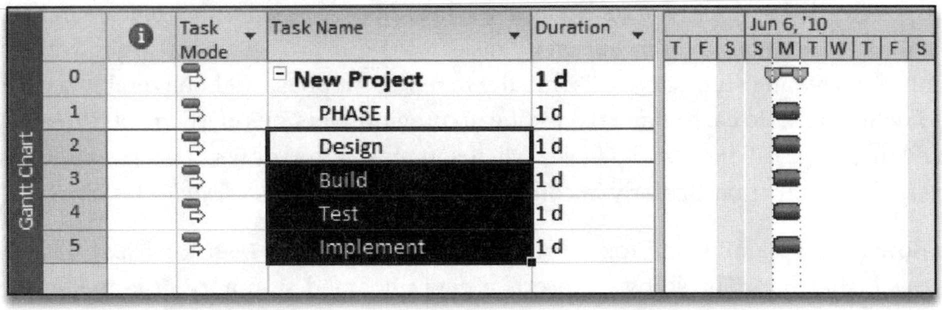

Figure 5 - 11: Prepare to make PHASE I a summary task

After I click the *Indent* button in the *Schedule* section of the *Task* ribbon, the software makes the four selected tasks subtasks of the PHASE I summary task. Figure 5 - 12 shows the result of this procedure.

	ⓘ	Task Mode	Task Name	Duration	Jun 6, '10
0			⊟ **New Project**	**1 d**	
1			⊟ **PHASE I**	**1 d**	
2			Design	1 d	
3			Build	1 d	
4			Test	1 d	
5			Implement	1 d	

Figure 5 - 12: PHASE I summary task with four subtasks

Notice in Figure 5 - 12 how Project Professional 2010 displays summary tasks and subtasks:

- It formats PHASE I in bold.

- It shows an outline indicator (+ sign) in front of the PHASE I task name.

- It changes the Gantt bar shape for PHASE I.

- It indents the Design task through the Implement task one level to the right of PHASE I.

Converting an existing task to a summary task causes the system to roll up information from the subtasks to the summary task. This changes the behavior of the summary task, but it does not change any underlying data that you previously entered in the existing task before you converted it to a summary task. If you convert the summary task back to a regular task, any previously entered data reappears. Because this can cause surprising schedule changes, MSProjectExperts recommends that you create all of your summary tasks **from new tasks** rather than by converting tasks in which you previously entered work or duration values.

Inserting Summary Tasks

The other method for creating summary tasks is to use the new *Insert Summary Task* feature in Project Professional 2010. This new feature allows you to insert summary tasks into your project. Many organizations like to do "top down" task planning by creating summary tasks initially to represent phase and deliverable sections in the project, and then they add regular tasks to each summary section. In previous versions of Microsoft Project, "top down" task planning was difficult. In the 2010 version, however, Microsoft makes "top down" task planning easier by using the new *Insert Summary Task* feature, particularly in combination with *Manually Scheduled* tasks.

To perform "top down" task planning in Project Professional 2010, click the *Insert Summary Task* button 🚚 in the *Insert* section of the *Task* ribbon. The software inserts a new unnamed summary task and subtask, as shown in Figure 5 - 13.

	ⓘ	Task Mode	Task Name	Duration
1		⇨	⊟ **\<New Summary Task\>**	**1 day**
2		🖈?	\<New Task\>	

**Figure 5 - 13: Newly Inserted Summary Task during
"top down" task planning process**

After inserting the new summary task and subtask pair, you should edit the name of the summary task, replacing the default value with the name of the phase or deliverable section it represents. Similarly, you eventually edit the name of the subtask and add additional subtasks as needed. You can leave the name of the subtask with its original \<New Task\> name as a placeholder for a future subtask until you are ready to add detail tasks to the summary section.

If you insert a summary task below another summary task or a subtask, Project Professional 2010 automatically indents the new summary task at the same level of indenture as the task immediately preceding it. This is the default behavior of the tool, and you cannot change it. For example, Figure 5 - 14 shows a new summary task and subtask pair inserted after the Design task. Notice that the system indented the new summary task at the same level as the Design task preceding it. To resolve the indenting situation shown in Figure 5 - 14, select the new summary task and then click the *Outdent Task* 🔙 button in the *Schedule* section of the *Task* ribbon.

	ⓘ	Task Mode	Task Name	Duration
1		⇨	⊟ **Phase I**	**1 day**
2		🖈?	Design	
3		⇨	⊟ **\<New Summary Task\>**	**1 day**
4		🖈?	\<New Task\>	

**Figure 5 - 14: New summary task indented at same
level as the Design task preceding it**

In addition to inserting summary tasks during "top down" task planning, Project Professional 2010 also makes it easier to insert a summary task for a selected group of subtasks. For example, consider the set of four tasks shown in Figure 5 - 15. I want to show that each of these four tasks is a subtask in the Phase I section of the project.

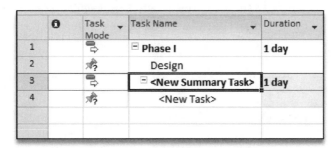

	ⓘ	Task Mode	Task Name	Duration
1		⇨	Design	1 day?
2		⇨	Build	1 day?
3		⇨	Test	1 day?
4		⇨	Implement	1 day?

**Figure 5 - 15: Four tasks ready for inclusion
as subtasks of Phase I**

171

To make these tasks a subtask in the Phase I section of the project, select the four tasks and then click the *Insert Summary Task* button on the *Task* ribbon. Project Professional 2010 automatically inserts a new unnamed summary task and indents the four tasks as subtasks of the summary section, as shown in Figure 5 - 16. You can then rename the new summary task as desired.

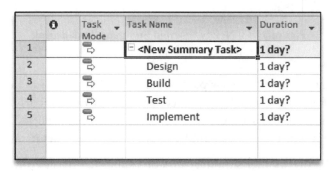

Figure 5 - 16: Four tasks inserted as subtasks
below the new unnamed summary task

Creating a Manually Scheduled Summary Task

In addition to creating *Manually Scheduled* tasks, Project Professional 2010 also allows you to create *Manually Scheduled* summary tasks. For example, Figure 5 - 17 shows a project with a *Manually Scheduled* summary task with *Manually Scheduled* subtasks. Notice in Figure 5 - 17 that the software displays a different type of summary Gantt bar for *Manually Scheduled* summary tasks than it does for *Auto Scheduled* summary tasks.

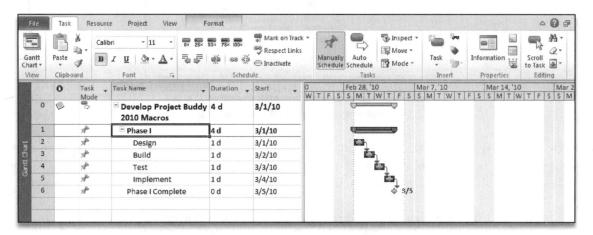

Figure 5 - 17: Phase I as a *Manually Scheduled* summary task

The behavior of *Manually Scheduled* summary tasks is similar to the behavior of *Manually Scheduled* tasks, but with a few differences, including:

- Project Professional 2010 formats the summary Gantt bar to show schedule *Warnings* about schedule conflicts.

- Project Professional 2010 shows a schedule *Warning* in the *Finish* column of every task causing the schedule conflict with the *Manually Scheduled* summary task.

Notice in Figure 5 - 18 that the software formats the summary Gantt bar for the Phase I summary task to show a schedule *Warning*, indicating that the duration of the subtasks now exceeds the duration of the *Manually Scheduled* summary task. The system also shows schedule *Warnings* in the *Finish* column for each subtask causing the schedule problem. To resolve the schedule problems, you can use the *Task Inspector* on the Phase I summary task, which offers the option to extend the duration of the *Manually Scheduled* summary task. I discuss the *Task Inspector* feature later in this module.

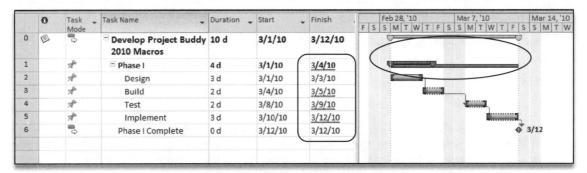

Figure 5 - 18: Schedule Warnings on a Manually Scheduled summary task and subtasks

Promoting a task to a summary task causes the system to rollup information from the subtasks. This changes the behavior of the task, but it does not change any underlying data that you previously entered. If you demote the summary task back to a normal task, any previously entered data reappears. This can cause surprising schedule changes so MsProjectExperts recommends that you create all of your summary tasks from new tasks rather than repurposing tasks in which you previously entered work or duration values.

Creating Milestones

In project management terms, we define a milestone as "a significant point in time" in a project that most typically indicates a point of completion. You may use a milestone to indicate the beginning point of a project, the ending point for a phase or a deliverable, or the ending point for an entire project. Most projects contain multiple milestones.

Project Professional 2010 offers you several ways to create milestone tasks. As with all previous versions of the software, you can create milestones by inserting a new task and then changing the value in the *Duration* column to *0 days*. Notice in Figure 5 - 19 that the *Gantt Chart* symbol for a milestone is a black diamond that displays the finish date of the milestone to the right of the black diamond.

		Task Mode	Task Name	Duration	Jun 6, '10
0			□ **New Project**	**1 d**	
1			□ **PHASE I**	**1 d**	
2			Design	1 d	
3			Build	1 d	
4			Test	1 d	
5			Implement	1 d	
6			Phase I Complete	0 d	◆ 6/7

Figure 5 - 19: Phase I Complete is a milestone task

In Figure 5 - 19, notice that indenture level for the Phase I Complete milestone task is the same as the PHASE I summary task. For ease of high-level reporting, MsProjectExperts recommends that you always outdent milestone tasks to the same level as the summary tasks they represent. With this structure in place, when you show and print Outline Level 1 tasks (the phase sections of your project), you see each phase and its corresponding milestone. The milestones show the finish date of each phase.

Warning: When you outdent milestone tasks at the same level as summary tasks, as recommended in the previous Best Practice note, the milestone tasks no longer move with their summary tasks. Before you attempt to move the entire summary task section to another location in the project, you should temporarily indent the milestone to the task level.

Project Professional 2010 allows you to create a milestone for a task with a *Duration* value *greater than 0 days* by completing the following steps:

1. Double-click the task to open the *Task Information* dialog.

2. Click the *Advanced* tab.

3. Select the *Mark task as milestone* option and then click the *OK* button.

Hands On Exercise

Exercise 5-3

Build the Work Breakdown Structure (WBS) and add milestones in your enterprise project.

1. Return to your Deploy Training Advisor Software project, if necessary.

2. Select task IDs #13-15, the *Design P3* through *Test P3* tasks.

3. Click the *Task* tab to display the *Task* ribbon, if necessary.

4. In the *Insert* section of the *Task* ribbon, click the *Insert Summary Task* button.

Notice how Project Professional 2010 created a dummy summary task named *<New Summary Task>* and indented the three selected tasks, making them subtasks of the new summary task.

5. Type the name *Phase III* in place of the name *<New Summary Task>* for the new summary task and then press the **Enter** key on your computer keyboard.

Warning: If the AutoComplete feature suggests the name *Phase III Complete* as you type the new name of the summary task, press the **Delete** key on your computer keyboard **after** you type the words *Phase III*, and then press the **Enter** key to complete the new name of the summary task.

6. Select task IDs #17-18, the *Phase III Complete* and *PROJECT COMPLETE* tasks.

7. In the *Properties* section of the *Task* ribbon, click the *Information* button.

8. In the *Multiple Task Information* dialog, enter *0d* in the *Duration* field and then click the *OK* button to enter a single *Duration* value simultaneously for the two selected tasks.

9. Click the *Save* button on the Quick Access Toolbar to save the changes to your enterprise project.

Adding Task Notes and Cell Background Formatting

Task notes are an important part of project documentation and are essential to understanding the historical information about any project. You can add notes to tasks at any time during the life of the project. To add a note to a task, use any of the following methods:

*   Select the task and then click the *Task Notes* button in the *Properties* section of the *Task* ribbon.

*   Double-click the task and then click the *Notes* tab.

*   Right-click on the task and then select the *Notes* item on the shortcut menu.

Using any of the preceding methods, the system displays the *Notes* tab in the *Task Information* dialog shown in Figure 5 - 20. Type the text of the note, add formatting as needed, and then click the *OK* button.

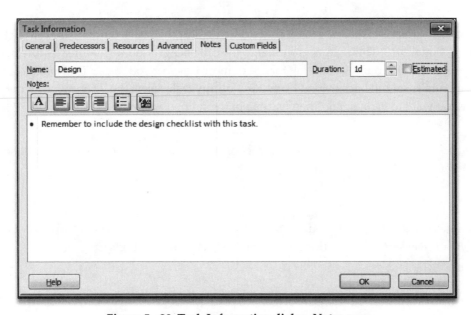

Figure 5 - 20: Task Information dialog, Notes page

MsProjectExperts recommends that you use "bulleted list" formatting for the text of your notes, as shown previously in Figure 5 - 20. When a task contains multiple notes, the bulleted list formatting makes the individual notes easier to read in the *Task Information* dialog, and when you print the project and include a *Notes* page at the end.

After you add a note to a task, Project Professional 2010 displays a note indicator in the *Indicators* column to the left of the task, as shown in Figure 5 - 21. You can read the text of the note by floating your mouse pointer over the note indicator.

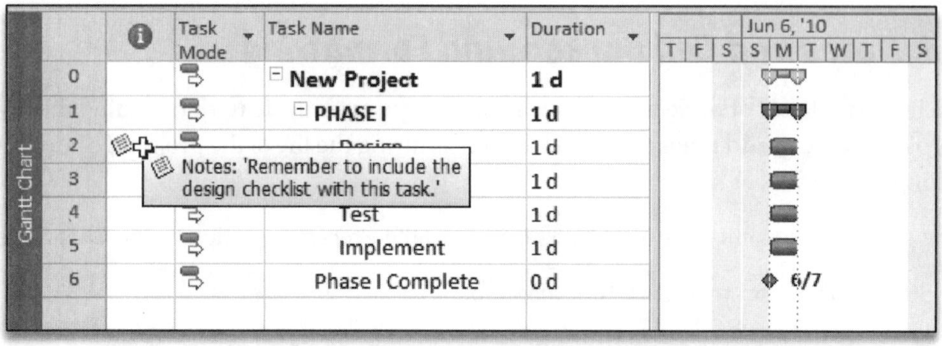

Figure 5 - 21: Notes indicator with screen tip text displayed

To easily identify tasks of interest, such as project milestones or slipping tasks, you can use cell background formatting in Project Professional 2010. This feature is similar to the cell background formatting feature in Microsoft Excel. You can manually set cell background formatting for one or more tasks, or you can set it automatically using a filter or a VBA macro. To manually set cell background formatting on any task, select the ID numbers of the tasks whose cell background color you want to format, and then use one of the following methods:

- Click the *Background Color* button in the *Font* section of the *Task* ribbon to format the cell background using the default yellow color.

- Click the *Background Color* pick list button in the *Font* section of the *Task* ribbon and select a color in either the *Theme Color* or *Standard Colors* sections of the pick list, as shown in Figure 5 - 22.

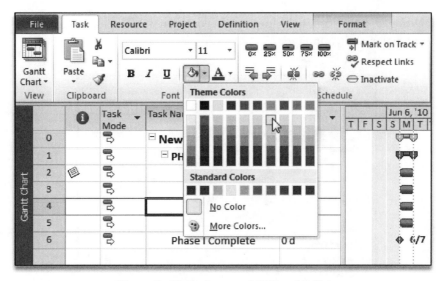

Figure 5 - 22: Background Color pick list

- Click the *Background Color* pick list button in the *Font* section of the *Task* ribbon and then click the *More Colors* item in the pick list. Select a color in the *Colors* dialog as shown in Figure 5 - 23 and then click the *OK* button.

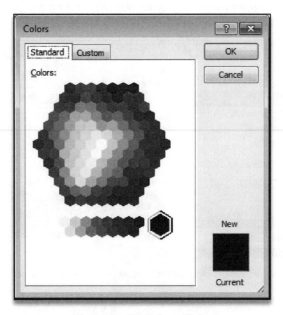

Figure 5 - 23: Colors dialog

- Click the *Font Dialog Launcher* icon in the lower right corner of the *Font* section of the *Task* ribbon. The system displays the *Font* dialog shown in Figure 5 - 24.

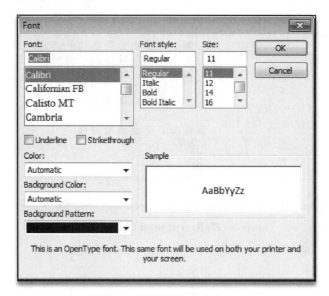

Figure 5 - 24: Font dialog

In the *Font* dialog, click the *Background Color* pick list and select the color of your background formatting. Click the *Background Pattern* pick list and select a pattern for the background color, if necessary. Click the *Color* pick list and select a different font color, if necessary. For example, if you select a dark color in the *Background Color* pick list, you should choose a lighter color in the *Color* pick list. Click the *OK* button when finished.

In the *Font* dialog shown in Figure 5 - 25, I selected the *Red, Darker 25%* color in the *Background Color* pick list and selected the *White* color in the *Color* pick list. Using contrasting colors between the *Color* pick list and the *Background Color* pick list helps users to more easily read the text of tasks with the cell background formatting applied.

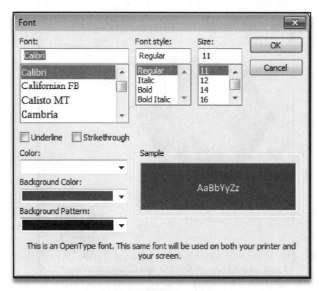

**Figure 5 - 25: Font dialog with cell
background formatting applied**

Warning: In the *Font* dialog, **do not** select the first pattern on the *Background Pattern* pick list (the white pattern). If you select this pattern, the system **does not** display any cell background formatting for the selected tasks.

Figure 5 - 26 shows the background cell formatting for the Test task in a project.

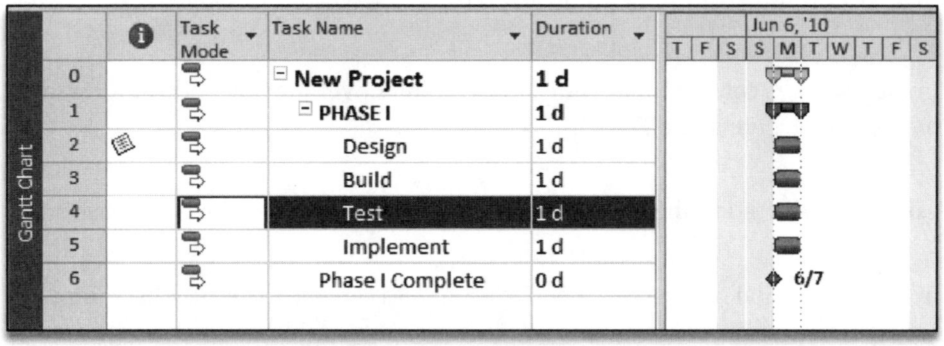

Figure 5 - 26: Cell background formatting for the Test task

Cell background formatting is an attribute of the view in which you apply the formatting. When you apply cell background formatting to a task, Project Profressional 2010 applies formatting to the task for all tables in the current view only. For example, if you apply the yellow color to a task displayed in the *Gantt Chart* view, the software applies the background formatting to the task in every task table you apply in the *Gantt Chart* view (such as the *Cost* and *Work* tables). However, if you display the *Tracking Gantt* view, the system does not apply any cell background formatting to the task in this view. This means that you can apply cell background formatting to different tasks in different views.

Hands On Exercise

Exercise 5-4

Add task notes and use cell background formatting in your enterprise project.

1. Return to your Deploy Training Advisor Software project, if necessary.

2. Double-click task ID #11, the *Rebuild P2* task.

3. In the *Task Information* dialog, click the *Notes* tab.

4. On the *Notes* page of the *Task Information* dialog, click the *Bulleted List* button.

5. Enter the following text in the *Notes* section of the page:

   New task added during task planning at request of team members.

6. Click the *OK* button to close the *Task Information* dialog.

7. In the *Indicators* column, float your mouse pointer over the note indicator for task ID #11 and read the text of the note in the ToolTip.

8. Click the row header (the ID number) for task ID #11 to select the entire task row.

9. In the *Font* section of the *Task* ribbon, click the *Background Color* pick list button.

10. In the *Background Colors* pick list, select the *Orange, Lighter 80%* item in the last column and second row of the *Theme Colors* section.

11. Click anywhere outside of the selected row so that you can see the cell background formatting color for task ID #11, the *Rebuild P2* task.

12. Click the *Save* button and then click the *Close* button on the Quick Access Toolbar to save and close your enterprise project.

Skills Review - Using Task Dependencies

After completing the initial steps in the task planning process, your next step is to determine the order in which tasks occur. This process requires you to determine and set task dependencies between tasks in the project.

Understanding Task Dependencies

When you set a dependency relationship between two tasks, Project Professional 2010 designates the first task as the **predecessor task** and designates the second task as the **successor task** in the dependency relationship. The software offers you the following four default task dependency types:

- Finish-to-Start (abbreviated as FS)
- Start-to-Start (SS)
- Finish-to-Finish (FF)
- Start-to-Finish (SF)

Figure 5 - 27 shows each of these four default dependency types.

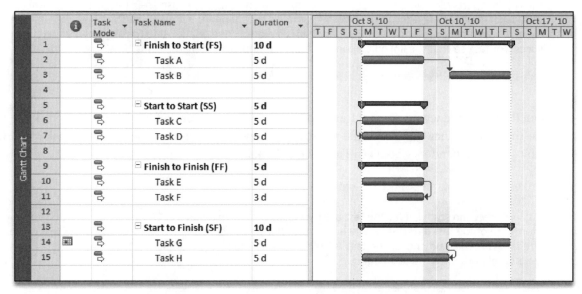

Figure 5 - 27: Four default task dependency types

A **Finish-to-Start (FS)** dependency means that the predecessor task must finish completely before the successor task can start. Figure 5 - 27 shows an FS dependency between Task A and Task B.

A **Start-to-Start (SS)** dependency means that the predecessor task must start before the successor task can start. Most people use this dependency to show that two tasks must start at the same time. Figure 5 - 27 shows an SS dependency between Task C and Task D.

 A Start-to-Start relationship does not mean that the predecessor and successor tasks **must** start at the same time. It simply means that the successor task may start any time **after** the predecessor task starts.

A **Finish-to-Finish (FF)** dependency means that the predecessor task must finish before the successor task can finish. Most people use this dependency to show that two tasks must finish at the same time. Figure 5 - 27 shows an FF dependency between Task E and Task F.

 A Finish-to-Finish relationship does not mean that the predecessor and successor tasks **must** finish at the same time. It simply means that the successor task may finish any time **after** the predecessor task finishes.

msProjectExperts recommends that you be cautious with using the Finish-to-Finish (FF) dependency because it is extremely difficult to force two or more independent events to finish at precisely the same time. A best practice is to use an FF dependency as a predictive relationship to tell you when to start the successor task so that the linked tasks **might finish** at approximately the same time.

A **Start-to-Finish (SF)** dependency means that the predecessor task must start before the successor task can finish. You should use this dependency whenever the start date of one task triggers when another task must finish. Figure 5 - 27 shows an SF dependency between Task G and Task H.

Taking a test and studying for the test are two tasks that have a Start-to-Finish (SF) dependency. The start date of the test determines when you must finish your studying. Therefore, taking the test is the predecessor and studying for the task is the successor. The SF dependency states that you must finish your studying before the test begins.

Setting Task Dependencies

To set a dependency in Project Professional 2010, complete the following steps:

1. Select two or more tasks that are dependent on each other.

2. Click the *Link Tasks* button in the *Schedule* section of the *Task* ribbon.

When you complete these steps, Project Professional 2010 sets a Finish-to-Start (FS) dependency on the selected tasks by default. To change the dependency type to any of the other three, continue with the following steps:

3. Double-click the link line between two dependent tasks. The system displays the *Task Dependency* dialog shown in Figure 5 - 28.

Figure 5 - 28: Task Dependency dialog

4. Click the *Type* pick list and select the desired dependency type.

5. Click the *OK* button.

Warning: Set task dependencies **only** on regular tasks and milestone tasks. **Do not** set dependencies on summary tasks, as doing this can lead to circular reference errors any time in the future. Circular reference errors are very difficult to troubleshoot and resolve, so it is better to avoid them by not setting task dependencies on summary tasks.

Warning: Be very careful when you use the *Control* key to select multiple tasks to link them. After selecting one task initially, when you press the *Control* key, Project Professional 2010 assumes the first task you selected is the predecessor task and all other tasks you select are successor tasks. This means that when using the *Control* key to select multiple tasks, the order in which you select the tasks is very important in the dependency planning process!

Linking Manually Scheduled Tasks

If you specify task dependencies by linking *Manually Scheduled* tasks with predecessor and successor tasks, Project Professional 2010 **initially schedules** each *Manually Scheduled* task as follows:

- If you do not enter duration, start, or finish values for a *Manually Scheduled* task, the software sets the duration of the task to the default value of *1d* and then calculates the start and finish dates accordingly, based on its dependency relationship with its predecessor task.

- If you enter an approximate duration on a *Manually Scheduled* task (such as *About 5 days*), the software maintains the approximate duration, but treats the task as if it has a duration value of *1 day*, and then calculates the start and finish dates accordingly.

- If you enter a numerical duration value on a *Manually Scheduled* task, the software maintains the valid duration, and then calculates the start and finish dates accordingly.

- If you enter an approximate start and/or finish date on a *Manually Scheduled* task (such as *Early October*), the software replaces the approximate date values for calculated dates in the *Start* and *Finish* columns.

- If you enter a valid start date on a *Manually Scheduled* task, the software **ignores** the start date and calculates the start date based on its dependency relationship with its predecessor task.

- If you enter a valid finish date on a *Manually Scheduled* task, the software honors the finish date, calculates the duration of the task based on the scheduled start date and the valid finish date, and then schedules the task accordingly.

To understand how the system initially schedules *Manually Scheduled* tasks when you link them with predecessor and successor tasks, first examine the *Manually Scheduled* tasks shown in Figure 5 - 29. Notice that Task A contains no duration, start, or finish information. Notice that Task B has an approximate duration while Task C has a valid duration value. Notice that Task D has an approximate start date, while Task E has a valid start date value. Notice that Task F has an approximate finish date, while Task G has a valid finish date value. Also notice the unusual bracket-shaped Gantt bars for the two tasks that have a valid start or finish date.

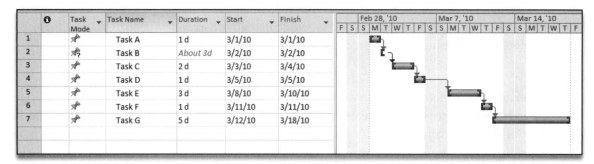

Figure 5 - 29: Manually Scheduled tasks BEFORE setting task dependencies

Now examine the same set of *Manually Scheduled* tasks after I link them with Finish-to-Start (FS) dependencies in Figure 5 - 30. Notice that the software behaves exactly as I described in the previous bulleted list. Take special notice of how the software scheduled Task G. The software calculated the start date of the task, honored the finish date of the task, and calculated a 5-day duration between these two dates.

Figure 5 - 30: Manually Scheduled tasks AFTER setting task dependencies

When you link *Manually Scheduled* tasks using task dependencies, the software calculates the **initial schedule** of each task. If you later change the duration, start, or finsh date of a *Manually Scheduled* task, Project Professional 2010 **does not** recalculate the schedule of the *Manually Scheduled* task. I discuss this behavior in the next section of this module.

Removing a Task Dependency

To remove a dependency relationship between two or more tasks, complete the following steps:

1. Select the tasks from which you wish to remove the dependencies.

2. Click the *Unlink Tasks* button on the *Standard* toolbar.

You can also remove a task dependency by double-clicking on the link line between the dependent tasks and then clicking the *Delete* button in the *Task Dependency* dialog.

Hands On Exercise

Exercise 5-5

Set each of the four types of task dependencies for *Auto Scheduled* and *Manually Scheduled* tasks.

1. Click the *Open* button on the Quick Access Toolbar.

2. Navigate to your *C:* drive and then to the folder containing the sample files for this class, and open the **Dependency Planning 2010.mpp** sample file.

You determine that Task A, Task B, Task C, and Task D are a "chain of events" that must occur sequentially. Link them with a Finish-to-Start (FS) dependency.

3. Select from *Task A* through *Task D* and then click the *Link Tasks* button in the *Schedule* section of the *Task* ribbon.

You determine that Task E and Task F must start at the same time, and that Task E is the "driving event" between these two tasks. Set a Start-to-Start (SS) dependency on these two tasks.

4. Select *Task E* and *Task F* and then click the *Link Tasks* button in the *Schedule* section of the *Task* ribbon.

5. In the Gantt chart, double-click the link line between the Gantt bars for *Task E* and *Task F* to display the *Task Dependency* dialog.

6. In the *Task Dependency* dialog, click the *Type* pick list, select the *Start-to-Start (SS)* item on the list, and then click the *OK* button.

You determine that Task G and Task H must finish at the same time, and that Task G is the "driving event" between these two tasks. Set a Finish-to-Finish (FF) dependency on these two tasks.

7. Select *Task G* and *Task H* and then click the *Link Tasks* button in the *Schedule* section of the *Task* ribbon.

8. In the Gantt chart, double-click the link line between the Gantt bars for *Task G* and *Task H* to display the *Task Dependency* dialog.

9. In the *Task Dependency* dialog, click the *Type* pick list, select the *Finish-to-Finish (FF)* item on the list, and then click the *OK* button.

Your professor scheduled a World History final examination for 8:00 AM on Friday, March 22. You believe you need two days to study for the exam. The date and time of the exam determines when you need to finish studying. Set a Start-to-Finish (SF) dependency between the *World History Final Exam* task and the *Study for the Exam* task.

10. Select the *World History Final Exam* and *Study for the Exam* tasks and then click the *Link Tasks* button in the *Schedule* section of the *Task* ribbon.

11. In the Gantt chart, double-click the link line between the Gantt bars for these two tasks to display the *Task Dependency* dialog.

12. In the *Task Dependency* dialog, click the *Type* pick list, select the *Start-to-Finish (SF)* item on the list, and then click the *OK* button.

13. Save but **do not** close the **Dependency Planning 2010.mpp** sample file.

Using Lag Time with Dependencies

Lag time is a delay in the start or finish date of a successor task. You can use *lag* time for a number of reasons, including situations such as the following:

- You need to plan for the delivery time delay between ordering equipment or supplies and receiving them in a FS dependency relationship.

- You require the completion of a portion (time or percentage) of the predecessor task before the successor task begins such as might be the case where you want to show that the painters can start painting after a portion of the dry wall work is complete in a SS dependency relationship.

You can enter *lag* time as either a time value, such as *5 days*, or as a percentage of the duration of the predecessor task, such as *50%*. To enter *lag* time on a dependency, complete the following steps:

3. Double-click the link line between two dependent tasks.

4. In the *Task Dependency* dialog, enter a **positive** value in the *Lag* field (either as a time unit, such as *days*, or as a percentage).

5. Click the *OK* button.

In the *Task Dependency* dialog shown in Figure 5 - 31, notice that I added *3d* of *lag* time to the FS dependency between the Design task and the Build task.

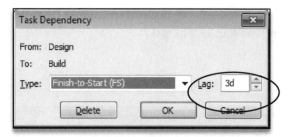

**Figure 5 - 31: Task Dependency dialog
with 3d lag time entered**

 You can also add *lag* time in the *Predecessors* column of the *Task Entry* table in any task view, such as the *Gantt Chart* view. Using notation such as *1FS+3d* means that task ID #1 is a predecessor to the selected task, with a Finish-to-Start (FS) dependency, and with *3 days* of *lag* time.

Figure 5 - 32 shows two different dependencies with *lag* time. To the FS dependency between Task A and Task B, I added *2 days* of *lag* time. This dependency means that Task B must start 2 days after Task A finishes, such as might be the case when cement needs to cure before additional building steps can begin. To the SS dependency between Task C and Task D, I added a *50% lag* time. This means that Task C starts, and when it is 50% completed, Task D starts.

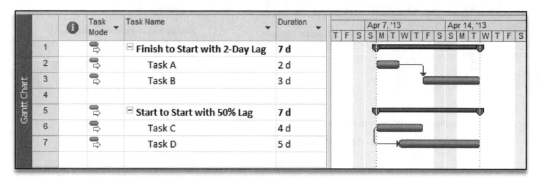

Figure 5 - 32: Lag time added to two different dependencies

Using Lead Time with Dependencies

Lead time is the opposite of *lag* time. Most people use *lead* time to create an overlap between two tasks linked with a Finish-to-Start (FS) dependency. To enter *lead* time on a task dependency, complete the following steps:

1. Double-click the link line between two dependent tasks.

2. In the *Task Dependency* dialog, enter a **negative** value in the *Lag* field (either as a time unit, such as *days*, or as a percentage).

3. Click the *OK* button.

In the *Task Dependency* dialog shown in Figure 5 - 33, notice that I added *2d* of *lag* time (-2d of *lead* time) to the FS dependency between the Test task and the Implement task.

**Figure 5 - 33: Task Dependency dialog
with 2d lead time added**

In an FS dependency, *2 days* of *lead* time means the successor task can start 2 days **before** the finish date of the predecessor task. Adding 2 days of *lead* time on an FS dependency creates an overlap between the dependent tasks as shown in Figure 5 - 34.

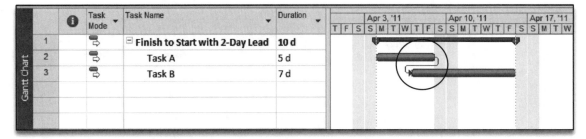

Figure 5 - 34: FS Dependency with 2 days of lead time

Warning: Project managers often use *lead* time to "fast track" a project by compressing the time it takes to complete a project schedule. Doing this is risky and can cause scheduling problems that result in an even later project finish date than originally scheduled. Because of this, msProjectExperts recommends that you be very careful when using *lead* time in your projects.

Hands On Exercise

Exercise 5-6

Add *lag* time and *lead* time on task dependencies.

1. Return to the **Dependency Planning 2010.mpp** sample file.

You determine that the Setup Equipment task cannot begin until 5 days after the Order Equipment task finishes. Set a Finish-to-Start (FS) dependency with *5 days* of *lag* time between the Order Equipment and Setup Equipment tasks.

2. Select the *Order Equipment* and *Setup Equipment* tasks and then click the *Link Tasks* button in the *Schedule* section of the *Task* ribbon.

3. In the Gantt chart, double-click the link line between the Gantt bars for these two tasks to display the *Task Dependency* dialog.

4. In the *Task Dependency* dialog, click the *Type* pick list, enter *5d* in the *Lag* field and then click the *OK* button.

5. Float your mouse pointer over the link line between these two tasks to see the screen tip indicating that the FS dependency includes 5 days of *lag* time.

You determine that the Decorate Rooms task cannot start until the Paint Rooms task reaches 50% completion. Set a Start-to-Start (SS) dependency with *50% lag* time on the Paint Rooms and Decorate Rooms tasks.

6. Select the *Paint Rooms* and *Decorate Rooms* tasks and then click the *Link Tasks* button in the *Schedule* section of the *Task* ribbon.

7. In the Gantt chart, double-click the link line between the Gantt bars for these two tasks to display the *Task Dependency* dialog.

8. In the *Task Dependency* dialog, manually type *50%* in the *Lag* field and then click the *OK* button.

9. Float your mouse pointer over the link line between these two tasks to see the screen tip indicating that the SS dependency includes *50% lag* time.

You determine that Task J must start 2 days before Task I finishes. Set a Finish-to-Start (FS) dependency with *2 days lead* time between Task I and Task J.

10. Select *Task I* and *Task J* and then click the *Link Tasks* button in the *Schedule* section of the *Task* ribbon.

11. In the Gantt chart, double-click the link line between the Gantt bars for *Task I* and *Task J* to display the *Task Dependency* dialog.

12. In the *Task Dependency* dialog, enter *-2d* in the *Lag* field and then click the *OK* button.

13. Float your mouse pointer over the link line between these two tasks to see the screen tip indicating that the FS dependency includes *2 days* of *lead* time.

You determine that your team must complete the Assemble Meeting Packets task 5 days before the Annual Shareholder Meeting task begins. Because the start date of the Annual Shareholder Meeting task drives the finish date of the Assemble Meeting Packets task, set a Start-to-Finish (SF) dependency between these two tasks with *5 days* of *lead* time.

14. Select the *Annual Shareholder Meeting* task and the *Assemble Meeting Packets* task, and then click the *Link Tasks* button in the *Schedule* section of the *Task* ribbon.

15. In the Gantt chart, double-click the link line between the Gantt bars for these two tasks to display the *Task Dependency* dialog.

16. In the *Task Dependency* dialog, enter *-5d* in the *Lag* field and then click the *OK* button.

17. Float your mouse pointer over the link line between these two tasks to see the screen tip indicating that the SF dependency includes 5 days of *lead* time.

18. Save but **do not** close the **Dependency Planning 2010.mpp** sample file.

Understanding Schedule Warnings and Suggestions

When you link *Manually Scheduled* tasks and then later change the project schedule, Project Professional 2010 recalculates the schedule for **only** *Auto Scheduled* tasks. It **does not** recalculate the schedule for *Manually Scheduled* tasks. Instead, the software calculates a likely start and finish date in the background, and then compares the current start and finish dates with the likely start and finish dates. If there is a schedule discrepancy, the software displays a *Warning* on that task by applying a red wavy underline to the date in the *Finish* column and by formatting the Gantt bar with a dotted outline. For example, in the schedule shown in Figure 5 - 35, I manually entered a duration value on the Design, Build, and Test tasks. This resulted in a schedule discrepancy on the Rebuild task, and *Warnings* from Project Professional 2010.

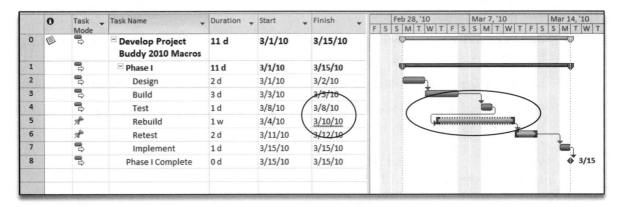

Figure 5 - 35: Schedule discrepancy Warning on a Manually Scheduled task

By default, Project Professional 2010 shows *Warnings* about schedule discrepancies on *Manually Scheduled* tasks; however, you can configure the software to show *Suggestions* about how to optimize your schedule as well. As I noted in Module 04, Project Definition, you can enable *Suggestions* by selecting the *Show task schedule suggestions* option on the *Schedule* page of the *Project Options* dialog. Remember that you can choose to apply this option only to the current project or for all new projects. If you did not select this option in the *Project Options* dialog, you can select this option for the current project by clicking the *Inspect* pick list button on the *Task* ribbon and then selecting the *Show Suggestions* item, as shown in Figure 5 - 36.

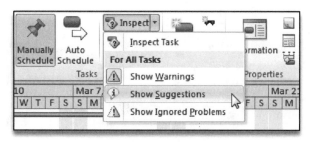

**Figure 5 - 36: Enable optimization Suggestions
for Manually Scheduled tasks**

When you enable *Suggestions* optimization, Project Professional 2010 examines the current start and finish date for each *Manually Scheduled* task and looks for opportunities to optimize the schedule with an earlier start or finish date. If the software finds an opportunity for you to improve your schedule, the system displays a *Suggestion* for that task by applying a green wavy underline to the date in the *Finish* column. For example, in the schedule shown in Figure 5 - 37, I manually entered a start date of Wednesday, March 10 on the Rebuild task. This caused a gap between the finish date of the Test task and the start date of the Rebuild task, and resulted in an optimization *Suggestion* from Project Professional 2010.

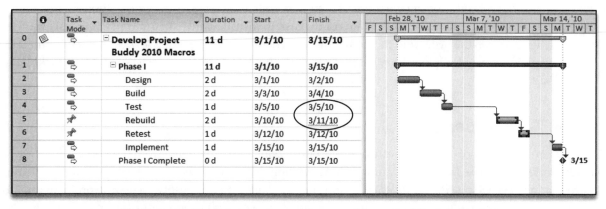

Figure 5 - 37: Optimization Suggestion on a Manually Scheduled task

When you float your mouse pointer over an optimization *Suggestion* in the *Finish* column, the system displays a tool tip with the words, *Potential scheduling optimization. Right-click to see options.* When you right-click in the *Finish* cell for the task with the optimization *Suggestion,* as suggested in the tool tip, the shortcut menu provides three options for acting on the *Suggestion,* including the *Fix in Task Inspector, Respect Links* and *Ignore Problems for this Task* items shown in Figure 5 - 38.

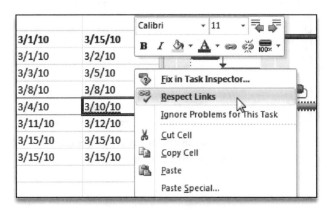

Figure 5 - 38: Respect Links item in
shortcut menu for a schedule Warning

Using the Respect Links Feature

Project Professional 2010 allows you to respond to schedule *Warnings* and optimization *Suggestions* using the new *Respect Links* feature. To use this feature, right click in any cell containing a *Warning* or a *Suggestion*. The system displays the shortcut menu shown previously in Figure 5 - 38.

When you click the *Respect Links* item on the shortcut menu for a schedule *Warning* or optimization *Suggestion,* Project Professional 2010 changes the start and finish dates of the task to the calculated start and finish dates, based on the task dependencies between the tasks, and then removes the schedule *Warning* or *Suggestion*. Keep in mind that this action might result in a new schedule *Warning* or optimization *Suggestion* on other *Manually Scheduled* tasks linked to the rescheduled task!

Using the Task Inspector

The *Task Inspector* is a newly revamped feature of Project Professional 2010 evolving from the *Task Drivers Pane* found in Microsoft Project 2007. The *Task Inspector* offers more functionality than its 2007 predecessor. You can use the *Task Inspector* to examine both *Manually Scheduled* tasks and *Auto Scheduled* tasks to resolve schedule problems and to determine the reason for the current scheduled start date of any task. To display the *Task Inspector,* click the *Inspect* button in the *Tasks* section of the *Task* ribbon. The system displays the *Task Inspector* on the left side of the application window as shown in Figure 5 - 39, Figure 5 - 40, and Figure 5 - 41.

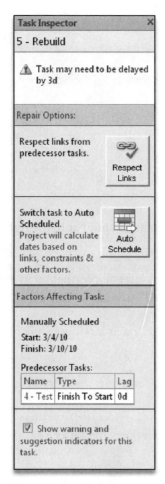

Figure 5 - 39: Task Inspector
for a task with a Warning

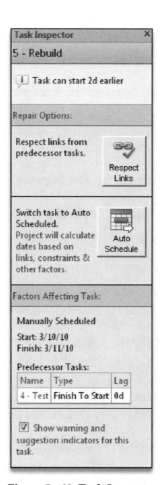

Figure 5 - 40: Task Inspector
for a task with a Suggestion

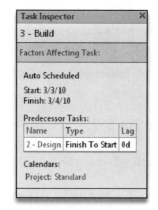

Figure 5 - 41: Task Inspector for
an *Auto Scheduled* task

Depending on the type of task you select, the *Task Inspector* includes either three sections or one section only. For example, Figure 5 - 39 shows the *Task Inspector* for a *Manually Scheduled* task with a schedule *Warning*. Notice that the first section displays the reason for the schedule *Warning* (the task needs to be delayed by 3 days). The *Repair Options* section offers the *Respect Links* button and the *Auto Schedule* button to resolve the schedule problem. The *Factors Affecting Task* section reveals the reason for the scheduled start date of the selected task.

Figure 5 - 40 shows the *Task Inspector* for a task with an optimization *Suggestion*. Notice that only the first section differs from the *Task Inspector* shown in Figure 5 - 39, and reveals the reason for the optimization *Suggestion* (the task can start 2 days earlier than currently scheduled). Figure 5 - 41 shows the *Task Inspector* for an *Auto Scheduled* task and contains only a single section, the *Factors Affecting Task* section. To close the *Task Inspector*, click the *Close* (**X**) button in the upper right corner of the pane.

For *Auto Scheduled* tasks, the *Task Inspector* tool reveals the reason for the current scheduled start date of any task. Possible reasons can include task dependencies, non-working time on a calendar, a task calendar applied to the task, constraints, and even leveling delays from leveling a resource overallocation.

Hands On Exercise

Exercise 5-7

Link *Manually Scheduled* tasks and then use the *Task Inspector* tool.

1. Return to the **Dependency Planning 2010.mpp** sample file.

2. Scroll down to the group of *Manually Scheduled* tasks and then drag the split bar to the right edge of the *Finish* column.

Notice that these seven *Manually Scheduled* tasks include a mix of different types of information in the *Duration*, *Start*, and *Finish* fields. Notice also the unusual Gantt bars for *Task M*, *Task O*, and *Task Q*.

3. Select from *Task K* to *Task Q* and then click the *Link Tasks* button in the *Schedule* section of the *Task* ribbon.

Notice how Project Professional 2010 calculates dates in the *Start* and *Finish* columns for every task, and calculates values in the *Duration* column for every task except *Task L*.

4. For *Task P,* change the value in the *Duration* column to *3d* and then press the **Enter** key.

Notice that the system displays a schedule *Warning* in the *Finish* column for *Task Q* (the red wavy underline below the date) and changes the Gantt bar shape for the task as well.

5. Float your mouse pointer over the schedule *Warning* for *Task Q* and read the tool tip.

6. Right-click in the schedule *Warning* for *Task Q* and then select the *Respect Links* item in the shortcut menu.

7. For *Task Q,* change the date in the *Start* column to *April 8, 2013* and then press the **Enter** key.

Notice that the system displays an optimization *Suggestion* in the *Finish* column for *Task Q* (the green wavy underline below the date).

8. Select *Task Q* again, then click the *Inspect* pick list button in the *Tasks* section of the *Task* ribbon, and select the *Inspect Task* item on the pick list.

9. In the *Task Inspector* sidepane, click the *Respect Links* button.

Notice how Project Professional 2010 removes the gap between the Gantt bars for *Task P* and *Task Q* by scheduling *Task Q* to start immediately after *Task P* finishes.

10. Close the *Task Inspector* sidepane.

11. Save and close the **Dependency Planning 2010.mpp** sample file.

Exercise 5-8

Set task dependencies in your enterprise project.

1. Click the *Open* button on your Quick Access Toolbar and reopen your Deploy Training Advisor Software project.

2. Select task IDs #10-12, from the *Test P2* task through the *Phase II Complete* task.

3. Click the *Unlink Tasks* button in the *Schedule* section of the *Task* ribbon to break the link between task IDs #10 and #12.

4. Click the *Link Tasks* button in the *Schedule* section of the *Task* ribbon to link all three tasks in a "chain of events."

5. Double-click the link line between the *Test P2* task and the *Rebuild P2* task.

6. In the *Task Dependency* dialog, select the *Start-to-Start (SS)* dependency in the *Type* pick list and enter *80%* in the *Lag* field.

7. Click the *OK* button to close the *Task Dependency* dialog and set the new dependency.

8. Select task IDs #14-18, from the *Design P3* task to the *PROJECT COMPLETE* milestone task.

9. Click the *Link Tasks* button in the *Schedule* section of the *Task* ribbon.

10. Select task ID #12, the *Phase II Complete* milestone task, press the **Control** key on your computer keyboard, and then select task #18, the *PROJECT COMPLETE* milestone task.

11. Release the **Control** key and click the *Link Tasks* button in the *Schedule* section of the *Task* ribbon.

12. Select task IDs #14-17, which includes the two *Manually Scheduled* tasks.

13. Click the *Auto Schedule* button in the *Tasks* section of the *Task* ribbon to convert these two *Manually Scheduled* tasks to *Auto Scheduled* tasks.

14. Click the *Save* button on the Quick Access Toolbar to save the changes to your enterprise project.

Skills Review - Setting Task Constraints and Deadline Dates

Project Professional 2010 offers you two options to constrain tasks in the project schedule:

- Constraints
- Deadline dates

A constraint is a restriction that you set on the start date or finish date of a task. When you set a constraint on a task in Project Professional 2010, you limit the software's ability to automatically reschedule the task's start date or finish date when the schedule changes on predecessor tasks. You can use constraints for all types of schedule limitations, including the following:

- **Contractual dates for task completion** when you have an obligation to complete a certain task in your project by a certain date.

- **Delivery dates for equipment and supplies** when a vendor guarantees delivery of equipment by a certain date.

- **Resource availability restrictions** when a resource cannot begin work on a task until after a certain date due to other project commitments.

Using a deadline date is a way to set a "soft target date" for the completion of a task. Unlike constraints, deadline dates **do not** limit the Project Professional 2010 scheduling engine, but the system does show an indicator if the task's finish date slips past the deadline date.

Setting Constraints

To set a constraint on a task, complete the following steps:

1. Double-click the task whose start or finish date you need to restrict.

2. In the *Task Information* dialog, click the *Advanced* tab.

Figure 5 - 42 shows the *Advanced* page in the *Task Information* dialog.

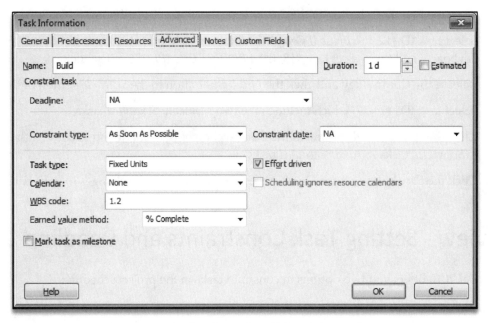

Figure 5 - 42: Task Information dialog, Advanced page

3. Click the *Constraint type* pick list and select a constraint.

4. Click the *Constraint date* pick list and select a date in the calendar date picker.

Notice in the *Task Information* dialog shown in Figure 5 - 43 that I selected the *Start No Earlier Than* constraint in the *Constraint type* pick list and selected the date *6/14/10* in the *Constraint date* field.

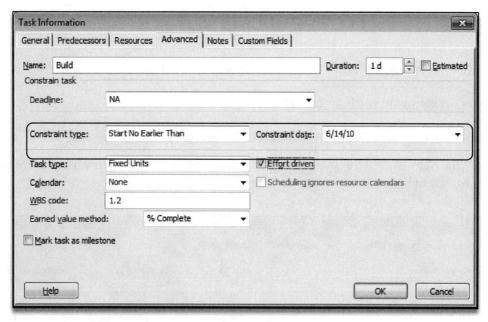

Figure 5 - 43: Task Information dialog with constraint set

5.   Click the *OK* button to set the constraint.

When you set a constraint on a task, Project Professional 2010 displays a constraint indicator in the *Indicators* column to the left of the task. If you see a blue dot in the constraint indicator, this means you set a **flexible** constraint. If you see a red dot in the constraint indicator, this means you set an **inflexible** constraint. A flexible constraint allows the software to reschedule the task as required, while an inflexible constraint limits or even stops the tool from using its normal scheduling behavior.

Adding Notes on Tasks with Constraints

When you set a constraint on a task, it is wise to add a note to the task to document the reason for the constraint. Adding a note makes it easier for others to understand why you set the constraint originally, and you can use this information later to evaluate the historical data in your project. To add a constraint note to a task, complete the following steps:

1.   Double-click the task with the constraint.

2.   In the *Task Information* dialog, click the *Notes* tab.

3.   Click the *Bulleted List* button.

4.   Click in the *Notes* text field and enter the body of your note.

5.   Click the *OK* button.

A good "shorthand" method for documenting a constraint is to include the following information in the body of the note:

- Abbreviation or acronym for the constraint type (such as *SNET*).

- The date of the constraint (such as *06/14/10*).

- The reason for setting the constraint (such as *Contractual delivery date for supplies*).

Figure 5 - 44 shows the *Notes* page of the *Task Information* dialog, with the note documenting the reason for the constraint shown previously in Figure 5 - 43.

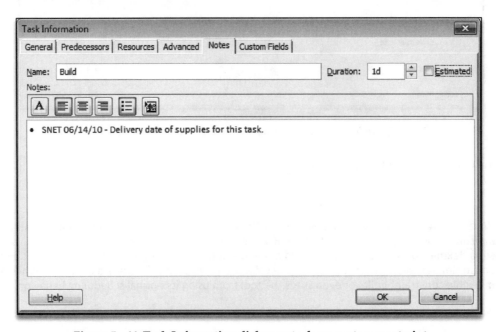

Figure 5 - 44: Task Information dialog, note documents a constraint

Understanding Planning Wizard Messages about Constraints

When you set a task constraint in a project scheduled from a start date, Project Professional 2010 displays a *Planning Wizard* message when the resulting situation meets both of the following conditions:

- The constraint is *inflexible*, such as a *Finish No Later Than* constraint.

- The constrained task is a successor task, meaning that it has one or more predecessors.

Project Professional 2010 also displays a *Planning Wizard* message that warns about a schedule conflict when you set either a *flexible* constraint or an *inflexible* constraint on a task that is a predecessor to one or more *Manually Scheduled* tasks. Because the system does not change the schedule of *Manually Scheduled* tasks automatically, it warns you of the potential scheduling conflict that may arise from this situation.

The *Planning Wizard* message, such as the one shown in Figure 5 - 45, is a warning that these two conditions can cause potential scheduling problems in your project.

**Figure 5 - 45: Planning Wizard message
warns about setting a constraint**

The default response in this dialog is the first choice, which is to cancel setting the constraint. If you truly want to set an *inflexible* constraint and risk potential scheduling problems, the *Planning Wizard* requires you to pick the third choice, *Continue*. The second option, by the way, makes no sense at all since selecting this option allows the software to change the constraint to a *flexible* constraint, an outcome that defeats the purpose of setting the *inflexible* constraint in the first place!

msProjectExperts recommends that you **do not** select the *Don't tell me about this again* checkbox to disable *Planning Wizard* messages about scheduling issues. Seeing warning messages of this type is a good way to confirm you selected the constraint you desire, especially if it is an *inflexible* constraint on a task that has predecessor tasks.

Understanding Task Scheduling Changes

One of the major changes in Project Professional 2010 is the way the software responds when you manually enter a date in either the *Start* or *Finish* column for a task. In previous versions of the software, when you manually entered a start date for a task, the system added a *Start No Earlier Than (SNET)* constraint on the task, using the date you entered as the constraint date. When you manually entered a finish date on a task, the system added a *Finish No Earlier Than (FNET)* constraint, using the date you entered as the constraint date. If you manually entered **both** a start date and a finish date on a task, the software sets either a *SNET* constraint or a *FNET* constraint, depending on which date you entered last.

In Project Professional 2010, when you manually enter a start date only on a task, the system continues to add a *Start No Earlier Than (SNET)* constraint on the task, using the date you entered as the constraint date. Likewise, when you manually enter only a finish date on a task, the system continues to add a *Finish No Earlier Than (FNET)* constraint on the task, using the date you entered as the constraint date.

The major change in behavior occurs when you manually enter **both** a start date and a finish date on a task. In this situation, Project Professional 2010 **calculates the duration of the task**. This behavior is a radical change from all previous versions of the software. As in previous versions of the software, when you manually enter both a start date and a finish date on a task, the software sets either a *SNET* constraint or a *FNET* constraint, depending on which date you entered last.

Hands On Exercise

Exercise 5-9

Set a constraint on a task in your enterprise project.

1. Return to your Deploy Training Advisor Software project, if necessary.

2. Double-click task ID #3, the *Build P1* task.

3. Click the *Advanced* tab in the *Task Information* dialog.

4. Click the *Constraint type* pick list and select the *Start No Earlier Than* constraint.

5. Click the *Constraint date* pick list and select the date of **Wednesday of the second week** of your enterprise project.

6. Click the *Notes* tab in the *Task Information* dialog.

7. Click the *Bulleted List* button and enter text documenting the reason for the constraint as resource availability issues, and then click the *OK* button.

8. Click the *Save* button on the Quick Access Toolbar to save the changes to your enterprise project.

Using Deadline Dates

In addition to constraints, Project Professional 2010 allows you to set deadline dates on tasks. Deadline dates are similar to constraints, but do not limit the scheduling engine. When you set a deadline date on a task, the software places a solid green arrow in the Gantt chart on the same line as the task's Gantt bar. To set a deadline date for any task, complete the following steps:

1. Double-click on the task.

2. In the *Task Information* dialog, click the *Advanced* tab.

3. Click the *Deadline* pick list and select a date in the calendar date picker.

4. Click the *OK* button.

Notice in Figure 5 - 46 that I set a deadline date of 6/23/10 on the Phase I Complete milestone task.

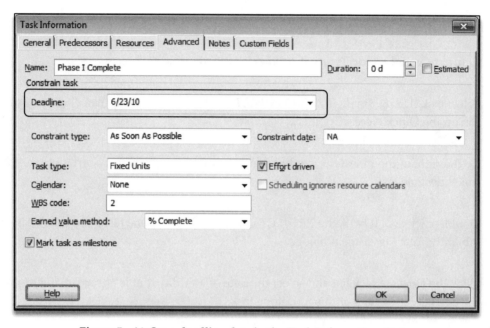

Figure 5 - 46: Set a deadline date in the Task Information dialog

Figure 5 - 47 shows how Project Professional 2010 displays the deadline date as a solid green arrow to the right of the milestone symbol in the Gantt chart for the Phase I Complete task.

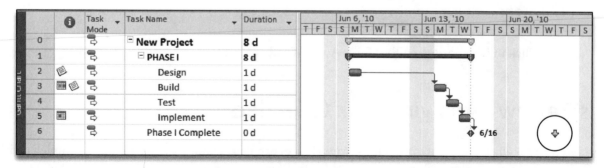

Figure 5 - 47: Deadline date indicator for the Phase I Complete milestone

Hands On Exercise

Exercise 5-10

Add a deadline date to a task in your enterprise project.

1. Return to your Deploy Training Advisor Software project, if necessary.

2. Select task ID #18, the *PROJECT COMPLETE* milestone task, and then click the *Scroll to Task* button on the Quick Access Toolbar.

3. To the right of the milestone symbol (black diamond) in the Gantt chart, note the *Finish* date of this milestone task.

4. Double-click task ID #18, the *PROJECT COMPLETE* milestone task, and then click the *Advanced* tab in the *Task Information* dialog.

5. Click the *Deadline* pick list and select the date of a Friday that is approximately **3 weeks later** than the current *Finish* date of this milestone task.

6. Click the *OK* button to close the *Task Information* dialog and set the deadline date on the selected task.

7. Scroll to the right in your Gantt chart until you can see the symbol for the deadline date on the *PROJECT COMPLETE* milestone task (the solid green arrow).

8. Select the Project Summary Task (task ID #0) and then the *Scroll to Task* button on the Quick Access Toolbar.

9. Click the *Save* button on the Quick Access Toolbar to save the changes to your enterprise project.

Skills Review - Applying Task Calendars

Apply a task calendar when you want to manually override the current schedule for any task with a completely different schedule defined in a custom calendar. In Figure 5 - 48, Project Professional 2010 schedules the Build task on a Monday and Tuesday, must only occur on only a Thursday or Friday. Because of this requirement, I need to apply a task calendar to override the schedule and let the Microsoft Project 2010 scheduling engine reschedule the task only on Thursdays and Fridays.

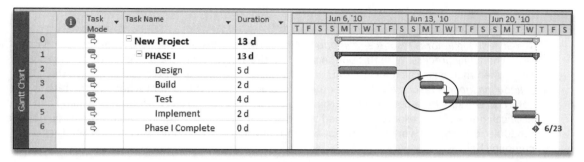

Figure 5 - 48: Build task scheduled for Monday and Tuesday

 By default, members of the Project Managers group in Project Server 2010 cannot create their own local base calendars. Therefore, before you can assign a task calendar, your Project Server administrator must create a new enterprise base calendar for this purpose.

To apply a task calendar to any task, complete the following steps:

1. Double-click the task you wish to manually reschedule.

2. In the *Task Information* dialog, click the *Advanced* tab.

3. Click the *Calendar* pick list and select a base calendar from the list, as shown in Figure 5 - 49.

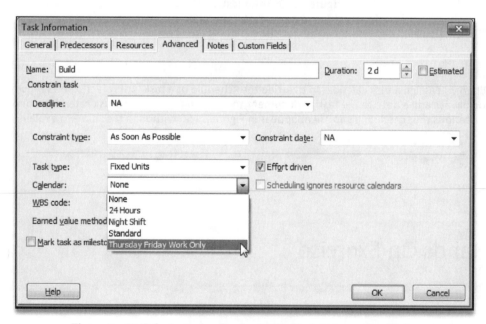

Figure 5 - 49: Select a task calendar in the Task Information dialog

4. Optionally, select the *Scheduling ignores resource calendars* option.

5. Click the *OK* button.

The *Scheduling ignores resource calendars* option forces the system to ignore resource calendars in the task scheduling process. With this option selected, the system schedules assigned resources to work even when their base calendars indicate that they are not available for work. If you leave the *Scheduling ignores resource calendars* option **deselected**, then the system schedules the task using the **common working time** between the project calendar (set in the *Project Information* dialog) and the base calendars of the resources assigned to the task. Selecting this option is useful when you need to schedule resources to work on days that are normally non-working time, such as weekends and company holidays.

Figure 5 - 50 shows the same project after assigning the *Thursday Friday Work Only* task calendar on the Build task. Notice how the software rescheduled the Build task from Monday and Tuesday to the next available Thursday and Friday. Notice also how Project Professional 2010 displays a special task calendar indicator in the *Indicators* column for the task.

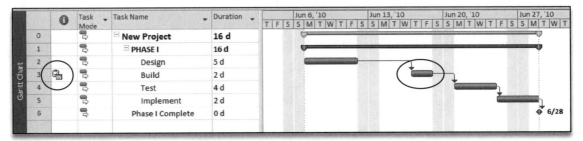

**Figure 5 - 50: Build task rescheduled
using a Task Calendar**

When you assign a task calendar to override the schedule of a task, MSProjectExperts recommends that you always add a note to the task to document the reason for using the task calendar. Think about how mysterious the scheduling gap might appear in Figure 5 - 50 without a task note to explain it!

Hands On Exercise

Exercise 5-11

In your enterprise project, the *Test P1* task must occur on a Saturday and/or Sunday only. Therefore, set a *Task Calendar* on this task to reschedule the task to the next available weekend.

1. Return to your Deploy Training Advisor Software project, if necessary.

2. Double-click task ID #4, the *Test P1* task.

3. In the *Task Information* dialog, click the *Advanced* tab, if necessary.

4. Click the *Calendar* pick list and select the *Weekend Work Only* calendar.

5. Select the *Scheduling ignores resource calendars* checkbox option.

6. Click the *Notes* tab and then click the *Bulleted List* button on the *Notes* page.

7. On the *Notes* page, enter the following text documenting the reason for scheduling this task on weekends only:

    Weekend Work Only calendar - Task must occur only on a Saturday and/or Sunday.

8. Click the *OK* button.

9. Notice in the Gantt chart how Project Professional 2010 rescheduled the task to the first available weekend.

10. Click the *Save* button on the Quick Access Toolbar to save the changes to your enterprise project.

Skills Review - Estimating Task Durations

After you create the task schedule, including setting task dependencies and constraints, you are ready to estimate task durations, wherever appropriate. According to Project Professional 2010, duration is "the total span of active working time for a task." Another way to think of duration is the "window of opportunity" during which the team members work on the task.

Many novice users of Project Professional 2010 wrongly assume that duration and work are interchangeable terms in a project. In some cases, this may be true, but in many cases, duration and work are two entirely different estimates. Consider the following examples:

*   A resource must perform 40 hours of work during a 10-day time period. The duration of this task, therefore, is 10 days because it is the "window" during which the resource performs the work (40 hours).

*   We allow an executive 5 days to approve a deliverable, but the executive will only perform 2 hours of actual work on the approval. The duration of this task, therefore, is 5 days because this is the "window" during which the executive performs the work (2 hours).

Notice in the two preceding examples that the duration or "window of opportunity" does not consider the amount of work performed on the task. The duration is simply the period of time during which team members perform the work, regardless of how much or how little work the task requires. There are several ways to determine a task duration estimate:

*   Get the estimate from the team member who will actually perform the work on the task. This allows you to tap the skills, knowledge, and experience of the team member, and this is a Project Management Institute best practice.

*   If you cannot get the duration estimate from a team member, then get an estimate from a team leader who has experience in this type of work.

- If you cannot get a duration estimate from a team leader, study your organization's repository of completed projects and get an estimate based on historical data for similar tasks.

- If you cannot use any of the previous methods, then set your own reasonable estimate, but validate your duration estimate later against the actual completion data for the task.

To enter duration values, simply type your estimate in the *Duration* column for each task. You may enter the duration value using any time unit, including hours, days, weeks, months, etc. By default, the system formats duration values in days.

Hands On Exercise

Exercise 5-12

Estimate *Duration* values for selected tasks in your enterprise project.

1. Return to your Deploy Training Advisor Software project, if necessary.

2. Enter the following *Duration* values for each of these tasks:

   - Rebuild P2   5 days

   - Design P3   3 days

   - Test P3   4 days

Notice how the system changes the cell background color to light blue for several tasks, indicating that you have changed the schedule of a predecessor task.

3. Leave the *Duration* value of the *Design P2* task at its default value of *1 day*.

4. Click the *Save* button on the Quick Access Toolbar to save the changes to your enterprise project.

Planning for Known Fixed Costs

The final step in the task planning process is to plan for known fixed costs on tasks. Examples of fixed costs include the cost of a building permit, the cost of a piece of equipment or hardware, or the cost of room rental. Most tasks do not have a fixed cost associated with them, but if a task does have a known fixed cost associated with it, you can enter the fixed cost amount by completing the following steps:

1. Apply any task view, such as the *Gantt Chart* view.

2. Right-click on the *Select All* button and select the *Cost table* on the shortcut menu.

3. Drag the split bar to the right side of the *Fixed Cost Accrual* column.

4. Enter the known fixed cost for the task in the *Fixed Cost* column.

5. Click the *Fixed Cost Accrual* pick list for the task and select the accrual method you want to use to allocate the fixed cost amount on the task.

6. Double-click the task and then select the *Notes* tab in the *Task Information* dialog.

7. Enter a notes text documenting the reason for the fixed cost and then click the *OK* button.

Step #5 above mentions that you need to select a *Fixed Cost Accrual* method for the task. The method you select determines how the software assesses the amount of the fixed cost on the task. The *Fixed Cost Accrual* column offers you three methods for accruing a fixed cost on a task in Project Professional 2010:

- The *Start* method causes the software to assess the entire fixed cost amount at the beginning of the task.

- The *End* method causes the software to assess the entire fixed cost amount at the end of the task.

- The *Prorated* method causes the software to distribute the fixed cost amount evenly over the duration of the task.

Figure 5 - 51 shows the *Cost* table for a construction project that contains a task called *Obtain construction permits*. This task has a known fixed cost associated with it, which is the cost of all the required construction permits. To plan for this known fixed cost, I entered *$4,350* in the *Fixed Cost* column, and selected the *End* option in the *Fixed Cost Accrual* column as well.

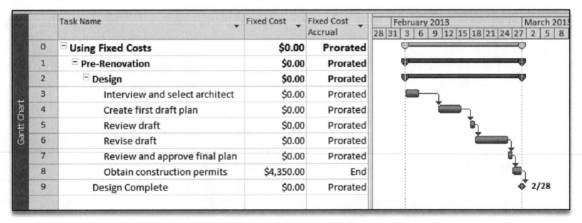

Figure 5 - 51: Enter Fixed Cost information in the Cost table

 When you enter actual progress for tasks during the execution stage of the project, you can also use the *Fixed Cost* column to show **unplanned** fixed costs for tasks. Planned fixed costs do not show as variance to the project, while unplanned fixed costs do show as variance to the project.

Hands On Exercise

Exercise 5-13

Plan for a known fixed cost (the cost of new testing equipment for the Phase I testing) in your enterprise project.

1. Return to your Deploy Training Advisor Software project, if necessary.

2. Right-click on the *Select All* button and select the *Cost* table on the shortcut menu.

3. Drag the split bar to the right side of the *Fixed Cost Accrual* column.

4. For task ID #1, the *Phase I* summary task, enter *$6,048* in the *Fixed Cost* column.

5. For the *Phase I* summary task, select the *Start* option in the *Fixed Cost Accrual* column.

6. Double-click the *Phase I* summary task and then select the *Notes* tab in the *Task Information* dialog.

7. On the *Notes* page, click the *Bulleted List* button and then enter the following note text:

   Fixed Cost of $6,048 for new testing equipment needed during Phase I only.

8. Click the *OK* button to close the *Task Information* dialog.

9. Right-click on the *Select All* button and select the *Entry* table on the shortcut menu.

10. Select the Project Summary Task (task ID #0) and then the *Scroll to Task* button on the Quick Access Toolbar.

11. Click the *Save* button on the Quick Access Toolbar to save the changes to your enterprise project.

In the preceding exercise, you added a known fixed cost for a summary task. Project Professional 2010 allows you to add known fixed costs in the *Fixed Cost* column for the Project Summary Task, for summary tasks, for regular tasks, and even for milestone tasks, as needed.

Module 06

Resource and Assignment Planning

Learning Objectives

After completing this module, you will be able to:

- Understand enterprise resources
- Use the Build Team dialog to build a project team
- Set the Booking type for project team members
- Use local resources as project team members
- Assign resources to tasks
- Assign Cost resources to your project
- Use the Resource Substitution Wizard
- Level resource overallocations

Inside Module 06

Understanding Enterprise Resources

The Enterprise Resource Pool in Project Server 2010 contains all of the enterprise resources needed to perform project work in your organization. Defined in simple terms, resources are the people, equipment, and materials required to execute a project. Defined in accounting terms, resources are the elements of project direct costs. Project Server 2010 defines enterprise resources in a variety of ways and organizes them in the Resource Organization Chart as shown Figure 6 - 1.

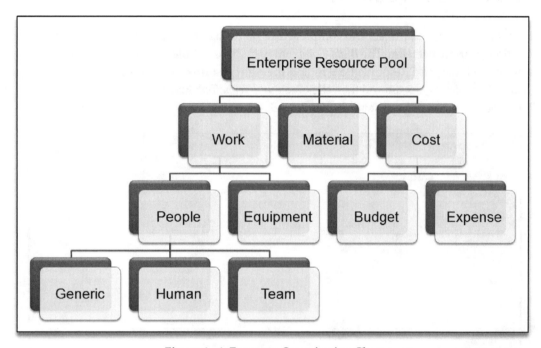

Figure 6 - 1: Resource Organization Chart

Project Server 2010 offers you three basic resource types: *Work, Material*, and *Cost*. You use *Work* resources to model people and equipment. You use *Material* resources to represent the supplies consumed during the project lifecycle. You use *Cost* resources to specify an overall budget and to track budget expenses unrelated to the *Work* resources assigned to tasks. *Work* resources affect both the schedule and the cost of the project, while *Material* and *Cost* resources affect only the project cost.

Project Server 2010 organizes *Work* resources into three groups: *Generic, non-Generic* (or *Human* resources), and *Team* resources. A *Human* resource is a specific individual you can identify by name. A *Generic* resource is a skill-based placeholder resource, such as an SQL Server DBA. *Generic* resources allow you to specify the skills required for a task assignment before you know which *Human* resources are available to work on the task. You can use skill-set matching and resource substitution to replace *Generic* resources with available *Human* resources who possess the same skills.

A *Team* resource is actually a special type of *Work* resource that represents a team of resources. You can only use *Team* resources if your organization uses dedicated project teams and the team members do not change from project to project. When you assign a *Team* resource to a task in a project and publish the project, any members of that team can self-assign the task, taking full ownership of the task, and can then report on the task in their Project Web App timesheets.

Warning: Project Server 2010 has no way to distinguish between *Work* resources that represent people and *Work* resources that represent equipment. Keep this fact in mind when you assign resources to tasks.

Building a Project Team

After you define a new enterprise project and complete task planning, you are ready to begin the resource planning process by building your project team. The *Build Team* dialog in Project Professional 2010 provides you with tools for searching through the Enterprise Resource Pool to find the right resources for your project team. To open the *Build Team* dialog, click the *Project Server* tab and then click the *Build Team from Enterprise* button in the *Plan and Publish* section of the *Project Server* ribbon. The system displays the *Build Team* dialog shown in Figure 6 - 2.

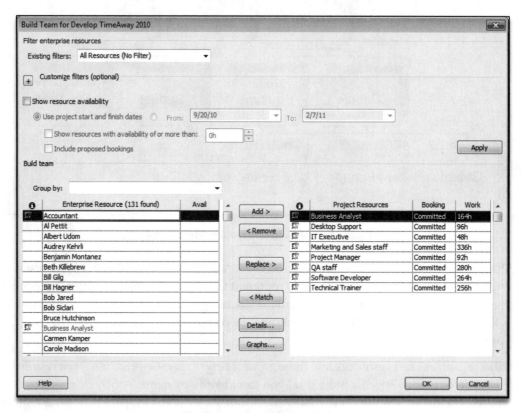

Figure 6 - 2: Build Team dialog

You can also access the *Build Team* dialog by clicking the *Resource* tab to display the *Resource* ribbon, then clicking the *Add Resources* pick list button and selecting the *Build Team from Enterprise* item on the list.

By default, Project Professional 2010 displays the *Build Team* dialog with the *Customize Filters* section collapsed each time you access the dialog. Click the *Expand (+)* button to the left of the *Customize Filters (optional)* section to expand it and show the complete dialog, as displayed in Figure 6-3.

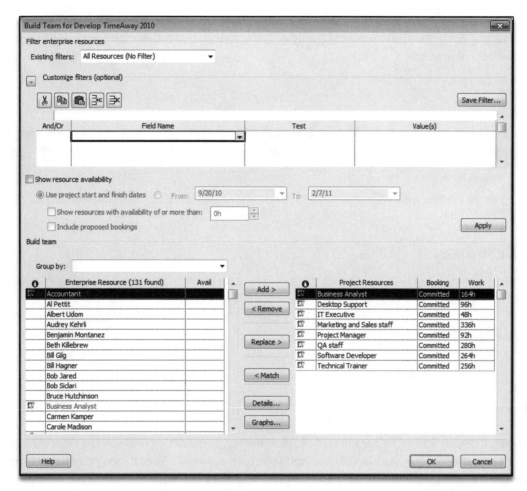

Figure 6 - 3: Build Team dialog with Customize Filters section expanded

The default permissions in Project Server 2010 allow members of the Project Managers group to see all resources in the Enterprise Resource Pool. Using features in the *Build Team* dialog, you can search through your Enterprise Resource Pool to identify resources with the skills, availability, and other criteria needed for the job. The other criteria you can use depend on the custom enterprise resource fields created by your Project Server administrator.

 If your Enterprise Resource Pool contains more than 1,000 resources, the system displays a pre-filter dialog to prompt you to filter the enterprise resource list. The system continues to prompt you to filter the list until the total number of resources displayed is less than 1,000.

The *Build Team* dialog consists of two sections. The *Filter Enterprise Resources* section in the top half of the dialog contains filtering tools to restrict the list of enterprise resources to those that meet your filter criteria. The *Build Team* section in the bottom half of the dialog consists of two resource lists: the *Enterprise Resource* list on the left displays the list of resources from the Enterprise Resource Pool, while the *Project Resources* list on the right displays the current list of resources on your project team. Notice in Figure 6 - 3 shown previously that my project team consists of eight *Generic* resources included in the project template and pre-assigned to tasks. Between the two lists the system provides a set of buttons to use for working with the two lists, such as the *Add, Remove, Replace,* and *Match* buttons.

Notice in Figure 6 - 3 shown previously that the *Enterprise Resource* list on the left includes both *Human* resources and two *Generic* resources, Accountant and Business Analyst. The system displays *Generic* resources with a double-headed icon in the *Indicators* column.

 When applicable, the system displays additional indicators to the left of each name in the *Build Team* dialog, such as overallocation indicators and *Note* indicators. Float the mouse pointer over any indicator to display information about the indicator.

Filtering Resources

Because the default permissions in Project Server 2010 allow you to see all of the resources in the Enterprise Resource Pool, the *Build Team* dialog offers three methods to filter the list of resources:

- Use an existing filter.

- Create your own ad hoc custom filter.

- Filter for availability within a date range.

To use an existing filter, click the *Existing filters* pick list at the top of the dialog and select a filter. The *Existing filters* pick list contains enterprise filters, standard filters, and your own personal filters. When you select a filter, the system applies your filter immediately and restricts the enterprise resources shown in the list on the left side of the dialog.

 Your Project Server administrator can build and save custom enterprise resource filters in the Enterprise Global file, which makes these enterprise filters available to all users on the *Existing filters* pick list.

To create your own ad hoc custom filter, use the data grid in the *Customize Filters* section. The data grid consists of four columns: the *Field Name, Test, Value(s),* and *And/Or* columns. In the *Field Name* column, you can select any resource field available in the system, including both standard and custom fields. Notice in Figure 6 - 4 that I am selecting the *Corporate Role (Enterprise)* field in the *Field Name* column.

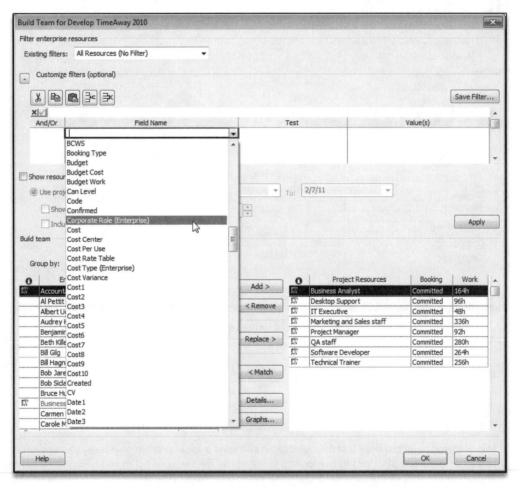

The *(Enterprise)* text to the right of the *Position Role* field name indicates that it is a custom enterprise resource field created by the Project Server administrator.

Figure 6 - 4: Select a field in the Field Name column

In the *Test* column, you must select the comparison test for your filter criteria. The tests available in this column include a set of common Boolean tests such as *does not equal, equals, contains, does not contain, contains exactly*, etc.

After you select values in the *Field Name* and *Test* columns, you must select or enter a comparison value in the *Value(s)* column. In this column, you can select another field with which to compare, or select a value from the list of values found in the resource field you selected in the *Field Name* column. Notice in Figure 6 - 5 that I am selecting the *Accounting* value from the list of values available in the *Corporate Role* field.

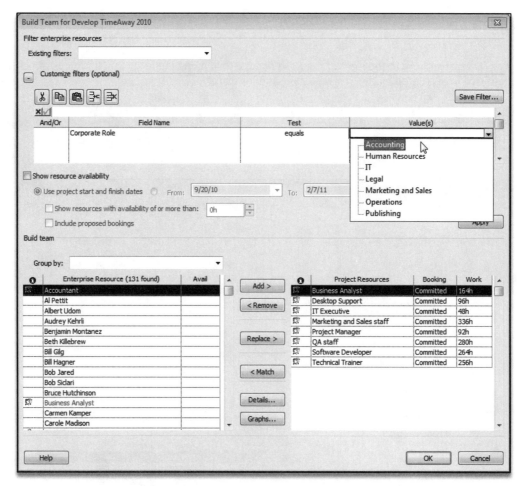

Figure 6 - 5: Select a field value in the Value(s) column

 If the field you select in the *Field Name* column contains a lookup table of values, the *Value(s)* column displays only the list of values in the lookup table. If the field you select in the *Field Name* column is a standard field, such as the *Cost* field, then the *Value(s)* column contains a list of other field names.

The *Customize Filters* data grid allows you to specify multiple criteria in your filter by using the *And/Or* column to add conditions to your custom filter using the Boolean *And* and *Or* functions. Notice in Figure 6 - 6 that I created a custom filter to locate resources whose *Corporate Role* field value is either *Accounting* or *Legal* using the *Or* option in the *And/Or* column.

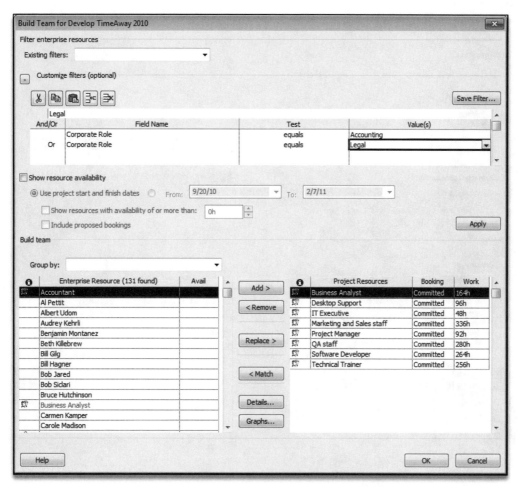

Figure 6 - 6: Custom filter with multiple filter criteria

When you complete your custom filter, click the *Apply* button to restrict the enterprise resources list using your filter. Figure 6 - 7 shows a filtered list of 12 enterprise resources that match my filter criteria: resources whose *Corporate Role* field value is either *Accounting* or *Legal*. Notice in Figure 6 - 7 that the filtered list contains two *Generic* resources called *Accounting* and *Legal staff*, along with 10 *Human* resources.

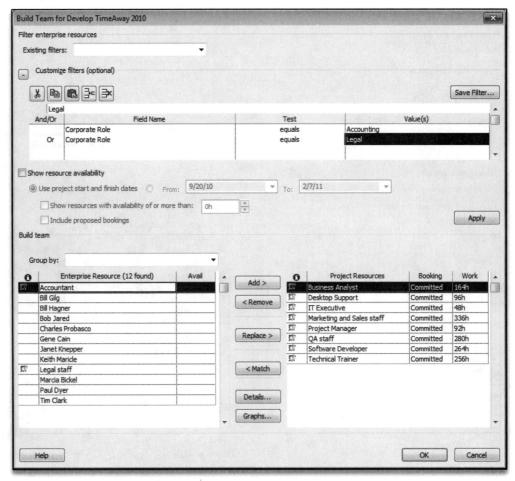

**Figure 6 - 7: Filtered enterprise resources list shows twelve
enterprise resources in Accounting or Legal**

After you create and test your custom filter, Project Server 2010 allows you to save it for future use by clicking the *Save Filter* button. The system displays the *Save Filter* dialog shown in Figure 6 - 8. Give your custom filter an original name and click the *OK* button to save it.

Figure 6 - 8: Save Filter dialog

MSProjectExperts recommends that you apply a naming convention to your personal custom filters so that you can easily distinguish them from both standard filters and enterprise custom filters. For example, you might preface the name of your filter with your initials. Using a naming convention, I might name the previous filter _DAH Accounting and Legal Resources. Using the underscore character at the beginning of the filter name forces it to sort to the top of the *Existing filters* pick list.

Warning: If you click the *Save Filter* button in the *Build Team* dialog, the system saves the filter in the **active project only**. To save your custom filter for use in all of your present and future projects, you must use the *Organizer* dialog (available in the *Info* page of the *Backstage*) to copy the filter to your Global.mpt file.

In addition to filtering resources using the *Existing filters* pick list and creating custom filters, you can restrict the enterprise resources list by testing for availability in a specific date range. To use availability filtering, select the *Show resource availability* option in the *Build Team* dialog. The system activates the options in this section of the dialog, as shown in Figure 6 - 9.

Figure 6 - 9: Show resource availability options

Select the *Use project start and finish dates* option to use the current scheduled start and finish dates in the project. Alternately, you can select the *From* option and enter a specific date range in the *From* and *To* fields.

If you select the *From* option, the system sets the *From* date to the *Start* date of the project, and sets the *To* date to the current scheduled *Finish* date of the project. You can change either date to filter during a specific date range.

Click the *Apply* button. Project Server 2010 calculates the availability for each resource shown in the *Enterprise Resource* list on the left side of the dialog and displays this information in the *Avail* column, as shown in Figure 6 - 10. The system calculates the availability for each resource using the following formula for the specified date range:

Availability = Capacity - Work

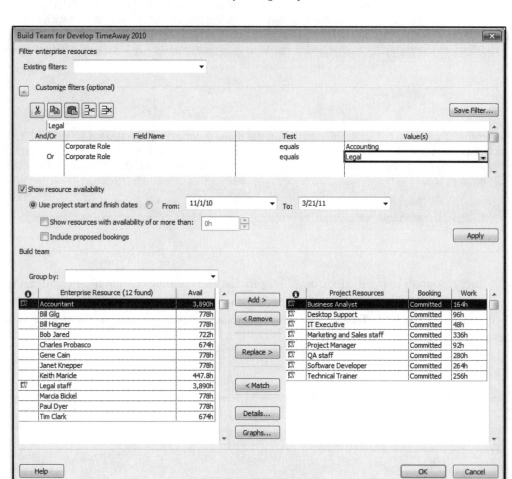

Figure 6 - 10: Availability calculation applied in the Build Team dialog

Notice in the *Enterprise Resource* list in Figure 6 - 10 that Keith Maricle has 447.8 hours of availability during the time span from 11/1/10 to 3/21/10, while Charles Probasco and Tim Clark each have 674 hours of availability during the same time span. If you see a resource with 0 hours of availability, this means the resource is completely booked on other projects during the time span of your project, and is not available to work on your project.

Warning: Even if a resource has 0 hours of availability to work on your project, Project Server 2010 allows you to add the resource to your project team and to assign the unavailable resource to tasks in your project. Doing so is unwise as this action creates a cross-project overallocation of the resource.

To continue filtering by availability by time period, select the *Show resources with availability of or more than* option and then enter the number of hours in the corresponding field. Click the *Apply* button to show only those resources with the minimum amount of availability for your project. For example, I want to filter for accounting and legal resources that have full-time availability (778 hours) to work on my project as shown in Figure 6 - 11.

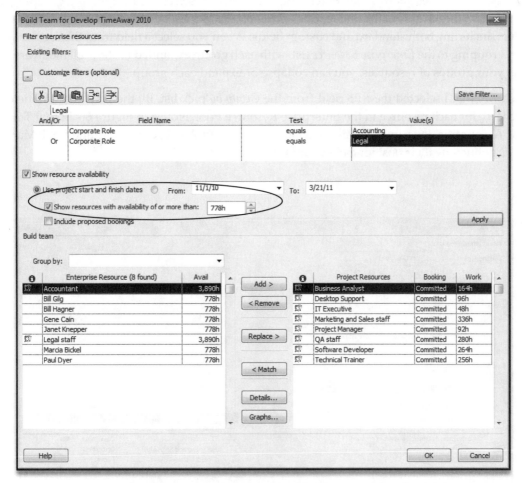

Figure 6 - 11: Filter for minimum availability in the Build Team dialog

When you filter for availability over a specific period, Project Server 2010 allows you to determine whether the system considers proposed bookings in the filtering process. A proposed booking indicates a tentative resource commitment to a project, while a committed booking (the default) indicates a firm commitment to a project. To include proposed bookings, select the *Include proposed bookings* option. To understand how this option works, consider the following example:

A fellow project manager books Mickey Cobb for 40 hours of work from October 15-19, 2012 as a proposed resource in an enterprise project. If you filter for availability and **select** the *Include proposed bookings* option, the system **subtracts** the 40 hours of proposed work from her availability. If you **do not** select the *Include proposed bookings* option, the system **does not subtract** the 40 hours of proposed work from her availability.

To remove all filtering from the list of enterprise resources, click the *Existing filters* pick list and select the *All Resources (No Filter)* item on the list.

Grouping Resources

The *Group by* pick list provides another way of refining your resource selections by applying grouping to the *Enterprise Resource* list of on the left side of the dialog. Click the *Group by* pick list and then select any resource field available in the system, including both standard and custom fields. When you select a field from the list, the system immediately applies grouping to the *Enterprise Resource* list, with each group expanded to show all members of the group. As you review your groups of resources, you can collapse or expand each group.

Figure 6 - 12 shows that I selected the *RBS* field from the *Group by* pick list. By the way, the *RBS* field defines the "pseudo org chart" for each resource in the Enterprise Resource Pool. Notice in Figure 6 - 12 that Tim Clark is the manager of the Accounting department, while Bill Hagner, Charles Probasco, Gene Cain, and Keith Maricle all report to Tim Clark, as defined by their position below Tim Clark in the *RBS* field.

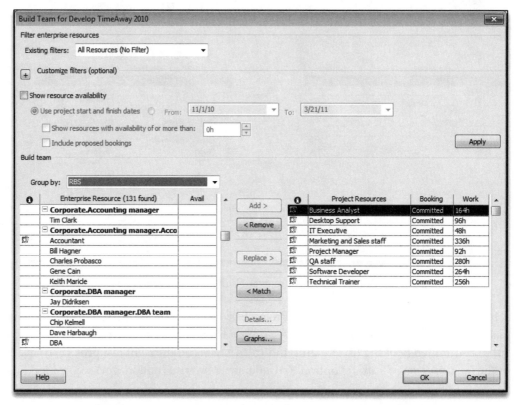

Figure 6 - 12: Apply grouping to the list of enterprise resources

To remove grouping from the *Enterprise Resource* list, click the *Group by* pick list and select the blank field at the top of the pick list.

Hands On Exercise

Exercise 6-1

Filter and group resources in the *Build Team* dialog.

1. If necessary, click the *Open* button on the Quick Access Toolbar and open the Deploy Training Advisor Software project in which you added tasks in Module 05.

2. Click the *Project Server* tab to display the *Project Server* ribbon.

3. Click the *Build Team from Enterprise* button in the *Plan and Publish* section of the *Project Server* ribbon.

Notice that the *Enterprise Resource* list on the left side of the *Build Team* dialog includes over 100 enterprise resources of all different types. Notice also that the *Project Resources* list on the right includes three local *Generic* resources named *PM*, *Resource 1* and *Resource 2*.

4. In the *Build Team* dialog, click the *Existing filters* pick list, then select and study the results of applying each of the following custom enterprise filters:

   - _msPE Cost Resources

   - _msPE Generic Resources

   - _msPE Material Resources

   - _msPE Human Resources

Notice how Project Professional 2010 displays a different set of resources as you apply each of these custom enterprise filters.

5. Click the *Existing filters* pick list and select the filter named *All Resources (No Filter)*.

6. Click the *Expand/Collapse* indicator (+ symbol) to expand the *Customize Filters (optional)* section at the top of the *Build Team* dialog.

7. Click the first blank line of the data grid in the *Field Name* column.

8. Click the pick list in the *Field Name* column and select *the IT Skill (enterprise)* field.

9. Click the pick list in the *Test* column and select the *contains* test.

10. Click the pick list in the *Value(s)* column and select the *Network* value.

11. Click the *Apply* button to apply the ad hoc filter.

Notice how Project Professional 2010 shows you the list of resources who work on the network team.

12. Select the *Show resource availability* option, leave the *Use project start and finish dates* option selected, and then click the *Apply* button again.

13. Examine the availability information shown in the *Avail* column for each resource.

14. Select the *Include proposed booking* option and click the *Apply* button again.

15. Look for any changes in the availability information for each resource.

16. Click the *Existing filters* pick list and select the filter named *All Resources (No Filter)*.

17. In the bottom half of the dialog, click the *Group by* pick list and select the *RBS* field.

18. Collapse the first blank group and then examine the *RBS* values for a number of resources in the *Enterprise Resource* list.

19. Click the *Group by* pick list again and then select the blank group at the very top of the pick list.

20. Leave the *Build Team* dialog open for the next Hands On Exercise.

Viewing Resource Information

Select any resource in the list of resources on either the left side or right side of the *Build Team* dialog, and then click the *Details* button to display the *Resource Information* dialog for the selected resource. Figure 6 - 13 shows the *Resource Information* dialog for Audrey Kehrli with the *General* tab selected.

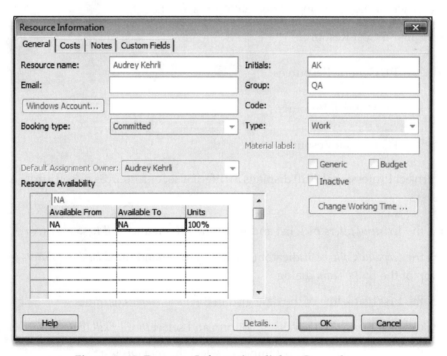

Figure 6 - 13: Resource Information dialog, General page

In the *Resource Information* dialog, examine the information shown for the selected resource on the *General*, *Costs*, *Notes*, or *Custom Fields* page. Click the *OK* button when finished.

You cannot change the resource information for any of the resources in the *Resource Information* dialog. Only the Project Server administrator can edit enterprise resource information.

Viewing Resource Availability

The *Build Team* dialog also gives you direct access to resource availability information using resource graphs. Select one or more resources in the list of resources on the right or left side of the dialog, and then click the *Graphs* button. Project Server 2010 launches a new Internet Explorer application window, navigates to the *Resource Availability* page in Project Web App, and displays the availability information for the selected resources. For example, notice in Figure 6 - 14 that the *Resource Availability* page shows availability information for Bob Jared and for the Business Analyst generic resource.

Figure 6 - 14: Resource Availability page in PWA

Warning: Microsoft Project 2010 allows you to select no more than 10 resources in the list of resources on either side of the dialog. This means that you cannot select more than 20 resources total (10 resources on the left side and 10 other resources on the right side). If you do select more than 10 resources total in the *Build Team* dialog, the *Resource Availability* page in PWA shows you only the first 10 resources you selected.

In the *Legend* section of the page, select or deselect the checkboxes for the selected resources to view availability information for each resource individually. In the *View Options* section of the page, set the date range and the time units (such as weeks) in which you want to view resource availability. If you want to include proposed work hours in the availability calculation, be sure to select the *Include proposed bookings* checkbox. Click the *Apply* button to view an availability graph for the selected resources.

In the *Details* section of the page, the system displays a data grid with numerical information about the selected resources. The data grid shows lines for *Capacity* and *Availability* data for each resource, along with the work assigned to each resource in every enterprise project. Close the Internet Explorer application window when you finish analyzing resource availability information.

For the purpose of brevity, I provide only an overview presentation of the *Resource Availability* page in Project Web App. However, I provide an in-depth presentation of this page in Module 15, *Working in the Resource Center*.

Hands On Exercise

Exercise 6-2

View resource information and resource graphs in the *Build Team* dialog.

1. In the *Build Team* dialog, select the name *Carmen Kamper* and then click the *Details* button.

2. In the *Resource Information* dialog, examine the resource information shown for *Carmen Kamper* on the *General*, *Costs*, *Notes*, and *Custom Fields* tabs.

3. Click the *OK* button to close the *Resource Information* dialog.

4. Select the name *Bob Siclari*.

5. Press and hold the **Control** key on your computer keyboard, and then select the names *Carole Madison*, *Larry McKain*, and *Sue Burnett*.

6. Release the **Control** key and then click the *Graphs* button at the bottom of the *Build Team* dialog.

Notice how the system displays the *Resource Availability* page in Project Web App.

7. In the *View Options* section of the *Resource Availability* page, enter *January 3, 2010* in the *Date Range* field.

8. Enter *December 29, 2012* in the *To* field.

9. Click the *Units* pick list and select the *Months* option.

10. Select the *Include proposed bookings* option, if selected, and then click the *Apply* button.

Notice how the chart on the *Resource Availability* page shows data columns for *Bob Siclari, Larry McKain*, and *Sue Burnett*, but shows no data bars for *Carole Madison*.

11. Select the *Include proposed bookings* option and then click the *Apply* button again.

Notice how the chart on the *Resource Availability* page now shows data bars for all four resources, with additional data bars for *Bob Siclari* to show his proposed work.

12. Scroll to the bottom of the *Resource Availability* page and examine the data shown in the *Details* data grid.

13. Close the Internet Explorer application window and return to the *Build Team* dialog in Project Professional 2010.

14. Leave the *Build Team* dialog open for the next Hands On Exercise.

Adding Resources to Your Project Team

To add resources to your project team, select one or more resources from the *Enterprise Resource* list on the left side of the *Build Team* dialog and then click the *Add* button. The system adds the selected resources to the *Project Resources* list on the right side of the dialog. To remove resources from your project team, select one or more resources from the *Project Resources* list on the right and then click the *Remove* button. When you add a resource to your project team, that particular resource appears as "grayed out" in the *Enterprise Resource* list on the left. In Figure 6 - 15, notice that I added two *Human* resources, Audrey Kehrli and Bob Jared, to the *Project Resources* list, and the system "grays out" both of these resources in the *Enterprise Resource* list on the left.

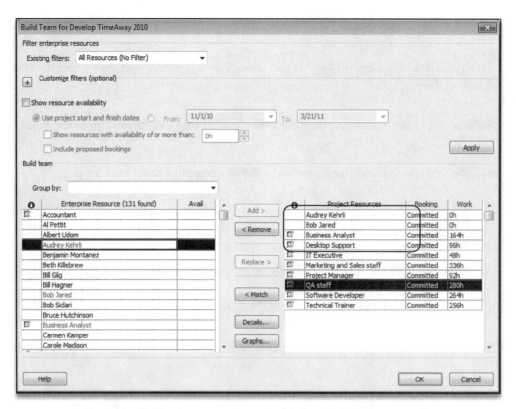

Figure 6 - 15: Two human resources added to Project Resources list

---

Using Team Resources

A *Team* resource is a special type of *Work* resource that represents a team of resources. If your Project Server 2010 system includes *Team* resources, you can add a *Team* resource to your project team and then assign the *Team* resource to tasks in your project. For example, suppose your Enterprise Resource Pool contains a *Team* resource named Desktop Support Team and this *Team* resource represents three resources named Bob Siclari, Larry McKain, and Susan Tartaglia. Suppose that you have a task in your schedule called Install Microsoft Office 2010 Client Software and any member of the team can perform this task, so long as it completes on time. You can add the *Desktop Support Team* resource to your project team and then assign the *Team* resource to this task.

When you publish this project, Project Server 2010 creates a *Team* task called *Install Microsoft Office 2010 Client Software* for all three of the team members (Bob, Larry, and Susan). These three team members can access this *Team* task using the *Insert Row* feature on the *Tasks* page in Project Web App. At any point, **one** of these three team members can self-assign this task and take over **sole ownership** of it. When that team member takes over ownership of the task, the system removes the task for the other two team members.

Team resources represent a way for you to assign a team to a task and to allow the team members to decide among themselves who should do the work on the task. Once a team member takes over ownership of the task, the system removes the task from the remaining team members and assigns it solely to that one team member.

Matching and Replacing Resources

If your Project Server administrator configured your Project Server 2010 system to support matching *Human* resources with *Generic* resources, you can use the *Match* button in the *Build Team* dialog. To match *Human* resources with a *Generic* resource, add the *Generic* resource to the *Project Resources* list on the right and then click the *Match* button. The system matches resources based on resource attributes such as skills, as defined by your Project Server administrator. For example, notice in Figure 6 - 16 that I matched the *Marketing and Sales* staff generic resource with *Human* resources who work in marketing and sales.

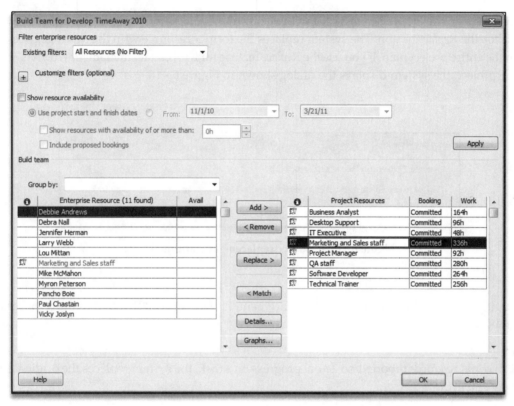

Figure 6 - 16: Match human resources with a Generic resource

When you use the *Match* feature in the *Build Team* dialog, the system applies a customized "contains" filter on the resources in the *Enterprise Resource* list using the matching attributes for the selected *Generic* resource. In our organization, the Project Server administrator configured the *RBS* field for matching *Human* resources with *Generic* resources. Notice in the *Customize Filters* grid shown in Figure 6 - 17 that the system created an ad hoc filter that displays any resource whose *RBS* field contains the value representing staff in the Sales and Marketing team.

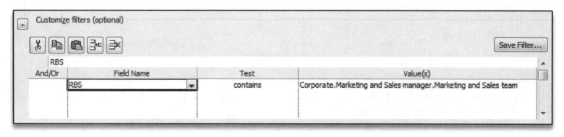

Figure 6 - 17: Customize filter data grid after a matching operation

229

In most cases, you use the *Match* button to match specific skills between *Generic* resources and *Human* resources. However, because the system shows all matches for a selected resource, including both *Generic* and *Human* resources, you can use the matching feature to make human-to-human matches as well.

To replace a resource on the *Project Resources* list with one from the *Enterprise Resources* list, select a resource in each list, and then click the *Replace* button. The system replaces the former resource with the new resource on every task assignment in the entire project plan. If you use the *Replace* feature for a project team member who has reported actual progress in the project, the system displays the dialog shown in Figure 6 - 18.

Figure 6 - 18: Resource replacement warning dialog

Click the *OK* button in the dialog to complete the replacement. Project Server 2010 handles the resource replacement operation as follows:

- If the original resource reported no actual progress on a task, the system replaces the original resource with the new resource.

- If the original resource reported some actual progress on a task, but has not completed the task, the system leaves the original resource on the task for historical purposes, and transfers all remaining work on the task to the new resource. This means that the system shows both the original resource and the new resource assigned to the task.

- If the original resource completed a task, the system leaves the original resource assigned and **does not** assign the new resource to the task.

If you want to replace a *Generic* resource with a *Human* resource on **completed tasks**, you must use the *Replace* feature in the *Assign Resources* dialog for this purpose. I discuss the *Assign Resources* dialog in the next topical section of this module.

Hands On Exercise

Exercise 6-3

Match and replace *Generic* resources with *Human* resources in the *Build Team* dialog.

1. In the *Build Team* dialog, select the name *Resource 1* in the *Project Resources* list on the right side.

2. Click the *Match* button.

Notice how the system displays a group of matching resources in the *Enterprise Resource* list on the left, including two *Generic* resources called *Technical Trainer* and *Technical Education Team*.

3. In the *Enterprise Resource* list on the left, select the name *Cher Zall* and then click the *Replace* button.

4. Select the name *Resource 2* in the *Project Resources* list on the right side and then click the *Match* button.

Notice how the system displays a new group of matching resources in the *Enterprise Resource* list on the left, including two *Generic* resources called *QA staff* and *Quality Assurance Team*.

5. In the *Enterprise Resource* list on the left, select the name *Myrta Hansen* and then click the *Replace* button.

6. Click the *Existing filters* pick list at the top of the dialog and select the *All Resources (No Filter)* item on the pick list.

7. In the *Enterprise Resource* list on the left, select the *C Sharp Software Developer* generic resource and then click the *Add* button.

8. In the *Project Resources* list on the right, select the *C Sharp Software Developer* generic resource and then click the *Match* button.

9. Scroll back up to the top of the *Enterprise Resource* list on the left.

Notice how the system displays a new group of matching resources in the *Enterprise Resource* list.

10. In the *Enterprise Resource* list on the left, select the name *David Erickson* and then click the *Replace* button.

11. Click the *Existing filters* pick list and select the filter named *All Resources (No Filter)*.

12. Select the name *PM* in the *Project Resources* list on the right side of the dialog.

13. In the *Enterprise Resource* list on the left, select *George Stewart* and then click the *Replace* button.

14. Leave the *Build Team* dialog open for the next Hands On Exercise.

Exercise 6-4

Add *Team, Material,* and *Cost* resources to your enterprise project team in the *Build Team* dialog.

1. In the *Enterprise Resource* list on the left side of the *Build Team* dialog, select the *Team* resource named *Software Development Team* and then click the *Add* button.

2. Click the *Existing filters* pick list at the top of the dialog and select the *_msPE Material Resources* filter.

3. In the *Enterprise Resource* list on the left, select the *Corporate Training Manuals* resource and click the *Add* button.

4. Click the *Existing filters* pick list at the top of the dialog and select the *_msPE Cost Resources* filter.

5. In the *Enterprise Resource* list on the left, select the *Project Budget* resource and click the *Add* button.

6. In the *Enterprise Resource* list on the left, select the *Computer Hardware* resource and click the *Add* button.

7. Leave the *Build Team* dialog open for the next Hands On Exercise.

Using Proposed vs. Committed Booking

The *Booking* column in the *Project Resources* list on the right side of the *Build Team* dialog allows you to specify a booking type for each team member you add to your team. You can book team members as either *Proposed* or *Committed*. A proposed booking indicates a tentative commitment for the resource, while a committed booking indicates a firm commitment.

The default *Booking* value for each project team member is *Committed,* unless specified otherwise by the Project Server administrator for any resource in the Enterprise Resource Pool. To change the *Booking* value for a project team member, click the *Booking* pick list for the resource and select the desired booking type. Notice in Figure 6 - 19 that I am setting the *Booking* value to *Proposed* for the resource *Audrey Kehrli*.

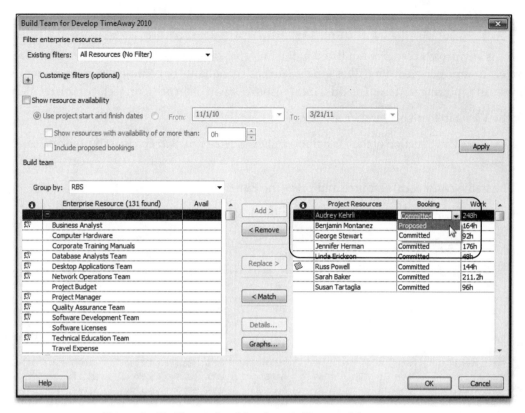

Figure 6 - 19: Change booking type to Proposed for a resource

When you book a team member as a proposed resource on a project, Project Server 2010 handles all task assignments in the project for the proposed resource as proposed assignments. The consequences of setting the *Booking* value to *Proposed* for a member of a project team are as follows:

- For proposed resources, published task assignments do not display on their *Tasks* page or their *Timesheet* page in Project Web App.

- On the *Resource Availability* page in PWA, you do not see projects assigned to a proposed resource unless you select the *Include proposed bookings* option on the page. Refer back to Figure 6 - 14 to see the *Resource Availability* page.

- On the *Resource Assignments* page in PWA, you do not see tasks assigned to a proposed resource.

- Booking type is a dimension of the OLAP cube and is available for use in views in the *Business Intelligence Center* page in PWA.

When you receive formal approval to begin the execution of your project, remember to change proposed bookings to committed bookings, or to replace proposed resources with committed resources.

Using Local Resources in a Project Team

A local resource is any project resource not listed in the Enterprise Resource Pool. You can use local resources in an enterprise project to represent temporary resources, such as consultants or contractors, who do not use the Project Web App timesheet reporting system. To add a local resource to an enterprise project, complete these steps:

1. Click the *View* tab to display the *View* ribbon.

2. In the *Resource Views* section of the *View* ribbon, click the *Resource Sheet* pick list button and select the *Resource Sheet* view.

3. Type the name of the local resource and press the **Enter** key.

Project Server 2010 displays a special indicator for the local resource in the *Indicators* column, as shown in Figure 6 - 20.

	①	Resource Name	Type	Material	Initials	Group	Max.	Std. Rate	Ovt. Rate	Cost/Use	Accrue	Base Calendar
1		Audrey Kehrli	Work		AK	QA	100%	$40.00/h	$60.00/h	$0.00	Prorated	US Work Schedule
2		Benjamin Montanez	Work		BM	BA	100%	$80.00/h	$120.00/h	$0.00	Prorated	US Work Schedule
3		George Stewart	Work		GS	PM	100%	$100.00/h	$150.00/h	$0.00	Prorated	US Work Schedule
4		Jennifer Herman	Work		JH	Marketing	100%	$40.00/h	$60.00/h	$0.00	Prorated	US Work Schedule
5		Linda Erickson	Work		LE	Exec	100%	$250.00/h	$375.00/h	$0.00	Prorated	US Work Schedule
6		Mike Andrews	Work		MA	TechEd	100%	$35.00/h	$55.00/h	$0.00	Prorated	US Work Schedule
7	📝	Russ Powell	Work		RP	SoftDev	100%	$60.00/h	$90.00/h	$0.00	Prorated	US Work Schedule
8		Sarah Baker	Work		SB	TechEd	100%	$35.00/h	$55.00/h	$0.00	Prorated	US Work Schedule
9		Susan Tartaglia	Work		ST	Desktop	100%	$30.00/h	$45.00/h	$0.00	Prorated	US Work Schedule
10	👤	SoftDev Contractor	Work		SC	Contractor	100%	$150.00/h	$225.00/h	$0.00	Prorated	US Work Schedule

Figure 6 - 20: Resource Sheet view shows a local resource

4. Enter general information for the local resource, as needed, such as information in the *Initials*, *Group*, *Max. Units*, or *Std. Rate*, and *Base Calendar* columns.

Hands On Exercise

Exercise 6-5

Set the *Booking* value for a project team member and then add a local resource to the project team.

1. In the *Project Resources* list on the right side of the *Build Team* dialog, click the pick list in the *Booking* field for *David Erickson* and select the *Proposed* value on the list.

2. Click the *OK* button to close the *Build Team* dialog.

3. Click the *Save* button on the Quick Access Toolbar to save your enterprise project.

4. Click the *View* tab to display the *View* ribbon.

5. In the *Resource Views* section of the *View* ribbon, click the *Resource Sheet* pick list button and select the *Resource Sheet* view.

Notice in the *Resource Sheet* view of your enterprise project that the system formats the name *Myrta Hansen* in red. This indicates that Project Professional 2010 considers her an overallocated resource. I discuss how to resolve resource overallocations later in this module.

6. In the first blank line of the *Resource Sheet* view, add a new resource named *Contract Labor*.

In the *Indicators* column, notice the unusual indicator for the new resource, showing that the new resource is a local resource and not an enterprise resource.

7. For the *Contract Labor* resource, enter the following additional information:

Field Name	Data
Initials	CL
Group	Contractor
Std. Rate	$100
Ovt. Rate	$150

8. In the *Task Views* section of the *View* ribbon, click the *Gantt Chart* button to reapply to the *Gantt Chart* view.

9. Click the *Save* button on the Quick Access Toolbar to save your enterprise project.

Assigning Resources to Tasks

After you build your project team in an enterprise project, you are ready to assign team members to tasks. Like all previous versions of the tool, Project Professional 2010 offers two powerful tools for assigning resources to tasks, but the method you use to apply these tools is different from all previous versions of the software. These two powerful resource assignment tools are:

*   *Task Entry* view

*   *Assign Resources* dialog

In addition to the *Task Entry* view and the *Assign Resources* dialog, Project Professional 2010 also includes a new *Team Planner* view that you can use to analyze resource assignments. I discuss each of these features in this module.

Warning: During the resource assignment process, **do not** assign resources to summary tasks, as this greatly increases the work hours and costs for your project. Instead, if you need to show a resource as the responsible person for a summary section of the project, use the built-in *Contact* field, or create a custom field and name it *Responsible Person*, or assign the resource to the milestone for the summary section of the project.

Assigning Resources Using the Task Entry View

The *Task Entry* view is the most powerful way to assign resources to tasks because it gives you total control over all of the attributes in the Project Professional 2010 scheduling engine. Using the *Task Entry* view, you can do all of the following in a single location:

- Assign multiple resources simultaneously, and specify different *Units* and *Work* values for each resource.

- Enter the *Duration* of the task.

- Set the *Task Type* for the task to determine whether the software fixes or "locks" the *Units*, *Work*, or *Duration* value for the task.

- Specify the *Effort Driven* status of the task to determine what happens when you add or remove resources on the task.

- Set the *Task Mode* for the task as either *Manually Scheduled* or *Auto Scheduled*.

 The only disadvantage of using the *Task Entry* view is that you cannot assign resources to multiple tasks simultaneously. This means that you cannot use the *Task Entry* view to assign resources to a *recurring* task, for example.

To display the *Task Entry* view, complete the following steps:

1. Click the *Task* tab and then click the *Gantt Chart* button (if you do not have the *Gantt Chart* view displayed already).

2. Click the *View* tab to apply the *View* ribbon.

3. Select the *Details* checkbox in the *Split View* section of the *View* ribbon. Project Professional 2010 displays the *Task Entry* view, shown in Figure 6 - 21.

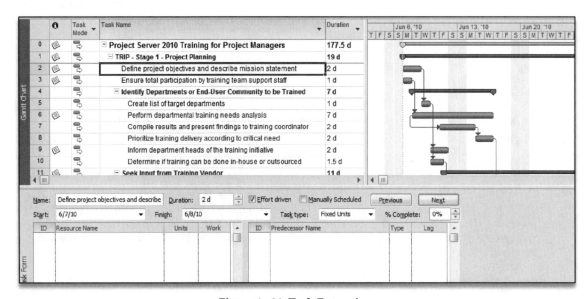

Figure 6 - 21: Task Entry view

If you have the *Timeline* view displayed along with the *Gantt Chart* view, Microsoft Project 2010 must close the *Timeline* view before it can display the *Task Entry* view.

The *Task Entry* view is a combination view consisting of two other views, each displayed in a separate pane. The *Task Entry* view includes the *Gantt Chart* view in the top pane and the *Task Form* view in the bottom pane. To assign a resource to a task using the *Task Entry* view, take the following steps:

1. Select a single task in the *Gantt Chart* pane.

2. In the *Task Form* pane, select the first blank cell in the *Resource Name* column and then click the pick list button in that cell. The software displays the list of resources you added to the *Resource Sheet* view, as shown in Figure 6 - 22.

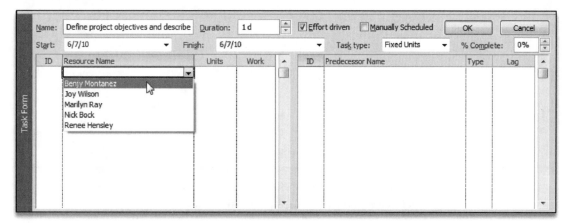

Figure 6 - 22: Task Entry view, select a resource

3. Click the first blank cell in the *Units* column and then select or enter a *Units* value for the selected resource.

In the *Units* column, you can use the spin control feature to select a value, but Microsoft Project 2010 displays only *Units* values in 50% increments (0%, 50%, 100%, etc.). For *Units* values you cannot select using the spin control feature, such as 25% or 75%, you must manually type the *Units* value you need.

4. Click in the first blank cell in the *Work* column and enter the estimated work hours for that resource.

5. Repeat steps #2-4 for each additional resource you wish to assign to the task.

6. Click the *OK* button.

Warning: Do not click the *OK* button in the *Task Form* pane until you finish selecting **all** of the resources you need and finish setting both the *Units* and *Work* values for each resource.

Project Professional 2010 assigns the resource to the task and then calculates the *Duration* value based on the *Units* and *Work* values you enter. Notice in Figure 6 - 23 that I assigned Benjy Montanez at *50% Units* and *16* hours of *Work*, and based on these two numbers, the software calculated a *Duration* value of *4 days* for the task. Notice also that the software changed the *OK* and *Cancel* buttons to the *Previous* and *Next* buttons. Using the *Previous* and *Next* buttons, you can navigate easily from task to task during the assignment process.

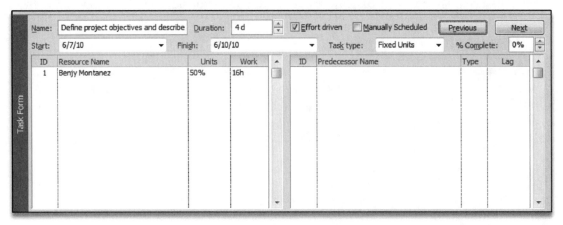

**Figure 6 - 23: Task Entry view, Duration calculated
after assigning a resource with Units and Work**

7. Click the *Next* button to select the next task in the project and to continue assigning resources to tasks.

To assign resources to a task for which you already entered an estimated *Duration* value, complete the following steps:

1. In the *Gantt Chart* pane, select the task with the estimated *Duration* value.

2. In the *Task Form* pane, select the name of a resource from the list in the *Resource Name* column.

3. Enter a *Units* value for the resource in the *Units* column.

4. **Do not** enter a *Work* value.

5. Repeat steps #2-4 for each additional resource you wish to assign to the task.

6. Click the *OK* button.

Project Professional 2010 calculates the *Work* value for each resource assigned to the task. Notice in Figure 6 - 24 that I assigned three resources to work full-time on the task with a *Duration* value of *10 days*, so the software calculated *80 hours* in the *Work* column for each resource.

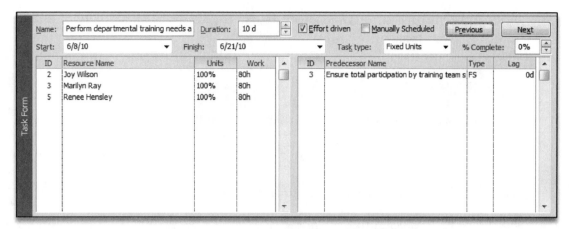

Figure 6 - 24: Task Entry view, Work calculated after assigning resources with Units and Duration

Hands On Exercise

Exercise 6-6

Assign resources to tasks using the *Task Entry* view.

1. Return to your Deploy Training Advisor Software project, if necessary.

2. Click the *Task* tab and then click the *Gantt Chart* button (if you do not have the *Gantt Chart* view displayed already).

3. Click the *View* tab to apply the *View* ribbon.

4. Select the *Details* checkbox in the *Split View* section of the *View* ribbon.

5. Select task ID #8, the *Design P2* task, in the *Gantt Chart* pane.

6. In the *Task Form* pane, click the *Resource Name* pick list and select *David Erickson*.

7. For the resource *David Erickson*, enter *50%* in the *Units* field and *40 hours* in the *Work* field.

8. Click the *OK* button in the *Task Form* pane.

Notice how Project Professional 2010 calculated a *Duration* value of *10 days* for this task. When you supply the *Units* value and the *Work* value, the system calculates the *Duration* value automatically for this *Fixed Units* task.

9. In the *Gantt Chart* pane, select task ID #11, the *Rebuild P2* task.

10. In the *Task Form* pane, select the following resources and then enter the *Units* value for each resource as shown below:

Resource Name	Units
Software Development Team	100%
Cher Zall	25%

11. Click the *OK* button to assign both resources to the task.

Notice how Project Professional 2010 calculated a *Work* value for the *Team* resource and for *Cher Zall*. When you supply the *Units* value and the *Duration* value, the system calculates the *Work* value automatically for each resource on this *Fixed Units* task.

12. Click the *View* tab to reapply the *View* ribbon and deselect the *Details* checkbox in the *Split View* section of the ribbon.

13. Click the *Save* button on the Quick Access Toolbar to save the changes to your project.

Assigning Resources Using the Assign Resources Dialog

The *Assign Resources* dialog is a second tool you can use in the assignment process. The *Assign Resources* dialog is ideal for assigning resources to recurring tasks, such as meetings, because it allows you to select and assign multiple resources to the recurring task. The *Assign Resources* dialog is also ideal for assigning one or more resources to multiple tasks simultaneously, and for replacing one resource with another on multiple tasks simultaneously. Although the *Assign Resources* dialog offers you a simple interface to assign resources to tasks quickly, keep in mind that it does not have all of the options available in the *Task Entry* view.

Using the *Assign Resources* dialog, you have no control over most of the attributes of the scheduling engine. This means you cannot specify the *Duration*, the *Work*, the *Task Type*, the *Effort Driven* status, or the *Task Mode* for a task. Furthermore, you cannot assign multiple resources to a task and individually select different *Units* values for each resource. To display the *Assign Resources* dialog, use one of the following methods:

- Click the *Resource* tab and then click the *Assign Resources* button in the *Assignment* section of the *Resource* ribbon.

- Right-click on any task and then select the *Assign Resources* item on the shortcut menu.

Project Professional 2010 displays the *Assign Resources* dialog, as shown in Figure 6 - 25.

In the *Assign Resources* dialog, the system sorts the resources in ascending order by the *Resource Name* column , and **not** in the order they appear on the *Resource Sheet* view of your project.

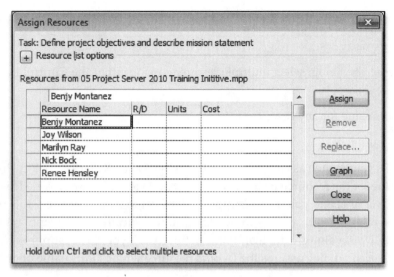

Figure 6 - 25: Assign Resources dialog

To assign a resource to tasks using the *Assign Resources* dialog, complete the following steps:

1. Select one or more tasks.

2. Select a single resource in the list of resources shown in the dialog.

3. Select or enter a *Units* value (if different than *100%* units).

4. Click the *Assign* button.

The *Assign Resources* dialog indicates that you assigned the resource to the selected tasks by moving the assigned resource to the beginning of the list, and by adding a checkmark indicator to the left of the resource's name. Notice in Figure 6 - 26, for example, that I assigned Nick Bock to work full time (*100%* units) on the selected task. If you previously entered cost rates for your resources in the *Std. Rate* column of the *Resource Sheet* view, Project Professional 2010 also calculates a cost value in the *Cost* column of the *Assign Resources* dialog for each assigned resource. Notice in Figure 6 - 26 that Nick Bock's assignment on the selected task costs the project *$800*, as indicated in the *Cost* column.

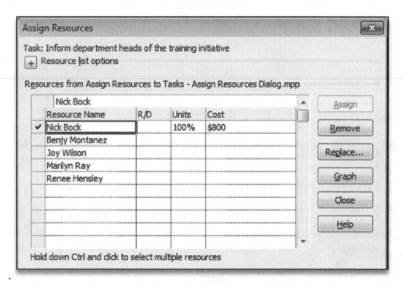

**Figure 6 - 26: Assign Resources dialog
with one resource assigned to a task**

241

To assign multiple resources to tasks using the *Assign Resources* dialog, complete the following steps:

1. Select one or more tasks.

2. In the *Assign Resources* dialog, select multiple resources using either the **Control** key or the **Shift** key on your computer keyboard.

3. **Do not** set a *Units* value for any resource.

4. Click the *Assign* button.

If you do not enter a *Units* value when assigning a resource in the *Assign Resources* dialog, Project Professional 2010 enters the *Max. Units* value for the resource from the *Resource Sheet* view of your project. This means that if the *Max. Units* value for a resource is *50%*, and you do not supply a *Units* value when assigning this resource, the *Assign Resources* dialog assigns the resource with a *Units* value of *50%* automatically. The exception to this rule is for *Generic* resources that have a *Max. Units* value greater than 100%. In this case, if you do not supply a *Units* value for the *Generic* resource, the *Assign Resources* dialog assigns the *Generic* resource with a *Units* value of only *100%* automatically.

Warning: Do not use the *Assign Resources* dialog to assign multiple resources to a task that requires using a different *Units* value for each resource. The software assigns the first resource at the *Units* value you select and then adds each of the other resources as **helpers** on the task using *Effort Driven* scheduling, decreasing the *Duration* of the task accordingly. This behavior is one of the major reasons that new users find Microsoft Project 2010 so frustrating! Instead, use the *Task Entry* view when you need to assign multiple resources with different *Units* values.

Hands On Exercise

Exercise 6-7

Assign resources to tasks using the *Assign Resources* dialog.

1. Return to your Deploy Training Advisor Software project, if necessary.

2. Click the *Assign Resources* button on the Quick Access Toolbar to open the *Assign Resources* dialog.

3. Select task ID #14, the *Design P3* task, press and hold the **Control** key on your computer keyboard, and then select task ID #16, the *Test P3* task.

4. In the *Assign Resources* dialog, select the *Contract Labor* resource and enter *100%* in the *Units* field for this resource.

5. Click the *Assign* button in the *Assign Resources* dialog to assign the *Contract Labor* resource to both of the selected tasks simultaneously.

6. Select task ID #15, the *Build P3* task.

7. In the *Assign Resources* dialog, select *George Stewart* and click the *Assign* button **without** setting a *Units* value for this resource.

If you do not specify a *Units* value when assigning a resource to a task, the system enters the *Max. Units* value as the *Units* value for the resource assignment automatically. In this case, since your *Max. Units* value is *100%* in the *Resource Sheet* view, the system enters *100%* in the *Units* field automatically.

Note: After assigning *George Stewart* to the *Build P3* task, notice that Project Professional 2010 displays a "burning man" indicator in the *Indicators* column to the left of the *Design P1* and *Build P3* tasks. The "burning man" indicator reveals that you accidentally overallocated *George Stewart* on these two tasks. I discuss resource overallocations and leveling later in this module, so for the moment, leave *George Stewart* as an overallocated resource on these two tasks.

8. Click the *Close* button to close the *Assign Resources* dialog.

9. Click the *Save* button on the Quick Access Toolbar to save the changes to your enterprise project.

10. Click the *Close* button on the Quick Access Toolbar and check in your enterprise project when prompted.

Understanding Other Factors in Assignment Planning

During the assignment planning process, three factors affect how you assign resources in Project Professional 2010. These factors are:

- **Duration Equation** - The system uses the Duration Equation to calculate the *Duration, Work,* or *Units* value when you assign a resource to a task.

- **Task Type** - You use the *Task Type* option to fix or "lock" the *Duration, Work,* or *Units* value when you assign a resource to a task.

- **Effort Driven Scheduling** - You use *Effort Driven* scheduling to reduce the *Duration* value on a task by adding one or more helpers to the task.

I discuss each of these factors individually as sub-topics in this section of the module.

Understanding the Duration Equation

When you assign a resource to a task using the *Task Entry* view, and you enter a *Units* value and a *Work* value for the resource, Project Professional 2010 calculates the *Duration* value for the task automatically. How does the software calculate duration? The software uses a simple formula known as the **Duration Equation**, written as follows:

$$\textbf{Duration} = \textbf{Work} \div (\textbf{Hours Per Day} \times \textbf{Units})$$

or

$$D = W \div (HPD \times U)$$

The default *Hours Per Day* value is 8 hours per day. You can locate this value by clicking the *File* tab and then clicking the *Options* item in the *Backstage* menu. In the *Project Options* dialog, click the *Schedule* tab. You find the *Hours per day* option in the *Calendar options for this project* section, as shown in Figure 6 - 27.

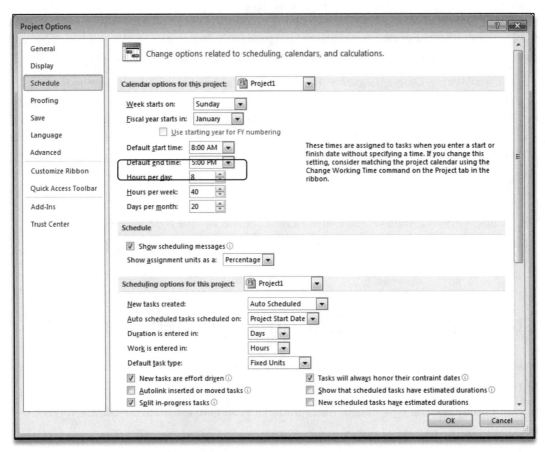

**Figure 6 - 27: Project Options dialog, Schedule tab
shows the Hours per day setting**

To demonstrate how the Duration Equation works, I assign a resource to a task at *50% Units* and *40 hours* of *Work*. Using the Duration Equation, Project Professional 2010 calculates the *Duration* value at *10 days* as follows:

$$D = W \div (HPD \times U)$$

$$D = 40 \div (8 \times 50\%)$$

$$D = 40 \div 4 = 10 \text{ days}$$

When you assign a resource to a task and enter *Duration* and *Units* values (rather than *Units* and *Work* values), Project Professional 2010 calculates the *Work* value. How does the software calculate work? The software uses a modified version of the Duration Equation, rewritten to solve for the *Work* variable as follows:

$$\textbf{Work} = \textbf{Duration} \times \textbf{Hours Per Day} \times \textbf{Units}$$

or

$$W = D \times HPD \times U$$

For example, I assign a resource to work *50% Units* on a task with a *Duration* value of *10 days*, Project Professional 2010 calculates *40 hours* of *Work* as follows:

$$W = D \times HPD \times U$$

$$W = 10 \times 8 \times 50\%$$

$$W = 10 \times 4 = 40 \text{ hours}$$

You can also rewrite the Duration Equation to solve for the *Units* variable as follows:

$$\text{Units} = \text{Work} \div (\text{Duration} \times \text{Hours per Day})$$

or

$$U = W \div (D \times HPD)$$

For example, I assign a resource *40 hours* of *Work* on a task with a *Duration* value of *10 days*, Project Professional 2010 calculates a *Units* value of *50%* as follows:

$$U = W \div (D \times HPD)$$

$$U = 40 \div (10 \times 8)$$

$$U = 40 \div 80 = .5 \text{ or } 50\%$$

Understanding Task Types

You can specify the *Task Type* setting for any task to one of three types: *Fixed Units*, *Fixed Work*, or *Fixed Duration*. You can select **only one** *Task Type* setting for each task. The default *Task Type* setting for every task is *Fixed Units*, unless you specify otherwise in the *Project Options* dialog. To specify the *Task Type* setting for any task, select the task and then use one of the following methods:

- Apply the *Task Entry* view. In the *Task Form* pane, click the *Task Type* pick list and select the desired *Task Type* setting.

- Double-click the task and then click the *Advanced* tab in the *Task Information* dialog. Click the *Task Type* pick list and select the desired *Task Type* setting.

- Click the *Information* button in the *Properties* section of the *Task* ribbon and then click the *Advanced* tab in the *Task Information* dialog. Click the *Task Type* pick list and select the desired *Task Type* setting.

- Right-click on the task and then select the *Information* item on the shortcut menu. In the *Task Information* dialog, click the *Advanced* tab. Click the *Task Type* pick list and select the desired *Task Type* setting.

You can also specify the *Task Type* setting for multiple tasks simultaneously by selecting a group of tasks first. Click the *Information* button in the *Properties* section of the *Task* ribbon and then click the *Advanced* tab in the *Multiple Task Information* dialog. Click the *Task Type* pick list and select the desired *Task Type* setting for the selected tasks.

Specify the *Task Type* setting for tasks using the following information as your guide:

- **Fixed Units** – Project Professional 2010 locks the *Units* value for all resources assigned to a *Fixed Units* task. Set the *Task Type* option to *Fixed Units* when a resource has a known availability to perform work on tasks in your project. For example, you assign a resource to work on a task at *50% Units* because the resource also works half time on the Help Desk. Use the *Fixed Units* task type on this task to guarantee that the software does not recalculate the *50% Units* value if you change either the *Work* or *Duration* values on the task.

- **Fixed Work** – The software locks the *Work* value for all resources assigned to a *Fixed Work* task. Set the *Task Type* option to *Fixed Work* when you are certain about the number of hours to complete a task. For example, you hire a consultant to work on a project task, and the work is set at 40 hours by contract. Use the *Fixed Work* task type on this task to guarantee that Project Professional 2010 does not recalculate the *40 hours* of *Work* if you change either the *Units* or *Duration* values on the task.

- **Fixed Duration** – The software locks the *Duration* value on a *Fixed Duration* task. Set the *Task Type* to *Fixed Duration* when you are certain of the *Duration* value for a task, such as when you have a known "window of opportunity" to complete the task. For example, you have a task called Shareholder Conference and the conference lasts 3 days. Use the *Fixed Duration* task type on this task to guarantee that the software does not recalculate the *Duration* value of *3 days* if you change either the *Units* or *Work* values on the task.

Based on the *Task Type* setting you select, the system fixes or "locks" one of the three variables in the Duration Equation for the selected task. When you change one of the two non-fixed variables, Project Professional 2010 calculates the other non-fixed variable automatically. Table 6 - 1 shows the behavior of all three Task Types when you change the non-fixed variable, and when you change the fixed variable as well.

Task Type	Fixed Value	You Change	Recalculated Value
Fixed Units	Units	Work	Duration
Fixed Units	Units	Duration	Work
Fixed Work	Work	Units	Duration
Fixed Work	Work	Duration	Units
Fixed Duration	Duration	Units	Work
Fixed Duration	Duration	Work	Units
Fixed Units	Units	Units	Duration
Fixed Work	Work	Work	Duration
Fixed Duration	Duration	Duration	Work

Table 6 - 1: Task Type behavior

The only exception to the Task Type behavior documented in Table 6 - 1 occurs when you initially assign a resource to a *Fixed Duration* task and enter a value in the *Work* field. In this situation, Project Professional 2010 does the following:

- In the *Units* field in the *Task Form* pane, the software enters the *Max. Units* value for the resource from the *Resource Sheet* view of your project.

- In the background, the software calculates the correct *Units* value, but does not display it in the *Units* field in the *Task Form* pane. Instead, the software stores this value in the *Peak* field, which you cannot see in the *Task Form* pane.

- The software assigns the resource using the correctly calculated *Units* value stored in the *Peak* field.

If you want to see the values in the *Units* and *Peak* fields, you can add the *Assignment Units* field and the *Peak* field to the *Task Usage* view of your project. At this point, however, do not despair. I provide an in-depth discussion of the behavior of the *Assignment Units* and *Peak* fields in the next section of this module.

When you change a non-fixed variable for any task type, Project Professional 2010 automatically recalculates the other non-fixed variable. When you change the **fixed** variable, however, the software invokes one of the programming decisions implemented by the Microsoft Project software development team many years ago. For example, which variable should the software recalculate when you change the *Units* value on a *Fixed Units* task, or change the *Work* value on a *Fixed Work* task, or change the *Duration* value on a *Fixed Duration* task?

We refer to the decisions made by the software development team as the Microsoft Project programming biases. These programming biases are as follows:

- If you change the *Units* variable on a *Fixed Units* task, Project Professional 2010 **always** recalculates the *Duration* variable.

- If you change the *Work* variable on a *Fixed Work* task, Project Professional 2010 **always** recalculates the *Duration* variable.

- If you change the *Duration* variable on a *Fixed Duration* task, Project Professional 2010 **always** recalculates the *Work* variable.

As you can see, Project Professional 2010 has a bias to calculate changes in *Duration* rather than to *Work* or *Units*. If the software cannot change *Duration*, it has a bias to calculate changes in *Work* rather than *Units*.

 Hands On Exercise

Exercise 6-8

Learn more about *Task Types* by changing the variables in the Duration Equation for tasks with different *Task Types*.

1. Click the *Open* button on the Quick Access Toolbar.

2. Navigate to your *C:* drive and then to the folder containing the sample files for this class, and then open the **Understanding Task Types.mpp** sample file.

3. In the *Task Usage* pane, select the *Fixed Units 1* task.

4. Click the *Scroll to Task* button on the Quick Access Toolbar to show the timephased *Work* hours in the timephased grid (right side of the view).

5. In the *Task Form* pane, change the *Work* value to *48h* and then click the *OK* button.

6. Click the *Next* button in the *Task Form* pane to select the *Fixed Units 2* task.

7. In the *Task Form* pane, change the *Duration* value to *8d* and then click the *OK* button.

For a *Fixed Units* task, notice that when you change the *Work* variable, Project Professional 2010 recalculates the *Duration* variable, and when you change the *Duration* variable, the system recalculates the *Work* variable.

8. Click the *Next* button in the *Task Form* pane to select the *Fixed Units 3* task.

9. In the *Task Form* pane, change the *Units* value to *100%* and then click the *OK* button.

For this *Fixed Units* task, notice that when you change the *Units* variable, Project Professional 2010 recalculates the *Duration* variable. This behavior is the first of three programming biases I discussed in the previous topical subsection.

10. Click the *Next* button in the *Task Form* pane to select the *Fixed Work 1* task.

11. In the *Task Form* pane, change the *Units* value to *100%* and then click the *OK* button.

For this *Fixed Work* task, notice that when you change the *Units* variable, Project Professional 2010 recalculates the *Duration* variable.

12. Click the *Next* button in the *Task Form* pane to select the *Fixed Work 2* task.

13. In the *Task Form* pane, change the *Duration* value to *5d* and then click the *OK* button.

14. Scroll down to view the assignment information for *Debbie Kirkpatrick* on the *Fixed Work 2* task, if necessary.

Notice in the *Task Usage* pane that Project Professional 2010 now includes **two fields** relating to the assignment units: the *Assignment Units* field and the *Peak* field. The *Units* value you see in the *Task Form* pane is actually the *Assignment Units* field, which shows the **original** *Units* value on the task (*50%*). The *Peak* field contains the **new** *Units* value after you changed the *Duration* value on the *Fixed Work* task. Notice that the *Peak* field shows the **correct** *Units* value of *100%*. Notice also in the timephased grid on the right side of the view that the system schedules the *Work* hours correctly at 8 hours per day based on the 100% *Units* value in the *Peak* field. Therefore, even though the *Units* value does not seem to be correct in the *Task Form* pane (*50%*), the software **does schedule the task correctly** using the value shown in the *Peak* field (*100%*).

11. Click the *Next* button in the *Task Form* pane to select the *Fixed Work 3* task.

12. In the *Task Form* pane, change the *Work* value to *32h* and then click the *OK* button.

For this *Fixed Work* task, notice that when you change the *Work* variable, Project Professional 2010 recalculates the *Duration* variable. This behavior is the second of three programming biases I discussed in the previous topical subsection.

13. Click the *Next* button in the *Task Form* pane to select the *Fixed Duration 1* task.

14. In the *Task Form* pane, change the *Units* value to *100%* and then click the *OK* button.

For this *Fixed Duration* task, notice that when you change the *Units* variable, Project Professional 2010 recalculates the *Work* variable.

15. Click the *Next* button in the *Task Form* pane to select the *Fixed Duration 2* task.

16. In the *Task Form* pane, change the *Work* value to *60h* and then click the *OK* button.

For this *Fixed Duration* task, notice that when you change the *Work* variable, Project Professional 2010 **did not seem** to recalculate the *Units* variable. Once again, examine the *Task Usage* pane and notice that the *Peak* field contains the expected value of *75%*. Notice also in the timephased grid that the system schedules the *Work* hours correctly at 6 hours per day based on the *75%* value in the *Peak* field.

17. Click the *Next* button in the *Task Form* pane to select the *Fixed Duration 3* task.

18. In the *Task Form* pane, change the *Duration* value to *6d* and then click the *OK* button.

For this *Fixed Duration* task, notice that when you change the *Duration* variable, Project Professional 2010 re-calculates the *Work* variable. This behavior is the final of three programming biases I discussed in the previous topical subsection.

19. Save and close the **Understanding Task Types.mpp** sample file.

Understanding Effort Driven Scheduling

In Project Professional 2010, you can designate each task individually as either an *Effort Driven* task or a *non-Effort Driven* task. The *Effort Driven* status of any task determines how the software responds when you add or remove resources from a task to which you previously assigned one or more resources. The default setting for every task in Project Professional 2010 is *Effort Driven*.

To assign additional resources as helpers to a task using *Effort Driven* scheduling, complete the following steps:

1. Select a task to which you previously assigned at least one resource.

2. Apply the *Task Entry* view.

3. In *Task Form* pane, select the *Effort driven* option, if not already selected.

4. Select one or more additional resources in the *Resource Name* column, and set a *Units* value for each additional resource.

5. **Do not** enter a *Work* value for any of the additional resources.

6. Click the *OK* button.

When you add a resource to an *Effort Driven* task, the software keeps the *Remaining Work* value constant and allocates the *Remaining Work* proportionately to each resource based on each resource's *Units* value. Consider the following examples of how Project Professional 2010 distributes the *Remaining Work* based on the *Units* values of each resource:

- I assign Ann Dyer to the Design task at 100% units and 80 hours of work, and the software calculates a duration of 10 days for the task. Using *Effort Driven* scheduling, I add Kevin Holthaus to the task at 100% units. Project Professional 2010 shortens the duration to 5 days and allocates the 80 hours of *Remaining Work* evenly between the two resources (40 hours each to Ann Dyer and to Kevin Holthaus), as shown in Figure 6 - 28.

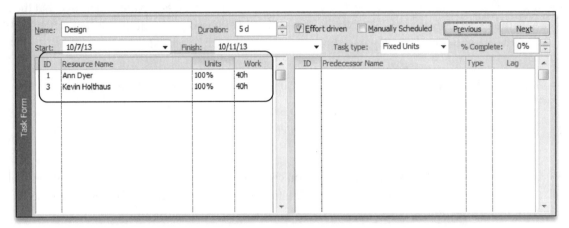

Figure 6 - 28: Using Effort Driven scheduling with identical Units values

- I assign Ann Dyer to the Design task at 100% units and 80 hours of work, and the software calculates a duration of 10 days for the task. Using *Effort Driven* scheduling, I add Kevin Holthaus to the task at **50% units**. In this situation, Project Professional 2010 shortens the duration to 6.67 days and allocates the 80 hours of *Remaining Work* **proportionately** between the two resources (53.33 hours to Ann Dyer and 26.67 hours to Kevin Holthaus), as shown in Figure 6 - 29.

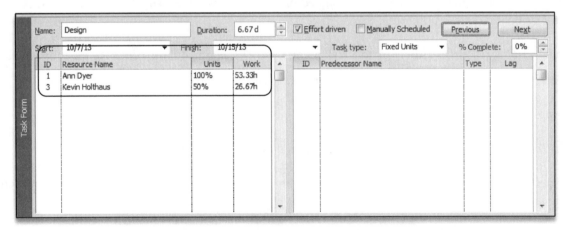

Figure 6 - 29: Effort Driven scheduling with different Units values

How does Project Professional 2010 actually determine the proportionate split of the original 80 hours of work? Ann Dyer's *Units* value of *100%* is two-thirds of the total units of *150%* for both resources (100/150 = 2/3), so the system allocates Ann Dyer two-thirds of the total work, which is 53.33 hours (80 x 2/3 – 53.33). Kevin Holthaus' *Units* value of *50%* is one-third of the total units value (50/150 = 1/3), so the system allocates Kevin Holthaus one-third of the total *Work*, which is 26.67 hours (80 x 1/3 = 26.67).

When you assign additional resources to an *Effort Driven* task, MSProjectExperts recommends that you also increase the *Work* hours for each resource in the range of **10% to 20%** to account for the increased communications overhead between the resources.

When you remove a resource from an *Effort Driven* task with multiple resources already assigned, Microsoft Project 2010 **increases** the *Duration* of the task and **increases** the *Remaining Work* value proportionately for each remaining resource. This behavior is also known as *Effort Driven* scheduling, although most people do not realize this.

Remember that when you assign additional resources to an *Effort Driven* task, Project Professional 2010 allocates the *Remaining Work* proportionately between all of the assigned resources. So how does the software respond when you add a helper to a task that already contains some completed work? Consider the following example:

- I assign Brian Harry to the Build task at 100% units and 80 hours of work, and the software calculates a duration of 10 days for the task. Brian completed 40 hours of actual work, which leaves 40 hours of remaining work. Using *Effort Driven* scheduling, I add Lisa Roach to the task at 100% units. Project Professional 2010 shortens the duration to 7.5 days and allocates the 40 hours of **remaining work** evenly between the two resources (20 hours each to Brian Harry and Lisa Roach), as shown in Figure 6 - 30.

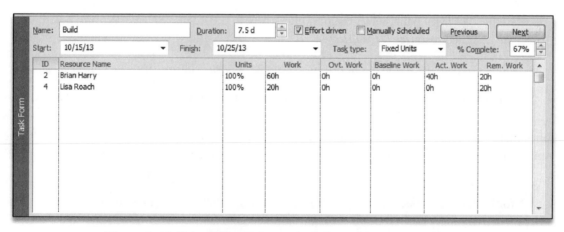

Figure 6 - 30: Using Effort Driven scheduling with completed work
Project Professional 2010 allocates Remaining Work

Figure 6 - 30 shows the *Task Form* view with the *Work* details applied. To view the *Work* details, right-click anywhere in the *Task Form* pane and then select *Work* on the shortcut menu. Notice in Figure 6 - 30 that the software holds the 40 hours of remaining work constant, which gives Brian Harry 60 hours of total work (40 hours of actual work + 20 hours of remaining work) and gives Lisa Roach 20 hours of total work (0 hours of actual work + 20 hours of remaining work).

On *Fixed Units* or *Fixed Work* tasks, assigning additional resources using *Effort Driven* scheduling **shortens the Duration** of the task. On a *Fixed Duration* task, however, assigning additional resources using *Effort Driven* scheduling **decreases the Units** for each assigned resource.

Hands On Exercise

Exercise 6-9

Use *Effort Driven* scheduling to shorten the duration of a task.

1. Click the *Open* button on the Quick Access Toolbar and reopen your Deploy Training Advisor Software project.

2. Select task ID #8, the *Design P2* task.

3. Click the *View* tab to apply the *View* ribbon.

4. Select the *Details* checkbox in the *Split View* section of the *View* ribbon.

5. In the *Task Form* pane, select the first blank row in the *Resource Name* column, below the name of the assigned resource *Dave Erickson*.

6. Click the pick list in the blank cell in the *Resource Name* column and select *Myrta Hansen*.

7. Enter *50%* in the *Units* field for *Myrta Hansen* and then click the *OK* button in the *Task Form* pane.

Notice that Project Professional 2010 reduces the *Duration* value to *5 days* and apportions the 40 hours of work evenly between the two assigned resources (20 hours for Dave Erickson and 20 hours for Myrta Hansen).

8. To account for the increased communications needs on this task, increase the *Work* value to *24h* for both *Dave Erickson* and *Myrta Hansen*, and then click the *OK* button in the *Task Form* pane.

Notice that Project Professional 2010 calculated *6 days* as the new *Duration* value for this task, based on the increased work hours you assigned to the two resources.

9. Click the *View* tab to display the *View* ribbon.

10. In the *Split View* section of the *View* ribbon, deselect the *Details* checkbox to close the *Task Form* pane.

11. Click the *Save* button on the Quick Access Toolbar to save the changes to your project.

Assigning Cost Resources

If your Project Server administrator included *Budget Cost* and *Expense Cost* resources in your Project Server 2010 system, it is important that you know how to assign each type of *Cost* resource. Because Microsoft does not include any type of standard view or table to use for assigning *Cost* resources, I also teach you how to create a custom view you can use to assign each type of *Cost* resource.

Assigning a Budget Cost Resource

When you use a *Budget Cost* resource in a project, Project Professional 2010 allows you to assign the resource to **only** the Project Summary Task (Task 0). This allows you to set a budget for the overall project as a whole, but it does not allow you to set a budget on phases, deliverables, or individual tasks. To specify an overall budget for your project, complete the following steps:

1. Click the *View* tab and then click the *Task Usage* button in the *Task Views* section of the *View* ribbon.

2. In your project, select the Project Summary Task (Task 0).

3. Click the *Resource* tab and then click the *Assign Resources* button in the *Assignments* section of the *Resource* ribbon.

4. In the *Assign Resources* dialog, select your *Budget Cost* resource and then click the *Assign* button.

5. Click the *Close* button to close the *Assign Resources* dialog.

Figure 6 - 31 shows that I assigned my *Budget Cost* resource to the Project Summary Task.

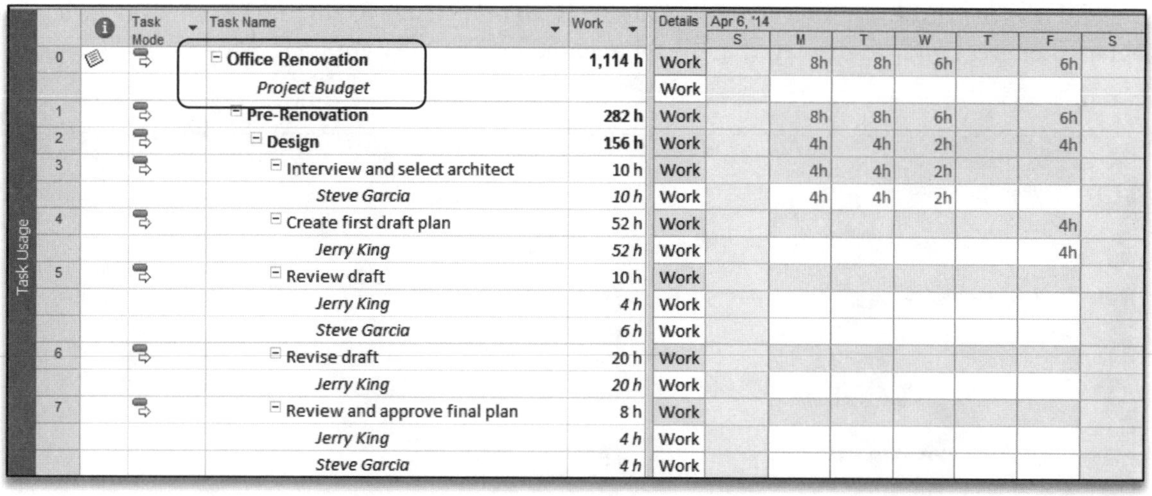

Figure 6 - 31: Budget Cost resource assigned to the Project Summary Task

6. Right-click on the *Select All* button and select the *Cost* table on the shortcut menu.

7. Right-click on the *Fixed Cost* column header, select the *Insert Column* item on the shortcut menu, and then select the *Budget Cost* column.

8. Right-click anywhere in the timephased grid and then select the *Detail Styles* item in the shortcut menu.

9. In the *Detail Styles* dialog, select the *Budget Cost* field and click the *Show* button to add the field to the *Show these fields* list.

Figure 6 - 32 shows the *Detail Styles* dialog with the *Budget Cost* field added to the *Show these fields* list.

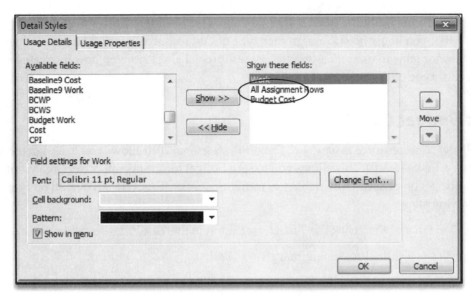

Figure 6 - 32: Detail Styles dialog with Budget Cost field added

10. Click the *OK* button to close the *Details Styles* dialog and insert the *Budget Cost* timephased field.

11. In the timephased grid, double-click the right edge of the *Details* column header to "best fit" the column width.

Figure 6 - 33 shows the *Task Usage* view with the *Budget Cost* column displayed in the *Cost* table on the left and with the timephased *Budget Cost* field displayed in the timephased grid on the right.

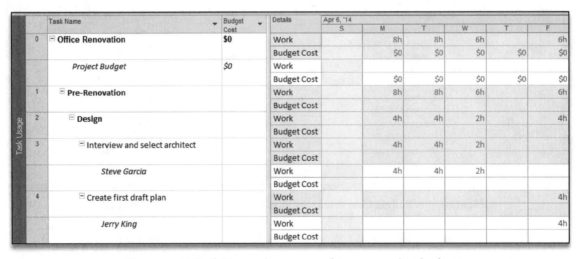

Figure 6 - 33: Task Usage view prepared to enter project budget

12. In the *Budget Cost* column for the *Budget Cost* resource assignment on the Project Summary Task, enter your planned budget for the entire project and then press the **Enter** key on your computer keyboard.

Figure 6 - 34 shows the *Budget Cost* value for my *Project Budget* cost resource assigned to the Project Summary Task.

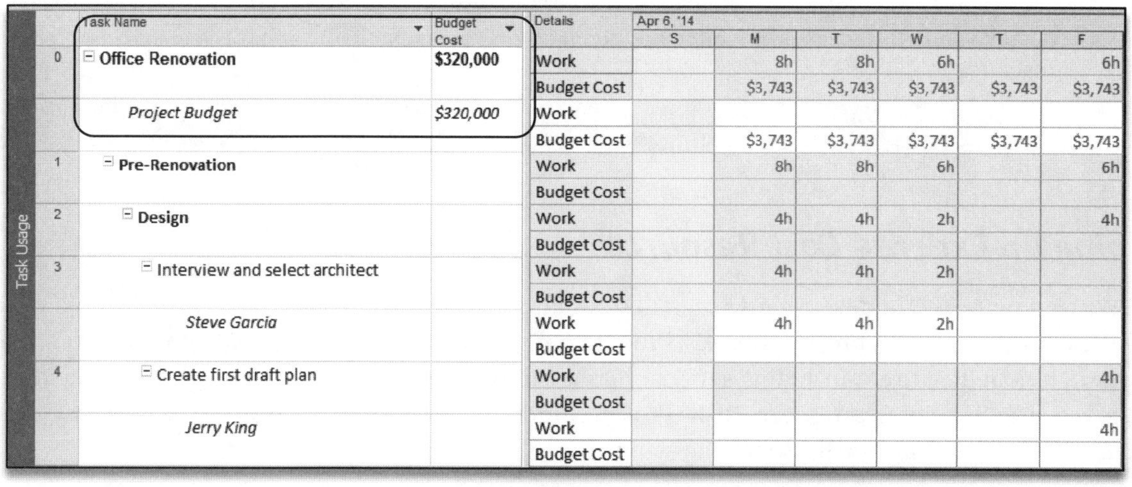

Figure 6 - 34: Budget Cost amount for entire project

If you set the *Accrue At* field value to *Prorated* for the *Budget Cost* resource in the *Resource Sheet* view of your project, then Project Professional 2010 apportions the *Budget Cost* amount evenly across the time span of the entire project. You see the timephased *Budget Cost* amounts in each day ($3,743 each day) of the timephased grid shown previously in Figure 6 - 34. If you wish to reapportion the *Budget Cost* information in another manner, such as on a monthly basis, then complete the following additional steps:

13. Click the *View* tab, click the *Zoom* button in the *Zoom* section of the *View* ribbon, and zoom the *Timescale* to the level of detail at which you wish to reapportion the *Budget Cost* amount.

14. In the timephased grid, enter your anticipated *Budget Cost* values in the *Budget Cost* cells for your *Budget Cost* resource assignment.

In Figure 6 - 35, notice that I entered my *Budget Cost* values on a monthly basis for my *Project Budget* cost resource, roughly timephased to correspond with the planned work hours for each month.

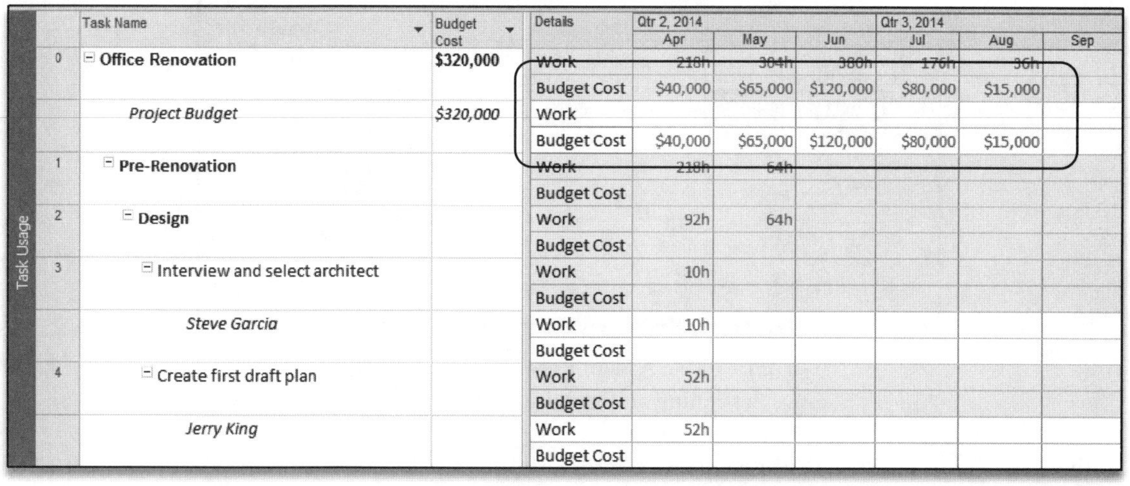

**Figure 6 - 35: Budget Cost information entered in
timephased grid for the Project Budget cost resource**

In addition to the *Budget Cost* field, Microsoft Project 2010 includes an additional budget field called *Budget Work*. This field allows you to set a budget for working hours for your project in addition to a cost budget.

Assigning an Expense Cost Resource

After you enter your project budget using a *Budget Cost* resource, you can assign *Expense Cost* resources to your project so that you can track additional project expenses. Project Professional 2010 allows you to assign *Expense Cost* resources to any type of task in the project, including summary tasks, subtasks, and milestone tasks. The software **does not** allow you to assign an *Expense Cost* resource to the Project Summary Task, however. To assign an *Expense Cost* resource to tasks in your project, complete the following steps:

1. Using the customized *Task Usage* view documented in the previous topical section, select any task in the project, including a regular task, a summary task, or a milestone task.

2. Click the *Resource* tab and then click the *Assign Resources* button in the *Assignments* section of the *Resource* ribbon.

3. In the *Assign Resources* dialog, select your *Expense Cost* resource and then click the *Assign* button.

Figure 6 - 36 shows the *Assign Resources* dialog after assigning an *Expense Cost* resource named *Travel Expense*. I want to use this resource to capture the travel expenses for my project so that I can report this amount as a line item expenditure.

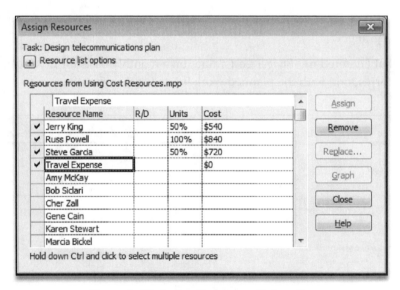

Figure 6 - 36: Assign Resources dialog after assigning an Expense Cost resource

4. In the *Cost* column for the *Expense Cost* resource in the *Assign Resources* dialog, enter the amount of **anticipated expenditure** and then press the **Enter** key on your computer keyboard.

Figure 6 - 37 shows the *Assign Resources* dialog after entering my estimated expenditure for travel expenses on the selected task. Notice that I anticipate the travel expenses to be *$1,525* for this task.

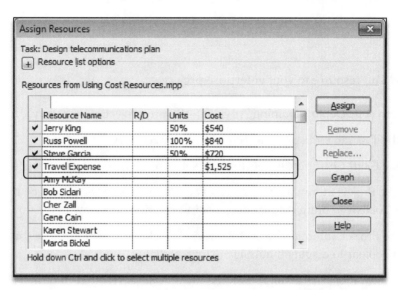

**Figure 6 - 37: Assign Resources dialog after
assigning an Expense Cost resource**

5.   Continue selecting tasks, assigning the *Expense Cost* resources, and entering anticipated expenditures until you finish.

6.   Click the *Close* button to close the *Assign Resources* dialog.

Recommendations for Using Cost Resources

Cost resources do have some limitations, so follow Microsoft's recommendations for using *Cost* resources effectively:

-   Do not assign a *Cost* resource on the same task as a *Work* resource if the resource reports actual progress from Project Web App.

-   Do not assign a *Task* calendar using 24-hour elapsed days (eDays) to a task assigned to a *Cost* resource.

-   Do not disable the *Actual costs are always calculated by Microsoft Project* option in your project. You find this option in the *Calculation options for this project* section of the *Advanced* page in the *Project Options* dialog.

-   Avoid using the *Undo* feature if you edit the *Remaining Duration* field for a task assigned to a *Cost* resource.

Hands On Exercise

Exercise 6-10

Assign a *Budget Cost* resource to your enterprise project.

1. Return to your Deploy Training Advisor Software project, if necessary.

2. Click the *Task* tab to display the *Task* ribbon, if necessary.

3. Click the *Gantt Chart* pick list button and select the *_msPE Cost Resources* custom enterprise view.

4. Select the Project Summary Task (task 0) and then click the *Scroll to Task* button on the Quick Access Toolbar to bring the planned cost information into view in the timephased grid.

5. With the Project Summary Task still selected, click the *Assign Resources* button on the Quick Access Toolbar to display the *Assign Resources* dialog.

6. In the *Assign Resources* dialog, select the *Project Budget* resource and then click the *Assign* button.

7. Click the *Close* button to close the *Assign Resources* dialog.

8. In the *Budget Cost* column for the *Project Budget* resource assignment, enter $50,000 and then press the **Enter** key on your computer keyboard.

9. Click the *Save* button on the Quick Access Toolbar to save the changes to your project.

Exercise 6-11

Assign an *Expense Cost* resource to your enterprise project.

1. Select task ID #8, the *Design P2* task.

2. Click the *Assign Resources* button on the Quick Access Toolbar to display the *Assign Resources* dialog.

3. In the *Assign Resources* dialog, select the *Computer Hardware* resource and then click the *Assign* button.

4. Click the *Close* button to close the *Assign Resources* dialog.

5. In the *Cost* column for the *Computer Hardware* resource assignment, enter $4,875 and then press the **Enter** key on your computer keyboard.

6. Scroll to the top of your project and select the Project Summary Task (task 0) again.

7. In the *View* section of the *Task* ribbon, click the *Gantt Chart* button to reapply the *Gantt Chart* view.

8. Click the *Save* button on the Quick Access Toolbar to save the changes to your enterprise project.

9. Click the *Close* button on the Quick Access Toolbar to close your enterprise project, and then check in your project when prompted.

Using the Team Planner View

At any point during the assignment planning process, you may want to display the new *Team Planner* view in Project Professional 2010. This new view allows you to analyze the current state of resource assignments in your project using a friendly graphical display. To apply the *Team Planner* view, click the *Resource* tab and then click the *Team Planner* button in the *View* section of the *Resource* ribbon. The system displays the *Team Planner* view for your project, as shown in Figure 6 - 38.

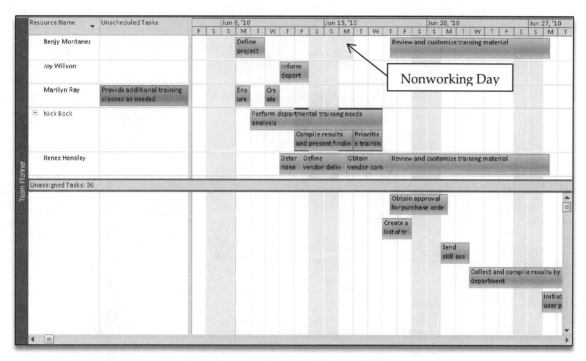

Figure 6 - 38: Team Planner view

 Warning: The first time you apply the *Team Planner* view in a project, the software always scrolls to the **current date** in the *Gantt Chart* area on the right side of the view. If you schedule your project to start in the future, you may not see any tasks in the *Unassigned Tasks* pane. To see tasks in the *Unassigned Tasks* pane, you must scroll the *Gantt Chart* to the start date of your project.

The *Team Planner* view displays resource and assignment information in two panes. The top pane is the *Resource* pane and shows resources from the *Resource Sheet* view of your project, sorted by ID number. Assigned tasks appear in the *Gantt Chart* area on the right side of the pane for each resource. Unlike the *Gantt Chart* view, however, the *Team Planner* view displays the Gantt bars arranged horizontally on a single line for each resource. *Unscheduled Tasks* (*Manually Scheduled* tasks with no *Duration, Start*, or *Finish* date) already assigned to a resource appear in the *Unscheduled Tasks* column to the right of the resource name.

The *Gantt Chart* area of the *Resource* pane also shows nonworking time for each resource, displayed as a gray shaded band for each time period. Nonworking time includes weekends and company holidays for all resources, plus vacation and planned sick leave for each resource individually. In the *Gantt Chart* area of the *Resource* pane shown previously in Figure 6 - 38, you can also see that Benjy Montanez has one day of nonworking time scheduled on Monday, June 14, indicated by the gray shaded band in the *Gantt Chart* area for this resource. To learn more about any person's nonworking time for any time period, double-click the gray shaded band for that time period. Project Professional 2010 displays the *Change Working Time* dialog shown in Figure 6 - 39. Notice in the *Change Working Time* dialog shown in Figure 6 - 39 that Benjy Montanez scheduled a Personal Day Off on June 14. Click the *Cancel* button to close the *Change Working Time* dialog for the selected resource.

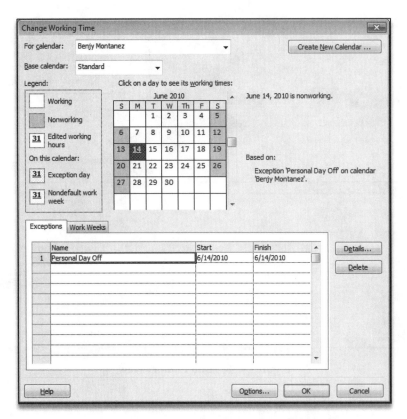

Figure 6 - 39: Change Working Time dialog,
Personal Day Off for Benjy Montanez

The bottom pane of the *Team Planner* view is the *Unassigned Tasks* pane and shows the list of tasks not yet assigned to any resource, sorted by task ID number. The *Gantt Chart* area on the right side of the *Unassigned Tasks* pane shows the current schedule for each unassigned task, based on the schedule specified in the *Gantt Chart* view of the project. The system zooms the *Gantt Chart* area to the *Weeks Over Days* level of zoom by default.

In the *Team Planner* view shown previously in Figure 6 - 38, notice that I already assigned tasks to each team member in the project, including one *Unscheduled Task* assigned to Marilyn Ray. To view additional information about any task, float your mouse pointer over the Gantt bar of the task. Project Professional 2010 displays a screen tip for the selected Gantt bar, as shown in Figure 6 - 40.

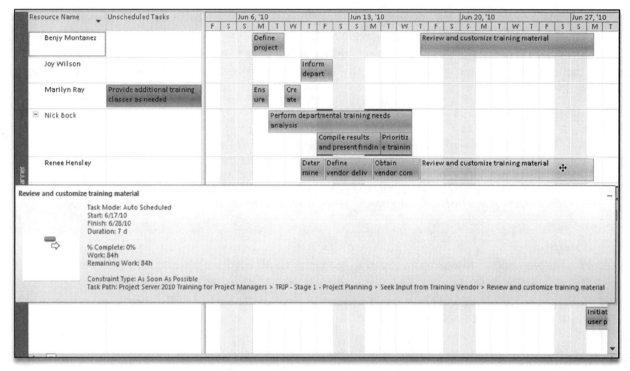

Figure 6 - 40: Schedule information for the selected task

The *Team Planner* view uses special colors and formatting to display task information for each assigned and unassigned task. The key to understanding the color formatting is as follows:

- Light blue Gantt bars represent unstarted *Auto Scheduled* tasks.

- Teal (turquoise) Gantt bars represent *Manually Scheduled* tasks.

- Dark blue in a Gantt bar represents task progress for both *Auto Scheduled* tasks and *Manually Scheduled* tasks.

- Gray Gantt bars represent external tasks in another project.

- Black Gantt bars with white text represent late tasks (tasks where the current *% Complete* progress does not extend to the *Status Date* of the project).

- Resource names formatted in red represent overallocated resources.

- Red borders on a Gantt bar represent the overallocated time periods for a resource.

For example, in Figure 6 - 38 and Figure 6 - 40 shown previously, the system formats Nick Bock's name in red, and displays red borders on his three assigned tasks. This indicates that Nick Bock is overallocated on these three tasks. In fact, he is overallocated specifically on June 11, 14, 15, and 16 on these three tasks.

Dragging Tasks in the Team Planner View

You can use the "drag and drop" functionality of the *Team Planner* view to do any of the following:

- Drag an assigned task to a different time period to reschedule the task.

- Drag an assigned task to a different resource.

- Drag an unassigned task to a resource.

261

To reschedule a task to a different time period, simply drag the task's Gantt bar to the new time period. Keep in mind, however, that when you reschedule a task by dragging it to a new time period, Project Professional 2010 sets a *Start No Earlier Than* (SNET) constraint on the task automatically. If you drag a task beyond the right edge of the *Team Planner* view, the system scrolls the view automatically so that you do not need to release the mouse button and scroll manually.

Warning: The software's use of SNET constraints in the *Team Planner* view may be contrary to the best interests of your scheduling model if you want to maintain a fully dynamic model. SNET constraints prevent a task from moving to an earlier start date if an earlier start becomes available. You can easily clear delays added by the built-in leveling tool with a press of a button, but you must manually remove constraints added by the *Team Planner*. I show you how to remove these constraints in Exercise 6-12.

To reassign a task to another resource, simply drag the task's Gantt bar from the assigned resource to the new resource and drop it on the desired time period. For example, Figure 6 - 41 shows the *Team Planner* view after I dragged two tasks assigned to Nick Bock and reassigned them to Marilyn Ray. These two tasks were the tasks causing the resource overallocation for Nick Bock.

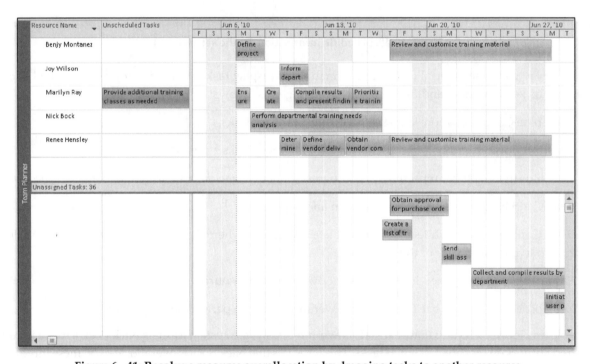

Figure 6 - 41: Resolve a resource overallocation by dragging tasks to another resource

You can also reassign a task to another resource by right-clicking on the Gantt bar for the task, choosing the *Reassign To* item on the shortcut menu, and then selecting the name of the new resource.

To assign an unassigned task to any resource using the *Team Planner* view, drag the task's Gantt bar from the *Unassigned Tasks* pane to the top pane and drop it in the time period during which you want to schedule the task for the selected resource. Keep in mind that when you assign a task to a resource using this method, Project Professional 2010 assigns the task to the resource at 100% Units automatically, indicating full-time work on the task.

To reassign or reschedule multiple tasks simultaneously, press and hold the **Ctrl** key to select multiple tasks, and then drag and drop the block of selected tasks. Microsoft Project 2010 **does not** allow you to drag and drop multiple **unassigned** tasks simultaneously in the *Team Planner* view, however.

Changing Schedule Information in the Team Planner View

As you analyze assignment information in the *Team Planner* view, at some point you may need to revise schedule information. Project Professional 2010 allows you to revise your project as follows in the *Team Planner* view:

- You can change the *Task Mode* option for a task by right-clicking on the Gantt bar for the task and choosing either the *Auto Schedule* or *Manually Schedule* item on the shortcut menu.

- You can set a task to *Inactive* status by right-clicking on the Gantt bar for the task and choosing the *Inactivate Task* item on the shortcut menu.

- You can change information for any task (such as setting a constraint or applying a task calendar) by double-clicking the Gantt bar for the task and entering the information in the *Task Information* dialog. You can also right-click on the Gantt bar for the task and choose the *Information* item on the shortcut menu.

- You can apply the *Task Details Form* in a split view arrangement with the *Team Planner* view by clicking the *Task* tab and then clicking the *Display Task Details* button in the *Properties* section of the *Task* ribbon. When you select the Gantt bar for any assigned task in the top pane, the *Task Details Form* in the bottom pane displays relevant information about the task and its assigned resources. Notice in Figure 6 - 42 that the *Task Details Form* displays information about the Perform Departmental Training Needs Analysis task whose Gantt bar I selected in the top pane. To close the *Task Details Form*, click the *Display Task Details* button again in the *Task* ribbon.

During the execution stage of your project, you can also enter progress against a task by right-clicking on the task's Gantt bar in the *Team Planner* view and then selecting a *% Complete* value on the *Mini Toolbar* section of the shortcut menu. The *Mini Toolbar* offers you the *0%, 25%, 50%, 75%,* and *100%* buttons with which to enter the progress on a task quickly.

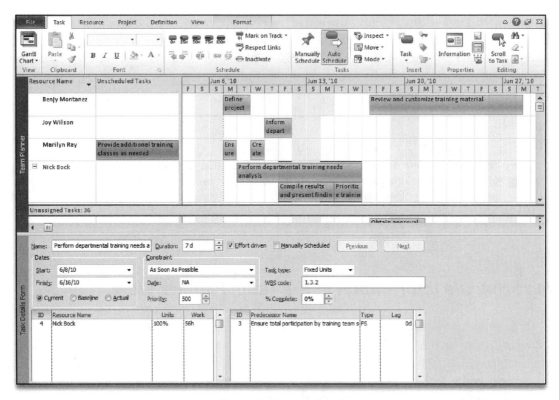

Figure 6 - 42: Task Details Form applied in a split-screen
arrangement with the Team Planner view

Hands On Exercise

Exercise 6-12

Use the *Team Planner* view to analyze resource assignments, to reassign tasks from one resource to another, and to assign unassigned tasks to a resource.

1. Click the *Open* button on the Quick Access Toolbar.

2. Navigate to your *C:* drive and then to the folder containing the sample files for this class, and then open the **Using the Team Planner View.mpp** sample file.

3. Click the *Resource* tab and then click the *Team Planner* button in *View* section of the *Resource* ribbon.

4. Scroll to the right, as needed, and examine the tasks currently assigned to each resource.

Notice that some of the Gantt bars include red borders, representing the overallocated time periods for an overallocated resource.

5. Scroll to the week of September 22, 2013 for *Dan Morton* and look for the week of nonworking time in the *Gantt Chart* area (gray shaded cells).

6. Double-click in the gray shaded cells during the week of nonworking time for *Dan Morton* to display the *Change Working Time* dialog and reveal the reason for the nonworking time.

Notice that Dan Morton has a week of educational leave scheduled for the week of September 22, 2013.

7. Click the *Cancel* button to close the *Change Working Time* dialog.

8. Select the resource, *Marilyn Ray,* and then examine the Gantt bars for her tasks during the week of September 22, 2013.

Notice that the system formats the Marilyn Ray's name using the red font color, indicating she is an overallocated resource. Also, notice the red borders on some of the Gantt bars for Marilyn Ray, indicating her overallocated time periods.

9. Drag the Gantt bar for the *Initiate End-User Placement Matrix* task from *Marilyn Ray* to *Cassie Endicott*. **Note:** Be sure to keep the **same time schedule** for the task when you drag the Gantt bar to *Cassie Endicott*.

10. Scroll to the week of *September 29, 2013* and locate tasks not yet assigned to any resource in the *Unassigned Tasks* pane.

11. Drag the Gantt bar for the *Determine course dates, start and end times, and locations* task to *Dan Morton*. **Note:** Be sure to keep the **same time schedule** for the task when you drag the Gantt bar to Dan Morton.

12. Click the *Task* tab and then click the *Gantt Chart* button to apply the *Gantt Chart* view.

13. Scroll to task ID #25, the *Determine course dates, start and end times, and locations* task you assigned to *Dan Morton*.

In the *Indicators* column, notice that Project Professional 2010 applied a *Start No Earlier Than (SNET)* constraint on this task after you assigned it to Dan Morton. This is the consequence of dragging and dropping task Gantt bars in the *Team Planner* view. If a task already has task dependencies set, you should remove the constraint created by the system when you drag a task to another resource in the *Team Planner* view.

14. In the *Gantt Chart* view, double-click task ID #25, the *Determine course dates, start and end times, and locations* task.

15. In the *Task Information* dialog, click the *Advanced* tab.

16. On the *Advanced* page of the *Task Information* dialog, click the *Constraint type* pick list and select the *As Soon As Possible* constraint on the list.

17. Click the *OK* button to close the *Task Information* dialog.

18. Click the *Resource* tab and then click the *Team Planner* button in *View* section of the *Resource* ribbon to reapply the *Team Planner* view.

19. In the *Team Planner* view, scroll to the week of September 1, 2013.

20. Save and close the **Using the Team Planner View.mpp** sample file.

Understanding Resource Overallocation

During the resource assignment process, you may accidentally overallocate one or more resources in the project. An overallocation occurs when you assign more work to a resource than the resource can do during the working time available, resulting in a *Units* value that exceeds the *Max. Units* value for the resource. Each of the following situations results in an overallocated resource:

- You assign a resource to work 32 hours in a single day.

- You assign a resource to work 160 hours in a single week.

- You assign a resource to work 30 minutes in a 15-minute time period.

Leveling is the process you use to resolve resource overallocations so that your project resources are no longer overallocated. The third bullet point reveals an important truth about leveling overallocated resources:

Not all overallocations are worth leveling.

You should definitely level the overallocations I describe in the first two bulleted items above, because either situation would likely cause your project finish date to slip. The third situation is not worth leveling, however, as the amount of time spent leveling this overallocation is not worth the bother.

In addition to the three previous examples, you can also overallocate a resource by assigning the resource to a task at a *Units* value of *200%* when the *Max. Units* value for the resource is *100%*. You cannot resolve this type of overallocation using the built-in leveling tool in Microsoft Project 2010. Instead, you must manually resolve this type of overallocation by reducing the *Units* value for the resource's assignment on the task.

Locating Resource Overallocations

The easiest way to locate overallocated resources is to use the *Resource Usage* view. To apply this view, click the *Resource* tab to display the *Resource* ribbon, click the *Team Planner* pick list button, and then select the *Resource Usage* view from the list. Because Microsoft Project 2010 formats overallocated resources with the red font color, look for any resource names formatted in red. To determine the time periods during which a resource is overallocated, select an overallocated resource and then click the *Next Overallocation* button in the *Level* section of the *Resource* ribbon. When you click the *Next Overallocation* button, Microsoft Project 2010 scrolls the timephased grid and selects the start of the first resource overallocation, as shown in Figure 6 - 43.

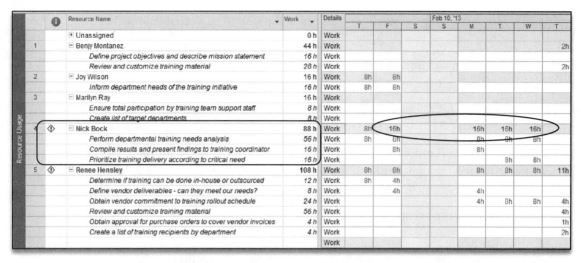

Figure 6 - 43: Resource Usage view shows first overallocation

In Figure 6 - 43, notice that I assigned Nick Bock to work 16 hours each day in a four-day period during the weeks of February 3 and 10, 2013. I accidentally caused this overallocation when I assigned Nick to work on three overlapping tasks, each of which requires full-time work. In addition, notice that I also overallocated Renee Hensley. In Figure 6 - 43, you can see the start of one of her overallocations on the right side of the timephased grid.

As you continue to click the *Next Overallocation* button, Microsoft Project 2010 selects the start of each successive overallocation. When the software cannot locate any more resource overallocations, it displays the dialog shown in Figure 6 - 44.

Figure 6 - 44: No more resource overallocations

Leveling Overallocated Resources

As I previously stated, leveling is the process you use to resolve resource overallocations. There are many ways to level overallocated resources, including each of the following:

- Substitute an available resource for the overallocated resource.

- Increase the availability of overallocated resources.

- Schedule overtime for the overallocated resource.

- Manually delay tasks with overallocated resources.

- Delay the start of a resource assignment on a task.

- Adjust the project schedule using task constraints to eliminate resource assignment conflicts.

- Split tasks by interrupting the work on a task to make resources available for other assignments.

- Adjust dependencies and add *Lag* time.

- Add resources to an *Effort Driven* task to shorten the duration of the task.

- Look for potential overlapping work opportunities, such as Finish to Start dependencies that do not have a true "finish to start" relationship.

- Negotiate with your project sponsor or customer to delay the finish date of the project.

- Negotiate with your project sponsor or customer to reduce the feature set (scope) of the project.

- Use the built-in leveling tool in Microsoft Project 2010.

Notice that using the built-in leveling tool in Microsoft Project 2010 appears last on the preceding list! Each of the preceding leveling methods is powerful and useful for leveling overallocated resources; however, most users assume the only way to level is to use the built-in leveling tool found in Microsoft Project 2010. Given the complexity of using the software's leveling capabilities, the average user of Microsoft Project 2010 is far better off using any of the other manual leveling methods. The key to using any method for resource leveling is to remember that you must take **complete control** of all leveling decisions.

Using a Leveling Methodology

Many Microsoft Project 2010 users attempt to level all of their overallocated resources simultaneously in the *Gantt Chart* view using the built-in leveling tool. Although this approach can work in some situations, most often it leads to frustration. This approach does not give you insight into how the software leveled the overallocations, and can lead to failure because you did not take control over the leveling process. A much better approach is to level overallocated resources using the following methodology:

1. Level each overallocated resource individually in the *Resource Usage* view.

2. Study the results of the leveling process in the *Leveling Gantt* view.

3. Clear unacceptable leveling results and then level the overallocated resource using any other method.

4. Repeat steps #1-3 for each overallocated resource.

Setting Leveling Options

Before you begin the process of leveling overallocated resources in the *Resource Usage* view, you should specify your leveling options by clicking the *Leveling Options* button in the *Level* section of the *Resource* ribbon. The system displays the *Resource Leveling* dialog shown in Figure 6 - 45.

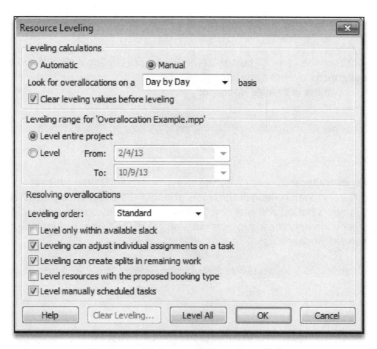

Figure 6 - 45: Resource Leveling dialog

In the *Resource Leveling* dialog, there are several options in the *Resource overallocations* section of the dialog that you may want to change from their default setting. These options include:

- Set the *Leveling order* option to the *Priority, Standard* value. By selecting this option, you force the software to consider first the *Priority* number of each task in the software's algorithm of five leveling factors. The other factors include predecessor task relationships, the start date of each task, the *Total Slack* value for each task, and whether the task has an inflexible constraint.

- Select the *Level only within available slack* option to guarantee that the leveling operation does not change the finish date of your project. With this option selected, Microsoft Project 2010 levels overallocations until it reaches the point where it must delay the finish date of your project. At this point, the system discontinues the leveling process and displays a warning dialog. From this point forward, you must select an alternate method for leveling remaining overallocations.

- If your project contains *Manually Scheduled* tasks with overallocated resources, and you want to manually reschedule the tasks to resolve these overallocations, then you should **deselect** the *Level manually scheduled tasks* option. If you leave this option selected, Microsoft Project 2010 delays or splits any *Manually Scheduled* tasks with overallocated resources assigned to them.

Warning: MSProjectExperts recommends that you never select the *Automatic* option in the *Leveling Calculations* section of the *Resource Leveling* dialog. When applied, the *Automatic* leveling option causes Microsoft Project 2010 to level all overallocated resources automatically in all open projects without asking your permission!

After you select your leveling options in the *Resource Leveling* dialog, click the *OK* button. Microsoft Project 2010 saves your option selections in this dialog so that you do not need to reselect them every time you want to level resource overallocations.

Warning: Do not click the *Level All* button in the *Resource Leveling* dialog. If you click the *Level All* button, you lose control over the leveling process because the software levels **all** of the overallocated resources in your project in a single operation.

Prior to leveling overallocated resources, MSProjectExperts recommends that you exit Project Professional 2010 and then re-launch the application. In the *Login* dialog, **deselect** the *Load Summary Resource Assignments* option and click the *OK* button. With this option deselected, the system focuses the leveling process on only those projects currently open and does not include assignments from other projects not currently open.

Warning: If you want to level an overallocated resource across multiple projects in the Project Server database, you must open each of these enterprise projects before you begin the leveling process.

Leveling an Overallocated Resource

To start the process of leveling overallocated resources, select the most critical resource in the project. Your most critical resource is the one whose skills and availability are the most limited in your organization. After selecting this resource, click the *Level Resource* button in the *Level* section of the *Resource* ribbon. Microsoft Project 2010 displays the *Level Resources* dialog shown in Figure 6 - 46.

**Figure 6 - 46: Level
Resources dialog**

The *Level Resources* dialog selects the same resource you selected in the *Resource Usage* view. Click the *Level Now* button in the dialog to level the overallocations for the first selected resource using the leveling options you set in the *Resource Leveling* dialog. When you use the built-in leveling tool to level an overallocated resource, Microsoft Project 2010 resolves the overallocation using one or both of the following methods:

- The software delays tasks or assignments.
- The software splits tasks or assignments.

To see the results of leveling the first overallocated resource, you must apply the *Leveling Gantt* view.

Viewing Leveling Results

The best way to apply the *Leveling Gantt* view is to open a new window containing this view by completing the following steps:

1. Click the *View* tab to display the *View* ribbon.

2. Click the *New Window* button in the *Window* section of the *View* ribbon. Microsoft Project 2010 displays the *New Window* dialog shown in Figure 6 - 47.

Figure 6 - 47: New Window dialog

3. Click the *View* pick list button and select the *Leveling Gantt* item on the list.

4. Click the *OK* button. The software displays the *Leveling Gantt* view shown in Figure 6 - 48.

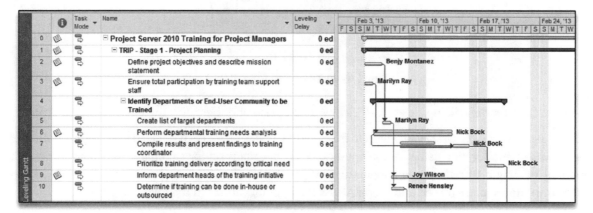

Figure 6 - 48: Leveling Gantt view

The *Leveling Gantt* view includes the *Delay* table on the left and the *Leveling Gantt* chart on the right. The symbols used in the *Leveling Gantt* view are as follows:

- The **tan Gantt bars** represent the pre-leveled schedule for each task you assigned to the overallocated resource. Figure 6 - 48 shows that I created the resource overallocation for Nick Bock accidentally by assigning him to work full-time on three parallel tasks (task ID numbers #6, 7, and 8).

- The **light blue Gantt bars** represent the schedule of the tasks after the software levels the resource overallocation. Figure 6 - 48 shows that Microsoft Project 2010 delayed task ID #7 (which then delayed task ID #8 due to a Finish-to-Start dependency relationship with task ID #7), which resolved Nick Bock's resource overallocation.

- The **brown underscore** to the left of any Gantt bar represents the amount of delay applied to the task schedule to level the resource overallocation. Figure 6 - 48 shows the delay symbol to the left of the Gantt bar for task ID #7.

- The **teal underscore** to the right of any Gantt bar represents the amount of time you can delay the task without delaying the finish date of the entire project.

The *Delay* table contains the *Leveling Delay* column to the right of the *Task Name* column. This column shows the amount of delay the software applies to a task to level a resource overallocation. By default, Microsoft Project 2010 measures the amount of *Leveling Delay* in **elapsed days** (displayed as **edays** or **ed**). Each elapsed day is a 24-hour calendar day that ignores nonworking time, such as weekends and holidays. In Figure 6 - 48, notice that the software delayed task ID #7 six elapsed days (6 ed).

Clearing Leveling Results

As you study the results of leveling an overallocated resource, you may find that Microsoft Project 2010 did not level the overallocation as you wished. In these situations, you must clear the unacceptable leveling and then level using another method. To clear an unacceptable overallocation, complete the following steps:

1. Click the *Resource* tab to display the *Resource* ribbon.
2. Select any tasks leveled in an unacceptable manner.
3. Click the *Clear Leveling* button in the *Level* section of the *Resource* ribbon. Microsoft Project 2010 displays the *Clear Leveling* dialog shown in Figure 6 - 49.

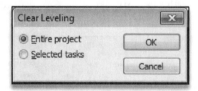

Figure 6 - 49: Clear Leveling dialog

4. In the *Clear Leveling* dialog, select the *Selected tasks* option and then click the *OK* button.

The software sets the *Leveling Delay* value back to the default value to *0d* for each selected task. At this point, you must level the resource overallocation using another method. You have many options available to you, including using one of the manual leveling methods I previously discussed. Another option is to set a *Priority* number on tasks showing the relative importance of each task, and then re-level the overallocations in the *Resource Usage* view.

Setting Task Priority Numbers

When you set a task *Priority* number, Microsoft Project 2010 levels the resource overallocation based on the task *Priority* numbers you assign. The software delays tasks with lower *Priority* numbers while maintaining the original schedule of the task with the highest *Priority* number. To set a *Priority* number on tasks with overallocated resources, complete the following steps:

1. Double-click a task assigned to an overallocated resource. Microsoft Project 2010 displays the *Task Information* dialog shown in Figure 6 - 50.

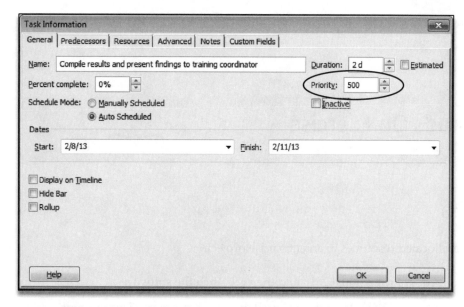

Figure 6 - 50: Task Information dialog – Set a Priority number

2. Click the *General* tab, if necessary.

3. Set a value between 0 and 1000 in the *Priority* field.

Remember that 0 signifies the lowest priority and 1000 signifies the highest priority for any task.

4. Click the *OK* button.

5. Repeat steps #1-4 for each task to which you assigned the overallocated resource.

When setting *Priority* numbers on multiple tasks, be sure to specify a **different** priority number on each task.

An alternate method for setting *Priority* numbers to tasks is to insert the *Priority* field temporarily in the *Leveling Gantt* view by completing the following steps:

1. Right-click on the *Leveling Delay* column header.

2. Select the *Insert Column* item on the shortcut menu.

3. In the pick list of available fields, select the *Priority* field.

4. Enter values in the *Priority* column for each task with an overallocated resource assigned.

After setting task *Priority* numbers, return to the *Resource Usage* window and then level the overallocated resource again.

Not only can you set a *Priority* number at the task level, Project Professional 2010 also allows you to set a *Priority* number at the project level. To level across multiple projects, open each project, display the *Project Information* dialog, and specify a value in the *Priority* field for the project.

Hands On Exercise

Exercise 6-13

Locate overallocated resources in an enterprise project.

1. Exit Project Professional 2010 and then relaunch the software.

2. In the *Login* dialog, **deselect** the *Load Summary Resource Assignments* option and then click the *OK* button.

Note: The preceding step is **vital** to the leveling process to force Project Professional 2010 to level overallocations only in any projects you open. I documented this step in a Best Practice note immediately prior to the *Leveling an Overallocated Resource* section of this module.

3. Click the *Open* button on the Quick Access Toolbar and re-open the Deploy Training Advisor Software project.

4. Click the *Resource* tab to display the *Resource* ribbon, if necessary.

5. Click the *Team Planner* pick list button and select the *Resource Usage* view.

Notice how Project Professional 2010 formats the names of two resources, *George Stewart* and *Myrta Hansen*, using the red font color. This indicates that the system believes both of them are overallocated resources.

6. Select *George Stewart* and then click the *Scroll to Task* button on the Quick Access Toolbar to scroll the timephased grid to the beginning of the project.

7. Click the *Next Overallocation* button in the *Level* section of the *Resource* ribbon.

Notice how the system highlights the overallocated time period for *George Stewart*.

8. Click the *Next Overallocation* button in the *Level* section of the *Resource* ribbon.

Notice how the system highlights the overallocated time period for *Myrta Hansen*.

9. Click the *Next Overallocation* button in the *Level* section of the *Resource* ribbon until you see the dialog indicating that there are no more overallocated resources in your enterprise project.

10. Click the *OK* button to close the informational dialog.

11. Click the *Save* button on the Quick Access Toolbar to save the latest changes to your enterprise project.

Exercise 6-14

Set resource leveling options and then level an overallocated resource in an enterprise project.

1. Return to your Deploy Training Advisor Software project, if necessary.

2. Click the *Leveling Options* button in the *Level* section of the *Resource* ribbon.

3. In the *Resource Leveling* dialog, set the following options:

   - Click the *Leveling Order* pick list and select the *Priority, Standard* item on the list, if not already selected.

   - Select the *Level only within available slack* option.

   - Leave all other options as they already appear.

4. Click the *OK* dialog to close the *Resource Leveling* dialog.

5. Select *George Stewart* and then click the *Scroll to Task* button on the Quick Access Toolbar to bring the resource's work into view in the timephased grid.

6. Click the *Level Resource* button in the *Level* section of the *Resource* ribbon.

7. Click the *Level Now* button in the *Level Resources* dialog.

Notice that Project Professional 2010 no longer formats *George Stewart's* name using the red font color, indicating that the system leveled the resource overallocation successfully.

8. Click the *View* tab to display the *View* ribbon.

9. Click the *New Window* button in the *Window* section of the *View* ribbon.

10. In the *New Window* dialog, click the *View* pick list and select the *Leveling Gantt* view, and then click the *OK* button.

11. In the *Leveling Gantt* view, widen the task name column and then drag the split bar to the right edge of the *Leveling Delay* column.

12. Select the Project Summary Task (task 0) and then click the *Scroll to Task* button on the Quick Access Toolbar.

Notice that Project Professional 2010 leveled the overallocation for *George Stewart* by delaying task ID #15, the *Build P3* task. Notice that the system delayed this task 4 elapsed days (4 ed), as shown in the *Leveling Delay* column for the task.

13. Double-click task ID #15, the *Build P3* task, and then click the *General* tab in the *Task Information* dialog.

14. Enter a value of *600* in the *Priority* field and then click the *OK* button.

15. Click the *Save* button on the Quick Access Toolbar to save the changes to your enterprise project.

16. Click the *Close* button on the Quick Access Toolbar and check in your enterprise project when prompted.

Leveling an Overallocated Resource in the Team Planner View

Project Professional 2010 allows you to use the *Team Planner* view to resolve resource overallocations several different ways, including the following:

- Level the resource overallocation using the built-in leveling tool in the software.

- Reschedule a task that is causing an overallocation by dragging it to a different time period.

- Reassign a task that is causing an overallocation by dragging the task to a different resource.

To level a resource overallocation using the built-in leveling tool in Project Professional 2010, complete the following steps:

1. Select the name of an overallocated resource in the *Resource* pane.

2. In the *Level* section of the *Resource* ribbon, click the *Leveling Options* button. The system displays the *Resource Leveling* dialog shown previously in Figure 6 - 45.

3. In the *Resource Leveling* dialog, select the options you want to use for leveling the selected resource and then click the *OK* button.

The *Resource Leveling* dialog in Microsoft Project 2010 contains all of the leveling options available in the 2007 version of the software, plus one new option: the *Level Manually Scheduled Tasks* option. The system selects this option by default, and you must deselect it if you do not want the leveling operation to level *Manually Scheduled* tasks.

Warning: Do not click the *Level All* button in the *Resource Leveling* dialog. If you click the *Level All* button, you lose control over the leveling process because the software levels **all** of the overallocated resources in your project in a single operation.

4. Click the *Level Resource* button in the *Level* section of the *Resource* ribbon.

Remember that when you use the built-in leveling tool to level an overallocated resource, Project Professional 2010 resolves the overallocation using one or both of the following methods:

*   The software delays tasks or assignments.

*   The software splits tasks or assignments.

You can prevent resource overallocations in your project by clicking the *Format* tab and then clicking the *Prevent Over-allocations* button in the *Format* ribbon. With this option selected, the software levels all existing overallocations in the project immediately, and levels any future resource overallocation when it occurs, such as when you drag a task or assign a task that causes a resource overallocation. In the *Team Planner* view, Project Professional 2010 indicates that you selected this option by highlighting the *Prevent Overallocations* button and by displaying a *Prevent Overallocations: On* indicator at the left end of the Status bar at the bottom of the application window, as shown in Figure 6 - 51.

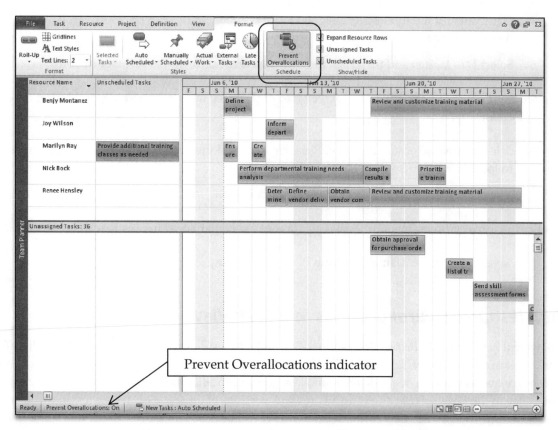

Figure 6 - 51: Prevent Overallocations option selected

Remember that if you prefer to use a manual approach to level a resource overallocation, Project Professional 2010 allows you to reschedule a task by dragging it to a different time period, or dragging a task to a different resource.

Hands On Exercise

Exercise 6-15

Use the *Team Planner* view to level resource overallocations.

1. Click the *Open* button on the Quick Access Toolbar.

2. Navigate to your *C:* drive and then to the folder containing the sample files for this class, and then re-open the **Using the Team Planner View.mpp** sample file.

3. Click the *Resource* tab and then click the *Team Planner* button in the *View* section of the *Resource* ribbon, if necessary.

4. In the *Resource* pane, scroll to the week of September 8, 2013 and notice the red borders on the Gantt bars for the three tasks assigned to *Dan Morton*, indicating he is an overallocated resource on these three tasks.

5. Select *Dan Morton* and then click the *Level Resource* button in the *Resource* ribbon

Notice that Project Professional 2010 delayed two of the three tasks assigned to Dan Morton to resolve the overallocation.

6. Select the overallocated resource, *Renee Hensley*, and then scroll to the week of September 15, 2013 to locate her resource overallocation.

7. Click the *Level Resource* button in the *Resource* ribbon.

Notice that Project Professional 2010 delayed a task assigned to Renee Hensley to resolve the overallocation.

8. Save and close the **Using the Team Planner View.mpp** sample file.

Leveling Resource Overallocations in a Task View

Another powerful new feature in Project Professional 2010 helps you to detect and level resource overallocations on a task-by-task basis in any task view, such as the *Gantt Chart* view. Previous versions of the software did not allow you to detect resource overallocations in a task view, displaying overallocation information and indicators only in a resource view, such as the *Resource Usage* view. In all previous versions of the software, the system allowed you to level resource overallocations in a task view, but it leveled the overallocations for all resources simultaneously, which meant you lost control over the leveling process.

To detect a resource overallocation in a task view using Project Professional 2010, apply any task view, such as the *Gantt Chart* view. Look in the *Indicators* column for any task with a "burning man" indicator, as this indicator identifies the task as assigned to an overallocated resource. For example, Figure 6 - 52 shows the *Gantt Chart* view of my project. Notice the special indicator in the *Indicators* column for task IDs #6, #7, and #8, indicating that I have an overallocated resource assigned to these three tasks. In this situation, the overallocated resource is Nick Bock. The overallocation is a consequence of assigning Nick Bock at *100% Units* on three tasks that run in parallel. Because he cannot work full-time on three tasks simultaneously, the system shows that Nick Bock is an overallocated resource on these three tasks.

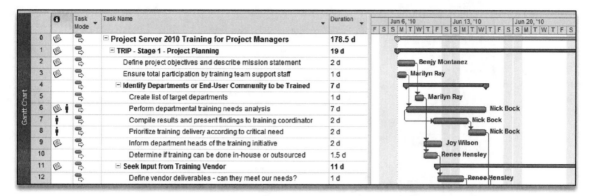

Figure 6 - 52: Three tasks with an overallocated resource assigned

As you already know, Project Professional 2010 allows you to level resource overallocations in the *Resource Usage* view for each resource individually. This method continues to offer you the most control over the leveling process. However, the 2010 version of the software does allow you to effectively level on a task-by-task basis in the *Gantt Chart* view, providing you with more control over the leveling process than in any other version. To level on a task-by-task basis, right-click in the *Indicators* column on any cell containing a "burning man" indicator. The system displays the shortcut menu shown in Figure 6 - 53, and offers three methods for dealing with the overallocation.

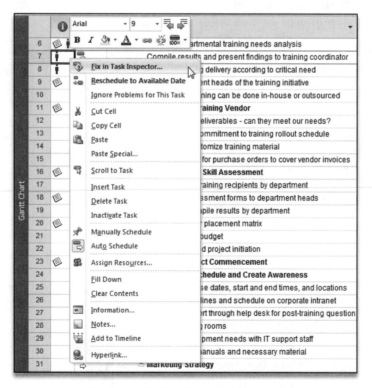

Figure 6 - 53: Shortcut menu for a task
assigned to an overallocated resource

The first item in the shortcut menu is the *Fix in Task Inspector* option. If you select this option, the system opens the *Task Inspector* sidepane on the left side of the *Gantt Chart* view, as shown in Figure 6 - 54.

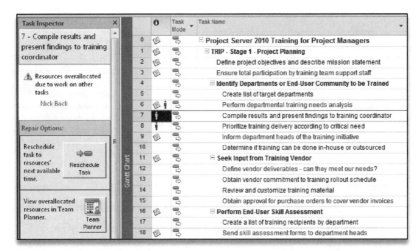

Figure 6 - 54: Task Inspector for a task assigned to an overallocated resource

The *Task Inspector* sidepane offers two options in the *Repair Options* section for resolving the resource overallocation. Click the *Reschedule Task* button to delay the task to the first available time period that resolves the overallocation. Click the *Team Planner* button to apply the *Team Planner* view, in which you can level the resource using any of the methods I discussed in the previous section of this module.

The second item in the shortcut menu is the *Reschedule to Available Date* option. If you select this option, Project Professional 2010 delays the task to the first available time period that resolves the overallocation. Selecting this option is the same as clicking the *Reschedule* button in the *Task Inspector* sidepane.

Lastly, you can use the third item on the shortcut menu, *Ignore Problems for This Task*. If you select this option, the system hides the "burning man" indicator for that task in the *Indicators* column, but does nothing to resolve the resource overallocation.

Hands On Exercise

Exercise 6-16

Locate and resolve resource overallocations in the *Gantt Chart* view.

1. Click the *Open* button on the Quick Access Toolbar.

2. Navigate to your *C:* drive and then to the folder containing the sample files for this class, and then open the **Level Overallocations in a Task View.mpp** sample file.

3. Scroll down through the list of tasks and look for any task that shows the "burning man" indicator in the *Indicators* column, indicating the task has an overallocated resource assigned to it.

Note: You should see that task IDs #6, 7, 8, 13, 14, 15, 19, and 20 have an overallocated resource assigned to them.

4. Float your mouse pointer over the overallocation indicator for task ID #7, the *Compile Results and Present Findings to Training Coordinator* task, and read the text in the ScreenTip.

5. Right-click in the *Indicators* cell for task ID #7, and then select the *Fix in Task Inspector* item on the shortcut menu.

6. In the *Task Inspector* sidepane, read the available information about the resource overallocation on this task.

7. Click the *Reschedule Task* button in the *Task Inspector* sidepane to resolve the resource overallocation on this task.

Notice that this action resolved the resource overallocation on task IDs #6 and #8 as well.

8. Select task ID #14, the *Review and Customize Training Material* task, and then click the *Reschedule Task* button in the *Task Inspector* sidepane.

Notice that this action resolved the resource overallocation on task IDs #13 and #15 as well.

9. Close the *Task Inspector* sidepane.

10. Right-click in the *Indicators* column for task ID #20, the *Initiate End-User Placement Matrix* task, and then select the *Reschedule To Available Date* item on the shortcut menu.

Without using the *Task Inspector* sidepane, notice that you resolved the resource overallocation on task IDs #19 and #20.

11. Save and close the **Level Overallocations in a Task View.mpp** sample file.

Exercise 6-17

Disable warning messages for a task assigned to an overallocated resource in an enterprise project.

1. Click the *Open* button on the Quick Access Toolbar and reopen your Deploy Training Advisor Software project.

2. Click the *Task* tab to display the *Task* ribbon.

3. Click the *Gantt Chart* pick list button and select the *Gantt Chart* view.

Notice the "burning man" indicator in the *Indicators* column for task ID #4, the Test P1 task. This indicates that Project Professional 2010 considers the assigned resource, Myrta Hansen, overallocated on this task because you assigned her to a task occurring on a weekend. In reality, she is not overallocated, so you must disable warning messages about resource overallocations on this task.

4. Right-click in the *Indicators* cell for task ID #4, the *Test P1* task, and then select the *Fix in Task Inspector* item on the shortcut menu.

5.   Scroll to the bottom of the *Task Inspector* sidepane and then **deselect** the *Show warnings and suggestion indicators for this task* option.

6.   Close the *Task Inspector* sidepane.

7.   Click the *Save* button on the Quick Access Toolbar to save the changes to your enterprise project.

8.   Click the *Close* button on the Quick Access Toolbar, and check in your Deploy Training Advisor Software project when prompted.

Using the Resource Substitution Wizard

The *Resource Substitution Wizard* is an automation tool that can substitute resources in one project plan or across many project plans. You can use this wizard to substitute *Human* resources for assigned *Generic* resources, or even to substitute other *Human* resources for assigned *Human* resources.

The *Resource Substitution Wizard* bases resource substitutions on skill code, availability, and other criteria defined for the resources in the Enterprise Resource Pool by your Project Server administrator. The *Resource Substitution Wizard* algorithm uses the following criteria:

*   **Skill Set** – The wizard's primary purpose is to substitute *Human* resources for *Generic* resources based on a skill set. In order to work correctly, there must be at least one enterprise custom field with a Lookup Table defined with the *Use this code for matching generic resources* option selected. In addition, every resource must have a value specified for this field.

*   **Availability** – The wizard substitutes resources based on availability. To get the best results from the wizard, you may want to try leveling the plan first before running the wizard.

*   **Request/Demand** – The wizard substitutes resources based on the *R/D* value specified for each resource assignment in the project. The wizard substitutes resources on assignments that you mark as *Request*, based on the most available matching resource. The wizard respects all resource assignments you mark as *Demand* and **does not** substitute resources on these assignments.

*   **Priority** – The wizard weights assignments by the *Priority* number of each project identified by you at run time. The wizard gives projects with a higher *Priority* number first consideration when matching resources.

*   **Pool Selection** – The wizard confines its resource selection to the restriction you set at run time. You may select specific resources or only resources defined in the selected projects.

*   **Resource Freeze Horizon** – The wizard does not make resource substitutions on assignments that occur before the Resource Freeze Horizon date.

Preparing a Project for the Resource Substitution Wizard

Before you attempt to use the *Resource Substitution Wizard*, you should carefully prepare your project. This means that you should assign *Generic* and/or *Human* resources to each task in the project. If you assign *Human* resources to any tasks, make sure you use the *Assign Resources* dialog to set the *R/D* field value for each *Human* resource's task assignments to either *Request* or *Demand*. For example, notice in Figure 6 - 55 that I specified the *Demand* value in the *R/D* column for a resource named *Genea Mallow* who I assigned to the *Determine project scope* task.

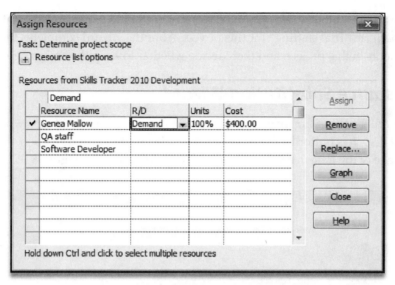

Figure 6 - 55: Human resource set to Demand in the Assign Resources dialog

If you specify the *Request* value in the *R/D* field for a resource's assignment on a task, the wizard **may** substitute another resource in place of the assigned resource. If you specify the *Demand* value in the *R/D* field, the wizard **does not** substitute another resource for the assigned resource. If you do not specify a value in the *R/D* field, the system assumes a *Request* value in the field and **may** substitute another resource in place of the assigned resource.

Figure 6 - 56 shows a project in which I intend to use the *Resource Substitution Wizard*. Because the start date of this project does not occur until February 2013, I assigned *Generic* resources to most of the tasks in the project. The exception is tasks assigned to the project manager, *Genea Mallow*. Notice in Figure 6 - 56 that I assigned two *Generic* resources to this project: *C Sharp Software Developer* and *QA staff*. By assigning these particular *Generic* resources, I indicate to the *Resource Substitution Wizard* what skills I require for the resources assigned to each task.

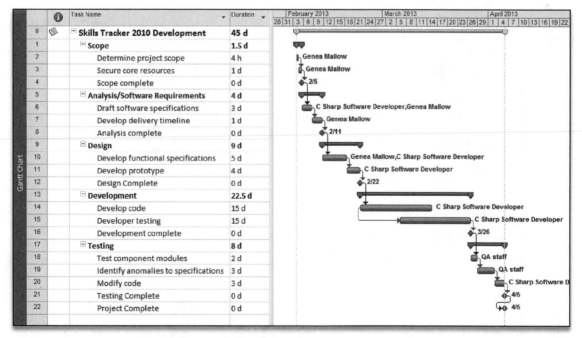

Figure 6 - 56: Project staff includes Generic and Human
resources; ready for the Resource Substitution Wizard

When today's date is less than a month away from the planned start date of the project, I intend to use the *Resource Substitution Wizard* to perform "trial staffing" for this project. After the wizard completes the substitution process, I can review the assignments in this project, and then decide whether to keep the assignments or revise them.

Running the Resource Substitution Wizard

To run the *Resource Substitution Wizard,* open one or more enterprise projects in which you want to run the wizard and then click the *Substitute Resources* button in the *Assignments* section of the *Resource* ribbon. Project Professional 2010 displays the *Welcome* page of the *Resource Substitution Wizard* dialog shown in Figure 6 - 57.

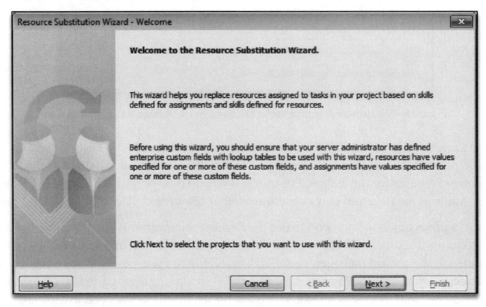

Figure 6 - 57: Resource Substitution Wizard dialog, Welcome page

Click the *Next* button to continue. The system displays step 1 of the wizard, the *Choose Projects* page, as shown in Figure 6 - 58.

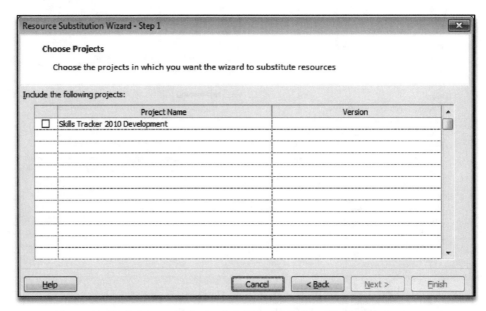

Figure 6 - 58: Resource Substitution Wizard dialog, Choose Projects page

When you run the *Resource Substitution Wizard,* the system assumes that you want to make resource substitutions on any projects you currently have open, even including a totally blank project. Select the check boxes for the projects in which you want the wizard to substitute resources and then click the *Next* button. The system displays step 2 of the wizard, the *Choose Resources* page shown in Figure 6 - 59.

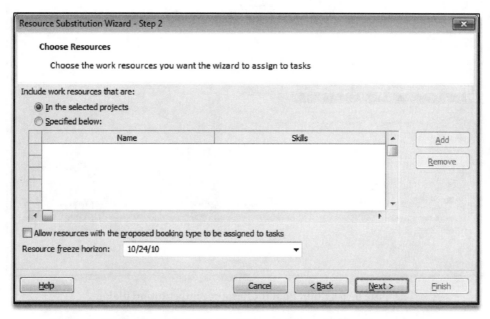

Figure 6 - 59: Resource Substitution Wizard dialog, Choose Resources page

On the *Choose Resources* page, you must select the resources for the wizard to consider during the substitution process. This page offers two resource substitution options:

- Select the *In the selected projects* option to indicate that you previously built a candidate project team of *Human* resources in each of the selected projects. When you choose this option, the system uses only resources specified in the selected projects.

- Select the *Specified below* option to select specific resources from the Enterprise Resource Pool.

If you select the *Specified below* option, then click the *Add* button. The system opens the *Build Pool for Resource Substitution* dialog shown in Figure 6 - 60.

The *Build Pool for Resource Substitution* dialog offers an ideal situation for using skill matching. Begin by adding the *Generic* resources assigned in the project to the substitution pool. Select the first *Generic* resource and click the *Match* button. From the list of matching resources, add the resources you want to the substitution pool, and then remove the first *Generic* resource. Repeat this process for every *Generic* resource you add to the substitution pool.

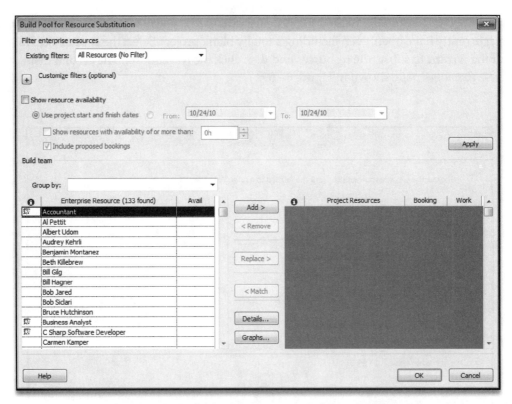

Figure 6 - 60: Build Pool for Resource Substitution dialog

In the *Build Pool for Resource Substitution* dialog, add *Human* resources to the substitution pool, and then click the *OK* button. The system displays the selected resources in the *Choose Resources* page of the *Resource Substitution Wizard* dialog, as shown in Figure 6 - 61. Notice the information shown in the *Skills* column for each resource. The system uses this information to match *Human* resources with *Generic* resources.

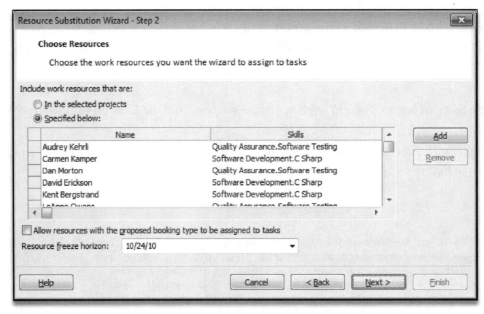

Figure 6 - 61: Resource Substitution Wizard dialog,
Choose Resources page with pool resources added

In addition to the two options available at the top of the page, the dialog offers two additional options at the bottom of the *Choose Resources* page. Select the *Allow resources with the proposed booking type to be assigned to tasks* option to force the wizard to consider resources with the *Proposed* booking type during the substitution process. Enter or select a date in the *Resource freeze horizon* field to specify a date **before** which the wizard cannot substitute resources. Using the date that you enter in the *Resource freeze horizon* field, the system performs resource substitution on task assignments occurring **after** that date, but not before that date.

The date in the *Resource Freeze Horizon* field defaults to the current date.

After you specify your options on the *Choose Resources* page, click the *Next* button to continue the substitution process. The system displays step 3 of the wizard, the *Choose Related Projects* page, shown in Figure 6 - 62.

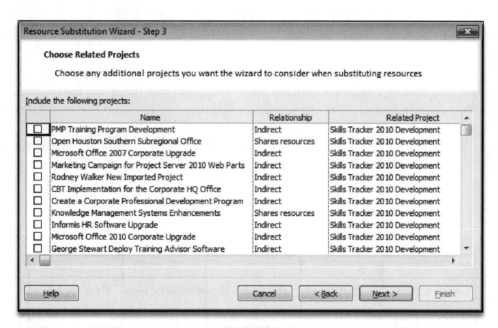

Figure 6 - 62: Resource Substitution Wizard dialog, Choose Related Projects page

The *Choose Related Projects* page displays a list of projects that have a relationship with one or more of your selected projects. The system determines related projects in two ways: either through cross-project dependencies between the projects, or through the sharing of common resources between the projects. The system displays the type of relationship between projects in the *Relationship* column.

When projects share common resources, the system describes the relationship as either a direct or an indirect relationship. A direct relationship exists between two or more projects when they share one or more of the same resources. The system denotes a direct relationship between projects by displaying *Shares resources* in the *Relationship* column. When projects have a direct relationship, resource substitutions made in one project can directly affect all other projects whose relationship is direct.

An indirect relationship exists between your selected projects and other projects when the other projects share one or more resources with a project that has a direct relationship with one of your selected projects. In other words, the relationship is "second cousin" in nature. The system denotes an indirect relationship between projects by displaying *In-*

direct in the *Relationship* column. To understand the indirect relationship between projects, consider the example shown in Table 6 - 2.

Project A	Project B	Project C
Jay Didriksen	Jay Didriksen	Jerry King
Sue Burnett	Sue Burnett	Marcia Bickel
Randy Parker	Linda Erickson	Linda Erickson
Jim Short	Terry Uland	Terry Uland

Table 6 - 2: Project C has an Indirect relationship to Project A

In Table 6 - 2, Project A has a direct (shares resources) relationship to Project B through the two common resources, Jay Didriksen and Sue Burnett. Project B has a direct (shares resources) relationship to Project C through two other shared resources, Linda Erickson and Terry Uland. Because Project A is directly related to Project B, and Project B is directly related to Project C, then Project C is indirectly related to Project A. You can visualize this relationship in Figure 6 - 63.

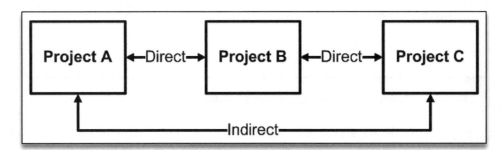

Figure 6 - 63: Project A has an indirect relationship with Project C

You may be wondering why it is necessary for the *Resource Substitution Wizard* to determine whether a project has any kind of relationship with your selected projects. Project Professional 2010 does this to alert you that your resource substitutions could have a "ripple effect" on the related projects. With this information in mind, select any related projects in which you want the wizard to perform resource substitutions and then click the *Next* button to continue. The system displays step 4 of the wizard, the *Choose Scheduling Options* page, as shown in Figure 6 - 64.

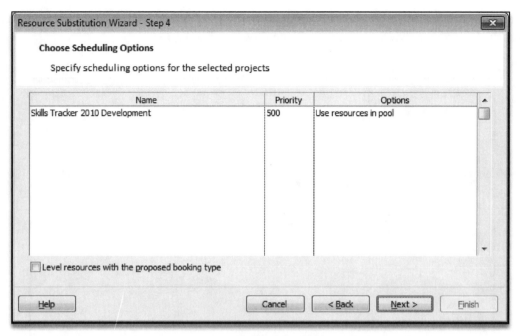

Figure 6 - 64: Resource Substitution Wizard dialog
Choose Scheduling Options page

Step 4 of the *Resource Substitution Wizard* dialog allows you to set the relative priority for each selected project by increasing or decreasing the *Priority* number of each project in relationship to the others. You can set the *Priority* number of each project from 0 (lowest priority) to 1000 (highest priority). The wizard uses the *Priority* value for each project to determine which project has first rights to an available resource, with the highest priority projects taking precedence.

You may specify a value in the *Options* column for each project to determine whether to substitute resources from the substitution pool you selected in the *Choose Resources* page or from the team in the selected project only. In addition, you may also select the *Level resources with the proposed booking type* option to level *Proposed* resources that may become overallocated during the substitution process.

In the *Options* column, select the *Use resources in project* option if you want to optimize the use of resources in your project team for one or more projects. Select the *Use resources in pool* option if you want to staff your project with the most available resources for one or more projects.

289

After you select your options on the *Choose Scheduling Options* page, click the *Next* button to continue. The system displays step 5 of the wizard, the *Substitute Resources* page shown in Figure 6 - 65.

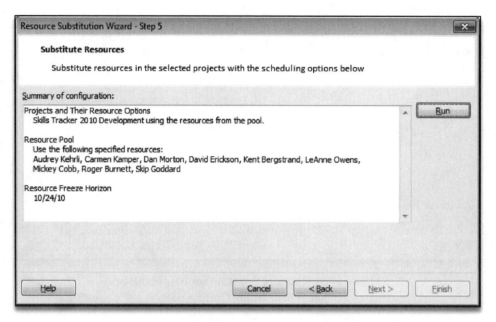

Figure 6 - 65: Resource Substitution Wizard, Substitute Resources page

The *Substitute Resources* page displays a summary of the substitution options you selected during the previous steps. If you notice a mistake here, you can either cancel the operation or step back through the pages to make changes. When you are satisfied with your selections, click the *Run* button to make the resource substitutions. After you click the *Run* button, click the *Next* button. The system displays step 6 of the wizard, the *Review Results* page shown in Figure 6 - 66.

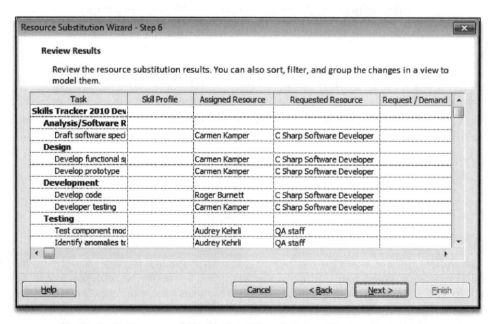

Figure 6 - 66: Resource Substitution Wizard dialog, Review Results page

The system displays the results of the resource substitution process for each task. The *Review Results* page contains the task name, the skill set used for the substitution, the name of the new resource assigned by the wizard, the name of the original resource, and the *Request/Demand* setting of the original assignment.

Notice in Figure 6 - 66 that the wizard substituted *Carmen Camper* for the *C Sharp Software Developer* generic resource on every task **except** for the *Develop code* task, in which the wizard substituted *Roger Burnett* instead. Why did the wizard substitute *Roger Burnett* instead of *Carmen Kamper* on this task only? In the project plan, the system schedules the *Develop code* task from February 22, 2013 to March 15, 2013. Examining the resource calendar for *Carmen Kamper*, the *Change Working Time* dialog shown in Figure 6 - 67 reveals that she has one week of planned vacation from February 25 to March 1, 2013. This means she is not available to work full-time on the *Develop code* task, so the *Resource Substitution Wizard* selects the first available resource with the right skills, *Roger Burnett*.

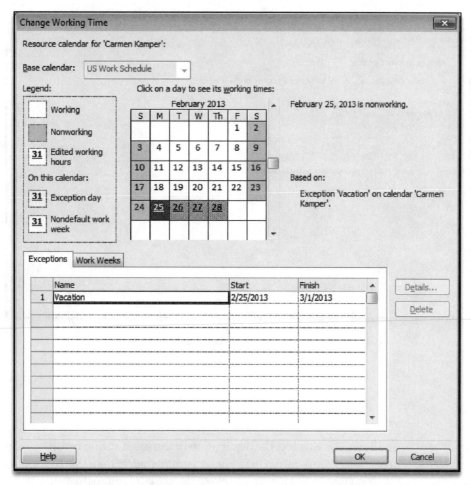

**Figure 6 - 67: Change Working Time dialog for Carmen Kamper
shows a week of planned vacation in February 2013**

MsProjectExperts recommends that you thoroughly review the results of the substitution process. Before moving on to the next page of the dialog, confirm that the resource substitutions are acceptable to your resource planning needs. If the results of the resource substitution process are not acceptable, click the *Cancel* button and then make modifications to your projects and/or to the resource assignments in the projects.

In the *Review Results* page, review the results of the resource substitution process and click the *Next* button when you are satisfied with the results. The system displays step 7 of the wizard, the *Choose Update Options* page, shown in Figure 6 - 68.

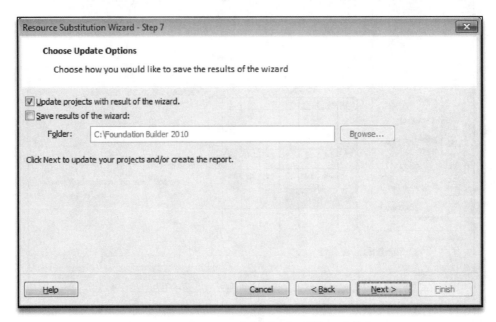

Figure 6 - 68: Resource Substitution Wizard dialog
Choose Update Options page

The *Choose Update Options* page allows you to select the destination of the substitution results. To update the selected projects with the chosen resources, select the default *Update projects with result of the wizard* option. To save the results of the substitution process for later review, select the *Save results of the wizard* option, then click the *Browse* button and select a location. The system saves the results in an HTML file in the location you designate. Click the *Next* button to continue. The system displays step 8 of the wizard, the *Finish* page, as shown in Figure 6 - 69.

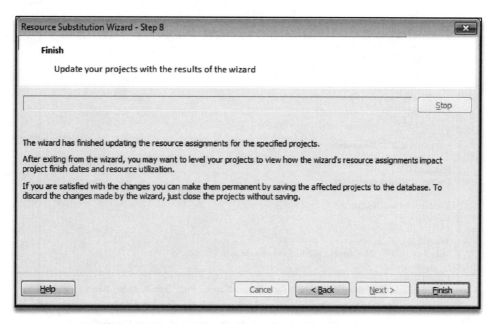

Figure 6 - 69: Resource Substitution Wizard, Finish page

The *Finish* page is the final step in the *Resource Substitution Wizard* process where the system makes several suggestions before you proceed. The wizard suggests leveling the plan to resolve any remaining resource overallocations. If you are satisfied with the changes, you can make them permanent by saving the affected projects to the database. The wizard also informs you that you can still abandon the resource substitution changes to any project simply by not saving the project plan to the database. Click the *Finish* button to complete the process.

If you elected to save the results of the substitution process as a file, navigate to the folder where you saved the file. The system saves the substitution information in an HTML file that you can open using the Internet Explorer software or any HTML-enabled software such as Microsoft Word. The system names the HTML file using the text *Resource Substitution Results on,* appended with the **date** (expressed as **yyyymmdd**) and **time** (expressed in military time) you performed the substitution. This means that if the *Resource Substitution Wizard* completed the substitution process on October 24, 2010 at 8:02 PM, the system appends *20101024 2002* to the file name. Figure 6 - 70 shows the text in the HTML file from the substitution process documented in this section of the module.

Resource Substitution Wizard Results Summary

Run Date:
10/24/10

Run Time:
8:02 PM

Projects:
Skills Tracker 2010 Development, Selected

Resources:
Use the specified resources.

Resource Freeze Horizon:
10/24/10

Scheduling Options:
Skills Tracker 2010 Development, 500, Use resources in pool.

Project Teams:
Skills Tracker 2010 Development, Genea Mallow, Carmen Kamper, Roger Burnett, Audrey Kehrli

Figure 6 - 70: HTML file saved by the Resource Substitution Wizard

Warning: Use extreme caution when using the *Resource Substitution Wizard*. This tool is not a "magic pill" that can solve all of your resource allocation issues, nor can it prevent resource overallocations from occurring in your projects.

MSProjectExperts recommends that you use the *Resource Substitution Wizard* as a means to do "trial resource loading" on a group of future planned projects for analysis of resource allocation issues. For the most part, you should use the two manual methods for making resource assignments to tasks, which are the *Task Entry* view and the *Assign Resources* dialog.

Hands On Exercise

Exercise 6-18

Prepare your enterprise project to use the *Resource Substitution Wizard*.

1. Click the *Open* button on the Quick Access Toolbar.

2. In the *Open* dialog, double-click the *Retrieve the list of all projects from Project Server* item at the top of the project list.

3. Select the **Resource Substitution Wizard Practice** project and click the *Open* button.

4. Click the *File* tab and then click the *Save As* item in the *Backstage* menu.

5. In the *Save to Project Server* dialog, enter the following new name for this project:

    Your First Name Your Last Name Resource Substitution Wizard Practice

6. Click the *Save* button to save this new enterprise project.

7. Click the *Assign Resources* button on the Quick Access Toolbar to open the *Assign Resources* dialog.

8. Select task ID #5, the *Perform Server Stress Test* task.

9. Click the *R/D* cell for *Myrta Hansen* and select the *Demand* item in the pick list.

10. Select task ID #9, the *Verify Connectivity* task.

11. Click the *R/D* cell for *Myrta Hansen* and select the *Request* item in the pick list.

12. Click the *Close* button in the *Assign Resources* dialog.

13. Click the *Save* button on the Quick Access Toolbar to save the changes to your enterprise project.

Exercise 6-19

Run the *Resource Substitution Wizard* and substitute *Human* resources for *Generic* resources.

1. Click the *Project Server* tab to display the *Project Server* ribbon, if necessary.

2. In the *Plan and Publish* section of the *Project Server* ribbon, click the *Substitute Resources* button.

3. On the *Welcome* page of the *Resource Substitution Wizard* dialog, click the *Next* button.

4. On the *Choose Projects* page of the wizard, select your Resource Substitution Wizard Practice project and then click the *Next* button.

5. On the *Choose Resources* page of the wizard, select the *Specified below* option and then click the *Add* button.

6. In the *Build Pool for Resource Substitution* dialog, click on the dropdown menu in the *Existing filters* field and select the *All Resources (No Filter)* item from the pick list.

7. Add the following resources to the pool team:
   - Cher Zall
   - Jeff Holly
   - Jim Short
   - Joy Wilson
   - Mary Kay Harry
   - Melena Keeth
   - Mike Andrews
   - Sarah Baker

8. Click the *OK* button to close the *Build Pool for Resource Substitution* dialog and then click the *Next* button on the *Choose Resources* page of the wizard.

9. On the *Choose Related Projects* page, click the *Next* button.

10. On the *Choose Scheduling Options* page, click the *Next* button.

11. On the *Substitute Resources* page, click the *Run* button and then click the *Next* button.

12. On the *Review Results* page, widen the *Task* column and scroll down to the *Create Training Materials* section of the task list.

Notice how the system substituted *Sarah Baker* for all of the tasks with the *Technical Training* skill profile, **except for** the *Create Training Module 02* and *Create Training Module 03* tasks. On these two tasks only, the *Resource Substitution Wizard* substituted *Joy Wilson* instead. This is because *Sarah Baker* has non-working time defined on her resource calendar during the time span of these two tasks.

13. On the *Review Results* page, click the *Next* button.

14. On the *Choose Update Options* page, click the *Next* button.

15. On the *Finish* page of the *Resource Substitution Wizard* dialog, click the *Finish* button.

16. Click the *View* tab to display the *View* ribbon.

17. In the *Resource Views* section of the *View* ribbon, click the *Resource Sheet* button.

18. Double-click the name *Sarah Baker* and then click the *Change Working Time* button in the *Resource Information* dialog.

19. If you see a warning dialog, click the *OK* button to close the warning dialog and then notice that *Sarah Baker* has two weeks of non-working time in July 2013.

20. Click the *OK* button to close the *Change Working Time* dialog and then click the *OK* button to close the *Resource Information* dialog.

21. Click the *Save* button on the Quick Access Toolbar to save the project.

22. Click the *Close* button on the Quick Access Toolbar and then check in the project when prompted.

Module 07

Project Execution

Learning Objectives

After completing this module, you will be able to:

- View the Critical Path
- Save and view a baseline for a project
- Understand the results of publishing a project
- Set publishing options for a project
- Publish a project
- Change the Status Manager for selected tasks in a published project
- Use the Delegate feature to allow another manager to take over your project
- Change permissions on a published project
- Manage project Deliverables

Inside Module 07

Analyzing the Critical Path

Project Professional 2010 defines the **Critical Path** as "The series of tasks that must be completed on schedule for a project to finish on schedule." Every task on the Critical Path is a **Critical task**. By default, all tasks on the Critical Path have a *Total Slack* value of 0 days, which means they cannot slip without delaying the project *Finish* date. If the *Finish* date of any Critical task slips by even 1 day, the project *Finish* date slips as well.

Project Professional 2010 defines a **non-Critical task** as any task that is 100% complete or any task with a *Total Slack* value greater than 0 days. A non-Critical task can slip by its amount of *Total Slack* before it impacts the *Finish* date of the project. For example, if a task has 5 days of *Total Slack*, the task can finish 5 days late before the resulting slippage would change the project *Finish* date. To manage your project well, you should be aware of the non-Critical tasks in your project, but you should focus your energy on managing the tasks on the Critical Path.

Project Professional 2010 automatically calculates the *Total Slack* field value for each task to determine the Critical Path of the project. To view the *Total Slack* for any task, apply the *View* ribbon, click the *Tables* button in the *Data* section of the *View* ribbon, and then select the *Schedule* table. The *Total Slack* column is the last column on the right side of the *Schedule* table.

In Project Professional 2010, the Critical Path may run from the *Start* date to the *Finish* date of the project, or it may begin anywhere in the project and run to the *Finish* date of the project. This behavior is a key difference from the traditional Critical Path Method (CPM) definition of the Critical Path.

If you make changes to your project, either by entering actual progress or by making plan revisions, keep in mind that the Critical Path may change in response.

Although there are a number of ways to determine the Critical Path in a project in Project Professional 2010, the simplest method is to format the *Gantt Chart* view to display red Gantt bars for Critical tasks. To format the *Gantt Chart* view to show the Critical Path, complete the following steps:

1. Click the *View* tab and then click the *Gantt Chart* button in the *Task Views* section of the *View* ribbon.

2. Click the *Format* tab to display the *Format* ribbon.

3. Select the *Critical Tasks* checkbox in the *Bar Styles* section of the *Format* ribbon.

4. Optionally select the *Slack* checkbox as well.

In the formatted *Gantt Chart* view shown in Figure 7 - 1, notice that Project Professional 2010 displays the following:

- **Red bars** represent Critical tasks on the Critical Path. These tasks have a Total Slack of 0 days.

- **Blue bars** represent non-Critical tasks. These tasks are completed tasks or have a Total Slack greater than 0 days.

- A **black stripe** to the right of any Gantt bar represents the amount of Total Slack for the task.

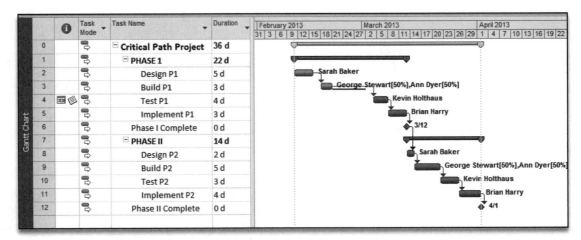

Figure 7 - 1: Gantt Chart formatted to show the Critical Path and Total Slack

Warning: Because of an unfixed bug in the release (RTM) version of Project Professional 2010, when you select the *Critical Tasks* checkbox on the *Format* ribbon, the system **removes** the names of assigned resources displayed to the right of Gantt bars for Critical tasks. To display the names of your assigned resources, double-click anywhere in the white part of the Gantt chart to display the *Bar Styles* dialog. Scroll to the bottom of the list, select the *Critical* item, and then select the *Text* tab. On the *Text* tab, click the *Right* pick list and select the *Resource Names* field. Click the *OK* button when finished.

You can also view the Critical Path in any project by applying the *Tracking Gantt* view. Be aware, however, that the *Tracking Gantt* view displays Gantt bars for both the Critical Path and for the baseline schedule of the project. Remember that red Gantt bars show Critical tasks, blue Gantt bars show non-Critical tasks, and gray Gantt bars show the original baseline schedule of each task.

Viewing the "Nearly Critical" Path

In Project Professional 2010, you can change the software's definition of a Critical task by clicking the *File* tab and then clicking the *Options* item in the *Backstage* menu. In the *Project Options* dialog, select the *Advanced* tab and then scroll down to the *Calculation options for this project* section of the dialog. To change the software's definition of a Critical task, change the *Tasks are critical if slack is less than or equal to* option to a value greater than *0 days*, and then click the *OK* button.

Using this technique is a helpful way to see the "nearly Critical tasks" that are not on the true Critical Path, but are close enough to impact the *Finish* date of the project if they slip by an amount greater than their *Total Slack* value. For example, I have a task with only 1 day of *Total Slack*, so this task is not a true Critical task since it has a *Total Slack* value greater than 0 days. However, if this task slips only 2 days, the *Finish* date of the project slips as well. Therefore, it is not a bad idea to identify the "nearly Critical tasks" in any enterprise project.

Hands On Exercise

Exercise 7-1

Display the Critical Path in your enterprise project and then display "nearly Critical tasks" as well.

1. Click the *Open* button on the Quick Access Toolbar and reopen your Deploy Training Advisor Software project.

2. Click the *Format* tab and then select the *Critical Tasks* checkbox in the *Bar Styles* section of the *Format* ribbon.

Notice that Project Professional 2010 displays Critical tasks with red Gantt bars and non-Critical tasks with blue Gantt bars. Because of a bug in the release (RTM) version of the software, notice also that the resource names no longer appear to the right of the red Gantt bars.

3. In the *Bar Styles* section of the *Format* ribbon, click the *Format* pick list button and select the *Bar Styles* item on the list.

4. In the *Bar Styles* dialog, scroll down to the bottom of the list and select the *Critical* item.

5. In the lower left corner of the *Bar Styles* dialog, click the *Text* tab.

6. Click the *Right* pick list and select the *Resource Names* field.

7. Click the *OK* button.

8. Right-click on the *Select All* button (above the ID number for the Project Summary Task) and then select the *Schedule* table.

9. Pull the split bar to the right so that you can view the *Total Slack* column on the far right side of the *Schedule* table.

Notice that the *Total Slack* value for every Critical task is *0 days*, indicating that these tasks cannot slip without delaying the project *Finish* date. Notice also that several other tasks have a *Total Slack* value greater than *0 days*, indicating that they are non-Critical tasks.

10. Right-click on the *Select All* button and select the *Entry* table again.

11. Dock the split bar on the right edge of the *Duration* column.

12. Click the *File* tab and then click the *Options* item in the *Backstage* menu.

13. In the *Project Options* dialog, select the *Advanced* tab and then scroll down to the *Calculation options for this project* section of the dialog.

14. Change the *Tasks are critical if slack is less than or equal to* option value to *2 days*, and then click the *OK* button.

Notice that Project Professional 2010 now displays a red Gantt bar for the *Design P1* task in the Phase I section of the project, indicating that this task is a "nearly Critical task" as well. You can use this technique at any time to see "nearly Critical tasks" in any project.

15. Click the *Undo* button in your Quick Access Toolbar to redisplay only the true Critical Path in the project.

16. Click the *Save* button on the Quick Access Toolbar to save your enterprise project.

Working with Project Baselines

Prior to executing a project, you should save a baseline for your project. All of the variance measurements that Project Professional 2010 calculates for you are dependent on the existence of a baseline. A baseline represents a snapshot of the work, cost, and schedule estimates as represented in your initial project plan. Your baseline should represent the schedule your stakeholders approved before you begin tracking progress. Saving a project baseline provides you with a way to analyze project variance by comparing the current state of the project against the original planned state of the project (the baseline).

When you save a baseline in Project Professional 2010, the software captures the current values for five important task fields and two important resource fields, and then saves these values in a corresponding set of Baseline fields. Table 7 - 1 shows the original fields and their corresponding Baseline fields.

Data Type	Field	Baseline Field
Task	Duration	Baseline Duration
Task	Start	Baseline Start
Task	Finish	Baseline Finish
Task	Work	Baseline Work
Task	Cost	Baseline Cost
Resource	Work	Baseline Work
Resource	Cost	Baseline Cost

Table 7 - 1: Baseline information

In addition to the five important task fields captured in the baseline, Project Professional 2010 also captures some additional task information as well. This information includes:

- Extra task cost information in the *Fixed Cost* and *Fixed Cost Accrual* fields, saving this information in the *Baseline Fixed Cost* and *Baseline Fixed Cost Accrual* fields, respectively.

- Estimated task schedule information in the *Scheduled Duration*, *Scheduled Start*, and *Scheduled Finish* fields, saving this information in the *Baseline Estimated Duration*, *Baseline Estimated Start*, and *Baseline Estimated Finish* fields, respectively. Remember that Project Professional 2010 uses these estimated schedule fields primarily with the new *Manually Scheduled* tasks feature.

- Task and resource budget information in the *Budget Cost* and *Budget Work* fields, saving this information in the *Baseline Budget Cost* and *Baseline Budget Work* fields, respectively.

- Baseline information for the start and finish dates associated with deliverables in the *Baseline Deliverable Start* and *Baseline Deliverable Finish* fields.

Project Professional 2010 also saves the timephased values for both tasks and resources in the timephased *Baseline Work* and *Baseline Cost* fields as well. You can view these timephased values in the timephased grid portion of either the *Task Usage* or *Resource Usage* views.

Saving a Project Baseline

To save a baseline for the entire project in Project Professional 2010, complete the following steps:

1. Click the *Project* tab to display the *Project* ribbon.

2. In the *Schedule* section of the *Project* ribbon, click the *Set Baseline* pick list button and select the *Set Baseline* item on the list. The system displays the *Set Baseline* dialog shown in Figure 7 - 2.

Figure 7 - 2: Set Baseline dialog

3. Select the *Set Baseline* option.

4. Leave the *Baseline* item selected in the *Set Baseline* pick list.

5. In the *For:* section, leave the *Entire project* option selected.

6. Click the *OK* button.

To view the task baseline information in any project, right-click on the *Select All* button and select the *More Tables* item on the shortcut menu. In the *More Tables* dialog, select the *Baseline* table and then click the *Apply* button.

MSProjectExperts recommends that you save an original baseline for the entire project only once during the life of the project. After a change control procedure that adds new tasks to your project, you may save a baseline for only the new tasks. This maintains the integrity of your original project baseline.

Saving Over a Previous Baseline

To determine whether you previously saved an original baseline in a project, click the *Set Baseline* pick list button in the *Schedule* section of the *Project* ribbon and select the *Set Baseline* item on the list. Project Professional 2010 indicates whether you previously saved a baseline displaying the date on which you saved it, as displayed in Figure 7 - 3.

**Figure 7 - 3: Last saved on date
in the Set Baseline dialog**

If you attempt to save baseline information over your original baseline, Project Professional 2010 warns you with the message in the dialog shown in Figure 7 - 4.

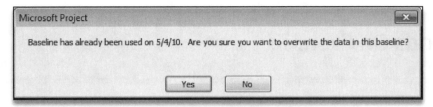

Figure 7 - 4: Warning dialog
Overwrite original baseline

Clearing the Project Baseline

You may need to clear the baseline information for a project, such as when management decides to delay the start of your project indefinitely. In a situation like this, your baseline information is invalid when your executives finally determine a new project start date. To clear the baseline values for your project complete the following steps:

1. In the *Schedule* section of the *Project* ribbon, click the *Set Baseline* pick list button and select the *Clear Baseline* item on the list. Project Professional 2010 displays the *Clear Baseline* dialog shown in Figure 7 - 5.

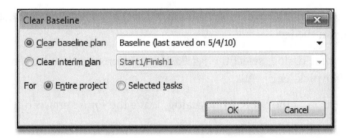

Figure 7 - 5: Clear Baseline dialog

2. Select the *Clear baseline plan* option.

3. On the *Clear baseline plan* pick list, leave the *Baseline* item selected.

4. Select the *Entire project* option.

5. Click the *OK* button.

You can clear the baseline for selected tasks only by choosing the *Selected tasks* option in the *Clear Baseline* dialog.

Hands On Exercise

Exercise 7-2

Save a baseline in an enterprise project.

1. Return to your Deploy Training Advisor Software project, if necessary.

2. Right-click on the *Select All* button and select the *More Tables* item on the shortcut menu.

3. In the *More Tables* dialog, select the *Baseline* table and click the *Apply* button.

4. Drag the vertical split bar to the right side of the *Baseline Cost* column so that you can see all of the columns in the *Baseline* table.

5. Click the *Project* tab to display the *Project* ribbon.

6. In the *Schedule* section of the *Project* ribbon, click the *Set Baseline* pick list button and select the *Set Baseline* item on the list.

7. In the *Set Baseline* dialog, select the *Set Baseline* option and then leave the *Baseline* item selected in the *Set Baseline* pick list.

8. In the *For:* section of the *Set Baseline* dialog, leave the *Entire project* option selected.

9. Click the *OK* button.

Notice the software saved baseline values for every task in the project in the five baseline columns shown in the *Baseline* table.

10. Right-click on the *Select All* button again and reapply the *Entry* table.

11. Drag the vertical split bar back to the right edge of the *Duration* column.

12. In the *Schedule* section of the *Project* ribbon, click the *Set Baseline* pick list button and select the *Set Baseline* item on the list again.

Notice that the *Set Baseline* pick list displays the date you saved the baseline for this project.

13. Click the *Cancel* button to exit the *Set Baseline* dialog.

14. Click the *Save* button on the Quick Access Toolbar to save your enterprise project.

Understanding Publishing

When you are ready to "go live" with an enterprise project, you must publish the project. When you publish a project for the very first time, the Project Server 2010 system performs a number of major operations. In the simplest sense, the system performs each of the following:

- The system saves the project data in both the *Published* and *Reporting* databases.

- The system sends an e-mail to all team members in the project, notifying them of tasks in a new project.

- The system creates a *Project Site* for the project in SharePoint. The Project Site allows all interested parties to collaborate together to manage risks, issues, documents, and deliverables associated with the project.

The result of the publishing operation is that all interested parties can now see information about the project in Project Web App. For example, executives can now see the project in the *Project Center* page, resource managers can see resource assignment information on the *Resource Availability* page, and team members can see their task assignments on both the *Tasks* and *Timesheet* pages.

The act of publishing a project for the first time also determines who receives task updates from team members working on the project. Project Server 2010 designates the user who publishes the project initially as the *Status Manager* for every task in the project. The person designated as the *Status Manager* is the one who receives task updates from team members assigned to the tasks. I discuss this feature a little later in this module.

Setting Publishing Options

Project Server 2010 gives you very limited control over the options used when publishing an enterprise project. To view these publishing options, click the *File* tab and then click the *Options* item in the *Backstage* menu. In the *Project Options* dialog, click the *Advanced* tab as shown in Figure 7 - 6. You can find the first of two publishing options in the *Project Web App* section of the dialog, the *Allow team members to reassign tasks* option. When selected for an enterprise project, this option allows a team member to delegate tasks to other team members in the project. When deselected, this option prevents team members from delegating tasks to other team members. Specify your option setting in the *Project Web App* section of the *Advanced* page, if necessary, and then click the *OK* button.

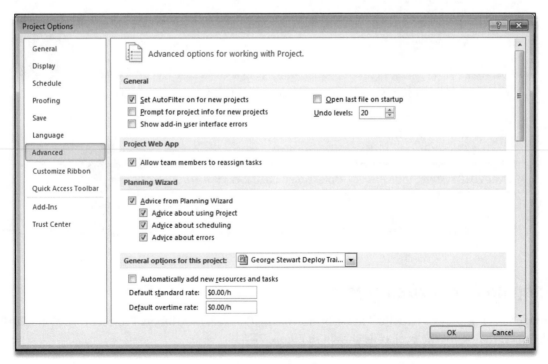

Figure 7 - 6: Advanced page in the Project Options dialog

To find the other publishing option, click the *File* tab to display the *Backstage*. On the right side of the *Information* page in the *Backstage*, the system displays a *Tracking Method* pick list as shown in Figure 7 - 7. If your Project Server 2010 system allows you to specify the default method of tracking for each enterprise project individually, select one of the items on the *Tracking Method* pick list. Select the *Actual/Remaining* method to track progress by capturing actual work and remaining work from team members. Select the *Percent Complete* method to track progress by capturing a percentage of completion value from team members. Select the *Specify Hours* option to capture actual work on a daily or weekly basis from team members. Otherwise, leave the *Server Default* item selected on the *Tracking Method* pick list to use the method specified for your organization by your Project Server administrator.

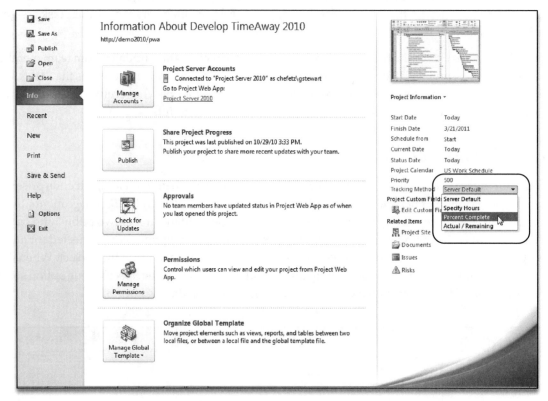

Figure 7 - 7: Specify the Tracking Method option in the Backstage

If your Project Server administrator locked the default method of tracking progress in your Project Server 2010 system, then Project Professional 2010 locks the *Tracking Method* pick list on the *Information* page of the *Backstage*.

Publishing an Enterprise Project

To publish an enterprise project, click the *Publish* button on the *Project Server* ribbon. Project Professional 2010 displays the *Publish Project* dialog for the project as shown in Figure 7 - 8.

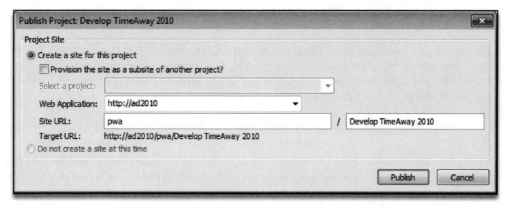

Figure 7 - 8: Publish Project dialog for a project

 You can also publish an enterprise project by clicking the *File* tab and then clicking the *Publish* item in the *Backstage* menu. You can also click the *Publish* button on either the *Information* page or the *Save & Send* page in the *Backstage* as well.

In the *Publish Project* dialog, you can select the default *Create a site for this project* option and the system automatically creates a new Project Site for the project in SharePoint. If your project is part of a larger program of projects that must share a single Project Site, then select the *Provision the site as a subsite of another project* option. The system activates the *Select a project* pick list in the *Publish Project* dialog as shown in Figure 7 - 9.

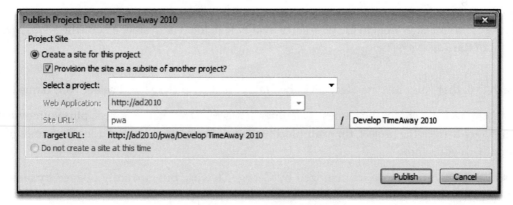

Figure 7 - 9: Publish Project dialog set to create a sub-workspace for a project

Click the *Select a project* pick list and select the Project Site under which to create the new subsite. Regardless of how you decide to create the Project Site, you can also change the site display name for the project displayed in the *Site URL* field in the lower right corner of the dialog.

Notice in the two preceding figures that the system disables the *Do not create a site at this time* option in the lower left corner of the *Publish Project* dialog. This is because our organization's Project Server administrator selected an option requiring Project Server 2010 to create a Project Site at the time a manager initially publishes a project.

After you set your publishing options in the *Publish Project* dialog, click the *Publish* button. As the system publishes your project and creates the Project Site, it displays progress information in the *Status* bar at the bottom of the Project Professional 2010 application window. When the publishing operation completes, the system displays a *Publish completed successfully* message in the *Status* bar.

Changing the Status Manager for Task Assignments

As I stated earlier, Project Server 2010 specifies the *Status Manager* on each task in an enterprise project as the manager who publishes the project initially. The system allows you to take over as the *Status Manager* of one or more tasks in another manager's project, either **temporarily** (such as when the other manager is on vacation) or **permanently** (such as when the other manager leaves the company). To take over as the *Status Manager* of another manager's project, complete the following steps:

1. Open the enterprise project in question.

2. Apply any task view, such as the *Gantt Chart* view.

3. Right-click on the column header to the right of the *Task Name* column and select the *Insert Column* item on the shortcut menu.

4. Select the *Status Manager* field in the pick list of available fields. The system inserts the *Status Manager* field to the right of the *Task Name* field.

5. For each task that you must manage, click the *Status Manager* pick list and select your name from the list.

The *Status Manager* pick list includes the names of all other *Status Managers* in the project, plus your own name. If you are the third manager to open the project, for example, the *Status Manager* pick list includes the names of the first two managers, along with your name.

Figure 7 - 10 shows an enterprise project managed by George Stewart, but currently opened by another manager named Genea Mallow. Genea needs to take over as the *Status Manager* for all of the tasks in the *Scope* and *Analysis/Software Requirements* sections of the project. To accomplish this, Genea must select her name in the *Status Manager* column for every subtask in those two summary task sections of the project.

To speed up the entry process, enter your name in the *Status Manager* column for a task and then use the **Fill Handle** in the selected cell to copy your name to other successive tasks in the project. You can also click the *Fill* pick list button in the *Editing* section of the *Task* ribbon and select the *Down* item on the pick list.

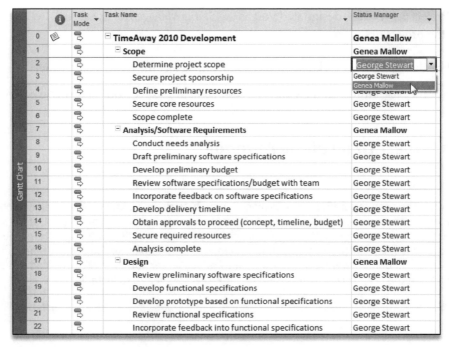

**Figure 7 - 10: Select a Status Manager value in the
Gantt Chart view of an enterprise project**

After setting yourself as the *Status Manager* for one or more tasks in the enterprise project, save and publish the project. As the new *Status Manager* for the selected tasks, Project Server 2010 redirects task updates for those tasks from the previous manager to you as the new *Status Manager*.

Hands On Exercise

Exercise 7-3

Publish an enterprise project and then view the Status Manager for each task.

1. Return to your Deploy Training Advisor Software project, if necessary.

2. Click the *Project Server* tab to display the *Project Server* ribbon.

3. In the *Plan and Publish* section of the *Project Server* ribbon, click the *Publish* button.

4. In the *Publish Project* dialog, leave all of the default settings in place and then click the *Publish* button.

5. As the system publishes the project, observe the publishing status on the *Status* bar at the bottom of the Project Professional 2010 application window.

6. Click the *Task* tab to display the *Task* ribbon.

7. Click the *Gantt Chart* pick list button and select the *_msPE Publishing* view on the pick list.

Note that Project Server 2010 designated you as the *Status Manager* for every task in the project because you published the project first.

8. Click the *Gantt Chart* pick list button again and select the *Gantt Chart* view.

9. Click the *Save* button on the Quick Access Toolbar to save your enterprise project.

Delegating a Project to a Fellow Manager

 Warning: The default permissions in Project Server 2010 **do not** allow you to delegate your work to another project manager using the new *Manage Delegates* feature. If your organization wants to allow project managers to manage their own delegations, your Project Server administrator must set the *Manage Resources' Delegates* permission to *Allowed* for members of the Project Managers group. For the purpose of demonstrating this feature, our Project Server administrator enabled this permission for members of the Project Managers group in our Project Server 2010 instance.

A new feature in Project Server 2010 allows you to delegate your work to another project manager temporarily, such as when you are on vacation and another manager must approve timesheets. To use this feature, log in to Project Web App for your organization's Project Server 2010 instance. Click the *Personal Settings* link in the *Quick Launch* menu and then click the *Manage Delegates* link on the *Personal Settings* page. The system displays the *Manage Delegates* page shown in Figure 7 - 11.

Figure 7 - 11: Manage Delegates page

On the *Manage Delegates* page of Project Web App, click the *New* button in the *Delegate* section of the *Delegations* ribbon. The system displays the *Add Delegation* page shown in Figure 7 - 12.

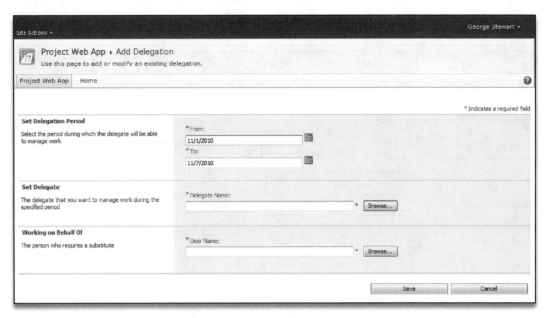

Figure 7 - 12: Add Delegation page

To add a new delegation, begin by setting a date range during which the delegation is effective using the *From* and *To* fields. Next, click the *Browse* button in the *Set Delegate* section of the page. The system displays the *Choose Name* dialog shown in Figure 7 - 13. Select the name of a fellow manager and then click the *OK* button. For example, in the *Choose User* dialog, I delegate my work to *Genea Mallow* temporarily.

Figure 7 - 13: Choose User dialog

Finally, use the *Browse* button in the *Working on Behalf of* section of the page. The system displays the *Choose User* dialog shown previously in Figure 7 - 13. Select your own name in the *Choose User* dialog and then click the *OK* button. Click the *Save* button to complete the temporary delegation to a fellow manager. The system displays the temporary delegation to *Genea Mallow* from *George Stewart* on the *Manage Delegates* page as shown in Figure 7 - 14.

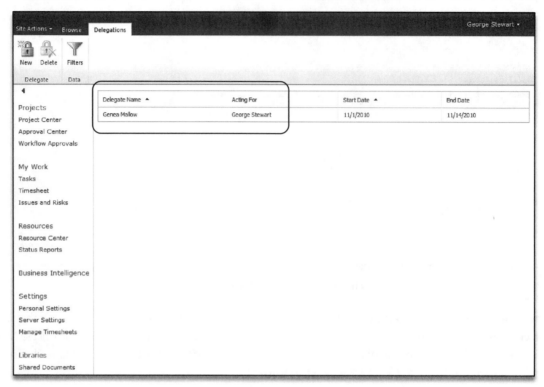

**Figure 7 - 14: Temporary delegation to Genea Mallow
shown on the Manage Delegates page**

To remove a temporary delegation to another project manager, select the delegation item on the *Manage Delegates* page and then click the *Delete* button on the *Delegations* ribbon. The system displays the warning dialog shown in Figure 7 - 15. Click the *OK* button to delete the delegation.

**Figure 7 - 15: Confirmation message to
delete a delegation to another manager**

Acting as a Delegate for another Project Manager

When another manager delegates his/her work to you, you act on the delegation by navigating to the *Personal Settings* page in Project Web App. Click the *Act as a Delegate* link and the system displays the *Act as a Delegate* page. For example, Figure 7 - 16 shows the *Act as a Delegate* page for the project manager named *Genea Mallow*. Notice that the page shows the delegation to *Genea Mallow* from her fellow manager, *George Stewart*, for the period from November 1-14, 2010. During this time period, Project Server 2010 allows *Genea Mallow* to work as a delegate on behalf of *George Stewart*. After that time period expires, the system **prevents** *Genea Mallow* from working as *George Stewart's* delegate.

Figure 7 - 16: Act as a Delegate page

To begin acting as a delegate for a fellow manager, select the delegation item in the *Acting For* column on the *Act as a Delegate* page, and then click the *Start Delegate Session* button on the *Delegations* ribbon. The system refreshes the top of the *Act as a Delegate* page to show that you are acting as a delegate on behalf of your fellow manager, as shown in Figure 7 - 17.

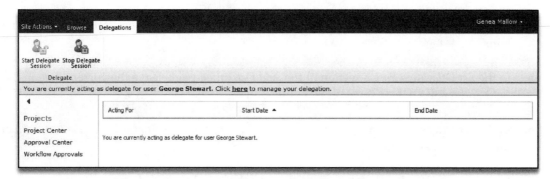

Figure 7 - 17: Act as a Delegate page with delegation session started

Notice in Figure 7 - 17 that the system displays a yellow band across the page just below the *Delegations* ribbon, indicating that the delegation session is active. This warning band remains across every page in Project Web App while you are act as a delegate to remind you that you are now working with Project Web App on behalf of your fellow manager.

After you complete your work on behalf of the other user, you stop your delegate session by returning to the *Act as a Delegate* page by clicking on the *Click here* link in the yellow band, or by navigating to the page from the *Personal Settings* page. Click the *Stop Delegate Session* button in the *Delegations* ribbon. The system exits the delegate session and the page displays the *You are not currently acting as anyone's delegate* message, as shown previously in Figure 7 - 16.

Warning: Delegation does not appy to all features. For instance, Project Server 2010 does not include delegation for features supported by SharePoint only, such as Project Sites and the *Business Intelligence Center* in Project Web App. Delegation does not apply to Project Professional 2010 or to editing project schedules with Project Professional 2010.

Hands On Exercise

Exercise 7-4

Use the *Delegation* feature in Project Web App to delegate your work to a fellow project manager.

1. Launch your Internet Explorer and then log into Project Web App for the Project Server 2010 instance used for this class.

2. Click the *Personal Settings* link in the *Settings* section of the *Quick Launch* menu.

3. Click the *Manage Delegates* link on the *Personal Settings* page.

4. On the *Manage Delegates* page, click the *New* button in the *Delegate* section of the *Delegations* ribbon.

5. In the *Set Delegation Period* section of the *Add Delegation* page, leave the current date in the *From* field and enter a date two weeks from today in the *To* field.

6. In the *Set Delegate* section of the *Add Delegation* page, click the *Browse* button at the right end of the *Delegate Name* field.

7. In the *Choose User* dialog, select any fellow manager and then click the *OK* button.

8. In the *Working on Behalf Of* section of the *Add Delegation* page, click the *Browse* button at the right end of the *User Name* field.

9. In the *Choose User* dialog, select your own name and then click the *OK* button.

10. Click the *Save* button at the bottom of the *Add Delegation* page.

11. Select anywhere on the delegation line, except for the name in the *Delegate Name* column.

12. In the *Delegate* section of the *Delegations* ribbon, click the *Delete* button to remove the delegation.

13. When prompted in a confirmation dialog, click the *OK* button to delete the delegation.

14. Close your Internet Explore application window and return to your Project Professional 2010 application window.

Setting Custom Permissions for a Project

After you publish a new enterprise project for the first time, Project Server 2010 allows you to designate special permissions for the project. For example, the default permissions in the system allow project managers to see and edit their own projects only, and do not allow project managers to see and edit any project they do not own or manage. Suppose that I need a fellow project manager named *Genea Mallow* to be able to see and edit a new enterprise project using Project Professional 2010, but I do not need her to see and edit the project in Project Web App. To set special permissions such as this for an enterprise project, open the enterprise project and then click the *File* tab. On the *Information* page of the *Backstage*, click the *Manage Permissions* button, as shown in Figure 7 - 18.

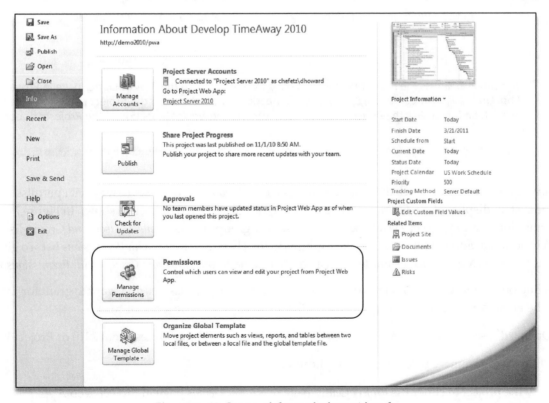

Figure 7 - 18: Set special permissions using the
Manage Permissions button in the Backstage

The system displays the *Project Permissions* page for the enterprise project, as shown in Figure 7 - 19.

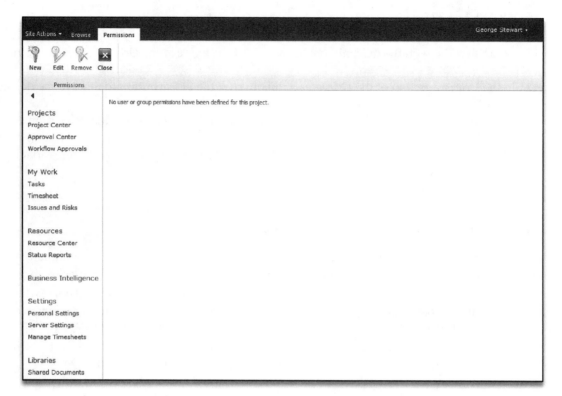

Figure 7 - 19: Project Permissions page for the Develop TimeAway 2010 project

You can also access the *Project Permissions* page by navigating to the *Project Center* page in Project Web App. On the *Project Center* page, click the row header at the left end of the project name to select the project, and then click the *Project Permissions* button in the *Navigate* section of the *Projects* ribbon.

On the *Project Permissions* page, click the *New* button in the *Permissions* ribbon to set new special permissions for the project. The system displays the *Edit Project Permissions* page for the selected project, as shown in Figure 7 - 20. To set special permissions for the project, select one or more users or groups in the *Available Users and Groups* list and then click the *Add* button to add the selected users and groups to the *Users and Groups with Permissions* list. To give special permissions to Genea Mallow, for example, I must add her name to the *Users and Groups with Permissions* list.

After selecting one or more users and groups, next select the specific permissions you want to grant for the selected project in the *Permissions* section of the page. The available permissions allow a user to:

- Open, edit, save, and publish an enterprise project in either Project Professional 2010 or Project Web App.

- Edit project summary fields in either application.

- View the project in either the *Project Center* page or *Project Details* page in Project Web App.

- View the Project Site.

To meet my special permissions needs for Genea Mallow, I select the following permissions **only**:

- *Open the project within Project Professional or Project Web App*

- *Edit and Save the project within Project Professional or Project Web App*

- *Publish the project within Project Professional or Project Web App*

By selecting the preceding options, I allow Genea Mallow to open, edit, save, and publish the project in Project Professional 2010. Because Genea cannot see the project in the *Project Center* page in Project Web App, she cannot edit the project using Project Web App, nor can she access the Project Site for the project.

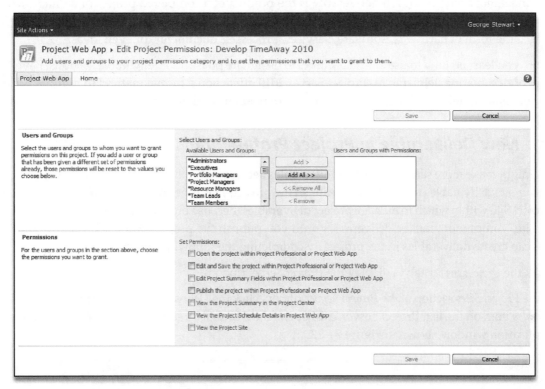

Figure 7 - 20: Edit Project Permissions page for the Develop TimeAway 2010 project

When you finish selecting special permissions for the selected users and groups, click the *Save* button. The system refreshes the *Project Permissions* page as shown in Figure 7 - 21. Notice that the *Project Permissions* page shows the special permissions I granted to Genea Mallow.

Figure 7 - 21: Project Permissions page for the Develop TimeAway 2010 project

319

To edit the special permissions for a project, select the checkbox for the special permissions and then click the *Edit* button in the *Permissions* ribbon. To remove the special permissions for a project, select the checkbox for the special permissions and then click the *Remove* button in the *Permissions* ribbon. To navigate away from the *Project Permissions* page, click the *Close* button in the *Permissions* ribbon. The system returns to the *Project Center* page shown previously in Figure 7 - 18.

Managing Project Deliverables

In project management terminology, a **deliverable** is the product of a completed project or an intermediate result within a project, such as at the end of each phase or deliverable section of the project. In the world of projects, deliverables can take the form of hardware, software, services, processes, documents, or even ideas.

In Module 05, you learned how to use summary tasks to designate phase and deliverable sections. Beyond this "informal" way of designating deliverables, Project Server 2010 offers you a formal method to indicate project deliverables, their negotiated delivery dates, and any external dependencies that may influence the delivery dates.

Adding a New Deliverable in Project Professional 2010

Although it might make more sense to manage deliverables before you publish a project, Project Server 2010 does not allow you to create deliverables until **after** you publish the project. This is because your project must have an accompanying Project Site within which to manage project deliverables. Because publishing for the first time actually creates the Project Site, you cannot manage deliverables until you publish the project. After you publish your enterprise project, you can create deliverables in the project by completing the following steps:

1. Click the *Project Server* tab to display the *Project Server* ribbon.

2. In the *Project Sites* section of the *Project Server* ribbon, click the *Deliverable* pick list and select the *Manage Deliverables* item on the list. Project Server 2010 opens the *Deliverables* sidepane in the Project Professional 2010 application window shown in Figure 7 - 22.

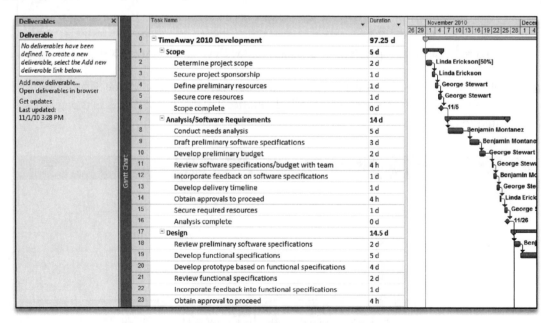

Figure 7 - 22: Deliverables sidepane in a published project

You can also display the *Deliverables* sidepane by clicking the *Task* tab to display the *Task* ribbon. In the *Insert* section of the *Task* ribbon, click the *Manage Deliverables and Dependencies* pick list and select the *Manage Deliverables* item on the pick list.

Notice in Figure 7 - 22 that the system informs me that I have not yet created any deliverables for the active project.

3. Select a task to which you want to link a deliverable.

4. Click the *Add new deliverable* link in the *Deliverables* sidepane.

5. Select the *Link to selected task* option in the *Add Deliverable* sidepane. The system imports the task name into the *Title* field, imports the task's start date into the *Start* field, and imports the task's finish date into the *Finish* field in the *Add Deliverable* sidepane, as shown in Figure 7 - 23.

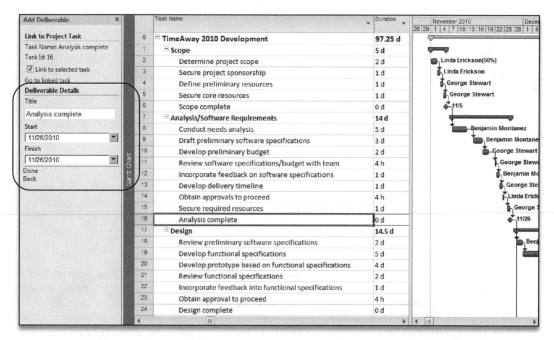

Figure 7 - 23: Deliverable information imported from a selected task

6. Edit the information in the *Title*, *Start*, and *Finish* fields of the *Add Deliverable* sidepane, as needed.

7. Click the *Done* link at the bottom of the *Add Deliverable* sidepane. The system displays the new deliverable at the top of the *Deliverables* sidepane, as shown in Figure 7 - 24.

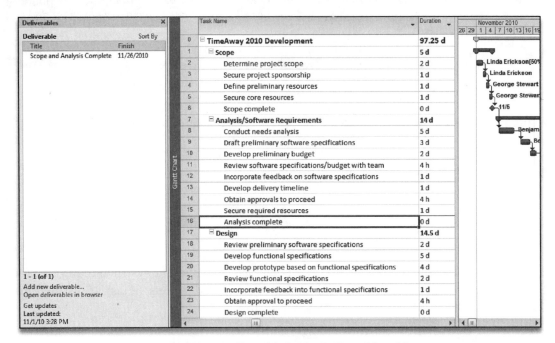

Figure 7 - 24: New Deliverable in the Deliverables sidepane

To display the full name of the deliverable shown in the preceding figure, I widened the *Deliverables* sidepane by clicking and holding the right edge of the sidepane to "grab" it, then moving the mouse pointer to the right, and releasing the mouse button.

By default, Project Professional 2010 sorts deliverables in ascending order by title in the *Deliverables* sidepane. To change the sorting, click the *Sort By* pick list in the upper right corner of the *Deliverables* sidepane and then select either the *Start Date* or *Finish Date* item on the pick list. You can also change the sort order to descending by **deselecting** the *Ascending* item on the pick list.

Warning: If you want to track variance on deliverable dates, **you must rebaseline your project** by clicking the *Set Baseline* pick list on the *Project* ribbon and selecting the *Set Baseline* item on the pick list. In the *Set Baseline* dialog, click the *OK* button to rebaseline the project. When prompted in a warning dialog, click the *Yes* button to update the baseline with the deliverable information. Project Server 2010 saves baseline information for each deliverable in the *Baseline Deliverable Start* and *Baseline Deliverable Finish* fields.

You can also create a new deliverable rapidly without using the *Deliverables* sidepane to change the information in the *Title, Start,* or *Finish* fields. Before you use this technique, first select the task on which you want to attach a deliverable, then click the *Create Deliverables* item on the *Deliverable* pick list in the *Project Sites* section of the *Project Server* ribbon. The system creates the new deliverable on the selected task using the task name, start, and finish information from the task, without every displaying the *Deliverables* sidepane.

> **Warning:** Before you use the preceding technique to create deliverables quickly, make absolutely sure that you **do not** select the Project Summary Task (row 0 or task 0). If you create a deliverable on the Project Summary Task accidentally, you cannot delete the deliverable in the *Deliverables* sidepane, as the system displays a continuous series of script error dialogs when you attempt to delete the deliverable. The only way to delete the deliverable is to access the Project Site for the project and delete the deliverable in the *Deliverables* section of the *Home* page.

Editing and Deleting Deliverables in Project Professional 2010

To edit a deliverable in Project Professional 2010, display the *Deliverables* sidepane and then float your mouse pointer over the name of the deliverable you want to edit. The system displays a "fly out" to the right of the deliverable with information about the deliverable, and displays a pick list arrow button at the right end of the deliverable name, as shown in Figure 7 - 25.

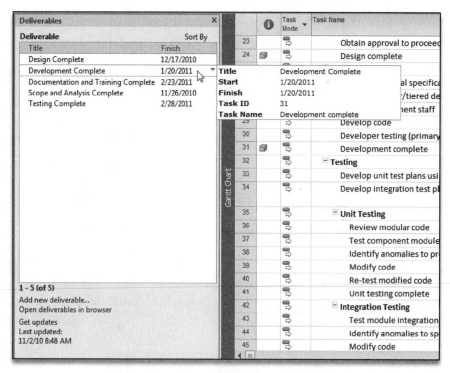

Figure 7 - 25: Prepare to edit a deliverable

Click anywhere on the deliverable name and the system displays a pick list menu of items, as shown in Figure 7 - 26. The items on the pick list allow you to edit the deliverable in Project Professional 2010, to edit the deliverable in the Project Site using your Internet Explorer application, to delete the deliverable, or to accept changes made to the deliverable in the Project Site.

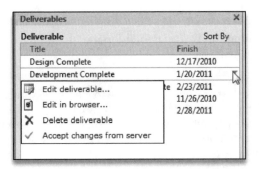

**Figure 7 - 26: Click on a deliverable
to edit its information**

Click the *Edit deliverable* item on the pick list to edit the deliverable. The system displays the *Edit Deliverable* sidepane shown in Figure 7 - 27. In the *Edit Deliverable* sidepane, you have the option to link or delink the deliverable with a specific task, or to edit the information in the *Title, Start,* and *Finish* fields. You can also click the *Go to selected task* link to select the task linked to the deliverable. When finished, click the *Done* link at the bottom of the sidepane.

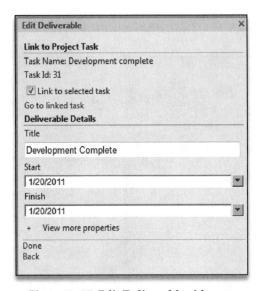

Figure 7 - 27: Edit Deliverable sidepane

To delete a deliverable, click anywhere on the deliverable name and, and then select the *Delete deliverable* item on the pick list menu. The system displays the confirmation dialog shown in Figure 7 - 28. Click the *OK* button to complete the deletion process.

**Figure 7 - 28: Delete deliverable
confirmation dialog**

When you delete a deliverable in Project Professional 2010, the system moves the deliverable to the *Recycle Bin* in the Project Site for your enterprise project. The deliverable remains in the *Recycle Bin* for 30 days, after which the system deletes the deliverable permanently. At any time during the 30 days, you can navigate to the *Recycle Bin* in the Project Site and restore the deliverable.

Hands On Exercise

Exercise 7-5

Add new deliverables in an enterprise project using Project Professional 2010.

1. Return to your Deploy Training Advisor Software project and display the *Gantt Chart* view, if necessary.

2. Click the *Project Server* tab to display the *Project Server* ribbon.

3. In the *Project Sites* section of the *Project Server* ribbon, click the *Deliverable* pick list and select the *Manage Deliverables* item on the list.

4. Select task ID #6, the *Phase I Complete* milestone task.

5. Click the *Add new deliverable* link in the *Deliverables* sidepane.

6. Select the *Link to selected task* option in the *Add Deliverable* sidepane.

Notice how Project Professional 2010 imports the task name into the *Title* field, imports the task's start date into the *Start* field, and imports the task's finish date into the *Finish* field in the *Add Deliverable* sidepane.

7. Click the *Done* link at the bottom of the *Add Deliverable* sidepane.

8. Click and hold the right edge of the *Deliverables* sidepane and widen it until you can see the full name and date of the new deliverable.

9. Select task ID #12, the *Phase II Complete* milestone task.

10. Click the *Add new deliverable* link in the *Deliverables* sidepane.

11. Select the *Link to selected task* option in the *Add Deliverable* sidepane.

12. Click the *Done* link at the bottom of the *Add Deliverable* sidepane.

Notice the special deliverable indicator shown in the *Indicators* column to the left of task ID #6 and #12.

13. Float your mouse pointer over one of the deliverable indicators to read the tooltip for the indicator.

14. Select task ID #17, the *Phase III Complete* milestone task.

15. In the *Project Sites* section of the *Project Server* ribbon, click the *Deliverable* pick list and select the *Create Deliverables* item on the list.

16. Notice how the system creates the deliverable automatically without allowing you to edit the *Title*, *Start*, or *Finish* fields.

17. Click the *Save* button on the Quick Access Toolbar to save your enterprise project.

18. Click the *Publish* button in the *Plan and Publish* section of the *Project Server* ribbon.

Exercise 7-6

Edit an existing deliverable in an enterprise project using Project Professional 2010.

1. In the *Deliverables* sidepane, float your mouse pointer over the *Phase II Complete* deliverable and then read the information about this deliverable in the tooltip.

2. Click the *Phase II Complete* deliverable and then select the *Edit deliverable* item on the pick list menu.

3. In the *Edit Deliverable* sidepane, add **1 week (5 working days)** to the date in the *Finish* field.

4. Click the *Done* link at the bottom of the *Edit Deliverable* sidepane.

5. Click the *Save* button on the Quick Access Toolbar to save your enterprise project.

6. Click the *Publish* button in the *Plan and Publish* section of the *Project Server* ribbon.

Managing Deliverables in Project Web App

In addition to using the Project Professional 2010 client, you can also manage deliverables in Project Web App by using the Project Site of the selected project. To view, create, edit, or delete deliverables in Project Web App, complete the following steps:

1. In the *Deliverables* sidepane in Project Professional 2010, click the *Open deliverables in browser* link at the bottom of the sidepane. The system launches a new Internet Explorer application window and displays the *Deliverables* page of the Project Site, as shown in Figure 7 - 29.

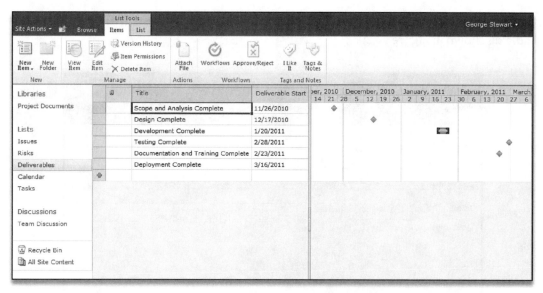

Figure 7 - 29: Deliverables page in the Project Site for the selected project

Notice that the *Deliverables* page shown in Figure 7 - 29 shows the six deliverables created so far for the selected project. The system represents each deliverable using either a milestone symbol or a Gantt bar in the *Gantt Chart* portion of the *Deliverables* page. The system uses a Gantt bar, by the way, when the *Deliverable Finish* date is later than the *Deliverable Start* date, such as when a deliverable has an "acceptable" date range for delivery of the product.

2. Widen the *Title*, *Deliverable Start*, or *Deliverable Finish* columns, as needed, and drag the split bar to the desired location on the page.

3. Click the *List* tab to display the *List* ribbon.

4. In the *Gantt View* section of the *List* ribbon, click the *Zoom Out* button until you see all of the deliverables for the project.

The *Deliverabes* page shown in Figure 7 - 25 reflects the changes I made to the page following steps #2-4 above.

Adding a New Deliverable in Project Web App

To create a new deliverable in Project Web App, navigate to the *Deliverables* page shown previously in Figure 7 - 29 and then complete the following steps:

1. Click the *Items* tab to display the *Items* ribbon.

2. In the *New* section of the *Items* ribbon, click the *New Item* button. The system displays the *Deliverables - New Item* dialog shown in Figure 7 - 30.

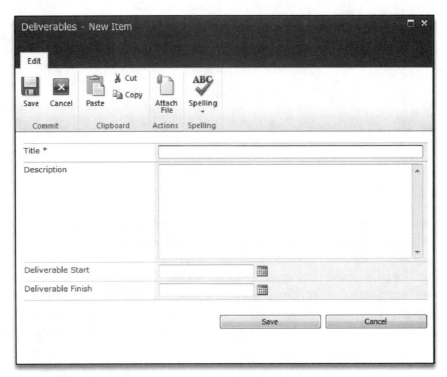

Figure 7 - 30: Deliverables - New Item dialog

3. Enter information in the *Title, Description, Deliverable Start*, and *Deliverable Finish* fields, as per your requirements.

4. If you want to attach a file to the deliverable, click the *Attach file* button in the *Edit* ribbon at the top of the dialog. Project Server 2010 displays the *Deliverables: New Item* dialog with the option to select an existing file, as shown in Figure 7 - 31.

Figure 7 - 31: Attach a file in the Deliverables - New Item dialog

5. Click the *Browse* button and navigate to the appropriate folder in the *Choose File to Upload* dialog, as shown in Figure 7 - 32.

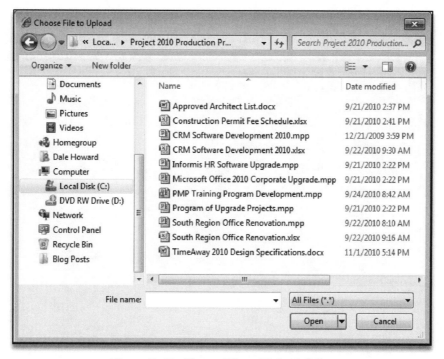

Figure 7 - 32: Choose File to Upload dialog

6. In the *Choose File to Upload* dialog, select a document, and then click the *Open* button. The system redisplays the *Deliverables: New Item* page for the document,

7. In the *Deliverables - New Item* page for the attached document, click the *OK* button. The system redisplays the *Deliverables - New Item* dialog as shown in Figure 7 - 33.

If you change your mind and want to delete the attached file, click the *Delete* link to the right of the file name in the *Attachments* section at the bottom of the *Deliverables - New Item* dialog.

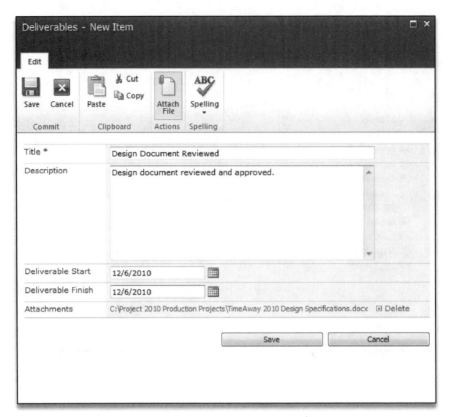

**Figure 7 - 33: Deliverables - New Item page with
information for the new Deliverable**

8.   Click the *Save* button to create the new deliverable. Figure 7 - 34 shows the new deliverable on the *Deliverables* page of the Project Site for the selected project.

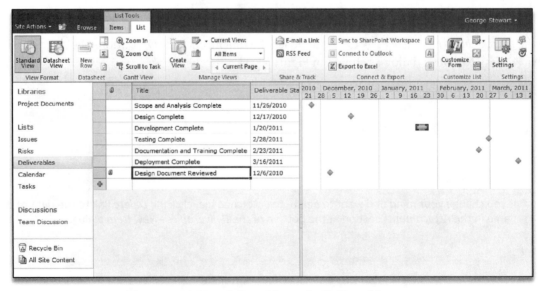

Figure 7 - 34: New deliverable on the Deliverables page

Warning: When you create a new deliverable from the Project Site using Internet Explorer, Project Server 2010 **does not** allow you to link the deliverable to a task in the project. Because of this limitation, you may want to create all deliverables in your enterprise projects using Project Professional 2010 instead.

Viewing Deliverable Information in Project Web App

Notice in Figure 7 - 34 that the system displays a paperclip icon to the left of the deliverable name, indicating that the deliverable has at least one file attached to it. To view the information about any deliverable, click the *Browse* tab at the top of the page and then click the name of the project. The system displays the *Home* page of the Project Site, as shown in Figure 7 - 35. Notice that the *Home* page includes a *Deliverables* section at the top of the main content area of the page.

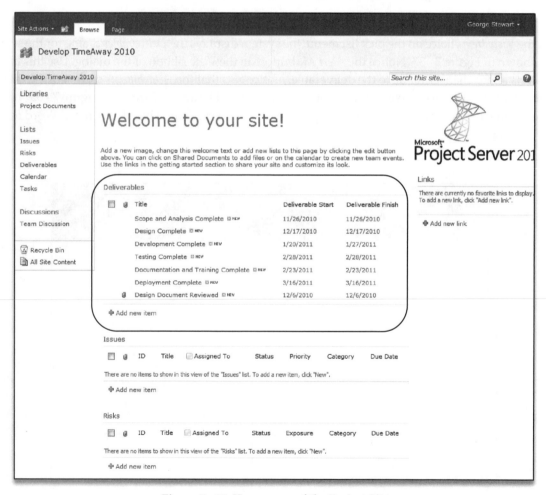

Figure 7 - 35: Home page of the Project Site

If you float your mouse pointer over a deliverable in the *Deliverables* section of the *Home* page, the system displays a pick list arrow button similar to what you see in the *Deliverables* sidepane in Project Professional 2010. When you click the pick list for a deliverable, the system displays the pick list menu shown in Figure 7 - 36.

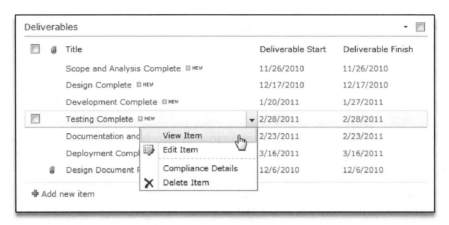

Figure 7 - 36: Pick list menu for a deliverable in the Project Site

If you click the *View Item* choice on the pick list menu, the system displays the *Deliverables* dialog for the selected deliverable, as shown in Figure 7 - 37. Notice the *Alert Me* button on the *View* ribbon of the dialog. Use this button to set up e-mail alerts about changes made to the deliverable. Notice also that the *Attachments* section of the dialog shows the document I attached to this deliverable previously, as shown in Figure 7 - 30 through Figure 7 - 33. You can click the document name to open the document in the application used to create it, which is Microsoft Word for the document shown in Figure 7 - 37.

Figure 7 - 37: Deliverables dialog for a deliverable

Editing and Deleting a Deliverable in Project Web App

To edit the selected deliverable, click the *Edit Item* choice on the pick list shown previously in Figure 7 - 36. The system opens the *Deliverables* dialog in editing mode, as shown in Figure 7 - 38. Edit the information in the *Title*, *Description*, *Deliverable Start*, and *Deliverable Finish* fields as needed. Click the *Attach File* button on the *Edit* ribbon to attach a file to the deliverable, if needed. When you finish editing the deliverable, click the *Save* button in the *Deliverables* dialog.

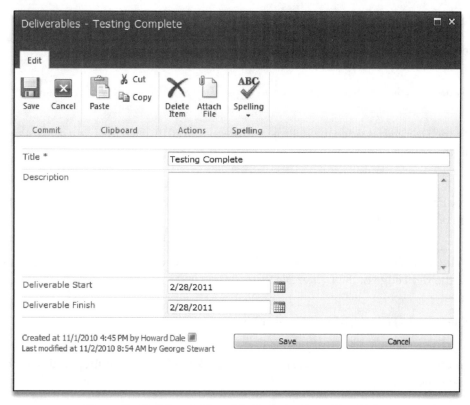

Figure 7 - 38: Edit a deliverable in the Deliverables dialog

To delete the selected deliverable, click the *Delete Item* button on the pick list shown previously in Figure 7 - 36. The system displays the confirmation dialog shown in Figure 7 - 39. Click the *OK* button to complete the deletion. When you delete a deliverable using Project Web App, the system moves the deleted deliverable to the *Recycle Bin* for the Project Site, where it remains for 30 days. Any time during the 30 days after deletion, you can navigate to the *Recycle Bin* and undelete the deliverable to restore it to the list of deliverables for the project.

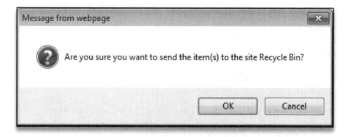

Figure 7 - 39: Confirmation dialog to delete
a deliverable in Project Web App

Hands On Exercise

Exercise 7-7

Add a new deliverable to an enterprise project using Project Web App.

1. Return to your enterprise project and apply the *Gantt Chart* view, if necessary.

2. In the *Deliverables* sidepane in Project Professional 2010, click the *Open deliverables in browser* link at the bottom of the sidepane.

Notice how Project Server 2010 launches a new Internet Explorer application window and displays the *Deliverables* page of the Project Site for your enterprise project.

3. Widen the *Title*, *Deliverable Start*, or *Deliverable Finish* columns, as needed, and drag the split bar to the right edge of the *Deliverable Start* column.

4. Click the *List* tab to display the *List* ribbon.

5. In the *Gantt View* section of the *List* ribbon, click the *Zoom Out* button until you see all of the deliverables for the project.

Notice that the *Deliverables* page shows the three deliverables you created in your enterprise project. Notice that the system represents each deliverable using either a milestone symbol or a Gantt bar in the *Gantt Chart* portion of the *Deliverables* page.

6. Click the *Items* tab to display the *Items* ribbon.

7. In the *New* section of the *Items* ribbon, click the *New Item* button.

8. In the *Deliverables - New Item* dialog, enter the text *Training Advisor Rollout Complete* in the *Title* field.

9. Do not enter any information in the *Description*, *Deliverable Start*, or *Deliverable Finish* fields.

10. Click the *Save* button to create the new deliverable in Project Web App.

11. Click the *Browse* tab and then click the name of your class project at the top of the *Home* page for your Project Site.

In the *Deliverables* section of the *Home* page, notice the four deliverables you created in both Project Professional 2010 and in Project Web App.

12. Close your Internet Explorer application window and return to your Project Professional 2010 application window.

Updating Deliverables in Project Professional 2010

If you create a new deliverable or edit an existing deliverable in Project Web App, and then reopen the enterprise project for these deliverables, Project Server 2010 **does not** automatically update the deliverable information in the project. Instead, Project Professional 2010 displays a red exclamation point icon to the left of the name of the new or changed deliverable in the *Deliverables* sidepane, as shown in Figure 7 - 40.

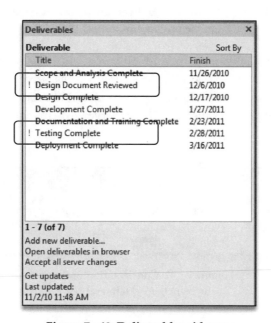

**Figure 7 - 40: Deliverables sidepane
shows new or changed deliverables**

Notice in Figure 7 - 40 that the *Deliverables* sidepane shows two deliverables with a red exclamation point to the left of the deliverable name. To learn more about any new or changed deliverable, float your mouse pointer over the name of the deliverable. The system displays a tooltip that provides information about this new deliverable, as shown in Figure 7 - 41. Notice that the red exclamation point icon means that the deliverable information in the project is "out of synch" with the information in Project Web App.

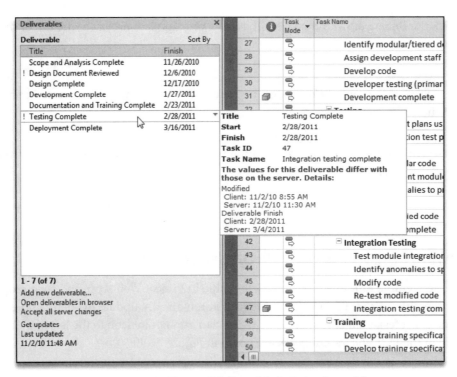

**Figure 7 - 41: Changed deliverable is "out of synch"
between the project and Project Web App**

To "synch up" any new or changed deliverable individually, float your mouse pointer over the deliverable, click anywhere on the deliverable name, and then select the *Accept changes from server* item on the pick list menu. To "synch up" all new and changed deliverables between the enterprise project and Project Web App, click the *Accept all server changes* link at the bottom of the *Deliverables* sidepane. Project Server 2010 displays the confirmation dialog shown in Figure 7 - 42.

**Figure 7 - 42: Confirmation dialog
to "synch up" Deliverables**

The confirmation dialog tells you how many deliverables are "out of synch" and asks you to confirm the update. Click the *OK* button to update all deliverables. After you finish managing deliverables for your enterprise project, click the *Close* button (**X**) in the upper right corner of the *Deliverables* sidepane.

To make sure you can see the current state of every deliverable, you may want to click the *Get updates* link at the bottom of the *Deliverables* sidepane before you click the *Accept all server changes* link. This guarantees you can see and accept all changes made in Project Web App.

Hands On Exercise

Exercise 7-8

Accept deliverable changes from Project Web App to deliverables in your enterprise project.

1. Return to your enterprise project and display the *Deliverables* sidepane, if necessary.

2. At the bottom of the *Deliverables* sidepane, click the *Get updates* link.

3. Click and hold the right edge of the *Deliverables* sidepane and widen it until you can see the full name of the new deliverable.

4. Float your mouse pointer over the *Training Advisor Rollout Complete* deliverable and read the information shown in the tooltip for this deliverable.

Note: Do not despair when you see red text stating, *Accepting the changes for this deliverable will add it to the client project*, since this is exactly what you need to do.

5. Click the *Accept all server changes* link at the bottom of the *Deliverables* sidepane.

6. When prompted in a confirmation dialog, click the *OK* button.

7. Click the *Training Advisor Rollout Complete* deliverable and select the *Delete deliverable* item on the pick list menu.

8. When prompted in a confirmation dialog, click the *OK* button to delete the new deliverable.

9. Click the *Close* button (**X**) in the upper right corner of the *Deliverables* sidepane to close the sidepane.

10. Click the *Save* button on the Quick Access Toolbar to save your enterprise project.

11. Click the *Publish* button in the *Plan and Publish* section of the *Project Server* ribbon.

Adding a New Deliverable Dependency

In the world of enterprise project management, it is entirely possible for dates in one project to be dependent on dates in one or more other projects. Because of this, a task in one project may be dependent on a deliverable in another project. To address this situation, you can specify a task dependency on an external deliverable in another project. To create a deliverable dependency, complete the following steps:

1. Click the *Project Server* tab to display the *Project Server* ribbon.

2. In the *Project Sites* section of the *Project Server* ribbon, click the *Deliverable* pick list and select the *Manage Dependencies* item on the list. Project Server 2010 opens the *Dependency* sidepane in the Project Professional 2010 application window shown in Figure 7 - 43.

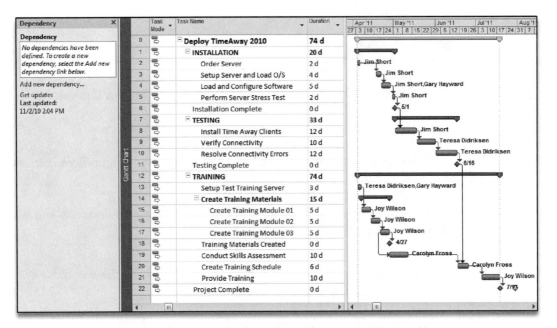

Figure 7 - 43: Dependency sidepane for an enterprise project

Figure 7 - 43 shows the *Dependency* sidepane for the Deploy TimeAway 2010 project. The first task in this project, *Order Server*, is dependent on the final deliverable in the Develop TimeAway 2010 project, since we cannot deploy the software until the developers actually create it. Notice in Figure 7 - 43 that the system informs me I have not yet created any deliverable dependencies for the active project.

3. Click the *Add new dependency* link in the *Dependency* sidepane. The system displays the *Add Dependency* sidepane.

4. In the *Add Dependency* sidepane, click the *Select project* pick list and choose a project on which the active project is dependent, as shown in Figure 7 - 44.

The *Select project* pick list shows all of the enterprise projects which you have permission to access, and which contain at least one deliverable.

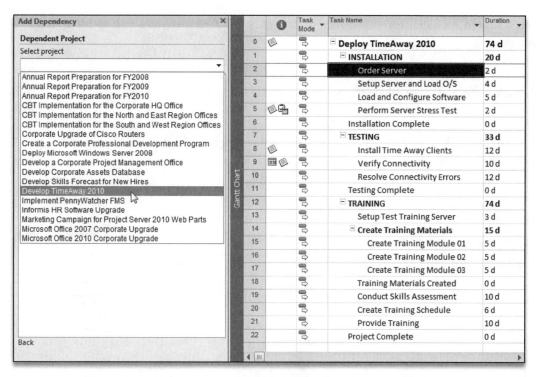

Figure 7 - 44: Select an enterprise project in the Select project pick list

Figure 7 - 45 shows the *Add Dependency* sidepane after I selected the Develop TimeAway 2010 project. Notice that the sidepane displays all of the deliverables in that enterprise project.

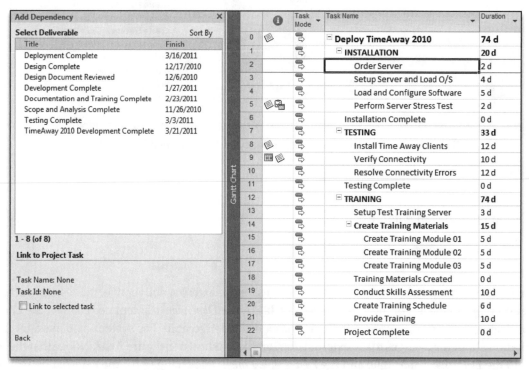

**Figure 7 - 45: Add Dependency sidepane shows
dependencies in the Develop TimeAway 2010 project**

5. Select a task in your enterprise project and then click the *Link to selected task* option in the *Add Dependency* sidepane.

6. Select an external deliverable in the *Select Deliverable* list in the *Add Dependency* sidepane.

7. Click the *Done* link when finished. The system displays the external deliverable dependency in the *Dependency* sidepane as shown in Figure 7 - 46.

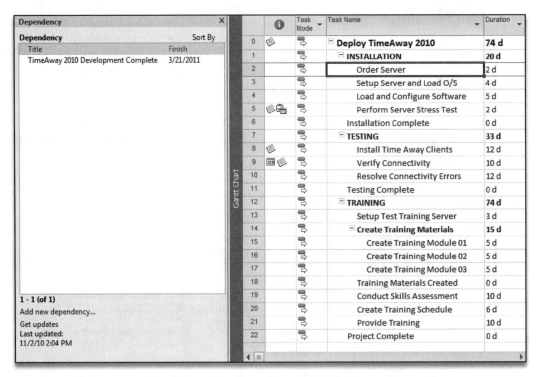

Figure 7 - 46: New deliverable dependency added in Dependency sidepane

8. Save and publish your enterprise project.

If the *Deliverable Start* date or *Deliverable Finish* date changes for the external deliverable, the system warns you with a red exclamation point to the left of the external deliverable in the *Dependency* sidepane. To view the changes to the external deliverable, float your mouse pointer over the external deliverable. The system displays a tooltip that provides information about the changes to the external deliverable, as shown in Figure 7 - 47. Notice that the tooltip indicates that both the *Deliverable Start* date and the *Deliverable Finish* date changed for the external deliverable.

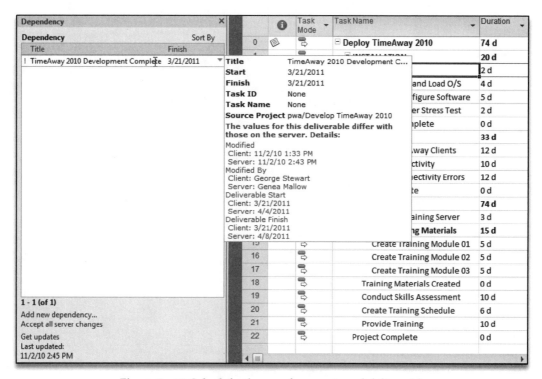

Figure 7 - 47: Schedule changes for an external deliverable

To update the project with the external deliverable information, click the *Accept all server changes* link at the bottom of the *Dependency* sidepane. The system displays the confirmation dialog shown in Figure 7 - 48. Click the *OK* button to update the deliverable dependency information. After updating the deliverable dependency, be sure to save and publish your enterprise project.

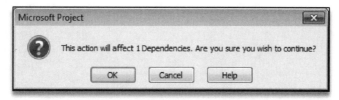

**Figure 7 - 48: Confirmation dialog to
update a deliverable dependency**

Module 08

Tracking Time and Task Progress

Learning Objectives

After completing this module, you will be able to:

- Create a new timesheet
- Report time on the My Timesheet page
- Plan and submit Administrative Time
- Create a Surrogate Timesheet for another resource
- Report progress on the Tasks page
- Use the Task Center
- Submit task updates from Outlook

Inside Module 08

Tracking Time in Project Web App

Project Server 2010 allows you to track both time and task progress using the Project Web App interface. Your organization can use a daily timesheet to track hours on all types of work, including both project and non-project work. Using the timesheet system, you can also track non-working time such as vacation or sick leave. Using the Timesheet system in Project Server 2010 allows your organization to account for every hour of work every day for all of your resources.

Your organization can also track task progress in enterprise projects using the default method of tracking progress defined by your Project Server administrator. Table 8 - 1 outlines the potential uses of Timesheets and Tasks Status tracking.

The first major topical section of the module reviews how to track time using the *Timesheets* page in Project Web App. The second major topical section of this module discusses how to track task progress using the *Tasks* page in Project Web App.

Function	Single Entry Mode	Double Entry Mode	Timesheet Stand Alone Mode	Tasks Stand Alone Mode
Timesheets	Timesheets track: • Billable hours • Non-billable hours • Administrative time • Project task progress Automatic data exchange with tasks	Timesheets track • Billable hours • Non-billable hours • Administrative time • Project task progress User initiated data exchange with tasks	Timesheets track • Administrative time No data exchange with tasks	Not used
Tasks	Work routing using Team tasks, Reassign task Management of Material resources	Tasks track of project task progress. User initiated data exchange with timesheets	Not used	Tasks track project task progress No data exchange with timesheets

Table 8 - 1: The Different Uses of Timesheets and Task Status Tracking

Single Entry Mode

Single Entry Mode enables you to enter your time once and have it feed both timesheets and task updates. Environments where tracking of project tasks and administrative time is important will typically use this mode as shown in Figure 8 - 1.

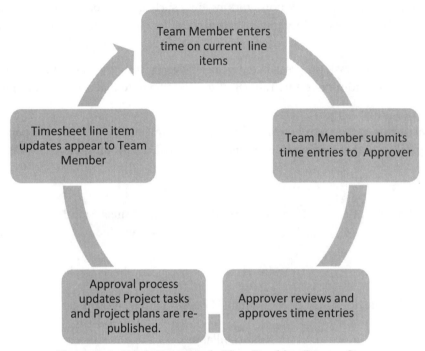

Figure 8 - 1: Single Entry Mode Time Tracking Process Steps

Double Entry Mode

Double Entry Mode enables you to separate task updates from timesheet entries. This capability is desirable in situations where customer billing uses timesheet data and task updates to keep the project plan up to date. For example, if you have a fixed bid contract, your billing must match a given number regardless of the actual number of hours invested in the project.

Standalone Modes

Standalone Modes indicate that you are using either timesheets or tasks but not using them together. Environments that have no billing need will likely not need timesheet capabilities. Environments that are only tracking time will not need task status capabilities.

The time tracking process is typically a repeated process that happens on a regular schedule. Many organizations have weekly time tracking reporting periods. The needs of your organization determine your time tracking reporting period length.

Timesheet Items Tracked

Timesheets help organizations determine where it is investing its efforts and whether there is sufficient capacity to maintain those efforts. Timesheets capture three types of data to fulfill this information need.

Project Tasks

This timesheet item represents your planned activities for a given time period to support the outcomes of the associated project.

Administrative Time Categories

This timesheet item represents a capture mechanism to reflect the number of hours you spend on non-project work. The default Project Server configuration has categories for *Administrative time, Sick Leave* and *Vacation*. Your Project Server administrator can add additional categories to meet your organization's specific needs.

Personal Tasks

Sometimes, your work does not fit in your project tasks or your administrative time categories. In this case, Project Server provides the ability to add personal tasks to your timesheet to capture this time.

Accessing Your Timesheet

To navigate to your timesheet, use any of the following methods as shown in Figure 8 - 2.

- To go to your current period timesheet, do the following:

    - Click the *Timesheet* link in the *My Work* section of the *Quick Launch* menu.

- To go to the *Manage Timesheets* page, do one of the following:

    - Click the *Manage Timesheet* link in the *Settings* section of the *Quick Launch* menu

    - Click the *Timesheets* link in the *Reminders* section of the page.

    - Click the ___ *unsubmitted timesheet* link in the *Reminders* section of the page (if available).

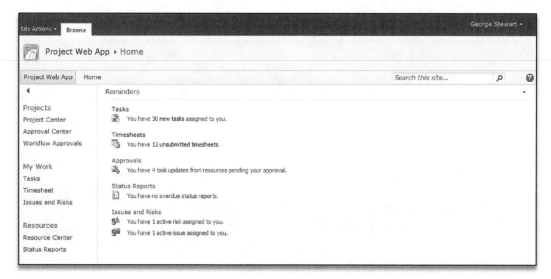

Figure 8 - 2: Project Web App Home Page

Understanding the Timesheet Page

The *Timesheet* page enables you to capture your time spent on all planned and administrative activities for the current time reporting period. New in Project Server 2010, when you first access the *Timesheet* link, Project Server automatically creates your timesheet for the current time reporting period.

To access your timesheet, click the *Timesheet* link in the *My Work* section of the Project Web App *Quick Launch* menu. When selected, you see the page similar to that appearing in Figure 8 - 3 . If you need more room horizontally to see your timesheet, click the *Triangle* button at the top of the *Quick Launch* menu, as highlighted in Figure 8 - 3.

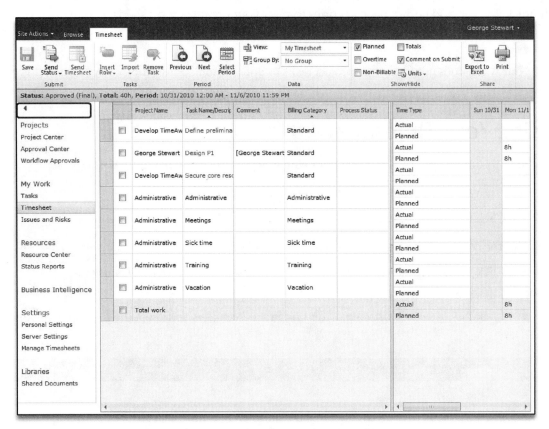

Figure 8 - 3: Project Server 2010 Timesheet

 You can collapse the *Quick Launch* menu to provide more horizontal room for the timesheet by selecting the *Triangle* button at the top of the *Quick Launch* menu.

Timesheet Ribbon

The *Timesheet* ribbon is new in Project Server 2010. This module covers all aspects of the *Timesheet* ribbon functionality. The initial items covered are the display control options. The default display of the *Timesheet* page includes these columns.

- Project Name

    - For administrative time categories, this column contains the term *Administrative*.

- Task Name/Administrative Time Description

    - Descriptive name of the timesheet line item

- Comment

    - Data field for you to add a comment related to this timesheet line item entry

- Billing Category

    - This optional field enables you to designate a billing category for a particular timesheet line item. For example, if the administrator set up a *Merger* billing category, you can set this value to designate a line item as a *Merger* effort.

- Process Status

    - Data field that informs you of the current state of the timesheet line item in regards to the approval cycle.

- To the right of the *Approval Status* column, you also see a timesheet grid containing one week of daily cells for reporting your work.

> The default settings in Project Server 2010 configure the *My Timesheet* page to allow the daily entry of work. Your Project Server administrator can change the configuration to allow users to enter an entire week of work for a seven-day period in a single cell.

Time Types

Each task in the timesheet includes two *Time* types by default, which is *Actual* and *Planned*. You use the first line to enter actual work hours. The second line displays the planned or scheduled work hours for the task. When you enter actual work hours for a task, Project Server 2010 assumes all hours are billable regular (non-overtime) work and it calculates the task cost using the *Standard Rate* value from the Enterprise Resource Pool. Some organizations, however, need to track overtime work in addition to regular work, and to differentiate between billable and non-billable work.

To add an additional *Time* type to track overtime work for each project task, click the *Overtime* checkbox in the *Show/Hide* section of the *Timesheet* ribbon as shown in Figure 8 - 4. For *Non-Billable* time, click the *Non-Billable* checkbox. These time types appear in the time phased entry grid on the right. Notice that *Overtime* and *Non-Billable Time* types only apply to project tasks.

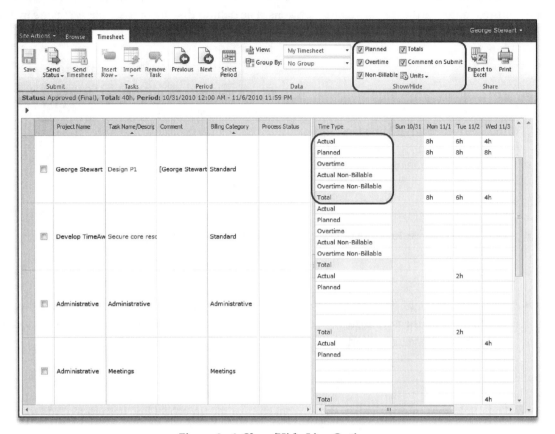

Figure 8 - 4: Show/Hide Line Options

To remove the lines for overtime work and non-billable work, click the appropriate checkboxes on the *TImesheet* ribbon.

Other Show/Hide Options

The *Show/Hide* section of the *Timesheet* ribbon also contains two other options. The *Comment on Submit* option determines whether a pop-up box into which you can enter timesheet level comments appears when you submit your timesheet. While the system enables this option by default, you can change it by unchecking the checkbox. The *Units* pick list enables you to decide the display formats of *Work, Duration* and *Date* fields on the page. For example, if you want to enter your updates as number of days, change the *Units* value for *Work* to *Days*.

The default unit used (minutes, hours, days, weeks) for time entered in the time phased grid is controlled by the *Units* pick list in the *Timesheet* ribbon.

Information Bar

The *Information* bar beneath the ribbon shows you information about the current timesheet period, the total number of hours entered and the current status of the timesheet. It turns *Yellow* when you make changes to the timesheet. This visual indicator helps remind you to save or submit your entries.

Period Selectors

By default, the timesheet opens in the current time reporting period. However, you may have cause to navigate to another time reporting period. As shown in Figure 8 - 5, you can either use the *Previous* and *Next* buttons to change periods or you can choose a specific period from the *Select Period* pick list.

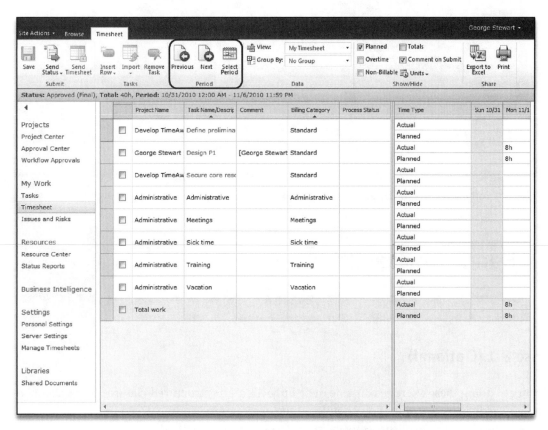

Figure 8 - 5: Period Navigation Ribbon Buttons

Changing Views and Grouping

The *View* pick list shown in Figure 8 - 6 enables you to select which *Timesheet* view to use. Your Project Server administrator determines the views that appear in this list.

The *Group By* pick list enables you to group your timesheet lines by process status or by project. Use *Process Status* grouping when you have a number of entries that are in progress or rejected so that you can see all of a given status together. Use *Group By Project* grouping when you are entering time for a number of project-related tasks.

Figure 8 - 6: Ribbon View/Grouping Options

Hands On Exercise

Exercise 8-1 (Optional)

If you are doing these exercises outside of MSProjectExperts structured classroom environment, and more than a week has passed since you completed the exercises in Module 07, complete this exercise to update your Deploy Training Advisor Software project to synchronize with the rest of the exercises in this module.

1. Using Project Professional 2010, connect to Project Server.

2. Open your Deploy Training Advisor Software project.

3. Click the *Project* tab to display the *Project* ribbon and in the *Schedule* section of the ribbon, click the *Move Project* button.

4. In the *Move Project* dialog, change the *New project start date* field to the date of the Monday following today's date and click the *OK* button. Click the *OK* button in the subsequent warning dialog.

5. Click the *File* tab and select the *Publish item* from the menu. Close your project and check it in.

Exercise 8-2

1. Log in to Project Web App and click the *Timesheet* link in the *My Work* section of the *Quick Launch* menu. If necessary, from the *Period* section of the *Timesheet* ribbon, click the *Next* button to advance to the period that includes the Monday date that you entered in Exercise 8-1.

2. Examine the *Planned* work and *Actual* work (if any) for both *Project* tasks and *Administrative* tasks during the reporting period.

3. Deselect the *Overtime* and *Non-Billable* items in the ribbon to hide the *Overtime Work* and *Non-Billable Work* lines from your timesheet.

4. Navigate to the *Manage Timesheets* page from the link in the *Settings* section of the *Quick Launch* menu and examine the time periods for existing timesheets, if any.

5. Click the *View* pick list in the ribbon and apply each of the available views.

Entering Time in the Timesheet

On the *Timesheet* page, you enter actual time spent on project and non-project work. There are a number of ways to enter time, including each of the following:

- Enter actual work manually in the daily timesheet grid for each of the items listed.

- Add a new line to the timesheet to enter time on an item not listed.

- Import the planned work as the actual work.

- If you are in Double Entry mode, you can import task progress from the *Tasks* page.

Entering actual work manually in the daily timesheet grid is simple. At the end of each day, enter the amount of time you spent that day on any task listed in the timesheet. In addition, you may want to add a comment in the *Comment* field for any task requiring additional information. After you enter your time each day, click the *Save* button to save the latest changes to your timesheet.

Figure 8 - 7 shows George Stewart's timesheet for the week of October 31. Notice that George entered a combination of task work and administrative time for the week. The *Information* bar shows that George has entered a total of 40 hours for the week.

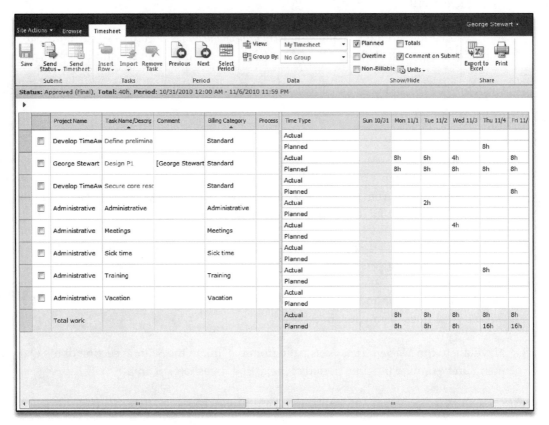

Figure 8 - 7: Timesheet Showing Tasks and Administrative Time

A final step for entering time on the *Timesheet* page may include adjusting the *Remaining Work* value according to your organization's methodology for submitting time. By default, the *Timesheet* view does not include the *Remaining Work* field. Instead, you should change your view to *My Work* to see this data column or have your administrator add this field to the *My Timesheet* view. The system displays the *Remaining Work* value according to the units you set as mentioned earlier in this section. Enter your remaining work for the task, if appropriate.

Warning: You can only edit the value in the *Remaining Work* column if your organization uses the *Only allow task updates via Tasks and Timesheets* option in Project Server 2010.

With this option enabled, you must enter all time and task progress in either the *Timesheet* page or the *Tasks* page. If your organization does not use this option, the system locks the *Remaining Work* column on the *My Timesheet* page.

Adding a New Line to a Timesheet

You may occasionally work on an assignment that is either not listed on your timesheet or is of a category of work that needs special tracking. Figure 8 - 8 shows the three kinds of work items that Project Server enables you to add to your timesheet. The *Timesheet Items Tracked* section of this document describes these items at a high level. Let us review an example of how to add each item type and the reasons for the addition.

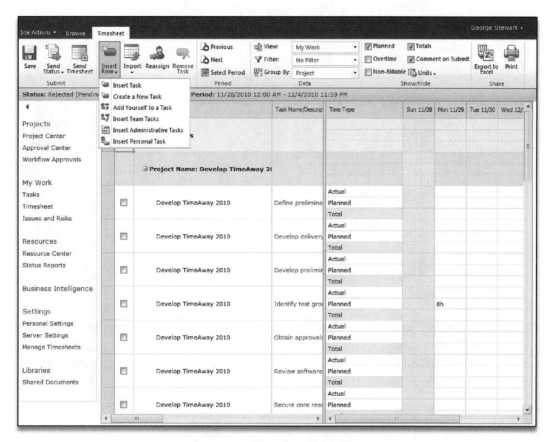

Figure 8 - 8: Timesheet Insert Row

For example, on Friday, November 12, George Stewart worked 2 hours on documenting "Lessons Learned" on the TimeAway 2010 project, as he wanted to include some lessons from recent issues. His assignment for this task is not for the current week. Because his organization requires resources to log all activities performed, George captures this time by adding a new line on his timesheet. To add a new timesheet line, click the *Add Lines* button. Project Server 2010 displays the *Select Task* dialog shown in Figure 8 - 9.

In the *Add an Existing Task* dialog, you can choose a task assignment from any project in which you have a current assignment. Click the *Project* pick list to select the project from which to retrieve the task. Click the *Task Hierarchy* pick list to narrow down the task selection. The *Task Hierarchy* field reads all Outline Level 1 tasks in the project plan as a fair number of Project Managers use these top-level tasks to denote project phases. Finally, select one of the tasks in the *Select from Existing Assignments* pick list. At the bottom of the dialog, you can add a comment as to why you are adding the task.

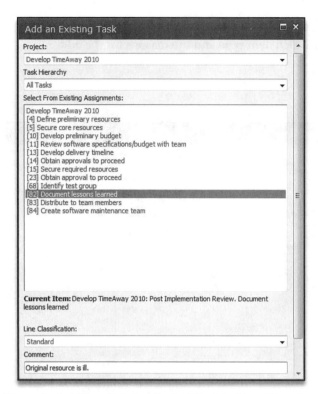

Figure 8 - 9: Add an Existing Project Task to Your Timesheet

George was an unplanned participant in a training class this week. His organization considers training as *Administrative* time ; therefore, he adds this time to his timesheet using the *Insert Administrative Tasks* option from the *Timesheets* ribbon. Figure 8 - 10 shows the dialog that appears once you select that option. You select the *Administrative Time* category on which to apply the time and add a description of the activity. Click the *OK* button to add it to the timesheet.

Figure 8 - 10: Add an Administrative Task to Your Timesheet

George Stewart also participates on a Merger System selection team as his company recently acquired another company. For tax accounting reasons, George's company tracks all merger activities. George attended a merger meeting for someone else and needs to account for this time. A personal task fulfills this need.

Selecting the *Insert Personal Task* option from the *Timesheet* ribbon yields the dialog shown in Figure 8 - 11. George types a name for this line, sets the category to *Merger* and adds a comment. Once he clicks the *OK* button, the line appears in his timesheet and he can enter time against this item.

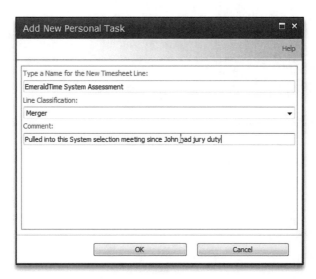

Figure 8 - 11: Add a Personal Task to Your Timesheet

Removing a Line from a Timesheet

When you need to remove a timesheet line, select the option checkbox at the left end of the line, and then click the *Remove Task* button. Project Server 2010 immediately removes the line from the timesheet.

> You are not prompted prior to removing a timesheet line so use this option carefully.

> If you accidentally delete a timesheet line, the only way to restore it is to delete the entire timesheet and recreate it. When you recreate the timesheet, the system restores the deleted line and restores all of the actual work hours you previously entered. I discuss how to delete a timesheet later in this section of the module.

Replacing Actual Work with Planned Work

Another method for entering time in your timesheet is to enter planned work as actual work for one or more selected tasks scheduled during the selected timesheet period. This feature enables you to enter your time rapidly on a large number of tasks. You then make manual adjustments only for those tasks where planned and actual values do not match. Since this feature works on the selected task, you can select the tasks upon which to perform this action. To perform it on all tasks, select the *Selector* column heading and select the *Select All* option prior to selecting the *Replace Actual with Planned* option. Figure 8 - 12 shows the *Timesheet* page showing the planned work for two tasks scheduled this week.

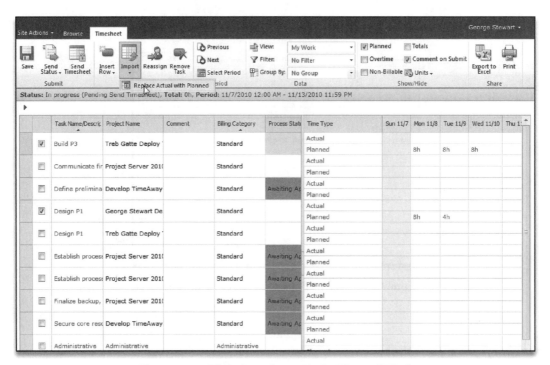

Figure 8 - 12: Timesheet shows Tasks Planned Work

To replace actual work with planned work, select the option checkbox to the left of each task you want to update and then click the *Replace Actual with Planned* button. The system updates the actual work using the planned work for each day, as shown in Figure 8 - 13. Note the *Information* bar will appear *Yellow* after performing this option and the *Process Status* values will change to *Not Submitted*, indicating that you have not yet submitted this information to the approver.

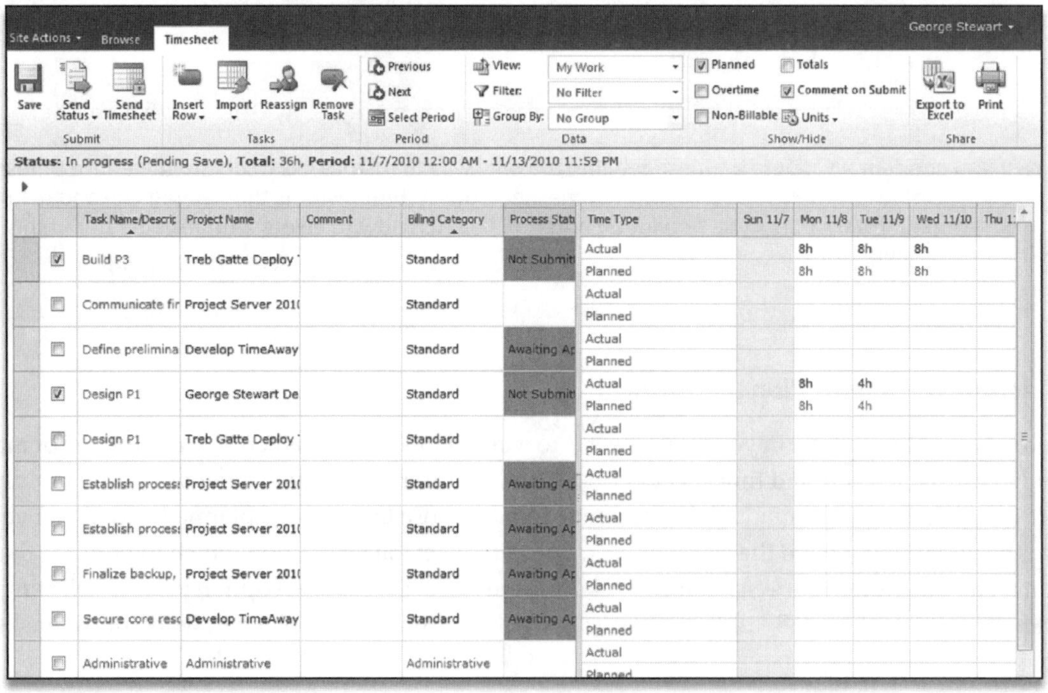

Figure 8 - 13: Replace actual work using planned work in the timesheet

After you replace the actual work using planned work, remember to click the *Save* button to save your timesheet.

Warning: Updating actual work from planned work is a quick way to enter time in your timesheet, but it is not a good way to enter accurate information. In the real world, rarely does actual work ever match planned work for a task.

Importing Task Progress

This section is only applicable if your organization uses Double Entry mode.

If you already entered progress for a task on the *Tasks* page or the *Assignment Details* page, you can import the progress from either page to the *Timesheet* page.

For example, Figure 8 - 14 shows the *Tasks* page for George Stewart's assignment during the week of November 7. Notice that George entered his daily Actual Work in the timesheet grid for the Design P1 task that week.

The *Imported Task Progress* function only works for Saved or Sent time entries on the *Tasks* page.

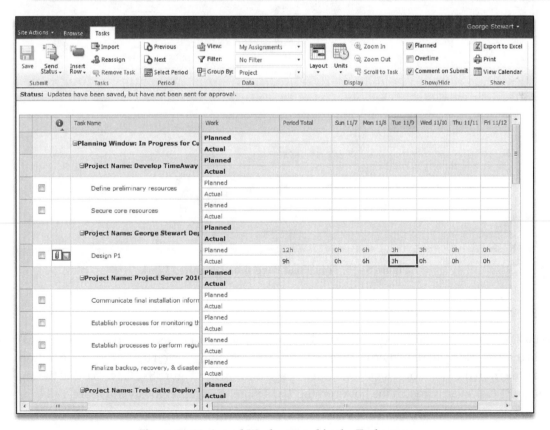

Figure 8 - 14: Actual Work entered in the Tasks page

Figure 8 - 15 shows George Stewart's timesheet for the week of November 7. Notice that the *Planned* work for the Design P1 task differs from the *Actual* work he entered on the *Tasks* page.

 The *Import Task Progress* function only works on Saved timesheet entries on the *Timesheet* page. Attempting to import task progress on a modified but not saved timesheet entry will result in updated planning time but no change in actual time.

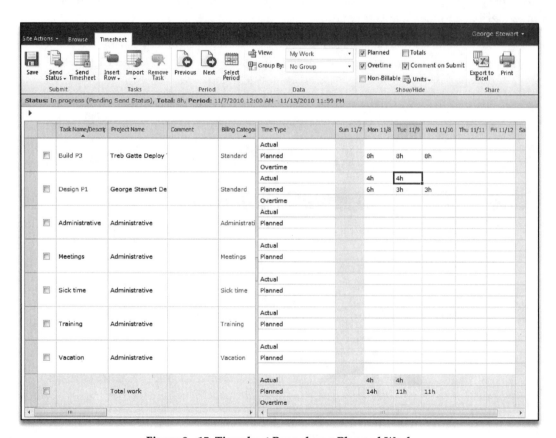

Figure 8 - 15: Timesheet Page shows Planned Work

To import task progress from the *Tasks* page or the *Assignment Details* page, select the option checkbox to the left of the task name in the *Timesheet* page and then click the *Import Task Progress* option on the *Import* menu button. The system imports the time from the *Tasks* (or *Assignment Details*) page as shown in Figure 8 - 16. Notice that the imported hours for the Design P1 task exactly match the hours on the *Tasks* page shown previously in Figure 8 - 14.

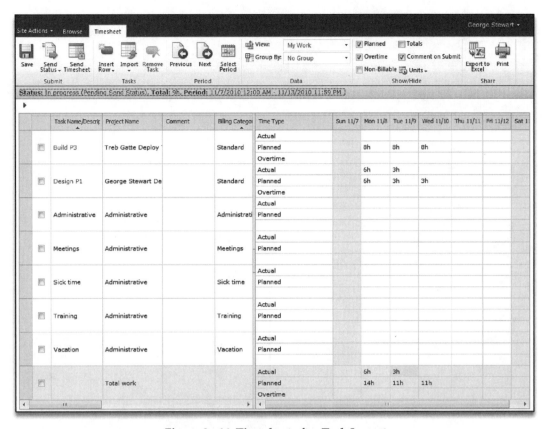

Figure 8 - 16: Timesheet after Task Import

After you import task progress to your timesheet, remember to click the *Save* button to save your timesheet.

Managing Timesheets

The *Manage Timesheets* page shown in Figure 8 - 17 enables you to create new timesheets, review timesheet submission status and delete your timesheets. The *Manage Timesheets* page shows the list of timesheets you already submitted, timesheets that are currently in-progress, and timesheets ready to create. I cover each of these functions in detail in later sections of this module.

The *Manage Timesheet* page lists timesheets in descending order by timesheet period. Therefore, your current timesheet always appears at the top of the page.

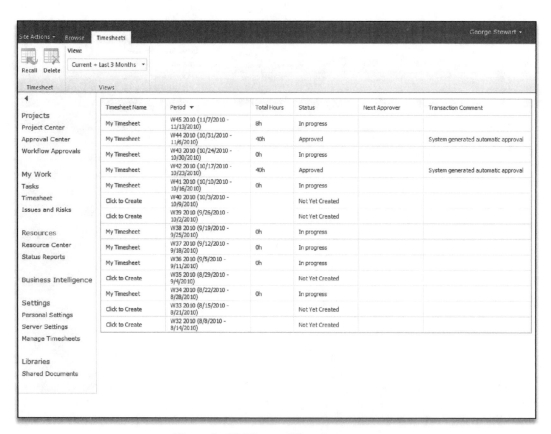

Figure 8 - 17: Manage Timesheets page

The *Manage Timesheets* ribbon includes a *View* pick list containing a list of views available for the page. The first time you access the *Manage Timesheets* page, the default view is *Current + Last Three Months*. If you click the *View* pick list, the system offers you the following views that control what timeframe the system uses to filter your list of timesheets:

- Current + Last 3 Months

- Next 6 Months + Last 3 Months

- Last 6 Months

- Last 12 Months

- All Timesheets

- Created and in progress

The view names explain each view, so further detail is not necessary. For most users, the default *Current + Last 3 Months* view suffices. The system reapplies this view if you navigate to another page in PWA and then return to the *Manage Timesheets* page.

The fastest way to create a new timesheet for a past or current time period is to click the *Click to create* link to the left of the timesheet period in the grid. Project Server 2010 creates your new timesheet using the default information specified by your Project Server administrator, which is set to display all tasks scheduled during the selected time period, plus any administrative tasks required by your organization.

Planning Time Away from Work

The default settings in Project Server 2010 prevent resources from booking unapproved vacation time. Instead, the system imposes a formal process for submission and approval of vacation time. Note, your Project Administrator can choose to extend this approval process requirement to other administrative time categories.

 Administrative time categories that require approval should be planned.

Entering Planned Administrative Time

George decides to visit New York City from December 5 to December 11 to meet his brother and to do some holiday shopping. This requires George to request a week of vacation.

To submit his vacation time request for approval by his timesheet manager, George clicks the *Manage Timesheets* link on the *Quick Launch* menu. The system displays a screen similar to Figure 8 - 18.

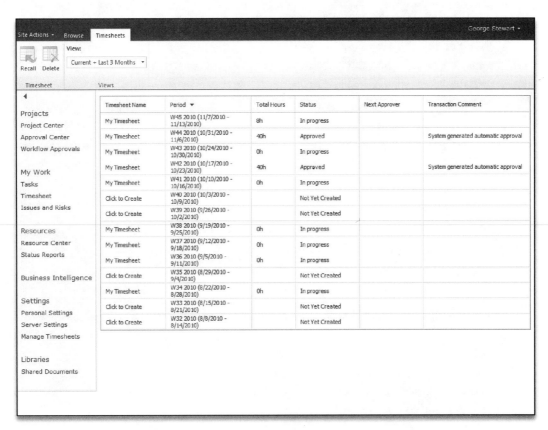

Figure 8 - 18: Initial Manage Timesheets page

George's timesheet for December 5 is not visible. George then selects the *Next 6 Months + Last 3 Months* value in the *Views* pick list to change the period. He clicks the *Click to Create* link to create the timesheet for the week of December 5 as shown in Figure 8 - 19.

Since the vacation time falls in a timesheet period for an uncreated timesheet, Project Server automatically sets the timesheet's status as *In Progress*. This status will not change until you submit actual time entries for that week.

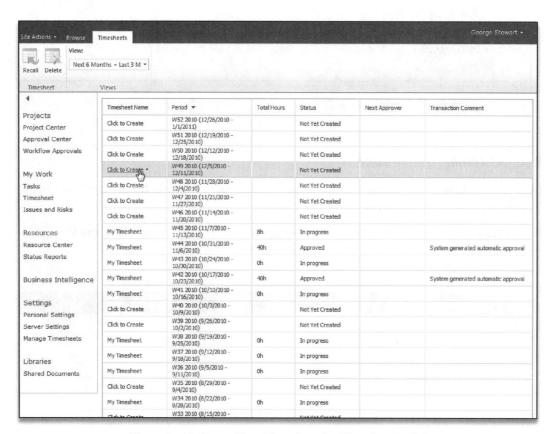

Figure 8 - 19: Create New Timesheet for Planning Period

 Warning: Do not enter the planned vacation time on the *Actual* line. Doing so will mark this time as *Actual* work rather than *Planned* work.

George enters 8hrs for each workday for the week as shown in Figure 8 - 20. He also enters *"Off to New York"* in the *Comments* column so that his timesheet approval manager knows why he is requesting this time. You may need to move the splitter bar to see this column in the left grid.

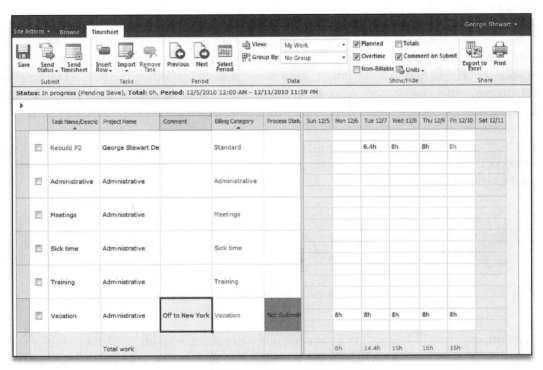

Figure 8 - 20: Enter Planned Vacation Time

The *Process Status* column shows the current state of the entry. *Not Submitted* indicates that you have not sent the status to a manager yet. Check the *Vacation Administrative* line and click the *Send Status* menu button to select the *Selected Tasks* option as shown in Figure 8 - 21. If you checked the *Comment on Submit* option in the ribbon, you see a comment box prior to final submission. Click the *OK* button to submit the planned time to your timesheet approval manager for review and approval.

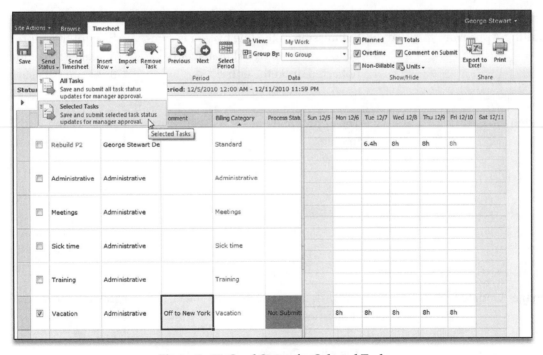

Figure 8 - 21: Send Status for Selected Tasks

Viewing the Submission Status

The *Process Status* column captures the current submission status of a *Timesheet* line. This column replaces the graphical status indicators of Project Server 2010 with an easier to understand text value. The field is blank normally when the current status requires no user action. When Project Server has a process status that requires user attention, the system adds a text status and color highlight to draw your attention.

To view the current approval status of the vacation request, click the *Manage Timesheets* link in the *Quick Launch* menu and click the link of the timesheet containing the vacation request. The system displays the timesheet for the selected period. Table 8 - 2 shows the *Process Status* values that indicate the current state of George's request.

Process Status Value	Color	What it means	User Action Required
[Blank]	None	Timesheet line is in an approved state.	None
Not Submitted	Red	You have not saved or submitted your change to this timesheet line.	Perform one of the following actions: Save Send Status Send Timesheet
Awaiting Approval	Red	Submission of the line by you is complete but the approval manager has not acted upon the entry.	Prompt the approval manager for action if this state persists.
Rejected	Red	The approval manager rejected your update.	Make changes to the entry and resubmit. OR Accept the rejection and remove the line.
Manager Updated	Red	The task manager changed the task properties.	Review the task.

Table 8 - 2: Process Status values

Hands On Exercise

Exercise 8-3

Enter time in a new timesheet.

1. Navigate to your *Timesheet* page by clicking the *Timesheet* link in the *My Work* section of the *Quick Launch* menu. If necessary, from the *Period* section of the *Timesheet* ribbon, click the *Next* button to advance to the period that includes the Monday date that you entered in Exercise 8-1.

2. For the timesheet currently displayed, enter the following *Actual* work for the Design P1 task for your Deploy Training Advisor Software project:

   - Monday – 8 hours
   - Tuesday – 6 hours
   - Wednesday – 4 hours
   - Thursday – 0 hours
   - Friday – 8 hours

3. Enter 2 hours of time for *Administrative* work on Tuesday.

4. Enter 4 hours for meetings on Wednesday.

5. Delete the *Sick Time* timesheet line.

6. Enter 8 hours of training time for Thursday.

7. In the *Show/Hide* section of the *Timesheet* ribbon, select the *Totals* checkbox if it is not already selected. Examine the total hours entered in the *Total* field in the information bar under the ribbon.

8. Click the *Save* button to save your current timesheet information.

9. Click the *Browse* tab in the ribbon.

10. Click the Project Web App link to return to the home page.

Exercise 8-4

Plan and submit vacation time for a future time reporting period.

1. Click the *Manage Timesheets* link from the *Settings* section of the *Quick Launch* menu.

2. Change the view to *Next 6 Months + Last 3 Months*.

3. Click the *Click to Create* link for the topmost timesheet.

4. In the *Show/Hide* section of the *Timesheet* ribbon, select the *Planned* checkbox.

5. Enter 8 hours of planned time for each day of the week in the *Vacation* line item in the *Administrative* items at the bottom of the timesheet.

6. Click the *Send Timesheet* button. In the *Send Timesheet* dialog, click the *Browse* button to select Linda Erickson in the *Sent Timesheet to* field, if she is not the default recipient.

Submitting a Timesheet for Approval

After you enter your time for the week, you must submit your timesheet for approval to the person designated as your timesheet approver. Before you submit your timesheet, however, remember that you use the timesheet to submit actual hours worked on tasks and on hours spent on administrative time.

Project Server does not prevent you from entering actual time for tasks that you did not plan for this period. Life sometimes has a way of interfering with your plans and Project Server provides flexibility in these cases. It is the duty of the timesheet approver to approve or reject your timesheet entry.

George Stewart's car broke down on the way back to the office after a late lunch and he missed two hours of the workday. In Figure 8 - 22, he logs two hours of vacation time on his timesheet although there is no planned time for this activity.

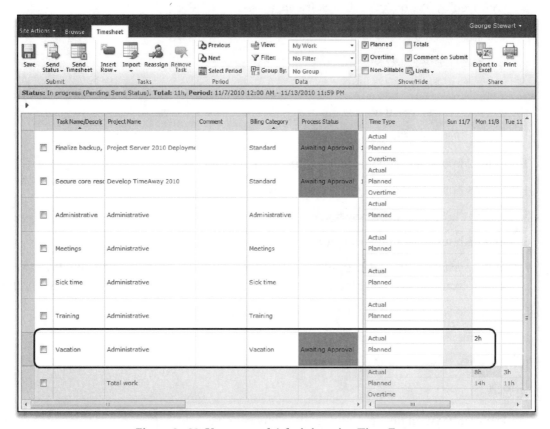

Figure 8 - 22: Unapproved Administrative Time Entry

 If your tracking routine includes importing time from your timesheet to the *My Tasks* page, import your time to the *My Tasks* page before you submit your timesheet.

To submit a timesheet, click the *Send Timesheet* button. Project Server 2010 displays the *Send Timesheet* dialog, shown in Figure 8 - 23. By default, the person shown in the *Send Timesheet to* field is the person designated as your timesheet manager by your organization's Project Server administrator.

Figure 8 - 23: Send Timesheet dialog

 If your Project Server administrator specified you as your own timesheet manager, you do not see the *Send Timesheet to* field in the *Send Timesheet* dialog.

If the person shown in the *Send Timesheet to* field is not correct, click the *Browse* button. The system displays the *Pick Resource* dialog shown in Figure 8 - 24. This dialog contains the names of users who have permission to approve your timesheet.

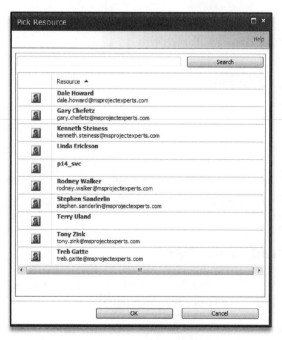

Figure 8 - 24: Pick Resource dialog

The *Pick Resource* dialog displays only twenty names at a time in the dialog. If your organization has more than twenty users who can approve timesheets, scroll to the bottom of the dialog and click the *Next* link in the lower right corner of the dialog to see more users.

In the list of possible timesheet approvers, double-click the name of your timesheet approver. The system enters the selected user's name in the *Send Timesheet to* field in the *Send Timesheet* dialog. Enter any additional comments about the timesheet in the *Comments* field and then click the *OK* button to complete your timesheet submission.

To view the current approval status of a timesheet, click the *Manage Timesheets* link in the *Quick Launch* menu. Project Server 2010 displays the *Manage Timesheets* page as shown in Figure 8 - 25. Refer back to Table 8 - 2 where I cover Process Status definitions.

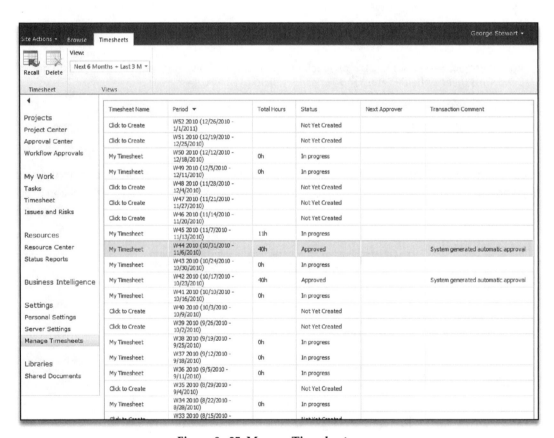

Figure 8 - 25: Manage Timesheets page

Responding to a Rejected Timesheet

In the normal flow of timesheet approvals, your timesheet manager approves your timesheets. However, a timesheet manager could reject a timesheet for a variety of reasons, such as:

- You submit a timesheet containing a factual error, such as when you fat finger the number 23 when you intended to type the number 3.

- You report work that totals greater than 24 hours in a single day.

- You create a new line of timesheet information to document time that does not fit into any of the tasks on your timesheet, but your timesheet manager needs you to add the time to the administrative task instead.

- You fail to report time on a day when you actually worked.

In situations like this, your timesheet manager may reject your timesheet and ask you to correct the troublesome information. For example, in the timesheet shown in Figure 8 - 26, George Stewart removed 20 hours of vacation time from his timesheet, but failed to enter any actual work in its place. Because his company requires resources to submit at least 40 hours of actual work each week results in the rejection of George Stewart's timesheet for the week of November 7.

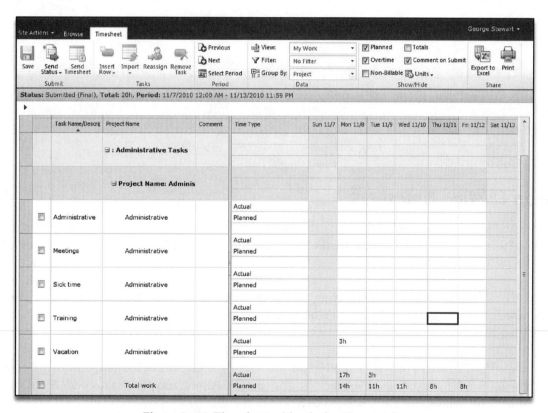

Figure 8 - 26: Timesheet with missing time entries

When a timesheet manager rejects a timesheet, Project Server automatically sends an e-mail message to notify the resource of the rejection, assuming your Project administrator enabled notifications. The system also shows the timesheet status as *Rejected* on the *Timesheets* page, as shown in Figure 8 - 27.

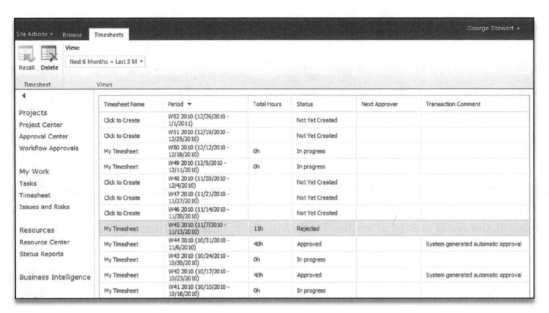

Figure 8 - 27: Rejected Timesheet

To respond to a rejected timesheet, click the *My Timesheet* link to the left of the rejected timesheet on the *Manage Timesheets* page. The system opens the *Timesheet* page for the rejected timesheet. Correct the timesheet information that shows a *Rejected* process status to address the reason for the rejection. Click the *Send Timesheet* button when you complete your entries.

Editing an Existing Timesheet

If you entered and saved your timesheet hours yesterday, you know that you must return to the timesheet today to add your actual work for the day. To edit the current time reporting period's timesheet, click the *Timesheet* link in the *Quick Launch* menu.

If the timesheet is not for the current time reporting period, click the *Manage Timesheets* link in the *Quick Launch* menu to access the *Manage Timesheets* page shown previously in Figure 8 - 27. Find the correct time reporting period and click the *My Timesheet* link for that timesheet.

Project Server 2010 loads the *Timesheet* page for the selected timesheet. Use any of the methods discussed previously to enter your actual work for today and then click the *Save* button. After the system saves your timesheet, click the *Manage Timesheets* link in the *Quick Launch* menu to return to the *Manage Timesheets* page.

New to Project Server 2010: If your Project Manager publishes a new task that is assigned to you for the current period, the system automatically adds the new task to your timesheet.

Recalling a Submitted Timesheet

There may come a time when you need to edit information on a timesheet that you previously submitted, such as to correct a mistake or make changes. By default, Project Server 2010 does not allow you to edit a submitted timesheet and locks all of the cells normally open for data entry. Before you can edit a submitted timesheet, you must recall it. To recall a timesheet do the following:

- Click the *Manage Timesheets* link in the *Quick Launch* menu.

- Select the row of the timesheet to recall.

- Click the *Recall* button on the ribbon.

- The system displays the confirmation dialog shown in Figure 8 - 28.

- Click the *OK* button to recall the timesheet.

- Project Server 2010 displays the *Timesheet* page for the selected timesheet.

Figure 8 - 28: Timesheet recall confirmation dialog

After recalling the timesheet, Project Server 2010 unlocks all data entry cells and resets the status of the timesheet to *In Progress*.

 You can recall timesheets with a *Submitted* or *Approved* status.

 Recalling and resubmitting your timesheet has no effect on any task progress you may have reported through this timesheet period.

Deleting a Timesheet

There may come a time when you need to delete an entire timesheet and recreate it. This can result from a variety of situations, such as when you totally "mess up" a timesheet and want to start over.

Do the following to delete a timesheet:

- Click the *Manage Timesheets* link in the *Quick Launch* menu.

- Select the row of the timesheet to recall.

- Click the *Delete* button on the ribbon.

- The system displays the confirmation dialog shown in Figure 8 - 29.

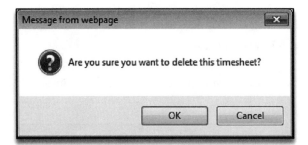

Figure 8 - 29: Confirmation dialog to delete a timesheet

- Click the *OK* button to delete the timesheet.

- Project Server 2010 deletes the timesheet and changes the timesheet name for that period to *Click to Create*.

- To recreate the timesheet, click the *Click to Create* link for the designated timesheet period.

Hands On Exercise

Exercise 8-5

Work with an existing timesheet.

1. Click the *Manage Timesheets* link from the *Settings* section of the *Quick Launch* menu. On the *Manage Timesheets* page, click the name of the timesheet you used in Exercise 8-2. Note that this timesheet shows an *In progress* value in the *Status* field and contains 40 hours of actual work.

2. Click the *Send Timesheet* button.

3. In the *Send Timesheet* dialog, notice the name listed in the *Send Timesheet to* field. Click the *Browse* button and select Linda Erickson from the *Pick Resource* dialog and click the *OK* button. Enter a comment in the *Comment* section, and then click the *OK* button.

4.   From the *Settings* section of the *Quick Launch* menu, click the *Manage Timesheets* link and select the same timesheet that you just submitted, but do not click on the name.

5.   In the *Timesheet* section of the *Timesheets* ribbon, click the *Recall* button and click the *OK* button in the confirmation dialog.

6.   From the *Manage Timesheets* page, click the name of the timesheet that you just recalled. Then, on the *Timesheet* page click the *Send Timesheet* button.

7.   Click the *Browse* tab on the ribbon and click the name of the Project Web App to return to the home page.

Tracking Task Progress in Project Web App

In most organizations, the purpose for tracking time in Project Server 2010 is to track task progress as well. Task progress information directly affects the enterprise projects in your Project Server 2010 database. The system offers your organization four methods for tracking task progress. The difference between each tracking method is the information that the system collects, as detailed below:

- **Percent of Work Complete** allows resources to enter % Work Complete and a Remaining Work estimate on each task assignment.

- **Actual Work Done and Work Remaining** allows resources to enter the cumulative Actual Work value and to adjust the Remaining Work estimate on each task assignment.

- **Hours of Work Done per Period** allows resources to enter the hours of Actual Work completed for the current time period and to adjust the Remaining Work estimate on each task assignment.

- **Free Form** allows resources to enter their work using whichever of the previous three methods is most convenient and Project Server calculates the requisite values.

Percent of Work Complete is the system default method of tracking progress unless your organization selects another method.

I discussed each of these tracking methods in Module 01 and demonstrated how each method controls how Project Server 2010 displays both the *Tasks* page and the *Assignment Details* page. Refer back to Module 01 to review this information.

Understanding the Tasks Page

To begin the process of tracking task progress, launch your Internet Explorer application and navigate to your Project Web App Home page. As you see in Figure 8 - 30, George Stewart has 30 new tasks assigned to him.

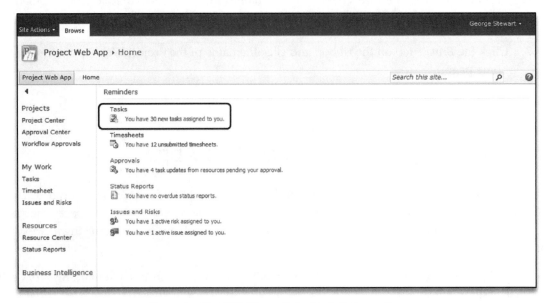

Figure 8 - 30: PWA Home Page Task Information

To navigate to the *Tasks* page, use any of the following methods:

- Click the *Tasks* link in the *My Work* section of the *Quick Launch* menu.

- Click the *Tasks* link in the *Reminders* section of the page.

- Click the ___ *new tasks* link in the *Reminders* section of the page (if available).

Project Server 2010 displays the *Tasks* page, shown in Figure 8 - 31.

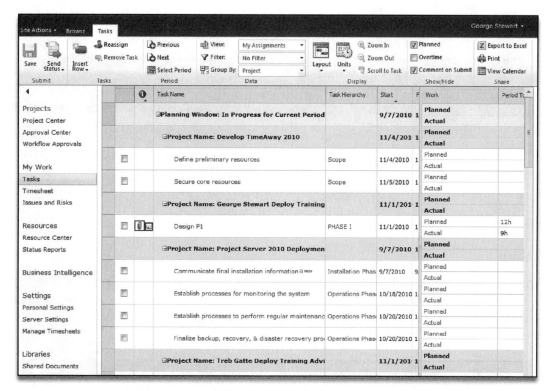

Figure 8 - 31: Tasks Page

Tasks Ribbon

The *Tasks* ribbon is new in Project Server 2010. This module covers all aspects of the *Tasks* ribbon functionality.

Show/Hide Options

The *Show/Hide* ribbon section also contains options that control the information presentation. Checking a box indicates you want to see that information.

The first two options relate to which time types the system displays. Each task includes two time types by default, which is *Actual* and *Planned*. You use the second line to enter actual work hours. The first line displays the planned or scheduled work hours for the task.

To add an additional time type to track overtime work for each project task, click the *Overtime* checkbox in the *Show/Hide* section of the *Tasks* ribbon as shown in Figure 8 - 32. All selected types now appear in the time phased entry grid on the right.

The *Comment on Submit* option determines whether a pop-up box where you enter timesheet level comments appears when you submit your timesheet. You can change the default option to show this dialog by unchecking the checkbox.

Figure 8 - 32: Tasks Show/Hide Options

The default unit used for time (minutes, hours, days, weeks) entered in the time phased grid is controlled by the *Units* pick list on the *Tasks* ribbon.

Period Selectors

By default, the *Tasks* page opens in the current time reporting period. However, you may have cause to navigate to another time reporting period. As shown in Figure 8 - 33, you can either use the *Previous* and *Next* buttons to change periods <u>or</u> you can choose a specific period from the *Select Period* pick list.

Figure 8 - 33: Period Selectors

View Calendar

The *View Calendar* option enables the user to see their tasks visualized as a calendar. Clicking the *View Calendar* button as shown in Figure 8 - 34 takes you to the page shown in Figure 8 - 35.

Figure 8 - 34: View Calendar button

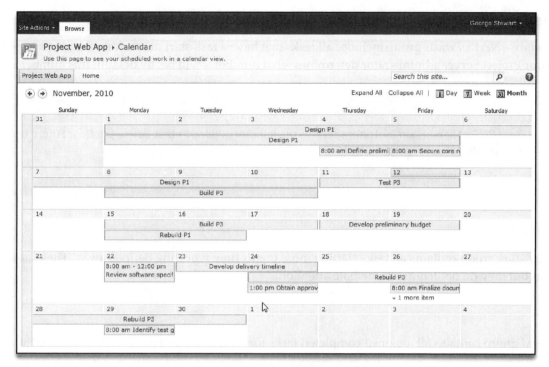

Figure 8 - 35: View Calendar page

The calendar can display by day, week or month. Clicking an individual task takes you to the *Assignment Details* page for that task.

Grouping and Views

By default, the system displays all tasks in the *Planning Window* grouping with tasks sorted by task start date. The *Planning Window* groups all of your tasks into four groups to facilitate your focus on the immediate tasks:

- In Progress for Current Period

- Near Future - Next x Periods

- Distant Future

- Completed

In Progress for Current Period

The *In Progress for Current Period* group includes all incomplete tasks which either have a task start date or task finish date less than or equal to the last day of the current period. Project 2010 no longer deems tasks as late; but rather is not currently complete. They appear at the top of the *Tasks* page to ensure they get proper attention.

Near Future – Next x Periods

The *Near Future – Next x Periods* group includes all tasks that have a task start date within the next x time reporting periods. Your Project Server administrator determines what number x will be. By default, this number is two.

> Your Project Server administrator specifies the number of periods that define the Near Future task group. The default value is 2 periods.

Distant Future

The *Distant Future* group contains all tasks starting more than x time reporting periods away. These tasks are your assignments but they do not require immediate attention.

Completed

The *Completed* group contains all assigned completed tasks for your use if you need to reference this information.

Fields

By default, Project Server 2010 displays the following columns in the *Tasks* page:

- Information

- Task Name

- Start

- Finish

- Remaining Work

- % Work Complete

- Work

- Actual Work

- Process Status

-

The *Information* column includes icons to denote task notes using a yellow note icon and a paperclip icon to denote linked issues, risks and documents.

Process Status

The *Process Status* column captures the current submission status of a *Task* line. This column replaces the graphical status indicators of Project Server 2010 with an easier to understand text value. The field is blank normally when the current status requires no user action. When Project Server has a Process Status that requires user attention, the system adds a text status and color highlight to draw your attention as shown in Table 8 - 3.

Process Status Value	Color	What it means	User Action Required
[Blank]	None	Timesheet line is in an approved state.	None
Not Submitted	Purple	You have not saved or submitted your change to this timesheet line.	Perform one of the following actions: • Save • Send Status • Send Timesheet
Awaiting Approval	Red	Submission of the line by you is complete but the approval manager has not acted upon the entry.	Prompt the approval manager for action if this state persists.
Rejected	Red	The approval manager rejected your update.	Make changes to the entry and resubmit. OR Accept the rejection and remove the line.
Manager Updated	Red	The task manager changed the task properties	Review the task.
Save Needed	Purple	You changed a task value but have not yet saved the change.	Save or exit without saving

Table 8 - 3: Process Status values

To rearrange the order of the fields, click and hold on the column header and drag the column to the desired location. The cursor changes to a four arrow cross to indicate the proper placement for dragging as shown in Figure 8 - 36.

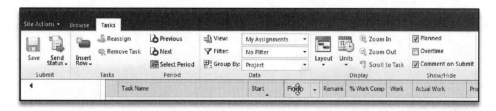

Figure 8 - 36: Example of Cursor Change for Column Rearrangement

Units

The *Units* pick list enables you to decide the display formats of *Work, Duration* and *Date* fields on the page as shown in Figure 8 - 37. For example, if you want to enter your updates as number of days, change the *Units* value for *Work* to *Days*.

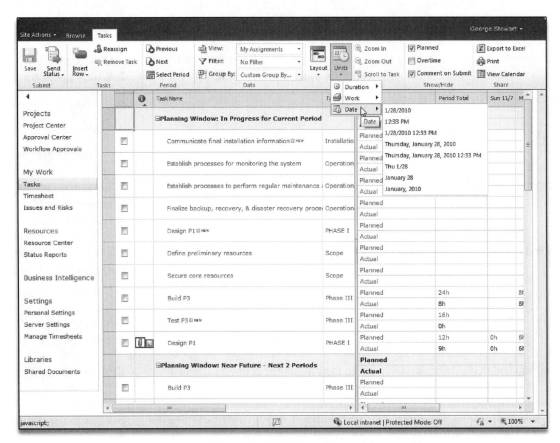

Figure 8 - 37: Units selector

 The default unit used for time (minutes, hours, days, weeks) entered in the time phased grid is controlled by the *Units* pick list in the *Task* ribbon.

Using the Timephased Data Layout

The *Tasks* page offers three screen layouts for your use. By default, the *Tasks* page displays the *Timephased Data* layout as shown in Figure 8 - 38. The right side of the page contains a data entry grid organized by day or week, where the user can enter actual and overtime data. This layout is best for hours per day or hours per week time entry.

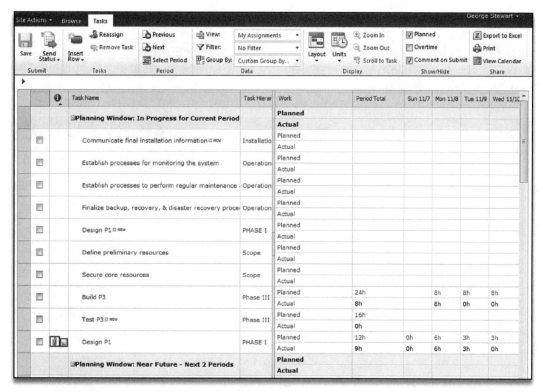

Figure 8 - 38: Timephased Data layout

Using the Gantt Chart Layout

The *Gantt Chart* layout, shown in Figure 8 - 39, provides the user with a way to visualize the relationships between their tasks. There are times where no graphics will show. Remember the current period is always the default so you may need to scroll to the appropriate place in the Gantt chart to see your tasks. The *Scroll to Task* button provides a quick way to do this. Select the desired task, then click the *Scroll to Task* button on the ribbon. The Gantt Chart graphics for that task come into view. The *Zoom In/Out* buttons also enable you to change the timescale used for the Gantt chart. By default, the view is at the day level. However, you can zoom out to see items at the month level.

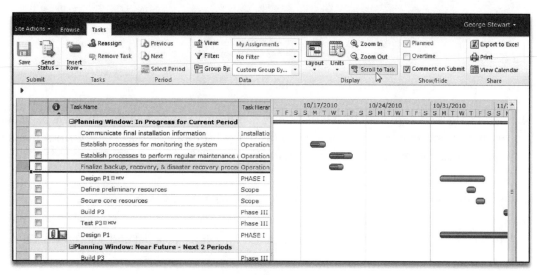

Figure 8 - 39: Gantt layout

Using the Sheet Layout

The *Sheet* layout shown in Figure 8 - 40, provides a simple list view of your tasks by removing the right side time-phased data entry grid. This layout best serves organizations that are using % Complete tracking and do not need the detail provided by the data entry grid.

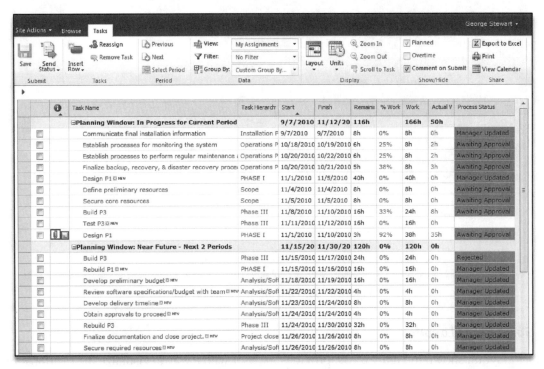

Figure 8 - 40: Sheet Layout

Hands On Exercise

Exercise 8-6

Learn about progress reporting in the Tasks page.

1. In the *My Work* section of the *Quick Launch* menu, click the *Tasks* link. When the page displays, study the information shown in each of the default columns. If necessary, change the period display to include the date that you entered in Exercise 8-1.

2. Click the triangle above the *Quick Launch* menu to collapse the menu.

3. In the *Display* section of the *Tasks* ribbon, click the *Layout* pick list and select the *Sheet* item.

4. Drag the *Process Status* column next to the task name.

5. Using the *Layout* pick list, change the layout to *Timephased Data*.

6. In the *Show/Hide* section of the *Tasks* ribbon, uncheck the *Planned Time* type.

7. In the *Display* section of the *Tasks* ribbon, click the *Units* pick list and select the *Duration* item and select *Days* from the fly out menu.

8. Use the *Layout* pick list to apply the *Gantt Chart* layout.

9. Select the row header for the third task in the *Display* section of the *Tasks* ribbon; click the *Scroll to Task* button.

10. In the *Share* section of the *Tasks* ribbon, click the *View Calendar* button and review the *View Calendar* page.

11. Close the calendar page when you complete your inspection.

Understanding the Assignment Details Page

To navigate to the *Assignment Details* page from the *Tasks* page, simply click the name of a task. Project Server 2010 displays the *Assignment Details* page for the selected task, shown in Figure 8 - 41.

The *Assignment Details* page displays complete information for the selected task assignment. Notice in Figure 8 - 41that the *Assignment Details* page includes the following sections:

- **General Details** – Enter progress update information in this section, such as the Start date, Percent Complete, Remaining Work, or Finish date.

- **Recent Task Changes** – If your task spans more than the current time period, use this section to review the history of task changes, task updates, and comments that you or your project manager added.

- **Attachments** – From this section, you can view risks, issues, or documents associated with the task.

- **Contacts** – Use this section to see the names of your project manager, approval manager, and your fellow team members.

- **Related Assignments** – Use this section to see predecessor and successor tasks related to the selected task.

- **Notes** – From this section, you can add a note to the task.

Design P1

| Recalculate | Save | Send | Back |

⊟ General Details
View and update status on this assignment

Task Progress

| Total work: | 4.75d |
| Timephased work: | 4.38d of 4.75d (92%) |

Task Properties

Start:	11/1/2010
Finish:	11/10/2010
Remaining Work:	3h

⊟ Recent Task Changes
View the history of task changes, updates, and approvals.

Approved: 11/3/2010 3:10 PM <George Stewart>
[CHEFETZ\gstewart: 11/3/2010]
Update accepted: 11/9/2010 11:29 AM
Details: Actual Work On 11/8/2010 → 7h
Actual Work On 11/9/2010 → 4h
Submitted: 11/9/2010 11:28 AM <George Stewart>
Approved: 11/9/2010 11:29 AM <George Stewart>
[CHEFETZ\gstewart: 11/9/2010]
Update pending: 11/10/2010 7:24 PM
Details: Actual Work On 11/8/2010 → 6h
Actual Work On 11/9/2010 → 3h
Submitted: 11/10/2010 7:24 PM <George Stewart>
[George Stewart: 11/10/2010]

⊟ Attachments
View, add or edit related information such as documents, issues, or risks.

Issues

Title	Due Date	Status

Risks

Title	Due Date	Status
Key engineering resource may leave		(1) Active

Documents

Title	File Name	Status

⊟ Contacts
Contact your project manager, others assigned to this task, or project team members.

| Project manager: | George Stewart |
| Approval manager: | George Stewart |

Assigned to this task	**Project Team**
George Stewart	Cher Zall
Mickey Cobb	Computer Hardware
	Contract Labor
	Corporate Training Manuals
	David Erickson
	George Stewart
	Mickey Cobb

⊟ Related Assignments
View related assignments with enterprise resources assigned. To view contact options, click on the resource name.

Tasks scheduled to finish before this task can start:

Task name:	Start	End	Status	Assigned To

Tasks dependent on this task's finish date:

Task name:	Start	End	Status	Assigned To
Build P1	11/10/2010	11/15/2010	0%	Cher Zall

⊟ Notes
To the right, you can Create, Edit and View notes for this task assignment. In the top section you can view a chronological listing of individual note entries. The lower section is for you to enter and edit notes you wish to add to this task.

Notes:
Click here to download this note in RTF format.

[George Stewart]
Increased Remaining Work from 14h to 24h because I have to redo work previously done.

Increased Remaining Work from 14h to 24h because I have to redo work previously done.

| Recalculate | Save | Send | Back |

Figure 8 - 41: Assignment Details page

Hands On Exercise

Exercise 8-7

Report progress using the Assignment Details page.

1. Click the name of any task shown on the *Tasks* page.

2. On the *Assignment Details* page, study your organization's progress tracking method, as shown in the *General Details* section.

3. Click the *Back* button to return to the *Tasks* page.

Reporting Progress from the Tasks Page

As I stated earlier, Project Server 2010 offers your organization four different methods for tracking progress, one of which enables you to use any of the three described here. The information you enter on the *Tasks* page varies with the method of tracking your organization uses. Your organization can choose to use the default layout of the *Tasks* page, or can use a modified layout recommended by MSProjectExperts. Because of this flexibility, I discuss each method of tracking progress, using both the default layout and the custom MSProjectExperts layout of the *Tasks* page.

Using Percent of Work Complete

Although you can report progress from the *Tasks* page using the Percent of Work Complete method of tracking progress, Project Server 2010 accepts only a limited amount of information with the default layout of the *Tasks* page. If your organization requires you to enter task progress from the *Tasks* page, use the following methodology to report progress on a task using this method of tracking:

1. Click in the *% Work Complete* field and enter your estimate of the percentage of work completed to date on the task. The *Process Status* field value changes to *Save Needed* and the *Information* bar appears under the ribbon with the message: *Status: There are unsaved updates.*

When you enter 100% complete on a task, Project Server 2010 assumes that you started and finished the task as **originally scheduled**. The system has no way of knowing that you started or finished a task early or late compared to the original schedule.

2. To adjust the remaining work (also known as the ETC or Estimated Time to Completion) for the task, click in the *Remaining Work* field and enter your remaining work estimate.

3. To add a note to the task, click on the task name and scroll to the bottom of the *Assignment Details* page as shown in Figure 8 - 42. Enter your note and click the *Save* button.

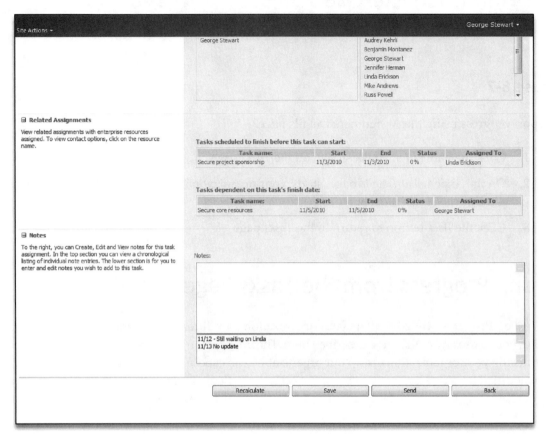

Figure 8 - 42: Add a Task Note

 If your project manager enters a note on a task in the actual Microsoft Project plan, the note text appears in the top half of the Project Web App *Assignment Notes* dialog. The top half of the dialog also contains notes that you previously submitted and which the project manager updated into the Microsoft Project plan.

 MSProjectExperts recommends that you train team members to "date stamp" their notes text, as shown in the note in Figure 8 - 42. Project Server 2010 "name stamps" each note to show who submitted the note, but does not "date stamp" the note to show when the team member submitted the note..

Project Server 2010 displays your attached note with an indicator to the left of the task name, as shown in Figure 8 - 43.

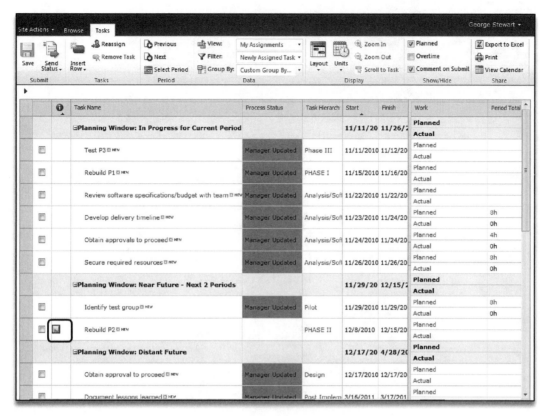

Figure 8 - 43: Task note indicators

To adjust the scheduled *Start* or *Finish* date for a future task, click in the *Start* or *Finish* field and change the date on the calendar date picker. This alerts your project manager that the actual start or finish is different from the current schedule in the project plan.

4. Click the *Save* button to save your task progress changes if you are not ready to submit them to your project manager for approval. When you save the changes, Project Server changes the line's *Process Status* value to *Not Submitted* and the *Information* bar shows the message: *Status: Updates have been saved, but have not been sent for approval* as shown in Figure 8 - 44.

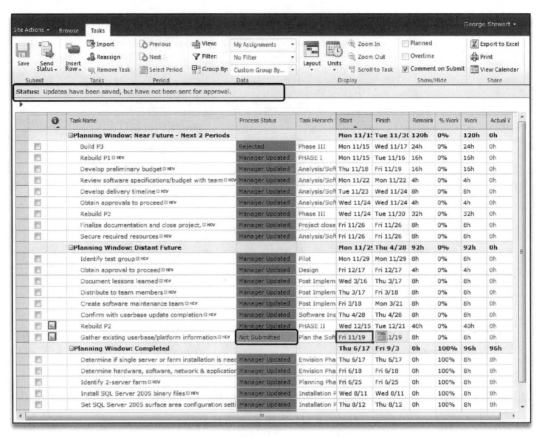

Figure 8 - 44: Saved Unsubmitted Tasks

5. When you are ready to submit the task changes to your project manager, select the *Send Status* menu button on the ribbon. The *All Tasks* option sends all changed tasks information for approval. The *Selected Tasks* option only sends the tasks that you selected in the list.

6. Project Server 2010 displays the *Submit Changes* dialog shown in Figure 8 - 45. Enter an optional comment about the update in the *Submit Changes* dialog and then click the *OK* button to submit the update to your project manager.

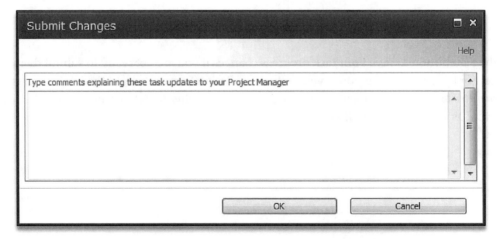

Figure 8 - 45: Comment on Submit dialog

Project Server 2010 displays the *Submit Changes* dialog as the *Show/Hide* option to *Comment on Submit* option is selected by default. To suppress the system prompt to add a comment each time you submit task progress, deselect the *Comment on Submit* option.

Project Server 2010 redisplays the *Tasks* page with a confirmation message in the *Information* bar indicating that the system submitted your updates for approval as shown in Figure 8 - 46.

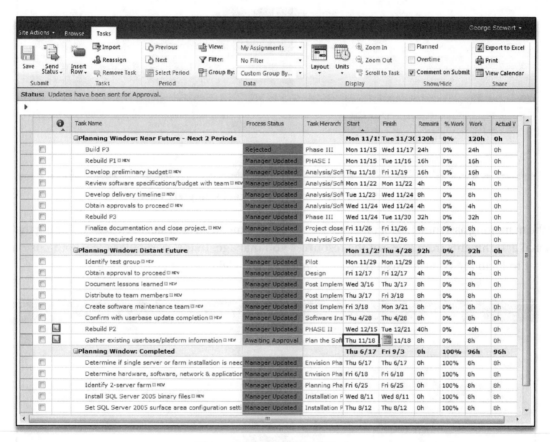

Figure 8 - 46: Submitted Tasks

Best Practice: Using Percent of Work Complete

MSProjectExperts recommends that your Project Server administrator create a custom view of the *Tasks* page to optimize your data entry experience. This view controls the data columns that are on the page; however you are in control of other aspects such as grouping.

The custom view contains the following columns: *Project Name, Task Name, Process Status, Task Hierarchy, Health, Actual Start, % Work Complete, Remaining Work, Actual Finish,* and *Resource Name*. Optional fields are *Start, Finish, Work* and *Comments*. These fields enable you to see the original dates as well as see any comments. I recommend the *Sheet* layout for this tracking method. The recommended grouping is by Project. Figure 8 - 47 shows the *Tasks* page with the custom view and MSProjectExperts recommended settings.

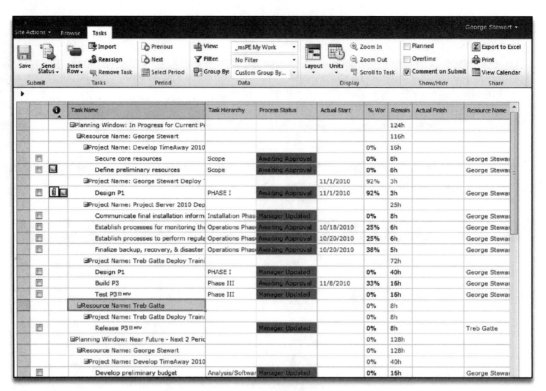

Figure 8 - 47: Recommended Percent Complete view

If you are the managing assignments for other resources, I recommend an alternative custom grouping that segregates your personal assignments from those of the resources you manage. In this particular case, your custom grouping values are set to *Planning Window, Resource Name, Project Name,* yielding the view in Figure 8 - 48.

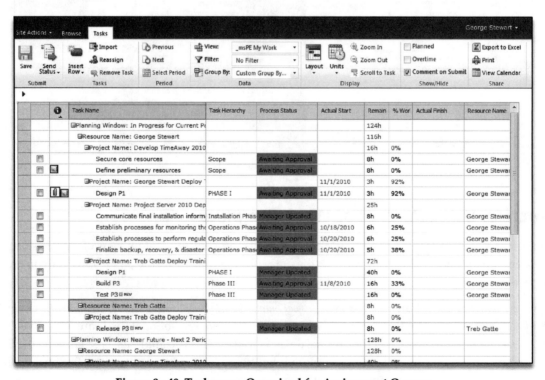

Figure 8 - 48: Tasks page Organized for Assignment Owners

The Administrator instructions for creating the custom layout are included in the download package for this book. See the download page following the book's Introduction for download details.

To enter progress using the Percent of Work Complete method of tracking with the custom layout of the *Tasks* page, use the following methodology:

1. When you start a new task, click in the Actual *Start* field for the selected task and enter the date you began work on the task.

2. Click in the *%Work Complete* field and enter your estimate of the percentage of work completed to date on the task.

3. Enter your estimated amount of Remaining Work (or ETC) in the *Remaining Work* field.

4. When you complete a task, click in the *Finish* field for the selected task and enter the date you finished work on the task.

5. To add a note to the task, either:

    5.1. Enter your note into the *Comments* field if it is present.

    5.2. Enter your note on the *Assignment Details* page.

       5.2.1. Save all changes.

       5.2.2. Click the name of the task to navigate to the *Assignment Details* page.

       5.2.3. Enter your note text at the bottom of the page.

       5.2.4. Click the *OK* button.

6. Click the *Save* button to save your task progress changes if you are not ready to submit them to your project manager for approval.

7. When you are ready to submit the task changes to your project manager, select the option checkbox to the left of each task that you want to submit and click the *Submit Selected* button. Alternately, you can also click the *Submit All* button to submit all task changes automatically.

Although this method of tracking requires a little more work on the part of team members, entering an Actual Start and Actual Finish date gives the project manager much more accurate scheduling information. This helps the project manager to better forecast schedule slippage due to a late Actual Start date or late Actual Finish date on a task and all successor tasks.

Using Actual Work Done and Work Remaining

In this tracking method, you are entering the amount of time spent on the task and the amount of work remaining. This method of time accrual enables you and your management to gauge progress toward the task outcome and the quality of the initial work estimate. This method also minimizes the somewhat subjective nature of % Work Complete tracking by forcing focus on the level of effort expended versus planned.

In Project Server 2010, the layout of the *Tasks* page does not automatically reconfigure based on the tracking method. The assumption is that your Project Server administrator configured the view previously.

Best Practice: Using Actual Work Done and Work Remaining

MSProjectExperts recommends that your Project Server administrator create a custom view of the *Tasks* page to optimize your data entry experience as shown in Figure 8 - 49. This view ensures that data columns are on the page; however you are in control of other aspects such as grouping.

The custom view contains the following columns: *Project Name, Task Name, Process Status, Task Hierarchy, Health, Actual Start, Actual Work, Remaining Work, Actual Finish*, and *Resource Name*. Optional fields are *Start, Finish, Work* and *Comments*. These fields enable you to see the original dates as well as any comments.

I recommend the *Sheet* layout for this tracking method. The recommended grouping is by Project.

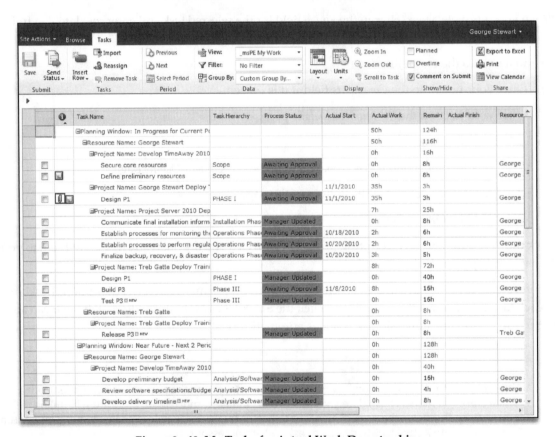

Figure 8 - 49: My Tasks for Actual Work Done tracking

 As a courtesy, your Project Server administrator may also include the *Start* and *Finish* fields so that team members can see the scheduled dates for tasks to start and finish.

To enter progress using the Actual Work Done and Work Remaining method of tracking with the *Tasks* page custom layout, use the following methodology:

1. When you start a new task, click in the Actual *Start* field for the selected task and enter the date you began work on the task.

2. Click in the *Actual Work* field and enter the total amount of work completed to date (measured in hours) on the task.

> If you enter a total amount of work that equals the planned work on a task (indicating you completed the task), Project Server 2010 assumes that you started and finished the task as **originally scheduled**. The system has no way of knowing that you started or finished a task early or late compared to the original schedule.

3. Enter your estimated amount of Remaining Work (or Estimated Time to Completion/ETC) in the *Remaining Work* field.

4. When you complete a task, click in the *Finish* field for the selected task and enter the date you finished work on the task.

5. Click the *Save* button to save your task progress changes if you are not ready to submit them to your project manager for approval.

6. When you are ready to submit the task changes to your project manager, select the option checkbox to the left of each task that you want to submit and click the *Submit Selected* button. Alternately, you can also click the *Submit All* button to submit all task changes automatically.

> To adjust the scheduled *Start* or *Finish* date for a future task, click in the *Start* or *Finish* field and change the date on the calendar date picker. This alerts your project manager that the actual start or finish is different from the current schedule in the project plan.

7. If you see the *Submit Changes* dialog, enter an optional comment about the update and then click the *OK* button to submit the update to your project manager.

> Although this method of tracking requires a little more work on the part of team members, entering an Actual Start and Actual Finish date gives the project manager much more accurate tracking information. This helps the project manager to better forecast schedule slippage due to a late Actual Start date or late Actual Finish date on a task and their successor tasks.

Using Hours of Work Done per Period

Organizations that use the Hours of Work Done per Period method of tracking progress need the finer level of detail, typically to meet billing requirements or the more rigorous requirements of a mature Project Management process. The *Tasks* page typically requires the timephased data entry grid for entries by day using this tracking method.

The *Tasks* page shown in Figure 8 - 50 includes a scroll bar at the bottom of the data grid. On lower screen resolutions, such as my current 1024 x 768 resolution, the data grid is too wide to fit on the page, and the system displays the scroll bar. At higher screen resolutions, such as at 1280 x 1024, the system displays the entire data grid without a scroll bar.

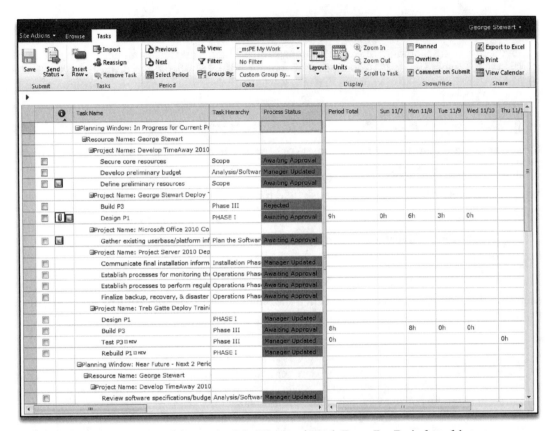

Figure 8 - 50: Tasks organized for Hours of Work Done Per Period tracking

Best Practice: Using Hours of Work Done per Period

MSProjectExperts recommends that your Project Server administrator create a custom view of the *Tasks* page to optimize your data entry experience as shown in Figure 8 - 51. This view ensures that data columns are on the page; however you are in control of other aspects such as grouping.

The custom view contains the following columns: *Project Name, Task Name, Process Status, Task Hierarchy, Health, Remaining Work, Actual Finish,* and *Resource Name.* Optional fields are *Start, Finish, Work* and *Comments.* These fields enable you to see the original dates as well as any comments.

I recommend the *Timephased Data* layout for this tracking method. The recommended grouping is by Project.

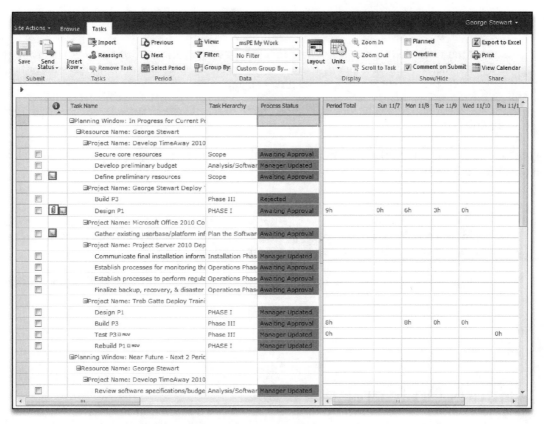

Figure 8 - 51: Tasks organized for Hours of Work Done tracking

To enter progress using the Hours of Work Done method of tracking with the custom layout of the *Tasks* page, use the following methodology:

1. On a daily basis, enter the hours you worked on each task in the timesheet grid.

2. Add notes as needed for each task, either:

    2.1. Enter your note in the *Comments* field if it is present.

    2.2. Enter your note on the *Assignment Details* page.

        2.2.1. Save all changes.

        2.2.2. Click the name of the task to navigate to the *Assignment Details* page.

        2.2.3. Enter your note text at the bottom of the page.

        2.2.4. Click the *OK* button.

3. Click the *Save* button to save your current progress at the end of each day.

4. On the last day of the reporting period, enter your estimated amount of Remaining Work (or Estimated Time to Completion/ETC) in the *Remaining Work* field for any tasks that require adjustment.

5. Add a note to any task that you adjust.

6. When you are ready to submit the task changes to your project manager, select the option checkbox to the left of each task that you want to submit and click the *Submit Selected* button. Alternately, you can also click the *Submit All* button to submit all task changes automatically.

To adjust the scheduled Start or Finish date for a future task, click in the *Start* or *Finish* field and change the date on the calendar date picker. This alerts your project manager that the actual start or finish is different from the current schedule in the project plan.

7. If you see the *Submit Changes* dialog, enter an optional comment about the update and then click the *OK* button to submit the update to your project manager.

As a best practice, MSProjectExperts recommends that you enter actual progress on a daily basis and update progress to your project manager on a weekly basis.

Hands On Exercise

Exercise 8-8

Enter and submit task progress from the Tasks page.

1. In the *My Work* section of the *Quick Launch* menu, click the *Tasks* link. In the *Data* section of the *Tasks* ribbon, use the *View* pick list to select the _msPE Work view. Pull the splitter bar to the right or apply the *Sheet* layout as you prefer.

2. For the Design P1 task, click the *Health* field for the in-progress task and select a value from the pick list.

3. Enter 40 hours in the *Actual Work* field and change the *Remaining Work* value to *24h*.

4. Click in the *Comment* field and enter a note on the task documenting a reason for the increase. (*Resource has to redo work previously done.*)

5. Click the *Save* button to save your task progress changes.

6. Notice the status message in the *Information* bar at the top of the tasks data grid.

7. Click the refresh button in your browser or press the **F5** key to refresh the screen. Select the option checkbox to the left of the in-progress task and then click the *Send Status* menu button, then select the *Selected Tasks* option.

8. Enter a comment about the update in the *Submit Changes* dialog and then click the *OK* button to submit the update to your project manager.

Reporting Progress from the Assignment Details Page

An alternate method for entering task progress is to use the *Assignment Details* page. Because this page contains so much more information about each task than the *Tasks* page, using the *Assignment Details* page is helpful if your organization uses the default layout of the *Tasks* page. That said, the *Assignment Details* page does not provide the same full update capabilities as the primary view. Depending on the tracking method, you can update the following values on the *Assignment Details* page as shown in Table 8 - 4.

Updatable Fields	% Complete	Actual Work / Remaining Work	Hours of Work Done
Completed Work		X	
Finish Date	X	X	X
Percent Complete	X		
Remaining Work	X	X	X
Start Date	X	X	X

Table 8 - 4: Updatable Fields on Assignment Details page

To access the *Assignment Details* page for any task, click the name of the task on the *Tasks* page. Figure 8 - 52 shows the layout of the *Assignment Details* page using the Percent of Work Complete method of tracking progress. Notice that the *Task Progress* section of the page includes the *Percent Complete* field.

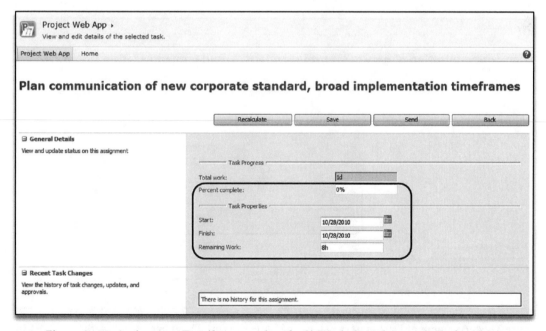

Figure 8 - 52: Assignment Details page using the % Work Complete method of tracking

Figure 8 - 53 shows the layout of the *Assignment Details* page using the Actual Work Done and Work Remaining method of tracking. Notice that the *Task Progress* section includes the *Completed work* field, measured in days.

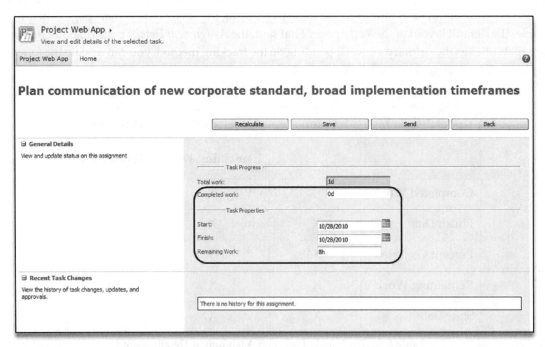

Figure 8 - 53: Assignment Details page using the Actual Work Done and Work Remaining method of tracking

Figure 8 - 54 shows the layout of the *Assignment Details* page using the Hours of Work Done per Period method of tracking. Note, in this tracking mode, you must use the primary *Tasks* view to enter time.

Figure 8 - 54: Assignment Details page using the Hours of Work Done per Period method of tracking

To report task progress from the *Assignment Details* page, use the same methodologies I presented earlier in this module for the method of tracking progress used by your organization. From this page, you can enter progress, adjust Remaining Work or add a note. When finished, click the *Save* button. From the *Tasks* page, submit the update to your project manager by clicking either the *Submit Selected* button or the *Submit All* button.

Importing Progress from the My Timesheet Page

Regardless of which hourly method your organization uses to track task progress, if you enter work hours in the *Timesheet* page, you can import the hours directly into the tasks shown on the *Tasks* page. To import timesheet hours, click the *Import* button on the *Tasks* page. Project Server 2010 displays the *Import Timesheet* page for the current time period, as shown in Figure 8 - 55.

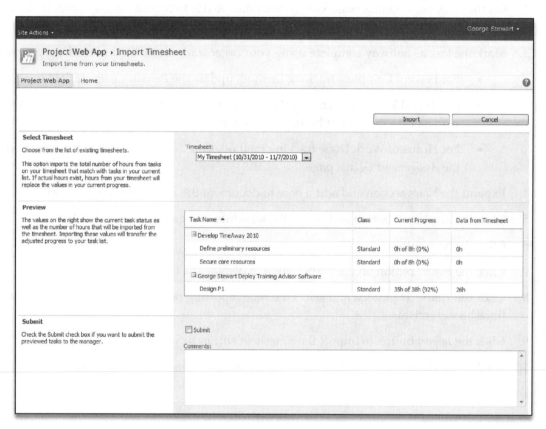

Figure 8 - 55: Import Timesheet page

To import a timesheet from a different time reporting period, click the *Timesheet* pick list at the top of the page and select the time reporting period you want to import. The system refreshes the page to show an updated *Import Timesheet* page. Click the *Import* button to import the timesheet data to the tasks shown on the *Tasks* page. When finished, add task comments as needed, and then submit the update to your project manager, following the methods detailed in the previous sections of this module.

Hands On Exercise

Exercise 8-9

Enter and submit task progress from the Assignment Details page.

1. If necessary, return to the *Tasks* page by clicking the *Tasks* link from the *My Work* section of the *Quick Launch* menu. On the *Tasks* page, click the Build P3 task assignment in the enterprise project used for this class.

2. On the *Assignment Details* page, enter a *Start* date that is two business days later than its currently scheduled *Start* date.

3. Mark the task as halfway complete using your organization's method of tracking progress.

   - For Percent Complete tracking method, update the *Percent Complete* field to *50%*.

   - For Actual Work / Remaining Work tracking method, update the *Completed Work* field with half the number of hours or days in the *Total Work* field.

   - For Hours of Work Done tracking method, skip this step, as this action is not possible on the *Assignment Details* page.

4. Expand the *Notes* section and add a note to document the reason for the late start.

5. Click the *Recalculate* button and notice the schedule changes in the *General Details* section.

6. Click the *Save* button.

7. Click the *Import* button on the *Tasks* ribbon to display the *Import Timesheet* page.

8. Click the *Timesheet* pick list and select the time reporting period under which you performed the timesheet exercises.

9. Click the *Import* button to import the timesheet entries to your *Tasks* page.

10. On the *Tasks* page, click the *Send Status* menu button and select the *All Tasks* item to submit all updates.

Managing Tasks

Along with reporting progress, other important task-related activities on the *Tasks* page include the following:

- Reassigning work to another resource

- Self-assigning Team tasks

- Creating new tasks

- Deleting tasks

I cover each activity in detail in the sections that follow.

Reassigning Work to another Resource

After a project manager assigns you to a task, Project Server 2010 offers you the option of reassigning the task to another resource. You might find this feature useful if you serve as a team leader to whom the project manager assigns tasks, and you are responsible for reassigning tasks to members of your team.

To reassign a task to another resource, navigate to the *Tasks* page, select one or more tasks to reassign and then click the *Reassign* button on the *Task* ribbon. Project Server 2010 displays the *Task Reassignment* page shown in Figure 8 - 56.

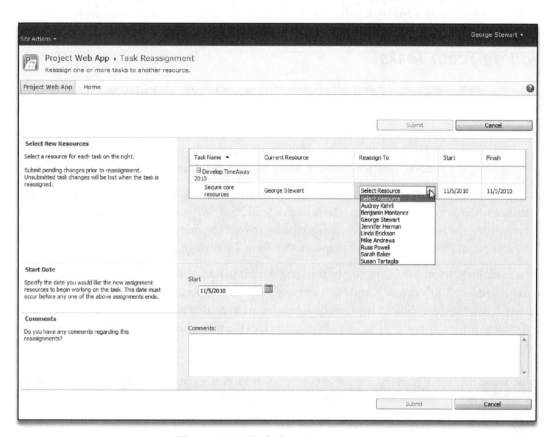

Figure 8 - 56: Task Reassignment page

The *Select New Resource(s)* section of the *Task Reassignment* page shows you a list of all your selected task assignments from the *Tasks* page. The *Reassign To* column in the data grid allows you to select the resource to which you want to reassign a task. Click the *Reassign To* field for the task you want to reassign and then click the pick list. The system displays the list of all resources that you have permission to see within the system.

The default permissions in Project Server 2010 allow you to see only members of your project team. If you need to reassign a task to someone outside your project team, your project manager must first add the new resource to the project team in the project plan.

After you select the resources to which you want to reassign one or more tasks, click the *Start* pick list in the *Start Date* section of the *Task Reassignment* page. Select the date on which the system reassigns the selected tasks. The date in the *Start* field defaults to the current date. You must select a date that is before the *Finish* date of the selected tasks. Generally, you want the system to reassign the tasks immediately, which means you should keep the current date selected.

In the *Comments* field, enter any relevant comment text you want to add. When you complete your entries, click the *Submit* button. Project Server 2010 displays the *Tasks* page and removes the task(s).

The new resource can immediately enter time against the reassigned task. This enables team members to manage their own work to a certain extent in situations when the project manager is unavailable. However, the task reassignment is not final until the project manager approves the reassignment. When you click the *Submit* button, a task reassignment request automatically appears for the project manager to approve in the Approval Center.

Self-Assigning Team Tasks

A team resource acts as an assignment proxy for all members of your team. This enables project managers to assign tasks to teams without knowing the specific resource to assign initially.

There are two primary ways to use team tasks. The team lead, if properly configured, can reassign team tasks to specific team members. The second is that any member of the team can self-assign a team task. For example, if your team services work requests, then self-assignment of team tasks may be of interest.

If you are a member of a group of resources represented by a team resource, and the project manager assigns the team resource to a task, Project Server 2010 refers to the task as a team task. After the project manager publishes the enterprise project containing the team task, you can assign the team task to yourself by clicking the *Self-assign Team Tasks* button on the *Tasks* page. Project Server 2010 displays the *Team Tasks* page, as shown in Figure 8 - 57.

To self-assign a team task, select the *Insert Row* button on the ribbon and select the *Insert Team Tasks* option. You then see the page in Figure 8 - 57. Select a task and click the *Assign to me* button on the ribbon. Project Server removes the task from the list. Click the *Tasks* link in the *Quick Launch* menu to return to the *Tasks* page. When you self-assign a team task to you from an enterprise project, the system removes the task immediately from the *Team Tasks* page of all other resources.

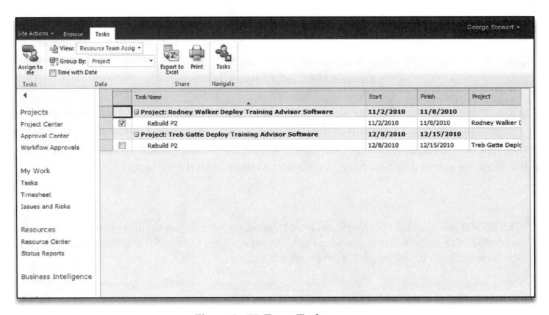

Figure 8 - 57: Team Tasks page

When you self-assign a team task, Project Server 2010 automatically approves the task reassignment.

Hands On Exercise

Exercise 8-10

Reassign work and self-assign team tasks from the Tasks page.

1. On the *Tasks* page, select the *Rebuild P1* task.

2. In the *Tasks* section of the *Tasks* ribbon, click the *Reassign* button.

3. Click the *Reassign To* pick list and select Cher Zall on the project team.

4. In the *Comments* field, add descriptive text to document the reason for the reassignment.

5. Click the *Submit* button.

6. (If enabled on your system) From the *Tasks* section of the *Tasks* ribbon, click the *Insert Row* pick list and select the *Insert Team Tasks* option.

7. Select the option checkbox for the *Rebuild P2* task and then click the *Assign task to me* button.

8. From the *My Work* section of the *Quick Launch* menu, click the *Tasks* link. Notice that the system adds the team task to your *Tasks* page.

Creating a New Task

In a collaborative project management environment, project team members may discover unplanned work and need to propose new tasks to their project manager. Proposed new tasks might include tasks related to tasks on which a resource is already working, but which were not included in the project plan, or future tasks that the team member anticipates.

To propose a new task, click the *Insert Row* menu button and select the *Create a New Task* option. Project Server 2010 displays the *New Task* page shown in Figure 8 - 58.

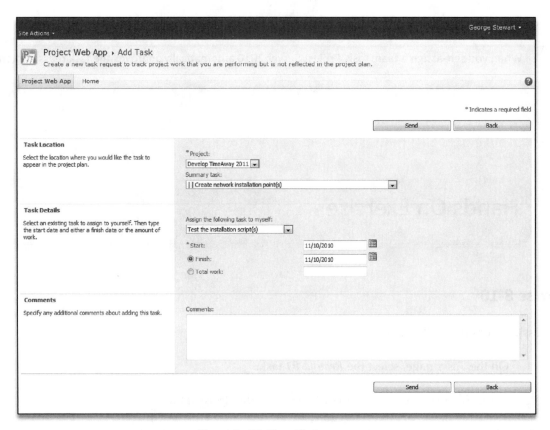

Figure 8 - 58: New Tasks page

To create the proposed task, begin by clicking the *Project* pick list and selecting the project in which to create the new task. The *Project* pick list contains only those projects in which you are a team member. Click the *Summary task* pick list and pick the level in the Work Breakdown Structure (WBS) at which to create the new task.

The first item on the *Subordinate to Summary task* pick list represents the highest level in the project. Selecting this item creates the new task at Outline Level 1, outside of any phase or deliverable sections in the project. The other items in the *Subordinate to Summary task* pick list include summary tasks that represent phase and deliverable sections in your project. Selecting one of these items creates the new task as a subtask of the selected phase or deliverable.

In the *Task Details* section of the *New Task* page, enter the new task name in *Task name* field. The *Start* field defaults to today's date but you should edit to reflect the actual anticipated start date. Lastly, either enter the anticipated finish date in the *Finish* field, the estimated work for the task in the *Total work* field or mark the task as a milestone.

 After your project manager approves the new task request, Project Server 2010 adds the new task to the enterprise project and sets a Start No Earlier Than (SNET) constraint on the task using the date you enter in the *Start* field.

In the *Comments* field, add any additional documentation for your project manager. Additional comments might help your project manager to decide whether to approve the proposed task. Click the *Send* button when you finish. Project Server 2010 displays the *Tasks* page with the new proposed task added to the task list, as shown in Figure 8 - 59.

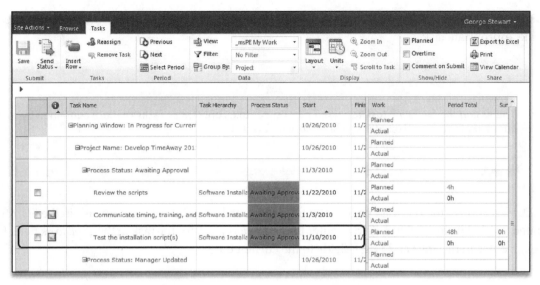

Figure 8 - 59: New Task Awaiting Approval

Add Yourself to a Task

Beyond the need for proposing new tasks, project team members might also need to add themselves to an existing task when enlisted by a fellow team member. Project Server 2010 allows a team member to add themselves to an existing task. To self-assign a task, click the *Insert Row* menu button and select the *Add Yourself to a Task* option. Project Server 2010 displays the *Add Task* page shown in Figure 8 - 60.

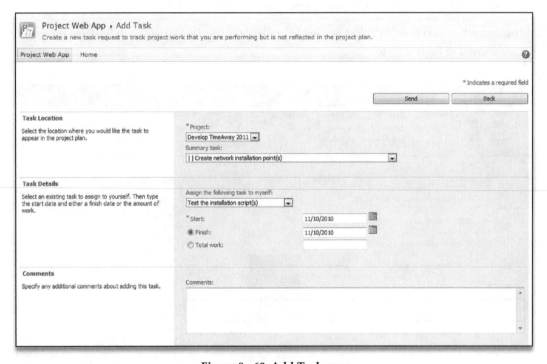

Figure 8 - 60: Add Task page

To begin, click the *Project* pick list and select the project containing the task you want to join. The *Project* pick list contains only those projects in which you are a team member. Click the *Summary task* pick list and pick the level in the

Work Breakdown Structure (WBS) to which the task belongs. Lastly, click the *Assign the following task to myself* pick list and select the appropriate task.

The *Assign the following task to myself* pick list contains only those tasks that are contained by the summary task you selected in the *Summary task* pick list.

In the *Task Dates* section of the *Add Task* page, enter the anticipated start date of the new task in the *Start* field. Enter the anticipated finish date in the *Finish* field or enter the estimated work for the task in the *Total work* field. By default, the system sets dates in the *Start* and *Finish* fields to the current date.

After your project manager approves the new task request, Project Server 2010 adds the new task to the enterprise project and sets a Start No Earlier Than (SNET) constraint on the task using the date you enter in the *Start* field.

In the *Comments* field, add any additional documentation for your project manager. Additional comments might help your project manager to decide whether to approve the proposed task.

Click the *Send* button when you finish. Project Server 2010 displays the *Tasks* page with the new proposed task added to the task list, as shown in Figure 8 - 61.

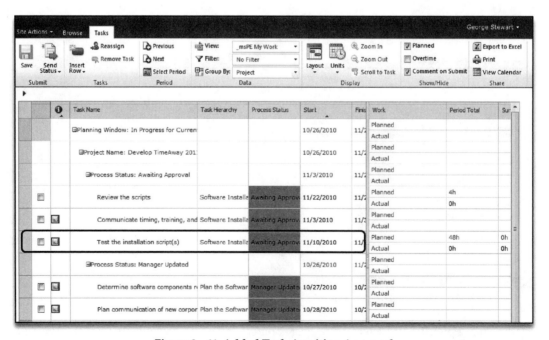

Figure 8 - 61: Added Task Awaiting Approval

When you click the *Send* button at the bottom of the *Add Task* page, Project Server 2010 immediately submits a new task request to your project manager for approval. If the project manager approves the proposed task, the task remains on the *Tasks* page and you can enter and submit progress for the task. If your project manager rejects the proposed task, the system changes the Process Status to *Rejected* as shown in Figure 8 - 62.

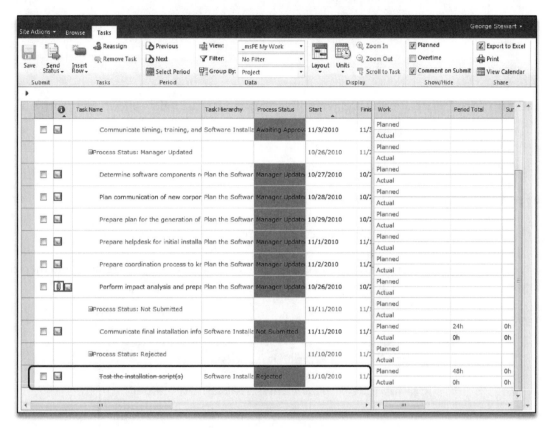

Figure 8 - 62: Tasks page shows rejected Add Task

If your project manager rejects your Add Task request, the system prevents you from entering progress against the task. Therefore, you should removal the rejected task from the *Tasks* page using the steps detailed below.

Removing Tasks

Project Server 2010 allows you to request removal of task assignments from the *Tasks* page. The *Remove* action creates a removal request that the project manager reviews and approves. Good targets for removal include rejected tasks, such as the rejected task shown previously in Figure 8 - 62.

Warning: Do not delete any other type of task from the *Tasks* page. If you attempt to delete a completed task, an in-progress task, or a future task, and your project manager accidentally approves your deletion request, the system **removes you from the task** in the Microsoft Project 2010 plan. You should delete future tasks only if your project manager gives you specific permission to do so, and intends to assign someone else to the tasks.

To remove tasks from the *Tasks* page, you and your project manager must follow a four-step process as follows:

1. You select and remove the tasks.

2. You submit the task removal request to your project manager.

3. Your project manager approves the removal.

4. Your project manager publishes the changes in the project.

To begin the task removal process, select the option checkbox to the left of each task to remove and then click the *Remove Task* button. Project Server 2010 displays the confirmation dialog shown in Figure 8 - 63.

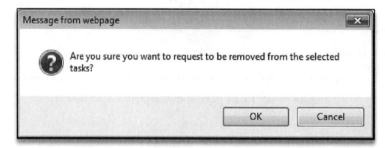

Figure 8 - 63: Task Removal confirmation dialog

Click the *OK* button to complete the task removal process on the *Tasks* page. The system refreshes the *Tasks* page and does the following:

- Changes the task Process Status to *Save Needed*.

- Strikes through the task name.

- Retains the selection status of the task

Notice in Figure 8 - 64 that the system formats the removed task with strikethrough text.

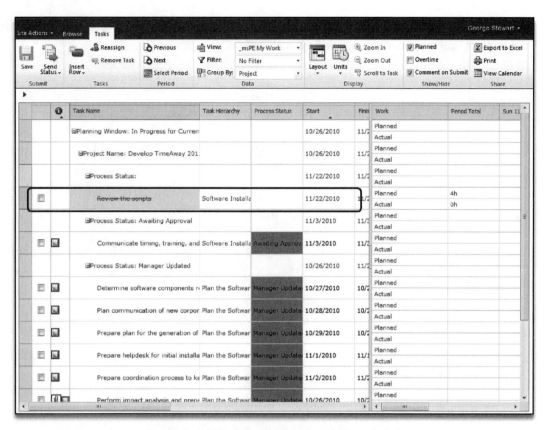

Figure 8 - 64: Tasks page showing Removed Task

Click the *Send Status* menu button and then select *Selected Tasks* or *All Tasks* options to submit the removal request to your project manager. Project Server 2010 sends your project manager a *Remove Assignment* request for each of the tasks you select. After your project manager approves the task removal and publishes the changes to the project, the task no longer appears on the project plan. However, the system does not remove the tasks from the *Tasks* page.

Hands On Exercise

Exercise 8-11

Create and submit a new task to your project manager. Remove one of your tasks.

1. If necessary, from the *My Work* section of the *Quick Launch* menu, select the *Tasks* link to return to the *Tasks* page. Click the *Insert Row* pick list and select the *Create a New Task* item.

2. Click the *Project* pick list and select your *Deploy Training Advisor Software* project.

3. Click the *Summary task* pick list and select the *Phase III* item.

4. Enter *Rebuild P3* as the name for the task in the *Task Name* field.

5.   In the *Task Dates* section, enter dates in the *Start* and *Finish* fields. Use a start date later than the current time period you are working with.

6.   Enter a comment.

7.   Click the *Send* button. The system redisplays the *Tasks* page.

8.   On the *Tasks* page, select the row selection check box for the *Build P3* task.

9.   Click the *Remove Task* button.

10.   Click the *OK* button in the confirmation dialog.

11.   Click the *Send Status* menu button, and then select the *All Tasks* item to send your updates.

12.   Click the *OK* button in the *Submit Changes* dialog.

Exercise 8-12

Assign yourself to a new task.

1.   From the *Tasks* page, click the *Insert Row* menu button and select the *Add Yourself to a Task* item.

2.   Click the *Project* pick list and select the Deploy Training Advisor project.

3.   Click the *Summary task* pick list and select the *Phase III* summary task.

4.   Click the *Assign the following task to myself* pick list, and select the *Test P3* task from the pick list.

5.   In the *Comments* field, add descriptive text to explain why you assigned yourself to an existing task.

6.   Click the *Send* button.

Updating tasks through Outlook

If your Project Server administrator configured Exchange synchronization for your system, your resources can update their tasks through Outlook. Each time that you publish task assignments, the system kicks off a synchronization job for tasks in your project, synchronizing Project Server assignments with the Outlook tasks list for each user in the schedule that has the *Synchronize Tasks* option selected in their Project Server user record. The synchronization process supports synchronization to the Outlook task list only, and your resources can enter percent complete only. Exchange synchronization does not support collecting time against tasks. Figure 8 - 65 shows a project assignment displayed in an Outlook task form.

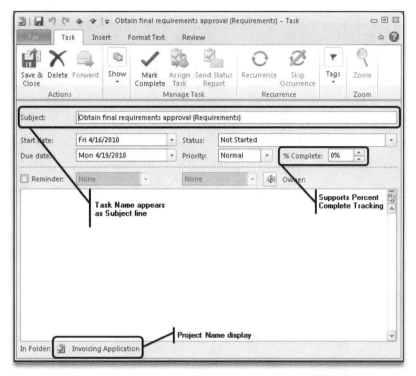

Figure 8 - 65: Project assignment as Outlook 2010 task

Notice in the figure that the task name appears as the *Subject* in the task form. Notice also that the task contains the planned start and end dates and the project name displays in the *In Folder* space at the lower left hand area of the task form. To report progress on the task, enter a percentage of completion in the *% Complete* field to show partial completion or use the *Mark Complete* button in the *Manage Task* section of the *Task* ribbon and adjust your dates accordingly. To commit your change click the *Save & Close* button on the ribbon. When you save your change, the system sends the update to Project Server via Exchange Server.

Exchange synchronization runs a full synchronization job nightly. In addition, a range of events trigger point synchronizations, including adding, deleting and modifying tasks in Outlook; modifying tasks in the *Tasks* page; and accepting and rejecting task updates in the Approval Center. Project actions such as deleting a published project, deleting a resource, activating or deactivating resources, and enabling and disabling the site-level exchange setting also trigger a synchronization event. Exchange synchronization supports users who work with the Outlook desktop client as well as Outlook Web App.

413

Module 09

Approving Time and Task Progress

Learning Objectives

After completing this module, you will be able to:

- View unsubmitted timesheets for resources
- View and adjust timesheets submitted by a resource
- Approve timesheets submitted by a resource
- Recall an approved timesheet
- Approve administrative time submitted by a resource
- Accept or reject task updates submitted by a resource
- Reschedule uncompleted work from the past into the current reporting period
- Set and run rules for automatically accepting updates from resources
- Manually update cost resource information
- Close tasks to updates

Inside Module 09

Approvals

Approvals are a key process for you if you are responsible for managing projects, timesheets or time-off requests. Any changes to these items require your approval. As a project manager, you are the gatekeeper for task updates. Timesheet managers ensure that timesheet submissions contain correct data. Administrative time requests can affect project schedules; therefore, approvers need to be aware of dependencies.

The Approvals Center in Project Server 2010 combines all requests into one page. In many companies, a few people approve all requests for the various categories. Therefore, presenting you with all transactions requiring approval is easier to process. This module introduces the Approval Center and details the approval process for each transaction type.

Home Page

The Project Web App home page contains a synopsis of outstanding transactions that require your approval. The specific sections that appear are dependent on the security rights granted to you by your Project Server administrator. Figure 9 - 1 shows the Approval reminders that appear on the Home page. Click the link to see the transactions.

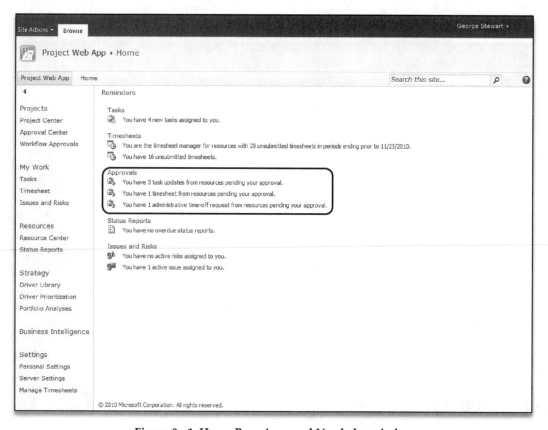

Figure 9 - 1: Home Page Approval Needed reminders

Approval Center

Figure 9 - 2 shows the *Approval Center* page that is your focal point for all approval related information and activity. You can see all *Task, timesheet* and *Administrative* time submissions in one list. You access the *Approval Center* page by clicking the *Approval Center* link in the *Quick Launch* menu.

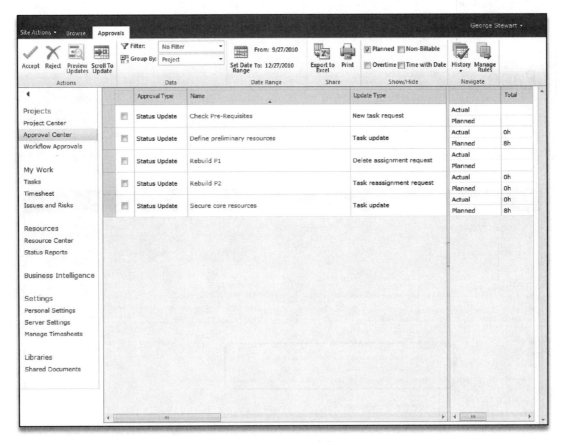

Figure 9 - 2: Approval Center

Approval Center Information

The *Approval Center* page contains the following data columns. You can customize the page to meet your particular needs by dragging columns into the order in which you want to see them and by applying custom grouping and filtering. You can perform grouping up to three levels using the fields as outlined in Table 9 - 1.

Field	Definition
Health	Recommended field for tasks/timesheets that enables team members to record task health.
Approval Type	This value indicates the transaction type of the line. - Status Update is a task transaction - timesheet is a timesheet transaction - Administrative time is an administrative time transaction
Name	Name of the task, timesheet line or administrative time category
Project	For tasks updates, this is the name of the project. Value is blank for all other transactions.
Update Type	For tasks, indicates the nature of the transaction. - *New Task Request* indicates a new task requested by a team member - *Task Reassignment request* indicates a changed to the assigned resource - *Task Update* indicates that a task data change was sent. This column is blank for timesheet and administrative time transactions.
Resource	Name of the resource to which the transaction applies
Owner	Assignment owner of the resource. This is blank for timesheet and administrative time transactions.
Transaction Comment	Comment entered by resource to provide more context to the transaction.
Sent Date	Date on which you sent the transaction.
Start	Start date of the transaction.
Finish	Finish date of the transaction.
Total	Total hours entered for the transaction. This applies if the transaction updated hours worked or remaining work. Otherwise, it will be zero.
% Complete	Task completion percentage. This is blank for timesheet and administrative time transactions.
Remaining Work	Task remaining work. This is blank for timesheet and administrative time transactions.
Task Hierarchy	This is the flattened task hierarchy for the task. The task hierarchy provides a breadcrumb trail of where the task is within the project plan. This is blank for timesheet and administrative time transactions

Table 9 - 1: List of Approval Page data fields

By default, the system displays *Actual* work for each transaction. The *Show/Hide* section of the *Approval Center* ribbon has checkboxes that you can select to show *Planned* work, *Overtime* work, *Non-Billable* work and *Dates with Time*. *Showing Planned, Overtime* and *Non-Billable* work increases the height of each row and reduces the number of rows appearing on the page.

By default, the system shows all transaction types. You use the *Filter* pick list in the ribbon to restrict visible transactions to a specific type. Available filters are *Administrative Time, Status Updates, timesheet Lines* and *timesheets*.

The system does not group transactions by default. You use the *Group By* pick list to group by any field in the view. The *Custom Group...* option enables you to group the list by up to three different view fields.

The system also enables you to set a date range for viewed transactions. To change the date range, click the *Set Date Range* button on the ribbon. Figure 9 - 3 shows the dialog that appears where you can change the *From* and *To* dates of transactions to appear.

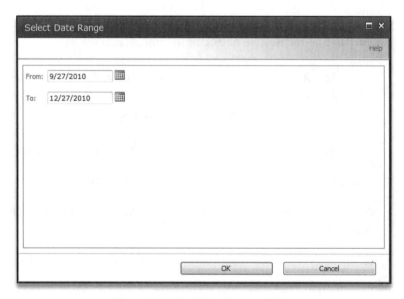

Figure 9 - 3: Set Date Range dialog

Approving timesheets

Project Server 2010 offers you two methods for approving or rejecting submitted timesheets:

- Approve/reject high-level timesheet information on the *Approval Center* page.

- Approve/reject detailed timesheet information for individual timesheet lines on the *Review Timesheet Detail* page.

The difference between the two methods is the amount of timesheet data you must view and approve. The first method is much quicker, but may not be as accurate. The second method takes more time, but allows you to review the time submitted for all lines in every timesheet.

MSProjectExperts recommends that your organization develop a standard process for approving timesheets and then train each resource manager how to follow this process.

Approving a timesheet using Summary Data

If you wish to approve each timesheet using only the high-level data shown on the *Approval Center* page, do the following:

- Apply the *Timesheets* filter, as shown in Figure 9 - 4.

- Select the option checkbox to the left of each timesheet you want to approve.

- Click the *Accept* button when you are ready to approve the selected timesheets.

- Enter documentation in the *Confirmation* dialog as you determine necessary when prompted.

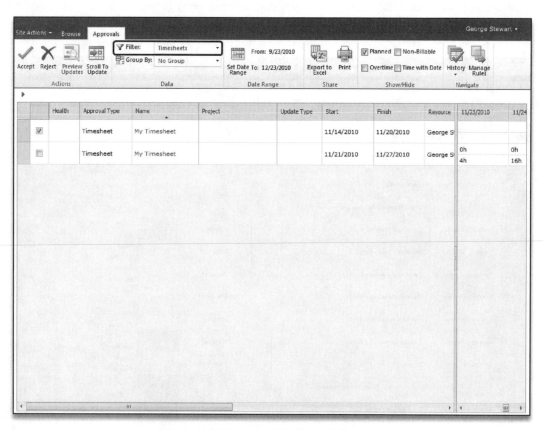

Figure 9 - 4: Approve High Level timesheet

Rejecting a timesheet using Summary Data

In some situations, such as when a resource enters erroneous information on the timesheet, you may need to reject a submitted timesheet. To reject timesheets, select the option checkbox to the left of each timesheet you want to reject, and then click the *Reject* button. Project Server 2010 sends the resource an e-mail message about the timesheet rejection and marks the *Status* field to *Rejected* for the rejected timesheet on the resource's *Manage timesheets* page. On the *Timesheet* page, the information bar on the rejected timesheet will show a *Rejected(Pending Send timesheet* status). The resource must correct the timesheet errors and then resubmit the timesheet to you for approval.

Approve Timesheet Lines using Detailed Data

To approve detailed timesheet information, click the *Timesheet* name link. The system displays the *Review Timesheet Detail* page grouped by project shown in Figure 9 - 5. Examine the data submitted for each timesheet line then click the *Approve* button.

Note: The *Approve* button approves the entire timesheet. You cannot select specific line items and only approve those. Timesheet approval is all or nothing.

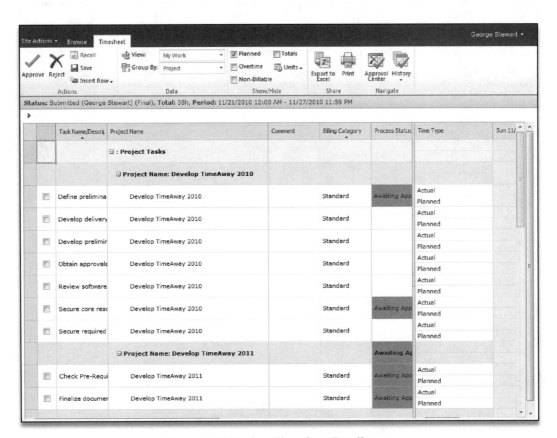

Figure 9 - 5: Review Timesheet Detail page

Enter additional information in the *Comment* field and then click the *OK* button. The *Approval Center* page appears and the timesheet no longer appears in the list.

Reject Timesheet Lines using Detailed Data

To reject a timesheet, examine the data submitted for each timesheet line as shown in Figure 9 - 5 then click the *Reject* button. Project Server 2010 displays the *Submit Timesheet* dialog. Enter additional information in the *Comment* field and then click the *OK* button. The *Approval Center* page appears and the timesheet no longer appears in the list. Project Server 2010 sends the resource an e-mail message about the timesheet rejection and marks the *Status* field to *Rejected* for the timesheet on the resource's *Timesheets* page. On the *Timesheet* page, the information bar on the rejected time-sheet will show a *Rejected (Pending Send timesheet)* status. The resource must correct the timesheet errors and then re-submit the timesheet to you for approval.

Recalling an Approved Timesheet

From time to time you may accidentally approve a timesheet that you should have rejected or vice versa. To address this situation, you must recall the timesheet and then take the intended action. To recall a previously approved time-sheet, do the following:

- Navigate to the *Approval Center* page

- On the *Approval Center* ribbon, click the *History* menu button, then select the *Timesheets* option.

- Select the *Approved By Me* option at the top of the *Timesheet Approvals History* page and then click the *Apply* button.

  - The system displays the history of your approved timesheets.

- Select the desired timesheet by clicking the area to the right of the name to select the row.

- Click the *Recall* button

Project Server 2010 returns the timesheet to your *Approval Center* page. Follow the procedures discussed previously to take the appropriate action for approval or rejection.

Hands On Exercise

Exercise 9-1

Approve pending timesheets using both summary timesheet data and detailed timesheet data.

1. Log on to Project Web App using your timesheet manager account.

2. Click the *Approval Center* link in the *Quick Launch* menu.

3. On the *Approval Center* page, click the name of the *My Timesheet* timesheet transaction to navigate to the *Review Timesheet Detail* page.

4. Select the checkbox for the Design P1 task line item, and select the checkbox for the Administrative Training item.

5. Review the data found on each timesheet line.

6. From the *Actions* section of the *Timesheet* ribbon, click the *Approve* button to accept the line item detail.

7. Enter information in the *Confirmation* dialog and then click the *OK* button.

Viewing Unsubmitted Timesheets

It is a good practice to determine which resources have not submitted their current timesheet to you. Project Server 2010 shows you the number of unsubmitted timesheets for your resources in the *Timesheets* section in the main content area of the Home page in Project Web App, as shown in Figure 9 - 6.

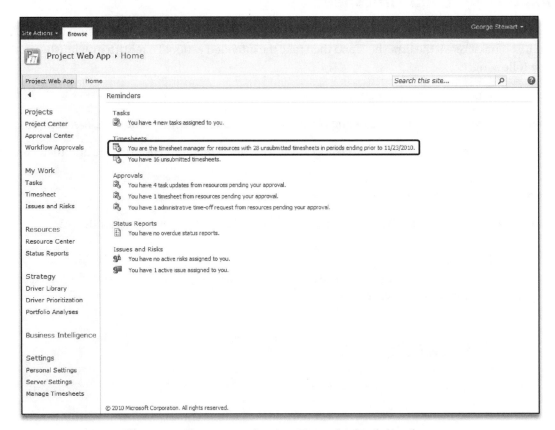

Figure 9 - 6: Home page showing 28 unsubmitted timesheets

To view the unsubmitted timesheets for your resources as shown in Figure 9 - 7, do the following:

- Click the ___ *unsubmitted timesheets* option on the first line of the *Timesheets* section of the Home page. Project Server 2010 displays the *Approval Center* page.

- Click the *History* menu button and then select the *Timesheet* option to see the *Timesheet Approvals History* page.

- Select the *My Resources Unsubmitted Timesheets* option and click the *Apply* button.

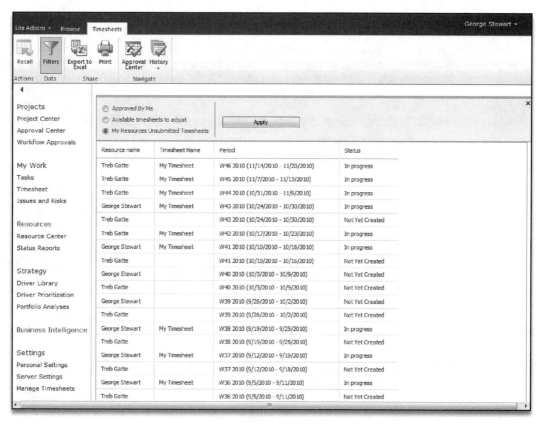

Figure 9 - 7: Timesheet Approvals History page

By default, the system displays unsubmitted timesheets sorted in descending order by timesheet period.

Notice in Figure 9 - 7 that the entries have of either a *In progress* or *Not Yet Created* status. *In progress* status happens when a resource creates a timesheet, enters time in it, but forgets to click the *Submit Timesheet* button.

Not Yet Created status happens for many reasons. Sometimes resources are out of town or away from the corporate network, and cannot create their own timesheets. Other causes can be resource forgetfulness or a simple neglect of the organization's time reporting obligation to create and submit timesheets in a timely manner.

Project Server 2010 also provides the *Timesheet Actuals* sample report that enables you to see what time you have reported and where it is in the approval process. In Module 17, I discuss how you can customize the built-in reports to meet your organization's specific needs.

During the early stages of a Project Server 2010 implementation, resources routinely forget to create and submit timesheets because they are simply not yet in the habit. msProjectExperts recommends that you use positive encouragement and feedback to help your resources establish good reporting habits with the system.

MSProjectExperts recommends that you develop a standard process for timesheet creation and submittal. This presents a training and performance issue for your resources. Train them how to create and submit timesheets and then hold them accountable for this performance. Deal appropriately with any resource who continually fails to submit timesheets.

Hands On Exercise

Exercise 9-2

You are a timesheet approver in your organization and must review unsubmitted timesheets for resources that report to you.

1. Log in as your timesheet manager and navigate to the Home page in Project Web App using your browser.

2. In the *Timesheets* section of the Home page, look for information that shows you how many re-sources have unsubmitted timesheets.

3. If you have resources with unsubmitted timesheets, click the ___ *unsubmitted timesheets* link in the *Timesheets* section.

4. On the *Approval Center* page, click the *History* menu button and then select the *Timesheet* option to see the *Timesheet Approvals History* page.

5. Select the *My Resources Unsubmitted Timesheets* option and click the *Apply* button.

6. Return to the Home page in Project Web App when finished.

Viewing and Adjusting Submitted Timesheets

On the Home page in Project Web App, the system notifies you about timesheets that need your approval by display-ing a link in the second line of the *Approvals* section in the main content area of the page. For example, notice in Figure 9 - 6, shown previously, that there is one timesheet awaiting approval.

To view submitted timesheets from your resources, click the *Timesheet* link in the *Approvals* section of the *Quick Launch* menu or click the ___ *timesheets from resources* option in the *Approvals* section of the main content area. When you click either link, the system displays the *Approval Center* page. You then click the *History* menu button and then select the *Timesheet* option to see the *Timesheet Approvals History* page. Lastly, select the *Available timesheets to adjust* option and click the *Apply* button. You see a page similar to Figure 9 - 8.

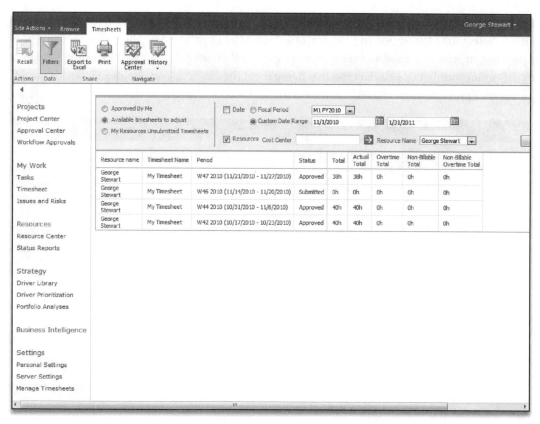

Figure 9 - 8: Timesheet Approvals History page with submitted timesheets

The *Timesheet Approvals History* page contains a section at the top that allows you to display different types of time-sheets and to filter the list of timesheets shown in the page. For example, you can select each of the following types of timesheet lists by selecting the appropriate option at the top:

- Approved By Me

- Available timesheets to adjust

- My Resources Unsubmitted Timesheets

To change the timesheets shown on the page, select one of the three options and click the *Apply* button. Select the *Approved By Me* option to see your past history of timesheet approvals. Select the *Available timesheets to adjust* option to see timesheets for which you have permission to edit the submitted actuals. Select the *My Resources Unsubmitted time-sheets* option to view timesheets that are due but which your resources have not yet submitted to you for approval.

 Warning: By default, members of the Resource Managers group do not have the Adjust Timesheet permission. If you need this capability, ask your Project Server administrator to allow this permission for the My Direct Reports category in the Resource Managers group.

The *Timesheet Approvals History* page contains a filter pane that allows you to filter the list of timesheets shown on the selected page, such as when the page displays a very large list of timesheets and you need to locate the timesheets for one particular resource. To filter the list of timesheets, select one or more filter options in the filter pane and then click the *Apply* button. Select the *Date* option to filter by date. Select the *Fiscal Period* option and choose a period from the *Fiscal Period* pick list, or select the *Custom Date Range* option and then set a date range. Select the *Resources* option and then enter a cost center number or select a resource name from the *Resource Name* pick list. For example, Figure 9 - 9 shows the *Timesheet Approvals* page filtered for a resource named George Stewart.

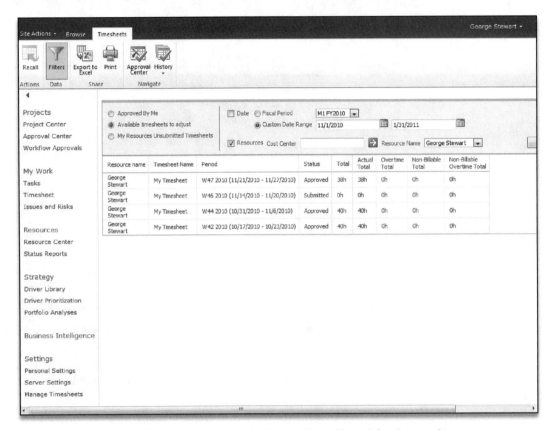

Figure 9 - 9: Timesheet Approvals History Page filtered for George Stewart

 If you do not see the filter pane at the top of the *Timesheet Approvals History* page, click the *Filter* button on the ribbon.

 To view all timesheets again, deselect the *Date* and *Resource* options and then click the *Apply* button.

By default, the *Timesheet Approvals* page contains the following columns:

- Resource Name

- Timesheet Name

- Period

- Status

- Total

- Actual Total

- Overtime Total

- Non-billable Total

- Non-billable Overtime Total

Depending on your organization's timesheet reporting method, the last four columns may or may not contain information. For example, if you do not track *Overtime* work, then the *Overtime Total* column is irrelevant.

Your Project Server administrator must set timesheet approvers in Project Server 2010 by designating the *Timesheet Manager* value for each resource and each timesheet approver. For example, for each of the resources who report to Marilyn Ray, the Project Server administrator specified Marilyn Ray in their *Timesheet Manager* field. Todd Chia is the Timesheet Manager for Marilyn Ray and the value is set accordingly.

To view the complete timesheet for a resource, click the *My Timesheet* link to the right of the resource's name for the desired reporting period. Project Server 2010 displays the *Review Timesheet Detail* page shown in Figure 9 - 10.

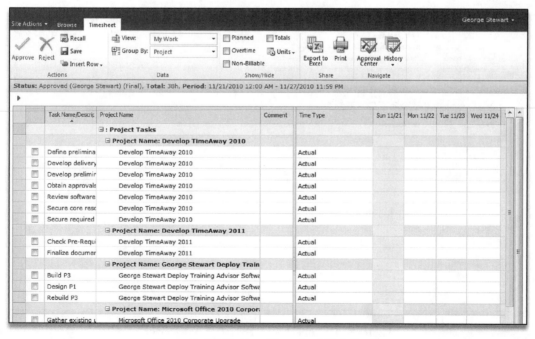

Figure 9 - 10: Review Timesheet Detail page

Adjusting Timesheet Updates

Occasionally, team members make a mistake entering data in the timesheet grid. For example, in Figure 9 - 11, George Stewart accidentally entered 23 hours of administrative time for Oct 28. Because you realize that George Stewart did not work 23 hours that day, you contact him and find out that he only worked 3 hours on that task. Therefore, you must adjust the timesheet to show the correct value. To adjust the timesheet entry, click in the cell containing the mistake; then enter the correct value and click the *Approve* button to save the changes.

Remember that members of the Resource Managers group do not have the Adjust Timesheet permission. If you need this capability, ask your Project Server administrator to allow this permission for the My Direct Reports category in the Resource Managers group.

If you want your resources to make their own corrections, select the option checkbox to the left of the timesheet line containing the mistake and then click the *Reject* button. The system automatically sends the resource an e-mail message requesting that the resource correct the rejected timesheet line.

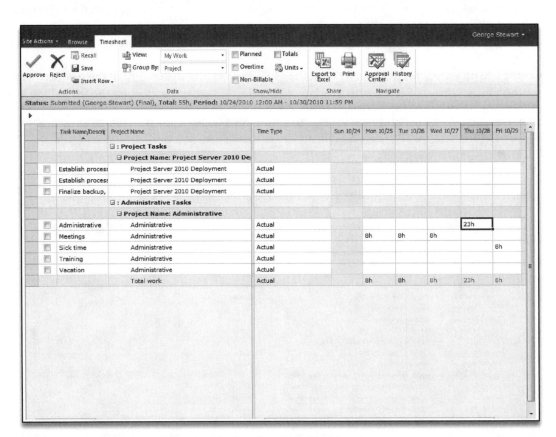

Figure 9 - 11: Timesheet Detail with entry error

Hands On Exercise

Exercise 9-3

You are a timesheet approver in your organization and must examine pending timesheets from resources that report to you.

1. Log on to Project Web App as your timesheet manager.

2. On the Home page in Project Web App, click the *Approval Center* link in the *Quick Launch* menu.

3. On the *Approval Center* page, click the *History* menu button and then select the *Timesheet* option to see the *Timesheet Approvals History* page.

4. On the *Timesheet Approvals History* page, click the *Filter* button on the ribbon to display the filter pane, if it is not already visible.

5. Select the *Approved By Me* option in the filter pane and then click the *Apply* button.

6. Reselect the *Available timesheets to adjust* option in the filter pane and then click the *Apply* button to return to the list of timesheets available for adjustment.

7. Experiment with the various options in the filter pane and apply different types of filtering to the submitted timesheets.

8. Click the *My timesheet* link to the right of a resource's name to examine the detailed timesheet from the resource.

9. On the *Review Timesheet Detail* page, adjust the timesheet information, and then click the *Accept* button to return to the *Approval Center* page.

Managing Administrative Time Requests

Project Server 2010 provides a formal approval process for administrative time requests such as vacation or educational leave. Your Project Server administrator must configure the system to determine the types of administrative time subject to approval. If your organization requires you to approve administrative time requests from your resources, you see these requests in the third line of the *Approvals* section in the main content area of the Project Web App Home page as shown in Figure 9 - 12.

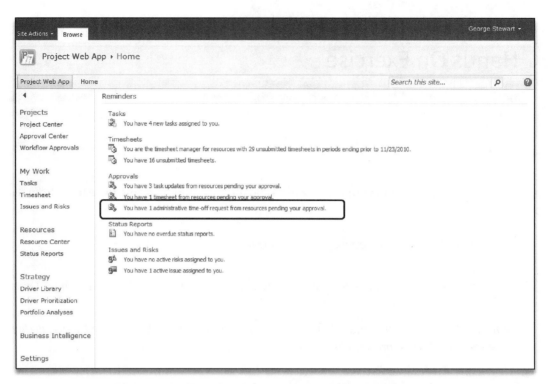

Figure 9 - 12: Home page shows administrative time requests

Click the *Approval Center* link in the *Quick Launch* menu or click the ___ *administrative time-off requests from your resources* link in the third line of *Approvals* section. The system displays the *Approval Center* page shown in Figure 9 - 13.

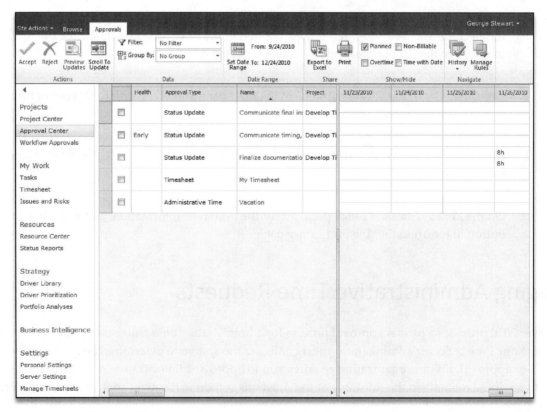

Figure 9 - 13: Approval Center page with Administrative time to approve

If you do not see the time entered for administrative time immediately, select the row selector to the left of the request and click the *Scroll to Update* button on the ribbon. This will show you the first instance of related hours for the selected transaction.

Approve Administrative Time Requests

To approve administrative time requests, select the option checkbox to the left of each request you want to approve and then click the *Accept* button. Enter any approval comments if prompted. The system redisplays the *Approval Center* page and removes the approved requests from the page. The approved administrative time shows up on the resource's timesheet as planned work for vacation line for the designated period as shown in Figure 9 - 14.

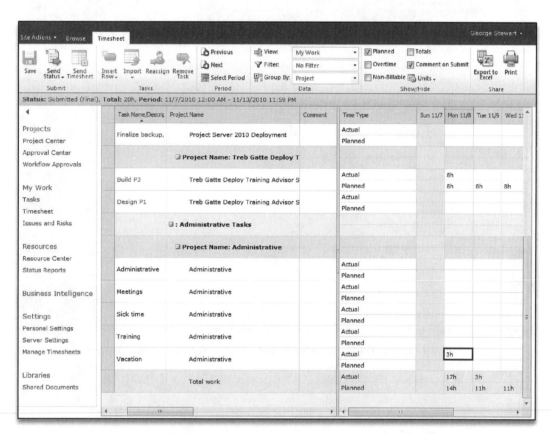

Figure 9 - 14: Timesheet page showing approved Administrative time

Rejecting Administrative Time Requests

To reject an administrative time request, select the requests to reject, and then click the *Reject* button. The system removes the administrative time request from the *Administrative Time* page and notifies the resource of the rejection with an e-mail message. Project Server 2010 displays the rejected administrative time with a *Rejected* status on the resource's timesheet for the designated period and shows a *Rejected* status in the *Information* bar beneath the ribbon as shown in Figure 9 - 15.

Unlike the *Timesheet Approvals* page, Project Server 2010 does **not** show you a history of approved and rejected administrative time requests.

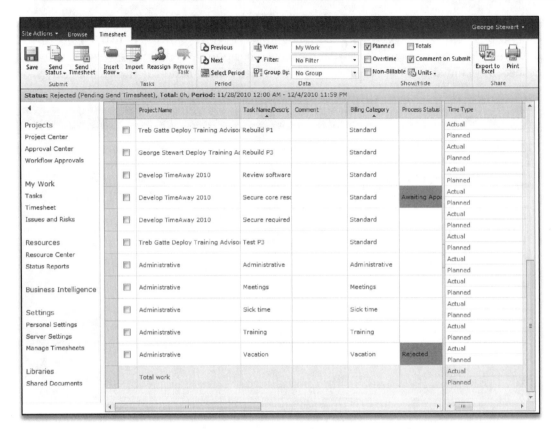

Figure 9 - 15: Timesheet showing Rejected Administrative Time request

Hands On Exercise

Exercise 9-4

Examine and approve administrative time requests for your resources.

1. Log in as your timesheet manager and navigate to the Home page in Project Web App.

2. In the *Approvals* section, look for information about administrative time-off requests pending your approval.

3. Click the *Approval Center* link in the *Project* section of the *Quick Launch* menu.

4. Select the option checkbox for the administrative time request and then click the *Accept* button.

5. Return to the Home page in Project Web App.

Viewing Task Updates

As project manager, you must approve or reject task updates from your resources, in addition to approving time-sheets and administrative time. Project Server 2010 indicates the number of task updates pending your approval in the *Approvals* section of the Project Web App Home page. For example, Figure 9 - 16 shows that the project manager, George Stewart, has 10 pending task updates from his resources.

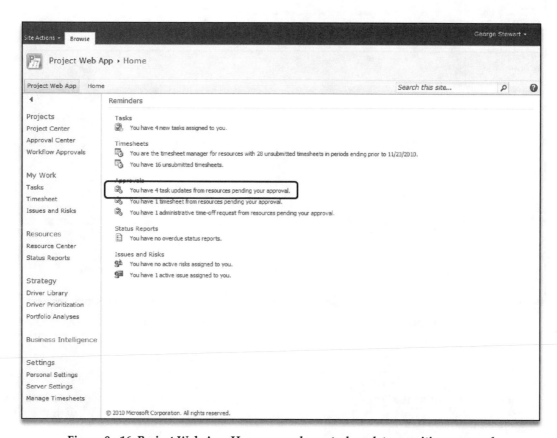

Figure 9 - 16: Project Web App Home page shows task updates awaiting approval

To view the task updates awaiting your approval, click the ___ *task updates from resources* link in the *Approvals* section of the Home page, or click the *Approval Center* link in the *Projects* section of the *Quick Launch* menu. The system displays the *Approval Center* page shown in Figure 9 - 17.

The display of planned and overtime work influences the row height of each update. Later, I discuss how to enable or disable these settings.

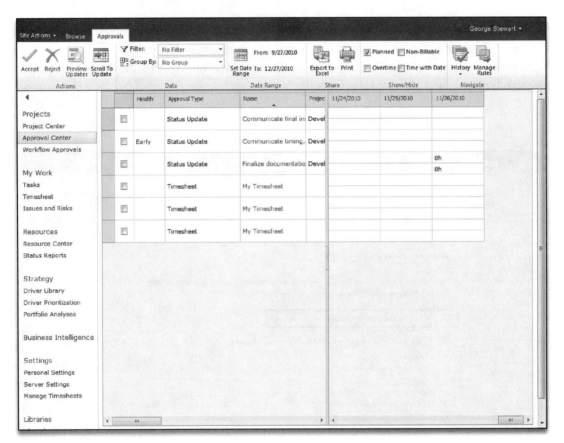

Figure 9 - 17: Approval Center page with three task updates

 For best results using the *Task Updates* page, MsProjectExperts recommends that you select the *Planned* option to display planned work. This option allows you to compare the **planned** work with the **actual** work for each task update.

If you click the hyperlink for any update in the *Name* field, Project Server 2010 displays a summary of the update information in the *Task Details* dialog, as shown in Figure 9 - 18. The *Task Details* dialog does not offer any additional information beyond that presented and is not modifiable.

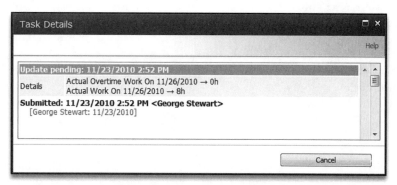

Figure 9 - 18: Task Details dialog for a selected task update

Hands On Exercise

Exercise 9-5

View and analyze task updates from your team members.

1. Log in as yourself.

2. On the Home page in Project Web App, look for task updates information in the *Approvals* section.

3. Click the *Approval Center* link in the *Projects* section of the *Quick Launch* menu.

4. Horizontally scroll to the left side of the grid and examine the information in each column shown for transactions with a *Status Update* approval type.

5. Change the *Filter* pick list value to *Status Updates*.

6. If it is not already checked, select the *Planned* Show/Hide option to view *Planned* work.

7. Click the hyperlink for any update in the *Name* field, examine the information shown in the *Task Details* dialog, and then close the dialog.

Task Update Processing

Successfully processing task updates requires the following process steps shown in Figure 9 - 19. You must repeat this process for each reporting cycle.

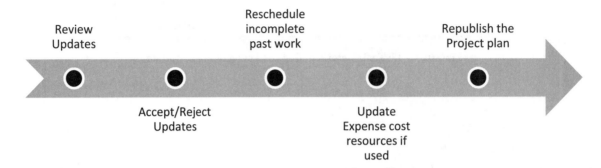

Figure 9 - 19: Task Update processing steps

The *Task Updates* page displays up to five types of updates, each of which you can see in Figure 9 - 20.

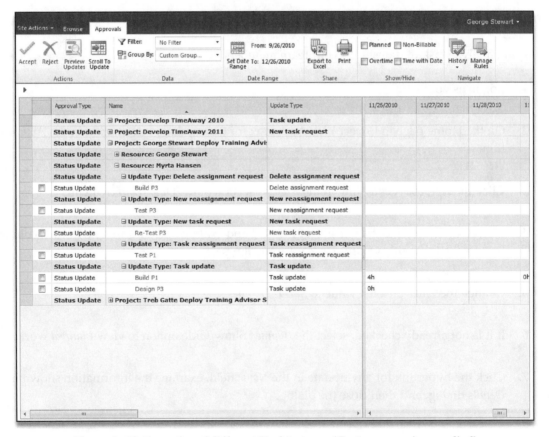

Figure 9 - 20: Examples of different Update types (Custom grouping applied)

The custom grouping of *Project, Resource, Update* type enables the illustrated view. Table 9 - 2 lists each *Update* type, with the action that creates it and what happens when you approve the transaction.

Action by Team Member	Resulting Update Type	What Does It Mean?
Updated task status	*Task update*	If approved, reported progress applies to the project plan
Updated task status and changed information such as Remaining Work	*Task update* with changed information shown in red, if present	If approved, reported progress and other changes apply to the project plan
Add themselves to an existing task	*New reassignment request*	If approved, the system creates a new assignment on the task for the requesting resource, enabling them to log time against the task.
Resource reassigned their assignment to another resource	*Task reassignment request*	If approved, the system transfers remaining work of the assignment to the new resource
Resource requests removal from a task.	*Delete assignment request*	If approved, the system removes the resource from the assignment
Resource requests a new task	*New Task Assignment*	If approved, the system adds the new task and assignment to the project plan.

Table 9 - 2: Task Update types

Warning: msProjectExperts recommends that you **never** accept a Delete Assignment request from a resource because this action automatically removes the resource from the task in the Project Professional 2010 plan. A better approach is to reject the Delete Assignment request and to ask the resource to delegate the task to another team member. If this is not possible, then reject the request and then manually replace the resource on the task in the Project Professional 2010 plan.

Review Task Updates

It is your responsibility as project manager to accept or reject all updates submitted by your resources. Accepting a task update automatically transfers the updated task information into the appropriate project plan. Rejecting a task update triggers an automatic e-mail message to the resource and may require the resource to take the appropriate action in response to your rejection. This process guarantees that you, the project manager, always serve as the "gatekeeper" between updates from your project team members and the actual Project Professional 2010 plan.

Project Server 2010 does not allow the system to bypass you and automatically update task progress from your team members into the Project Professional 2010 plan. Because the system requires your participation in the updates process, you must provide minimal oversight to all updates, preventing the system from updating "dirty data" into your Project Professional 2010 plan.

Before you process updates, pay special attention to any task update that includes a note in the *Comments* column. You can also click the *Name* link to view the details of the transaction as shown in Figure 9 - 21. A note attached to a task update usually indicates that your team members are trying to give you additional information about their task updates. In this case, the team member discovers a missing task and requests the addition of the task to their tracked work.

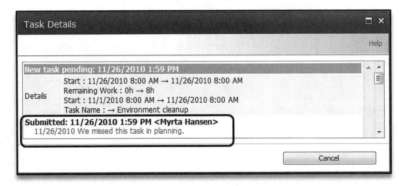

Figure 9 - 21: Update detail dialog with submission note

After reviewing the note, click the *Cancel* button to close the dialog and return to the *Task Updates* page.

MSProjectExperts strongly recommends that you take the time to read all notes included with task updates. If your team member took the time to write a note, you need to take the time to read the note!

Reject Task Updates

This process assumes you discovered updates in your review that you are not accepting. To begin the process of rejecting task updates, select the option checkbox to the left of each update to reject and then click the *Reject* button. Project Server 2010 displays the confirmation dialog into which you can enter rejection notes, as shown in Figure 9 - 22. Project Server 2010 removes the update from the *Task Updates* page.

Figure 9 - 22: Confirmation dialog to enter notes regarding selected action

You might reject a task update when a resource accidentally types an incorrect *Actual* work value, forgets to update *Remaining* work, or fails to annotate a new task request. You might also reject a *Task Assignment* request or a *Task Reassignment* request that is not appropriate. As indicated previously, you should always reject a *Delete Assignment* request.

If your organization uses single entry mode for timetracking, Rejected tasks show only in the *Tasks* page with a *Rejected* value. The *Timesheet* page only shows current approved tasks.

If you reject a task update because the resource made a data entry error, the resource must complete the following steps to see your rejection comments:

1. Click the name of the rejected task on the *Tasks* page.

2. On the *Assignment Details* page, expand the *Transaction Comments* and *Task History* section.

Approve Task Updates

To begin the process of approving task updates, select the option checkbox to the left of each update to approve. If all task updates are from the same project, you may want to click the *Select All* button to select all of the updates. If you want to preview the impact of the updates on the selected project, click the *Preview Updates* button. Project Server 2010 opens a separate Internet Explorer window and displays the *Approval Preview* page, shown in Figure 9 - 23.

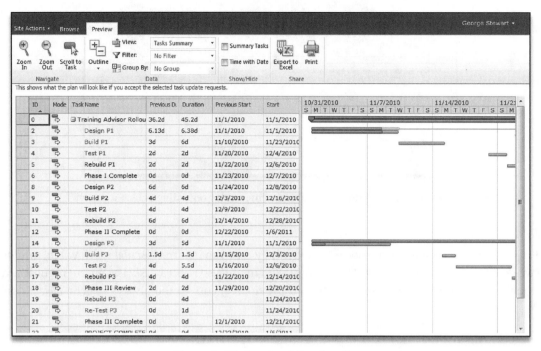

Figure 9 - 23: Approval Preview Page

The system indicates your selected task updates by displaying a hyperlink in the *Task Name* column. The *Approval Preview* page displays the *Tasks Summary* view for the project, and shows the post-approval state of the project before you actually approve the task updates. The information shown in the *Approval Preview* page is similar to the *Tracking Gantt* view available in Project Professional 2010.

The Gantt Chart portion of the view shown in the *Approval Preview* page allows you to compare current task progress against the original baseline schedule for each task. The system displays this information as follows:

- The **gray Gantt Bar** represents the baseline schedule of each task.

- The **blue Gantt Bar** represents the current schedule of each task after updates.

- The **filled part of each Gantt bar** represents the % Complete (current progress) on each task.

- The **gray diamond** represents the baseline schedule for each milestone task.

- The **black diamond** represents the current baseline schedule for each milestone task.

The table portion of the view shown in the *Approval Preview* page contains columns you can use to assess the current schedule. The default columns in the *Approval Preview* page include the following:

- Indicators

- ID

- Task Mode

- Task Name

- Previous Duration (the pre-approval Duration)

- Duration (the post-approval Duration)

- Previous Start (the pre-approval Start date)

- Start (the post-approval Start date)

- Previous Finish (the pre-approval Finish date)

- Finish (the post-approval Finish date)

- Previous % Complete

- % Complete

- Work

- Resource Names

When you see a task *Duration* value that is greater than the *Previous Duration* value, it indicates that the task is slipping. If you see a task *Finish* date later than the *Previous Finish* date, it also indicates that the task is slipping.

In the *Approval Preview* page ribbon, click the *View* pick list selector to see a list of views available in the *Approval Preview* page. The list contains a list of default detailed project views that ship with Project Server 2010, as well as any custom views created by your Project Server administrator. From the *View* pick list, choose and apply any additional views you want to use for the project in its pre-approval state. Click the *Window Close* button in the upper right corner of the window to close the window when finished.

After you examine the project in the **Approval Preview** page, click the *Accept* button to approve your selected updates. The system displays the confirmation dialog shown previously in Figure **9 - 22: Confirmation dialog to enter notes regarding selected action**

. Enter any additional information in the confirmation dialog and then click the *OK* button. Project Server 2010 transfers the updated information into the project and then removes the updates from the *Task Updates* page. Once you complete processing your updates, **publish the project plan** to update to the latest information state for all involved parties.

 MSProjectExperts recommends that you accept task updates for only one project at a time. This allows you to study the impact of the updates in the enterprise project, reschedule uncompleted work, make plan revisions, and publish schedule changes before you process updates for the next project.

Approving Task Updates in Project Professional 2010

In addition to using the *Task Updates* page in Project Web App, Project Server 2010 also allows you to process task updates within the Project Professional 2010 client. When you open an enterprise project in Project Professional 2010 and the project has pending unapproved task updates, the system displays the dialog shown in Figure 9 - 24.

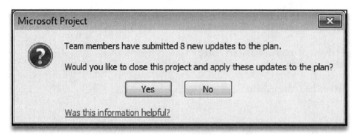

Figure 9 - 24: Enterprise project has outstanding task updates

Your choice is either to process outstanding updates now or later. Clicking the *Yes* button opens the *Approval Center* page for you to process task updates as covered previously. Clicking the *No* button opens the project plan for editing.

Be cognizant of changing the schedule when there are pending updates. If you anticipate schedule or work change, it is better to accept the updates so that the plan is at a known agreed state between you and the team members prior to making subsequent changes.

Hands On Exercise

Exercise 9-6

Approve updates from your team members using the Task Updates page in Project Web App.

1. Log in as yourself

2. Navigate to your *Approval Center* page by clicking the *Approval Center* link in the *Projects* section of the *Quick Launch* menu.

3. Select the *Rebuild P3* task and from the *Actions* section of the *Approvals* ribbon, click the *Accept* button. Type a comment and click the *OK* button in the *Confirmation* dialog.

4. Review any comments on the updates.

5. Select the task updates for the *Deploy Training Advisor Software* project

6.   Click the *Preview Updates* button on the ribbon.

7.   From the *View* pick list in the *Approval Preview* window, select and review the *Task Schedule* view, then select and review the *Tasks Work* view.

8.   Click the *Window Close* button to close the *Approval Preview* window.

9.   Verify the selection of the task updates.

10.   Click the *Accept* button, enter explanatory text in the confirmation dialog, and then click the *OK* button to complete the approval process.

11.   Leave your Internet Explorer application open to the *Approval Center* page in Project Web App.

Exercise 9-7

Review applied task updates in an enterprise project in Project Professional 2010.

1.   Launch Project Professional 2010 and log in to Project Server as yourself.

2.   Open the *Deploy Training Advisor Software* project (it should not contain pending updates).

3.   Review the impact of the updated task information from Exercise 9-6.

4.   Save and publish the latest schedule changes.

5.   Leave the *Deploy Training Advisor Software* project open for use with the next Hands-On Exercise.

Rescheduling Uncompleted Work in Past Reporting Periods

After accepting task updates, you should always examine the project in Project Professional 2010 to locate and reschedule uncompleted tasks that remain scheduled to occur in the past. These tasks mostly comprise unstarted tasks and in-progress tasks for which the assigned resource performed no work at all during the last reporting period. When a resource reports progress on a task, and you subsequently update the progress into the plan, the system automatically reschedules the incomplete work to begin after the update status date. The system **does not** automatically reschedule work on current tasks not updated by resources, as the system takes no action on them.

Figure 9 - 25 shows a project that contains uncompleted work that I scheduled to occur prior to the *Project Status Date*. By default, the *Project Status Date* found on the *Project* tab is today unless the project manager manually changes this date.

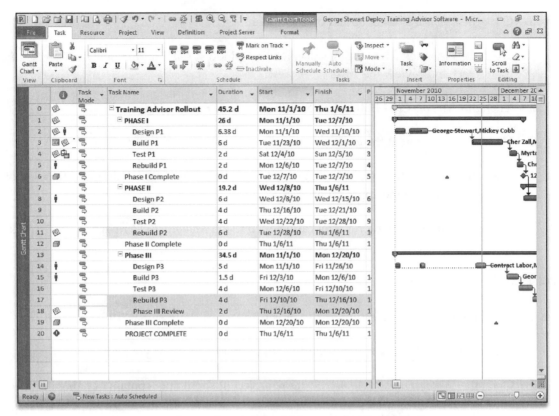

Figure 9 - 25: Enterprise project with uncompleted work in the past

To reschedule uncompleted work from a past reporting period into the current reporting period, complete the following steps:

1. Select specific tasks with uncompleted work in a past reporting period if you only want to reschedule those tasks.

   1.1. The *Late Tasks* view filter can help determine what tasks to reschedule.

   1.2. Otherwise, skip to step 2 to do this over all tasks with past work.

2. On the *Project* tab in Project Professional, click the *Update Project* button.

3. Project Professional 2010 displays the *Update Project* dialog. The *Update work as complete through* setting is the default setting. Change the settings as follows:

4. Select the *Reschedule uncompleted work to start after* option.

5. Click the *Reschedule uncompleted work to start after* pick list and select a date at least one day **before** the work must resume on the uncompleted tasks.

6. Select the *Selected tasks* option if you selected tasks in step 1. Otherwise, leave *Entire Project* selected.

7. Figure 9 - 26 illustrates the proper dialog settings. Review your settings and continue to the next step.

8. Click the *OK* button

9. The dialog closes and the uncompleted work moves to begin on the date selected in step 5.

If you select the *Entire project* option in the *Update Project* dialog, Project Professional 2010 reschedules any task with uncompleted work in the past. This option is very useful for large projects with hundreds or thousands of tasks.

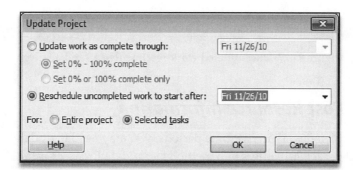

Figure 9 - 26: Update Project dialog set to reschedule uncompleted work

Figure 9 - 26 shows the *Update Project* dialog set to reschedule tasks to start on Monday, November 29. Notice that I selected Friday, November 26, 2010 as the date in the *Reschedule uncompleted work to start after* option, forcing the selected tasks to start November 29.

Figure 9 - 27 shows how Project Professional 2010 reschedules tasks with unstarted and uncompleted work from past reporting periods into the current reporting period by setting a Start No Earlier Than (SNET) constraint on the selected tasks. If the task is in-progress, then Project Professional 2010 splits the task and moves only the uncompleted portion to the current reporting period.

Because the *Design P1* task is a predecessor task to *Build P1* task of the project, delaying this task affects the schedule of a chain of other dependent tasks. Notice that the *Change Highlighting* feature shows every task impacted by the rescheduled task.

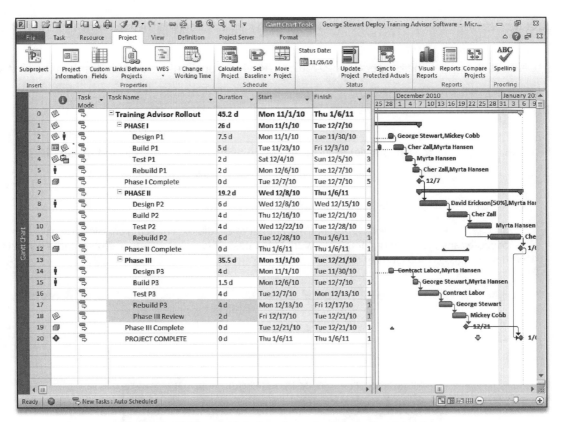

Figure 9 - 27: Uncompleted work rescheduled after date given

Updating Expense Cost Resource Information

After you reschedule uncompleted work in past time periods, you may need to update project expenditures for *Expense Cost* resources. Project Server 2010 offers two methods to update *Expense Cost* resource information:

- Programmatically update the *Expense Cost* resources from a third-party financial system.

- Manually enter the *Expense Cost* information.

If you use the programmatic approach, you do not need to take any action since the system automatically updates the *Expense Cost* resource information from your financial system.

To update the *Expense Cost* resource information manually, complete the following steps:

1. In Project Professional 2010, click the *Task Usage* menu button on the *View* tab.

2. Click the *Tables* menu button and select the *Cost* item to apply the *Cost* table.

3. Pull the split bar to the right of the *Remaining Cost* column. Compare your screen to Figure 9 - 28.

4. Enter the cost in the *Actual Cost* column for the *Expense Cost* resource assignment you want to expense.

5. Reduce the *Remaining Cost* value to $0.00, if necessary.

Figure 9 - 28 shows that I assigned the *Expense Computer Hardware* resource to the *Design P2* task in the second phase of my project. This is because I intend to track this expense in that project phase. The view is already set up to enable you to enter *Actual Cost* values for the *Expense Computer Hardware* resource.

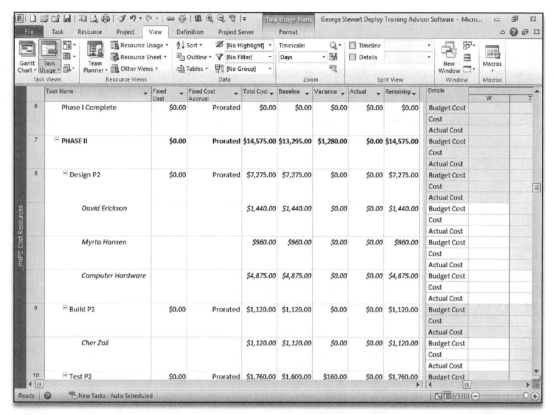

Figure 9 - 28: Expense Computer Hardware assigned to tasks in the second phase

You should reduce the Remaining Cost to $0.00 if the Actual Expense is less than the planned expense shown in the *Cost* column.

Figure 9 - 29 shows the *Task Usage* view with the timephased grid setup to enter *Actual Cost* information for the *Expense Travel* resource. Notice that the *Task Usage* view shows $812.50 of *Actual Cost* for the *Expense Computer Hardware* resource, timephased across the 6 days of the *Design P2* task.

Project Professional 2010 distributes the *Actual Cost* evenly across the duration of the task in the timephased grid. In reality, the expense likely accrued on a specific day due to payment of an invoice or the filing of an expense report. To reallocate the *Actual Cost* to a specific day or days, complete the following additional steps:

1. Pull the split bar back to the edge of the *Fixed Cost* column to expose the timephased grid (gray timesheet on the right side of the view).

2. If costs are not visible, right-click anywhere in the timephased grid and select the *Cost* item, right-click again and select the *Actual Cost* item, and then right-click one more time and deselect the *Work* item.

3. Edit the Actual Cost information in the timephased grid.

Warning: Enter 0 for any days that scheduled expenses that will no longer occur. Otherwise, Project Server 2010 attempts to reschedule the existing timephased cost which can lead to double counting. The total cost column can indicate if your entries are correct.

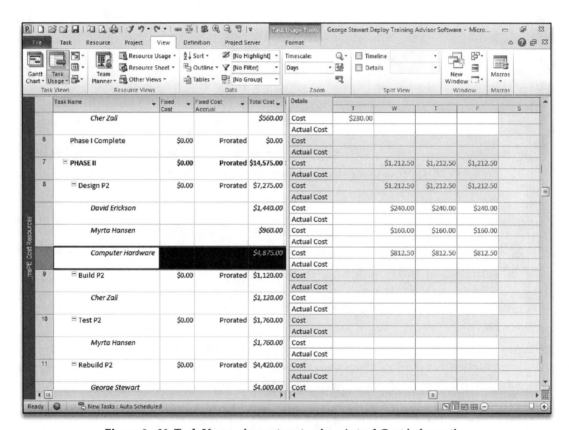

Figure 9 - 29: Task Usage view set up to view Actual Cost information

Notice in Figure 9 - 30 that I entered all of the $4875.00 of *Actual Cost* for the *Expense Computer Hardware* resource on Friday as the receipt of the computer hardware occurred on that day.

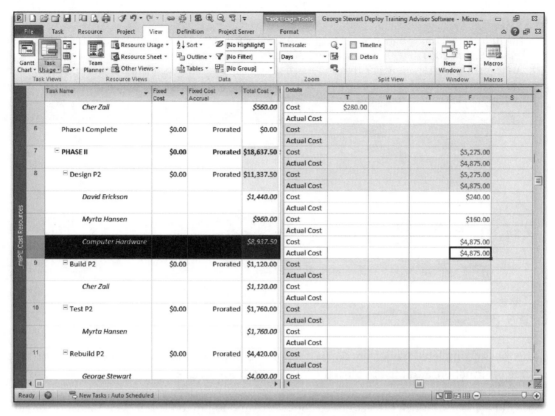

Figure 9 - 30: Task Usage view shows all $4875.00 of Actual Cost on Friday

Publishing the Latest Schedule Changes

After you update task progress into your project, reschedule uncompleted work, and update *Cost* resource information, you must **always** save the project and then publish the latest schedule changes. This step is extremely important, as it updates the latest schedule information on the *Tasks* page of each team member in the project. To publish the latest schedule changes, click *File* tab, then click the *Publish* button in the *Backstage*. The system updates the Project Server 2010 database with the current information for the project, making the current schedule visible everywhere in Project Web App.

Warning: If you fail to publish the latest schedule changes after updating a project, your project becomes "out of synch" between the Project Professional 2010 plan and Project Web App. "Out of synch" project information adversely affects your project team members, as they cannot see the current task schedule on the *Tasks* page. Remember that you must **always** publish your enterprise project after updating it with task progress.

The default publishing behavior for Project Server 2010 is different from the publishing behavior in Project Server 2003. If your organization upgraded from the 2003 version to the 2010 version, MsProjectExperts recommends that you make project and task publishing a training and performance issue. Teach your project managers to publish their enterprise project after every round of task updates, and then hold them accountable for this performance.

Hands On Exercise

Exercise 9-8

Reschedule uncompleted work from the past reporting period into the current reporting period, update Cost resource information, and then publish the latest schedule changes.

1. If necessary, launch Project Professional 2010 and log in to Project Server as yourself, and open the *Deploy Training Advisor Software* project.

2. On the *View* tab, click the *Tables* menu button and select the *Tracking* item.

3. Set the *Percent Complete* value for *Design P3* task to *50%*.

4. With *Design P3* task as the current selection, click the *Task* tab, then the *Notes* icon in the *Properties* section of the ribbon.

5. Add a note to indicate the contractor called in sick in the middle of the week and click the *OK* button.

6. With *Design P3* task as the current selection, click the *Project* tab, then click the *Update Project* button.

7. Select the *Reschedule uncompleted work to start after* option and set the selected *Design P3* task to start after the upcoming Sunday. Select the *Selected Tasks* option in the *For* section and click the *OK* button.

8. Select the *Test P3* and *Phase III Complete* tasks using **Ctrl + Mouse** click.

9. On the *Tasks* tab, in the *Schedule* section, click the *Unlink* button to break the existing links between the tasks.

10. With the tasks from step 9 still selected, click the *Link* button on the *Tasks* tab in the *Schedule* section to relink the tasks.

11. Save your project and then click the *File* tab, then the *Publish* button in the *Backstage* to publish the latest schedule changes.

12. Close and check-in your enterprise project and then exit Project Professional 2010.

Using Status Updates History Page and Approval Rules

The next topical sections relate to the *Status Updates History* page and automatic approval rule setup. You use these two functions together to make the management of projects that track processes or ad hoc tasks easier. For example, you use a project plan as a way of allocating resources to a repetitive process, like customer setup. The template assigns the standard tasks to team generic resources. Team leads then reassign the work to actual work resources. The status of each task is paramount to the actual schedule as customer setup is a known process with well-known time-lines. Automatic approval rules allow you to direct the system to accept all updates to these plans. You use the *Status Updates History* page to monitor for new updates and to republish the project plan on the server.

Viewing Status Updates History Page

Project Server 2010 maintains a history of all task updates that you accept and reject. To view the history of in-progress updates, on the *Approval Center* page, click the *History* menu button and select the *Status Updates* item. The system displays the *Status Updates History* page shown in Figure 9 - 31.

The action column indicates the *Transaction* approval status as either *Accepted* or *Rejected*. The *Status* column indicates the publish state of the transaction as *Published, Unpublished* or *Pending* if a project is checked out and the change cannot be applied yet.

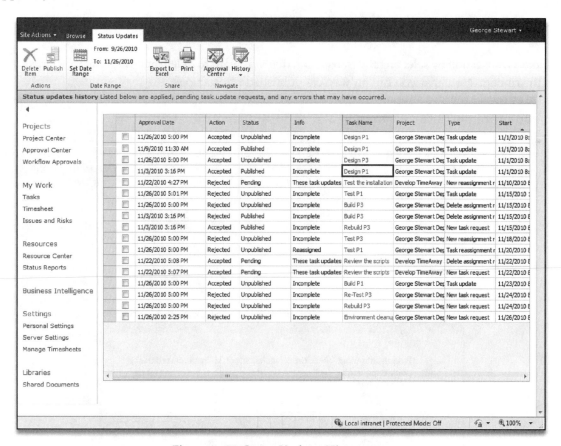

Figure 9 - 31: Status Updates History page

Normally the *Reviewed Task Update Requests* page should appear **empty** and **should not** show any task updates. However, if you attempt to accept or reject task updates in a project checked out to someone else, Project Server 2010 cannot complete the update process, and then displays them as reviewed updates on the *Reviewed Task Update Requests* page. If you navigate to this page and find any task updates, close the enterprise project indicated in the *Project* column so that Project Server 2010 can complete the update process. After completing the updates, the system removes the reviewed task updates from the *Reviewed Task Update Requests* page.

To clear transactions on the *Reviewed Task Update Requests* page, do one of the following three actions:

1. Check in any project that has transactions in a *Pending* status.

    1.1. This enables the system to apply outstanding changes.

    1.2. Note, perform project check-in from the Project Center.

2. Publish the project.

    2.1. Select any transaction from a project and then click the *Publish* button to process all outstanding transactions for that project.

    2.2. Publish presents the prompt in Figure 9 - 32.

3. Delete a transaction by selecting the transaction that you want to delete and then click the *Delete Item* button on the ribbon. Note that you can only delete published transactions.

Warning: The *Delete* function **DOES NOT** give you a confirmation prompt before executing the delete. Ensure this is really what you want to do prior performing the delete. Use the *Delete* functionality carefully as you are deleting published data. You should republish the project after a delete to ensure that the project plan and the server data are in sync.

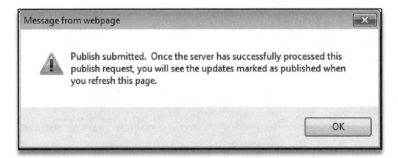

Figure 9 - 32: Publish transaction prompt

Hands On Exercise

Exercise 9-9

View the history of task updates.

1. Log in as yourself and navigate to your *Approval Center* page by clicking the *Approval Center* link in the *Projects* section of the *Quick Launch* menu.

2. Click the *History* menu button and select the *Status Updates* option.

3. If you see any unpublished updates, select the unpublished transaction and click the *Publish* button.

4. Click the *Approval Center* button to return to the *Approval Center* page.

Managing Rules for Accepting Task Updates

The *Rules* feature in Project Server 2010 allows you to create logical rules for quickly approving task updates into your projects. When you apply a rule, the system approves only those task changes that meet the criteria defined in the rule. Rules can also execute automatically if you desire. However, rules never automatically publish the projects for which transactions are accepted or rejected.

Access the *Rules* feature by clicking the *Manage Rules* button from the *Approval Center* page. The system displays the *Rules* page shown in Figure 9 - 33.

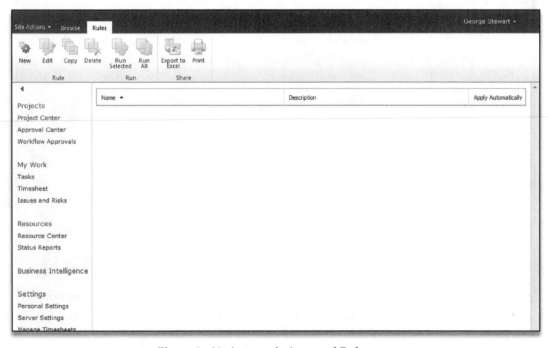

Figure 9 - 33: Automatic Approval Rules page

Create a New Rule

Click the *New Rule* button to begin the process of creating the new rule. The system displays the *Edit/Create Rule* page shown in Figure 9 - 34.

Enter a name for the new rule in the *Name* field and enter an optional description in the *Description and comments for team members* field. Select the *Automatically run this rule* option if you want Project Server 2010 to run the rule automatically or when you click the *Run All Rules* button on the *Rules* page. Leave the option deselected if you want to run the rule manually. If you run the rule automatically, you can monitor the transactions resulting from the rule execution on the *Status Updates History* page.

Figure 9 - 34: Edit/Create Rule page

In the *Request Types* section, select the type of updates you wish to process with the rule as shown in Table 9 - 3.

Setting	Action
All new task and assignment requests	Select the option to process updates for which a resource proposes a new task or assigns himself to an existing task.
All task reassignment requests	Select the option to process updates for which a resource delegates a task to another team member, or assigns himself to a task previously assigned to a team resource.
All assignment deletion requests	Select the option to process updates for resource rejected task assignments.
Task updates	Select the option to process task progress updates from your resources.

Table 9 - 3: List of Request Types

If you select the *Task updates* option as shown previously in Figure 9 - 34, you must select one of the three options, which follow. Select the *All Updates* option to process all progress updates from your resources.

If you select the *Where updated field matches a field in the published project* option, Project Server 2010 expands the *Request Types* section with additional options, as shown in Figure 9 - 35. In the expanded *Request Types* section, create a custom filter by specifying values from the *Updated Field, Operator,* and *Published field* pick lists. For example, you can enable automatic approval of updates where *Assignment Actual Work* is equal to *Assignment Baseline Work.*

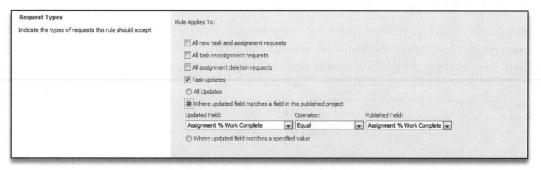

Figure 9 - 35: Request Type custom filter based on field value match

If you select the *Where updated field matches a specific value* option, Project Server 2010 expands the *Request Types* section with additional options, as shown in Figure 9 - 36. In the expanded *Request Types* section, create a custom filter by specifying values from the *Updated Field* and *Operator* pick lists, and enter a value in the *Value* field. For example, you can enable automatic approvals for all updates where the assignment *% Work Complete* value is equal to *100.*

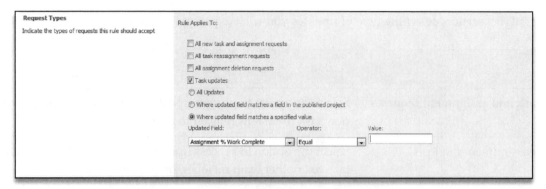

Figure 9 - 36: Request Type custom filter based on specific value match

In the *Projects* section of the page, select an option to determine to which projects the rule must apply. Select the *All my current and future projects* option to apply the rule to all current and future projects. If you select the *Specific projects* option, the system expands the *Projects* section, as shown in Figure 9 - 37.

Figure 9 - 37: Expanded Projects section allows selection of specific projects

From the *Available Projects* list, select one or more projects and then click the *Add* button to add your selections to the *Selected Projects* list. If you want the rule to process future projects in addition to the selected projects, select the *All projects in the future* option as well.

In the *Resources* section, select an option to determine the resources to which the rule applies. Select the *All my current and future resources* option to apply the rule to updates from all current and future resources. If you select the *Specific resources* option, the system expands the *Resources* section, as shown in Figure 9 - 38.

Figure 9 - 38: Expanded Resources section allows selection of specific resources

From the *Available Resources* list, select one or more resources and then click the *Add* button to add them to the *Selected Resources* list. If you want the rule to process updates from future resources in addition to the selected resources, select the *All resources in the future* option as well.

> If you select the *All task assignment requests* option in the *Request Types* section of the page, the system adds two additional options in the *Resources* section. These options allow you to select the specific resources for task reassignment.

Figure 9 - 39 shows my completed rule that automatically approves progress updates from all resources for all projects when the task assignment is not completed. The new rule ignores all task updates that complete a task assignment, requiring the project manager to approve such updates manually. The rule also ignores all other types of updates as well.

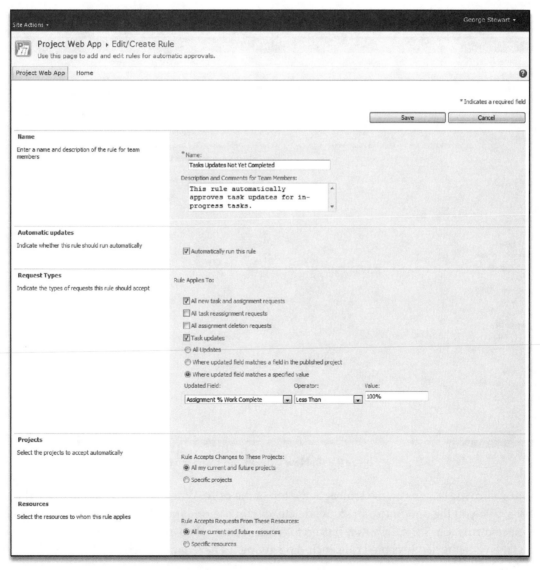

Figure 9 - 39: New rule created to approve task updates

Click the *Save* button to save the new rule. Figure 9 - 40 shows three rules on the *Rules* page in Project Web App. These rules are as follows:

- **Any Update from PMO Team Members** automatically approves any type of update in any project from a resource in the PMO.

- **Task Reassignment Updates from Team Leaders** automatically approves task reassignment requests from resources designated as a team leader.

- **Task Updates Not Yet Completed** automatically approves task updates for in-progress assignments, but ignores updates that complete work on a task assignment.

Use these three rules as examples for creating your own rules.

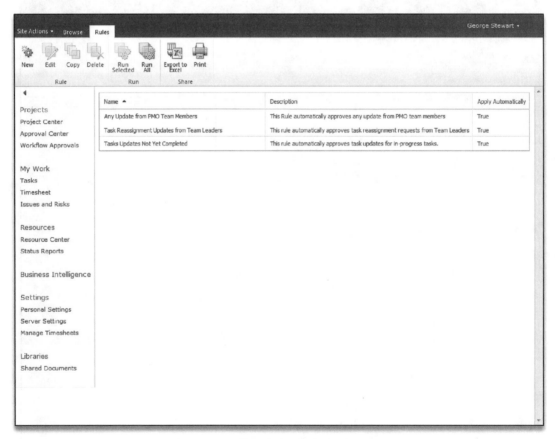

Figure 9 - 40: New rule on the Rules page

In Figure 9 - 40, notice the buttons on the toolbar at the top of the page. When you select a rule in the data grid, these toolbar buttons give you the option to edit, copy, delete, or run the rule individually. Click the *Edit Rule* button to modify the selected rule. Click the *Copy Rule* button to create a new rule based on the selected rule. After copying a rule, you must then edit the newly copied rule, including giving it a new name. Click the *Delete Rule* button to remove the selected rule.

Select a rule in the data grid and then click the *Run Rule* button to run only the selected rule. To run all rules in a single operation, click the *Run All Rules* button. Project Server 2010 approves all updates indicated in the rules for which the *Apply Automatically* option is set to *True*. If the *Apply Automatically* option is set to *False*, then you must run the rule individually by selecting it and clicking the *Run Rule* button.

Hands On Exercise

Exercise 9-10

Create a new rule for processing task updates and then apply the rule to any pending task updates.

1. Log in as yourself and navigate to your *Approval Center* page by clicking the *Approval Center* link in the *Projects* section of the *Quick Launch* menu.

2. From the *Navigate* section of the *Approvals* ribbon, click the *Manage Rules* button.

3. On the *Rules* page, click the *New Rule* button.

4. On the *Edit/Create Rule* page, create a new rule using the following options:

   - Give your new rule a name

   - Select the *Automatically run this rule* item in the *Automatic* Updates section.

   - Select the Where updated field matches a specified value option and set the Updated Field value to *Assignment % Work Complete,* the *Operator* value to *Less Than,* and the *Value* value to 100

     - Set the value in the *Project* section to *All my current and future projects* and set the *Resources* section option to *All my current and future resources.*

5. Click the *Save* button when finished.

6. From the *Rules* page, click the *Run All Rules* button if you currently have pending task updates.

7. Return to the Home page in Project Web App.

Closing Tasks to Update

Project Server 2010 allows you to close tasks to prevent team members from entering progress against them. You might want to close tasks that are completed or cancelled. To close tasks to updates, click the *Project Center* link in the *Quick Launch* menu. The system displays the *Project Center* page shown in Figure 9 - 41. Select the row for the desired project and click the *Close Tasks to Update* button in the ribbon.

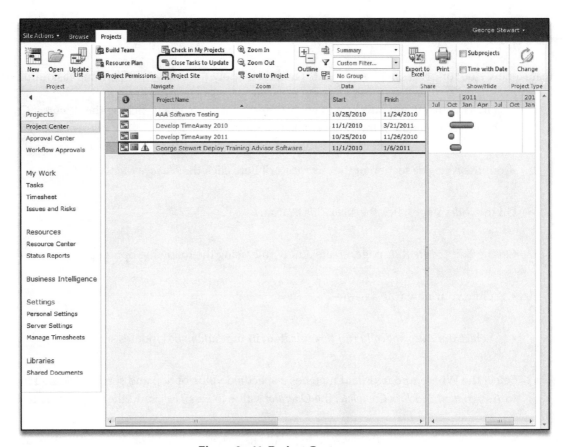

Figure 9 - 41: Project Center page

The system opens the *Close Tasks to Update* page as shown in Figure 9 - 42.

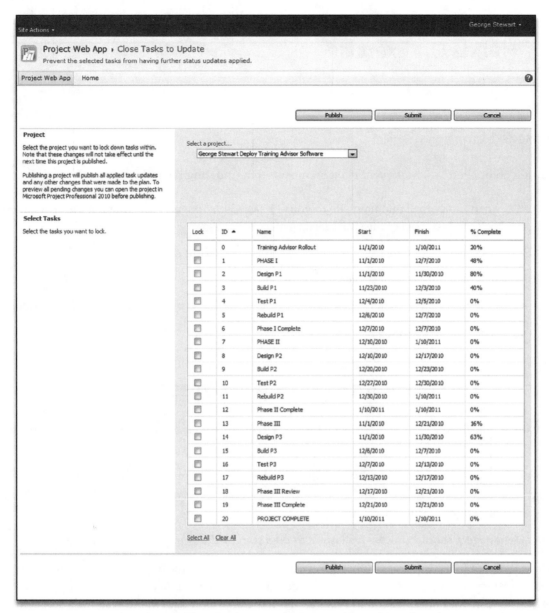

Figure 9 - 42: Close Tasks to Update page with project selected

Select the option checkboxes to the left of the tasks you wish to close and then click the *Publish* button. If you are not ready to publish the latest schedule changes in the project, you may click the *Submit* button instead. After publishing your project, the system locks the closed tasks to prevent team members from entering and submitting progress against the closed tasks.

Once you close a task to update, the task no longer appears as a task in the *Tasks* page nor will it appear on new time-sheets.

Hands On Exercise

Exercise 9-11

Close a completed task to prevent team members from updating the task.

1. Log in as yourself and navigate to your *Project Center* page by clicking the *Project Center* link in the *Projects* section of the *Quick Launch* menu.

2. Select the row for the Deploy Training Advisor Software project.

3. Click the *Close Tasks to Update* button on the ribbon.

4. In the *Select Tasks* section of the page, select the option checkbox to the left of a completed task.

5. Click the *Publish* button.

Axioms for Success with Tracking Progress

To be successful in tracking project progress using Project Server 2010, your organization should keep the following in mind:

- Everyone in your organization who is responsible for reporting progress should enter their time and send their updates on a standard day and time whether this is daily, weekly, semi-weekly or other predictable and appropriate reporting standard.

- Project managers should process task updates on a standard day each reporting period.

- Managers should deal appropriately with anyone who is responsible for reporting progress, but who fails to cooperate or participate fully in the process. You must take all necessary steps to ensure the full participation of everyone in your organization in order to validate the project data in the system.

- Your organization should track and manage the absence of resources during each update cycle. If necessary, you can create delegates to manage timesheets for absent resources.

- Your organization should also track and manage the absence of managers during each update cycle. For updating purposes, other managers can take over tasks owned by absent managers and process the updates.

- Stay current with progress reporting and updates to make sure that you are managing your projects with current data.

Module 10

Variance Analysis, Plan Revision, and Reporting

Learning Objectives

After completing this module, you will be able to:

- Understand the different types of project variance
- Define plan revision and change control
- Revise a project plan to bring it back on schedule
- Use change control procedures to add a new task to a project
- Baseline a project after adding new tasks
- Use the Timeline view with the Gantt Chart view
- Use Visual Reports with Microsoft Excel and Microsoft Visio

Inside Module 10

Understanding Variance

At the end of every reporting period, you should analyze project variance by comparing actual progress and remaining estimates against the original project baseline. This is the way you determine schedule slippage and overruns, as well as identifying existing and/or potential problems with your project schedule. Analyzing variance is the first step in revising the project plan to bring it back on track with its original goals and objectives.

Understanding Variance Types

In Module 07, I stated that when you save a baseline in Project Professional 2010, the software baselines the current values for five important task fields. These fields include the *Duration, Start, Finish, Work,* and *Cost* fields. Because the system saves five task values in a project baseline, the system calculates five types of task variance:

- Duration variance
- Start variance
- Finish variance
- Work variance
- Cost variance

About Those Extra Task Baseline Fields

In Module 07, I noted that in addition to the five important task fields captured in the baseline, Project Professional 2010 also captures extra baseline information in several other task fields. The software captures the extra baseline information in the following fields: the *Baseline Fixed Cost* and *Baseline Fixed Cost Accrual* fields; the *Baseline Estimated Duration, Baseline Estimated Start,* and *Baseline Estimated Finish* fields; and the *Baseline Budget Cost* and *Baseline Budget Work* fields.

Even though Project Professional 2010 captures the extra task baseline information in these seven fields, the software **does not** include any corresponding variance fields for them. This means that if you want to analyze *Fixed Cost* variance, for example, there is no default field called *Fixed Cost Variance*. So, if you want to analyze *Fixed Cost* variance, you must create a custom task field containing a formula to calculate this variance. The same is true for the other six extra baseline fields as well.

Calculating Variance

To calculate variance, Project Professional 2010 uses the following formula:

Variance = (Actual Progress + Remaining Estimates) - Baseline

In Project Professional 2010, a positive variance is unfavorable to the project, and means that the project schedule is late, or that work and/or cost are over budget. Negative variance is favorable to the project, and means that the project is ahead of schedule, or that work and/or cost are under budget.

For example, suppose that the actual work for a task is 60 hours, the remaining work estimate is 40 hours, and the baseline work for the task is 80 hours. Using the formula above, Project Professional 2010 calculates the work variance as:

> Work Variance = (Actual Work + Remaining Work) – Baseline Work
>
> Work Variance = (60 hours + 40 hours) – 80 hours
>
> Work Variance = 100 hours - 80 hours
>
> Work Variance = 20 hours

The resulting 20-hour work variance is unfavorable to the project because the total work hours exceed the original baseline work budget.

Analyzing Project Variance

Project Professional 2010 offers you the following locations from which to analyze project variance:

- *Tracking Gantt* view
- *Variance* table
- *Work* table
- *Cost* table

The *Tracking Gantt* view and the *Variance* table allow you to analyze start and finish variance for tasks. The *Work* and *Cost* tables allow you to analyze work and cost variance, respectively.

> Microsoft Project 2010 does not offer a default table from which to analyze *Duration* variance. If you want to see *Duration* variance, you must create your own custom table for this purpose. Later in this module, I teach you how to use the custom duration slippage view included in the Project Server 2010 system used with this course.

Analyzing Date Variance

Date variance is a major concern for every project manager because many projects have an inflexible project finish date. You can analyze *Date* variance graphically by applying the *Tracking Gantt* view. To apply the *Tracking Gantt* view, use one of the following methods:

- On the *Task* ribbon, click the *Gantt Chart* pick list button and select the *Tracking Gantt* view from the list.
- On the *Resource* ribbon, click the *Team Planner* pick list button and select the *Tracking Gantt* view from the list.
- On the *View* ribbon, click the *Gantt Chart* pick list button and select the *Tracking Gantt* view from the list.

Project Professional 2010 applies the *Tracking Gantt* view shown in Figure 10 - 1.

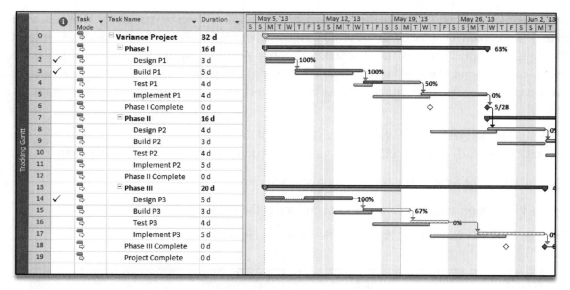

Figure 10 - 1: Tracking Gantt view

Following is a description of the symbols shown in the *Gantt Chart* screen on the right side of the *Tracking Gantt* view:

- Light red Gantt bars represent planned work for tasks on the Critical Path.

- Light blue Gantt bars represent planned work for tasks not on the Critical Path.

- Light teal Gantt bars represent planned work for *Manually Scheduled* tasks not on the Critical Path.

- Dark red Gantt bars represent completed work for tasks on the Critical Path.

- Dark blue Gantt bars represent completed work for tasks not on the Critical Path.

- Dark teal Gantt bars represent completed work for *Manually Scheduled* tasks not on the Critical Path.

- Gray Gantt bars represent the baseline schedule for each task.

- Black solid diamonds represent the current schedule for each milestone task.

- Teal solid diamonds represent the current schedule for *Manually Scheduled* milestone tasks.

- Hollow diamonds represent the baseline schedule for each milestone task.

- The percentage value at the right end of each Gantt bar represents the *% Complete* field value for each task.

- The tan bar on the bottom half of each summary task Gantt bar represents the cumulative *% Complete* field value for all of the subtasks for the summary task.

To see every possible symbol that Microsoft Project 2010 can display in the *Tracking Gantt* view, double-click anywhere in the white part of the *Gantt Chart* screen on the right side of the view. The system displays the *Bar Styles* dialog, which shows you the definition for every symbol used in the *Tracking Gantt* view.

The *Tracking Gantt* view allows you to see slippage graphically in your project by comparing blue, red, and teal Gantt bars with their accompanying gray Gantt bars (the baseline schedule for each task). If a blue, red, or teal Gantt bar slips to the right of its gray Gantt bar, then the task is slipping. Additionally, if a black or teal diamond slips to the right of its hollow diamond, then the milestone task is slipping. Using the *Tracking Gantt* view to analyze date variance makes it easy to see the slippage in all phases of the project, as well as the overall slippage for the final project finish date.

Use the *Variance* table to view the *Date* variance in a numerical format, such as in days. To apply the *Variance* table, display any task view (such as the *Tracking Gantt* view) and then use either of the following methods:

- Right-click on the *Select All* button and then select the *Variance* table in the shortcut menu.

- In the *View* ribbon, click the *Tables* pick list and select the *Variance* table in the list.

Project Professional 2010 displays the *Variance* table shown in Figure 10 - 2.

	Task Mode	Task Name	Start	Finish	Baseline Start	Baseline Finish	Start Var.	Finish Var.
0		⊟ **Variance Project**	**5/6/13**	**6/19/13**	**5/6/13**	**6/14/13**	**0 d**	**3 d**
1		⊟ **Phase I**	**5/6/13**	**5/28/13**	**5/6/13**	**5/22/13**	**0 d**	**3 d**
2		Design P1	5/6/13	5/8/13	5/6/13	5/8/13	0 d	0 d
3		Build P1	5/9/13	5/15/13	5/9/13	5/14/13	0 d	1 d
4		Test P1	5/16/13	5/21/13	5/15/13	5/16/13	1 d	3 d
5		Implement P1	5/22/13	5/28/13	5/17/13	5/22/13	3 d	3 d
6		Phase I Complete	5/28/13	5/28/13	5/22/13	5/22/13	3 d	3 d
7		⊟ **Phase II**	**5/29/13**	**6/19/13**	**5/23/13**	**6/14/13**	**3 d**	**3 d**
8		Design P2	5/29/13	6/3/13	5/23/13	5/29/13	3 d	3 d
9		Build P2	6/4/13	6/6/13	5/30/13	6/3/13	3 d	3 d
10		Test P2	6/7/13	6/12/13	6/4/13	6/7/13	3 d	3 d
11		Implement P2	6/13/13	6/19/13	6/10/13	6/14/13	3 d	3 d
12		Phase II Complete	6/19/13	6/19/13	6/14/13	6/14/13	3 d	3 d
13		⊟ **Phase III**	**5/6/13**	**6/3/13**	**5/6/13**	**5/30/13**	**0 d**	**2 d**
14		Design P3	5/6/13	5/14/13	5/6/13	5/10/13	0 d	2 d
15		Build P3	5/16/13	5/20/13	5/13/13	5/16/13	3 d	2 d
16		Test P3	5/21/13	5/24/13	5/17/13	5/22/13	2 d	2 d
17		Implement P3	5/28/13	6/3/13	5/23/13	5/30/13	2 d	2 d
18		Phase III Complete	6/3/13	6/3/13	5/30/13	5/30/13	2 d	2 d
19		Project Complete	6/19/13	6/19/13	6/14/13	6/14/13	3 d	3 d

Figure 10 - 2: Variance table applied in the Tracking Gantt view

To analyze *Date* variance, examine each value in the *Start Variance* and *Finish Variance* columns. Figure 10 - 2 shows that the *Finish Variance* value for the Project Summary Task (Row 0) equals *3 days*, revealing that this project is 3 days late on its finish date, caused by the late finish for the tasks in Phase I. Because of the 3 days of *Finish Variance* in Phase I, all of the tasks in Phase II are 3 days late as well. Notice also that the tasks in Phase III are each 2 days late on their finish date due to the late finish of the Design P3 task.

Analyzing Work Variance

Use the *Work* table to analyze *Work* variance and to determine when project work exceeds its original planned work budget. To apply the *Work* table, display any task view (such as the *Tracking Gantt* view) and then use either of the following methods:

- Right-click on the *Select All* button and then select the *Work* table in the shortcut menu.

- In the *View* ribbon, click the *Tables* pick list and select the *Work* table in the list.

Project Professional 2010 displays the *Work* table shown in Figure 10 - 3.

	Task Name	Work	Baseline	Variance	Actual	Remaining	% W. Comp.
0	Variance Project	456 h	432 h	24 h	176 h	280 h	39%
1	Phase I	168 h	136 h	32 h	120 h	48 h	71%
2	Design P1	24 h	24 h	0 h	24 h	0 h	100%
3	Build P1	80 h	64 h	16 h	80 h	0 h	100%
4	Test P1	32 h	16 h	16 h	16 h	16 h	50%
5	Implement P1	32 h	32 h	0 h	0 h	32 h	0%
6	Phase I Complete	0 h	0 h	0 h	0 h	0 h	0%
7	Phase II	152 h	152 h	0 h	0 h	152 h	0%
8	Design P2	32 h	32 h	0 h	0 h	32 h	0%
9	Build P2	48 h	48 h	0 h	0 h	48 h	0%
10	Test P2	32 h	32 h	0 h	0 h	32 h	0%
11	Implement P2	40 h	40 h	0 h	0 h	40 h	0%
12	Phase II Complete	0 h	0 h	0 h	0 h	0 h	0%
13	Phase III	136 h	144 h	-8 h	56 h	80 h	41%
14	Design P3	40 h	40 h	0 h	40 h	0 h	100%
15	Build P3	24 h	32 h	-8 h	16 h	8 h	67%
16	Test P3	32 h	32 h	0 h	0 h	32 h	0%
17	Implement P3	40 h	40 h	0 h	0 h	40 h	0%
18	Phase III Complete	0 h	0 h	0 h	0 h	0 h	0%
19	Project Complete	0 h	0 h	0 h	0 h	0 h	0%

Figure 10 - 3: Work table applied in the Tracking Gantt view

To analyze work variance, examine each value in the *Variance* column. In Figure 10 - 3, the *Variance* value for the Project Summary Task (Row 0) reveals that this project is currently 24 hours over budget. Phase I is currently 32 hours over its work budget. Build P1 is 16 hours over budget, and the task is complete; therefore, Build P1 shows actual variance. Test P1 is also 16 hours over budget, but the task is only 50% complete; therefore, Test P1 shows estimated variance. Phase III is 8 hours **under** its work budget, indicated by the negative value in the *Variance* column.

In the *Work* table, the real name of the *Variance* column is *Work Variance*. Microsoft uses the shorter name as the title of this column for display purposes only. You can see the real name of the column by floating your mouse pointer over the *Variance* column header. The system displays a tooltip that shows the title of the column, followed by the real name of the column in parentheses.

Analyzing Cost Variance

Use the *Cost* table to analyze *Cost* variance and to determine when project costs exceed its original planned cost budget. To apply the *Cost* table, display any task view (such as the *Tracking Gantt* view) and then use either of the following methods:

- Right-click on the *Select All* button and then select the *Cost* table in the shortcut menu.

- In the *View* ribbon, click the *Tables* pick list and select the *Cost* table in the list.

Project Professional 2010 displays the *Cost* table shown in Figure 10 - 4.

	Task Name	Fixed Cost	Fixed Cost Accrual	Total Cost	Baseline	Variance	Actual	Remaining
0	⊟ **Variance Project**	**$0.00**	**Prorated**	**$25,300.00**	**$21,600.00**	**$3,700.00**	**$11,300.00**	**$14,000.00**
1	⊟ **Phase I**	**$0.00**	**Prorated**	**$10,900.00**	**$6,800.00**	**$4,100.00**	**$8,500.00**	**$2,400.00**
2	Design P1	$0.00	Prorated	$1,200.00	$1,200.00	$0.00	$1,200.00	$0.00
3	Build P1	$2,500.00	Prorated	$6,500.00	$3,200.00	$3,300.00	$6,500.00	$0.00
4	Test P1	$0.00	Prorated	$1,600.00	$800.00	$800.00	$800.00	$800.00
5	Implement P1	$0.00	Prorated	$1,600.00	$1,600.00	$0.00	$0.00	$1,600.00
6	Phase I Complete	$0.00	Prorated	$0.00	$0.00	$0.00	$0.00	$0.00
7	⊟ **Phase II**	**$0.00**	**Prorated**	**$7,600.00**	**$7,600.00**	**$0.00**	**$0.00**	**$7,600.00**
8	Design P2	$0.00	Prorated	$1,600.00	$1,600.00	$0.00	$0.00	$1,600.00
9	Build P2	$0.00	Prorated	$2,400.00	$2,400.00	$0.00	$0.00	$2,400.00
10	Test P2	$0.00	Prorated	$1,600.00	$1,600.00	$0.00	$0.00	$1,600.00
11	Implement P2	$0.00	Prorated	$2,000.00	$2,000.00	$0.00	$0.00	$2,000.00
12	Phase II Complete	$0.00	Prorated	$0.00	$0.00	$0.00	$0.00	$0.00
13	⊟ **Phase III**	**$0.00**	**Prorated**	**$6,800.00**	**$7,200.00**	**($400.00)**	**$2,800.00**	**$4,000.00**
14	Design P3	$0.00	Prorated	$2,000.00	$2,000.00	$0.00	$2,000.00	$0.00
15	Build P3	$0.00	Prorated	$1,200.00	$1,600.00	($400.00)	$800.00	$400.00
16	Test P3	$0.00	Prorated	$1,600.00	$1,600.00	$0.00	$0.00	$1,600.00
17	Implement P3	$0.00	Prorated	$2,000.00	$2,000.00	$0.00	$0.00	$2,000.00
18	Phase III Complete	$0.00	Prorated	$0.00	$0.00	$0.00	$0.00	$0.00
19	Project Complete	$0.00	Prorated	$0.00	$0.00	$0.00	$0.00	$0.00

Figure 10 - 4: Cost table applied in the Tracking Gantt view

To analyze cost variance, examine each value in the *Variance* column. In Figure 10 - 4, the *Variance* value for the Project Summary Task (Row 0) reveals that the project is currently $3,700 over budget. This variance is because Phase I is currently $4,100 over budget while Phase III is currently $400 **under** budget. Notice that a significant part of the *Cost* variance in Phase I arises from the $2,500 in the *Fixed Cost* column for the Build P1 task. Remember that you can use the *Fixed Cost* column to track unanticipated task costs.

In the *Cost* table, the real name of the *Variance* column is *Cost Variance*. Microsoft uses the shorter name as the title of this column for display purposes only. You can see the real name of the column by floating your mouse pointer over the *Variance* column header. The system displays a tooltip that shows the title of the column, followed by the real name of the column in parentheses.

Hands On Exercise

Exercise 10-1

Analyze schedule variance, along with date, work, cost, and duration variance in your enterprise project.

1. Click the *Open* button on the Quick Access Toolbar and reopen your Deploy Training Advisor Software project, if necessary.

2. Click the *View* tab to display the *View* ribbon.

3. In the *Task Views* section of the *Task* ribbon, click the *Gantt Chart* pick list button and select the *Tracking Gantt* view.

4. Compare the blue and red Gantt bars (the current schedule) with their corresponding gray Gantt bars (the original Baseline schedule) for every task in the project.

Notice the schedule slippage for all tasks in the Phase I, Phase II, and Phase III sections of the project. Notice also that the *Rebuild P3* task does not have a gray bar because you have not baselined this new task yet.

5. In the *Data* section of the *View* ribbon, click the *Table* pick list and select the *Variance* table.

6. Pull your split bar to the right edge of the *Finish Variance* column.

Notice the amount of schedule slippage for each task in the project, as indicated in numbers displayed in the *Finish Variance* column.

7. In the *Data* section of the *View* ribbon, click the *Table* pick list and select the *Work* table.

Notice the total amount of work over budget for each task in the project, as shown in the *Variance* column. Remember that a positive number in this column has a negative impact to the project. By the way, the real name of this column is *Work Variance*.

8. In the *Data* section of the *View* ribbon, click the *Table* pick list and select the *Cost* table.

Notice the total amount of cost over budget for each task in the project, as shown in the *Variance* column. Remember that a positive number in this column has a negative impact to the project. By the way, the real name of this column is *Cost Variance*.

9. In the *Data* section of the *View* ribbon, click the *Table* pick list and select the *Entry* table.

10. Drag your split bar to the right edge of the *Duration* column.

11. In the *Task Views* section of the *View* ribbon, click the *Gantt Chart* pick list button and select the *_msPE Duration Variance* view.

Note: This special custom view, which includes a custom table and filter, allows you to analyze the fifth type of variance, which is *Duration* variance. Tasks highlighted with the yellow cell background color indicate tasks whose current *Duration* value exceeds their original *Baseline Duration* value. Examine the values shown in the *Duration Variance* column. Remember that a positive number in this column has a negative impact to the project.

12. In the *Task Views* section of the *View* ribbon, click the *Gantt Chart* pick list button and select the *Gantt Chart* view.

Revising a Project Plan

After completing variance analysis, you may need to revise your project plan to bring it "back on track" against its original goals, objectives, and schedule. There are a number of strategies for revising a project plan, but each one requires careful consideration before you make the revision. You should perform a "what-if" analysis before making plan revisions, especially if you need formal approval to make the revisions.

Project Professional 2010 offers a number of methods for revising a project plan. These methods include:

- Add resources to *Effort Driven* tasks.

- Ask project team members to work overtime or on weekends.

- Increase project team availability for your project.

- Modify mandatory dependencies, including reducing or removing *Lag* time, or adding *Lead* time.

- Reduce the scope of the project.

- Renegotiate the project finish date.

Potential Problems with Revising a Plan

Prior to employing any of the preceding techniques, you should be aware of potential problems that may arise when you implement the revisions. Some of the potential problems include:

- Adding resources to an *Effort Driven* task can increase the total work on the task due to increased communication needs between the team members.

- Asking team members to work overtime on a regular basis can increase your employee turnover rate.

- Increasing team member availability for your project reduces their availability for projects managed by other project managers, causing those projects to slip.

- Reducing *Lag* time on task dependencies can create an overly optimistic project schedule.

- Adding *Lead* time on task dependencies can create a scheduling crisis when the predecessor task must finish completely, thus negating the intent of adding the *Lead* time.

- The scope of your project may be non-negotiable.

- The finish date of your project may be non-negotiable.

Hands On Exercise

Exercise 10-2

Add a new team member to your enterprise project to help on *Effort Driven* tasks.

1. Return to your Deploy Training Advisor Software project, if necessary.

2. Click the *Project Server* tab to display the *Project Server* ribbon.

3. In the *Plan and Publish* section of the *Project Server* ribbon, click the *Build Team from Enterprise* button.

4. In the *Build Team* dialog, click the *Existing Filters* pick list and select the *All Resources (No Filter)* item on the pick list, if not already selected.

5. In the *Project Resources* list on the right side of the dialog, select the name *David Erickson* and then click the *Match* button.

6. In the *Enterprise Resource* list on the left side of the dialog, scroll up to the top of the list of matching resources, if necessary.

7. In the *Enterprise Resource* list on the left, select the name *Mickey Cobb* and then click the *Add* button to add her to the list on the right (**do not** click the *Replace* button).

8. Click the *OK* button to close the *Build Team* dialog.

9. Click the *Save* button on your Quick Access Toolbar to save the changes to your enterprise project.

Exercise 10-3

Revise your enterprise project to bring it back on schedule.

1. Click the *View* tab to display the *View* ribbon.

2. In the *Task Views* section of the *View* ribbon, click the *Gantt Chart* pick list button and select the *Tracking Gantt* view.

3. In the *Split View* section of the *View* ribbon, **select** the *Details* checkbox.

4. In the *Gantt Chart* pane, select task ID #2, the *Design P1* task.

Use *Effort Driven* scheduling to shorten the duration of the *Design P1* task by adding a helper to assist with the remaining work on the task.

5. In the *Task Form* pane, add the name *Mickey Cobb* below your name.

6. Set the *Units* value to *100%* for *Mickey Cobb* and then click the *OK* button.

Notice how Project Professional 2010 shortened the *Duration* value. The software did not shorten the *Duration* value by half, as you might have expected, because you completed some actual work on the. Because of this, the software can only distribute the remaining work on the task between *you* and *Mickey Cobb*.

7. Right-click anywhere in the *Task Form* pane and then select the *Work* details on the shortcut menu.

Because you completed some actual work on the task in the previous week, the software can only redistribute the remaining work on the task. Notice in the *Remaining Work* column of the *Task Form* pane that Project Professional 2010 distributed the hours of remaining work evenly between the two resources.

8. Select task ID #10, the *Test P2* task and then click the *Scroll to Task* button on your Quick Access Toolbar to bring the task's Gantt bar into view.

9. In the *Task Form* pane enter *8 hours* in the *Ovt. Work* column for *Myrta Hansen* and then click the *OK* button.

Adding planned overtime work is another way to shorten the duration of tasks. Notice that the system shortened the *Duration* value of the task from *5 days* to *4 days* since the resource will work longer days to complete the task.

10. Click the *Save* button on your Quick Access Toolbar to save the changes to your enterprise project.

Exercise 10-4

Revise project deliverables as needed.

1. Click the *View* tab to display the *View* ribbon, if necessary.

2. In the *Split View* section of the *View* ribbon, **deselect** the *Details* checkbox.

3. Select, the *Phase III Complete* milestone task, and then click the *Scroll to Task* button on your Quick Access Toolbar.

4. Scroll the Gantt chart back to the left until you can see the symbol for the deliverable you created on this task.

Notice that the deliverable symbol is earlier than the milestone symbol for this task (the solid black diamond), indicating you may miss the agreed upon deliverable date on this task.

5. Click the *Project Server* tab to display the *Project Server* ribbon.

6. In the *Project Sites* section of the *Project Server* ribbon, click the *Deliverable* pick list and select the *Manage Deliverables* item on the pick list.

7. In the *Deliverables* sidepane, click the *Phase III Complete* deliverable and select the *Edit Deliverable* item on the pick list menu.

8. In the *Deliverables* sidepane, change the dates in the *Start* and *Finish* fields to the date shown to the right of the milestone symbol in the Gantt chart.

9. Click the *Done* link at the bottom of the sidepane.

Notice that Project Professional 2010 moved the deliverable symbol to the milestone symbol on the Gantt chart part of the *Tracking Gantt* view.

10. Click the *Close* button (**X**) in the upper right corner of the *Deliverables* sidepane.

11. Select the Project Summary Task (row 0) and then click the *Scroll to Task* button on your Quick Access Toolbar to bring the beginning of your project into view.

12. Click the *Save* button on your Quick Access Toolbar to save the changes to your enterprise project.

13. In the *Plan and Publish* section of the *Project Server* ribbon, click the *Publish* button to publish the changes to your enterprise project.

Using a Change Control Process

Change control is the process of managing requested changes in your project. Change requests can arise from a variety of sources, including your customer, your project sponsor, your project stakeholders, your company's executives, your fellow project managers, and even from your project team members. Because each change can result in schedule slippage and cost overruns, it is important that you manage all changes in your project. Remember the old project management saying, "Either you manage change, or change manages you!"

Your change control process should identify and maximize the benefits of change, and should avoid all changes that offer no benefit to the project or that impact the project negatively. Document your change management process in both the Statement of Work document and in the "rules of engagement" with your project sponsor and/or client. Following is an example of a change management process:

- Use a paper or electronic change request form to initiate the change request.

- Perform an impact analysis to assess the impact of the change on the project. Determine who does the impact analysis and how they report the results.

- Calculate the cost of the impact analysis and determine who pays for it. Remember that an impact analysis is never free!

- Enlist the support of an executive in your organization with the authority to accept or reject the change request.

- Apply a procedure for implementing an approved change request.

- In your project plan, indicate the tasks you changed or added because of the change request.

Inserting New Tasks in a Project

The most common change request is to add new tasks to a project. When you insert a new task between two dependent tasks, the *Autolink* feature of Project Professional 2010 determines whether the software automatically adds dependency links to the new task. If you disabled the *Autolink* feature in the *Project Options* dialog, per my directions in Module 04, *Creating Enterprise Projects*, the software **does not** automatically link the new task to the existing tasks in the project. However, if you did not disable the *Autolink* feature, then Project Professional 2010 handles the task linking operation as follows:

- If the dependent tasks have a Finish-to-Start (FS) dependency, the software automatically links the new task to the existing tasks using the Finish-to-Start FS dependency.

- If the dependent tasks have any other type of dependency (SS, FF, or SF), then Project Professional 2010 **does not** automatically link the new task to the existing tasks. Instead, the software leaves the new task unlinked.

Because you should always make task dependency decisions, and not the software, MSProjectExperts recommends that you either disable the *Autolink* feature in the *Project Options* dialog, or you break the task dependency links between tasks in the section where you intend to insert new tasks. After inserting the new tasks, establish appropriate task dependencies for tasks in that section of your project plan.

Reminder: To disable the *Autolink* feature of Microsoft Project 2010, click the *File* tab and then click the *Options* item in the *Backstage*. In the *Project Options* dialog, click the *Schedule* tab. In the *Scheduling options for this project* section, deselect the *Autolink inserted or moved tasks* option, and then click the *OK* button.

When you add new tasks to a project through a change control process, MSProjectExperts recommends that you format the new tasks with a unique color. You can format the font, the cell background color, and/or the Gantt bar color, as needed. Keep in mind that you can see these formatting changes only in the view in which you apply the formatting.

Hands On Exercise

Exercise 10-5

Through a change control process, add a new task to your enterprise project at the request of project team members.

1. Return to your Deploy Training Advisor Software project, if necessary.

2. Click the *Task* tab to display the *Task* ribbon.

3. In the *View* section of the *Task* ribbon, click the *Gantt Chart* pick list button and select the *Gantt Chart* view on the list.

4. Select the Project Summary Task (row 0) and then click the *Scroll to Task* button on your Quick Access Toolbar to bring the beginning of your project into view.

5. Click the *Zoom Out* button on your Quick Access Toolbar to zoom your timescale to the *Months Over 3-Day Time Periods* level of zoom.

6. Select the *Phase III Complete* milestone task.

7. Press the **Insert** key on your computer keyboard to insert a new blank row above the *Phase III Complete* milestone task.

8. In the new blank row, enter the text *Phase III Review* and then press the **Enter** key on your computer keyboard.

Because you have the *Autolink* feature disabled for this project, notice that Project Professional 2010 **did not** link the new task with the tasks immediately above and below it.

9. Enter *2 days* in the *Duration* column for the new *Phase III Review* task and then press the **Enter** key on your computer keyboard.

10. Select tasks from the *Build P3* task to the *Phase III Complete* milestone task.

11. Click the *Unlink Tasks* button on your Quick Access Toolbar to remove the existing link.

12. Click the *Link Tasks* button to link all three tasks into a chain of events.

13. Select the new *Phase III Review* task, and then click the *Assign Resources* button on your Quick Access Toolbar.

14. In the *Assign Resources* dialog, select the name *Mickey Cobb*, enter *100%* in the *Units* column for *Mickey Cobb*, and then click the *Assign* button.

15. Click the *Close* button in the *Assign Resources* dialog.

16. Select the row headers for, the *Rebuild P3* and *Phase III Review* tasks, to select the entire task rows.

17. In the *Font* section of the *Task* ribbon, click the *Background Color* pick list and select the *Olive Green, Lighter (60%)* color (third item in the *Olive Green* column) in the *Theme Colors* area of the gallery.

18. Double-click the new *Phase III Review* task, and then click the *Notes* tab in the *Task Information* dialog.

19. Click the *Bulleted List* button and then enter the following text in the notes field:

New task added through change control at request of project team members.

20. Click the *OK* button to close the *Task Information* dialog.

21. Click the *Save* button on your Quick Access Toolbar to save the changes to your enterprise project.

22. Click the *Project Server* tab to display the *Project Server* ribbon.

23. In the *Plan and Publish* section of the *Project Server* ribbon, click the *Publish* button to publish the changes to your enterprise project.

Rebaselining Your Project

After you add new tasks to your project through change control, you must rebaseline your project. Although there are several methodologies for rebaselining a project, I recommend you use one the two following methods:

- Back up your current baseline into one of the ten additional sets of baseline fields, and then baseline only the new tasks in the project using the default *Baseline* set of fields.

- Rebaseline all tasks in the project using one of the ten additional sets of baseline fields (the *Baseline 1* through *Baseline 10* sets of fields). If you want to use this technique, you must change the baseline that Project Professional 2010 uses to calculate variance. You must also change how the system displays the baseline schedule, shown by gray Gantt bars, in the *Tracking Gantt* view of your project.

I discuss each of these rebaselining methodologies separately.

The default *Baseline* set of fields includes the following: *Baseline Start, Baseline Finish, Baseline Duration, Baseline Work*, and *Baseline Cost*. The ten additional sets of baselines, named *Baseline 1* through *Baseline 10*, include a corresponding set of fields. For example, the *Baseline1* set of fields includes the following: *Baseline 1 Start, Baseline 1 Finish, Baseline 1 Duration, Baseline 1 Work*, and *Baseline 1 Cost*.

Backing Up an Original Baseline

Before you rebaseline your project after a change control procedure, it is wise to back up the current baseline data stored in the default *Baseline* set of fields. This is true, regardless of how you rebaseline your project. As you know by now, Project Professional 2010 offers you 11 sets of fields in which to save baseline data. These sets of fields include the default *Baseline* set of fields, plus the *Baseline 1* through *Baseline 10* sets. You can use any of these ten sets of alternate baseline fields to back up the current baseline before you rebaseline your project. To back up your current baseline values, use the *Interim Plan* feature of Project Professional 2010 by completing the following steps:

1. Click the *Project* tab to display the *Project* ribbon.

2. In the *Schedule* section of the *Project* ribbon, click the *Set Baseline* pick list button and then click the *Set Baseline* item on the menu. Project Professional 2010 displays the *Set Baseline* dialog shown in Figure 10 - 5.

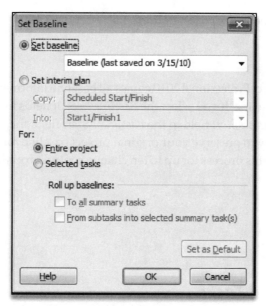

Figure 10 - 5: Set Baseline dialog

3. In the *Set Baseline* dialog, select the *Set interim plan* option.

4. Click the *Copy* pick list and select the *Baseline* item.

5. Click the *Into* pick list and select the next available set of baseline fields into which you want to back up the current baseline of the project, as shown in Figure 10 - 6.

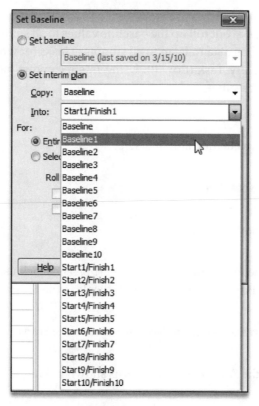

Figure 10 - 6: Back up the current baseline into the Baseline 1 set of fields

6. In the *For:* section, select the *Entire project* option.

7. Click the *OK* button.

When you use this procedure, Project Professional 2010 copies all baseline information from the *Baseline* set of fields to the set of fields for the alternate baseline. If you select the *Baseline 1* set of fields in the *Into* pick list, the system copies the values for every task in the *Baseline Start* field to the *Baseline 1 Start* field, the *Baseline Finish* field to the *Baseline 1 Finish* field, etc. This is a useful way to preserve your original project baseline for historical purposes before you re-baseline your project. You can use this process for up to ten change control procedures, at which point you run out of alternate sets of baseline fields.

Baselining Only Selected Tasks

An ideal method for rebaselining a project after adding new tasks through a change control procedure is to baseline **only** the new tasks you added to the project. Project Professional 2010 offers you two methods for baselining only selected tasks:

*   Baseline only the selected tasks, but do not roll up the baseline values to any summary tasks in the project. Using this technique, new tasks show as variance against the original project baseline.

*   Baseline only the selected tasks, but roll up the baseline values to all summary tasks in the project. When you choose this option, the baseline data rolls up to all summary tasks for which the selected tasks are subtasks, including the Project Summary Task (Row 0). Using this technique, new tasks do not show as variance against the original project baseline.

To baseline only selected tasks, complete the following steps:

1. Select the tasks you want to baseline.

2. Click the *Project* tab to display the *Project* ribbon.

3. In the *Schedule* section of the *Project* ribbon, click the *Set Baseline* pick list button and then click the *Set Baseline* item on the menu. Project Professional 2010 displays the *Set Baseline* dialog.

4. Select the *Set baseline* option and select the *Baseline* value in the *Set baseline* pick list.

5. In the *For:* section, choose the *Selected tasks* option, as shown in Figure 10 - 7.

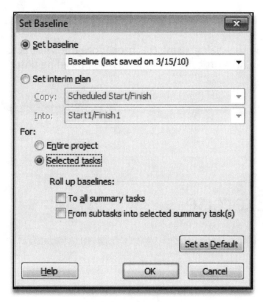

**Figure 10 - 7: Set Baseline dialog
to baseline selected tasks**

6. If you wish to roll up the baseline values to summary tasks, choose one of the following options in the *Roll up baselines* section:

    - Select the *To all summary tasks* option if you want the software to roll up the baseline values to all summary tasks for which the selected tasks are subtasks and to the Project Summary Task as well.

    - Select the *From subtasks into selected summary tasks* option if you want the software to roll up the baseline values to only the summary tasks currently selected (you must select these summary tasks before you begin the baselining process).

 If you do not want to roll up the baseline values to any summary tasks, **do not** select either of the checkboxes in the *Roll up baselines* section of the dialog. This means that the selected tasks continue to show as variance against the current project baseline.

7. To save the current options in the *Roll up baselines* section of the dialog, click the *Set as Default* button.

8. Click the *OK* button. Project Professional 2010 warns you about overwriting the baseline data in the warning dialog shown in Figure 10 - 8.

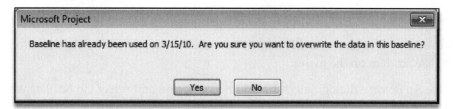

Figure 10 - 8: Warning dialog about overwriting baseline data

9. When warned about overwriting the original baseline, click the *Yes* button in the warning dialog.

> In spite of the warning in the dialog, using this procedure does not actually "overwrite" the data in your original baseline. Instead, this procedure "appends" the baseline data from the new tasks to the current project baseline.

Hands On Exercise

Exercise 10-6

Back up the original project baseline information in the *Baseline1* set of fields for an enterprise project.

1. Return to your Deploy Training Advisor Software project, if necessary.

2. Click the *Project* tab to display the *Project* ribbon.

3. In the *Schedule* section of the *Project* ribbon, click the *Set Baseline* pick list button and then click the *Set Baseline* item on the menu.

4. In the *Set Baseline* dialog, select the *Set interim plan* option.

5. Click the *Copy* pick list and select the *Baseline* item.

6. Click the *Into* pick list and select the *Baseline1* item.

7. In the *For:* section, select the *Entire project* option.

8. Click the *OK* button.

9. Click the *Save* button on your Quick Access Toolbar to save the changes to your enterprise project.

Exercise 10-7

Rebaseline only the new tasks in an enterprise project.

1. Select task IDs #17 and #18, the *Rebuild P3* and *Phase III Review* tasks.

2. In the *Schedule* section of the *Project* ribbon, click the *Set Baseline* pick list button and then click the *Set Baseline* item on the menu.

3. In the *Set Baseline* dialog, select the *Set baseline* option and select the *Baseline* value in the *Set baseline* pick list.

4. In the *For:* section of the dialog, choose the *Selected tasks* option.

5. In the *For:* section of the dialog, select the *To all summary tasks* option as well.

6. Click the *OK* button.

7. When warned about overwriting the original baseline, click the *Yes* button in the warning dialog.

8. Click the *Save* button on your Quick Access Toolbar to save the changes to your enterprise project.

9. Click the *Project Server* tab to display the *Project Server* ribbon.

10. In the *Plan and Publish* section of the *Project Server* ribbon, click the *Publish* button to publish the changes to your enterprise project.

11. Click the *Close* button on your Quick Access Toolbar and then check in your enterprise project when prompted.

Rebaselining the Entire Project Using an Alternate Baseline

To rebaseline an entire project using one of the ten alternate sets of baseline fields, such as the *Baseline 1* set of fields, complete the following steps:

1. Click the *Project* tab to display the *Project* ribbon.

2. In the *Schedule* section of the *Project* ribbon, click the *Set Baseline* pick list button and then click the *Set Baseline* item on the menu. Project Professional 2010 displays the *Set Baseline* dialog.

3. In the *Set Baseline* dialog, click the *Set baseline* pick list and choose one of the ten alternate sets of baseline fields, such as the *Baseline 1* item shown in Figure 10 - 9.

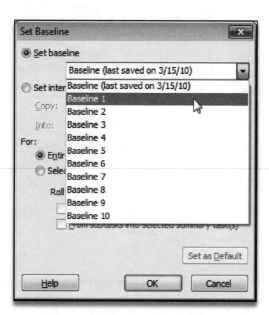

**Figure 10 - 9: Set Baseline dialog,
select the Baseline 1 set of fields**

4. In the *For:* section, select the *Entire project* option.

5. Click the *OK* button.

After you rebaseline your project using one of alternate sets of baseline fields, you must change the baseline Project Professional 2010 uses to calculate variance. To make this change, complete the following steps:

6. Click the *File* tab and then click the *Options* item in the *Backstage*.

7. In the *Project Options* dialog, click the *Advanced* tab.

8. In the *Earned Value options for this project* section of the dialog, click the *Baseline for Earned Value Calculation* pick list and select the alternate set of baselines used during the rebaselining process, as shown in Figure 10 - 10.

9. Click the *OK* button.

When you change the *Baseline for Earned Value Calculation* option in the *Project Options* dialog, you change how Project Professional 2010 calculates variance in your project. When you change this option, the system now uses the new set of baseline fields to calculate all variance in the project. This affects the *Start Variance, Finish Variance, Duration Variance, Work Variance,* and *Cost Variance* fields, and you see the results in the task *Work, Cost,* and *Variance* tables. For example, if you selected the *Baseline 1* set of fields in step #3 above, the system calculates the values in the *Work Variance* field for every task using the following formula: **Work Variance = Work – Baseline 1 Work**.

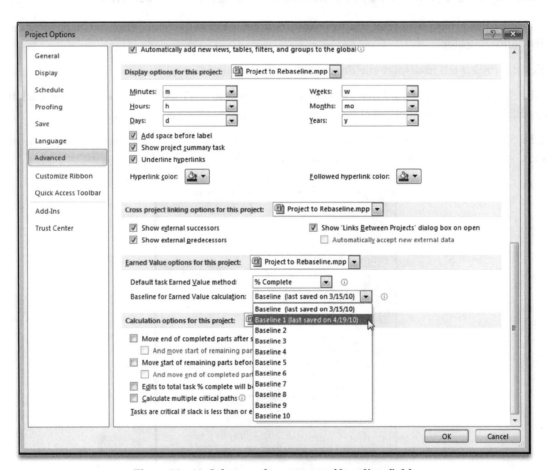

Figure 10 - 10: Select an alternate set of baseline fields

In addition to changing the set of baseline fields used to calculate variance in Project Professional 2010, you must also change the baseline schedule shown in the *Tracking Gantt* view. To change this view, complete the following additional set of steps:

1. Using the *Gantt Chart* pick list button on either the *Task* ribbon or the *View* ribbon, apply the *Tracking Gantt* view.

2. Click the *Format* tab to display the *Format* ribbon.

3. In the *Bar Styles* section of the *Format* ribbon, click the *Baseline* pick list button, and then select the alternate set of baseline fields, as shown in Figure 10 - 11.

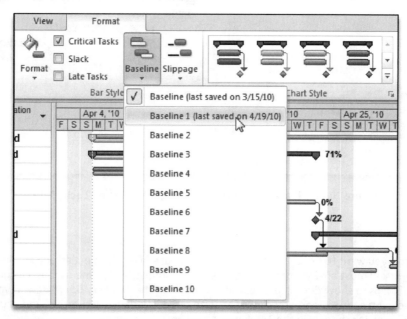

Figure 10 - 11: Select the alternate set of baseline fields for the Tracking Gantt view

For example, Figure 10 - 12 shows the default *Tracking Gantt* view for a project after a change control procedure added a new task to the project, and after the project manager rebaselined the project using the *Baseline 1* set of fields. Because the *Tracking Gantt* view uses the default *Baseline* set of fields to create the gray Gantt bars, the baseline schedule shown with the gray Gantt bars is not correct.

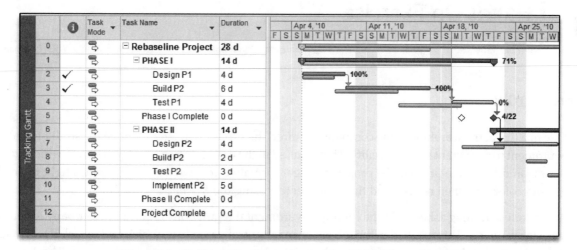

Figure 10 - 12: Tracking Gantt view using the Baseline schedule

Figure 10 - 13 shows the *Tracking Gantt* view after the project manager selected the *Baseline 1* set of fields in the *Baseline* pick list on the *Format* ribbon. The *Tracking Gantt* view now uses the *Baseline 1* set of fields to show the baseline schedule, which results in an accurate baseline schedule.

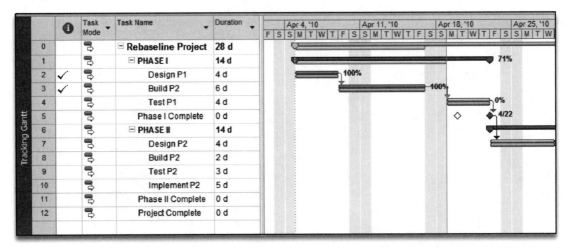

Figure 10 - 13: Tracking Gantt view using the Baseline 1 schedule

Warning: If you want to use this methodology for rebaselining a project after a change control procedure, you **must always** complete the steps to change the baseline used to calculate variance **and** the set of steps to show the correct baseline schedule in the *Tracking Gantt* view. If you fail to complete these two extra sets of steps, you cannot analyze project variance accurately, and you do not see the accurate baseline schedule in the *Tracking Gantt* view.

Hands On Exercise

Exercise 10-8

Due to a fire at the warehouse, the company required the project manager to move the stored furniture and equipment to a different storage facility. This resulted in the first change control procedure, which added task IDs #16 and #17 to the project. The project manager formatted the two new tasks using a light red cell background color, and then rebaselined the entire project using the *Baseline 1* set of fields.

As a result of finding asbestos in the ceiling, governmental regulations require the company to remove the asbestos properly. This resulted in the second change control procedure, which added task IDs #24, #26, and #27 to the project. The project manager formatted the three new tasks using a light green cell background color. After this second major change control procedure, rebaseline a project using the *Baseline 2* set of fields.

1.   Click the *Open* button on the Quick Access Toolbar.

2. Navigate to your *C:* drive and then to the folder containing the sample files for this class, and then open the **Rebaseline a Project.mpp** sample file.

3. Click the *Project* tab to display the *Project* ribbon.

4. In the *Schedule* section of the *Project* ribbon, click the *Set Baseline* pick list button and then click the *Set Baseline* item on the menu.

5. In the *Set Baseline* dialog, select the *Set baseline* pick list and select the *Baseline 2* item.

6. In the *For:* section, select the *Entire project* option.

7. Click the *OK* button.

Exercise 10-9

Configure Project Professional 2010 using the *Baseline 2* set of fields to calculate variance and then set up the *Tracking Gantt* view in Project Professional 2010 to show the *Baseline 2* schedule as gray Gantt bars.

1. Continue using the **Rebaseline a Project.mpp** sample file.

2. Click the *File* tab and then click the *Options* item in the *Backstage*.

3. In the *Project Options* dialog, click the *Advanced* tab.

4. In the *Earned Value options for this project* section of the dialog, click the *Baseline for Earned Value Calculation* pick list and select the *Baseline 2* set of fields.

5. Click the *OK* button.

6. Click the *Task* tab to display the *Task* ribbon.

7. Click the *Gantt Chart* pick list button and then select the *Tracking Gantt* view on the list.

8. Select task ID #24, the *Obtain asbestos removal permit* task, and then click the *Scroll to Task* button in the *Editing* section of the *Task* ribbon.

Notice that the *Tracking Gantt* chart shows no baseline schedule (no gray bars) for task IDs #24, #26, and #28. This is because the *Tracking Gantt* view currently shows the *Baseline 1* schedule for all tasks, and the *Baseline 1* schedule does not include these three tasks.

9. Click the *Format* tab to display the *Format* ribbon.

10. In the *Bar Styles* section of the *Format* ribbon, click the *Baseline* pick list button, and then select the *Baseline 2* schedule.

After the second change control procedure, which resulted in a second rebaselining of the project, Project Professional 2010 reset all variance to 0. You can see this reflected in the *Tracking Gantt* view, where the gray Gantt bars (the baseline schedule) now match the schedule of their accompanying blue or red Gantt bars (the current schedule of all tasks in the project).

11. Save and close the **Rebaseline a Project.mpp** sample file.

Using the Gantt with Timeline View

During project execution, you must report project progress to one or more stakeholder groups. These typically include your project sponsor, your customer, your company executives, and even your project team. Although Project Professional 2010 offers you a number of ways to report about your project, the *Timeline* view offers you a powerful new means of reporting on you projects.

Project Professional 2010 includes the new *Timeline* view that displays the current project schedule using a timeline presentation similar to what you see in Microsoft Visio or in any other timeline software application. You can modify the default *Timeline* view to show your current project schedule according to your reporting requirements. You can also export the *Timeline* view to other Microsoft Office applications, such as Microsoft PowerPoint.

The *Gantt with Timeline* view is the default view for every new project you create in Project Professional 2010. In fact, you see this view every time you launch the software, because the system always creates a new blank project on application launch. The *Gantt with Timeline* view is a split view that shows the *Timeline* view in the top pane and the *Gantt Chart* view in the bottom pane. Figure 10 - 14 shows the *Gantt with Timeline* view applied to an in-progress project.

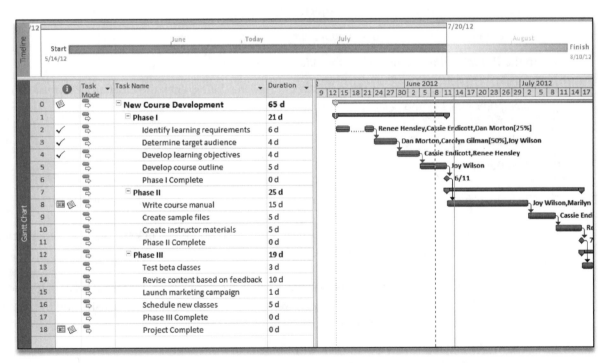

Figure 10 - 14: Gantt with Timeline view for an in-progress project

If you do not see the *Gantt with Timeline* view when you open a project, apply the *Gantt Chart* view and then click the *View* tab. In the *Split View* section of the *View* ribbon, select the *Timeline* option.

Depending on your level of zoom applied in your project, the *Timeline* view shows the following information by default:

- The gray *Timeline* bar represents the time span of the entire project, with the project *Start* date on the left end of the bar and the project *Finish* date on the right end of the bar. Notice in Figure 10 - 14 that the project runs from 5/14/12 to 8/10/12, indicated by the dates to the left and right of the gray *Timeline* bar.

- The system divides the *Timeline* bar into one-month segments using light blue tick marks, and displays the name of the month above each segment. Figure 10 - 14 shows that the project spans a partial month of May (not shown as a month name), plus the months of June, July, and August.

- The system indicates the current date with the word *Today* formatted with orange text above the *Timeline* bar and with an orange dashed line in the *Timeline* bar.

- The light blue *Pan and Zoom* bar above the *Timeline* bar represents the time span of the project currently visible in the *Gantt Chart* view. At the ends of the *Pan and Zoom* bar, the system displays the beginning and ending dates of the time span currently visible in the *Gantt Chart* view. Notice in Figure 10 - 14 that the gray *Timeline* bar extends only to 7/20/12, indicated by the date on the right end of the *Pan and Zoom* bar.

- The system uses light gray shading for the portion of the *Timeline* bar not visible in the *Gantt Chart* view. Figure 10 - 14 shows that project information is not visible past 7/20/12 in the *Gantt Chart* view, indicated by the light gray shading in the gray *Timeline* bar after that date.

As you scroll right or left in the *Gantt Chart* view, the *Pan and Zoom* bar scrolls with you to indicate the portion of the timeline currently visible in the Gantt Chart.

Adding a Task to the Timeline

To add any task to the *Timeline* view, right-click on the name of the task in the *Task Sheet* part of the *Gantt Chart* view and then click the *Add to Timeline* item on the shortcut menu. To add multiple tasks to the *Timeline* view, select a block of tasks, right-click anywhere in the selected block of tasks, and then click the *Add to Timeline* item on the shortcut menu. Project Professional 2010 adds the selected tasks to the *Timeline* view as shown in Figure 10 - 15. Notice that I added the Phase I and Phase II tasks to the *Timeline* view, along with the first three subtasks in the Phase II section of the project.

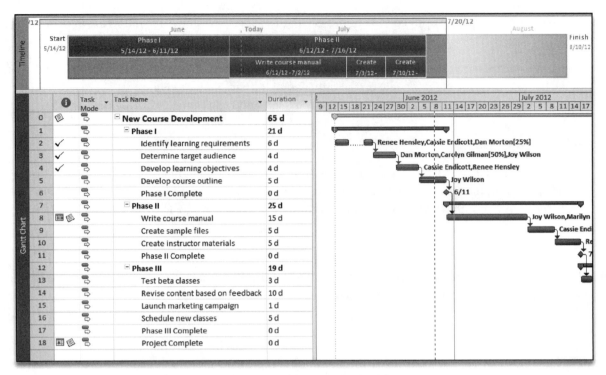

Figure 10 - 15: Tasks added to the Timeline view

You can also add a task in the *Timeline* view by double-clicking the task and then selecting the *Display on Timeline* option in the *General* page of the *Task Information* dialog. If you select multiple tasks, you can add a task in the *Timeline* view by selecting the *Task* ribbon and then clicking the *Information* button in the *Properties* section of the *Task* ribbon. In the *Multiple Task Information* dialog, select the the *Display on Timeline* option on the *General* page.

After you add tasks to the *Timeline* view, you can rearrange the tasks on the *Timeline* bar using any of the following techniques:

- Drag a task to a new row above or below its current position in the *Timeline* bar.

- Drag a task above or below the *Timeline* bar to display the task as a callout.

- Drag a block of tasks by selecting them while pressing and holding the **Control** key on your keyboard, and then dragging the block of the selected tasks to a new position.

- Right-click on any task in the *Timeline* bar and select the *Display as Callout* item on the shortcut menu.

- Drag a new callout from the top of the *Timeline* bar to a position below the *Timeline* bar.

- Convert a callout to a task bar by right-clicking on the callout and then clicking the *Display as Bar* item on the shortcut menu.

When you drag tasks into a new position in the *Timeline* bar, or create callouts above or below the *Timeline* bar, Project Professional 2010 adjusts the height of the *Timeline* view automatically to accommodate the new information. For example, Figure 10 - 16 shows my *Timeline* view after I created two callouts and dragged the Phase II task and its subtask to a new row in the *Timeline* bar.

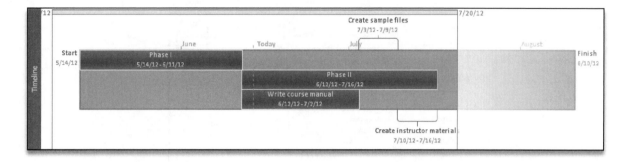

Figure 10 - 16: Rearranged tasks in the Timeline view

 To remove a task or a callout from the *Timeline* view, right-click the task or the callout and then click the *Remove from Timeline* item on the shortcut menu.

Formatting the Timeline View

To format the *Timeline* view, click anywhere in the *Timeline* view to select it and then click the *Format* tab. The system displays the contextual *Format* ribbon with the *Timeline Tools* applied, shown in Figure 10 - 17. The process for formatting the *Timeline* view is similar to the process of formatting the *Gantt Chart* view that you learned earlier in this module.

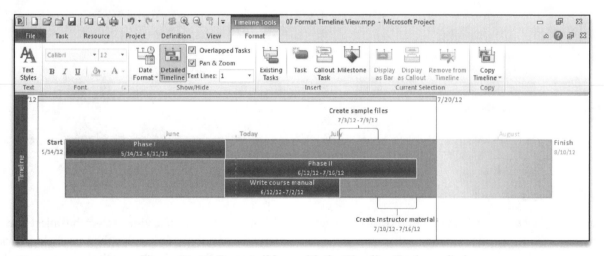

Figure 10 - 17: Format ribbon with the Timeline Tools applied

Using the Text Tools

To format the text for any set of objects shown in the *Timeline* view, click the *Text Styles* button in the *Text* section of the contextual *Format* ribbon. Project Professional 2010 displays the *Text Styles* dialog shown in Figure 10 - 18.

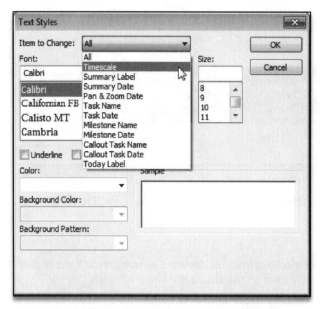

Figure 10 - 18: Text Styles dialog Item to Change pick list

 Notice in the previous figure that Microsoft Project 2010 does not allow you to change the *Background Color* or *Background Pattern* options in the *Text Styles* dialog for the *Timeline* view. The system limits you to changing only text formatting options such as the *Font* and *Color* items.

 You can also display the *Text Styles* dialog by right-clicking anywhere in the white part of the *Timeline* view and then clicking the *Text Styles* item on the shortcut menu.

Using Font Tools

To change the font or the cell background color of an individual object in the *Timeline* view, select the object and then change the formatting options in the *Font* section of the contextual *Format* ribbon. To display the *Font* dialog, click the *Font* dialog launcher icon in the lower right corner of the *Font* section of the ribbon. To change the background color of a task, for example, select the task and choose a new color on the *Background Color* pick list.

Using Show/Hide Tools

To change the date format of the dates shown in the *Timeline* view, click the *Date Format* pick list button in the *Show/Hide* section and select a new date format. By default, the *Timeline* view uses the date format specified in the *Date Format* field on the *General* page of the *Project Options* dialog. On the *Date Format* pick list, Project Professional 2010 also allows you to hide some of the dates shown by default on the *Timeline* view. To hide the dates shown for each task, click the *Date Format* pick list and deselect the *Task Dates* option. To hide the current date, deselect the *Current Date* option on the *Date Format* pick list. To hide the dates shown above the *Timeline* bar, deselect the *Timescale* option on the *Date Format* pick list.

To remove the details from the *Timeline* view, such as the names of tasks and task dates, deselect the *Detailed Timeline* option in the *Show/Hide* section of the contextual *Format* ribbon. The system completely removes all details from the *Timeline* view. As you can see in Figure 10 - 19, without the details, the *Timeline* view is probably not very useful to you.

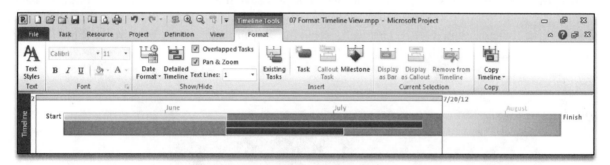

Figure 10 - 19: Timeline view with details removed

If your project contains parallel task sections, and you display overlapping tasks from these parallel sections in the *Timeline* view, the *Overlapped Tasks* option in the *Show/Hide* section works to your advantage. When selected, the *Overlapped Tasks* option displays each overlapping task in its own row in the *Timeline* view. For example, Figure 10 - 20 shows a different project with multiple parallel task sections and with each summary task section displayed in the *Timeline* view. Notice how Project Professional 2010 displays each overlapping section in its own task row in the *Timeline* view.

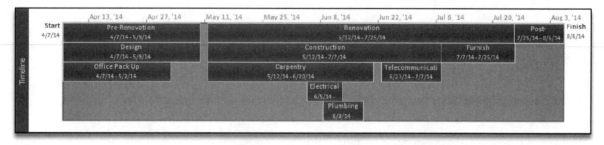

Figure 10 - 20: Timeline with Overlapped Tasks option selected

Figure 10 - 21 shows the same *Timeline* view with the *Overlapped Tasks* option deselected. Notice how the system displays all tasks in a single task row in the *Timeline* view, rendering the information all but impossible to read. For this reason, I recommend you leave the *Overlapped Tasks* option selected for the *Timeline* view when you build a timeline presentation containing numerous overlapping tasks.

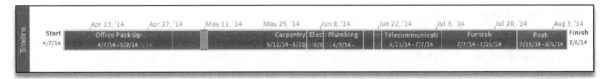

Figure 10 - 21: Timeline with Overlapped Tasks option deselected

In the *Show/Hide* section of the contextual *Format* ribbon, the *Pan & Zoom* option allows you to display or hide the light blue *Pan and Zoom* bar shown at the top of the *Timeline* view. If you select the *Pan & Zoom* option, the system displays the *Pan and Zoom* bar; if you deselect this option, the system hides the *Pan and Zoom* bar.

The final option in the *Show/Hide* section is the *Text Lines* option, which allows you to determine how many lines of text to display for every task shown in the *Timeline* view. By default, the system sets the *Text Lines* value to *1 line*. Because of this, the system truncates long task names when displayed in the *Timeline* view. For example, consider the *Timeline* view shown previously in Figure 10 - 15. Notice how the system truncates the names of the three subtasks shown in the Phase II section with the *Text Lines* value set to the default *1 line* value. Compare the same *Timeline* view shown in Figure 10 - 22 with the *Text Lines* value set to *3 lines*.

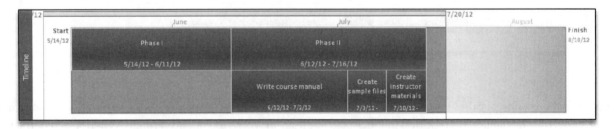

Figure 10 - 22: Timeline view with the Text Lines option set to 3 lines

Figure 10 - 23 shows the completed *Timeline* view after I formatted it using methods I documented in this section of the module. To format the *Timeline* view, I did the following:

- I added the Phase III task to the *Timeline* view.

- I changed the Create Instructor Materials task to a callout.

- I dragged the new callout to a position below the *Timeline* bar.

- I changed the *Date Format* option to the *Jan 28* format.

- I changed the *Background Color* setting for each task individually.

- Using the *Text Styles* dialog, I changed the *Font Color* setting to *Red* for the names of all callout items.

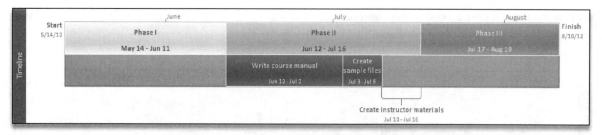

Figure 10 - 23: Timeline view after applying custom formatting

Notice in Figure 10 - 23 that the *Timeline* view no longer includes the light blue *Pan and Zoom* bar at the top of the view. This is because I zoomed the *Gantt Chart* view to show the complete time span of the project. When you zoom the *Gantt Chart* view to show the Gantt bars for all tasks in the project, Microsoft Project 2010 removes the *Pan and Zoom* bar from the *Timeline* view automatically.

To change the type of object displayed in the *Timeline* view, or to remove an object from the *Timeline* view, use the buttons in the *Current Selection* section of the contextual *Format* ribbon. For example, to change a callout to a task bar, select the callout and then click the *Display as Bar* button. To change a task bar to a callout, select the task bar and then click the *Display as Callout* button. To remove a task or a callout from the *Timeline* view, select the task or callout and then click the *Remote from Timeline* button.

Adding Tasks Using the Contextual Format Ribbon

In addition to the formatting options available on the contextual *Format* ribbon for the *Timeline* view, this ribbon also offers options for adding or removing tasks in the *Timeline* view. In the *Insert* section, Project Professional 2010 includes four buttons that allow you to add new tasks to the *Timeline* view. To add a new existing task to the *Timeline* view, click the *Existing Tasks* button. The system displays the *Add Tasks to Timeline* dialog shown in Figure 10 - 24. Select the checkbox to the left of the task name and then click the *OK* button.

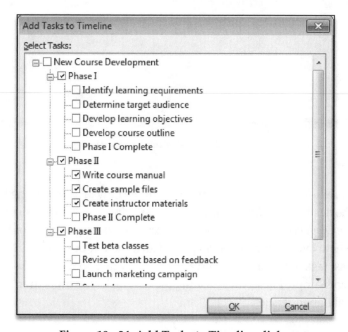

Figure 10 - 24: Add Tasks to Timeline dialog

The system adds the selected task(s) to the *Timeline* view. For example, notice in Figure 10 - 25 that I added the *Project Complete* milestone task to the *Timeline* view.

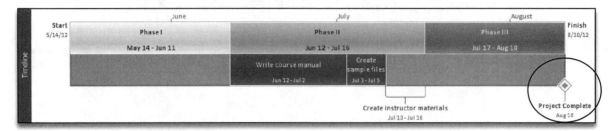

Figure 10 - 25: Milestone task added to the Timeline view

To add a completely new task to your project and add the new task to the *Timeline* view, click the *Task* button, the *Callout Task* button, or the *Milestone* button in the *Insert* section of the contextual *Format* ribbon. When you click any of these three buttons, Project Professional 2010 displays the *Task Information* dialog shown in Figure 10 - 26.

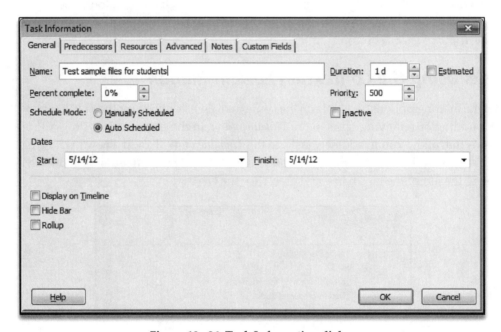

Figure 10 - 26: Task Information dialog

In the *Task Information* dialog, enter complete information about the new task, including information in the *Name* and *Duration* fields, and select the desired *Schedule Mode* option. Assuming you want to display the new task in the *Timeline* view, be sure to select the *Display on Timeline* option. If necessary, select predecessor tasks on the *Predecessors* page and assign resources to the new task on the *Resources* page. Click the *OK* button to finish. Project Professional 2010 creates the new task as the last task in the task list, and adds the new task to the *Timeline* view. Figure 10 - 27 shows a new task I added, Test Student Sample Files. After creating the new task, you must drag the task to the correct place in the project and set additional dependencies.

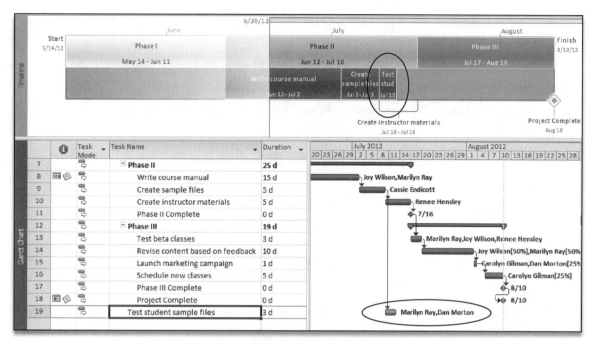

Figure 10 - 27: New task added to the project and to the Timeline view

You can also insert a new task in the project and add it to the *Timeline* view by right-clicking anywhere in the white part of the *Timeline* view, selecting the *Insert Task* menu item, and then clicking the *Callout Task*, *Task*, or *Milestone* item on the flyout menu.

Hands On Exercise

Exercise 10-10

Add tasks to the *Timeline* view.

1. Click the *Open* button on the Quick Access Toolbar.

2. Navigate to your *C:* drive and then to the folder containing the sample files for this class, and then open the **Format the Timeline View.mpp** sample file.

3. Click the *View* tab and then select the *Timeline* option in the *Split View* section of the *View* ribbon.

4. Grab the split bar along the bottom edge of the *Timeline* view and drag it down to approximately **triple** the height of the *Timeline* view.

5. Right-click on the name of the *Pre-Renovation* summary task and then click the *Add to Timeline* item on the shortcut menu.

Notice how Project Professional 2010 adds a bar to the *Timeline* view representing the *Pre-Renovation* summary task.

6. Using the **Control** key on your keyboard, select and highlight the following summary tasks as a group:

   - Renovation

   - Construction

   - Furnish

   - Post Renovation

7. Release the **Control** key, then right-click anywhere in one of the selected tasks and click the *Add to Timeline* item on the shortcut menu.

8. Using the **Control** key on your keyboard, select the three tasks highlighted with *Lime* as their cell background color (task IDs #22, 24, and 25).

9. Release the **Control** key, then right-click anywhere in one of the selected tasks and then click the *Add to Timeline* item on the shortcut menu.

10. In the *Timeline* view, right-click on the *Obtain asbestos removal permit* task bar and click the *Display as Callout* item on the shortcut menu.

11. In the *Timeline* view, right-click on the task bar for the *Asbestos removal inspection* task bar and click the *Display as Callout* item on the shortcut menu.

12. Grab the split bar along the bottom edge of the *Timeline* view and drag it down to add approximately one inch to the height of the *Timeline* view.

13. In the *Timeline* view, drag the *Remote asbestos in ceiling* task bar **below** the *Timeline* bar to display this task as a callout below the timeline.

14. Save but **do not** close the **Format the Timeline View.mpp** sample file.

Exercise 10-11

Customize the *Timeline* view.

1. Click anywhere in the *Timeline* view to select the view.

2. Click the *Format* tab to display the contextual *Format* ribbon with the *Timeline Tools* applied.

3. In the *Text* section of the *Format* ribbon, click the *Text Styles* button.

4. In the *Text Styles* dialog, click the *Item to Change* pick list and select the *Callout Task Name* item.

5. In the *Standard Colors* section of the dialog, click the *Color* pick list and select the *Red* color.

6. Click the *OK* button.

7. In the *Timeline* view, click the task bar for the *Construction* summary task.

8. In the *Font* section of the *Format* ribbon, click the *Background Color* pick list button and select the *Red* color in the first row of the *Theme Colors* section.

9. In the *Font* section of the *Format* ribbon, click the *Color* pick list button and select the *Yellow* color in the *Standard Colors* section.

10. In the *Show/Hide* section of the *Format* ribbon, click the *Date Format* pick list button and then **deselect** the *Timescale* item at the bottom of the pick list.

11. In the *Show/Hide* section of the *Format* ribbon, **deselect** the *Pan & Zoom* option.

12. In the *Insert* section of the *Format* ribbon, click the *Existing Tasks* button.

13. In the *Add Tasks to Timeline* dialog, select the checkbox for the *Project Complete* milestone task and then click the *OK* button.

14. Save but **do not** close the **Format the Timeline View.mpp** sample file.

Exporting the Timeline View

One additional feature of the new *Timeline* view allows you to export the entire *Timeline* view to any Microsoft Office application, such as Microsoft PowerPoint or Microsoft Visio. To copy the *Timeline* view, click the *Copy Timeline* pick list button in the *Copy* section of the contextual *Format* ribbon. The *Copy Timeline* pick list contains three choices, including *For E-Mail*, *For Presentation*, and *Full Size*.

If you select the *Full Size* item on the *Copy Timeline* pick list, Project Professional 2010 copies the full-size image of the *Timeline* view to your Windows clipboard. If you select the *For Presentation* item, the system optimizes the image for use in Microsoft PowerPoint by reducing the image size to approximately 90% of full size. If you select the *For E-Mail* item, the system optimizes the image for use in Microsoft Outlook by reducing the image size to approximately 60% of full size.

After copying the *Timeline* view to your clipboard, paste the image in one of the Microsoft Office applications. If you use an application that has image editing capabilities, such as Microsoft Word or Microsoft PowerPoint, you can continue to refine your *Timeline* view presentation. For example, Figure 10 - 28 shows the *Timeline* view after I pasted the image into a Microsoft PowerPoint presentation and applied additional formatting. Notice that I used the *Bevel* feature to give the tasks a 3-D appearance, and I used the *Glow* feature to alter the appearance of the *Project Complete* milestone task.

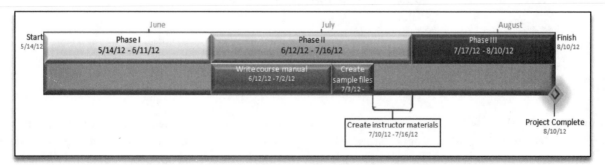

Figure 10 - 28: Timeline view formatted in Microsoft PowerPoint

You can also copy the *Timeline* view by right-clicking anywhere in the white part of the *Timeline* view, selecting the *Copy Timeline* item from the shortcut menu, and then clicking the *For E-Mail*, *For Presentation*, or *Full Size* item on the flyout menu.

Exercise 10-12

Export the *Timeline* view to another Microsoft Office application.

1. Return to the **Format the Timeline View.mpp** sample file, if necessary.

2. Click anywhere in the *Timeline* view to select it.

3. In the *Copy* section of the *Format* ribbon, click the *Copy Timeline* pick list button and then select the *For Presentation* item on the pick list.

4. Launch Microsoft PowerPoint and create a new blank slide with no placeholder information.

5. Click the *Paste* button in Microsoft PowerPoint.

6. Zoom your PowerPoint slide to the *100%* level of zoom.

7. Double-click one of the task bars in the timeline image to launch the *Drawing Tools* feature in Microsoft PowerPoint.

8. Using the **Control** key on your computer keyboard, select each of the task bars in the Timeline image, and then release the **Control** key.

9. Use any of the object formatting features in Microsoft PowerPoint to format the selected task bars in the Timeline image. For example, if you have Microsoft PowerPoint 2007, format the task bars using one of the *Bevel* items in the *Shape Effects* pick list.

10. Exit your Microsoft PowerPoint application and then return to your Project Professional 2010 application window.

11. Save and close the **Format the Timeline View.mpp** sample file.

Using Visual Reports

In addition to using the new *Timeline* view for project reporting, you can also use visual reports for this purpose. Microsoft introduced visual reports as a new feature in Project Professional 2007, and continues to offer improved visual report functionality in Project Professional 2010. Visual reports allow you to see your project data in a *PivotChart* and *PivotTable* in Microsoft Excel or in a *PivotDiagram* in Microsoft Visio. The software creates the visual report by building local OLAP (On Line Analytical Programming) cubes directly on your computer's hard drive. These local OLAP cubes provide a multi-dimensional summary of task and resource data in your project.

You can use the Excel Visual Reports with Microsoft Excel 2003, 2007, or 2010. To use the Visio Visual Reports, however, you must have Microsoft Visio **Professional** 2007 or 2010.

If you are a previous user of Microsoft Project 2007 and upgraded to the 2010 version, you might be interested in knowing the improvements to visual reports. Although these improvements are relatively minor, they include the following:

- You can add custom fields to the OLAP cubes used for the *Assignment Usage* and *Assignment Summary* visual reports.

- Visual reports now support custom field names of up to 100 characters, increased from 25 characters in Microsoft Project 2007.

Project Professional 2010 allows you to choose the fields to display in the visual report while viewing it and to make ad hoc modifications to the visual report without regenerating the underlying data. With this type of flexibility, visual reports offer you much greater flexibility than the default reports that ship with the software.

To access visual reports, click the *Project* tab and then click the *Visual Reports* button in the *Reports* section of the *Project* ribbon. The system displays the *Visual Reports – Create Report* dialog shown in Figure 10 - 29.

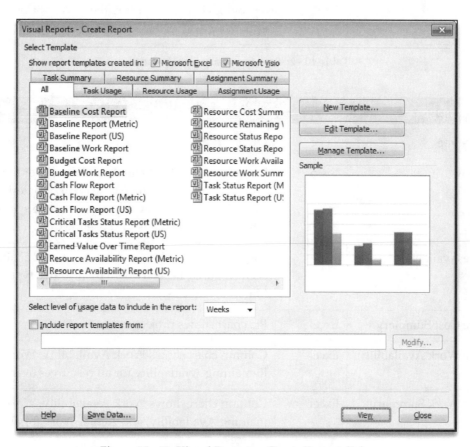

Figure 10 - 29: Visual Reports – Create Report dialog

The *Visual Reports – Create Report* dialog provides you with six categories of default visual reports for both Microsoft Excel and Microsoft Visio. The *Task Usage, Resource Usage,* and *Assignment Usage* categories display timephased task, resource, and assignment data, respectively. The *Task Summary, Resource Summary,* and *Assignment Summary* categories display task, resource, and assignment data without timephased data. Table 10 - 1through Table 10 - 6 describe the default visual reports included in each category.

Task Usage		
Report Name	**Type**	**Description**
Cash Flow	Excel	Combination column chart/line chart shows Cost (columns) and cumulative cost (lines) over time.

Table 10 - 1: Task Usage visual reports

Task Summary		
Report Name	**Type**	**Description**
Critical Tasks Status	Visio	Diagram shows Work, Remaining Work, and % Work Complete for both critical and non-critical tasks, with a progress bar representing the % Work Complete for each task.

Table 10 - 2: Task Summary visual reports

Resource Usage		
Report Name	**Type**	**Description**
Cash Flow	Visio	Diagram shows Cost and Actual Cost over time and broken down by resource type (Work, Material, and Cost). Diagram shows an orange triangle symbol when the Cost exceeds the Baseline Cost.
Resource Availability	Visio	Diagram shows Work and Remaining Availability for each resource, broken down by resource type (Work, Material, and Cost).
Resource Cost Summary	Excel	Pie chart shows project costs.
Resource Work Availability	Excel	Column chart shows Work Availability, Work, and Remaining Availability for all resources over time.
Resource Work Summary	Excel	Column chart shows Work Availability, Work, Remaining Availability, and Actual Work for all resources.

Table 10 - 3: Resource Usage visual reports

Resource Summary		
Report Name	**Type**	**Description**
Resource Remaining Work	Excel	Stacked column chart shows Actual Work and Remaining Work for all resources.

Table 10 - 4: Resource Summary visual reports

Assignment Usage		
Report Name	**Type**	**Description**
Baseline Cost	Excel	Column chart shows Baseline Cost, Cost, and Actual Cost for all tasks.
Baseline	Visio	Diagram compares Work and Cost with Baseline Work and Baseline Cost over time for all tasks. Displays a red stoplight when Work exceeds Baseline Work. Displays a yellow flag when Cost exceeds Baseline Cost.
Baseline Work	Excel	Column chart shows Baseline Work, Work, and Actual Work for all tasks.
Budget Cost	Excel	Column chart shows Budget Cost, Baseline Cost, Cost, and Actual Cost over time.
Budget Work	Excel	Column chart shows Budget Work, Baseline Work, Work, and Actual Work over time.
Earned Value Over Time	Excel	Line chart shows Earned Value (EV), Planned Value (BCWP), and Actual Cost (ACWP) over time through the *Status* date of the project.

Table 10 - 5: Assignment Usage visual reports

Assignment Summary		
Report Name	**Type**	**Description**
Resource Status	Visio	Diagram shows Work and Cost for each resource with color shading in each box representing % Work Complete. White shading represents 100% Work complete, dark purple represents 0% Work complete, and light purple represents % Work Complete greater than 0% and less than 100%.

Assignment Summary		
Report Name	**Type**	**Description**
Task Status	Visio	Diagram displays Work and Cost for all tasks. Diagram displays an orange progress bar representing % Work Complete for each task and also shows a yellow "unhappy face" when Work exceeds Baseline Work. The system shows a yellow "neutral face" when Work is equal to or less than Baseline Work.

Table 10 - 6: Assignment Summary visual reports

Each Visio visual report is available in either a metric version or US version. The versions refer to the measurement units applied to the horizontal and vertical ruler bars in the PivotDiagram. When you select the metric version, the software applies the **millimeter** measurement to the ruler bar. When you select the US version, the software applies the **inches** measurement.

If you used Project Professional 2007 previously before upgrading to the 2010 version, you see some changes to the default data displayed in most of the Excel visual reports. These changes include:

- The **Baseline Cost Report** no longer includes the *Tasks* dimension in the *Row Labels* drop area of the *PivotTable*.

- The **Baseline Work Report** no longer includes the *Tasks* dimension in the *Row Labels* drop area of the *PivotTable*.

- The **Earned Value Over Time Report** shows Earned Value data only through the *Status* date of the project. In Project Professional 2007, the report showed Earned Value data over the entire time span of the project, but the Earned Value dropped to 0 for every time period after the *Status* date of the project.

- The **Resource Cost Summary Report** no longer includes the *Type* dimension in the *Row Labels* drop area of the *PivotTable*.

- The **Resource Remaining Work Report** no longer includes the *Type* and *Resources* dimensions in the *Row Labels* drop area of the *PivotTable*.

- The **Resource Work Summary Report** no longer includes the *Type* and *Resources* dimensions in the *Row Labels* drop area of the *PivotTable*.

For the Visio visual reports, Microsoft made only one minor change to the default data shown in the **Resource Status Report,** which displays information for a new default resource named *Task's Fixed Cost.* This new resource displays any extra task costs you add to the *Fixed Cost* column.

Viewing a Visual Report

To view a visual report, complete the following steps:

1. Click the *Project* tab and then click the *Visual Reports* button in the *Reports* section of the *Project* ribbon.

2. In the *Visual Reports – Create Report* dialog, click the tab containing the visual report you want to view.

3. In the selected report section, select a visual report from the list.

4. Click the *Select level of usage data to include in this report* pick list and select the data granularity you want to use in the report, as shown in Figure 10 - 30.

 Microsoft Project 2010 generates the data in the local OLAP cubes using the granularity you select and then transfers the data to the visual report.

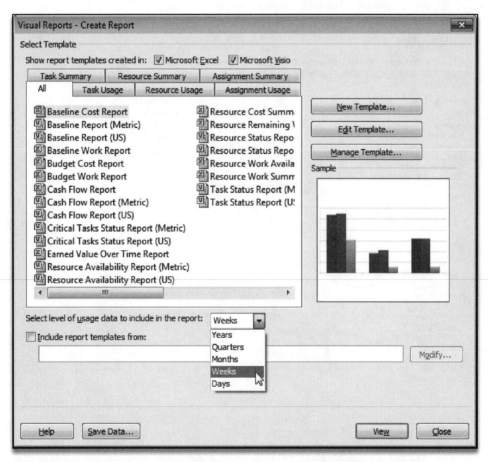

Figure 10 - 30: Visual Reports – Create Report dialog, select the
granularity for the Resource Work Availability Report

Based on the size of your project, Microsoft Project 2010 sets a recommended value in the *Select level of usage data to include in this report* pick list. For most projects, the recommended value is *Weeks*. For very large projects, the recommended value might be *Months*, *Quarters*, or even *Years*.

5. If you want to supplement the standard list of task and resource details included with the local OLAP cube, click the *Edit Template* button.

Project Professional 2010 displays the *Visual Reports – Field Picker* dialog shown in Figure 10 - 31. In the *Selected Fields* list on the right, you see the standard list of detail fields added to the local OLAP cube automatically. This list includes fields like *Task WBS* and *Task Percent Complete*, for example. If you want to supplement this list with additional fields, select one or more fields in the *Available Fields* list and click the *Add* button.

The *Available Custom Fields* list shows the list of custom fields available for inclusion in the local OLAP cube, and includes any custom fields you created in the project. For example, notice in Figure 10 - 31that the list includes two custom fields I created in this project: the *Accountable Person Task (dimension)* field and the *Cost Center ID Task (dimension)* field. To add any custom field to the local OLAP cube, select one or more fields in the *Available Custom Fields* list and click the *Add* button. Click the *Edit Template* button when finished.

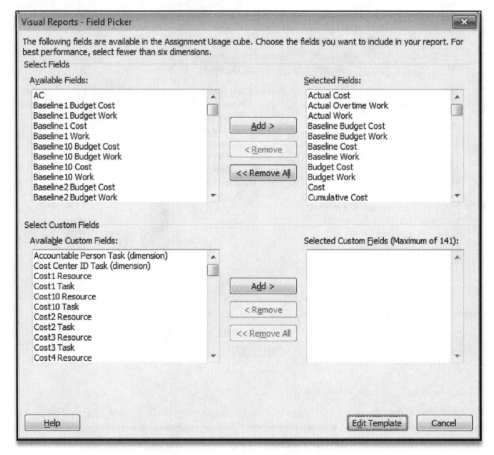

Figure 10 - 31: Visual Reports – Field Picker dialog

6. If you did not need to use step #5, click the *View* button to create the visual report.

Project Professional 2010 displays a progress indicator at the bottom of the dialog in which it indicates that it is gathering data for the report, building the local OLAP cubes, and then opening the visual report template for viewing. Figure 10 - 32 shows the completed *Baseline Cost* visual report in Microsoft Excel. Notice that the legend at the top of the chart explains the meaning of each column color.

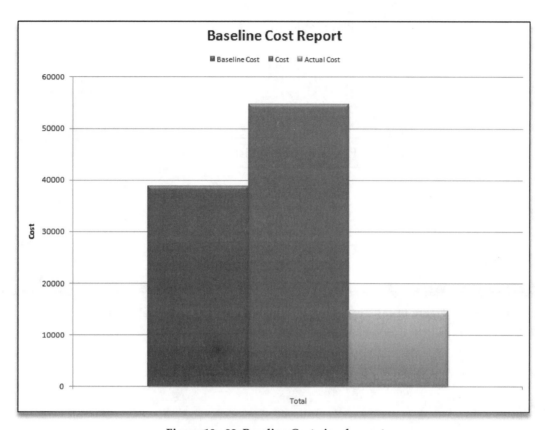

Figure 10 - 32: Baseline Cost visual report

7. Click the *Zoom Out* or *Zoom In* buttons to set the desired level of zoom.

In Microsoft Excel 2007 and 2010, the system sets the default level of zoom for each visual report to 125%. Depending on your monitor size and screen resolution, you may need to zoom out for every visual report you view.

The visual report in Microsoft Excel consists of two parts: the graphical *PivotChart*, shown previously in Figure 10 - 32, and the *PivotTable* containing the underlying data. To view the *PivotTable* data, click the *Task Usage*, *Resource Usage*, or *Assignment Usage* worksheet tab in the lower left corner of the application window. Figure 10 - 33 shows the *PivotTable* data on the *Assignment Usage* worksheet for the *Baseline Cost* visual report.

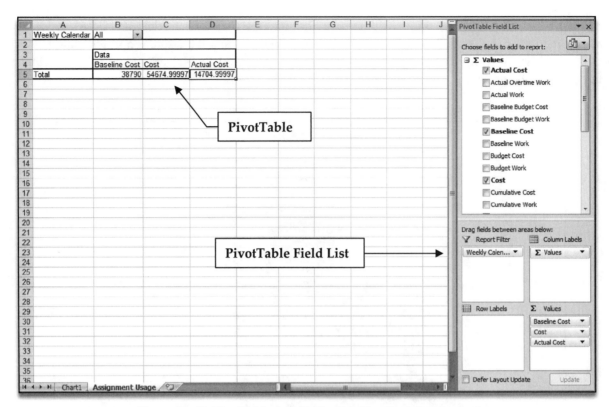

Figure 10 - 33: PivotTable data for the Baseline Cost visual report

The *Assignment Usage* worksheet consists of two parts. The worksheet displays the *PivotTable* in the upper left corner of the page, as shown in Figure 10 - 33. The *PivotTable* includes data areas for row fields, column fields, project filter fields, and total fields. The worksheet displays the *PivotTable Field List* sidepane on the right side of the page.

Figure 10 - 34 shows the *Task Status* visual report in Microsoft Visio. Because the default zoom level is set to display the entire page, you probably need to zoom in to see your visual report data clearly. Notice in Figure 10 - 34 that a visual report in Microsoft Visio consists of three parts: the *PivotDiagram*, the *PivotDiagram* sidepane on the left, and the floating *PivotDiagram* toolbar.

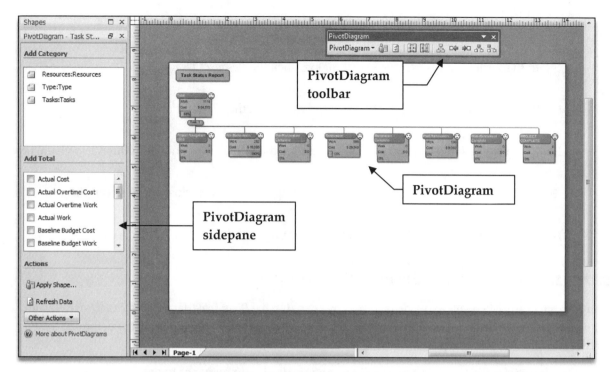

Figure 10 - 34: Task Status visual report

Hands On Exercise

Exercise 10-13

View visual reports in Project Professional 2010.

1. Click the *Open* button on the Quick Access Toolbar.

2. Navigate to your *C:* drive and then to the folder containing the sample files for this class, and then open the **Project Navigation 2010.mpp** sample file.

3. Click the *Project* tab and then click the *Visual Reports* button in the *Reports* section of the *Project* ribbon.

4. Click the *Assignment Usage* tab and select the *Baseline Work Report* item.

5. Click the *Select level of usage data to include in this report* pick list and select the *Days* level of data granularity.

6. Click the *View* button.

7. Examine the *PivotChart* shown on the *Chart1* worksheet and the *PivotTable* data shown on the *Assignment Usage* worksheet.

8. Close and **do not** save the Microsoft Excel workbook, but leave the Excel application running.

9. Return to the Project Professional 2010 application window.

10. In the *Visual Reports – Create Report* dialog, click the *Resource Usage* tab.

11. Select the *Cash Flow Report (US)* item and then click the *View* button.

12. Zoom to the *100%* level of zoom and examine the information shown in this Visio visual report.

13. Close and **do not** save the Microsoft Visio diagram, and then close the Visio application.

14. Return to your Project Professional 2010 application window.

Customizing a Microsoft Excel Visual Report

You can customize any Microsoft Excel visual report by changing the *PivotTable* data on the *Task Usage*, *Resource Usage* or *Assignment Usage* worksheet. For example, you can use any of the following methods to customize the *PivotTable* data in the *Baseline Cost* visual report:

- In the *PivotTable Field List* sidepane, deselect any fields you do not want to display, and select the fields you do want to display. The software adds the newly selected field(s) to the appropriate area in the sidepane. For example, notice in Figure 10 - 35 that I **deselected** the *Actual Cost* field in the *PivotTable Field List* sidepane, removing this field from both the *PivotTable* and the *PivotChart* as a consequence. Though not visible in Figure 10 - 35, I also selected the *Tasks* field for inclusion in the Excel visual report.

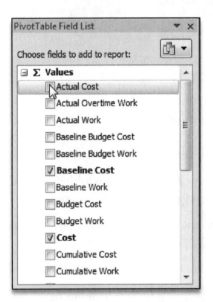

Figure 10 - 35: Deselect the Actual Cost field

- In the *PivotTable Field List* sidepane, drag and drop fields from the field list to the drop areas at the bottom of the pane. For example, I dragged the *Weekly Calendar* field from the *Report Filter* area to the *Row Labels* area, as shown in Figure 10 - 36. You can see the *Tasks* field in the *Row Labels* area as well.

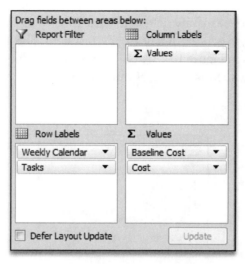

**Figure 10 - 36: Move the Weekly Calendar
field to the Row Labels area**

- In the *PivotTable*, click the *Expand* (**+**) or *Collapse* (**-**) buttons in any section on the left side to show the level details you want to see in the visual report. Notice in Figure 10 - 37 that I expanded the *Year* section to show *Quarters*, and I expanded the *Project Navigation 2010* task to show first-level tasks in the *Task 1* section.

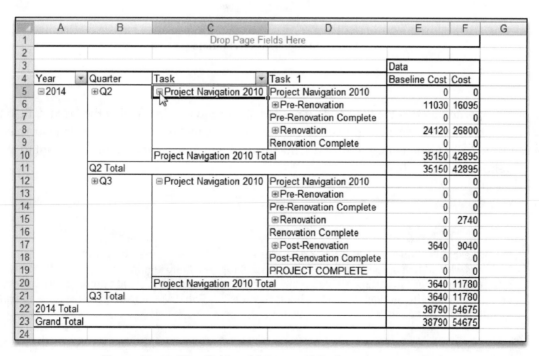

	A	B	C	D	E	F	G
1			Drop Page Fields Here				
2							
3					Data		
4	Year	Quarter	Task	Task 1	Baseline Cost	Cost	
5	⊟2014	⊞Q2	⊞Project Navigation 2010	Project Navigation 2010	0	0	
6				⊞Pre-Renovation	11030	16095	
7				Pre-Renovation Complete	0	0	
8				⊞Renovation	24120	26800	
9				Renovation Complete	0	0	
10			Project Navigation 2010 Total		35150	42895	
11		Q2 Total			35150	42895	
12		⊞Q3	⊟Project Navigation 2010	Project Navigation 2010	0	0	
13				⊞Pre-Renovation	0	0	
14				Pre-Renovation Complete	0	0	
15				⊞Renovation	0	2740	
16				Renovation Complete	0	0	
17				⊞Post-Renovation	3640	9040	
18				Post-Renovation Complete	0	0	
19				PROJECT COMPLETE	0	0	
20			Project Navigation 2010 Total		3640	11780	
21		Q3 Total			3640	11780	
22	2014 Total				38790	54675	
23	Grand Total				38790	54675	
24							

Figure 10 - 37: PivotTable with Year and Task sections expanded

- Select the details you want to see for any field in the *Row Labels* area by clicking the pick list arrow button in the field name. For example, to edit the details for the *Task* field, click the *Task* pick list. The system displays the *Select field* dialog shown in Figure 10 - 38. Using this dialog, you can select the specific task items you want to see in the *PivotTable*, such as first-level summary tasks that represent phases of the project.

Figure 10 - 38: Select field dialog

- Display properties fields in the *PivotTable*, if needed. If you add the *Task* field or the *Resource* field to the *Row Labels* area in any visual report, right-click on the *Task* or *Resource* field. In the shortcut menu, select the *Show Properties in Report* menu item, and then use the fly out menu to select the details you want to see in the report, as shown in Figure 10 - 39.

For this example, I do not include any properties fields in the *PivotTable*. In your own projects, be judicious with adding properties fields to your visual reports. Keep in mind that Microsoft Excel limits how much number formatting you can apply to properties fields, or prevents number formatting entirely. Beyond this, adding properties fields to your *PivotTable* can negatively impact the appearance of your *PivotChart* as well.

514

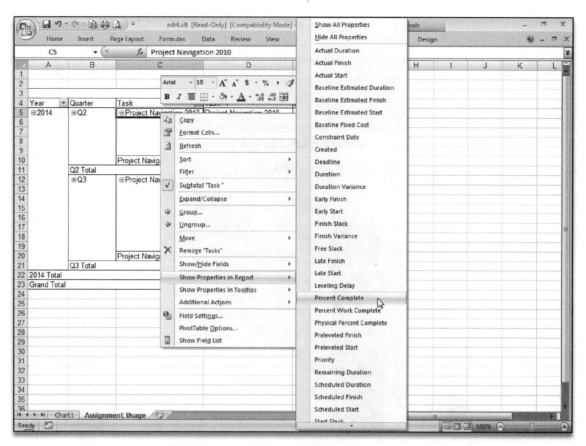

Figure 10 - 39: Add the Percent Complete details to the PivotTable

- Apply numeric formatting to the numbers in the *PivotTable*. For example, in Figure 10 - 40, I applied the *Accounting Number Format* numeric formatting to the data shown in the *PivotTable*, and then I clicked the *Decrease Decimal* button to reduce to *zero* the number of digits to the right of the decimal.

	A	B	C	D	E	F	G
1			Drop Page Fields Here				
2							
3					Data		
4	Year	Quarter	Task	Task 1	Baseline Cost	Cost	
5	⊟2014	⊞Q2	⊟Project Navigation 2010	⊞Pre-Renovation	$ 11,030	$ 16,095	
6				⊞Renovation	$ 24,120	$ 26,800	
7			Project Navigation 2010 Total		$ 35,150	$ 42,895	
8		Q2 Total			$ 35,150	$ 42,895	
9		⊞Q3	⊟Project Navigation 2010	⊞Pre-Renovation	$ -	$ -	
10				⊞Renovation	$ -	$ 2,740	
11				⊞Post-Renovation	$ 3,640	$ 9,040	
12			Project Navigation 2010 Total		$ 3,640	$ 11,780	
13		Q3 Total			$ 3,640	$ 11,780	
14	2014 Total				$ 38,790	$ 54,675	
15	Grand Total				$ 38,790	$ 54,675	
16							

Figure 10 - 40: PivotTable with numeric formatting applied

When you make changes to the data shown in the *PivotTable,* Microsoft Excel updates the changes immediately in the *PivotChart.* Figure 10 - 41 shows the updated *PivotChart* after making changes to the underlying data in the *PivotTable.* If you compare this updated *Baseline Cost* report with the original *Baseline Cost* report shown previously in Figure 10 - 32, you see dramatic changes in appearance after making only a few simple changes in the *PivotTable.*

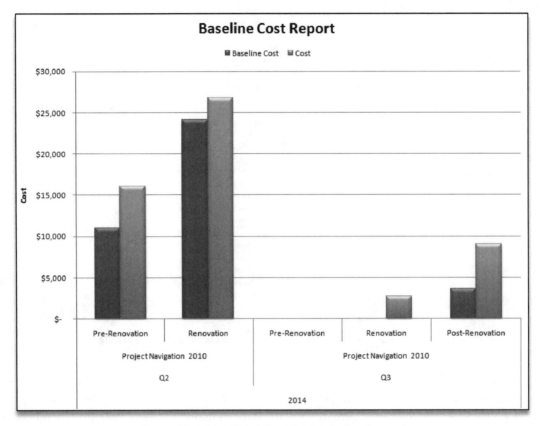

Figure 10 - 41: Updated Baseline Cost visual report

You can also modify the *PivotChart* by right-clicking anywhere in the area of the chart you want to change. When you right-click in the *Chart Area* of the *PivotChart,* Microsoft Excel displays the shortcut menu shown in Figure 10 - 42. Using the options on this shortcut menu, you can use any of the built-in chart formatting capabilities available in Microsoft Excel.

In Microsoft Excel 2007 and 2010, you can also double-click anywhere in the *PivotChart.* The system displays the contextual *Design* ribbon with the *PivotChart Tools* applied. Using the features on the *Design* ribbon, you can apply many different types of formatting to the *PivotChart.*

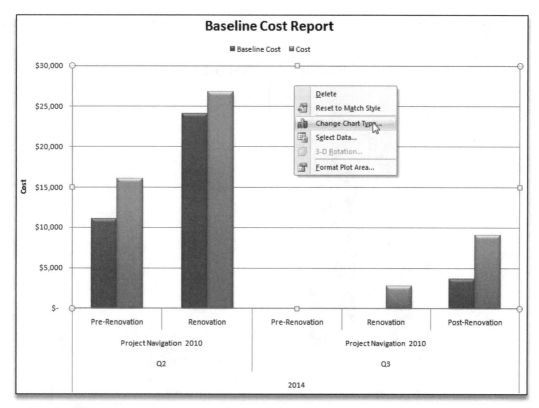

Figure 10 - 42: Right-click in the PivotChart to display the shortcut menu

If you select the *Change Chart Type* item on the shortcut menu, Microsoft Excel displays the *Change Chart Type* dialog shown in Figure 10 - 43. Select an alternate chart type in this dialog and then click the *OK* button.

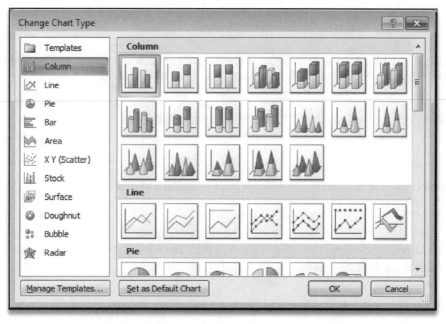

Figure 10 - 43: Change Chart Type dialog

Figure 10 - 44 shows the *PivotChart* after I applied the *Clustered Cylinder* chart type in the *Change Chart Type* dialog.

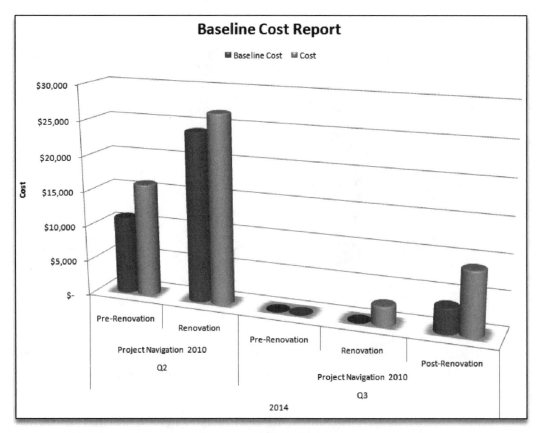

Figure 10 - 44: PivotChart formatted using the Clustered Cylinder chart type

Because this is not a course on Microsoft Excel, I do not provide an exhaustive discussion about how to format either the *PivotTable* or the *PivotChart* in an Excel visual report.

Within Microsoft Excel, you can also do the following after viewing a visual report:

- Save the workbook by clicking the *Save* button.

- Print the workbook by clicking the *Office* button in the upper left corner of the application window, and then click *Print* from the *Office* menu.

- Close the workbook without saving it and then exit the application.

Customizing a Microsoft Visio Visual Report

You can customize a Microsoft Visio visual report by using any of the following methods:

- Select one or more objects in the *PivotDiagram* and then change the options in the sidepane or on the floating toolbar.

- Manually delete objects in the *PivotDiagram*.

- Change the layout of objects in the *PivotDiagram*.

Notice in the *Task Status* visual report, shown previously in Figure 10 - 34, that the report displays only the first-level tasks representing the phases in the project. In this visual report, I want to show the second-level summary tasks for the *Renovation* phase to view the deliverables for that phase. To accomplish this, I must do the following:

1. Click the *Renovation* object to select it.

2. Click the *Tasks* pick list in the *Add Category* section of the sidepane and then select the *Task 2* item on the list, as shown in Figure 10 - 45.

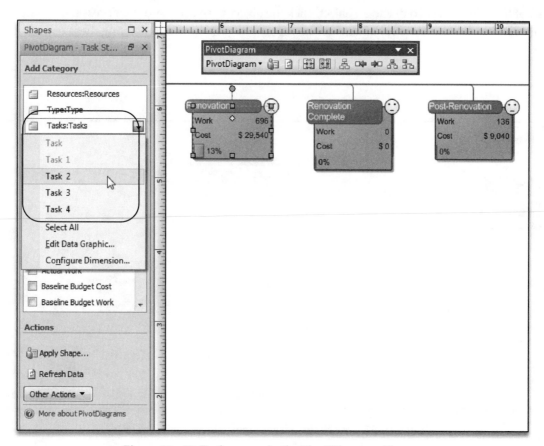

Figure 10 - 45: Tasks menu in the PivotDiagram sidepane

Figure 10 - 46 shows the *Task Status* visual report after adding the second-level summary task objects to the report.

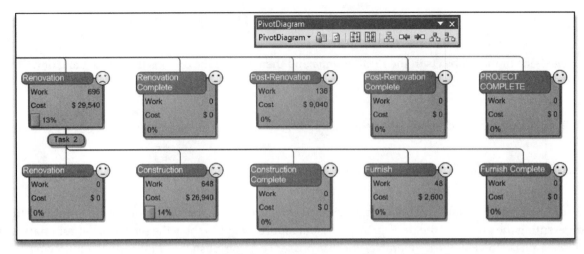

Figure 10 - 46: Task Status visual report with second-level summary tasks for the Renovation phase

In the *Task Status* visual report shown in Figure 10 - 46, I want to remove the objects representing the Project Summary Task and all of the milestones. To delete an object, click the object to select it and then press the **Delete** key on your keyboard. Figure 10 - 47 shows my *Task Status* visual report after selecting and deleting these objects.

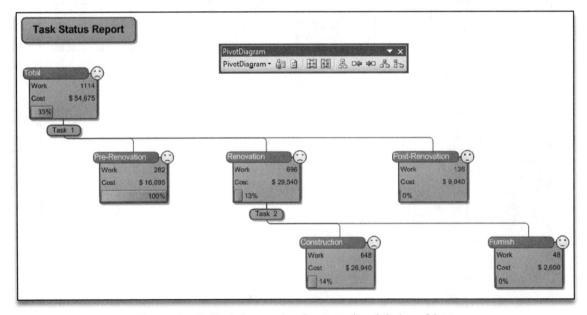

Figure 10 - 47: Task Status visual report after deleting objects

To change the layout of the objects, click the *Re-layout All* button on the floating *PivotDiagram* toolbar. You can also manually drag and drop objects anywhere on the *PivotDiagram*. Figure 10 - 48 shows the *Task Status* visual report after changing the layout of the *PivotDiagram* objects using the *Re-layout All* button.

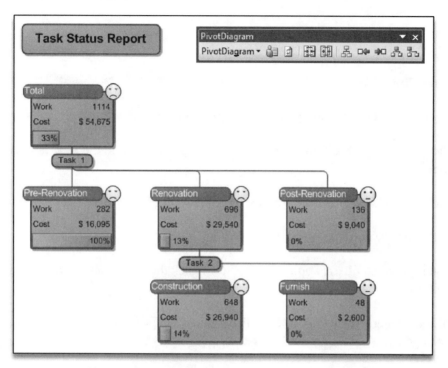

Figure 10 - 48: Task Status visual report after changing the layout

 Because this is not a course on Microsoft Visio, I do not provide an exhaustive discussion about how to format a *PivotDiagram*.

You can also do the following after viewing a visual report within Microsoft Visio:

- Save the visual report as a Drawing file.

- Print the visual report.

- Close the visual report without saving and then exit the application.

Hands On Exercise

Exercise 10-14

Customize the *PivotTable* in an Excel visual report.

1. Return to the **Project Navigation 2010.mpp** sample file, if necessary.

2. Click the *Project* tab and then click the *Visual Reports* button in the *Reports* section of the *Project* ribbon.

3. Click the *Assignment Usage* tab and select the *Baseline Work Report* item.

4. Click the *View* button.

5. In your Microsoft Excel application window, click the *Assignment Usage* worksheet tab to view the *PivotTable* data.

6. Click anywhere in the *PivotTable* to display the *PivotTable Field List* sidepane on the right side of the page.

7. In the *PivotTable Field List* sidepane, **deselect** the *Actual Work* item in the *Choose fields to add to report* section.

8. In the *Choose fields to add to report* section of the *PivotTable Field List* sidepane, scroll down so that you can see the last two sections on the list (*Time* and *Type*).

9. Select the *Tasks* item in the *Tasks* section, and then **deselect** the *Weekly Calendar* item in the *Time* section.

10. In the *PivotTable*, expand the *Project Navigation 2010* item in the *Task* section.

11. In the *PivotTable*, click the *Task* pick list.

12. In the *Select field* dialog, expand the *Project Navigation 2010* item to view summary tasks and milestone tasks.

13. In the *Select field* dialog, **deselect** the *(Select All)* option and then select only the following task items:

    - Pre-Renovation

    - Renovation

    - Post-Renovation

14. Click the *OK* button to close the *Select field* dialog.

15. Select all of the numbers in the *Baseline Work* and *Work* columns of the *PivotTable* and then format the numbers with the following number styles:

    • *Comma* style

    • Zero digits to the right of the decimal point

16. Click the *Chart1* worksheet tab and study the new information shown in the *PivotChart*.

Exercise 10-15

Customize the *PivotChart* in an Excel visual report.

1. Continue using the **Project Navigation 2010.mpp** sample file.

2. In the *Baseline Work* visual report, click anywhere in the *Chart Area* of the *PivotChart* and then close the *PivotTable Field List* sidepane that appears automatically on the right side of the screen.

3. Click and hold the right border of the *Chart Area (Plot Area)* and then drag it over to the right edge of the *PivotChart*.

4. Right-click anywhere in the *Chart Area* of the *PivotChart* and select the *Change Series Chart Type* item on the shortcut menu.

5. In the *Change Chart Type* dialog, select the *Clustered Pyramid* option (second icon in the third row of the *Column* charts) and then click the *OK* button.

6. Save the *Baseline Work* visual report as an Excel workbook file in your student folder and name it *Custom Baseline Work Report.xls*.

7. Close the *Baseline Work* visual report file and then exit your Microsoft Excel application.

8. Return to your Project Professional 2010 application window and click the *Close* button in the *Visual Reports - Create Report* dialog.

9. Save and close the **Project Navigation 2010.mpp** sample file.

Module 11

Managing Personal Settings

Learning Objectives

After completing this module, you will be able to:

- Set e-mail Alerts and Reminders for yourself
- Set e-mail Alerts and Reminders for resources that you manage
- Manage Queued jobs
- Set Delegations for yourself
- Act as a Delegate

Inside Module 11

Personal Settings Overview

Depending on your permissions within the system, Project Server 2010 offers you a number of personal settings that you can modify to suit your needs. Click the *Personal Settings* link in the Quick Launch menu to change your personal settings. The system displays the *Personal Settings* page shown in Figure 11 - 1.

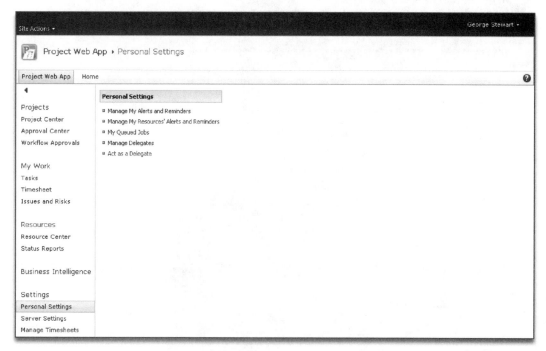

Figure 11 - 1: Personal Settings page in Project Web App

Depending on your permissions in Project Server 2010 and your method of authentication, the *Personal Settings* page may offer you some or all the following options:

- Manage My Alerts and Reminders

- Manage My Resource's Alerts and Reminders

- My Queued Jobs

- Manage Delegates

- Act as a Delegate

I discuss each of these options individually.

Managing Alerts and Reminders for Yourself

Project Web App allows you to set up a subscription to receive e-mail Alerts and Reminders from Project Server 2010. An Alert is an e-mail message that the system sends immediately when an event occurs, such as when the project manager publishes a new project in which you are a team member. A Reminder is an e-mail message that the system sends on a periodic cycle, usually once a day at midnight, to remind you of upcoming or overdue responsibilities, such as an overdue Status Report.

To manage your subscription for Alerts and Reminders, click the *Manage My Alerts and Reminders* link on the *Personal Settings* page. Project Server 2010 displays the *Manage My Alerts and Reminders* page shown in Figure 11 - 2.

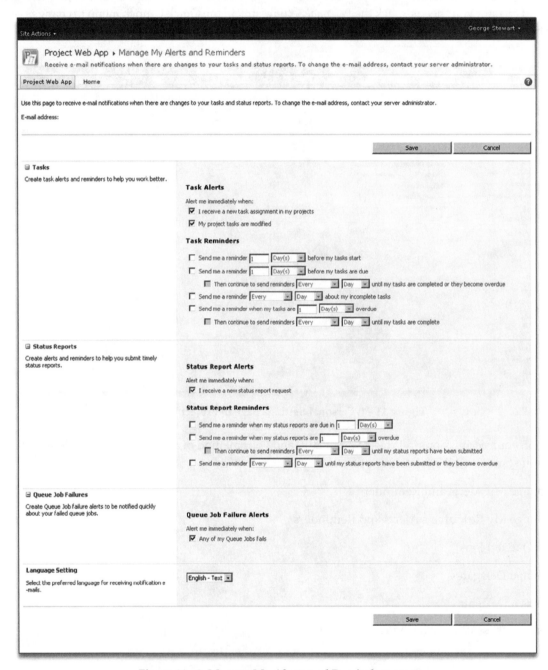

Figure 11 - 2: Manage My Alerts and Reminders page

Notice that the *Manage My Alerts and Reminders* page includes options in four sections. You set your alerts and reminders in the *Tasks* section and the *Status Reports* section. In the *Tasks* section, the default options trigger the system to send you an e-mail message whenever the following occurs:

- A project manager publishes a new project containing a task assigned to you, or the project manager assigns you to a new task in an existing project and then publishes the project.

- The schedule changes for one or more of your task assignments in an existing project.

Between the two default e-mail subscriptions for Alerts on tasks, the first is most valuable because you should always notify team members about new task assignments. The second e-mail subscription is problematic, however, because it can lead to a large number of e-mail messages sent to team members every time the project schedule changes. If team members receive too many e-mail messages from Project Server 2010, they may treat these messages as "spam" and create an Outlook rule to filter out all messages originating with Project Server.

> To reduce the number of e-mail messages that users receive from Project Server 2010, MSProjectExperts recommends that all project managers and team members deselect the *My project tasks are modified* option on the *Manage My Alerts and Reminders* page.

The second set of options in the *Tasks* section allows you to subscribe to e-mail reminders related to specific task criteria for project work. Each night the system tests your criteria and generates an email message containing the task reminders for your subscriptions. You receive an email only if you set reminder criteria and the system finds an appropriate match between your tasks in the system and your specified criteria. Think of these criteria as triggering conditions, which include each of the following:

- Before a task starts

- Before a task is due

- Until a task is complete or becomes overdue

- When you have an incomplete task

- When you have an overdue task

- Until an overdue task is complete

Notice in Figure 11 - 2 that the default settings include none of these options. If you select any of these options, you should also specify the frequency, as you do not have to receive these messages every day unless you prefer daily delivery.

The options in the *Status Reports* section are similar to those in the *Tasks* section. The default permission for alerts on Status Reports causes the system to send you an e-mail message immediately when a manager includes you in a new Status Report request. The second set of options allows you to subscribe to reminders for Status Reports.

The *Queue Job Failures* section of the *Manage My Alerts and Reminders* page includes only a single option. This option causes Project Server 2010 to send you an e-mail message immediately if any job you send to the Queue fails in the queuing process. For example, if you submit a timesheet or a task update, each of these constitutes a job sent to the Queue for processing. If the job fails, the system immediately sends you an e-mail message.

The *Language Setting* section contains a single option that allows you to set your language preference for e-mail messages sent to you by Project Server 2010. Select the language you want, if necessary, and then click the *Save* button to save the selections you specify.

Managing Alerts and Reminders for Your Resources

In addition to managing e-mail subscriptions for Alerts and Reminders for yourself, Project Server 2010 also allows you to manage e-mail subscriptions for your team members and your resources. The system defines "your team members" as those resources who are a team member in your projects and assigned to at least one task. The system defines "your resources" as any resource included in a Status Report request. To set e-mail subscriptions for your team members and resources, click the *Manage My Resource's Alerts and Reminders* link on the *Personal Settings* page. Project Server 2010 displays the *Manage My Resource's Alerts and Reminders* page shown in Figure 11 - 3.

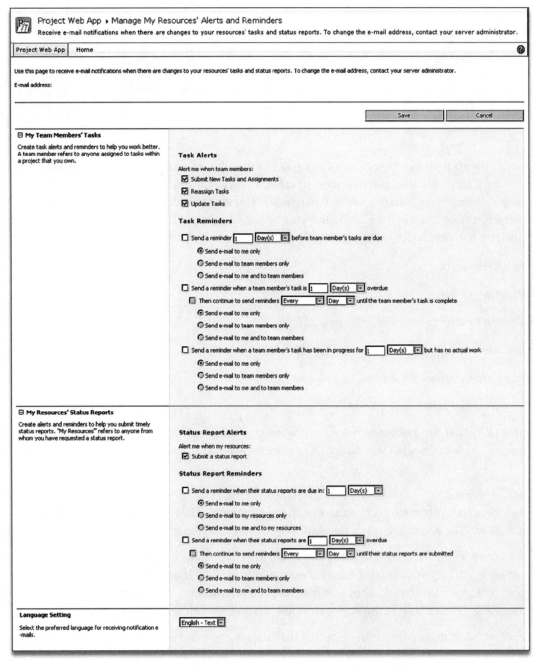

Figure 11 - 3: Manage My Resources' Alerts and Reminders page

Notice in Figure 11 - 3 that the *Manage My Resource's Alerts and Reminders* page layout is similar to the *Manage My Alerts and Reminders* page. In this case, the page consists of only three sections, with sections for My Team Member's Tasks, My Resource's Status Reports, and Language Settings. Notice also that the default options in the *Task Alerts* section of the page cause Project Server 2010 to send you an e-mail alert immediately when one of the following triggering events occurs:

- A team member submits a New Task request or a New Assignment request to you.

- A team member reassigns (delegates) a task to another team member.

- A team member submits task progress to you.

Because these three default options can lead to a high volume of e-mail messages sent to you by Project Server 2010, you may wish to deselect one or more of these options. Of the three, the *Update Tasks* option causes the system to send the most e-mail messages.

The *Task Reminders* section of the page allows you to set up subscriptions for e-mail reminders for your team members about their project work. When you set up reminder subscriptions for your team members, you may choose to have the reminder sent to you only, to the team members only, or to both you and your team members. Set the reminders for your team members and specify who receives the e-mail reminders.

The *Status Report Alerts* section contains only a single option, selected by default. This option causes Project Server 2010 to send you an e-mail alert immediately when a resource submits a Status Report to you. Again, because this option can lead to a flurry of e-mail messages, you may wish to deselect it.

The *Status Report Reminders* section allows you to set up subscriptions for e-mail reminders for those resources assigned in Status Report requests you create. Again, you may choose to have the reminders sent to you only, to the resources only, or to both you and your resources.

> If one of your team members or resources deselects a Reminder option on the *Manage My Alerts and Reminders* page, and you select the same reminder option for your team members or resources on the *Manage My Resource's Alerts and Reminders* page, your selection overrides the user's selection and sets the reminder.

In the *Language Setting* section, specify your language preference and then click the *Save* button to save your settings.

Hands On Exercise

Exercise 11-1

Set Alerts and Reminders for yourself, and for your team members and resources.

1. Launch your Internet Explorer and navigate to your organization's Project Web App Home page.

2. Click the *Personal Settings* link in the *Quick Launch* menu.

531

3. Click the *Manage My Alerts and Reminders* link on the *Personal Settings* page.

4. Set your options and then save your changes.

5. Click the *Manage My Resource's Alerts and Reminders* link on the *Personal Settings* page.

6. Set your options and then save your changes.

Managing My Queued Jobs

Every time you stand in line at a fast food restaurant, you are waiting in a "queue." In Project Server 2010, the Queue is a waiting line that is necessary whenever the number of service requests to the system is greater than the system's optimum serving capacity. When you save and submit a timesheet or a task update, the system places your job in the Queue for processing.

Project Server 2010 allows you to view the jobs in the Queue by clicking the *My Queued Jobs* link on the *Personal Settings* page. The system displays the *My Queued Jobs* page shown in Figure 11 - 4.

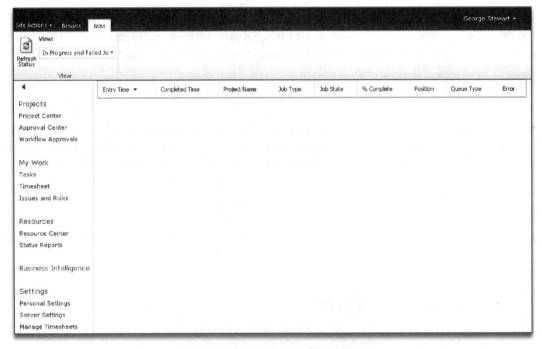

Figure 11 - 4: My Queued Jobs page

The *My Queued Jobs* page should normally appear blank, as shown previously in Figure 11-5. A blank page means, "no news is good news." This indicates that the Project Server 2010 system is running without errors. If you see a Queue job on the *My Queued Jobs* page, you can watch the job's progress in the system by clicking the *Refresh Status* button occasionally.

In addition to being able to view jobs currently processing in the Queue, Project Server 2010 also allows you to view the history of processed jobs. Click the *View* pick list in the *View* ribbon and select one of the following views:

- In Progress and Failed Jobs in the Past Week (the default view)

- All In Progress and Failed Jobs

- Successful Jobs in the Past Week

- All Successful Jobs

- All Jobs in the Past Week

- All Jobs

For example, Figure 11 - 5 shows the *My Queued Jobs* page with the *Successful jobs in the Past Week* view selected. Notice that the page shows a number of different job types.

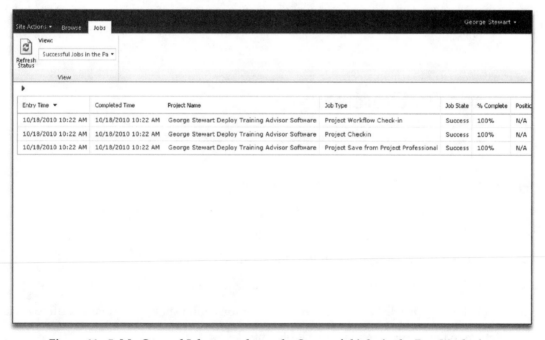

Figure 11 - 5: My Queued Jobs page shows the Successful jobs in the Past Week view

If you notice a job that the system simply does not process, or a job that failed, you should contact your Project Server administrator immediately for assistance. To help the Project Server administrator, you should click the *Click to view the error details* link in the *Error* column. The system displays the *Queue Job Error Details* dialog as shown in Figure 11 - 6.

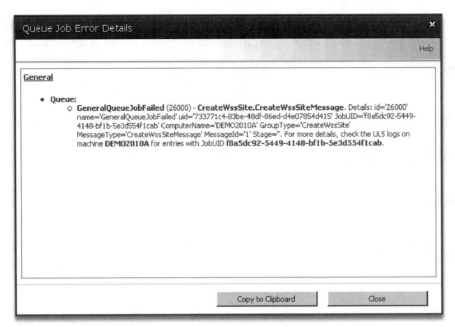

Figure 11 - 6: Queue Job Error Details dialog

The *Queue Job Error Details* dialog contains information valuable to help your Project Server administrator to diagnose and solve the Queue errors. To share the error information with your Project Server administrator, click the *Copy to Clipboard* button and paste the error contents into an email message.

Hands On Exercise

Exercise 11-2

Explore the *My Queued Jobs* page.

1. Click the *Personal Settings* link in the Quick Launch menu.

2. Click the *My Queued Jobs* link on the *Personal Settings* page.

3. Click the *View* pick list and study the Queue information shown for several different views.

4. Return to the *Home* page in Project Web App.

Manage Delegates

Project Server 2010 allows you to designate delegates who can act on your behalf in the system, such as when you know you will be away when timesheets are due. Using delegation in Project Server allows you to appoint a coworker to submit your timesheet for you. Click on the *Manage Delegates* link on the *Personal Settings* page and the system opens the *Manage Delegates* page shown in Figure 11 - 7.

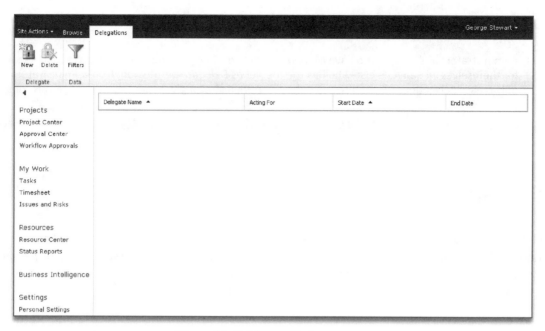

Figure 11 - 7: Manage Delegates page

To create a new delegation, click the *New* button in the *Delegate* section of the *Delegations* ribbon. The system displays the *Add Delegation* page shown in Figure 11 - 8.

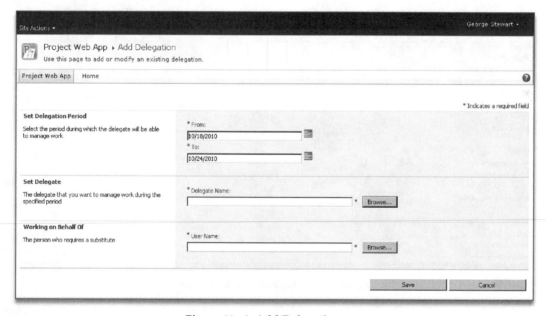

Figure 11 - 8: Add Delegation page

To add a new delegation, begin by setting a date range during which the delegation is effective using the *From* and *To* fields. Next, select the person who you would like to act as your delegate by clicking the *Browse* button and selecting the username from the list. Finally, use the *Browse* button in the *Working on Behalf of* section to select yourself from the list. Click the *Save* button when you complete your entries.

Administrators and others who have *Manage Resources' Delegates* permission can create delegations for themselves and anyone else who has the the *Act as Delegate* permission. Non-administrators may only create delegations for themselves unless an Administrator gives them additional permissions.

Act as Delegate

When another user selects you as a delegate by creating a delegation, you can act on behalf of that person to perform most functions within Project Web App. To act as a delegate, select the *Act as a Delegate* link from the *Personal Settings* page. The system displays the *Act as a Delegate* page shown in Figure 11 - 9.

Figure 11 - 9: Act as a Delegate page

If another user or an administrator created a delegation for you to act on behalf of another user, the *Act as a Delegate* page displays those delegations. Notice in Figure 11 - 9 that George Stewart has a delegation for Gary Chefetz effective October 18 through October 24, 2010. To start a delegate session, select the delegation you want to use by highlighting the row, and then click the *Start Delegate Session* button from the *Delegate* section of the *Delegations* ribbon. The page changes to indicate that the delegation session is active as shown in Figure 11 - 10.

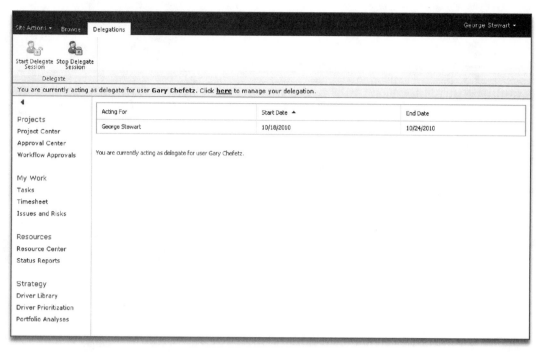

Figure 11 - 10: Act as Delegate page with delegation session in progress

Notice in Figure 11 - 10 that the screen changes by displaying a band across the page just beneath the ribbon indicating that the delegation session is active. This warning band remains across every page in Project Web App while you are acting as a delegate to remind you that you are now looking at Project Web App through someone else's eyes. After you complete your work on behalf of the other user, you end your delegate session by returning to the *Act as Delegate* page by clicking on the *Click here* link in the information band, or by navigating to the page from the *Personal Settings* page. Click the *Stop Delegate Session* button from the *Delegate* section of the *Delegations* ribbon. The system exits the delegate session and the page displays *You are not currently acting as anyone's delegate* in the message section.

Warning: Delegaton does not appy to all features. For instance, features supported by SharePoint only, such as Project Sites and the BI Center are not included in delegation. Delegation does not apply to Project Professional or editing project schedules with Project Professional.

Module 12

Collaborating with Project Sites

Learning Objectives

After completing this module, you will be able to:

- Understand the features available in a Project Site
- Track and manage project Risks
- Track and manage project Issues
- Share and manage project Documents
- Track and manage Action Items
- Track and manage Calendar events

Inside Module 12

540

Understanding Project Sites

When you publish a new enterprise project, Project Server 2010 automatically provisions a new Project Site in Windows SharePoint Services if your system options are set to automatic workspace creation. Project team members and other project stakeholders can collaborate using Project Site tools to do the following depending upon their permissions:

- Manage risks, issues, documents, and deliverables associated with the project.

- View a calendar of events and announcements related to the project.

- Create and/or work on tasks associated with the project but not included in the actual enterprise project plan.

- Participate in a discussion related to the project.

- Restore a deleted object from the Recycle Bin.

Once you open a Project Site, you are working mostly with the native capabilities of Windows SharePoint Services 3.0. The *Project Document* library contains customizations that handle linking documents to Project objects. The *Issues* and *Risks* lists feature custom web parts embedded in standard SharePoint lists to provide connectivity to Project Server. The *Deliverables* list also contains custom capabilities specific for use with Project Server. All of the other features that you encounter in your Project Sites are available to any SharePoint site. The skills you learn in this section apply to general SharePoint usage, not just Project Server. To access a *Project Site* for any project, from the Project Center, select the row header for the project and from the *Navigate* section of the *Projects* ribbon click the *Project Site* button. The system displays the homepage for your project site shown in Figure 12 - 1.

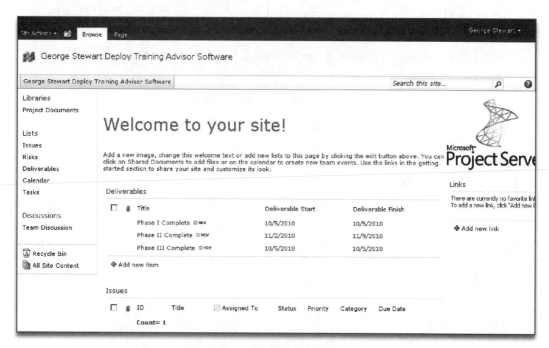

Figure 12 - 1: Project Site homepage

Notice in Figure 12 - 1 that the Project Site contains the following features:

- The *Quick Launch* menu on the left side of the page offers links that allow you to work with documents, issues, risks, deliverables, calendar events, tasks, and team discussions.

- The main content area in the middle of the page displays announcements and calendar events.

- The sidepane on the right side of the page displays links to additional information.

> To learn more about Deliverables, refer to Module 07, "Project Execution."

Hands On Exercise

Exercise 12-1

Navigate to and explore your Project Site.

1. From the *Project Center* page, select the row header for your Deploy Training Advisor Software project and from the *Navigate* section of the *Projects* ribbon click the *Project Site* button. The system displays the homepage for your Project Site.

2. Notice that the deliverables that you defined in Module 07 display in the *Deliverables* list near the center of the page.

3. Visit the *Project Documents* library, the *Risks* list, and the *Issues* list.

4. Return to the Project Site homepage.

Tracking Project Risks

The Project Management Institute defines a risk as "an uncertain event or condition that, if it occurs, has a positive or negative effect on a project objective." Risks have both causes and consequences. If a risk occurs, the consequence can be either negative or positive. Your organization's risk management methodologies may dictate that you log and document anticipated risks to your project work.

Creating a New Risk

To create a new risk in the Project Site, click the *Risks* link on the *Quick Launch* menu. Project Server 2010 displays the *Risks* list page for the project shown in Figure 12 - 2.

Figure 12 - 2: Risks page for the Deploy Training Advisor Software project

Click the *Add new item* link in the page. The system displays the *New Item* dialog for risks partially shown in Figure 12 - 3.

Figure 12 - 3: New Item dialog for risks

The *New Item* page for risks contains fields into which you can enter relevant information about the risk. The system requires you to enter information into only four fields: *Title, Status, Probability,* and *Impact*. Notice that the *Status* field defaults to a pick list entry "Active." This field determines the status of the risk for display in your reminders on the homepage, the Project Server reminder email, and on the *Issues and Risks* page. Project Server 2010 requires probability and impact entries to determine the *Exposure* value for the risk, which it calculates by multiplying the two numbers.

Project Server 2010 displays the *Exposure* field on the *Risks* page. You can use the exposure value to rank risks in descending order by severity. For example, your organization might establish a risk management methodology that requires you to create a risk management plan for the top four risks ranked by exposure.

Warning: Do not change the values for the *Status* field or you break some of the integration with Project Server.

In the *Title* field, enter a brief description. In the *Owner* field, enter the name of the individual who owns the new risk. If you manually type the name of the individual, click the *Check Names* button to the right of the field to confirm a valid name. If you enter an incorrect name, the system displays warning text below the *Owner* field. If you want to pick the name of the owner from a list, then click the *Browse* button to the right of the *Owner* field. Project Server 2010 displays the *Select People and Groups* dialog shown in Figure 12 - 4. Enter a full or partial name in the *Find* field and then click the *Search* button at the right end of the *Find* field. Select a name from the list and click the *OK* button.

Figure 12 - 4: Select People and Groups Webpage dialog

In the *Assigned To* field, enter the name of the person responsible for managing the risk. This is the person assigned to monitor risk conditions and enact a backup plan if the risk occurs. You may use the *Check Names* button and the *Browse* button to the right of the field, to assist your data input.

Click the *Status* pick list and select the status. This defaults to *Active* for new risks. The options include *Active, Postponed*, and *Closed*. The *Category* field is a field your organization should edit to display risk management information specific to your organization or your particular project. The default values in this field do not contain relevant identifiers, so unless you or your Project Server administrator modifies these values, you may ignore this field.

 I teach you how to customize Project Sites in Module 13, *Managing Project Sites*.

In the *Due Date* field, enter either the date on which you anticipate the risk may occur, or the date on which the *Assigned To* person must complete the risk management plan. Because this field is optional, your organization may use it any way you deem appropriate. You may also select a date and time for the *Due Date* field using the *Calendar* button and the *Time* pick lists to the right of the field.

In the *Probability* field, enter a percentage value between 0 and 100, representing the likelihood that the risk may actually occur. In the *Impact* field, enter a number between 1 and 10 to describe the magnitude of the consequences in the project should the risk occur. Remember that Project Server 2010 multiplies these two numbers to determine the *Exposure* value for the risk. In the *Cost* field, enter any additional cost incurred to the project if the risk occurs.

 Entering a value of 0% in the *Probability* field makes no sense. If there is no chance of risk there is no risk. Entering a value of 100% makes no sense either. If the risk is absolutely certain, it is not a risk, it is an issue.

Click into the *Description* field to activate the text editing buttons at the top of the field. Enter additional information about the risk, such as causes of the risk and consequences to the project, should the risk occur. Format the text using the formatting buttons at the top of the field.

Click into the *Mitigation Plan* field and enter your plan for reducing the likelihood of the risk occurring, or to reduce the impact of the risk should it occur. Click in the *Contingency Plan* field and enter your backup plan for action should the risk actualize.

Click into the *Trigger Description* field and enter the description of what triggers the risk and determines whether it is about to occur, is currently occurring, or has already occurred. If you want to enter additional trigger information, click the *Trigger* pick list button and select an item from the list. Alternately, you may also select the *Specify your own value* option and enter text in the accompanying field.

If you want to link the new risk to one or more project objects, scroll to the top of the page. To link the new risk to an existing file, click the *Custom Commands* tab to expose the *Custom Commands* ribbon. Click the *Link Items* button on the ribbon. The system displays the *Link Items* dialog shown in Figure 12 - 5.

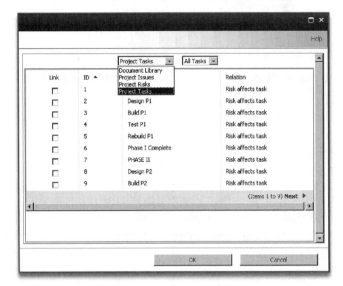

Figure 12 - 5: Link Items dialog

Notice in the figure that I expanded the *Object Type* pick list to display the various objects for which you can create links. These links drive the display of icons next to task rows in Project drilldown views and in the Project Center. Notice the *View* pick list next to the *Object Type* pick list. You use this context-sensitive pick list to limit the number of items displayed in the view. The list varies by object type and does not display when you select *Document Library* from the list.

To link the new risk to tasks, other risks or issues, or to documents in the document library associated with the project, select the check boxes for the linked items in the *Link* column, which behaves like a yes/no toggle, as shown previously in Figure 12 - 5.

In the RTM release of Project Server 2010, the *Link Item* dialog lacks control labels as well as a dialog label. The *Link Items* button in the *New Item* dialog is a leftover placeholder as well. This might be changed in later builds.

Figure 12 - 6 shows the completed *New Item* dialog for a risk scrolled to the bottom of the page. Notice at the bottom of the page that I linked the new risk to the Design P1 task in the project. Click the *Save* button to save the new risk.

Warning: You can also configure SharePoint to use web pages instead of popup dialog forms like the *New Item* dialog shown in this section. You learn how to configure these settings in Module 13. If your administrator changed this setting, your experience with the screens in this module will vary.

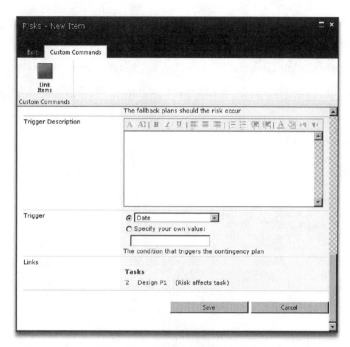

Figure 12 - 6: New Item dialog showing link information

Hands On Exercise

Exercise 12-2

Create a new risk and link it to a task.

1. From your Deploy Training Advisor Software Project Site homepage select the *Risks* link from the *Quick Launch* menu. The system displays the *Risks* homepage.

2. Click the *Add new item* link to launch the *New Item* dialog for risks. In the *New Item* dialog enter a name for your risk in the *Title* field. Enter or select your own user account in both the *Owner* and *Assigned To* pick lists by clicking on the *Browse* icon to the right of the field. In the *Select People and Groups Web Page* dialog, type a name into the *Find* field, click on the *Search* icon, select the name you typed in the field, and click the *OK* button.

3. Leave the default *Active* selection for the *Status* field and the default selection for the *Category* field. Set a value in the *Due Date* field for 10 days from today.

4. Enter 50% in the *Probability* field and enter 5 in the *Impact* field.

5. Enter a cost, description, optional mitigation plan, contingency plan, and trigger information in their respective fields.

6. Select the *Custom Commands* tab to display the *Custom Commands* ribbon and click the *Link Items* button. The system displays the *Link Items* dialog.

7. Select the check box for the Design P1 task. Select the *Risk affects task* item in the *Relation* pick list and click the *OK* button to link the risk to the task.

8. In the *New* Item dialog click the *Save* button to create your new risk.

9. Repeat this process at least two more times to define several risks for your project.

Working with Existing Risks

While working with existing risks, the system allows you to do the following:

- Apply a view to the *Risks* page.

- Sort the risks by the data in any column.

- View a risk.

- Edit a risk.

- Delete a risk.

- Subscribe to e-mail alerts about changes to a risk.

I cover each of these topics individually. Figure 12 - 7 shows the *Risks* page for the Deploy Training Advisor Software project. Notice the three active risks associated with the project.

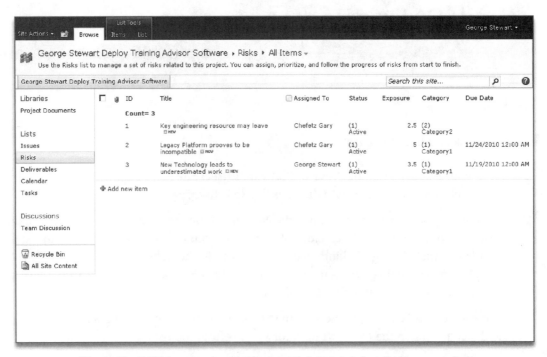

Figure 12 - 7: Risks page for the Deploy Training Advisor Software project

Working with Risk List Views

To apply a view to the *Risks* page, select the *List* tab, and from the *Manage Views* section, click the *Current View* pick list button and then select an available view as shown in the expanded pick list in Figure 12 - 8.

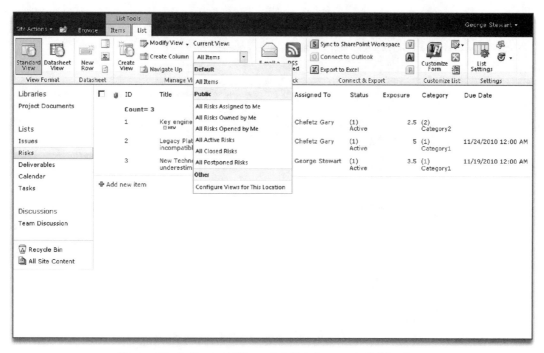

Figure 12 - 8: Current View pick list shows available views

The *Current View* pick list for the *Risks* page offers seven pre-defined *Public* views, including the following:

- All Items (the default View)

- All Active Risks

- All Closed Risks

- All Postponed Risks

- All Risks Assigned to Me

- All Risks Opened by Me

- All Risks Owned by Me

Project Server 2010 also allows you to modify views and to create new views. I discuss these two features in Module 13. After you apply a view from the *Current View* pick list, the system filters the list of risks as suggested in the view name. For example, Figure 12 - 9 shows the *Risks* page after applying the *Risks Owned by Me* view.

You use the *Configure Views for This Location* selection in the *Other* section when you use the *Locations* feature in SharePoint. For more information on this topic, see Microsoft's TechNet site.

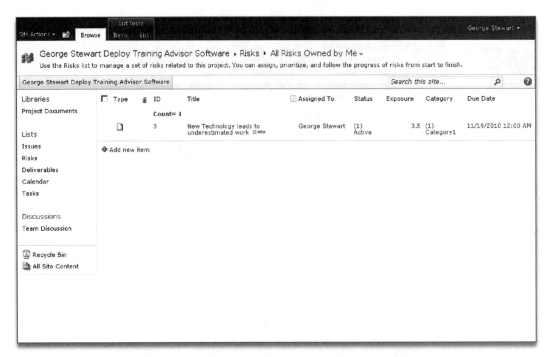

Figure 12 - 9: Risks Owned by Me view applied to the Risks page

Notice in Figure 12 - 9 that I am the owner for only one of the three risks for this project. To view all risks, reapply the *All Items* view. To sort the risks, click the name of the column header on which to sort the data. The system applies default sorting on the ID number column, sorted in the order users created the risks. For example, Figure 12 - 10 shows that you can change the sort order by floating your mouse pointer over the column header to reveal the pick list control, then select either the *Ascending* or *Descending* item from the pick list.

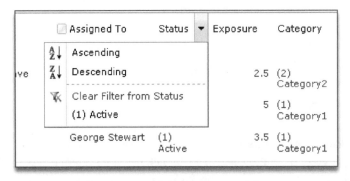

Figure 12 - 10: Selecting a sort order

Notice the downward-pointing arrow indicator to the right of the *Exposure* column name, indicating sorting in descending order in Figure 12 - 11. You can also see the list of *AutoFilter* options. Notice that the pick list for the *Exposure* column contains every value in the column, plus the options to sort in *Ascending* (Smallest on Top) or *Descending* (Largest on Top) order. Select an item from the pick list to AutoFilter the risks based on data contained in that column.

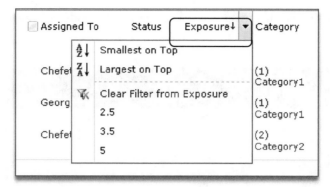

Figure 12 - 11: Sort order for the Exposure column

When you apply AutoFiltering to a column, Project Server 2010 indicates the AutoFiltered column by displaying a funnel indicator to the right of the column name. To remove AutoFiltering from a column, click the pick list button and select the *Clear Filter from* _____ item on the list

Viewing and Editing Existing Risks

To work with an existing risk, such as to view or edit it, float your mouse pointer over the name of the risk. Project Server 2010 displays a pick list button to the right of the risk name. Click the pick list button and the system displays the menu shown in Figure 12 - 12.

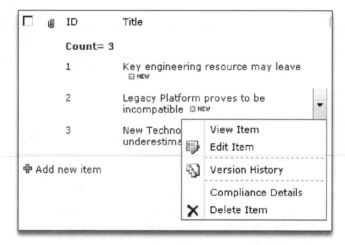

Figure 12 - 12: Pick list button and pick list for an existing risk

Notice that the menu allows you to select from *View Item*, *Edit Item*, or *Delete Item*, and view the *Version History* and *Compliance Details* for the list items. These concepts apply when using both the *Risks* list and the *Issues* list, and any other SharePoint list you work with. The *Version History* item applies only when you have this feature enabled in the system. I show you how to enable version control in Module 13. The *Compliance Details* feature is something you use when your system employs advanced types of SharePoint document management features including, among others, records compliance, content retention policies and content validation. These features are beyond the scope of this book.

Click the *View Item* item from the pick list to open a risk in view-only mode, as shown in Figure 12 - 13.

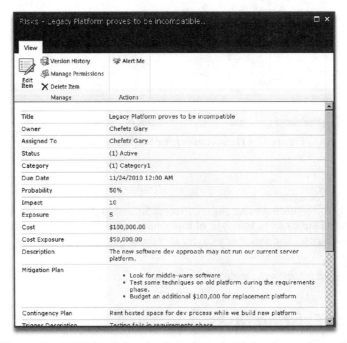

Figure 12 - 13: Risks dialog for the selected risk in view-only mode

You can also display a risk in view-only mode by clicking the name of the risk in the *Title* field.

To subscribe to e-mail alerts about changes to a risk or other list type item, from the *Actions* section of the *View* ribbon, click the *Alert Me* button. If you choose to receive e-mail messages about the risk, the system displays the *New Alert* dialog shown in Figure 12 - 14.

On the *New Alert* page, specify your options in each section of the page and then click the *OK* button. Notice that the <u>*New Alert*</u> page allows you to determine what type of change triggers the system to send an e-mail message to you, and that you can determine this change when the system sends the message.

Warning: Your SharePoint Server must be configured for email to use the *Alerts* feature in SharePoint.

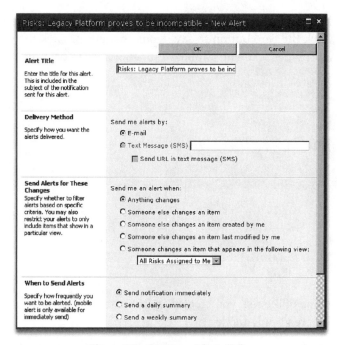

Figure 12 - 14: New Alert dialog

To edit the selected risk, from the *Manage* section of the *View* ribbon, click the *Edit Item* button or select the *Edit Item* option from the pick list menu shown previously in Figure 12 - 12. The system opens the risk for editing in the *Risk* dialog as shown in Figure 12 - 15.

Figure 12 - 15: Risks dialog for the selected risk in editing mode

Notice that the system hides the *View* ribbon and displays the *Edit* ribbon. Edit the data in any of the fields, or use item linking to update your risk. Click the *Save* button to save your changes or click the *Cancel* button to discard your changes. Notice that the menu provides you with clipboard functionality to support the rich editing tools in the text field areas.

Hands On Exercise

Exercise 12-3

Edit and work with an existing risk.

1. Click on the name of the risk you created in Exercise 12-2 on the *Risk* list homepage. The system opens the risk in read-only mode.

2. In the *Actions* section of the *View* ribbon, click the *Alert Me* button. The system opens the *New Alert* dialog.

3. In the *New Alert* dialog, explore the various options for configuring an alert. When finished, click the *Cancel* button unless your instructor guides you differently. The system closes the *New Alert* dialog and returns to the *Risks* homepage.

4. Again, click on the name of the risk you created in Exercise 12-2 on the *Risk* list homepage. The system opens the risk in read-only mode.

5. From the *Manage* section of the *View* ribbon, click the *Edit Item* button. The system opens the risk in edit mode.

6. Change the value of any field and in the *Commit* section of the *Edit* ribbon, click the *Save* button. The system saves and closes the risk.

Deleting a Risk

To delete a risk, from the *Actions* section of the *Edit* ribbon, you can click the *Delete Item* button or you may select the *Delete Item* option from the pick list menu shown previously in Figure 12 - 12. If you choose to delete a risk, Project Server 2010 displays the confirmation dialog shown in Figure 12 - 16. Click the *OK* button to delete the risk and send it to the Recycle Bin for the Project Site.

Figure 12 - 16: Confirmation dialog to delete a Risk

Restoring a Deleted Risk from the Recycle Bin

When you delete a risk, Project Server 2010 transfers the record to the Recycle Bin for the Project Site. If you accidentally delete a risk, Project Server 2010 allows you to restore it easily. Click the *Recycle Bin* link in the *Quick Launch* menu to begin the restoration process. The system displays the *Recycle Bin* page shown in Figure 12 - 17.

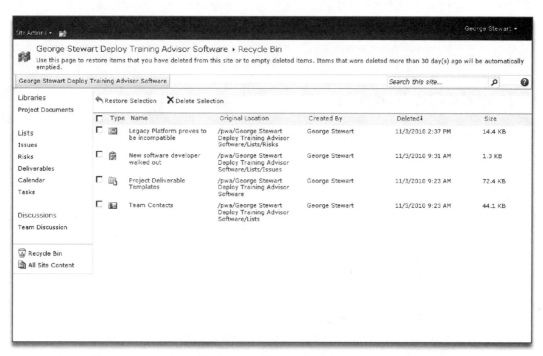

Figure 12 - 17: Recycle Bin page shows deleted items of various types

On the *Recycle Bin* page, select the option checkbox to the left of the item you want to restore, such as the deleted risk, and then click the *Restore Selection* link above the content area. Project Server 2010 displays the confirmation dialog shown in Figure 12 - 18.

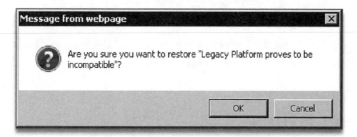

Figure 12 - 18: Restore item confirmation

Click the *OK* button and the system restores the deleted risk item from the Recycle Bin to the *Risks* list. You can delete and restore items in SharePoint lists and libraries using the same techniques. You can permanently delete an item by selecting it on the *Recycle Bin* page and then clicking the *Delete Selection* link next to the *Restore Selection* link.

SharePoint systems also have an administrative Recycle Bin that captures all deletions in the system. Therefore, it may be possible for your system administrator to restore items that you permanently delete from the user Recycle Bin depending upon the retention policies enforced by your organization.

Hands On Exercise

Exercise 12-4

Delete and restore a risk list item.

1. On the *Risks* list homepage, hover your mouse pointer over the name of one of your risks in the *Title* field to reveal the pick list button and click to expose the pick list.

2. Select the *Delete Item* selection and the system displays a confirmation to delete the item. Click the *OK* button in the confirmation warning to delete the item.

3. Click on the *Recycle Bin* link at the bottom of the *Quick Launch* menu. The system displays the *Recycle Bin* page.

4. Select the checkbox next to the item that you just deleted and then click the *Restore Selection* link above the content area. The system displays a restore item confirmation. Click the *OK* button in the confirmation dialog to complete the restore action.

5. Click the *Risks* link from the *Quick Launch* menu and the system displays the *Risks* list page. Confirm that your restored item appears on the page.

Managing Project Issues

An issue is any type of problem or concern you might experience and need to manage during the life of the project. Another way to think of an issue is to consider it a realized risk. Whether or not you predicted their occurrence through proactive risk management, issues are events that cause problems that require management. The issues management features in Project Server allow you to identify, track, and manage issues in collaboration with your project team and stakeholders. Examples of project issues include a shortage of resources or an unanticipated hardware upgrade requirement.

Creating a New Issue

The process for creating a new issue is nearly identical to creating a new risk, although the fields in the custom web parts for these are different. Click the *Issues* link in the *Quick Launch* menu of your Project Site and Project Server 2010 displays the *Issues* page, as shown in Figure 12 - 19.

Figure 12 - 19: Issues page for the Deploy Training Advisor Software project

Click the *Add New Item* link on the page. The system displays the *New Item* dialog for issues shown in Figure 12 - 20.

Figure 12 - 20: New Item dialog for Issues

The *New Item* dialog for issues contains only two required fields, the *Title* field and *Status* field. Enter a descriptive name for the issue in the *Title* field. The same caution about the *Status* field for risks applies to the *Status* field for issues. You must not alter the values in this field or you break the display of issue status in Project Web App. Use the same process described in the Creating a New Risk topical section of this module to enter data in the *Owner*, *Assigned To*, *Status*, and *Category* fields.

Click the *Priority* pick list and select an item from the list. Notice that the system allows you to set the priority of an issue as High, Medium, or Low. Enter a date in the *Due Date* field. In the *Discussion* field, enter preliminary discussion details to describe the issue, including potential resolutions for the issue. Do not enter any information in the *Resolution* field, unless you already have an idea about ways to resolve the issue. You use the same process described in the Creating a New Risk topical section to link your new issue to a file or to other issues, tasks, risks, and documents. Click the *Save* button to save and complete your new issue.

Hands On Exercise

Exercise 12-5

Create a new issue and link it to a risk.

1. From your Deploy Training Advisor Software Project Site homepage select the *Issues* link from the *Quick Launch* menu. The system displays the *Issues* homepage.

2. Click the *Add new item* link to launch the *New Item* dialog for issues. In the *New Item* dialog, enter a name for your issue in the *Title* field that closely relates to one of the risks you created earlier. Enter or select your own user account in both the *Owner* and *Assigned To* pick lists.

3. Leave the default *Active* selection for the *Status* field and the default *Category 2* selection for the *Category* field. Select a priority value in the *Priority* field. Set a value in the *Due Date* field for 10 days from today.

4. Enter an opening discussion in the *Discussion* field and assume that there is nothing to enter into the *Resolution* field at this time.

5. Select the *Custom Commands* tab to expose the *Custom Commands* ribbon and click the *Link Items* button. The system displays the *Link Items* dialog.

6. Select the *Project Risks* item from the *Item Type* pick list then select the risk that closely relates to your issue to create a "risk realized" issue. Click the *OK* button to link your new issue to your previously created risk.

7. In the *New Item* dialog click the *Save* button to create your new risk.

8. Repeat this process at least two more times to define several issues for your project linking them to other items rather than risks.

Viewing and Editing Existing Issues

Figure 12 - 21 shows the *Issues* page for my Deploy Training Advisor Software project. Notice that there are three active issues associated with the project. Notice also that I customized the values for the *Category* field. You learn how to customize this field in Module 13.

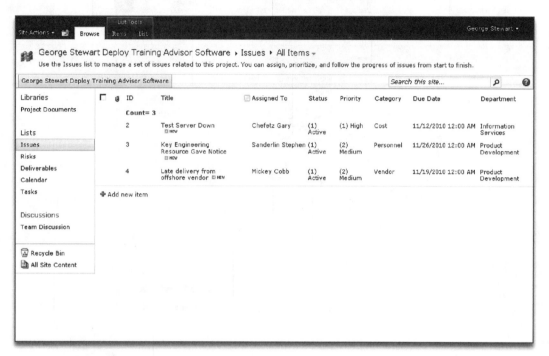

Figure 12 - 21: Issues page for the Deploy Training Advisor Software project

Similar to risks, the system allows you to do the following with existing issues:

- Apply a view to the *Issues* page.

- Sort the issues by the data in any column.

- AutoFilter the issues using the data in any column.

- View an issue.

- Edit an issue.

- Delete an issue.

- Subscribe to e-mail alerts about changes to an issue.

Because I described how to do each of these in the Working with Existing Risks topical section of this module, I do not repeat this information here except for editing an existing issue, because you need to know how to close an issue when it is resolved. I also cover viewing issue version history because I did not cover that in the risk topics.

To edit an existing issue, float your mouse pointer over the issue in the *Title* field, click the pick list button, and select the *Edit Item* option on the pick list. Project Server 2010 displays the *Issues* dialog for the selected issue, as shown in Figure 12 - 22.

Figure 12 - 22: Issues dialog for a selected Issue

To close the issue, click the *Status* pick list button and then select the *Closed* item from the list. In the *Resolution* field, enter text to describe how you resolved the issue. Click the *Save* button when finished.

Hands On Exercise

Exercise 12-6

Edit and close an issue.

1. Float your mouse pointer over one of the new issues you created in Exercise 12-5, and then click the pick list button.

2. Select the *Edit Item* item on the pick list menu. The system opens the *Issues* dialog.

3. Click the *Status* pick list button and select the *Closed* item from the list.

4. Enter text in the *Resolution* field to describe how you resolved the issue.

5. Click the *Save* button to save the closed issue.

6. Close the Internet Explorer application window for the *Project Site* page and return to the *Home* page in Project Web App.

Working with Version History

If your issues list, or any SharePoint list you may work with, has version control enabled, the system automatically creates a new version of list items each time someone edits them. To view the item history for a list item, you can select the *Version History* item by floating your mouse pointer over the *Title* field / column? for your issue, and selecting it from the pick list. The system displays the *Version History* dialog shown in Figure 12 - 23.

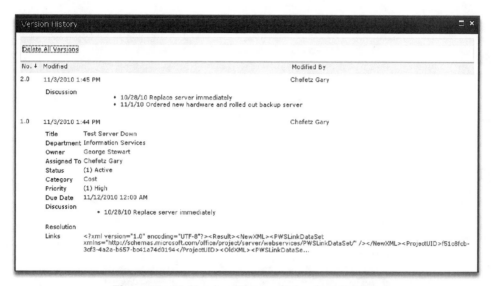

Figure 12 - 23: Version History dialog for a list item

Notice that the system creates a version record when you first create the item and then creates a version record every time someone edits the item, which displays the details for the version. To close the *Version History* dialog, click the *Close* **X** button.

Viewing Your Assigned Issues and Risks

Project Server 2010 offers you a quick way to view and manage the risks and issues assigned to you. Navigate to any page in Project Web App that displays the *Quick Launch* menu, and then click the *Issues and Risks* link in the *My Work* section. The system displays the *Issues and Risks* page, shown in Figure 12 - 24. The page displays issues and risks for George Stewart to whom the software assigned one active issue and one active risk, each of which belongs to its own project.

Warning: This page confuses many users. Notice the large gap between the two data table sections and the lack of header labels for data grid. Many users need to scroll to see the *Risks* section at the bottom of the page and leave the page before discovering this. You must remember that the software presents this page with issues in the top section and risks listed at the bottom. Your Project Server administrator can customize this page to make it more user-friendly.

Figure 12 - 24: Issues and Risks page for George Stewart

To access either the *Risks* page or the *Issues* page for one of the listed projects, click the project name in the *Issues* or *Risks* section of the page. Project Server 2010 displays the *Risks* or *Issues* page for the selected project applying the *All Risks Assigned to Me* view. Figure 12 - 25 shows George Stewart's *Risks* page for the Deploy Training Advisor Software project.

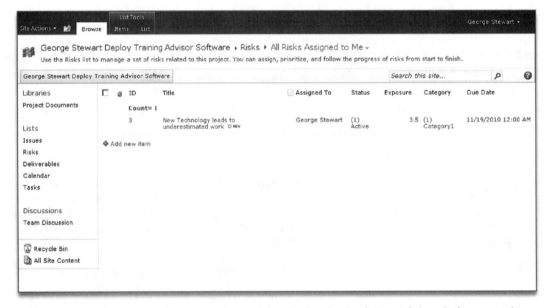

Figure 12 - 25: Risks page for George Stewart for the Deploy Training Advisor Software project

Notice that the page defaults to the *All Risks Assigned to Me* view. You can change the view by clicking on the pick list button next to the view name in the *Browse* area. You can apply any public view to this page by switching to the *List* ribbon and using the *View* selection tools from the ribbon.

Hands On Exercise

Exercise 12-7

View risks and issues assigned to you.

1. From any page that displays the *Quick Launch* menu in Project Web App, click the *Issues and Risks* link in the *My Work* section.

2. On the *Issues and Risks* page, notice the names of any projects containing issues or risks assigned to you.

3. Click the name of a project containing an issue or risk assigned to you.

4. Examine the *Issues* page or the *Risks* page for any items assigned to you.

5. Click the *Navigate Up* icon 📁 and use the bread crumb menu to return to the Project Web App homepage.

Managing Project Documents

During the typical project life cycle, you and your team create multiple documents associated with the project. During project definition, you might create a project charter and a statement of work document. During the execution stage of the project, you might create change control documents and expense reports. At project closure, you might create a lessons learned document to capture the knowledge gained during the project. Regardless of which type of project documents you create, each document is a part of your project's "electronic paper trail" and you can manage these documents within Project Server 2010 Project Sites.

Viewing and Creating Document Libraries

You learned in your introduction to Project Sites that each site contains a project document library for storing individual documents. Each Project Web App instance also has a general document library provided for the shared use of all Project Web App users, not just for members of specific projects. You can open the *Shared Documents* library by clicking the *Shared Documents* link from the *Libraries* section at the bottom of the standard *Quick Launch* menu. When you select the *Libraries* link, the system displays the *All Site Content* page listing all available document libraries in the PWA site as shown in Figure 12 - 26. Every PWA instance contains a single *Shared Documents* library for general use and a number of others that support other functionality in the system.

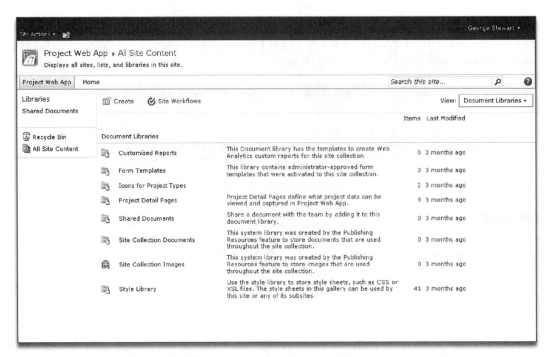

Figure 12 - 26: All Site Content page showing all PWA site Document libraries

When you click the same link from the homepage of your Project Site, the system displays the same page for your specific site as shown in Figure 12 - 27.

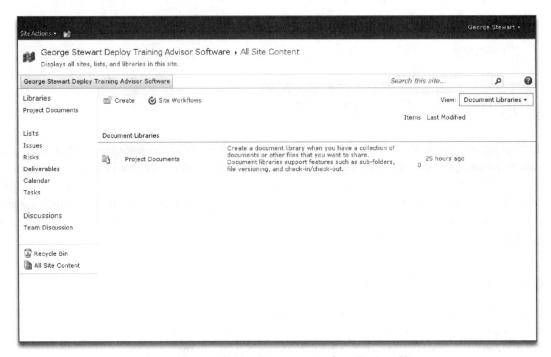

Figure 12 - 27: All Site Content page for a Project Site

Notice that the site contains a single *Project Documents* library. I teach you more about creating and managing document libraries in Module 13, *Managing Project Sites*.

> If you enable the versioning feature in a document library, the system creates a new version of a document every time a user edits and saves the document. If you need to reverse the changes made to a document, you can restore the previous version and then continue working with the document.

Uploading Documents to a Document Library

To begin the process of uploading an existing document to a document library, click the name of the library in the *Libraries* section of the *Quick Launch* menu. The system opens the *Project Document* library for the Deploy Training Advisor Software project as shown in Figure 12 - 28.

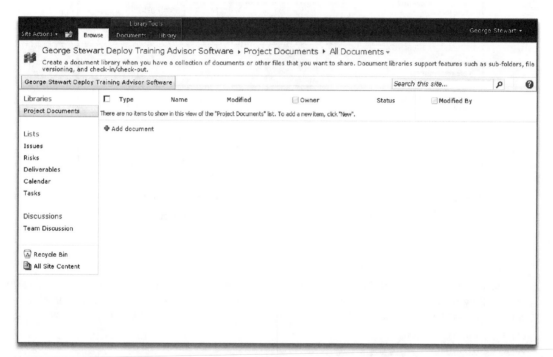

Figure 12 - 28: Project Documents library homepage

Project Server 2010 offers you three ways to upload documents to a document library:

- Upload one document at a time.

- Upload a batch of documents in a single operation.

- Use the Explorer view to copy documents from local folders and network shares.

To upload one document at a time, click the *Add document* link on the page, or click on the *Documents* tab to reveal the *Documents* ribbon, then click on the *Upload Document* pick list button and select the *Upload Document* item from the pick list. Project Server 2010 displays the *Upload Document* dialog for the selected document library, as shown in

Figure 12 - 29 with version control enabled, and in Figure 12 - 30 with version control disabled. Notice that the option in the *Upload Document* section below the *Name* field changes based on the version control setting.

 With Version Control: If your document library uses version control, leave the *Add as new version to existing files* option selected. Click the OK button.

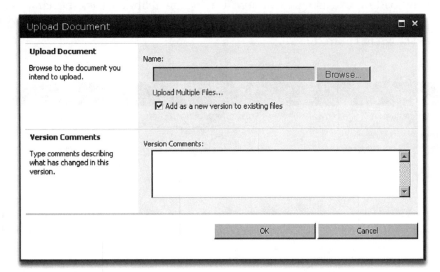

Figure 12 - 29: Upload Document dialog with version control

 Without Version Control: If the file currently exists in the document library, and you want to overwrite the existing file with the new file, then leave the default *Overwrite existing files* option selected. If you want to create a new version of the existing file, then deselect the *Overwrite existing files* option.

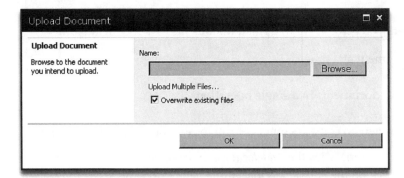

Figure 12 - 30: Upload Document dialog without version control

Click the *Browse* button. The system displays the *Choose File* dialog shown in Figure 12 - 31.

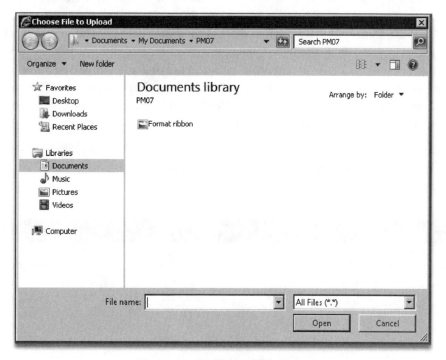

Figure 12 - 31: Choose File dialog

Navigate to the folder containing the file you want to upload, select the file, and then click the *Open* button. Project Server 2010 lists the path to the file in the *Name* field in the *Upload Document* dialog shown previously in Figure 12 - 29 and in Figure 12 - 30. The system may display a *Processing* message window as it uploads a copy of the selected document and then displays the *Edit Item* dialog shown in Figure 12 - 32.

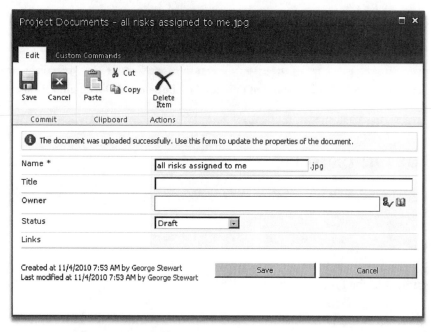

Figure 12 - 32: Edit Item dialog for the uploaded document

On the *Edit Item* page, the only required field is the *Name* field. You can rename the document by changing the text in the *Name* field. If you want to add a title for the document, enter a title in the *Title* field. Enter the name of the document owner in the *Owner* field, and use the *Check Names* and *Browse* buttons at the right end of the field, to locate names if necessary. Click the *Status* pick list button and select the status of the document. The default *Status* options include *Draft, Ready for Review,* and *Final.* From the *Commit* section of the *Edit* ribbon, click the *Save* button to complete the document upload process or click the *Cancel* button to cancel the upload. Notice that these buttons appear at the bottom of the dialog as well. Just like the *Edit Item* dialog for list items that you worked with earlier in this module, you can delete a document from this dialog, use clipboard tools, and select the *Custom Commands* ribbon to access the *Link Items* button and link the document to issues, risks, tasks and other documents.

Project Server 2010 displays the newly uploaded document in the document library, as shown in Figure 12 - 33. You can apply ribbons, views, sort, and AutoFilter the list of documents in the library the same way you can with risks, issues and other SharePoint lists.

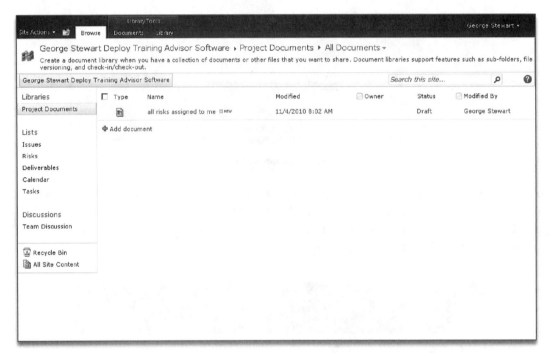

Figure 12 - 33: Existing document uploaded to the selected Document Library

 Hands On Exercise

Exercise 12-8

Upload a document to the Project Documents library.

1. Navigate to your Deploy Training Advisor Software Project Site homepage and click the *Project Documents* link in the *Quick Launch* menu.

2. Click on the *Documents* tab and in the *New* section click the *Upload Document* pick list button, then select the *Upload Document* item from the pick list. Alternately, click the *Add Document* link in the content area of the page. The system displays the *Upload Document* dialog.

3. Click the *Browse* button and the system displays the *Choose File to Upload* dialog. Select a Microsoft Word document from your PC's hard drive or from a network folder and click the *Open* button, then click the *OK* button. The system displays a processing message and then displays the *Edit Item* dialog.

4. In the *Edit Item* dialog, enter a unique title for the document in the *Title* field, enter your name in the *Owner* field, and specify a status for the document in the *Status* field. Click the *Save* button and the system returns to the library homepage.

5. Examine your new document in the *Project Documents* library.

You can upload multiple files as a batch from the *New* section of the *Document* ribbon by clicking the *Upload Document* pick list button and selecting the *Upload Multiple Documents* item from the pick list. If you have Office 2010 installed on your computer, Project Server 2010 displays the *Upload Multiple Documents* dialog shown in Figure 12 - 34. If you have Office 2007 installed, the system displays the *Upload Multiple Documents* dialog shown in Figure 12 - 35.

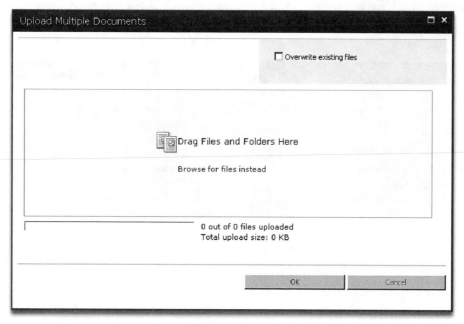

Figure 12 - 34: Upload Multiple Documents dialog with Office 2010

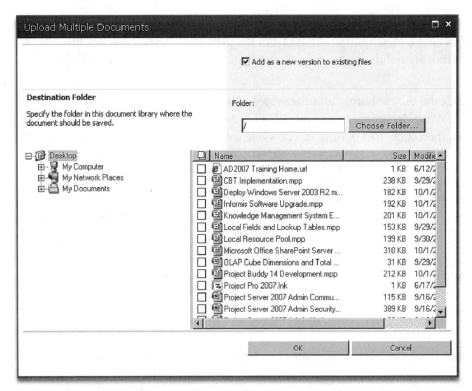

Figure 12 - 35: Upload Multiple Documents dialog with Office 2010

The dialog you see when using Office 2010 provides two methods for selecting files: **Drag and Drop** which allows you to drag files from an Explorer window or other location that supports file dragging or **File Select** which allows you to use a standard *Open* dialog to choose your files. I do not demonstrate the latter technique here. Figure 12 - 36 shows the *Upload Multiple Documents* dialog after dragging documents to the *Drag Files and Folders Here* area. Notice that you can remove files by clicking the *Remove* link in the *Status* column.

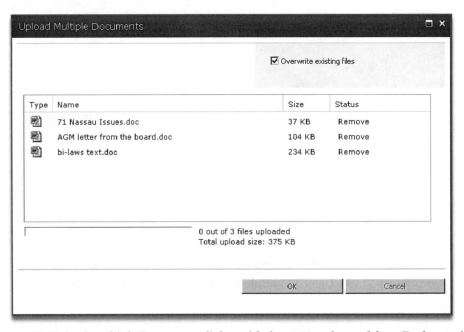

Figure 12 - 36: Upload Multiple Documents dialog with documents dragged from Explorer window

On the *Upload Multiple Documents* page, click the *OK* button when you complete your file selections. The system displays progress information in the dialog and updates the status of each document as shown in Figure 12 - 37.

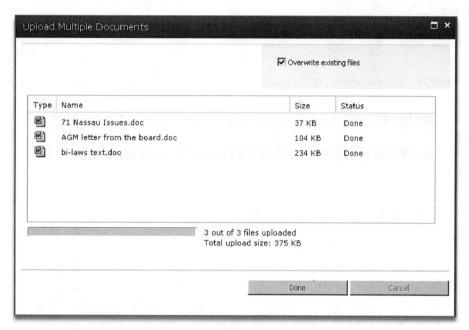

Figure 12 - 37: Upload Multiple Documents dialog with upload status updated

Click the *Done* button to close the dialog and return to your Project Site library homepage. When the system uploads the batch of files, it does not select a name in the *Owner* field for each document, and it sets the *Status* field value to *Draft* for each document. You can see this for the four uploaded documents in Figure 12 - 38. When you upload multiple files, the system does not present an *Edit Item* dialog for each item as it does for single file uploads.

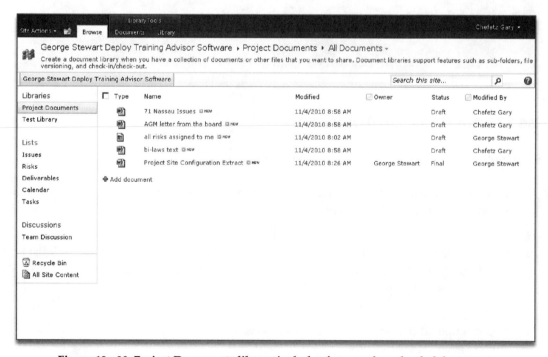

Figure 12 - 38: Project Documents library includes four newly-uploaded documents

To specify values in the *Owner* field and the *Status* field, you must edit the properties for each document.

The third method for copying documents to your documents library is to open your document library using Windows Explorer. You can do this only if you have the correct SharePoint permissions. Using the *Explorer* view allows you to treat the document library like any local file folder and drag, copy, and paste documents into it. To open the library in *Explorer* view, select the *Library* tab to expose the *Library* menu. In the *Connect &Export* section of the ribbon click the *Open with Explorer* button. The system launches the library in Windows Explorer. If you do not have permission to take this action, the system displays the warning shown in Figure 12 - 39.

Figure 12 - 39: Explorer View prohibited

Hands On Exercise

Exercise 12-9 for Office 2010 Users

Upload multiple documents to the Project Documents library.

1. Navigate to your Deploy Training Advisor Software Project Site homepage and click the *Project Documents* link in the *Quick Launch* menu.

2. Click on the *Documents* tab and in the *New* section click the *Upload Document* pick list button and select the *Upload Multiple Documents* item from the pick list. The system displays the *Upload Multiple Documents* dialog.

3. You can upload documents in one of two ways:

- Size your browser window so that you can drag files into the *Drag Files and Folders Here* area of the dialog from your desktop or Windows Explorer, and then click the *OK* button after dragging your selected files. After you click the *OK* button in the *Upload Multiple Documents* dialog, the system reports its progress in the dialog.

- Click the *Browse for files instead* link and the system displays the *Open* dialog. Select multiple documents from your PC's hard drive or from a network folder and click the *Open* button. Click the *OK* button in the *Upload Multiple Documents* dialog, the system reports its progress in the dialog.

4. When the system completes the upload, the *OK* button becomes a *Done* button. Click the *Done* button to close the dialog and return to the library.

5. Examine your new documents in the *Project Documents* library and verify the new additions.

Exercise 12-9 for Office 2007 Users

Upload multiple documents to the Project Documents library.

1. Navigate to your Deploy Training Advisor Software Project Site homepage and click the *Project Documents* link in the *Quick Launch* menu.

2. Click on the *Documents* tab and in the *New* section click the *Upload Document* pick list button and select the *Upload Multiple Documents* item from the pick list. The system displays the *Upload Multiple Documents* dialog.

3. Use the folder navigation tool to the left of the file selection pane to navigate to your source folder. After selecting a source folder, select multiple documents from that location by clicking the checkboxes next to the file names. Click the *OK* button and if the system prompts you with a confirmation dialog click the *Yes* button to continue. The system uploads your documents and then returns to the *Project Documents* library.

4. Examine your new documents in the *Project Documents* library and verify the new additions.

Creating a New Folder in a Documents Library

In addition to uploading existing documents to a document library, Project Server 2010 also allows you to organize your content by creating folders within the library.

> When you use folders to organize content in SharePoint libraries, you are not taking full advantage of the power of SharePoint. Always consider using content types and metadata with views and filters to organize content in SharePoint libraries and lists.

To create a new folder in your document library, display the *Documents* ribbon and in the *New* section click the *New Folder* button. The system displays the *New Folder* dialog shown in Figure 12 - 40.

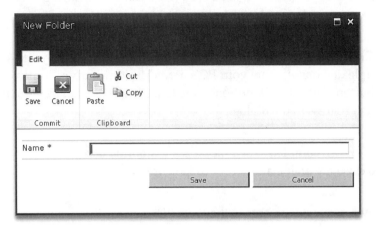

Figure 12 - 40: New Folder page

Enter the name of the new folder in the *Name* field and then from the *Commit* section of the *Edit* ribbon, or at the bottom of the dialog, click the *Save* button. Project Server 2010 displays the folder in your document library, as shown in Figure 12 - 41. Notice that I created a new folder called Archive.

Figure 12 - 41: Project Documents library with Archive folder

 When you add folders to SharePoint libraries, various SharePoint tools become aware of the folders. For instance, the *Upload Documents* dialog prompts for a *Destination Folder* value when it detects the presence of folders in the library.

Hands On Exercise

Exercise 12-10

Create a new folder in a document library.

1. In your *Project Documents* library, display the *Documents* ribbon and in the *New* section of the ribbon, click the *New Folder* button. The system displays the *New Folder* dialog.

2. Enter the name **Archive** for the new folder and click the *Save* button.

3. Notice your new folder in the *Project Documents* library.

Working with Existing Documents in a Documents Library

Depending on your permissions in the system, Project Server 2010 allows you to do the following to work with an existing document:

*   View the document properties.

*   Edit the document properties.

*   Edit the document in the Office application used to create it.

*   Check out the document.

*   View compliance details (configuration dependent)

*   Set alerts on the document

*   Send the document to another location or application.

*   Delete the document.

To perform any of the above actions with an existing document in a document library, float your mouse pointer over the name of the document and then click the pick list button, as shown in Figure 12 - 42.

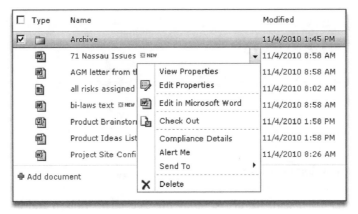

Figure 12 - 42: Options for working with an existing document

Viewing and Editing Document Properties

To view the properties for any document, float your mouse pointer over the name of the document, click the pick list button, and then click the *View Properties* item on the pick list. Project Server 2010 displays the *View Item* dialog for the selected document, as shown in Figure 12 - 43.

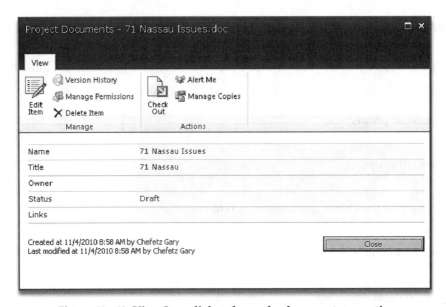

Figure 12 - 43: View Item dialog shows the document properties

Like the *View Item* dialog for list items, when you click to view only, you cannot edit any fields in the dialog until you click the *Edit Item* button in the ribbon. Notice that you can check out the item before you edit it.

 Whe a document library does not have version control enabled, it is up to the user to decide whether to check out the document prior to editing it. When you enable version control in a SharePoint library, the system enforces check out and check in rules for editing.

From the *Manage* section of the *View* menu in the *View Item* dialog, click the *Edit* button. Alternately, select the *Edit Properties* item from the pick list shown previously in Figure 12 - 42. The system displays the *Edit Item* dialog for documents shown in Figure 12 - 44.

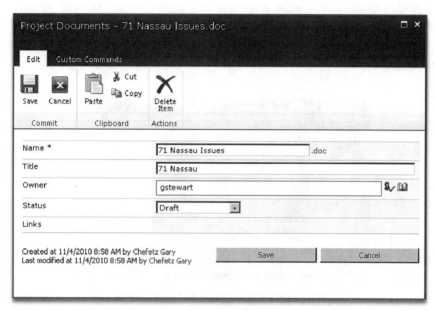

Figure 12 - 44: Edit Item dialog for a document

The editable properties for any document include *Name, Title, Owner, Status,* and *Links.* Just as you did with list items, you apply the *Custom Commands* ribbon to use the *Link* button. Notice that you can also delete a document from the dialog; however, there are more expedient ways to access this feature. Click the *Save* button to save your changes and close the dialog or click the *Cancel* button to close the dialog without saving.

Hands On Exercise

Exercise 12-11

View and edit properties for an existing document in the Project Documents library.

1. Float your mouse pointer over the name of a Microsoft Word document in the *Project Documents* library, click the pick list button, and select the *View Properties* item on the pick list.

2. Examine the properties for the selected document in the *View Item* dialog.

3. In the *Manage* section of the *View* ribbon, click the *Edit Item* button. The system opens the *Edit Item* dialog.

4. Enter your account in the *Owner* field and verify your entry.

5. Click the *Save* button at the bottom of the dialog to save your change

Checking Out a Document Manually

If you are using a Microsoft Office application earlier than the 2007 version, you cannot check out the document from within the Office application. Instead, you must manually check out the document from the document library. To check out a document, float your mouse pointer over the name of the document, click the pick list button, and then select the *Check Out* item on the pick list shown previously in Figure 12 - 42. Project Server 2010 displays the confirmation dialog shown in Figure 12 - 45.

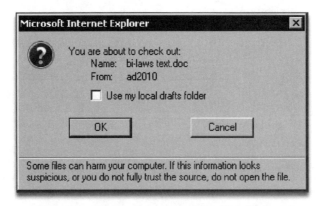

Figure 12 - 45: Confirmation dialog for check out

Click the *OK* button in the confirmation dialog to complete the check out. The system displays the checked-out status of the document by adding a green and white arrow logo to the lower right corner of the indicator for the selected document. Float your mouse pointer over the indicator to determine who currently has the document checked out, as shown in Figure 12 - 46. Alternately, you can modify the view to show the check-out information for each document.

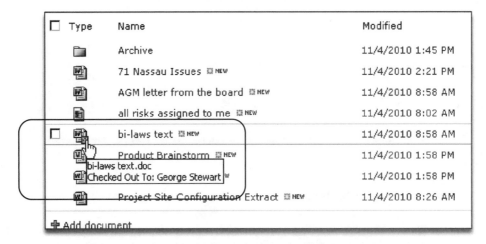

Figure 12 - 46: Selected document checked out to George Stewart

When you close the document after editing, you must manually check in the document by floating your mouse pointer over the name of the document, clicking the pick list button, and then selecting the *Check In* item on the pick list. After you check out a document, the selections on the item pick list change as shown in Figure 12 - 47.

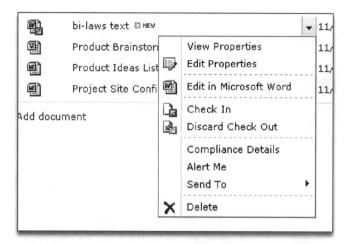

Figure 12 - 47: Pick list after document check out

Notice that you can choose from two options: *Check In* or *Discard Check Out*. Select the *Discard Check Out* option if you have not made any changes to the document; otherwise, select the *Check In* option on the menu and the system displays the *Check In* dialog shown in Figure 12 - 48.

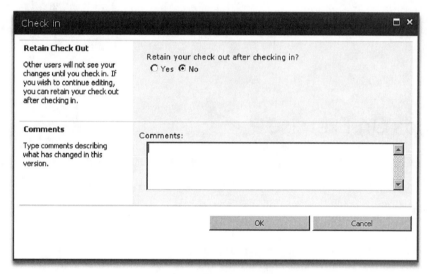

Figure 12 - 48: Check In dialog for a document

Enter information in the *Comments* field in the *Check In* dialog about your latest editing session and select whether to retain the checkout after checking in the current version, and then click the *OK* button. The system checks in the document and adds your comments to the *Version History* for the document if your document is version control enabled.

When you use document check out in a SharePoint library, any user who opens your document sees the document version in the state in which it was when you checked it out, even if you upload more current versions. MSProjectExperts recommends that you periodically check in interim versions of your document when editing over long periods, so that others can access the changes.

If you select the *Discard Check Out* item from the pick list, Project Server 2010 displays the confirmation dialog shown in Figure 12 - 49. Click the *OK* button to reverse the document check out and return it to a checked-in state.

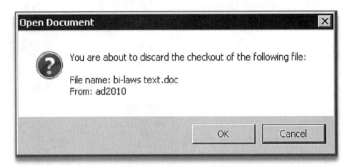

Figure 12 - 49: Confirmation dialog to discard a check out

If you check in a document after accidentally checking it out, the system creates an additional version of the document if you have versioning enabled. If you discard the check out, the system does not create an additional version of the document.

Hands On Exercise

Exercise 12-12

Open and check out an existing document for editing.

1. Float your mouse pointer over the name of a Microsoft Word document in the *Project Documents* library, click the pick list button, and select the *Check Out* item from the list.

2. When the system prompts, click the *OK* button to check out the document.

3. Float your mouse pointer over the name of the same Microsoft Word document in the *Project Documents* library, click the pick list button, and select the *Check In* item from the list.

4. Add a comment and click the *OK* button to check in your document.

Working with Document Copies

You can manage copies of a document from the *View Item* dialog for a document shown previously in Figure 12 - 43. In your project management environment, you might wish to create and manage multiple copies of a single document. For example, you might have a draft copy of a document, a copy that is in revision and a final completed copy as well. To manage additional copies of a document, from the *Actions* section of the *View* ribbon click the *Manage Copies* button. The system displays the *Manage Copies* dialog shown in Figure 12 - 50.

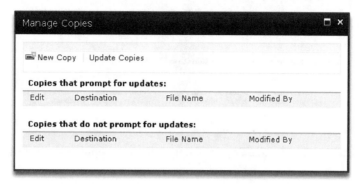

Figure 12 - 50: Manage Copies dialog for a document

To create a new copy of the selected document, click the *New Copy* button at the top of the page. The system displays the *Edit Copy* dialog shown in Figure 12 - 51.

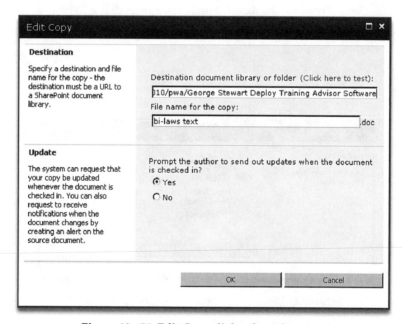

Figure 12 - 51: Edit Copy dialog for a document

Using the *Edit Copy* page, optionally enter an alternate location for the document in the *Destination document library or folder* field. Enter a name for the new copy of the document in the *File name for the copy* field. In the *Update* section of the page, select the *Yes* or *No* option to determine whether the document editor must send an update after editing and checking in the document copy. Click the *OK* button. Project Server 2010 redisplays the *Manage Copies* dialog as shown in Figure 12 - 52.

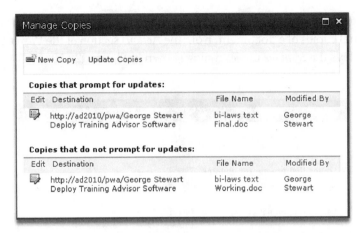

Figure 12 - 52: Manage Copies dialog shows two copies of a document

Notice that the *Manage Copies* dialog shows two new copies of the document. One copy represents the in-progress working copy of the document, and requires an update by the editor when checking in the edited document. The other copy represents the final draft of the presentation and does not require an update from the editor. To update one or more copies, click the *Update Copies* button at the top of the *Manage Copies* dialog. The system displays the *Update Copies* dialog shown in Figure 12 - 53.

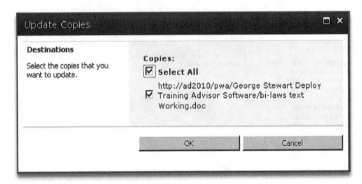

Figure 12 - 53: Update Copies dialog for a document

On the *Update Copies* dialog, select the option checkbox to the left of each copy you wish to update, or click the *Select All* option to select all copies. The system displays the *Copy Progress* dialog shown in Figure 12 - 54.

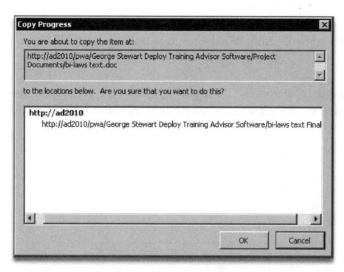

Figure 12 - 54: Copy Progress dialog for document copies

Click the *OK* button to complete the update process. After updating the copy, the system closes the *Manage Copies* dialog, unless you encounter an error.

Editing a Document

To edit a document in a document library, float your mouse pointer over the name of the document, click the pick list button, and then select the *Edit in Microsoft _____* item on the pick list. The system opens the document for editing in the application used to create it, such as Microsoft Word 2010 shown in Figure 12 - 55.

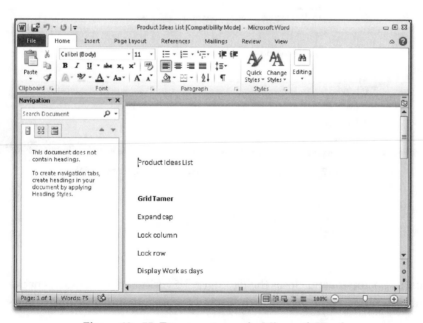

Figure 12 - 55: Document open in Microsoft Word

In an environment where multiple users may need to edit a document in a *Document* library, you should always check out the document after opening it for editing. When you check out a document, Project Server 2010 prevents all other users from opening the document for editing, thus preventing multiple unwanted versions of a document.

To check out a document using any Microsoft 2010 application, click the *File* tab and then select the *Info* tab on the left hand side of the *Backstage* as shown in Figure 12 - 56. At the bottom of the main area of the page, click the *Manage Versions* button to open the pick list shown in the figure. Select the *Check Out* item to check out the document.

Figure 12 - 56: Info Tab of the backstage in Microsoft Word

The system checks out the document and closes the *Backstage*. To verify that the system checked out your document form the SharePoint library, return to the *Info* tab in the *Backstage* and your information display should appear like the one shown in Figure 12 - 57.

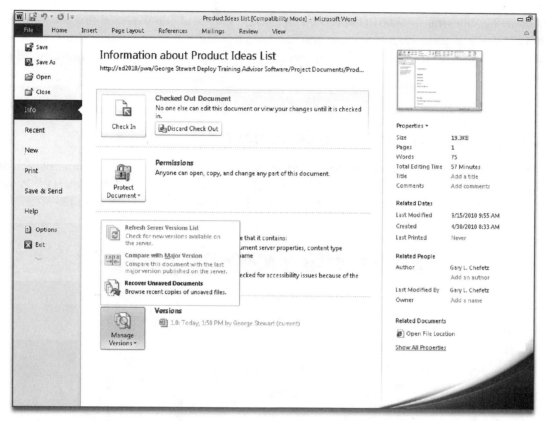

Figure 12 - 57: Backstage with checked out document information

Notice in the figure that the system displays *Checked Out Document* information at the top of the page with a prominent *Check In* button and a somewhat less prominent *Discard Check Out* button. Notice also that the *Manage Versions* pick list changes to reflect the current state of the document.

After you edit your document and save your changes, you must check in the document before others can view the changes. To check in a document using any Microsoft 2010 application, click the *Edit* button and select the *Info* tab in the *Backstage* to reveal the page shown previously in Figure 12 - 57. Click the *Check In* button and the system displays the *Check In* dialog shown in Figure 12 - 58.

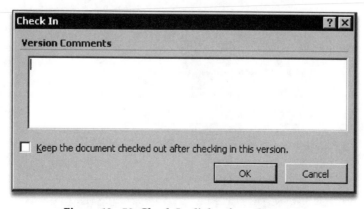

Figure 12 - 58: Check In dialog for a document

In the *Check In* dialog, enter information in the *Version Comments* field about your latest editing session and then click the *OK* button. The system checks in the document and adds your comments to the version history for the document if your system is version control enabled. After you check in the document, close the document and exit the Microsoft application.

Viewing the Version History for a Document

If you enabled versioning in your SharePoint document library, you can view the version history of each document. Float your mouse pointer over the name of the document, click the pick list button, and then select the *Version History* item on the pick list. Project Server 2010 displays the *Version History* dialog shown in Figure 12 - 59.

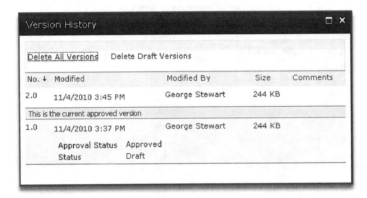

Figure 12 - 59: Version History dialog for a document

The *Version History* dialog shows you the running history for all versions of a document, sorted in descending order so that the latest version appears at the top of the list. Notice in Figure 12 - 59 that there are two versions of the selected document. Notice that the records include comments that users enter while checking in the document. These comments are very useful when people make a habit of entering them.

To manage the versions of the selected document, float your mouse pointer over the date and time of the version you wish to manage and then click the pick list button and select an action item as shown in Figure 12 - 60.

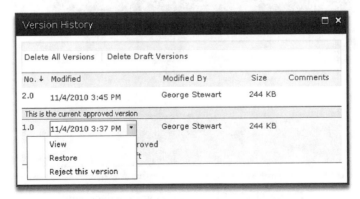

Figure 12 - 60: Working with the Version History dialog

The system offers you three options for managing a document version. Using these options, you can view, restore, or reject any version. If you select the *View* item from the pick list menu, the system displays the *View Item* dialog for the selected version, as shown in Figure 12 - 61. Notice that the dialog contains tools for working with versions.

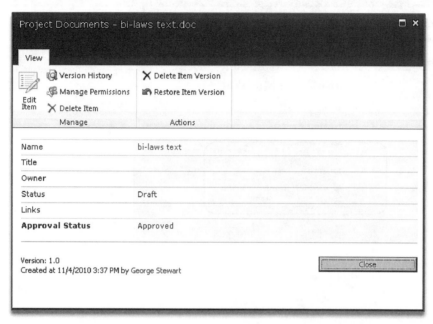

Figure 12 - 61: View Item page for a selected version of a document

Use the buttons in the *Actions* section of the ribbon to delete the selected version, restore it, or return to the *Version History* dialog. If you click the *Close* button, the system returns you to the *Document Library* page. You can restore any previous version and make it the current version of any document. To restore any previous version, select the *Restore* item from the pick list menu or click the *Restore Item Version* item on the ribbon. The system displays the confirmation dialog shown in Figure 12 - 62.

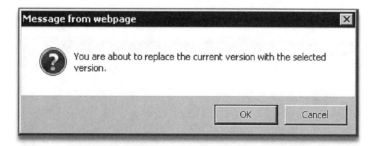

Figure 12 - 62: Confirmation dialog for restoring a previous version

Click the *OK* button to complete the process of restoring a previous version and make it the current version of any document. The system creates a new current version from the previous version, as shown in Figure 12 - 63.

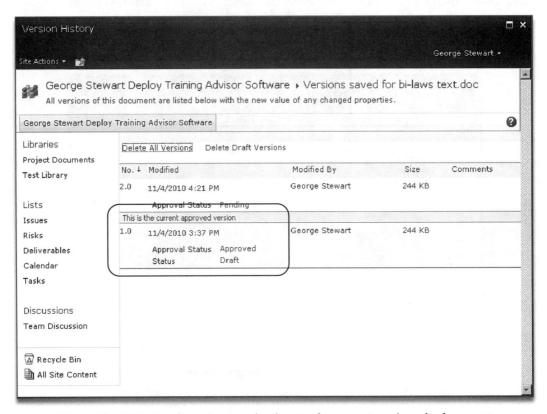

Figure 12 - 63: Restored previous version is now the current version of a document

 The system always opens the current version of a document when you select the *Edit in Microsoft* _____ item for any document in a *Document* library.

Project Server 2010 also allows you to deny any version of a document if you no longer want it to be active in the *Document* library but want to retain it in history. To deny a version, float your mouse pointer over the version you want to deny and then click the *Reject this Version* item from the pick list menu. The system displays the confirmation dialog shown in Figure 12 - 64.

Figure 12 - 64: Confirmation dialog
to delete a document version

Click the *OK* button to deny the version.

Deleting Documents and Document Versions

Notice at the top of the *Version History* dialog shown previously in Figure 12 - 63, that you can also delete versions. The system allows you to delete only draft versions of the document or delete all versions of the document except the current document version and send them to the recycle bin. To delete versions of a document in a *Document* library, click either the *Delete All Versions* link or the *Delete Draft Versions* link at the top of the page. The system prompts you with a warning similar to the one shown in Figure 12 - 65.

Figure 12 - 65: Warning about deleting versions

 The system does not delete a document that is checked out.

To delete the current version of a document and delete all the previous versions along with it, on the *Document Library* page, float your mouse pointer over the name of the document, click the pick list button, and then select the *Delete* item on the pick list. The system displays the confirmation dialog shown in Figure 12 - 66.

Figure 12 - 66: Confirmation dialog to delete a document

Click the *OK* button to complete the deletion. The system removes the deleted document and all of its versions from its *Document* library and transfers them to the Project Site Recycle Bin.

Sending a Document to another Location or Application

Project Server 2010 allows you to send a document and document information from a *Document* library to another location or application using the following methods:

- Send a copy of the document to the location of existing copies of the document.

- Send a copy of the document to a new folder in the WSS folder system.

- Send the URL of the document to others in an e-mail message.

- Download a copy of the document to your hard drive or to a network drive.

To send a document or document information to another location, float your mouse pointer over the name of the document, click the pick list button, and then select the *Send To* item on the pick list. The system displays the *Send To* submenu shown in Figure 12 - 67.

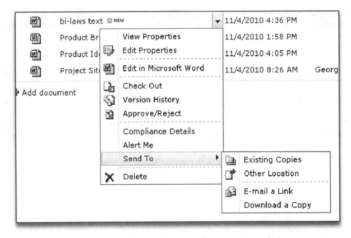

Figure 12 - 67: Send to submenu for a selected document

Select the *Existing Copies* submenu item to send the selected document to the location where you previously saved copies of the document. The system displays the *Update Copies* page shown previously in Figure 12 - 53. Select the *Other Location* submenu item to send the document to another location or to create additional copies of the document. The system displays the *Update Copies* page shown in Figure 12 - 68.

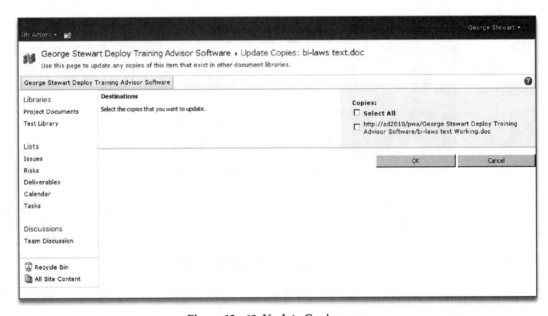

Figure 12 - 68: Update Copies page

The *Update Copies* page is similar to the *Update Copies* dialog you learned about previously. Refer to the Managing Document Copies section of this module for more information about creating and managing copies of a document. Select the *E-mail a Link* submenu item to send the URL for the document to others in an e-mail message. The system launches your default e-mail application, creates a new e-mail message, and then inserts the URL for the document in the body of the message. In the outgoing e-mail message, enter one or more addresses in the *To* field, enter a subject in the *Subject* field, and add additional information in the body of the message.

 Warning: Depending on your operating system and security settings, the system may prompt you to allow access to your e-mail application.

Select the *Download a Copy* submenu item to download a copy of the document to your hard drive or to a network drive. Project Server 2010 displays the *File Download* dialog shown in Figure 12 - 69.

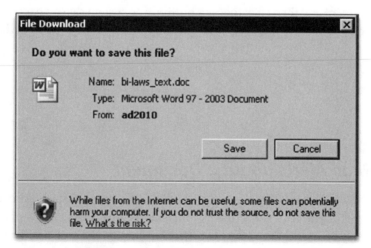

Figure 12 - 69: File Download dialog

Click the *Save* button to save the selected document. The system displays the *Save As* dialog shown in Figure 12 - 70.

Figure 12 - 70: Save As dialog

Select a location for the document and then click the *Save* button. The system saves a copy of the document to the designated location. From there, you can modify the document and upload a new version of the document into the *Document* library.

Subscribing to E-Mail Alerts about a Document

As with risks and issues, Project Server 2010 allows you to subscribe to e-mail alerts whenever a user changes a selected document in a *Document* library. To subscribe to e-mail alerts, float your mouse pointer over the name of the document, click the pick list button, and then select the *Alert Me* item on the pick list. The system displays the *New Alert* dialog shown in Figure 12 - 71.

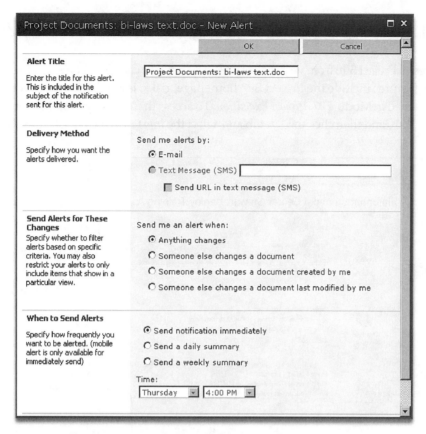

Figure 12 - 71: New Alert dialog for a selected document

In the *New Alert* dialog, specify your options in each section of the page and then click the *OK* button. Notice that the *New Alert* dialog allows you to determine what type of change triggers the system to send an e-mail message to you, and you can determine when the system sends the message.

Hands On Exercise

Exercise 12-13

Subscribe to an e-mail alert about changes to a document in the Project Documents library.

1. Float your mouse pointer over the name of a Microsoft Word document, click the pick list button, and then select the *Alert Me* item on the pick list.

2. In the *New Alert* dialog, select your options for the new e-mail alert.

3. Click the *OK* button to subscribe to the e-mail alert.

Accessing a Project Site from Project Professional 2010

Not only can you access a Project Site from within Project Web App, you can also access it indirectly using Project Professional 2010. These features include the Project Site homepage, risks, issues, and documents. You can also access deliverables as you learned in Module 07, *Project Execution*. To access these for any project, open the enterprise project in Project Professional 2010 and then click the *File* tab and select the *Info* tab in the *Backstage* as shown in Figure 12 - 72.

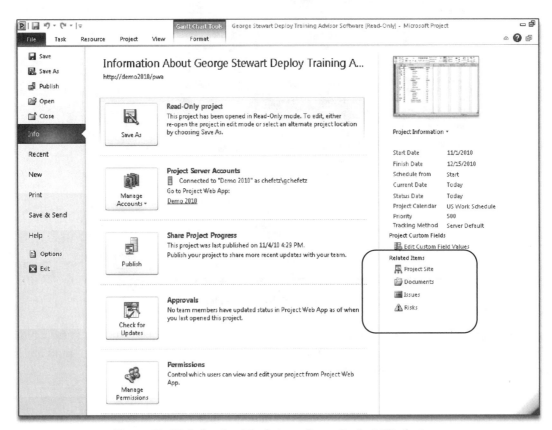

Figure 12 - 72: Info tab of Backstage shows Project Site features

Select the *Risks*, *Issues*, *Documents*, or *Project Site* item. The system spawns a new Internet Explorer window in the background and displays the selected page of the Project Site. Notice the new window on your task bar to switch to the displayed page.

Working with other SharePoint Lists

While the *Issues* list, *Risk* list, *Deliverables* list and the *Project Document Library* are customized SharePoint elements that provide specific management capabilities for your enterprise project management system, your Project Site also includes a number of provisioned SharePoint lists that you can use to enhance your team's collaboration experience. Additionally, you have the entire range of SharePoint sites and list types available to you in creating your own collaboration solutions. While covering all of these is beyond the scope of the book, the following sections teach you how to use the common SharePoint elements included in your Project Site.

Working with the Task List

In addition to the tasks you assign to resources in the Project Professional 2010 project plan, you can also create tasks and assign resources to them in the Project Site for your project. Typically, you use the *Tasks* list in the Project Site to define work associated with the project, but are too trivial to include in the actual project plan. For example, you have a weekly project status meeting with your project team. During this meeting, you generate a list of "action items" associated with the project that members of your team must complete by the next status meeting. Use the *Tasks* feature in the Project Site to create the list of "action items" and then assign them to the appropriate team members.

Creating New Tasks

To use the *Tasks* list in your Project Site, navigate to the Project Site for your project. Click the *Tasks* link in the *Lists* section of the *Quick Launch* menu. Project Server 2010 displays the *Tasks* page shown in Figure 12 - 73. Note that I selected the *Items* ribbon.

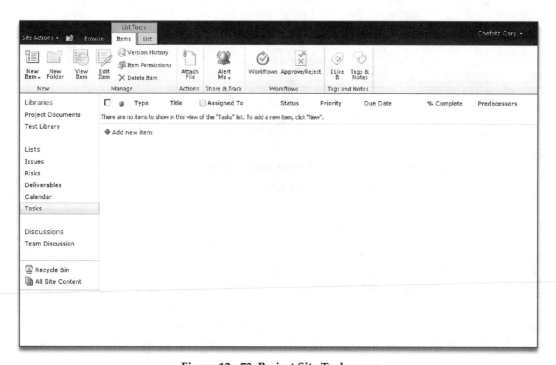

Figure 12 - 73: Project Site Tasks page

To create a new task, from the *New* section of the *Items* ribbon, click the *New Item* pick list button and select the *Task* item from the list. Notice that you can create a task or a summary task. The system displays the *New Item* dialog for the *Tasks* list shown in Figure 12 - 74.

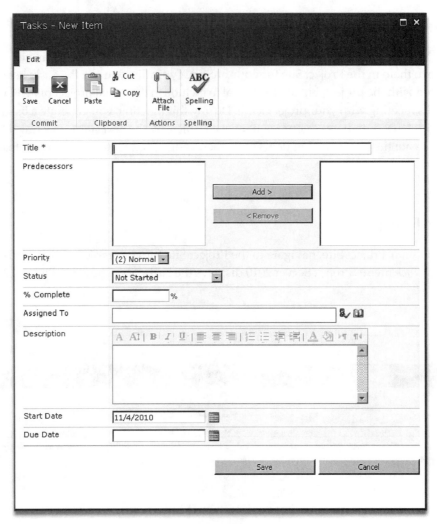

Figure 12 - 74: New Item dialog for Tasks

To create the new task, begin by entering a name for the task in the *Title* field, which is the only required field. Select a priority for the task from the *Priority* pick list. Your options in the *Priority* pick list include *High, Normal,* and *Low.* Leave the value in the *Status* pick list set to *Not Started,* because the resource assigned to the task must change the value in the pick list while performing the work. Items available in the *Status* pick list include *Not Started, In Progress, Completed, Deferred,* and *Waiting on Someone Else.* Leave the *% Complete* field blank because the resource assigned to the task must enter this information. Notice that you can define other tasks in the list as predecessors; however, this is the first entry in the list.

Enter the resource assigned to the task in *Assigned To* field, and use the *Check Names* and *Browse* buttons to the right of the field to locate or verify resource names. Enter additional information about the task in the *Description* field. In the *Start Date* field, enter the date that the resource must begin work on the task. In the *Due Date* field, enter the date the resource must complete the work on this task. From the *Actions* section of the *Edit* ribbon, click the *Attach File* button to optionally attach a file to the task. Click the *Save* button to finish. The system creates the new task and displays it on the *Tasks* list as shown in Figure 12 - 75

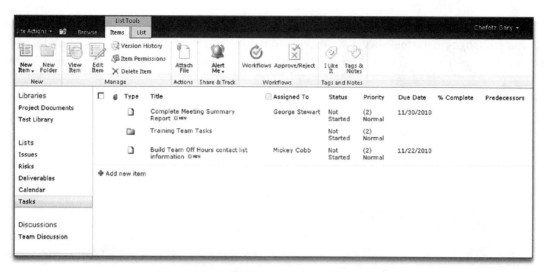

Figure 12 - 75: Tasks page shows three Tasks

Notice that the *Tasks* list shown in Figure 12 - 75 contains three tasks, one summary task and two individual tasks assigned to members of the project team. The system represents *Summary* tasks as folder items and you create subtasks by drilling down into the folder.

 Warning: Do not confuse tasks that you create in the Project Work Space with tasks in the enterprise project. The tasks you create in the Project Site are not part of the reporting cycle in Project Web App, they do not affect resource loading, and you cannot use any of the system's scheduling capabilities with these tasks.

Working with Existing Tasks

When a team member begins working on a task assigned in the Project Site, he or she must edit the task and enter progress. When complete, the team member must edit the task to indicate that it is complete. Working with an existing task is very similar to working with an existing risk or issue. Float your mouse pointer over the name of the task, click the pick list button, and select an item from the pick list menu, as shown in Figure 12 - 76.

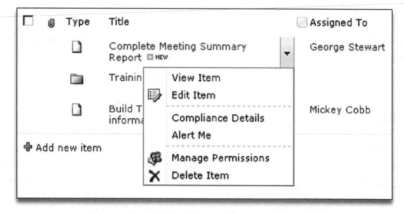

Figure 12 - 76: Working with an existing task

Notice on the pick list that Project Server 2010 allows you to view the task, edit the task, delete the task, or subscribe to e-mail alerts about changes to the task. Because I discussed these concepts previously in this module, I do not repeat this information here. Refer to previous sections in this module concerning risks and issues to review this information.

Hands On Exercise

Exercise 12-14

Create new tasks in the Project Site and assign them to project team members.

1. From your Project Site homepage, click the *Tasks* link in the *Lists* section of the *Quick Launch* menu. The system displays the *Tasks* list for your Project Site.

2. Select the *Items* tab and from the *New* section, click the *New Item* pick list button and select the *Task* item from the list. The system opens the *New Item* dialog.

3. Enter a name for the new task in the *Title* field, leave the *Predecessors* field blank, select a priority for the task in the *Priority* field, leave the *Status* and *% Complete* fields at their default values, and then enter your own name in the *Assigned To* field.

4. Enter a description for the task in the *Description* field, a *Start Date* value and a *Due Date* value, and then click the *Save* button.

5. Repeat steps #2-4 again and create two additional tasks, and assign each of them to another member of your project team.

Using the Calendar List

In the Project Site for your project, Project Server 2010 allows you to create a calendar of events related to the project. These events might include team meetings, project status meetings, training classes, client consultations, and perhaps even a project closure celebration party. To create a calendar event, click the *Calendar* link in the *Lists* section of the *Quick Launch* menu. The system displays the *Calendar* page shown in Figure 12 - 77.

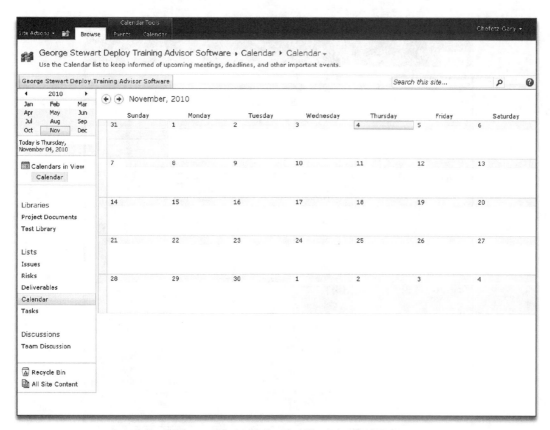

Figure 12 - 77: Calendar List homepage

Creating a New Calendar Event

To create a new calendar event, click on the *Events* tab to display the *Events* ribbon. In the *New* section click the *New Event* button and select the *Event* item from the list. The system displays the *New Item* dialog for the calendar, as shown in Figure 12 - 78.

Figure 12 - 78: New Item dialog for the Calendar

The *New Item* dialog for the calendar contains three required fields: the *Title, Start Time,* and *End Time* fields. Enter the name of the event in the *Title* field and the event location in the *Location* field. Enter the time of the event in the *Start Time* and *End Time* fields. Enter optional event description information in the *Description* field. To set the event as an all-day event, select the *Make this an all-day activity that doesn't start or end at a specific hour* option. When you select this option the system removes the time information from the *Start Time* and *End Time* fields. To make the event a recurring event, select the *Make this a repeating event* option. Project Server 2010 redisplays the *New Item* dialog to include recurrence information, as shown in Figure 12 - 79.

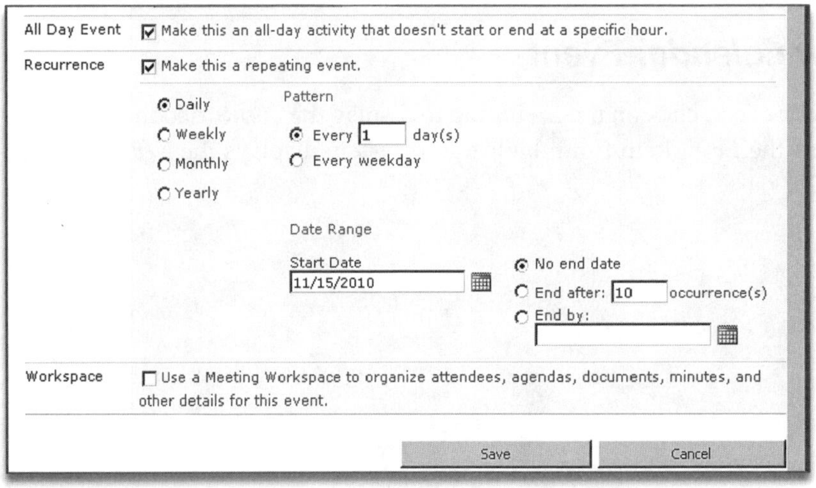

Figure 12 - 79: New Item page includes recurrence information

In the *Recurrence* section of the page, select the options necessary to define how your event recurs. Be sure to enter a date in the *Start Date* field and to specify how many events to create by selecting the *No end date* option, the *End after ___ occurrence(s)* option, or the *End by* option. If you want to use a Meeting Workspace to help organize the event, select the *Use a Meeting Workspace to organize...* option at the bottom of the page. Click the *OK* button to finish.

While creating a new event, if you select the *Use a Meeting Workspace to organize...* option at the bottom of the page, the system creates a New Meeting Workspace.

Project Server 2010 displays the new calendar event(s) as shown in Figure 12 - 80. Notice that I created a weekly Team Meeting event every Friday and one individual event on November 15, 2010.

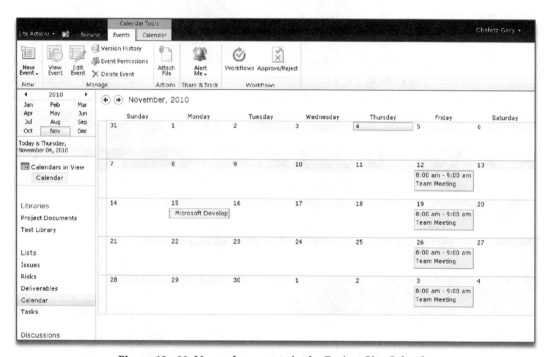

Figure 12 - 80: November events in the Project Site Calendar

Hands On Exercise

Exercise 12-15

Create Calendar events in the Project Site.

1. Click the *Calendar* link in the *Lists* section of the *Quick Launch* menu.

2. On the *Calendar* page, click the *Events* tab to display the *Events* ribbon and click the *New Event* pick list button and select the *Event* item from the list. The system displays the *New Event* dialog.

3. Enter a name for the event in the *Title* field, enter a location in the *Location* field, and enter date and time information in the *Start Time* and *End Time* fields. Ignore the remaining five fields.

4. Click the *Save* button to create the new event.

5. Repeat steps #2-4 to create another event, but make it a recurring event that occurs weekly every week on Wednesday, and ends after 12 occurrences.

6. Click the *Save* button to create the new recurring event.

7. Navigate through your *Calendar* page and examine your new events.

8. Click on the *Calendar* tab to display the *Calendar* ribbon and explore the *Manage Views* section. Explore the views selections in the *Scope* section on the left.

Creating a Meeting Workspace for an Event

When you create a new event and select the *Workspace* option at the bottom of the *New Item* dialog as shown previously in Figure 12 - 79, the system launches the *New Meeting Workspace* page, shown in Figure 12 - 81, after you click the *Save* button in the *New Item* dialog. I want to create a meeting workspace in which to plan the details of the Microsoft Developer Learning event that I am sending half my team to attend.

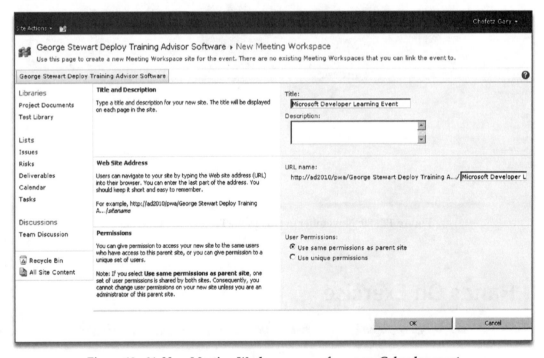

Figure 12 - 81: New Meeting Workspace page for a new Calendar event

In the *New Meeting Workspace* page, edit the information in the *Title* field and enter description information in the *Description* field. Project Server 2010 automatically enters a URL for the meeting workspace in the *URL name* field. In the *Permissions* section of the page, select the *Use same permissions as parent site* option to keep the same security as your Project Site. The *Permissions* option you specify determines what users can do in the Meeting Workspace site. The system allows you to specify the same permissions as the Project Site (the parent site) or to specify unique permissions.

Warning: Project Server 2010 does not allow you to create a Meeting Workspace site if you have only Project Manager permissions in the system. Therefore, if you attempt to create a Meeting Workspace, the system generates a Windows SharePoint Services error message. If you need to create a Meeting Workspace site, contact your Project Server administrator for assistance before you attempt to create it.

Click the *OK* button to finish. Project Server 2010 displays the *Template Selection* page shown in Figure 12 - 82.

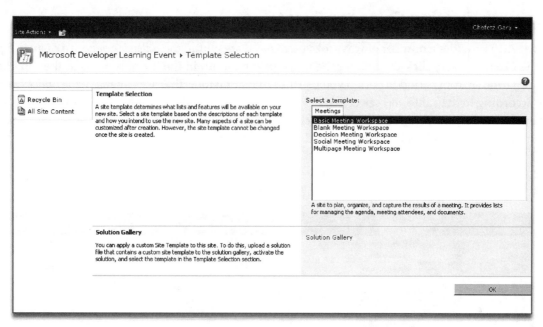

Figure 12 - 82: Template Selection page for a new Meeting Workspace

Select an appropriate site template from the list shown in the *Template Selection* field and then click the *OK* button. The system creates a new Meeting Workspace as a collaboration area for all users involved with the event, such as the Meeting Workspace shown in Figure 12 - 83.

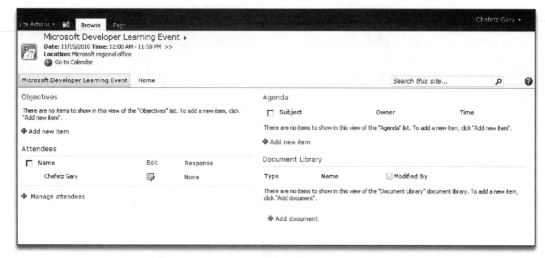

Figure 12 - 83: Meeting Workspace for the event

603

In the Meeting Workspace, you and your fellow users can collaborate to create a variety of items in the workspace, such as a list of event attendees, directions to the event, and a list of things to bring to the event. To return to the *Calendar* page in the Project Site, click the *Go to Calendar* link at the top of the page.

Working with Existing Calendar Events

Project Server 2010 provides a number of ways for you to navigate within the *Calendar* page. To display a particular month on the *Calendar* page, click the link for the name of the month in the list of months at the top of the *Quick Launch* menu. To move from period to period you use the navigation tools that appear above the *Quick Launch* menu. These vary according to the value you select in the *Scope* section of the *Calendar* ribbon. To apply a daily, weekly, or monthly view of the *Calendar* page, click the *Day, Week,* or *Month* button to set the scope of the *Calendar* page. For example, Figure 12 - 84 shows a weekly scope applied to the *Calendar* page.

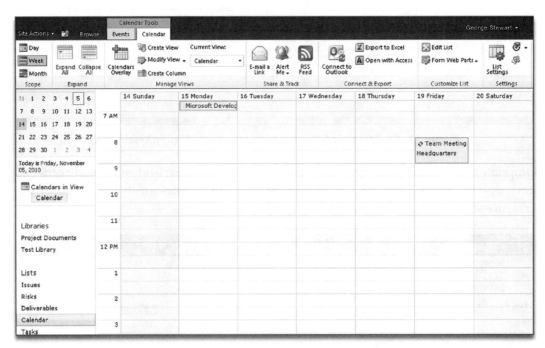

Figure 12 - 84: Calendar page with weekly scope

To view the information for any calendar event, click the link for the event. The system displays the information page for the selected event, as shown in Figure 12 - 85.

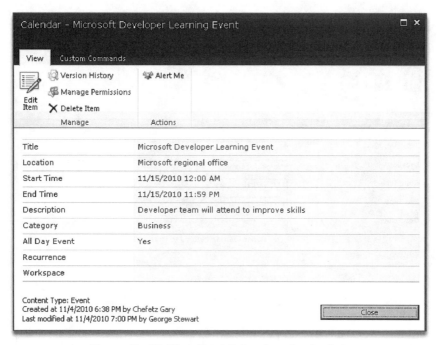

Figure 12 - 85: View Item dialog for calendar item

Notice in the figure that it displays the event information for the Microsoft Developer Learning Event. The *View Item* dialog contains all of the information for this event, including an optional *Workspace* link at the bottom for a Meeting Workspace if one is available. To edit the event, from the *Manage* section of the *View* menu, click the *Edit Item* button. The system displays the *Edit Item* dialog for the calendar item shown in Figure 12 - 86. To delete the event form the *View Item* dialog, click the *Delete Item* button. To subscribe to e-mail alerts about changes to the event, in the *Actions* section of the ribbon, click the *Alert Me* button.

Figure 12 - 86: Edit Item dialog for calendar item

Using the *Edit Item* dialog is identical to using the *New Item* dialog and similar to editing the other types of list items that you worked with earlier in this module.

Connecting SharePoint Calendars to Outlook

You can display SharePoint calendar lists in Microsoft Office Outlook just as you can display shared Outlook calendars that belong to other people. Once you connect your SharePoint calendar list to Outlook, you can work the calendar items using the appointment tools in Outlook. You can share events between calendars by copying and pasting, or dragging and dropping.

You connect your SharePoint calendar to Outlook by selecting the *Calendar* tab and from the *Connect & Export* section of the ribbon, click the *Connect to Outlook* button as shown in Figure 12 - 87.

Figure 12 - 87: Calendar ribbon

When you click the button, Outlook displays the warning dialog shown in Figure 12 - 88. The warning advises you to connect only to data sources that you trust.

Figure 12 - 88: Outlook security warning

Click the *Advanced* button in the warning dialog to open the *SharePoint List Options* dialog shown in Figure 12 - 89.

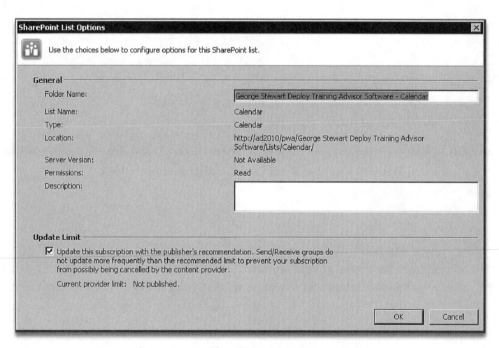

Figure 12 - 89: SharePoint List Options dialog

In the *SharePoint List Items* dialog, you can change the display name for the calendar and add a description. Notice the *Update Limit* section in the dialog. This option, selected by default, allows you to determine whether your copy of Outlook polls the SharePoint calendar each time it executes a send and receive action, or whether it respects a polling limit set for the SharePoint calendar administratively. Normally, you want to respect polling limits set in the source system. Click the *OK* button and the system transfers focus to Microsoft Outlook displaying your newly connected calendar as shown in Figure 12 - 90.

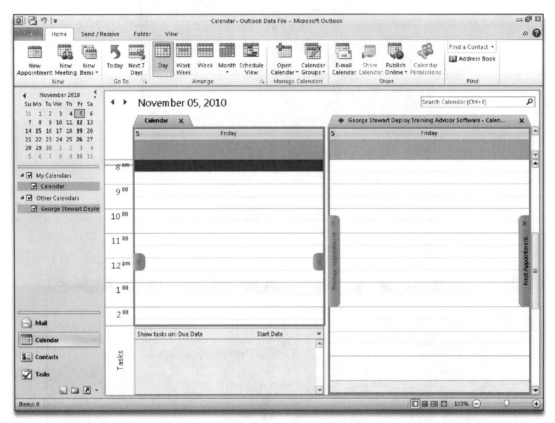

Figure 12 - 90: SharePoint Calendar displayed in Outlook

Notice that the SharePoint calendar appears in the *My Calendars* navigation section on the left and that the calendar itself displays the same way an Outlook calendar displays and that you can overlay SharePoint calendars with Outlook calendars.

Using Team Discussions

Because the Project Site represents a centralized collaboration area for everyone involved in a project, you can use the *Team Discussion* feature to create and log threaded discussion topics between all parties. To use the *Team Discussion* feature, from the *Discussions* section of the *Quick Launch* menu, click the *Team Discussion* link and the system displays the *Team Discussion* page shown in Figure 12 - 91.

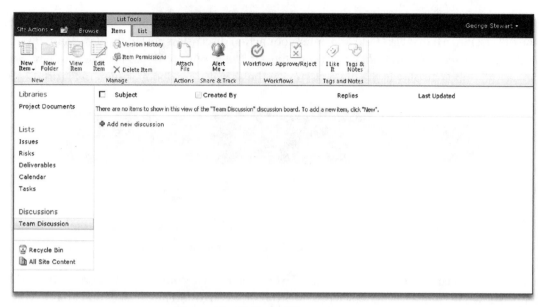

Figure 12 - 91: Team Discussion page

Creating a New Team Discussion

To create a new team discussion, click the *Items* tab to display the *Items* ribbon and from the *New* section, click the *New Item* pick list button and select the *Discussion* item. The system displays the *New Item* dialog for a team discussion as shown in Figure 12 - 92.

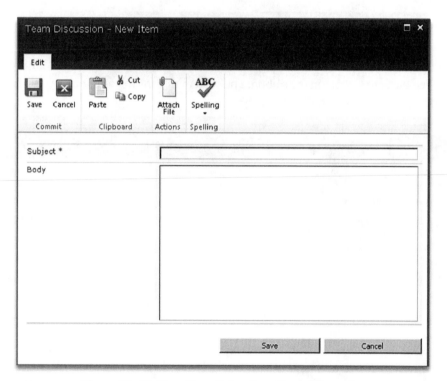

Figure 12 - 92: New Item dialog for a Team Discussion

609

Notice that the *Team Discussion* feature is simply another specialized SharePoint list. Use the *New Item* page to enter a subject for the discussion in the *Subject* field and enter your actual discussion post in the *Body* field. If you want to attach a file, in the *Actions* section of the *Edit* ribbon click the *Attach File* button. When you click into the *Body* field, the systems changes the ribbon display in the dialog to reveal the *Format Text* ribbon shown in Figure 12 - 93.

Figure 12 - 93: Format Text ribbon for discussions

You use familiar rich-text editing tools on the *Format Text* ribbon to style your post. Click on the *Insert* tab to display the *Insert* ribbon shown in Figure 12 - 94, which provides tools for you to add media, files and links to your discussion post.

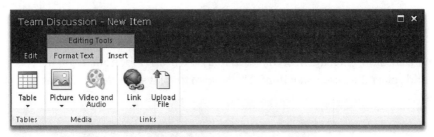

Figure 12 - 94: Insert ribbon for discussions

When you finish composing your discussion list post, click the *Save* button at the bottom of the dialog or navigate to the *Edit* ribbon and click the *Save* button on the ribbon. The system returns to your *Team Discussions* homepage, which now displays your first post as shown in Figure 12 - 95.

Figure 12 - 95: Team Discussion page with first post

610

Hands On Exercise

Exercise 12-16

Create a new Team Discussion in a Project Site.

1. In the *Discussions* section of the *Quick Launch* menu, click the *Team Discussion* link.

2. Click the *Items* tab to apply the *Items* ribbon and from the *New* section, click the *New Item* pick list button and select the *Discussion* item from the menu.

3. Enter a name for the discussion in the *Subject* field and enter a description of your post in the *Body* field.

4. Click the *Save* button to create the Team Discussion.

Working with a Team Discussion

To work with an existing discussion item, float your mouse pointer over the item in the *Subject* column and then click the pick list button. The system displays a pick list with available options, based on the permissions you have in the Project Site as shown in Figure 12 - 96.

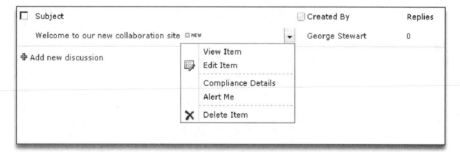

Figure 12 - 96: Pick list for working with discussions

The system presents pick list selections based on the permissions set by the project manager who created the discussion. If you want to view the original post, click the *View Item* option on the pick list. If you want to edit the original post, click the *Edit Item* option on the pick list and then edit the item. If you want to delete the existing discussion, click the *Delete Item* option on the pick list. If you want to subscribe to e-mail alerts about changes to the discussion, click the *Alert Me* option and set the alert options you want to use. To view the discussion, select the *View Item* selection from the list or simply click on the item's *Subject* link. The system displays the discussion as shown in Figure 12 - 97.

Figure 12 - 97: Discussion page displays discussion

Anyone with an interest in a project, and who has access to the Project Site, can add a reply or comments to an existing discussion. For example, a team member might add comments to the existing discussion shown in the figure by way of introduction to the team. To respond to a post, click the *Reply* button in the bar above the post at the far right. The system opens the *New Item* dialog to reply to a discussion as shown in Figure 12 - 98.

Figure 12 - 98: New Item dialog to reply to a post

Notice that the dialog for the reply reveals the author of the discussion (George Stewart) and shows the current text of the discussion. To add a reply, enter it in the *Body* section above the line that demarks the previous post. Click the *Save* button to complete the reply. Figure 12 - 99 shows the *Team Discussion* page displaying the original post and one reply using the *Threaded* option in the *Manage Views* section, *Current View* pick list.

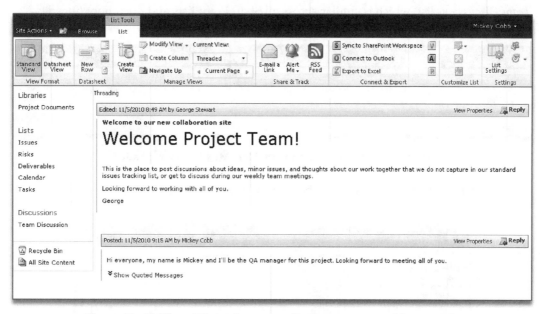

Figure 12 - 99: Team Discussions page displays one post with one reply

When you view the page, such as the one shown previously in Figure 12 - 97, the system applies the default *Flat* view to the page. The *Flat* view shows all of the comments, listed in date order from the earliest response to the latest response. You can also apply the *Threaded* view of the page to see the comments listed as a threaded discussion.

Hands On Exercise

Exercise 12-17

Reply to a team discussion post.

1. From the *Team Discussions* homepage click the name of the team discussion you created in Exercise 12-15.

2. On the *Team Discussion* page, click the *Reply* button in the upper right corner of the page.

3. Add your reply or comments in the *Body* field and then click the *Save* button.

4. On the *Team Discussion* page, click the *List* tab to display the *List* ribbon. In the *Manage Views* section of the *List* ribbon, click the *Current View* pick list button and select the *Threaded* item.

5. Examine the *Threaded* view.

Working with Alerts in SharePoint

In previous sections of this module, you learned how to set alerts on individual list and document items. When your SharePoint site is email enabled, you can also set alerts for entire lists and libraries. Figure 12 - 100 shows the *List* ribbon for the *Team Discussions* list, which is similar across all SharePoint lists and document libraries.

Figure 12 - 100: List ribbon with Alert Me pick list expanded

Select the *Set Alert on this list* item on the pick list. The system displays the *New Alert* dialog shown in Figure 12 - 101.

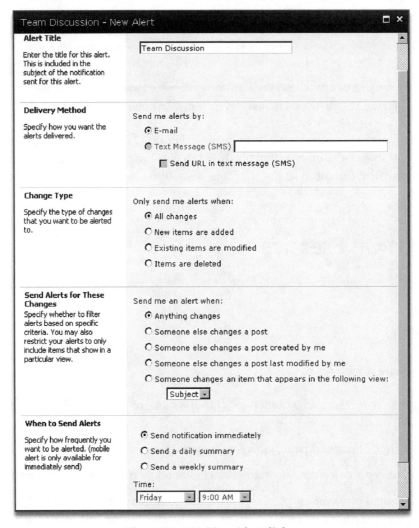

Figure 12 - 101: New Alert dialog

Notice that the *New Alert* dialog for an entire list or library looks very similar to the one for individual items. Here you can set alerts on a list-wide or library-wide basis rather than selectively for individual items or documents.

> SharePoint ribbon menu selections and picklist menu selections vary based on user, system configuration and other factors. In fact, as you increase the resolution on your system, many of the ribbons respond by expanding to display more detail and they contract intelligently when you reduce your resolution.

To manage your existing alerts, from any *List* ribbon or *Document* ribbon displaying the *Alert Me* pick list button, such as shown previously in Figure 12 - 100, select the *Manage My Alerts* item and the system displays the *Manage My Alerts* page for that particular site as shown in Figure 12 - 102.

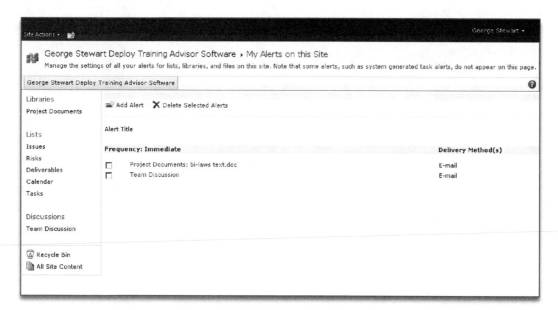

Figure 12 - 102: Manage My Alerts page

From this page, you can delete alerts that you previously created and add new list-wide or document-wide alerts. To remove an existing alert, select the checkbox to the left of the alert name, and click the *Delete Selected Alerts* button at the top of the page. To view an existing alert, click on the alert name. To set alerts across the entire site, click the *Add Alert* button at the top of the page. The system displays the *New Alert* page shown in Figure 12 - 103.

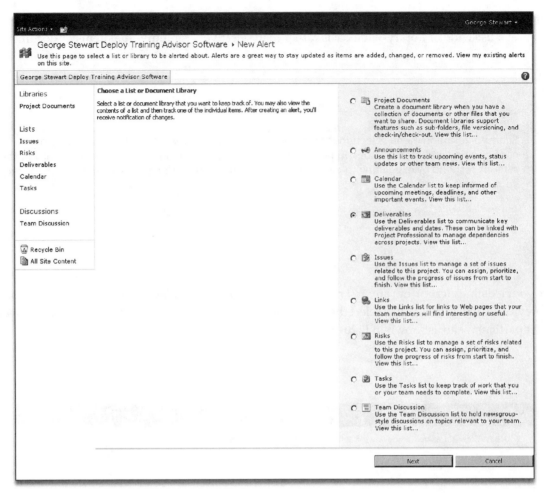

Figure 12 - 103: New Alert page

The *New Alert* page allows you to select any list or library contained in your site, and set a list-wide or library-wide alert.

Subscribing to an RSS Feed

Another option for sharing and tracking information about a SharePoint list or library is to use Really Simple Syndication (RSS) feeds. Each library and list automatically includes this capability. To setup an RSS subscription, from the *Share & Track* section of a *List* or *Document* ribbon, click the *RSS* button. The system displays the *RSS Feed* page for the selected document library or list as shown in Figure 12 - 104.

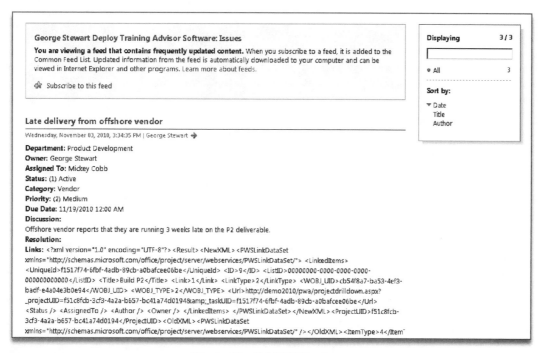

Figure 12 - 104: RSS Feed page

Notice that the page displays the feed in its native XML format. This is not a very good way to read the list! Instead, you want to connect the feed to an application like Microsoft Outlook that translates RSS raw feeds to human-readable form. Click the *Subscribe to the feed* link in the shaded area at the top of the page. The system displays the *Subscribe to this Feed* dialog shown in Figure 12 - 105.

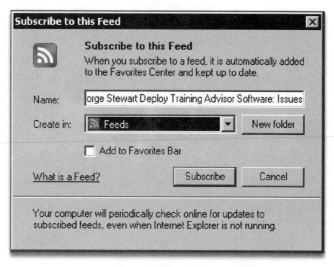

Figure 12 - 105: Subscribe to this Feed dialog

Notice that the system defaults to creating the feed link in your *Feeds* folder in Outlook. If you want to change the folder, you can create a new folder by clicking on the *New Folder* button. Click the *Subscribe* button to complete your subscription once you select or create the correct folder. Locate your new feed in your Outlook client.

Module 13

Managing Project Sites

Learning Objectives

After completing this module, you will be able to:

- Create and modify metadata for classifying Project Site content items
- Create and modify views of content items
- Modify the settings for a Project Site list or library
- Create new lists and libraries for storing items in the Project Site
- Create and modify the layout of pages in the Project Site
- Modify the settings for the overall Project Site

Inside Module 13

Introducing Project Site Management

As the owner of a project schedule in Project Server, you have many site ownership privileges giving you the ability to control the structure, behaviors, and appearance of the Project Site attached to that project. More specifically, you have the ability to:

- Capture additional pieces of data for each *Document, Issue,* or *Risk* stored in the Project Site, in addition to the data that Project Server already captures.

- Create custom views of items stored in a list or library to provide different perspectives on the data.

- Enable or disable features in any list or library within the Project Site.

- Create new list or library repositories to store various types of content in the Project Site.

- Create and modify *pages* allowing people to view, input, or otherwise interact with the data stored in the Project site.

- Enable or disable features in the overall Project Site.

- Modify the navigation menus and links within the Project Site.

- Control the color schemes used on the *Project Site* pages.

Important SharePoint Concepts

SharePoint is a family of tools for creating and managing websites for teams to collaborate and share many different types of information and content. Because Project Sites use SharePoint technology for storing, organizing, and providing access to project artifacts, it is important that you become familiar with some important SharePoint concepts before learning how to manage a Project Site.

SharePoint helps to organize structured and unstructured data and enables collaboration. Regardless of the type of data, there are several main concepts that recur throughout the system, including the following:

- Administration

- User Access

- Templates

- Metadata

- Version Control

- Workflow

Administration Areas

As a project owner, you will use two interfaces to configure various aspects of your Project Site:

- **Site settings:** An administrative area available within each Project Site that you use to manage configuration settings that apply to that site only. Examples include site-specific themes, navigation, and metadata management.

- **List and Library settings:** An administrative area available within each list or library in a SharePoint website that you use to manage configuration settings within that list or library only. Examples include list-specific version control, metadata management, and views.

You learn how to use each of these tools to perform various administrative functions throughout the remainder of this module.

User Access to a Project Site

Project Server manages security for your Project Site through a synchronization process built into the Project Server application. When a project stored in Project Server has a Project Site associated with it, the synchronization process runs automatically when the project manager republishes the project to PWA, as shown in Figure 13 - 1. The system then automatically grants project team members access to the Project Site.

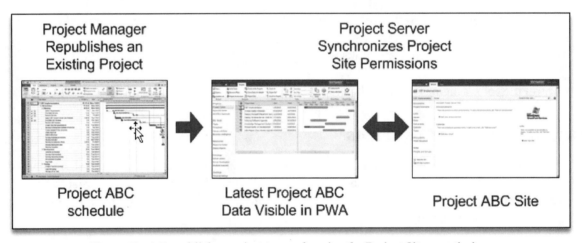

Figure 13 - 1: Republish a project to synchronize the Project Site permissions

Templates

SharePoint helps you streamline list and library creation by employing templates. If none of the built-in templates meets your needs, you can create your own custom templates, which you can use to create future lists or libraries within your Project Site. Examples of list and library templates included in SharePoint are:

- Announcements

- Contacts

- Discussion Board

- Links

- Calendar

- Tasks

- Survey

- Wiki Page Library

- Picture Library

- Slide Library

Metadata

SharePoint stores various types of structured and unstructured content. You can attach additional pieces of descriptive data to classify each item, whether the item is an expense report, a document, a calendar event, or a project issue. This additional data, also known as *metadata*, can be quite helpful for sorting, grouping, filtering, or searching for the content within the SharePoint content store.

For example, your team members are tracking a list of issues that are impeding the progress of your project. The core data entity is an issue, but you may also want to capture additional data that further classifies each issue, such as the date when you logged the issue, the person who is responsible for following the issue to resolution, and the date by which the issue must be resolved.

Version Control

SharePoint provides automatic version control, a mechanism for tracking updates contributed by members of a team. When you enable this functionality you can track major versions (1.0, 2.0, 3.0, etc.) for each item of structured content in a SharePoint list. Each time you make a change to an item stored in a list, the system automatically increments the version number and stores the previous version of the item for later review and retrieval. You can also track both major and minor versions (1.0, 1.1, 1.2, 2.0, etc.) for each unstructured content item that you store in a SharePoint library. When you enable minor versioning for files in a library, these minor versions are drafts. When you enable versioning for a list or library within a SharePoint site, the system includes all of the content items stored in that list or library.

Workflow

A workflow in SharePoint is an electronic representation of a business process. More specifically, it is a way of attaching business logic to content stored and managed in a SharePoint website. Whether you want to represent a review and approval process, an issue escalation process, or a project proposal process, you can break down each process into a set of activities or tasks that the SharePoint workflow engine represents, stores, and tracks. Each workflow can automatically perform actions on content stored in a SharePoint list or library, such as update a status field from "Submitted" to "Approved" or move an expense report from one location to another. Workflows can also initiate a request to a person to perform an action on an item, such as review a project issue and assign it to the appropriate team member for resolution. You can use a number of options and tools for creating workflows in SharePoint, including each of the following.

- **Built-in Workflows:** Because Project Server 2010 installs with Microsoft SharePoint Server, the system provides a number of built-in workflows for Project Server Lifecycle Management. You do not need to have custom code development capabilities to use and configure built-in workflows.

- **Microsoft SharePoint Designer:** This Microsoft desktop application has a convenient wizard-style interface for building workflows for non-developers. It allows you to represent sophisticated processes that may have several process steps and can contain conditional logic as well as perform several types of actions on the content stored in a SharePoint list or library. These workflows are limited, in that they can interact within the scope of only a single site.

- **Microsoft Visual Studio:** You can use this developer tool to build much more sophisticated SharePoint workflows, including custom interactive forms, interaction with multiple lists and libraries, and interaction with other applications or Line of Business systems. Leveraging this power and flexibility comes at a price: you must be proficient with the tool and have knowledge of .NET application development and deployment.

- **Third-Party Tools:** There are various third-party tools available for building SharePoint workflows. These tools combine the ease of use provided by SharePoint Designer with the power and flexibility of Visual Studio workflows.

I cover only the built-in workflows in this module. If you are interested in learning more about building workflows with SharePoint Designer, Visual Studio, or third-party tools, you should consider acquiring additional reference materials and training.

Creating and Modifying Project Site Columns

Each Project Site that the system creates for a project uses the *Microsoft Project Site* template that installs with Project Server 2010. Because every company, department, and team may follow different processes and therefore operate with different requirements, the features included in the built-in *Project Site* template may not meet all of your business process needs.

Fortunately, you can modify each Project Site to better map to your existing business processes. Your Project Server Administrator can also customize the site template that the system uses to generate new Project Sites, saving you the manual effort required to modify each newly provisioned Project Site. Project Server supports multiple site templates through the *Enterprise Project Type* feature.

Managing List and Library Metadata

SharePoint stores both structured content and unstructured content; SharePoint lists act as containers for structured content, and SharePoint libraries act as containers for unstructured content. A SharePoint list stores a collection of structured data items similar to a bulleted list of values, and a SharePoint library stores a collection of unstructured items in the form of files. Because the functionality and configuration options are so similar for lists and libraries, I primarily present instructions and examples for lists in this module, but the information I present typically applies to libraries as well, with only minor differences.

Regardless of whether it is in a list or library, each item stored in SharePoint has descriptive metadata to help classify the items for sorting, grouping, filtering, or otherwise locating specific items of interest. This is especially helpful when lists or libraries contain hundreds or thousands of items. SharePoint columns are the pieces of descriptive metadata that you can use to classify items in lists and libraries.

SharePoint columns are a fundamental building block for lists and libraries. In the event that your business process requires you to capture additional metadata to describe or categorize the items in a list or library, the system allows you to modify existing columns or create new custom columns in the Project Site for a selected project. Although Microsoft uses the word *column* to describe this feature, it is very similar to a custom *field* in Project Server.

Figure 13 - 2 displays a form for editing or logging a new project issue. You can see in this form that there are several metadata columns (*Title, Owner, Assigned To, Status*, etc.) that describe and classify the issue that you log in the *Issues* list:

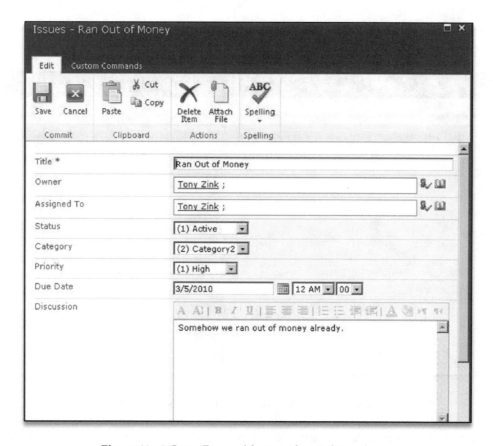

Figure 13 - 2: Issue Form with several metadata columns

Creating a New Column

To create a new column within a SharePoint list, navigate to the list, click the *List* ribbon tab, from the *Manage Views* section click the *Create Column* button as shown in Figure 13 - 3.

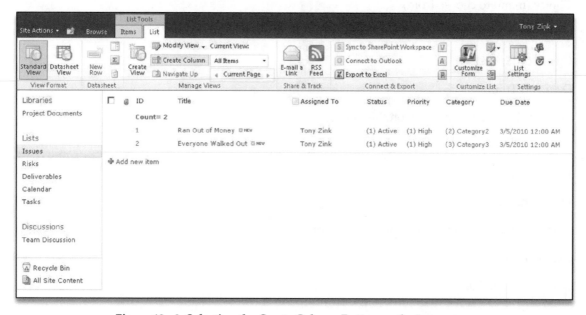

Figure 13 - 3: Selecting the Create Column Button on the Issues page

The system displays the *Create Column* form shown in Figure 13 - 4.

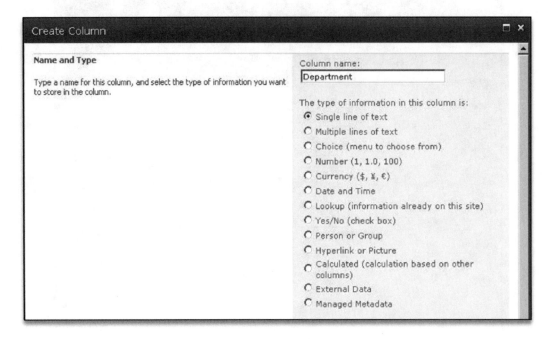

Figure 13 - 4: Create Column dialog for the Issues list

To create the new custom column, enter a descriptive name for the column in the *Column name* field, then select an option that describes the data type for the information in the column. The system offers a number of data types, including each of the following:

- Single line of text

- Multiple lines of text

- Choice (menu to choose from)

- Number (1, 1.0, 100)

- Currency ($, ¥, €)

- Date and Time

- Lookup (information already on this site)

- Yes/No (check box)

- Person or Group

- Hyperlink or Picture

- Calculated (calculation based on other columns)

- External Data

- Managed Metadata

When you select an option for the column data type, the system redraws the *Additional Column Settings* section of the form for the type of data you select. For example, Figure 13 - 5 shows the *Additional Column Settings* section after I selected the *Choice (menu to choose from)* option from the *The type of information in this column* section.

In the *Additional Column Settings* section of the form, select your options for the new custom column. For example, when using the *Choice* data type for the column, you must do the following:

- Enter an optional description for the column.

- Specify whether the field is required.

- Specify whether to enforce unique values.

- Enter the list of choices.

- Determine how the system displays the choices (as a pick list menu, as radio buttons, or as checkboxes).

- Determine whether to allow a user to append the list with additional choices.

- Specify a default value in the column.

- Determine whether to add the column to the default view.

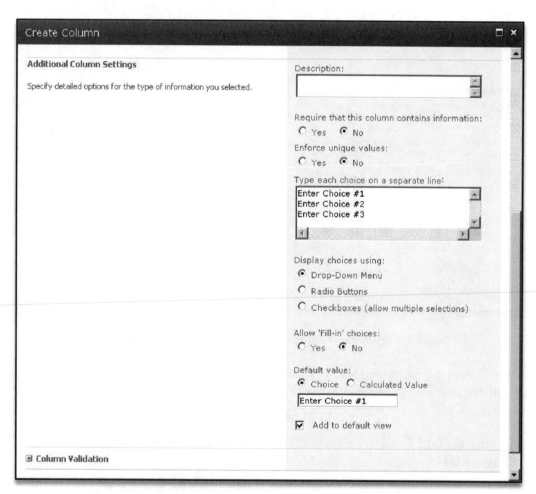

Figure 13 - 5: Additional Column Settings section for the Choice data type

Finally, there is an optional *Column Validation* section at the end of the *Create Column* form; you need to click the heading to expand this section. As shown in Figure 13 - 6, you may enter a validation formula that prevents people from entering incorrect data into the column. To enter a validation rule for data entered into this column, enter an expression into the *Formula* text box using similar syntax as you use for SharePoint calculated columns, based on Microsoft Excel formulas.

If a user enters data into the column that does not comply with the validation rule that you enter, SharePoint does not save the item and spawns an alert message to the user. You can determine this message when you enter a custom alert message into the *User message* text box.

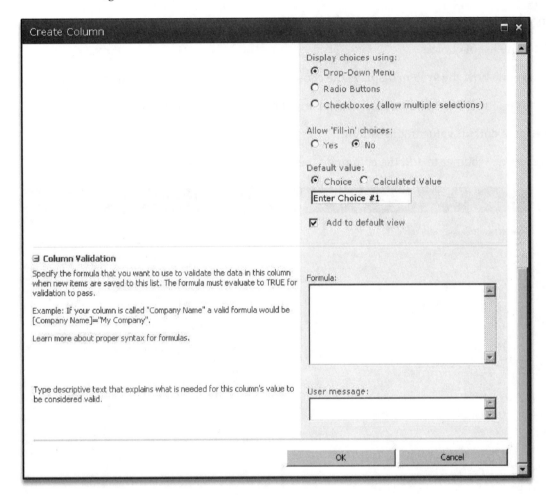

Figure 13 - 6: Column Validation options in the Create Column form

For example, one of your business process requirements states that the customer number for any item entered into the list must start with the text "Cust-". The validation formula for this scenario is:

$$=LEFT([Customer],5)="Cust-"$$

This formula tests that the left 5 characters of the data entered into the *Customer* column equals "Cust-". The user alert message for this scenario is:

You must begin the customer number with the text "Cust-".

It is unlikely that you would use this type of data validation with a *Choice (menu to choose from)* field, rather you would use this with a *Single line of text* field type.

Figure 13 - 7 shows a case of column validation failure; the user alert message appears below the *Customer* column:

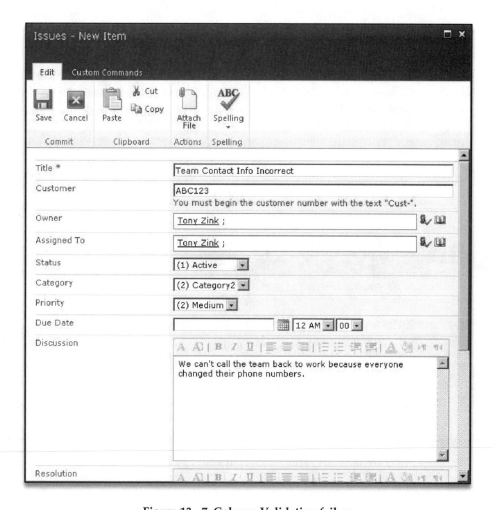

Figure 13 - 7: Column Validation failure

 A column validation formula cannot refer to any columns other than itself. For example, you cannot enter a column validation formula for the *Due Date* column that compares it against the *Created* column. You can accomplish this through list validation settings, which I cover later in this module.

Warning: Multiple columns within the same list can have unique column validation rules; be careful not to enter rules that conflict with one another, preventing people from entering any new items into the list.

After you configure all of the settings for the new custom column, click the *Save* button at the top of the form or the *OK* button at the bottom of the form. If you selected the *Add to default view* option, SharePoint adds the new custom column on the far right side of the default view for the selected list, the issues list in this example, as shown on the *Issues* page in Figure 13 - 8.

Figure 13 - 8: Department column added to the Issues page

When you add a new column to a list with existing records, and the column is not self-populating, then you must edit each of the items in the list to populate that new piece of metadata. For example, Figure 13 - 9 shows the new field at the bottom of the *Issues* edit form, along with the values available on the choice list.

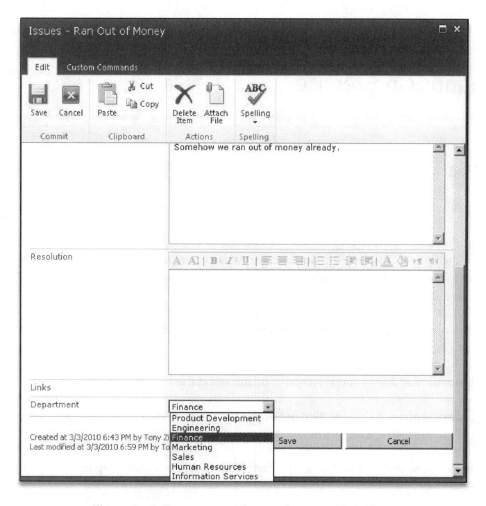

Figure 13 - 9: Department column at bottom of Issue form

A column that you create within a SharePoint list or library is available **only** to the list or library in which you create it. Later in this module, you learn how to create a *Site* column, which allows you to create a column that you can use in any list or library within that site.

MSProjectExperts recommends that if you have a generalized need for Project Site customizations, such as new or modified columns, your Project Server Administrator should modify the base template for Project Sites. If you are using the *Enterprise Project Types* feature in Project Server, each project type can utilize its own *Project Site* template that has unique customizations for that *Project Type*.

Hands On Exercise

Exercise 13-1

Create a new column for the Issues List.

1. In Project Web App, click the *Project Center* link in the *Projects* section of the *Quick Launch* menu. In the Project Center, select the header row for your Deploy Training Advisor Software project and from the *Navigate* section of the *Projects* ribbon click the *Project Site* button. The system launches a new window displaying your Project Site.

2. If necessary, expand your Project Site to full screen and click the *Issues* link in the *Lists* section of the *Quick Launch* menu.

3. From the *List Tools* context sensitive menu, select the *List* tab to display the *List* ribbon.

4. From the *Manage Views* section of the *List* ribbon, click the *Create Column* button. The system displays the *Create Column* form.

5. In the *Name and Type* section of the *Create Column* form, enter "Department" in the *Column Name* field.

6. In the *The type of information in this column is* selector, select the *Choice (menu to choose from)* option.

7. In the *Additional Column Settings* section of the *Create Column form*, enter a brief description in the *Description* field, accept the default *No* selection in the *Require that this column contains information* selector and the *Enforce unique values* selector. Enter the following choices in the *Type each choice on a separate line* field: Product Development, Engineering, Finance, Marketing, Sales, Human Resources, and Information Services.

8. Accept the default *Drop-Down Menu* option in the *Display choices using* selector and select the *No* option in the *Allow 'Fill-in' choices* selector. Leave the *Choice* option selected in the *Default value* selector and leave the *Add to default view* checkbox selected.

9. Click the *OK* button to save your new column. The system redisplays the *Issues* page of your Project Site. Notice that your new column displays on the far right.

Modifying or Deleting an Existing Column

To modify or delete an existing column within a SharePoint list, navigate to the list, click the *List* ribbon tab, then in the *Settings* section, click the *List Settings* button as shown in Figure 13 - 10.

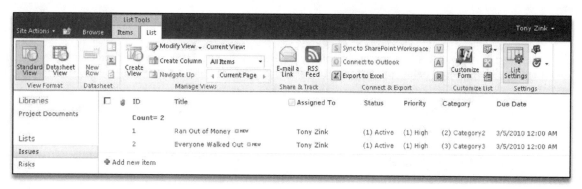

Figure 13 - 10: Selecting the List Settings Button on the Issues Page

The system displays the *List Settings* page shown in Figure 13 - 11, which contains links to all of the administrative configuration options for the list.

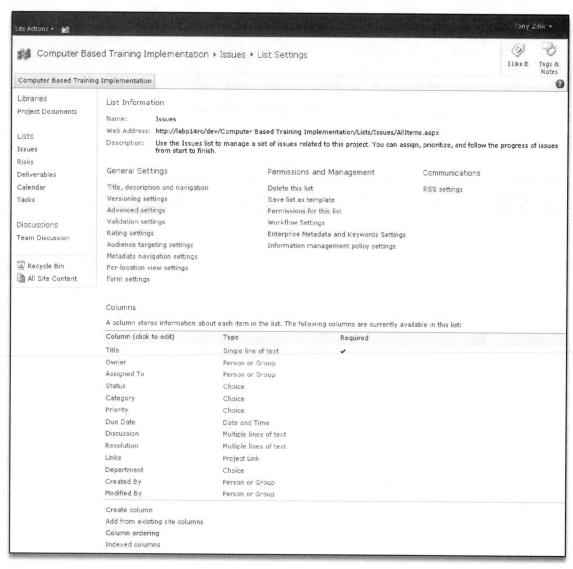

Figure 13 - 11: List Settings page for the Issues list

Notice that you can also create a new column by visiting the *List Settings* page, then clicking the *Create column* link, located below the list of columns in the *Columns* section of the page.

The *Columns* section of the *List Settings* page displays the entire list of columns for the selected list. To modify one of the existing columns, click on the name of the column in the list.

MSProjectExperts recommends that you modify the built-in *Category* column and enter choice values that are relevant to your organization's business processes.

The system displays the *Change Column* page as shown in Figure 13 - 12, which contains the same column configuration options that are available on the *Create Column* form shown in the previous section. When you finish modifying the behavior of the column, as shown in Figure 13 - 12 where I change the *Category* choice values, click the *OK* button at the bottom of the page. If you need to delete the column from the list, click the *Delete* button at the bottom of the page.

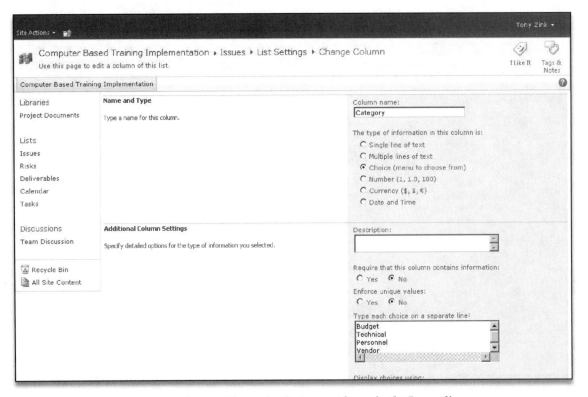

Figure 13 - 12: Modifying the Category column in the Issues list

> **Warning:** Do not delete any built-in columns from the *Risks, Issues, Deliverables* lists, or from the *Project Documents* library. Doing so will prevent Project Server from synchronizing properly with the Project Site.

Hands On Exercise

Exercise 13-2

Modify the Category column in the Issues list.

1. Return to the Project Site for your Deploy Training Advisor Software project. If necessary, navigate to the *Issues* list and select the *List* tab. From the *Settings* section of the *List* ribbon, click the *List Settings* button. The system displays the *List Settings* page.

2. Scroll down to the *Columns* section of the page and click on the *Category* column name. The system displays the *Change Column* page.

3. Scroll down to the *Additional Column Settings* section and locate the *Type each choice on a separate line* field as you did in the previous exercise.

4. Enter choice values that would be meaningful to your organization or enter the following generic values: Vendor, Quality, Cost, and Personnel. Click the *OK* button at the bottom of the page to save your changes. The system redisplays the *List Settings* page.

Creating a New Site Column

You may find that you need to add the same column to multiple lists and libraries within a Project Site; if you find yourself in this situation, then you can create a *Site* column centrally that acts as a reusable column throughout the entire site. You can then easily add this *Site* column to any list to capture metadata for classifying items within the site.

To create a new *Site* column, click the *Site Actions* menu from any page within the Project Site, then select the *Site Settings* item, as shown in Figure 13 - 13.

Figure 13 - 13: Opening the Site Actions menu

The system displays the *Site Settings* page as shown in Figure 13 - 14, which contains the links to all of the administrative configuration options for the Project Site available to project managers.

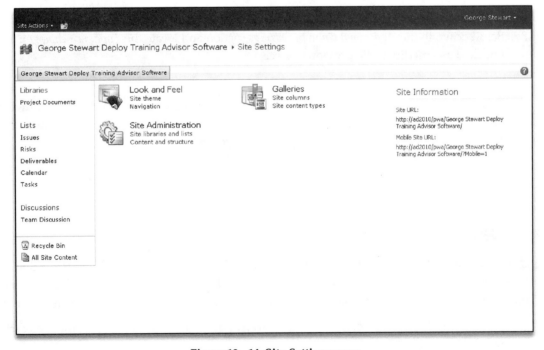

Figure 13 - 14: Site Settings page

In the *Galleries* section of the *Site Settings* page, click the *Site columns* link. The system displays the *Site Columns* page shown in Figure 13 - 15, which displays all of the *Site* columns for the Project Site.

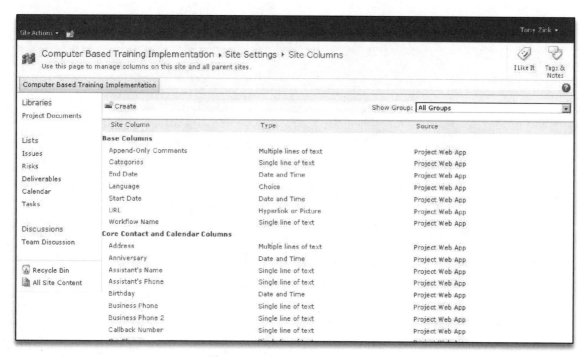

Figure 13 - 15: Site Columns page

Click the *Create* link, located near the top of the page, to create a new *Site* column. The system displays the *New Site Column* page shown if Figure 13 - 16. Here you see options very similar to those you saw when you created a new custom column for the issues list. The primary difference is the addition of the *Group* section of the page, which allows you to place your new *Site* column into a group when it appears on the *Site Columns* page. You may select from an existing group or create your own group as shown previously in Figure 13 - 15. When you finish specifying all of the options for the new *Site* column, click the *OK* button at the bottom of the page.

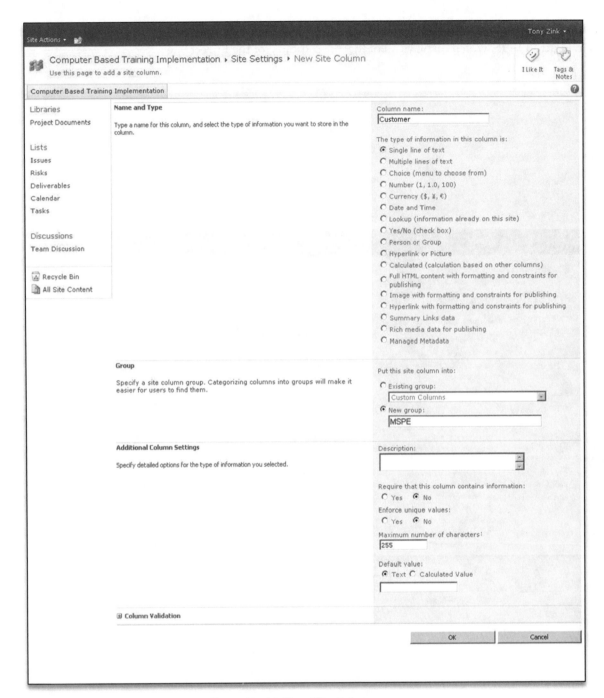

Figure 13 - 16: New Site Column page

 msProjectExperts recommends that you create a new group to categorize any new *Site* columns that you create in a Project Site. This will make it easier to separate and find your custom *Site* columns in the future.

The system displays the *Site Columns* page again, and you can scroll the page to find your new *Site* column listed in the group that you specified.

Modifying or Deleting an Existing Site Column

Although you cannot modify or delete any of the built-in *Site* columns from a Project Site, you may need to modify or delete a custom *Site* column that you previously created. To modify an existing custom column visit the *Site Columns* page in the Project Site as shown in the previous section. In the list, locate the *Site* column that you want to modify or delete, then click its name. The system displays the *Change Site Column* page shown in Figure 13 - 17, allowing you to make any modifications necessary to the selected *Site* column. Click the *OK* button at the bottom of the page, or if you need to delete the column entirely from the Project Site, click the *Delete* button at the bottom of the page.

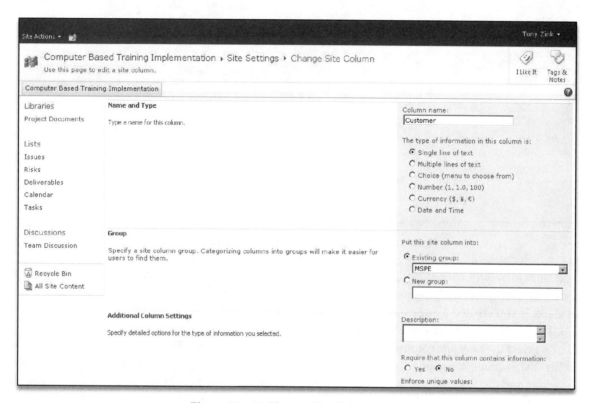

Figure 13 - 17: Change Site Column page

 Deleting a "parent" *Site* column from a Project Site will not remove any associated "child" columns from lists or libraries within the site. However, all "child" instances of the column become orphans and they will continue to function; but they will function independently of one another.

Adding a Site Column to a List

Once you create a new custom *Site* column for a Project Site, you can add that *Site* column to one or more lists or libraries within that site. To add a *Site* column to a list, navigate to the list, click the *List* tab, then click the *List Settings* button in the *Settings* section of the ribbon. On the *List Settings* page, scroll to the *Columns* section and click the *Add from existing site columns* link, located below the column listing. The system displays the *Add Columns from Site Columns* page, as shown in Figure 13 - 18.

639

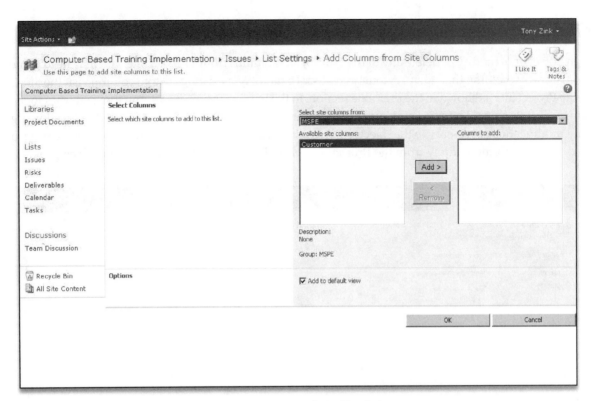

Figure 13 - 18: Add Columns from Site Columns page

The *Add Columns from Site Columns* page allows you to select your custom *Site* columns to add to the current list. The *Select site columns from* pick list displays all *Groups*; therefore all *Site* columns from all groups appear in the *Available site columns* list. If you created a *Site* column and placed it into a new custom group, select the group from the *Select site columns from* pick list. Your custom *Site* column appears in the *Available site columns* list, as shown previously in Figure 13 - 18. Select the new *Site* column and click the *Add* button. To add the *Site* column to the default view for the list, select the *Add to default view* option, then click the *OK* button at the bottom of the page. The system returns to the *List Settings* page and displays the newly-added *Site* column in the *Columns* section of the page. If you selected the *Add to default view* option, return to the list and view the *Site* column in the default view.

Removing a Site Column from a List

Removing a *Site* column from a list is similar to deleting a standard column. Navigate to the list, click the *List* tab, then click the *List Settings* button in the *Settings* section of the ribbon. On the *List Settings* page, scroll to the *Columns* section and click the name of the *Site* column that you need to remove.

The *List Settings* page does not indicate which columns were created from *Site* columns.

On the *Change Column* page, click the *Delete* button at the bottom of the page. A warning message appears, as shown in Figure 13 - 19; click the *OK* button to acknowledge the message and continue with the removal of the column.

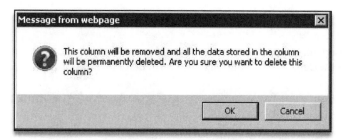

Figure 13 - 19: Delete column warning message

 Deleting a *Site* column from a list or library will not delete the *Site* column entirely from the Project Site. It will remain in any other lists or libraries that are using it.

Controlling Column Ordering in Forms

When you create new columns in a list or add columns from existing *Site* columns, the system adds new columns to the bottom of the *New Item* and *Edit Item* forms. Depending upon your business process requirements, you may need to change the order of the columns in these forms. To control column ordering in list and library forms, navigate to the list, click the *List* tab, then click the *List Settings* button in the *Settings* section of the ribbon. On the *List Settings* page, scroll to the *Columns* section and click the *Column ordering* link, located below the collection of columns. The system displays the *Change Field Order* page, as shown in Figure 13 - 20.

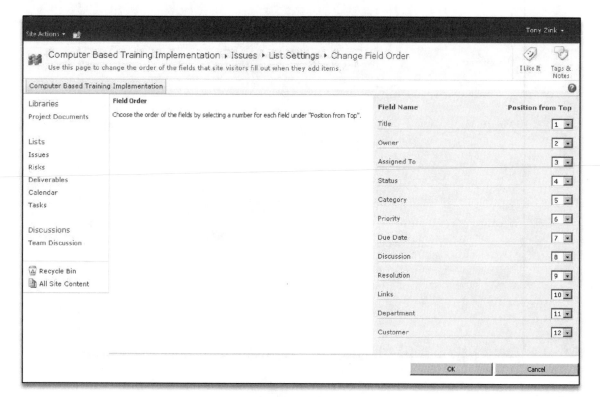

Figure 13 - 20: Change Field Order page

Don't be confused here! Even though this page refers to "*fields,*" you are working with SharePoint *columns* within the selected list or library. The term *Column* and the term *Field* are interchangeable.

The *Change Field Order* page displays all of the columns associated with the list in the order in which they displayed in the *New Item* and *Edit Item* forms. To change their order in the forms, select the appropriate numeric value next to each column; the system re-arranges the columns automatically to show the current order. Click the *OK* button at the bottom of the page to accept the column ordering.

Notice in Figure 13 - 21 that the columns displayed on the *New Item* form now reflect the new ordering selected on the *Change Field Order* page.

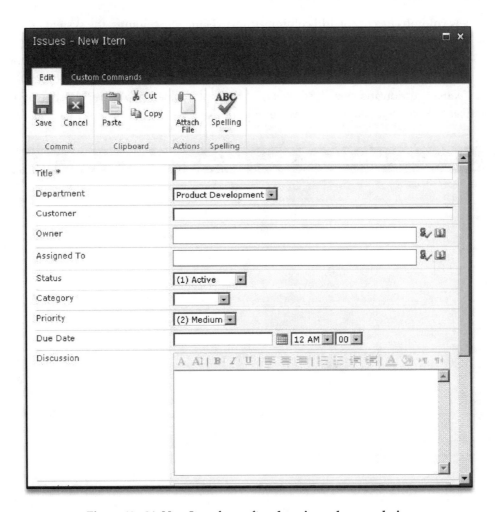

Figure 13 - 21: New Item form after changing column ordering

Hands On Exercise

Exercise 13-3

Change the order of the columns in the New and Edit forms.

1. Return to the *Issues* list in your Deploy Training Advisor Software Project Site.

2. Select the *List* tab and from the *Settings* section of the *List* ribbon, click the *List Settings* button. The system displays the *List Settings* page.

3. Scroll to the bottom of the *Columns* section and click on the *Column Ordering* link. The system displays the *Change Field Order* page.

4. At the bottom of the *Field Name* section, locate the *Department* field that you created in the previous exercise. Set the value for its *Position form the Top* selector to 2. Notice that the system immediately reorders the columns to reflect your change.

5. Click the *OK* button to save your ordering change. The system redisplays the *List Settings* page.

6. From the *Quick Launch* menu, select the *Issues* link. The system displays the *All Items* page.

7. Click the *Add new item* link and the system opens the *New Item* form. Notice that the *Department* field now occupies the second spot. From the *Commit* section of the *Edit* ribbon, click the *Cancel* button to close the form.

Managing List and Library Views

After people enter structured and unstructured content into a Project Site, SharePoint can display those content items in many ways, allowing project team members and stakeholders to review, analyze, and interact with the data in meaningful ways. Think of a view of a SharePoint list or library as an interactive report.

As I mentioned previously in this module, the system creates each new Project Site from a site template; this site template includes not only several lists and libraries in which to store project data, deliverables, and artifacts, but it also includes several built-in views for each list and library. In the event that your business process requires you to interact with the data differently, the system allows you to modify existing views or create new custom views in the Project Site for a selected project.

Figure 13 - 22 displays a view of the *Issues* list for a project; notice that the view displays a listing of issue items in table format, including a collection of columns that hold additional information describing each issue item.

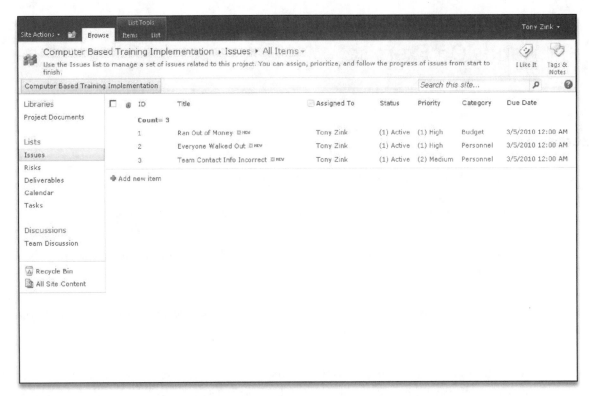

Figure 13 - 22: View of the Issues list

When customizing an existing view or creating a new view for a SharePoint list or library, you need to ask yourself or your stakeholders the following questions:

- Which items do you need to see? Should you see all items in the list or library, or only specific items of interest?

- When displaying items in a view, which columns of metadata do you need to see for each item, and in which order should the view display them?

- When displaying items in a view, should the view sort the rows into a specific order?

- When displaying items in a view, should the view create groupings of similar items?

The answers to these questions are useful when you define list and library views in a Project Site.

Modifying or Deleting an Existing View

To modify an existing view in a list, navigate to the list, click the *List* tab, in the *Manage Views* section of the ribbon, select the desired view from the *Current View* pick list, and then click the *Modify View* button. The system displays the *Edit View* page shown in Figure 13 - 23. Select the appropriate options as described below and then click the *OK* button.

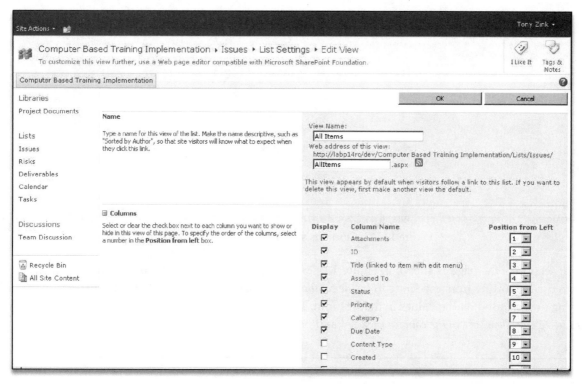

Figure 13 - 23: Edit View page

 You can also access the *Edit View* page by navigating to the list or library, clicking the *List* tab, and clicking the *List Settings* button in the *Settings* section of the ribbon. Once on the *List Settings* page, scroll to the *Views* section of the page and click on the name of the view.

In the *Name* section of the page as shown in Figure 13 - 24, rename the view or change the unique URL of the view as necessary. Enter a new name into the *View Name* text box, or enter a new URL ending into the *Web address of this view* text box.

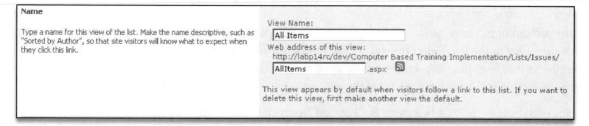

Figure 13 - 24: Name section of the Edit View page

In the *Columns* section of the page shown in Figure 13 - 25, change which columns appear in the view and the ordering of those columns. Select your desired columns by selecting the *Display* option next to each and then adjust the ordering of the selected columns by adjusting the *Position from Left* values next to each column.

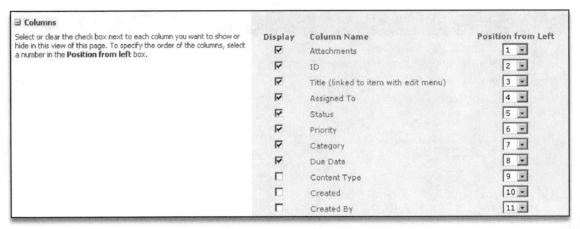

Figure 13 - 25: Columns section of the Edit View page

In the *Sort* section of the page as shown in Figure 13 - 26, change the sort order of the item rows in the view. Select a column to use for sorting from the *First sort by the column* pick list, then select whether the rows sort in ascending or descending order, based on the values in that column. To sort the rows based on multiple columns, select a second column using the *Then sort by the column* pick list and pick a sort order.

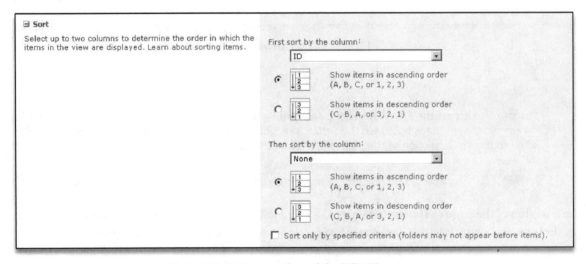

Figure 13 - 26: Sort section of the Edit View page

In the *Filter* section of the page as shown in Figure 13 - 27, display only specific items of interest in the view, rather than all of the items in the list. Select the *Show items only when the following is true* option and then configure one or more conditions that each item must meet before appearing in the view. To configure a conditional test, select a column from the first pick list, select a test from the second pick list, and enter a value in the text box.

For example, to show items that belong to the Human Resources Department, you may create a condition such as:

Column	Test	Value
Department	is equal to	Human Resources

To configure multiple conditional tests, select the appropriate *And / Or* option after the first conditional test, then configure a second conditional test using the second set of options in the *Filter* section. To configure more than two conditional tests, click the *Show More Columns* link.

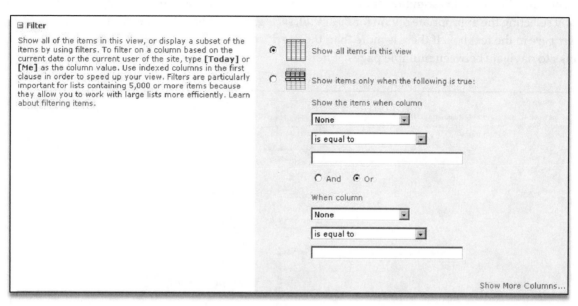

Figure 13 - 27: Filter section of the Edit View page

In the *Inline Editing* section of the page shown in Figure 13 - 28, you can enable quick inline editing in the view. Selecting the *Allow inline editing* option adds an editing button next to each row in the view and allows editing of the item on that row without leaving the page.

Figure 13 - 28: Inline Editing section of the Edit View page

In the *Tabular View* section of the page shown in Figure 13 - 29, you can allow people to select multiple item rows in the view for certain operations such as multi-item deletion. Select the *Allow individual item checkboxes* option to allow multi-item selection in the view.

Figure 13 - 29: Tabular View section of the Edit View page

647

In the *Group By* section of the page shown in Figure 13 - 30, you can rearrange the rows in the view to group similar items together under common headings. Select a column from the *First group by the column* pick list, then select whether the group headings sort in ascending or descending order. To create a second level of nested groupings within the first level of groupings, select another column using the *Then group by the column* pick list, then select whether the nested group headings sort in ascending or descending order. Select whether the groupings appear collapsed or expanded by selecting the appropriate option for *By default, show groupings*. Finally, enter a value for *Number of groups to display per page* in the text box. If there is more than the specified number of groupings in the view, SharePoint displays links to navigate between multiple pages of items.

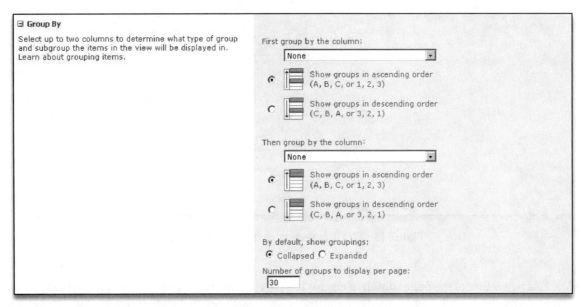

Figure 13 - 30: Group By section of the Edit View page

In the *Totals* section of the page shown in Figure 13 - 31, you can display totals at the bottom of any column in the view. The page displays a listing of all of the columns selected to appear in the view, as well as the option to display a total for each column. Select the appropriate option for each listed column.

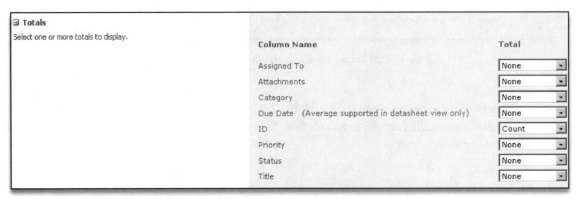

Figure 13 - 31: Totals section of the Edit View page

In the *Style* section of the page shown in Figure 13 - 32, you control the formatting of the items displayed in the view. Select the desired formatting option from the *View Style* pick list.

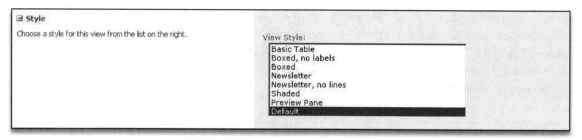

Figure 13 - 32: Style section of the Edit View page

In the *Folders* section of the page shown in Figure 13 - 33, you control whether folders appear in the view. Select the *Show items inside folders* option or the *Show all items without folders* option, depending on your requirements.

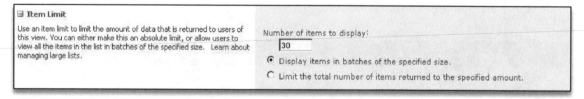

Figure 13 - 33: Folders section of the Edit View page

In the *Item Limit* section of the page shown in Figure 13 - 34, you control how many item rows appear on each page in the view. Enter a number into the *Number of items to display* text box, then select the *Display items in batches of the specified size* option or the *Limit the total number of items returned to the specified amount* option, depending on your requirements.

Figure 13 - 34: Item Limit section of the Edit View page

 A large number of items displayed in a view could have adverse effects on system performance.

In the *Mobile* section of the page shown in Figure 13 - 35, you can control mobile options for the view. Select the *Enable this view for mobile access* option to format the view optimally for mobile devices with small screens such as PDAs or mobile phones. Select the *Make this view the default view for mobile access* option to configure the view as the default mobile view. To limit the number of items displayed in the mobile view, enter a number in the *Number of items to display in list view web part for this view* text box.

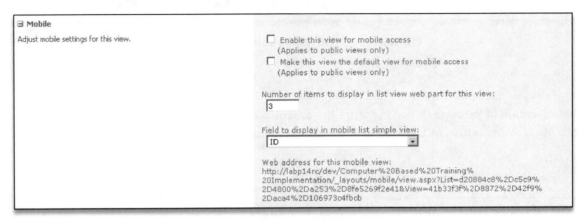

Figure 13 - 35: Mobile section of the Edit View page

 MSProjectExperts recommends that if you have a generalized need for Project Site customizations, such as new or modified views, your Project Server Administrator modify the base template for Project Sites. If you are using the *Enterprise Project Types* feature in Project Server, each project type can utilize its own *Project Site* template that has unique customizations for that Project Type.

Creating a New Standard View

A standard view is a basic SharePoint list view that displays items in table format with rows and columns. Figure 13 - 36 shows an example of a standard view.

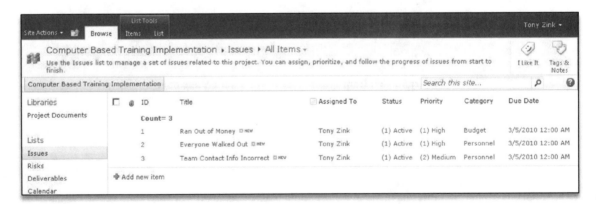

Figure 13 - 36: Example of a Standard view

To create a new standard view for a list, navigate to the list, click the *List* tab, then click the *Create View* button in the *Manage Views* section of the ribbon. In the *Choose a view format* section of the *Create View* page shown in Figure 13 - 37, click the *Standard View* option.

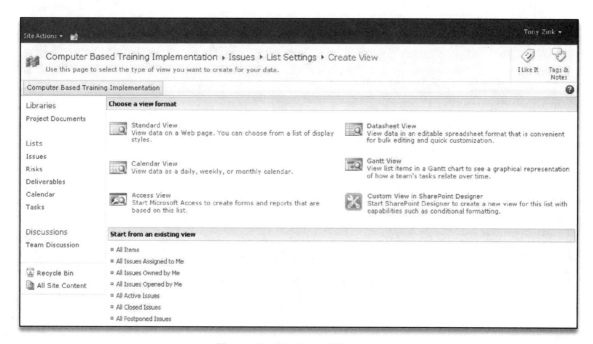

Figure 13 - 37: Create View page

The system displays the *Create View* page shown in Figure 13 - 38, which is very similar to the *Edit View* page shown previously. Enter a name for the new view in the *View Name* text box, and then select the *Make this the default view* option if you want this view to be the default view for everyone who visits the list. Next in the *View Audience* selector for the new view; to create a view that is visible only to you, select the *Create a Personal View* option, or to create a view that is visible to everyone, select the *Create a Public View* option. Select the other options on the page as described in the previous section, then click the *OK* button.

You can set only a Public View as the default view for a list or library.

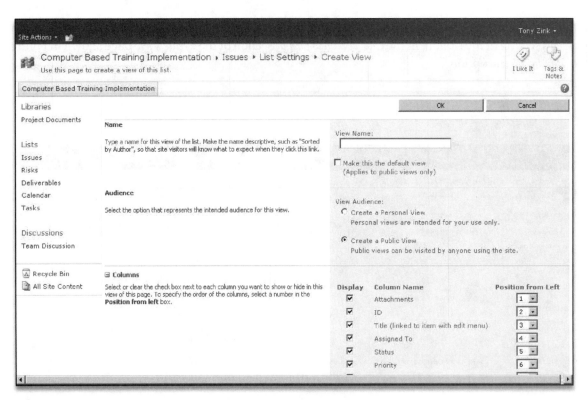

Figure 13 - 38: Create View page

You can also access the *Create View* page by navigating to the list or library, clicking the *List* or *Library* tab, and clicking the *List* or *Library Settings* button in the *Settings* section of the ribbon. Once on the *List* or *Library Settings* page, scroll to the *Views* section of the page and click the *Create view* link.

Creating a New Calendar View

A *Calendar* view is a SharePoint list view that displays items in monthly, weekly, or daily calendar format. Figure 13 - 39 shows an example of a *Calendar* view.

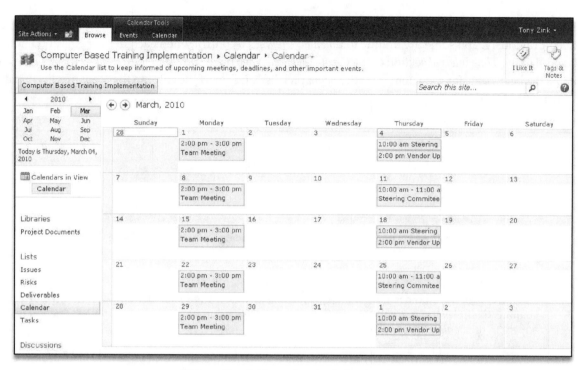

Figure 13 - 39: Example of a Calendar view

 Calendar views are most useful for viewing lists of tasks, events, or other date-driven items.

To create a new *Calendar* view for a list, navigate to the list, click the *List* tab, then click the *Create View* button in the *Manage Views* section of the ribbon. In the *Choose a view format* section of the *Create View* page, click the *Calendar View* option. The system displays the *Create Calendar View* page, shown in Figure 13 - 40. Select the appropriate options as described below and then click the *OK* button.

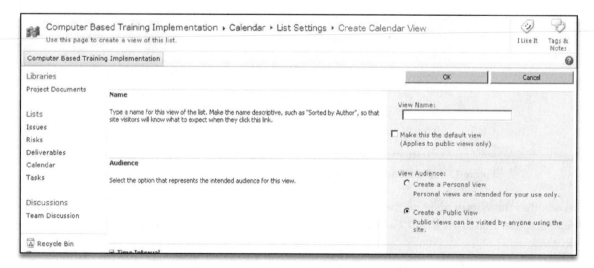

Figure 13 - 40: Create Calendar View page

The *Create Calendar View* page has several sections and options; some are similar to those for creating a standard view as described previously, and some are unique to *Calendar* views. To control when each item begins and ends on the timeline, scroll to the *Time Interval* section of the *Create Calendar View* page shown in Figure 13 - 41. Select the column that contains the begin date for each item from the *Begin* pick list, and select the column that contains the end date for each item from the *End* pick list.

Figure 13 - 41: Time Interval section of the Create Calendar View page

You **must** select a column in both the *Begin* and *End* pick lists. The system uses the dates in the selected columns to display items graphically on the calendar. Only columns that contain date information will appear in the *Begin* and *End* pick lists.

To control which columns of data appear for each item in the *Calendar* view, scroll to the *Calendar Columns* section of the *Create Calendar View* page shown in Figure 13 - 42. Because you can display a *Calendar* view in daily, weekly, or monthly format, you can configure a different column to appear as the title for each item in each of these types of views. To specify the title that appears for each item in the monthly *Calendar* view, select the appropriate column from the *Month View Title* pick list. To specify the title that appears for each item in the weekly *Calendar* view, select the appropriate column from the *Week View Title* pick list. To specify the title that appears for each item in the daily *Calendar* view, select the appropriate column from the *Day View Title* pick list. Optionally, select a sub-heading to appear for each item in the weekly *Calendar* view or the daily *Calendar* view by selecting the appropriate column in the *Week View Sub Heading* pick list and the *Day View Sub Heading* pick list.

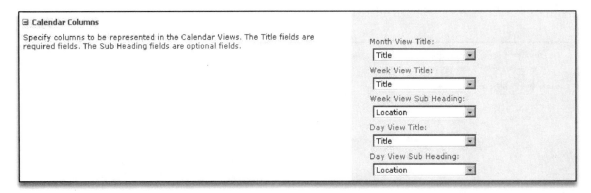

Figure 13 - 42: Calendar Columns section of the Create Calendar View page

To control whether the system displays the default *Calendar* view in daily, weekly, or monthly calendar format, scroll to the *Default Scope* section of the *Create Calendar View* page shown in Figure 13 - 43 and select the appropriate *Default scope* option.

Figure 13 - 43: Default Scope section of the Create Calendar View page

Creating a New Access View

An *Access* view allows you to create a report or an interactive form in Microsoft Access by creating a local Access database on your PC that is connected to the SharePoint list; you can then create custom reports or forms that draw data from the local database. The system also transfers any changes that you make to the local data to the original SharePoint list in the Project Site. Figure 13 - 44 shows an example of a report originated through an *Access* view, and Figure 13 - 45 shows an example of a data entry form originated through an *Access* view.

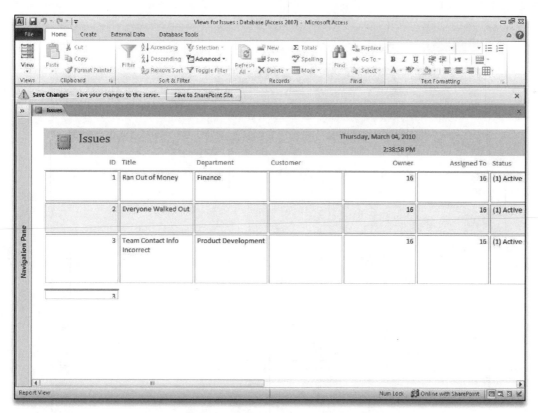

Figure 13 - 44: Example of an Access report

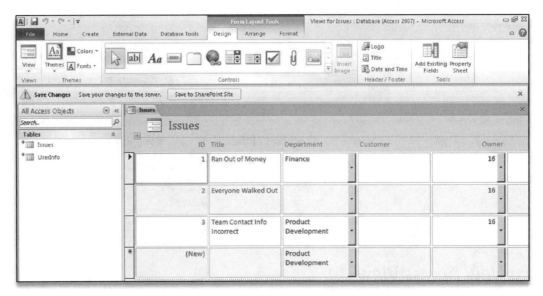

Figure 13 - 45: Example of an Access data entry form

To create a new *Access* view for a list, navigate to the list, click the *List* tab, then click the *Create View* button in the *Manage Views* section of the ribbon. In the *Choose a view format* section of the *Create View* page, click the *Access View* option. The system launches Microsoft Access on your desktop, which offers to create and save a new local database file, as shown in Figure 13 - 46; browse to a desired file location, enter a name for the new Access database file, and click the *Save* button.

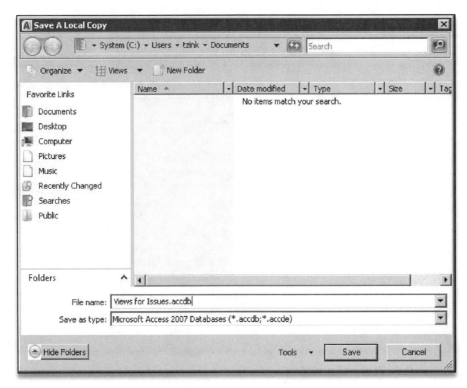

Figure 13 - 46: Microsoft Access Save a Local Copy dialog

You must have Microsoft Access 2010 installed on your computer in order to create an *Access* view.

Microsoft Access displays the *Create Access View* dialog shown in Figure 13 - 47 that presents options for creating a new report or interactive form based on the data from the Project Site. To create a new report, select the *Report* option, then click the *OK* button.

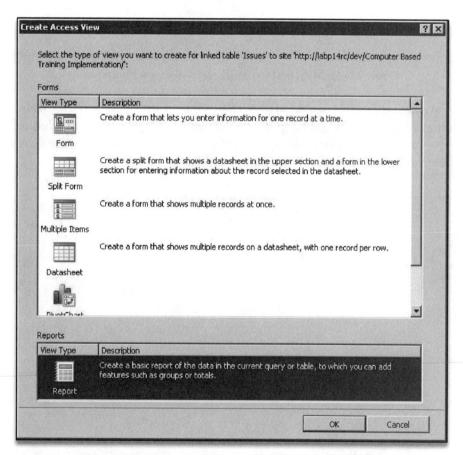

Figure 13 - 47: Microsoft Access Create Access View dialog

Microsoft Access displays the report designer, including live data from the Project Site that the system copied to the local database file, as shown in Figure 13 - 48.

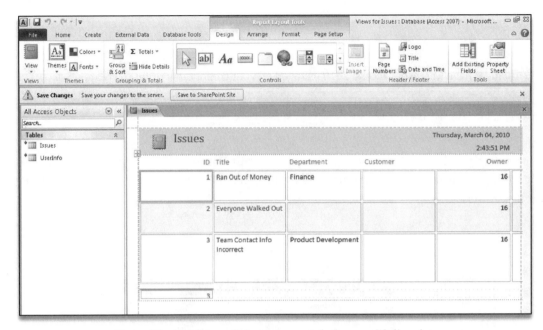

Figure 13 - 48: Microsoft Access report designer with live data

To create a new interactive form instead of a report, select one of the *Form* options in the *Create Access View* dialog, then click the *OK* button. Figure 13 - 49 shows a split form created in Microsoft Access, including live data from the Project Site that the system copied to the local database file. The system also transfers any data changes that you make locally through the form to the original SharePoint list in the Project Site.

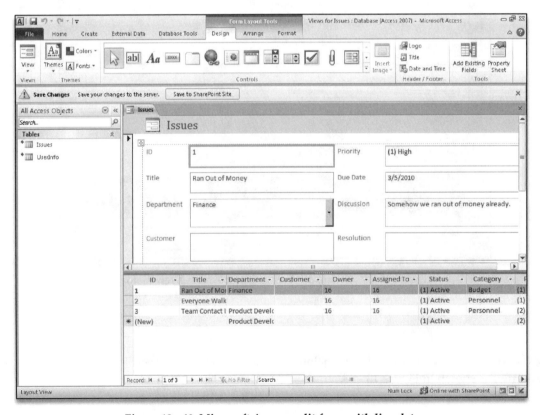

Figure 13 - 49: Microsoft Access split form with live data

Creating a New Datasheet View

A *Datasheet* view is an interactive SharePoint view that displays items in table format with rows and columns and allows in-page editing of the data, including the addition and deletion of items, as if you are working in an embedded spreadsheet. Figure 13 - 50 shows an example of a *Datasheet* view.

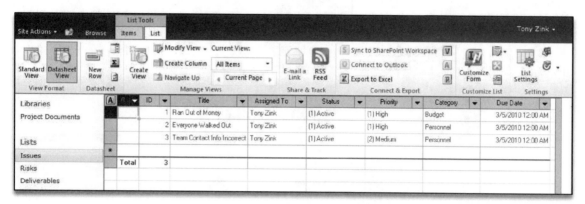

Figure 13 - 50: Example of a Datasheet view

To create a new *Datasheet* view for a list, navigate to the list, click the *List* tab, then click the *Create View* button in the *Manage Views* section of the ribbon. In the *Choose a view format* section of the *Create View* page, click the *Datasheet View* option. The system displays the *Create Datasheet View* page, as shown in Figure 13 - 51. The sections and options available to configure the view are nearly identical to those available for creating a standard view described previously. Select the appropriate options for the view and then click the *OK* button.

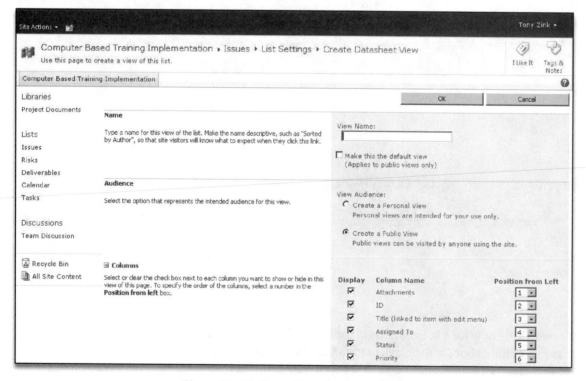

Figure 13 - 51: Create Datasheet View page

Creating a New Gantt View

A *Gantt* view is a SharePoint list view that displays items in Gantt chart format. Figure 13 - 52 shows an example of a *Gantt* view.

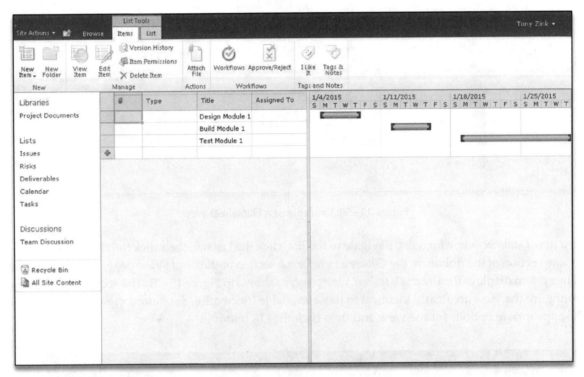

Figure 13 - 52: Example of a Gantt view

 Gantt views are most useful for viewing lists of tasks, events, or other date-driven items.

To create a new *Gantt* view for a list, navigate to the list, click the *List* tab, then click the *Create View* button in the *Manage Views* section of the ribbon. In the *Choose a view format* section of the *Create View* page, click the *Gantt View* option. The system displays the *Create Gantt View* page, as shown in Figure 13 - 53. Select the appropriate options as described below and then click the *OK* button.

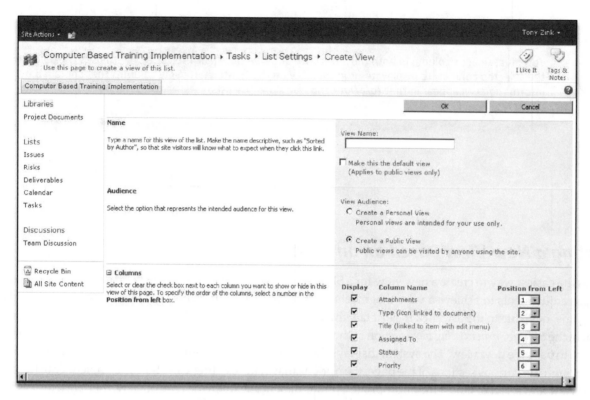

Figure 13 - 53: Create Gantt View page

The *Create Gantt View* page has several sections and options; some are similar to those for creating a standard view as described previously, and some are unique to *Gantt* views. To control which columns represent the title for each Gantt bar, the date when each item begins and ends on the timeline, as well as the progress and predecessors for each Gantt bar, scroll to the *Gantt Columns* section of the *Create Gantt View* page shown in Figure 13 - 54. Select the column that contains the title for each Gantt bar from the *Title* pick list, select the column that contains the begin date for each item from the *Start Date* pick list, and select the column that contains the end date for each item from the *Due Date* pick list. Optionally select the column that contains the progress value for each Gantt bar from the *Percent Complete* pick list, and optionally select the column that contains the predecessor information for each Gantt bar from the *Predecessors* pick list.

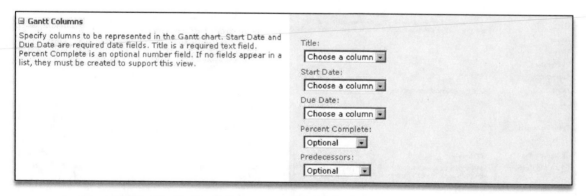

Figure 13 - 54: Gantt Columns section of the Create Gantt View page

You **must** select a column in both the *Start Date* and *Due Date* pick lists. The system uses the dates in the selected columns to display items graphically on the Gantt chart. Only columns that contain date information will appear in the *Start Date* and *Due Date* pick lists.

Creating a New View Based on an Existing View

Perhaps the easiest way to create a new view for a SharePoint list is by making a copy of an existing view, then making slight adjustments to achieve a view that meets your business requirements. To create a new view based on an existing one, navigate to the list, click the *List* tab, then click the *Create View* button in the *Manage Views* section of the ribbon. In the *Start from an existing view* section of the *Create View* page, click the name of the existing view upon which you want to base the new view. The system displays the *Create View* page, shown in Figure 13 - 55. Notice that if you scroll through the various sections of the page, the options match the existing view that you copied. Enter a name for the new view and select or adjust the appropriate options depending upon the type of view, then click the *OK* button.

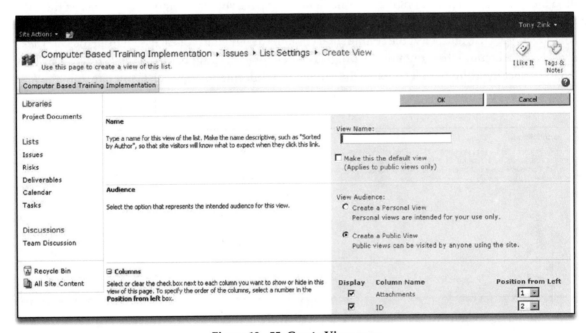

Figure 13 - 55: Create View page

Hands On Exercise

Exercise 13-4

Create a new list view from an existing view.

1. If necessary, return to the homepage of the *Issues* list for your Deploy Training Advisor Software project. Select the *List* tab to display the *List* ribbon

2. From the *Manage Views* section of the *List* ribbon, click on the *Create View* button. The system displays the *Create View* page.

3. From the *Start from an existing view* section, click on the *All Active Issues* item. The system displays the second *Create View* page.

4. In the *Name* section, enter a name for your view in the *View Name* field: **Active Issues by Category**

5. In the *Audience* section below the *View Audience* selector, leave the default *Create a Public View* option selected.

6. Scroll to the *Sort* section and select the *Due Date* item from the *First sort by the column* pick list. Leave the *Then sort by the column* pick list set to "None."

7. Scroll to the *Filter* section and notice that the *Show items only when the following is true* option is selected because this is the condition set in the original view that you copied.

8. Scroll to and expand the *Group by* section of the page. From the *First group by the column* pick list, select the *Category* item. For the *By default, show groupings* selector, select the *Expanded* option and leave the other settings at their default values.

9. Scroll to and expand the *Style* section, and select the *Newsletter* item from the *View Style* pick list. Click the *OK* button at the bottom of the page to save your new view.

10. Return to your *Issues* list, and select the *List* tab and apply your new view by selecting it in the *Current View* pick list.

Modifying List and Library General Settings

SharePoint organizes structured and unstructured content into list and library containers within a Project Site. You learned how to work with columns and views for these repositories, but there are additional ways you can control the behavior of lists and libraries affecting all of the items stored in them. To view and adjust the configuration settings for a list, navigate to the list, click the *List* tab, then click the *List Settings* button in the *Settings* section of the ribbon shown in Figure 13 - 56. I cover many of these topics but not all of them because you must have Administrator rights to fully leverage some of these. Some of these features require additional administrative setup and configuration.

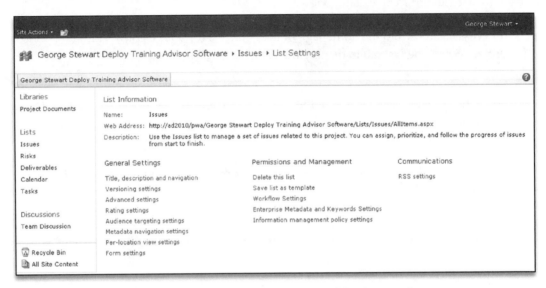

Figure 13 - 56: List Settings page General Settings section

Specifying Title, Description, and Navigation Settings

To change the name or description for a list or to control whether the list is easily accessible from the *Quick Launch* menu, click the *Title, description and navigation* link on the *List Settings* page, located below the *General Settings* heading. The system displays the *General Settings* page shown in Figure 13 - 57.

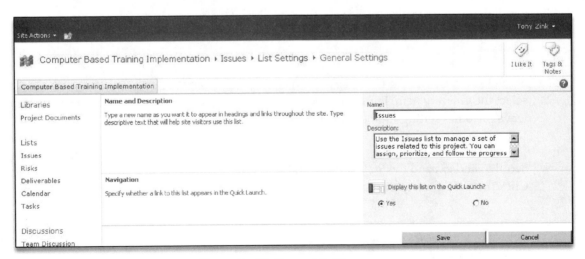

Figure 13 - 57: General Settings page

To change the name of the list, update the contents of the *Name* text box. To change the description of the list, update the contents of the *Description* text box. To control the *Quick Launch* navigation to the list, select the appropriate option for *Display this list on the Quick Launch*. Select the *Yes* option to display the list on the *Quick Launch* menu, or select the *No* option to prevent the list from appearing on the menu.

Removing the Quick Launch navigation to a list **does not** remove the list itself from the Project Site; there are more indirect ways to navigate to a list if it does not appear on the Quick Launch menu.

MsProjectExperts recommends that you rename the *Calendar* and *Tasks* lists that are available in the default Project Site, as these names can imply to some people that they contain project task information. Consider renaming the *Calendar* list to *Event Calendar* or similar, and consider renaming the *Tasks* list to *Action Items* or similar.

Specifying List Versioning Settings

For many organizations, the ability to automate version control for issues, risks and documents is a great advantage. You can take advantage of this feature by selecting the *Versioning Settings* link on the *List Settings* page, located below the *General Settings* heading. The system displays the *Versioning Settings* page shown in Figure 13 - 58.

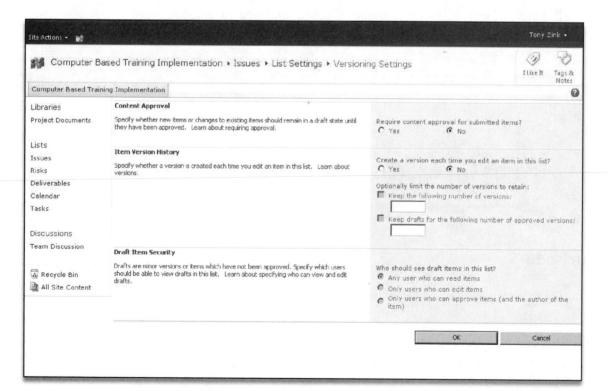

Figure 13 - 58: Versioning Settings page

In the *Content Approval* section of the page, you can select whether to require a designated person or group approve items before they become publicly visible in the list. Enabling content approval places a hold on all item submissions until someone with the appropriate permissions approves them. Submitted content items are not visible to the rest of the project team until approved. Select the *Yes* option to enable content approval for the list, or select the *No* option to disable content approval. When you select to enable the *Content Approval* option, the system enables the *Draft Item Security* section options at the bottom of the page where you can determine who can see the items in the list pending approval.

In the *Item Version History* section of the page, you can enable item version control. When you enable item versioning the system creates a new copy of an item each time someone edits the item. Select the *Yes* option for the *Create a version each time you edit an item in this list?* option to enable item versioning for the list, or select the *No* option to disable versioning. When you enable this option, you should set a version retention policy to limit the number of copies held by the system to avoid overusing your data storage capacity. This consideration is more important for libraries than for lists. Select the *Keep the following number of versions* option and then enter a number of versions into the text box. When you enable both content approval and version control, you can also specify the retention policy for draft versions in the *Keep drafts for the following number of approved versions* option.

MSProjectExperts recommends that you **do not** enable content approval in most cases for lists and libraries; doing so can impose an unnecessary process bottleneck, because project team members will not be able to see items such as new risks, issues, and project documents until they are approved.

MSProjectExperts recommends that you enable item version control and set a reasonable retention policy in lists and libraries; doing so can provide valuable historical information for artifacts stored in a Project Site.

Hands On Exercise

Exercise 13-5

Enable version control on an Issues list.

1. If necessary, navigate back to the *Issues* list for your Deploy Training Advisor Software project and select the *List* tab. From the *Settings* section of the *List* ribbon, click the *List Settings* button. The system displays the *List Settings* page.

2. In the *General Settings* section of the page, click the *Versioning Settings* link. The system displays the *Versioning Settings* page for the *Issues* list.

3. Leave the *Content Approval* option set to *No*.

4. In the *Item Version History* section, select the *Yes* option for the *Create a version each time you edit an item in this list* selector.

5. Select the checkbox for the *Optionally limit the number of versions to retain* selector and enter *25* in the *Keep the following number of versions* field.

6. Click the *OK* button to save your configuration and return to the *List Settings* page.

Specifying List Advanced Settings

To change several other behaviors for items stored in the list, such as item-level permissions, attachments, and search visibility, click the *Advanced Settings* link on the *List Settings* page, located below the *General Settings* heading. The system displays the *Advanced Settings* page shown in Figure 13 - 59.

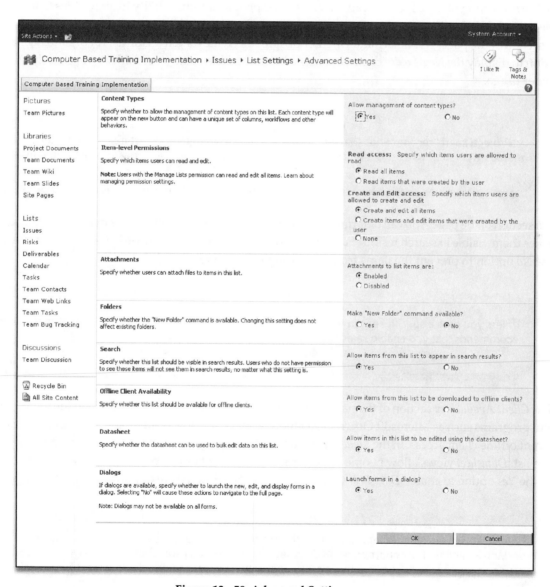

Figure 13 - 59: Advanced Settings page

Working with the *Content Types* section and other options on this page is out of the scope of this book; however there are some settings on this page of interest to a project manager who wants to employ advanced management techniques for a Project Site. In the *Item-level Permissions* section of the page, for instance, you can select options to control which items users can read and which items users can edit in the list. For *Read access*, there are two available options to control which items people can read: *Read all items* or *Read items that were created by the user*. For *Create and Edit access*, there are three available options you can use to control which items people are allowed to edit: *Create and edit all items*, *Create items and edit items that were created by the user*, or *None*.

MSProjectExperts recommends that you select *Read all items* for *Read access* and *Create and edit all items* for *Create and Edit access (Default values)* for *Issue* lists.

In the *Attachments* section of the page, you can select whether people have the ability to attach files to items stored in the list. Select the *Enabled* option to enable file attachments, or select the *Disabled* option to prevent file attachments. In the *Folders* section of the page, you determine whether people can create folders in the list for organizing items. Select the *Yes* option to display the *New Folder* command in the list and enable creation of folders, or select the *No* option to prevent folder usage.

MSProjectExperts recommends that you prevent people from organizing list items into folders. Attaching metadata columns to a list is a much better way to classify, organize, and locate items stored in a list.

In the *Search* section of the page, you can determine whether the SharePoint search engine indexes content items in the list and makes them visible in search results. Select the *Yes* option to allow items in the list to appear in search results, or select the *No* option to prevent the items from appearing in search results.

Unless you have a specific reason to exclude items from appearing in search results, MSProjectExperts recommends that you enable searching within a list.

In the *Offline Client Availability* section of the page, you determine whether users can download the items in the list to offline client programs such as Microsoft Office. Select the *Yes* option to allow offline client access, or select the *No* option to prevent offline client access. In the *Datasheet* section of the page, you select whether users can apply *Datasheet* views to the list. *Datasheet* views allow people to perform bulk editing of multiple items in a spreadsheet-like interface. Select the *Yes* option to enable *Datasheet* views for the list, or select the *No* option to prevent *Datasheet* views.

Datasheet views in SharePoint require that the proper Micrsoft Office components are installed on the desktop PC and that the appropriate ActiveX security permissions are enabled in the web browser. If your company has restrictions in these areas, then you may want to disable datasheet functionality.

In the *Dialogs* section of the page, you can set an option to disable the system from launching dialog forms for adding and editing items. If you disable dialogs, the system navigates to an entirely separate page each time people create new items, edit existing items, or display existing items in the list. Select the *Yes* option to enable form dialog functionality, or select the *No* option to disable dialog functionality. In most cases, you should leave the default *Yes* option selected.

Specifying Rating Settings

To enable 5-star content item ratings in the list, click the *Validation settings* link on the *List Settings* page, located below the *General Settings* heading. The system displays the *Rating Settings* page shown in Figure 13 - 60.

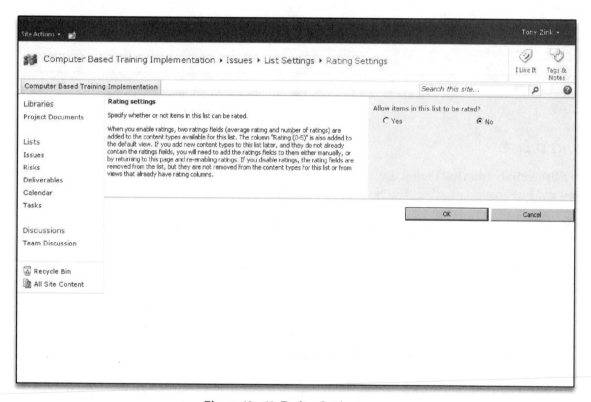

Figure 13 - 60: Rating Settings page

As Figure 13 - 61 shows, if you enable ratings in the list, the system adds two columns to the list, *Rating (0-5)* and *Number of Ratings*, as displayed on the *List Settings* page. SharePoint uses these two columns to store the average rating for each item in the list and the number of people who have rated each item.

Figure 13 - 61: Rating (0-5) and Number of Ratings columns on the List Settings page

If you enable ratings in the list, the system also adds the *Rating (0-5)* column to the default list view, as shown in Figure 13 - 62.

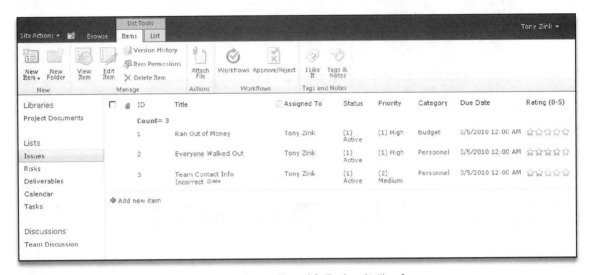

Figure 13 - 62: Issues list with Rating (0-5) column

Deleting a List

To delete a list entirely from the Project Site, click the *Delete this list* link on the *List Settings* page, located below the *Permissions and Management* heading. The system displays the confirmation dialog shown in Figure 13 - 63.

Figure 13 - 63: Warning dialog when deleting a list

Click the *OK* button to confirm the list deletion. The system then deletes the list, places it into the site recycle bin, and displays the *All Site Content* page.

Specifying RSS Settings

All SharePoint lists are capable of generating an RSS feed, which is an XML-based data feed that people or other systems can subscribe to and consume. An RSS feed for a SharePoint list contains the latest items added to that list.

To configure the RSS settings for a list, click the *RSS settings* link on the *List Settings* page, located below the *Communications* heading. The system displays the *Modify RSS Settings* page shown in Figure 13 - 64. The *Modify RSS Settings* page contains four sections: *List RSS, RSS Channel Information, Columns,* and *Item Limit*.

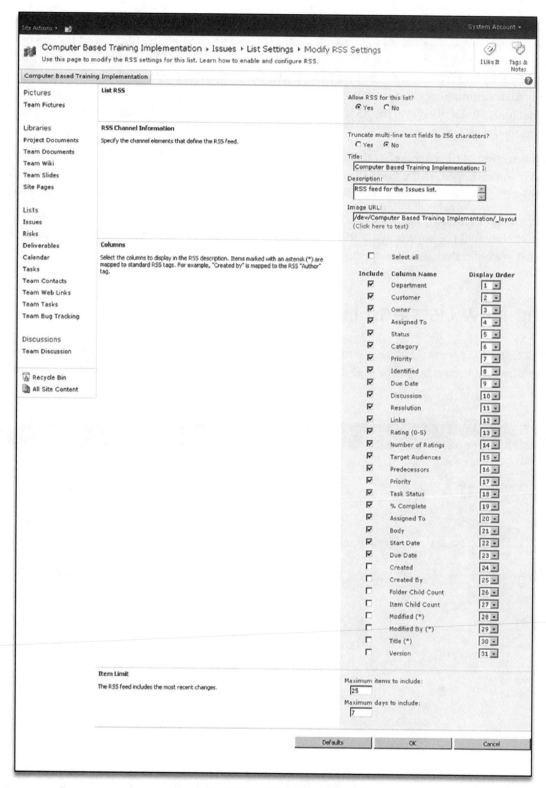

Figure 13 - 64: Modify RSS Settings page

In the *List RSS* section of the page, select whether the system should generate an RSS data feed for the list. Select the *Yes* option to enable the RSS feed, or select the *No* option to disable the RSS feed.

In the *RSS Channel Information* section of the page, specify general information about the list that the system embeds in the header of the XML feed. To prevent long text fields from appearing in the RSS feed, select the *Yes* option for the *Truncate multi-line text fields to 256 characters?* selector; to allow long text fields into the feed, select the *No* option. Enter a title for the RSS feed into the *Title* text box, and enter a brief description for the feed into the *Description* text box. Notice that the system automatically pre-populates this information. Each RSS feed can contain an image, such as a company logo, that is also embedded into the XML data feed. To specify a location for a custom image, enter the URL of the image into the *Image URL* text box.

In the *Columns* section of the page, select the *Include* option for each column of data to appear in the RSS data feed. Any selected columns appear in the body of each item in the RSS feed. To control the display order for the selected columns, adjust the *Display Order* pick list value next to each selected column that will appear in the feed.

In the *Item Limit* section of the page, enter an item limit in the *Maximum items to include* text box; if there are more items in the list, they will not appear in the RSS feed. Enter a time limit into the *Maximum days to include* text box; if items in the list are older than the time specified, they will not appear in the feed.

Creating New Lists and Libraries

Default Project Sites have several built-in list and library repositories for project team collaboration. To view a listing of the repositories for a Project Site, click the *Site Actions* menu and select the *View All Site Content* option, as shown in Figure 13 - 65.

Figure 13 - 65: Selecting View All Site Content from the Site Actions menu

The system displays the *All Site Content* page shown in Figure 13 - 66.

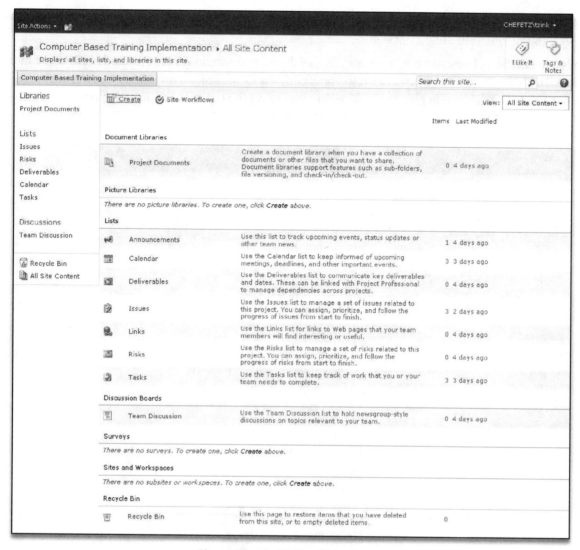

Figure 13 - 66: All Site Content page

The default Project Site includes the following content repositories:

- Project Documents

- Announcements

- Calendar

- Deliverables

- Issues

- Links

- Risks

- Tasks

- Team Discussion

Although Project Sites have several built-in lists and libraries for project team collaboration, you may need to add a new list or library in an individual Project Site.

In the following sections, I describe how to create some of the more common types of list and library repositories in a Project Site. To create a new repository in a Project Site, click the *Create* link on the *All Site Content* page. The system displays the *Create* page shown in Figure 13 - 67 where you select the type of repository to create.

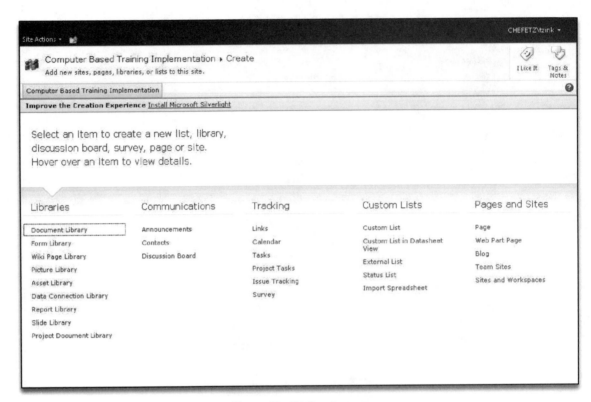

Figure 13 - 67: Create page

 As a shortcut to the *Create* page, you may also select *More Options* from the SharePoint *Site Actions* menu.

Creating a New Contacts List

A SharePoint contacts list is a repository for storing contact information to share with the Project Team. To create a new contacts list in a Project Site, navigate to the *Create* page in the Project Site and click the *Contacts* link, located below the *Communications* heading. The system displays the *New* page shown in Figure 13 - 68.

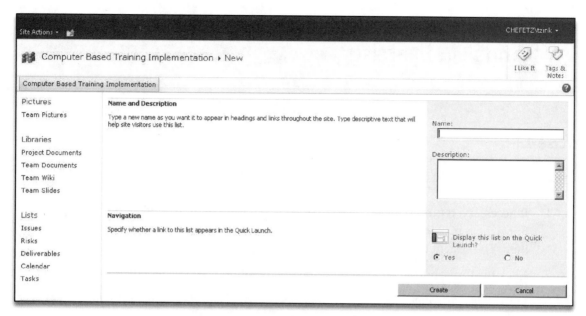

Figure 13 - 68: New contacts list page

In the *Name and Description* section of the page, enter a name for the new list into the *Name* text box, and enter a brief description for the new list into the *Description* text box. In the *Navigation* section of the page, select whether the new list appears in the Project Site *Quick Launch* menu. Select the *Yes* option to display a link to the new list in the *Quick Launch* menu, or select the *No* option to hide the list from the menu. Figure 13 - 69 shows a newly-created contacts list with contacts added.

Figure 13 - 69: New contacts list with contacts added

MsProjectExperts recommends that you visit the *List Settings* page and review the configuration of the new list and make adjustments based on your business requirements.

Hands On Exercise

Exercise 13-6

Create a new contacts list.

1. If necessary, return to the home page of your Deploy Training Advisor Software project. Click the *Site Actions* pick list in the upper left hand corner of the screen and select the *View all Site Content* item. The system displays the *All Site Content* page.

2. Click the *Create* button on the left just below the ribbon. The system displays the *Create* page.

3. In the *Communications* section of the page, select the *Contacts* link. The system displays the *New* page.

4. Enter "Team Contacts" in the *Name* field, enter an optional description and leave the *Yes* option selected in the *Navigation* section. Click the *Create* button to create your new contact list. The system displays the homepage for your new list with the *List* ribbon displayed.

5. Enter several contacts in your new list.

Creating a New Links List

A SharePoint links list is a repository for storing web links to share with the Project Team. To create a new links list in a Project Site, navigate to the *Create* page in the Project Site as described previously and click the *Links* link, located below the *Tracking* heading. The system displays the *New* page shown in Figure 13 - 70.

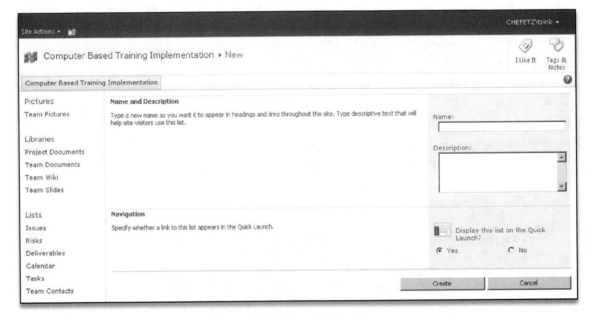

Figure 13 - 70: New links list page

In the *Name and Description* section of the page, enter a name for the new list into the *Name* text box, and enter a brief description for the new list into the *Description* text box. In the *Navigation* section of the page, select whether the new list appears in the Project Site *Quick Launch* menu. Select the *Yes* option to display a link to the new list in the *Quick Launch* menu, or select the *No* option to hide the list from the menu. Figure 13 - 71 shows a newly-created links list with web links added.

Figure 13 - 71: New links list with web links added

  MSProjectExperts recommends that you visit the *List Settings* page and review the configuration of the new list and make adjustments based on your business requirements.

Creating a New Project Tasks List

A SharePoint project tasks list is a repository for storing tasks and displaying them in Gantt Chart format to share with the Project Team. To create a new project tasks list in a Project Site, navigate to the *Create* page in the Project Site and click the *Links* link, located below the *Tracking* heading. The system displays the *New* page shown in Figure 13 - 72.

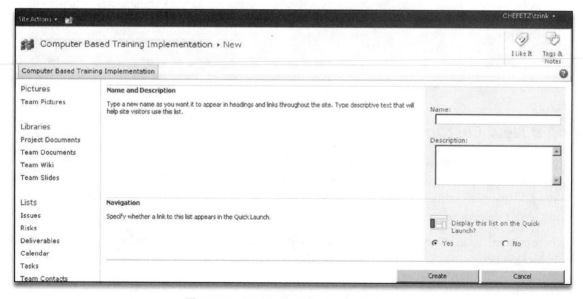

Figure 13 - 72: New project tasks list page

In the *Name and Description* section of the page, enter a name for the new list into the *Name* text box, and enter a brief description for the new list into the *Description* text box. In the *Navigation* section of the page, select whether the new list appears in the Project Site *Quick Launch* menu. Select the *Yes* option to display a link to the new list in the *Quick Launch* menu, or select the *No* option to hide the list from the menu. Figure 13 - 73 shows a newly-created project tasks list with a *Gantt* view and tasks added.

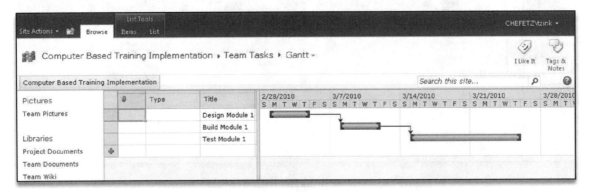

Figure 13 - 73: New project tasks list Gantt view with tasks added

MsProjectExperts recommends that you visit the *List Settings* page and review the configuration of the new list and make adjustments based on your business requirements.

As with a standard SharePoint tasks list, a Project tasks list is not intended to track work that is managed by Microsoft Project Server. Use tasks lists and Project tasks lists to track and manage action items, punch list items, and other items that are too small in scope or schedule to track in a Microsoft Project schedule.

Creating a New Custom List

At times, you may need to create a custom repository in a Project Site that does not fit into any of the provided template categories. For example, a project team may need a list for tracking directional decisions that may impede project progress if not addressed in a timely manner, or the team may need a list for tracking bugs discovered in a new software product under development.

To create a new custom list in a Project Site manually, navigate to the *Create* page in the Project Site and click the *Custom List* link, located below the *Custom Lists* heading. The system displays the *New* page shown in Figure 13 - 74.

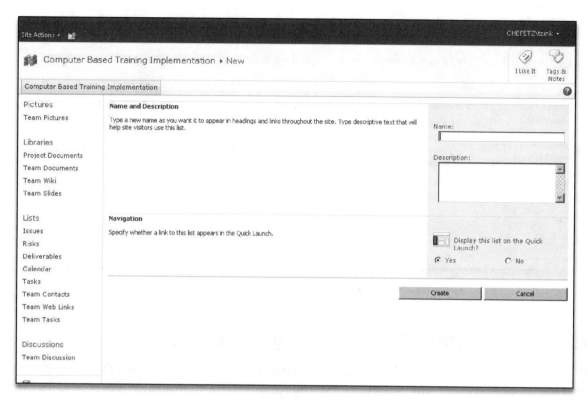

Figure 13 - 74: New custom list page

In the *Name and Description* section of the page, enter a name for the new list into the *Name* text box, and enter a brief description for the new list into the *Description* text box. In the *Navigation* section of the page, select whether the new list appears in the Project Site *Quick Launch* menu. Select the *Yes* option to display a link to the new list in the *Quick Launch* menu, or select the *No* option to hide the list from the menu.

Figure 13 - 75 shows a newly-created custom list. Depending upon your list requirements, you may need to add columns, enable version control, create views, and so forth. Click the *List Settings* button to navigate to the *List Settings* page and further configure the new custom list.

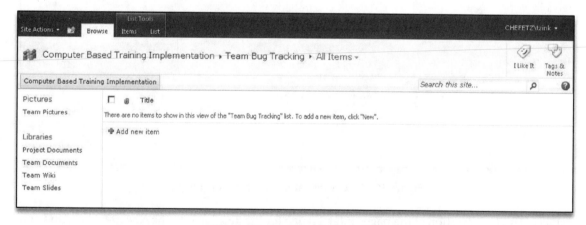

Figure 13 - 75: New Custom List

Figure 13 - 76 shows an example of a fully configured custom list for tracking software bugs discovered during the product development process.

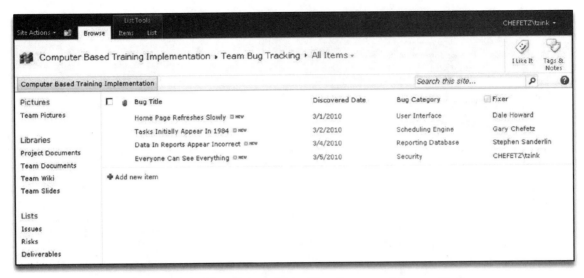

Figure 13 - 76: New Custom List with columns and items added

Creating a New Custom List by Importing a Spreadsheet

You can convert a Microsoft Excel spreadsheet into a SharePoint list in a Project Site to share the data with members of the project team. To create a new custom list in a Project Site by importing a spreadsheet, navigate to the *Create* page in the Project Site and click the *Import Spreadsheet* link, located below the *Custom Lists* heading. The system displays the *New* page shown in Figure 13 - 77.

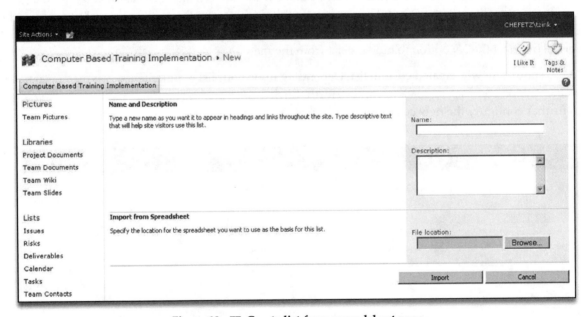

Figure 13 - 77: Create list from spreadsheet page

In the *Name and Description* section of the page, enter a name for the new list into the *Name* text box, and enter a brief description for the new list into the *Description* text box. In the *Import from Spreadsheet* section of the page, click the *Browse* button to browse for the Microsoft Excel spreadsheet on your local hard drive. The system displays the *Import* dialog, shown in Figure 13 - 78. Select the appropriate options in the dialog to select the data from the spreadsheet, and click the *Import* button.

Figure 13 - 78: Import dialog

 Warning: The selected data from the spreadsheet needs to include a header row, because SharePoint uses this information to create new columns in the list to hold the imported data.

The system creates a new custom list and imports the data from the spreadsheet into the list as new items, as shown in Figure 13 - 79.

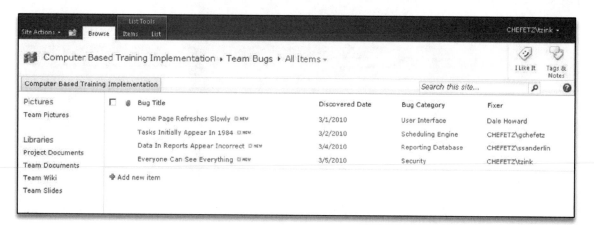

Figure 13 - 79: New custom list with columns and items added

 msProjectExperts recommends that you visit the *List Settings* page and review the configuration of the new list and make adjustments based on your business requirements.

Warning: Although SharePoint automatically creates new columns in the list to hold the imported data, you should visit the *List Settings* page, inspect the newly-created columns, and verify that they are configured correctly.

Warning: When using this method to create a custom SharePoint list, the system **does not** automatically create a link to the new list on the Quick Launch menu. To access the new list, you may visit the *All Site Content* page. You may then navigate to *List Settings* page and add a link to the Quick Launch menu.

Creating a New Document Library

A SharePoint document library is a repository for storing documents and other types of files to share with the Project Team. To create a new document library in a Project Site, navigate to the *Create* page in the Project Site as described previously, and click the *Document Library* link, located below the *Libraries* heading. The system displays the *New* page shown in Figure 13 - 80.

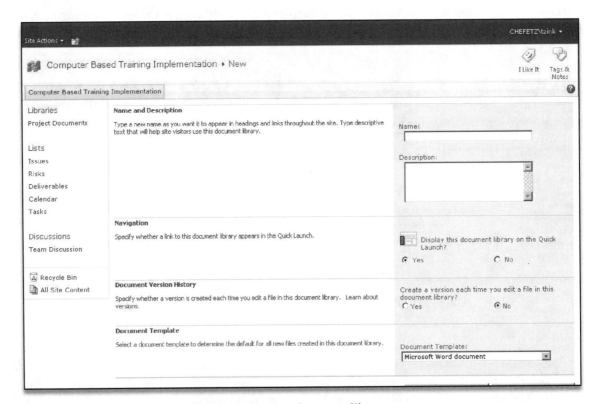

Figure 13 - 80: New document library page

The *New* page contains four sections: *Name and Description*, *Navigation*, *Document Version History*, and *Document Template*. In the *Name and Description* section of the page, enter a name for the new document library into the *Name* text box, and enter a brief description for the new library into the *Description* text box. In the *Navigation* section of the page, select whether the new library will appear in the Project Site *Quick Launch* menu. Select the *Yes* option to display a link to the new library in the *Quick Launch* menu, or select the *No* option to hide the library from the menu.

In the *Document Version History* section of the page, you can select whether to enable version control in the new library. Select the *Yes* option to enable versioning in the new library, or select the *No* option to disable versioning. In the *Document Template* section of the page, select a default file type that the system uses when people click the *New* button. Select one of the types from the *Document Template* pick list and click the *Create* button. Figure 13 - 81 shows a newly-created document library with documents added.

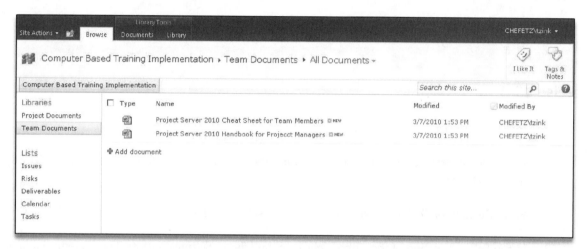

Figure 13 - 81: New Document Library with documents added

MSProjectExperts recommends that you visit the *Library Settings* page and review the configuration of the new library and make adjustments based on your business requirements.

Hands On Exercise

Exercise 13-7

Create a new document library.

1. From the *Site Actions* menu, select the *View all Site Content* item. The system displays the *All Site Content* page.

2. Click the *Create* button in the upper left below the ribbon. From the *Libraries* section on the left, select the *Document Library* link. The system displays the *New* page for a document library.

3. In the *Name and Description* section, enter "Project Templates" in the *Name* field. Enter an optional description for your library such as "Contains project deliverable templates."

4. In the *Navigation* section, leave the default *Yes* option selected.

5. In the *Document Version History* section, select the *Yes* option for the *Create a version each time you edit a file in this document library* selector.

6. Leave the default value for the *Document Template* field.

7. Click the *Create* button to create your new document library. The system displays your new library homepage.

Exercise 13-8

Change the settings on a document library.

1. From the *Libraries* section of the *Quick Launch* menu, select the *Project Documents* link. The system displays the *Project Documents* library.

2. From the *Library Tools* context sensitive menu, select the *Library* tab to reveal the *Library* ribbon.

3. In the *Settings* section of the ribbon, click on the *Library Settings* button. The system displays the *Library Settings* page.

4. In the *General Settings* section, click the *Versioning Settings* link. The system opens the *Versioning Settings* page.

5. In the *Document Version History* section, select the *Create major versions* option. Notice that for document libraries, you can also opt to create minor versions as well as major versions

6. In this same section, select the *Optionally limit the number of versions to retain* option and enter *15* in the *Keep the following number of major versions* field.

7. Scroll to the *Require Check Out* section and select the *Yes* option for the *Require documents to be checked out before they can be edited* selection.

8. Click the *OK* button to save your changes to the Project Documents library.

Creating a New Wiki Page Library

A SharePoint wiki page library is a set of connected and easily editable web pages to which the Project Team can contribute. To create a new wiki page library in a Project Site, navigate to the *Create* page in the Project Site and click the *Wiki Page Library* link, located below the *Libraries* heading. The system displays the *New* page shown in Figure 13-82.

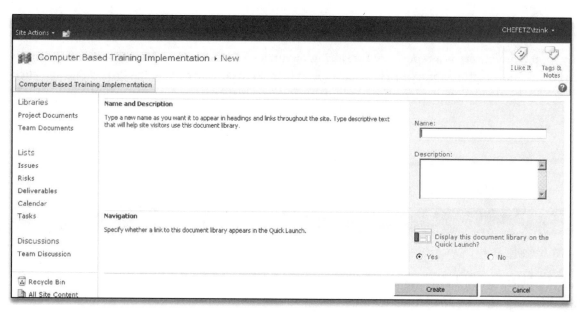

Figure 13 - 82: New wiki library page

In the *Name and Description* section of the page, enter a name for the new library into the *Name* text box, and enter a brief description for the new library into the *Description* text box. In the *Navigation* section of the page, select whether the new library appears in the Project Site *Quick Launch* menu. Select the *Yes* option to display a link to the new library in the *Quick Launch* menu, or select the *No* option to hide the library from the menu. Figure 13 - 83 shows a newly-created wiki library home page.

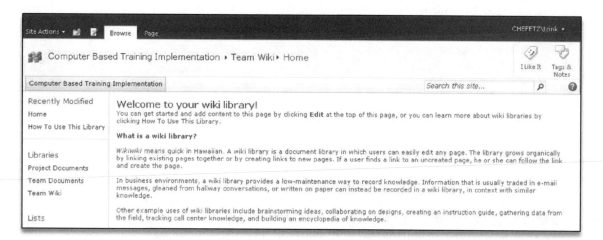

Figure 13 - 83: New Wiki Library home page

 MSProjectExperts recommends that you visit the *Library Settings* page and review the configuration of the new library and make adjustments based on your business requirements.

Creating a New Picture Library

A SharePoint picture library is a repository for storing pictures and other types of images to share with the Project Team. To create a new picture library in a Project Site, navigate to the *Create* page in the Project Site and click the *Picture Library* link, located below the *Libraries* heading. The system displays the *New* page shown in Figure 13 - 84.

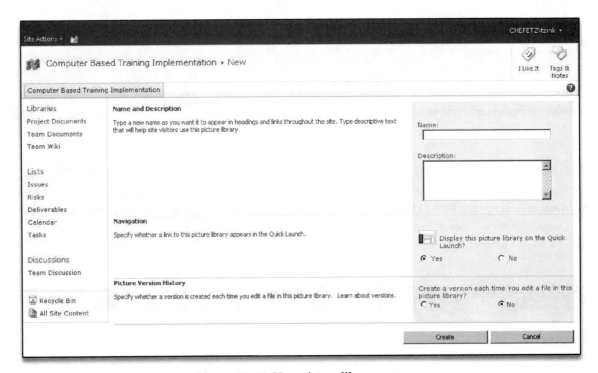

Figure 13 - 84: New picture library page

In the *Name and Description* section of the page, enter a name for the new library into the *Name* text box, and enter a brief description for the new library into the *Description* text box. In the *Navigation* section of the page, select whether the new library appears in the Project Site *Quick Launch* menu. Select the *Yes* option to display a link to the new library in the *Quick Launch* menu, or select the *No* option to hide the library from the menu. In the *Picture Version History* section of the page, select whether to enable version control in the new library. Select the *Yes* option to enable versioning in the new library, or select the *No* option to disable versioning. Figure 13 - 85 shows a newly-created picture library with pictures added.

Figure 13 - 85: New picture library with pictures added

 msProjectExperts recommends that you visit the *Library Settings* page and review the configuration of the new library and make adjustments based on your business requirements.

Creating a New Slide Library

A SharePoint slide library is a repository for storing Microsoft PowerPoint slides to share with the Project Team. To create a new slide library in a Project Site, navigate to the *Create* page in the Project Site and click the *Slide Library* link, located below the *Libraries* heading. The system displays the *New* page shown in Figure 13 - 86.

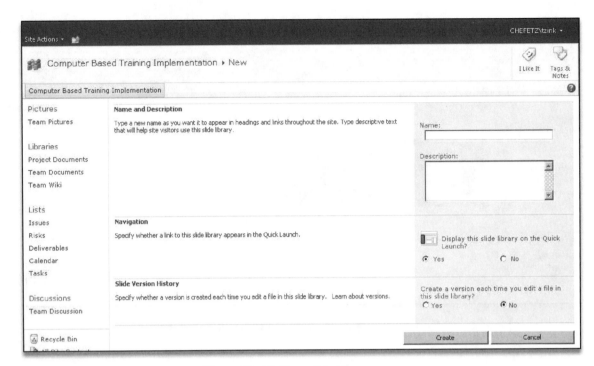

Figure 13 - 86: New slide library page

In the *Name and Description* section of the page, enter a name for the new library into the *Name* text box, and enter a brief description for the new library into the *Description* text box. In the *Navigation* section of the page, select whether the new library appears in the Project Site *Quick Launch* menu. Select the *Yes* option to display a link to the new library in the *Quick Launch* menu, or select the *No* option to hide the library from the menu. In the *Slide Version History* section of the page, select whether to enable version control in the new library. Select the *Yes* option to enable versioning in the new library, or select the *No* option to disable versioning. Figure 13 - 87 shows a newly-created slide library with Microsoft PowerPoint slides added.

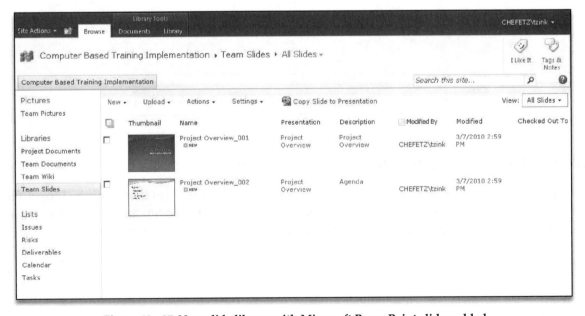

Figure 13 - 87: New slide library with Microsoft PowerPoint slides added

MSProjectExperts recommends that you visit the *Library Settings* page and review the configuration of the new library and make adjustments based on your business requirements.

Creating and Editing Pages

In addition to the list and library repositories that the system creates for storing and managing content within a Project Site, SharePoint also provides *pages* for presenting that content in an organized and meaningful manner to Project Site visitors. Each Project Site contains a single *Home* page that can act as a central landing page or dashboard, and you can create additional pages based on your business process needs.

SharePoint provides a user-friendly, web browser-based interface for creating and editing pages, and new pages reside in libraries, much like other types of unstructured SharePoint content. The exception is the *Home* page, which does not reside in a library.

Editing the Project Site Home Page

The Project Site *Home* page is a web part page, which allows placement of one or more web parts onto the page, organized into one or more web part zones. A web part is a page component that allows you to add content or functionality to a page; a web part zone is an area on the page where you may place one or more web parts. To edit the Project Site *Home* page in order to manipulate the web parts on the page, select the *Edit Page* item from the *Site Actions* menu, as shown in Figure 13 - 88.

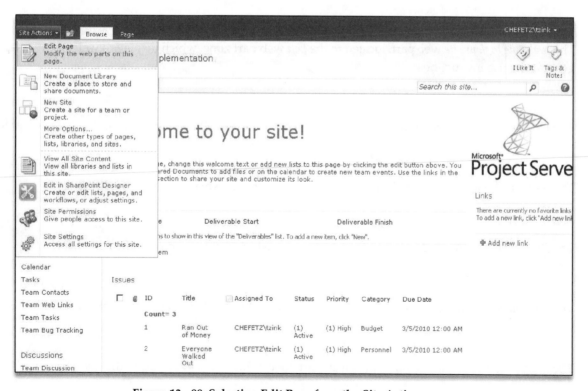

Figure 13 - 88: Selecting Edit Page from the Site Actions menu

You can also switch the page into editing mode by clicking the *Page* tab on the ribbon menu, then clicking the *Edit Page* button.

The system displays the *Home* page in editing mode as shown in Figure 13 - 89, allowing you to manipulate the contents of the page in any of the following ways:

- Add a web part to a web part zone

- Reposition a web part within a web part zone

- Move a web part to a different web part zone

- Remove a web part from the page

Notice that the *Home* page contains six web parts by default:

- The *Welcome to your site* web part, located in the *Left* web part zone, which displays a welcome message and general site use instructions

- The *Deliverables* web part, located in the *Left* web part zone, which displays items in the *Deliverables* list

- The *Issues* web part, located in the *Left* web part zone, which displays items in the *Issues* list

- The *Risks* web part, located in the *Left* web part zone, which displays items in the *Risks* list

- The *Site Image* web part, located in the *Right* web part zone, which displays a predefined image

- The *Links* web part, located in the *Right* web part zone, which displays items in the *Links* list

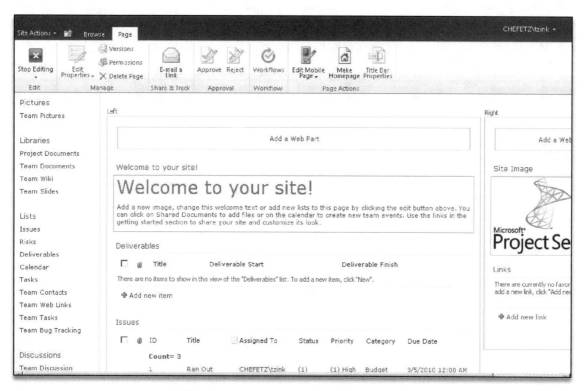

Figure 13 - 89: Home page in editing mode

To add a web part to the *Home* page, click the *Add a Web Part* link near the top of both the *Left* web part zone and the *Right* web part zone. The system displays a panel below the ribbon that lists web parts available to add to the page, as shown in Figure 13 - 90.

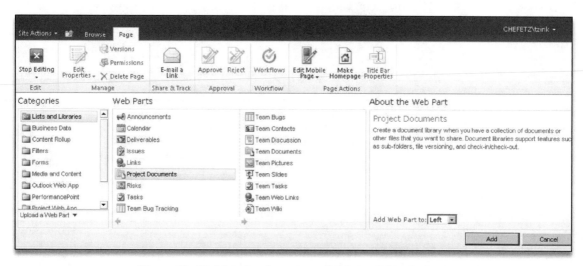

Figure 13 - 90: List of web parts available to add to the page

Select a web part type from the *Categories* listing, then select a web part from the *Web Parts* listing, then click the *Add* button. The system adds the web part to the top of the selected web part zone, as illustrated in Figure 13 - 91.

Figure 13 - 91: Page with Project Documents web part added to top of Left web part zone

To reposition a web part within a web part zone or to move it to a different zone, click the title bar of the web part and drag it into the desired position on the page, as shown in Figure 13 - 92. Notice that a blue bar indicates positions where you may drop the web part on the page.

Figure 13 - 92: Repositioning the Welcome web part on the page

The system displays the repositioned web part on the page, as shown in Figure 13 - 93.

Figure 13 - 93: Updated page with repositioned Welcome web part

To remove a web part from the page, float the mouse cursor over the web part title bar to activate the web part menu, indicated by a tiny downward-pointing arrow in the upper right corner of the web part. Click the arrow to open the web part menu and select the *Delete* option, as shown in Figure 13 - 94.

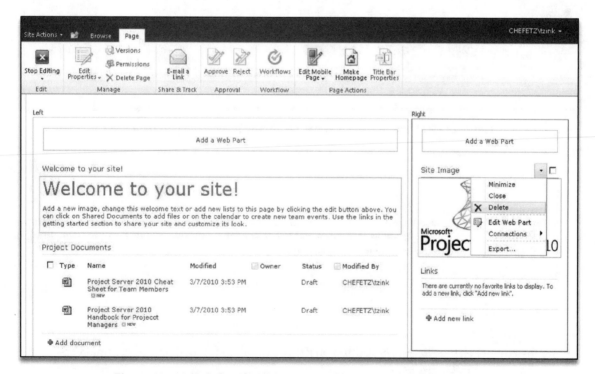

Figure 13 - 94: Deleting the Site Image web part via the web part menu

The system displays the warning dialog shown in Figure 13 - 95; click the *OK* button to acknowledge the message and proceed with the web part deletion.

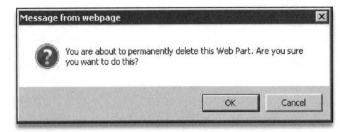

Figure 13 - 95: Web part deletion warning dialog

The system displays the updated web part page with the **web** part removed, as shown in Figure 13 - 96.

Figure 13 - 96: Updated web part page with Site Image web part removed

 Warning: Deleting a web part removes it **completely** from the page. Selecting the ***Close*** option from the web part menu or clicking the **X** in the upper right corner of the web part *hides* it on the page, but it still remains embedded in the underlying code of the page.

To stop editing the page, click the *Stop Editing* button on the ribbon. The system displays the final version of the page in viewing mode as shown in Figure 13 - 97.

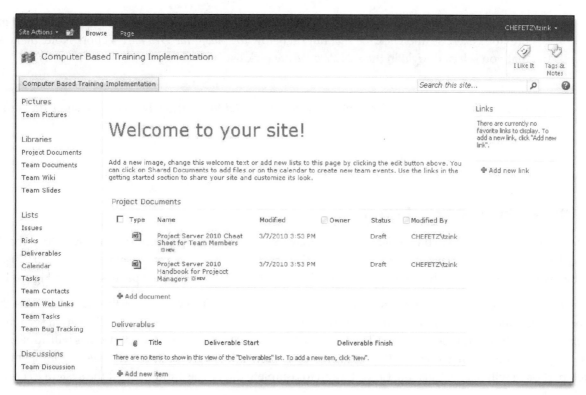

Figure 13 - 97: Updated web part page in viewing mode

Depending upon your last page editing action, you may need to click the *Page* tab on the ribbon to display the *Stop Editing* button.

Hands On Exercise

Exercise 13-9

Modify the Project Site homepage.

1. If necessary, navigate to the homepage of your Deploy Training Advisor Software project.

2. From the *Site Actions* menu, select the *Edit Page* item. The system puts the page into edit mode.

3. If necessary, scroll to reveal the *Right* zone of the page and click the *Add a Web Part* link.

4. From the *Web Parts* section below the ribbon, select the *Team Contacts* item that you created in a previous exercise and click the *Add* button below the *About the Web Part* section. Note: make sure that you selected *Right* in the *Add Web Part to* pick list.

5. In the *Edit* section of the *Page* ribbon, click the *Stop Editing* button. Notice the change on your homepage.

Creating a New Web Part Page

To create a new web part page in the Project Site to display information for the Project Team, navigate to the *Create* page by selecting the *More Options* item from the *Site Actions* menu. On the *Create* page, select the *Web Part Page* item located below the *Pages and Sites* heading. The system displays the *New Web Part Page* page, shown in Figure 13 - 98.

In the *Name* section of the page, enter a name for the new web part page. The system uses this name to create the file name for the page, and it displays this name on the page when people visit the Project Site. In the *Layout* section of the page, select an item from the *Choose a Layout Template* pick list to specify how many web part zones will appear on the page, as well as how to arrange them. In the *Save Location* section of the page, select the *Document Library* where the new web part page will reside. Click the *Create* button to complete the process and instruct the system to create the new web part page.

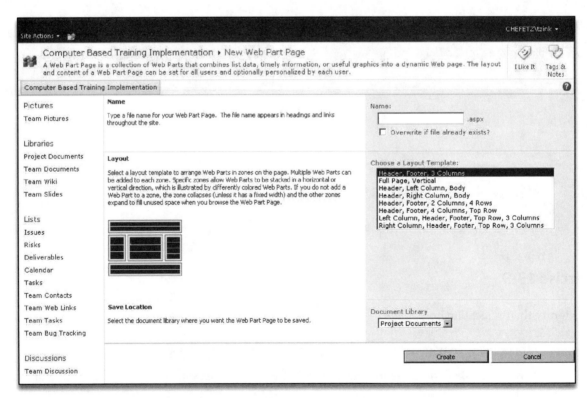

Figure 13 - 98: New Web Part Page page

You **must** specify where the new web part page will reside by selecting from the listing of **existing** document libraries. If you need to create a new library to contain the new web part page, then you should first manually create that library before proceeding through this process.

MSProjectExperts recommends that you create a library in the *Project Site* to contain any web part pages that may be created in that site; name the library *Web Part Pages* or similar, and select *Web Part page* as the default *Document Template*.

The system displays the new empty web part page in editing mode, as shown in Figure 13 - 99. You may add to, re-arrange, or otherwise edit and manipulate web parts on the page as described previously in this module. To stop editing the page, click the *Stop Editing* button on the ribbon.

Figure 13 - 99: New Web Part Page in editing mode

Creating a New Content Page

A SharePoint content page is similar to a web part page, except that you can also easily add formatted text, images, and other types of content in addition to web parts. Content pages function similarly to wiki pages, and therefore they reside in a wiki library that the system creates specifically for storing content pages.

To create a new content page in the Project Site, navigate to the *Create* page by selecting the *More Options* item from the *Site Actions* menu. On the *Create* page, select the *Page* item located below the *Pages and Sites* heading. The system displays the *Create Default Wiki Libraries* dialog, shown in Figure 13 - 100. Click the *Create* button to instruct the system to create a wiki library to house this and future content pages in the Project Site.

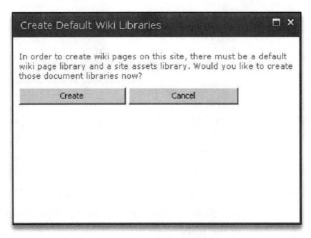

Figure 13 - 100: Create Default Wiki Libraries dialog

 The system also creates a *Site Assets* library to contain images, videos, and other types of content that you may upload to the site and insert into content pages.

The system displays the *New Page* dialog, shown in Figure 13 - 101. Enter a name for the new content page into the *New page name* text box, then click the *Create* button.

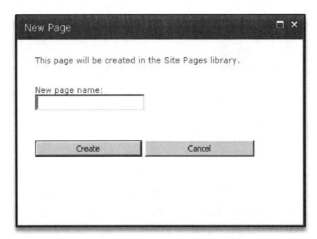

Figure 13 - 101: New Page dialog

The system displays a new empty content page in editing mode shown in Figure 13 - 102. Use the various text formatting, image, layout, and other tools on the ribbon to add and format content in the new page, then click the *Save* button on the ribbon to save your changes and stop editing the page.

Depending on your last page editing action, you may need to click the *Page* tab on the ribbon to display the *Save* button.

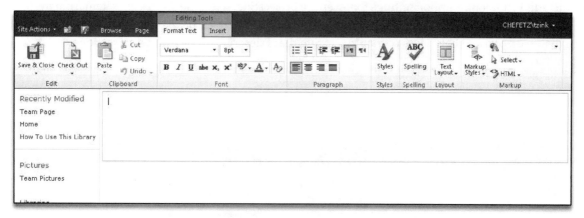

Figure 13 - 102: New Content Page in editing mode

Figure 13 - 103 shows an example of a content page with formatted text, an image, and a web part.

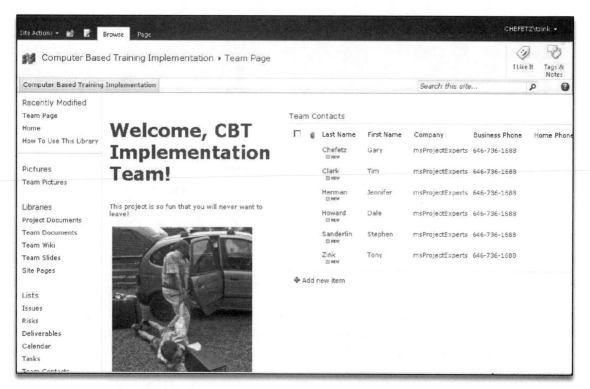

Figure 13 - 103: New Content Page with various types of content inserted

Managing Project Site Settings

As I described previously in this module, the SharePoint administration model provides the ability to manage list and library settings as well as overall site settings for an entire Project Site. List and library settings control the behavior of each individual repository within the site, but site settings control the behavior of the entire site and all repositories contained within it.

To view and adjust the configuration settings for an entire Project Site, select the *Site Settings* item from the *Site Actions* menu. The system displays the *Site Settings* page shown in Figure 13 - 104. The *Site Settings* page provides options to configure many aspects and behaviors of the Project Site that I describe in the following sections.

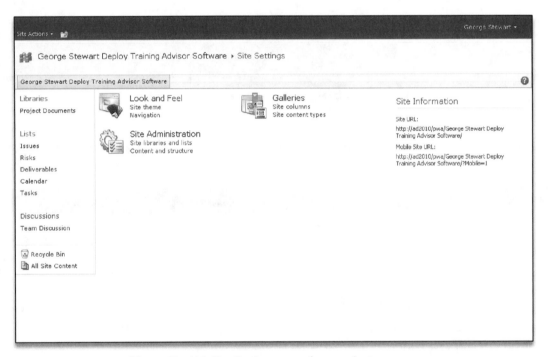

Figure 13 - 104: Site Settings page for a project manager

Specifying Site Navigation and Menu Settings

To change the global navigation tabs across the top of each *Project Site* page, as well as the links that appear in the *Quick Launch* menu on the left side of each page, navigate to the *Site Settings* page and click on the *Navigation* item located below the *Look and Feel* heading. The system displays the *Navigation Settings* page shown in Figure 13 - 105.

The *Navigation Settings* page contains five sections: *Global Navigation, Current Navigation, Sorting, Navigation Editing and Sorting,* and *Show and Hide Ribbon.* I describe each individual section separately.

In the *Global Navigation* section of the page, select whether the Project Site inherits the global navigation tabs from the parent PWA site, or whether it shows tabs for site or page destinations below the Project Site. The provided options are fairly self-explanatory. Select from the appropriate options provided in this section of the page.

In the *Current Navigation* section of the page, select whether the Project Site inherits the *Quick Launch* menu links from the parent PWA site, shows links for the current site pages and subsites, or shows links only for subsites. The provided options are self-explanatory. Select from the appropriate options provided in this section of the page.

In the *Sorting* section of the page, select whether the system sorts navigation links automatically or manually. To sort automatically, select the *Sort automatically* option. To sort manually, select the *Sort manually* option. Notice that if you select automatic sorting, an additional *Automatic Sorting* section appears on the page, allowing you to determine how the system automatically sorts the global and current navigation links. Select the appropriate option from the *Sort by* pick list, then select whether the system sorts the items in *ascending* or *descending* order.

In the *Navigation Editing and Sorting* section of the page, add, remove, and re-order the global and current navigation links as necessary. Notice that if you select the *Display the navigation items below the current site* option in the *Global Navigation* section of the page, global navigation links appear in this section for editing.

In the *Show and Hide Ribbon* section of the page, select whether people have the ability to show and hide the ribbon within the Project Site. To allow the show / hide functionality, select the *Yes* option, or to prevent the functionality, select the *No* option.

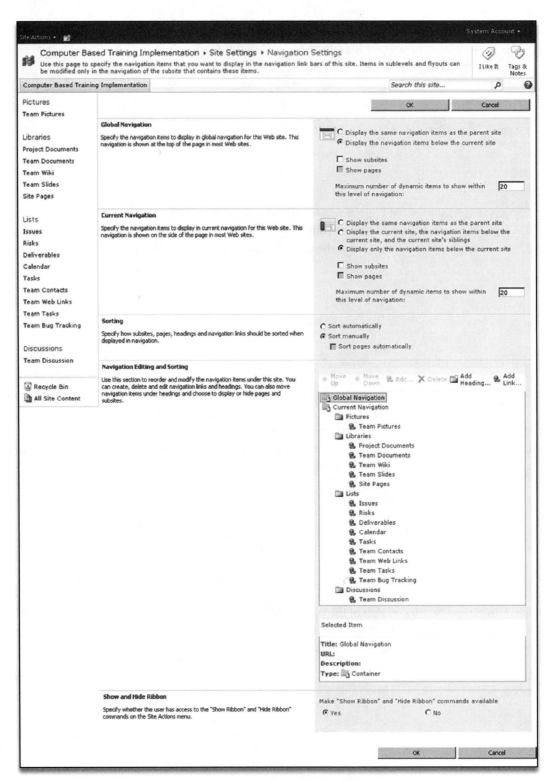

Figure 13 - 105: Site Navigation Settings page

To change whether the *Quick Launch* menu is visible in the Project Site and whether the system displays a tree-style version of the menu, navigate to the *Site Settings* page and click on the *Tree view* item located below the *Look and Feel* heading. The system displays the *Tree view* page shown in Figure 13 - 106.

Figure 13 - 106: Tree view page

The *Enable Quick Launch* section of the page enables the standard *Quick Launch* menu within the Project Site. To enable the menu, select the *Enable Quick Launch* option. The *Enable Tree View* section of the page enables a hierarchical tree-style version of the *Quick Launch* menu within the Project Site. To enable the tree-style menu, select the *Enable Tree View* option. Note that selecting both options displays **both** versions of the *Quick Launch* menu on the left side of pages within the Project Site. Figure 13 - 107 shows the Project Site with the standard *Quick Launch* menu disabled and the tree-style *Quick Launch* menu enabled.

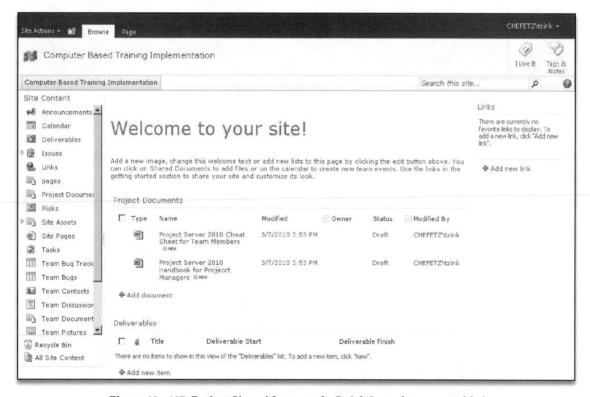

Figure 13 - 107: Project Site with tree style Quick Launch menu enabled

Warning: Select the standard Quick Launch menu or the tree-style Quick Launch menu, but do not select both, as this would confuse people who use the Project Site.

Specifying Site Theme Settings

To select or modify the color scheme of the Project Site, navigate to the *Site Settings* page and click on the *Site theme* item located below the *Look and Feel* heading. The system displays the *Site Theme* page shown in Figure 13 - 108.

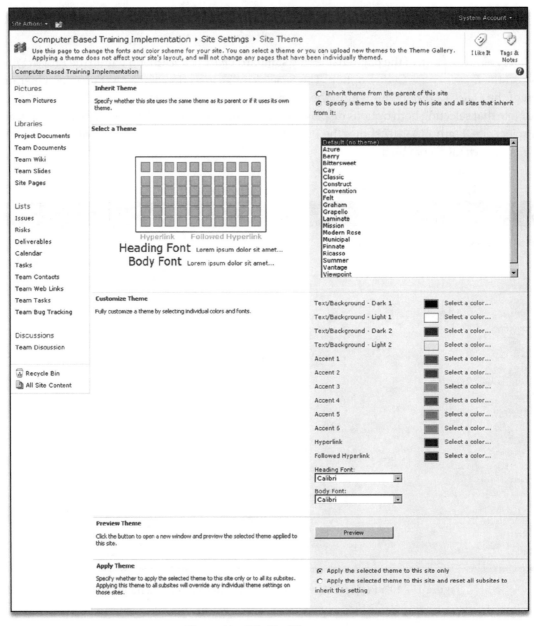

Figure 13 - 108: Site Theme page

The *Site Theme* page contains five sections: *Inherit Theme*, *Select a Theme*, *Customize Theme*, *Preview Theme*, and *Apply Theme*. I describe each individual section below.

In the *Inherit Theme* section of the page, select whether the Project Site inherits its theme from the parent PWA site. To inherit the theme, select the *Inherit theme from the parent of this site* option. To specify a unique theme for the Project Site, select the *Specify a theme to be used by this site and all sites that inherit from it* option.

In the *Select a Theme* section of the page, select a built-in site theme from the pick list. Notice that a preview color palette and some formatted text examples appear to the left of the pick list when you select a theme.

In the *Customize Theme* section of the page, select custom colors for each element of the color scheme. To select a different color for any type of item, click the *Select a color* link next to the item; the *Colors* dialog appears, as shown in Figure 13 - 109, allowing you to select a different color or enter a 6-character hexadecimal color code. When you are finished selecting a color or entering a new color code, click the *OK* button. To change the font style that the selected theme uses, select new values in the *Heading Font* and the *Body Font* pick lists.

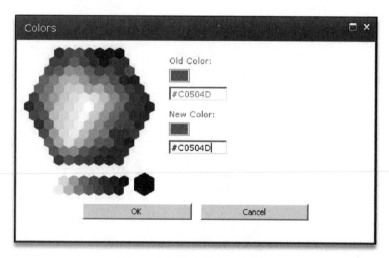

Figure 13 - 109: Colors dialog

In the *Preview Theme* section of the page, click the *Preview* button to launch the Project Site in a separate web browser session to preview the new theme. In the *Apply Theme* section of the page shown previously in Figure 13 - 108, select an option to either apply the new theme only to the current Project Site or to apply it to any subsites. To apply the theme to the current Project Site only, select the *Apply the selected theme to this site only* option.

Hands On Exercise

Exercise 13-10

Change the theme of your Deploy Training Advisor Software project.

1. From the *Site Actions* menu, select the *Site Settings* item. The system displays the *Site Settings* page.

2. From the *Look and Feel* section, select the *Site Theme* link. The system displays the *Site Theme* page.

3. Select the *Classic* item in the *Select a Theme* section of the page. Leave all other options at their default values and click the *Apply* button to apply the new theme to your site. The system processes the change and redisplays the *Site Settings* page with the new theme.

4. Explore the pages of your site with the 2010 version of the SharePoint classic theme applied.

Module 14

Working with Status Reports

Learning Objectives

After completing this module, you will be able to:

- Create and send a new status report request
- Edit and delete a status report
- Respond to a status report request
- Submit an unrequested status report
- View the status report archive
- View status report responses
- View unrequested status reports

Inside Module 14

Requesting a Status Report

Not only does Project Server 2010 provide time and task tracking, the system also allows managers to capture text-based information from resources using status reports. You can use the status reports feature to create periodic status reports due on a regular basis from specific resources or to request a one-time status report. To create a new *Status Report* request, click the *Status Reports* link in either the *Quick Launch* menu or the main content area of the *Home* page in Project Web App. The system displays the *Status Reports* page shown in Figure 14 - 1.

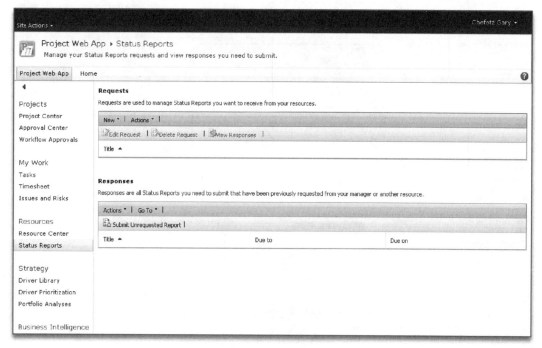

Figure 14 - 1: Status Reports page

 The *Request a Status Report* feature is dependent on permissions granted in groups in Project Web App. By default, this feature is available only to members of the following groups: Executives, Portfolio Managers, Project Managers, Resource Managers, Team Leads, and Administrators.

The *Status Reports* page includes two sections. Use the options in the *Requests* section to create and manage *Status Report* requests. Use the options in the *Responses* section to view and work with *Status Report* responses from your resources.

To create a new *Status Report* request, click the *New* pick list button in the *Requests* section and then click the *New Request* item on the pick list. Project Server 2010 displays the *Status Report Request* page shown in Figure 14 - 2.

Figure 14 - 2: Status Report Request page

On the *Status Report Request* page, enter a descriptive name for the *Status Report* request in the *Title* field. In the *Frequency* section, select the appropriate options to set the recurrence for the *Status Report* request. The system offers you a wide variety of options for setting a recurrence pattern, such as weekly, monthly, and yearly. Using the available options in the *Frequency* section, you can even create recurrences such as bi-weekly or quarterly. Click the *Start* pick list and select the starting date for the first reporting period.

Warning: Project Server 2010 does not allow you to select a Start date earlier than the current date. This means that you cannot create a monthly report in the middle of the month and set the Start date to the first day of the month!

In the *Available Resources* list, select the resources that must respond to your *Status Report* request and then click the *Add* button. Next, you set up the topical sections for the status report in the *Sections* part of the page. By default, the system offers three standard topical sections: *Major Accomplishments, Objectives for the Next Period,* and *Hot Issues*. You can delete, reorder, rename, add additional topical sections, add descriptions, or simply accept the default topical sections listed on the *Status Report Request* page.

When you complete your new *Status Report* request, click the *Send* button. Project Server 2010 sends an e-mail message to each resource, notifying them of the new *Status Report* request. The system displays your new *Status Report* request in the *Requests* section of the *Status Reports* page. Notice in Figure 14 - 3 that I created a monthly *Status Report* request for members of the Training team. Notice also that I included myself in the respondents list, so this new *Status Report* request displays in the *Responses* section as well.

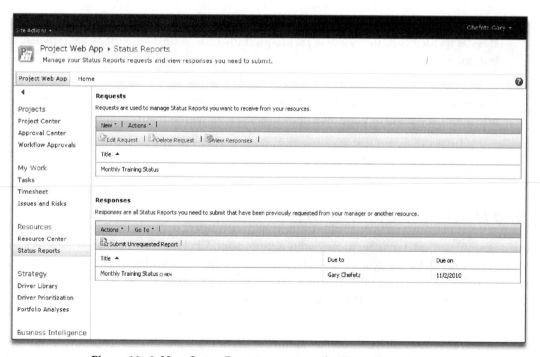

Figure 14 - 3: New Status Report request on the Status Reports page

Hands On Exercise

Exercise 14-1

Create a new status report request.

1. Navigate to the *Status Reports* page.

2. Click the *New* pick list button and select the *New Request* item from the pick list.

3. In the *Report Title* section of the *Status Report Request* page, enter a name for your new status report in the *Title* field followed by the phrase *Team Weekly Report*.

4. In the *Frequency* section of the *Status Report Request* page, set the *Recurrence* field to *weekly* due *every* week on *Thursday*.

5. In the *Start Date* section of the *Status Report Request* page, set the date to today's date.

6. In the *Resources* section of the *Status Report Request* page, add **yourself** and each member of your class as recipients of the *Status Report* request (include your instructor as well) by using the *Add* button.

7. In the *Sections* section of the *Status Report Request* page, keep the three default topical sections, but add a fourth section of your own choice by clicking on the *Insert Section* button.

8. Click the *Send* button when finished.

Editing and Deleting Status Reports

To edit an existing status report, navigate to the *Status Reports* page. Click the row header to the left of the *Status Report* request you want to edit and then click the *Edit Request* button. The system displays the *Status Report Request* page shown previously in Figure 14 - 2. Edit the information as you determine necessary and then click the *Send* button. You can also edit the *Status Report* request by clicking the *Actions* pick list button and selecting the *Edit Request* item on the list.

To delete a *Status Report* request, click the row header to the left of the *Status Report* request you want to delete and then click the *Delete Request* button. Project Server 2010 displays the confirmation dialog shown in Figure 14 - 4. In the confirmation dialog, click the *OK* button to complete the deletion.

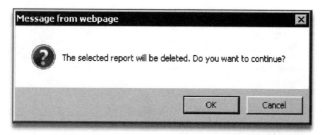

Figure 14 - 4: Delete a Status Report request confirmation

Responding to a Status Report Request

As I mentioned earlier in this module, when a manager sends a *Status Report* request, Project Server 2010 sends an e-mail message to each resource included in the *Status Report* request. Resources can see the *Status Report* request by clicking the *Status Reports* link in either the *Quick Launch* menu or the main content area of the *Home* page. The system displays the new *Status Report* request in the *Responses* area of the *Status Reports* page. For example, Figure 14 - 5 shows the Monthly Training status report on the *Status Reports* page for a resource named George Stewart.

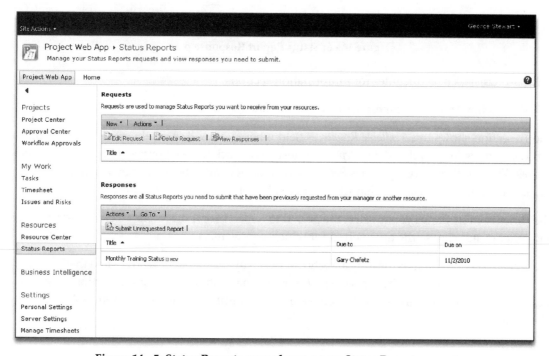

Figure 14 - 5: Status Reports page shows a new Status Report request

On the *Status Reports* page, resources may see multiple *Status Report* requests created by different managers. To respond to a *Status Report* request; click the link for the status report to which you want to respond. Project Server 2010 displays the *Status Report Response* page shown in Figure 14 - 6.

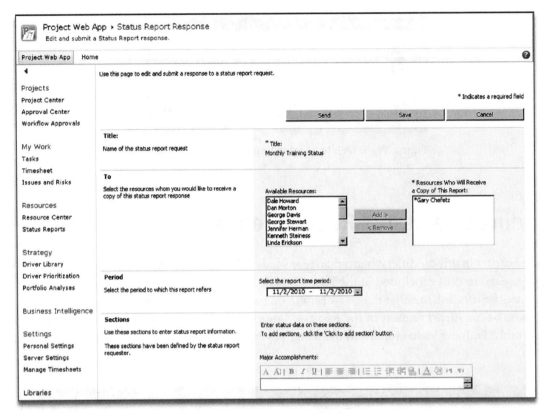

Figure 14 - 6: Status Report Response page

The *Status Report Response* page includes four information sections:

- The *Title* section shows the *Status Report* request name.

- The *To* section shows the *Available Resources* field where you will select the name(s) of the resource(s) who you want to respond to the *Status Report* request. You click the *Add* button to add these names to the *Resources Who Will Receive a Copy of This Report* field. This field also shows the name of the *Status Report* requestor, as indicated by an asterisk character (*) to the left of the manager's name.

- The *Period* section allows you to select the period to which the report refers. Click the *Select the report time period* pick list and choose the time period for which you want to respond.

- The *Sections* section contains the topical sections chosen by the manager who created the *Status Report* request. Notice in Figure 14 - 6 that the *Status Report* request image shows one topical sections: Major Accomplishments This Month. Not shown in the image are two additional default sections: Objectives for the Next Month and Hot Issues.

All three sections are not shown in the figure.

To enter information into any of the topical sections, click anywhere in the text field for the topic. Project Server 2010 activates the toolbar at the top of the text field giving you extensive formatting capabilities. For example,

Figure 14 - 7 shows the activated toolbar for the *Major Accomplishments* field. Notice that the toolbar gives you text-formatting options such as font size, font style, alignment, and numbered or bulleted lists.

Figure 14 - 7: Activated toolbar for Major Accomplishments field

In each of the topical sections, enter information required to complete the *Status Report* response. If you need to add an additional topical section, click the *Click to add section* button at the bottom of the page. The system displays the *Section Name* dialog shown in Figure 14 - 8.

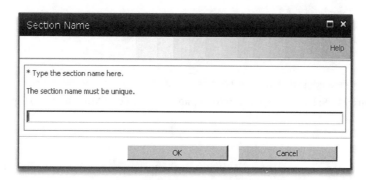

Figure 14 - 8: Section Name dialog

In the dialog, enter a unique name for the new section in the text field and then click the *OK* button. Enter additional information in the new topical section, as you require.

If you create a topical section that you no longer need, click the *Delete this section* button in the upper right corner of the section. You can delete any section that you add; however you cannot delete a section added by the requestor.

When you finish entering information in the topical sections, Project Server 2010 offers you two options:

- *Save the Status Report* response for additional editing and later submission.

- *Send the Status Report* response immediately.

If are working on an in-progress *Status Report* response and are not ready to send it to your manager, click the *Save* button. The system saves the *Status Report* response in your *Status Report Archive,* where you can edit it and send it at a later time. Project Server 2010 displays the *Status Report Archive* page with the saved *Status Report* response. For example, Figure 14 - 9 shows a *Status Report* response saved on October 19.

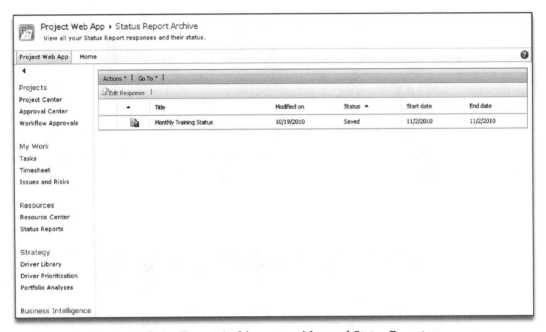

Figure 14 - 9: Status Report Archive page with saved Status Report response

 To update an in-progress *Status Report* response, navigate to the *Status Reports* page, click the *Go To* pick list button, and select the *Status Reports: Archive* item on the pick list. Click the name of the *Status Report* response to update, then update it, save it, or send it.

If you are ready to submit the *Status Report* response to your manager, click the *Send* button. The system saves the *Status Report* response in your *Status Report Archive* and sends your manager an e-mail message notifying her of your *Status Report* response.

Submitting an Unrequested Status Report

You can create and send an ad hoc status report without a manager request. To submit an unrequested status report, navigate to the *Responses* section of the *Status Reports* page and click the *Submit Unrequested Report* button. Project Server 2010 displays the *Unrequested Status Report* page shown in Figure 14 - 10.

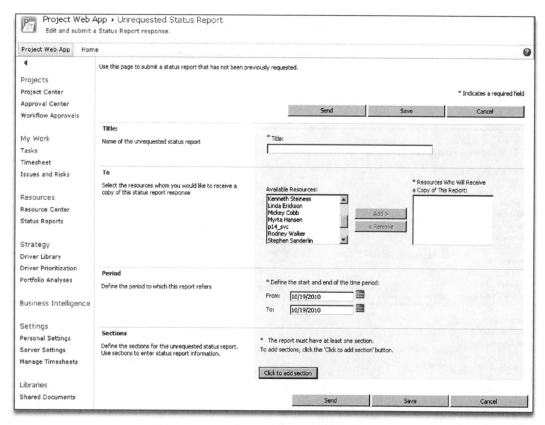

Figure 14 - 10: Unrequested Status Report page

To create the unrequested status report, enter the name of your status report in the *Title* field. In the *Available Resources* list, select the resources to which you want to send the unrequested status report and then click the *Add* button. In the *Period* section of the page, enter dates in the *From* and *To* fields to indicate the period for your report. Click the *Click to add section* button, enter a name for the topical section in the dialog, and then click the *OK* button. Enter data in the topical section and add additional topical sections until you complete your report and then click the *Send* button. The system adds your new unrequested status report to the status report Archive.

Viewing the Status Report Archive

The *Status Report Archive* page gives you access to your saved status reports and any previously submitted status reports. To access the *Status Report Archive* page, navigate to the *Status Reports* page, click the *Go To* pick list button in the *Responses* section, and then click the *Status Reports: Archive* item on the pick list. Project Server 2010 displays the *Status Report Archive* page shown in Figure 14 - 11.

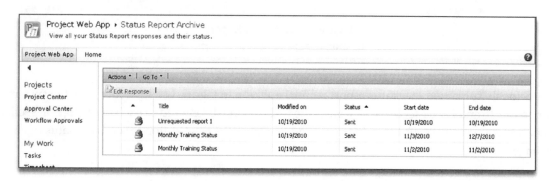

Figure 14 - 11: Status Report Archive page

Notice in Figure 14 - 11 that the user submitted two monthly status reports and one *Unrequested* status report. To edit an in-progress or previously submitted *Status Report* response, click the row header of the status report you want to edit and then click the *Edit Response* button. Project Server 2010 displays the *Status Report Response* page as shown in Figure 14 - 12.

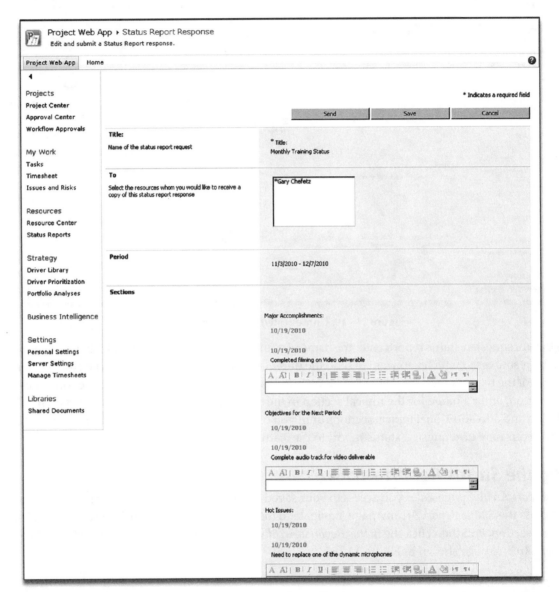

Figure 14 - 12: Status Report
Response page ready for editing

Because I previously submitted the status report response shown in Figure 14 - 12, notice how the system locks the information in the *To* and *Period* sections, as well as the text previously entered in each of the topical sections. Enter additional information in any of the topical sections and then click the *Send* button to send the status report response to your manager.

Hands On Exercise

Exercise 14-2

Respond to a status report request.

1. Click the *Status Reports* link in the *Quick Launch* menu to refresh your *Status Reports* page.

2. In the *Responses* section of the page, click the name of your own *Status Report* request.

3. In the *To* section of the page, select any two members of the class to receive copies of your response.

4. Make sure the setting in the *Period* section is for the current reporting period.

5. Enter report information in each of the topical sections and then click the *Send* button.

6. In the *Response* section of the *Status Reports* page, select the *Status Report* request from one of your fellow students and repeat steps #3-5.

7. From the *Responses* section of the *Status Reports* page, click the *Go To* pick list button, and then click the *Status Reports: Archive* item on the pick list.

8. Examine the two *Status Report* responses you sent during class.

Viewing Status Report Responses

When a resource sends you a *Status Report* response, Project Server 2010 automatically alerts you with an e-mail message. To view the *Status Report* responses from your resources, navigate to the *Status Reports* page and in the *Requests* section of the page click the name of the status report you want to view. The system displays the *View Responses* page for the selected status report. Figure 14 - 13 shows the *View Responses* page for my Monthly Training Status report.

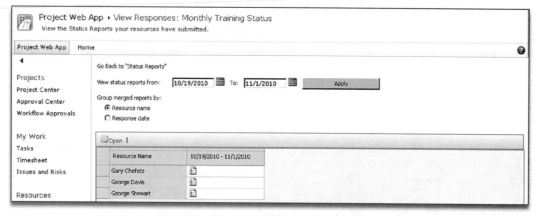

**Figure 14 - 13: View Responses page for the
Monthly Training Status Report**

The options at the top of the *View Responses* page allow you to view *Status Report* responses for specific reporting periods and to group the responses into a merged report. By default, the *View Responses* page shows the *Status Report* responses for each reporting period, with columns representing the current reporting period and all past periods. To display Status Responses for specific reporting periods, select the date range you want in the *From* and *To* fields and then click the *Apply* button.

If you select all of the cells, Project Server 2010 merges all selected *Status Report* responses into a merged team status report for each reporting period. The *Group merged reports by* option allows you to group by *Resource name* or *Response date*. Select the *Resource name* option to display the responses grouped by the name of each resource. Select the *Response date* option to display the responses grouped by the date each resource sent the response.

To view an individual *Status Report* response, click the cell to the left of the name of the person whose response you want to see and then click the *Open* button. To view the merged team *Status Report* response, select the names of all response cells and then click the *Open* button. The system displays the *Status Report Responses* page for the selected status report. Figure 14 - 14 shows the *Status Report Responses* page for the Monthly Training status report, grouped by resource name.

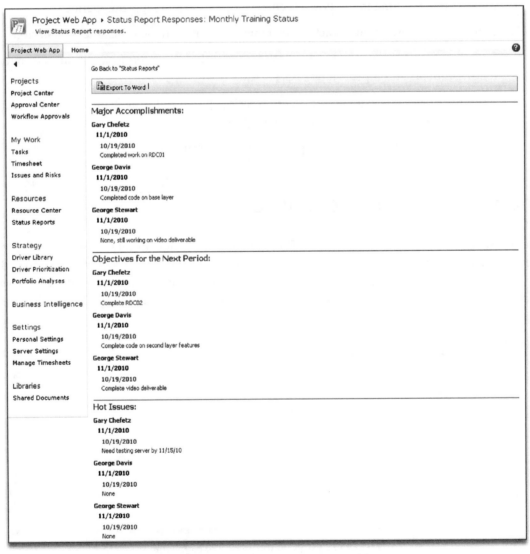

Figure 14 - 14: Status Report Responses page grouped by resource name

Beyond reading the responses on the *Status Report Responses* page, Project Server 2010 offers you one additional option; you can export the merged team status report to Microsoft Word. Click the *Export to Word* button and the system displays the *File Download* warning dialog shown in Figure 14 - 15.

If the merged team Status Report is associated with a particular project, MSProjectExperts recommends that you upload the saved copy of the merged team Status Report to the Document Library for that project. This allows you to share the Status Reports with the team and with other stakeholders.

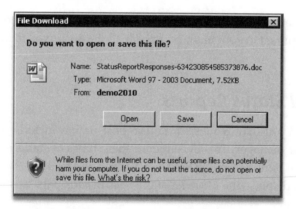

Figure 14 - 15: File Download warning

Click the *Save* button to save the Word document on your local computer or click the *Open* button in the dialog and the system opens Microsoft Word with the merged team status report in a new document. Figure 14 - 16 shows the Microsoft Word application with the top part of the merged team status report.

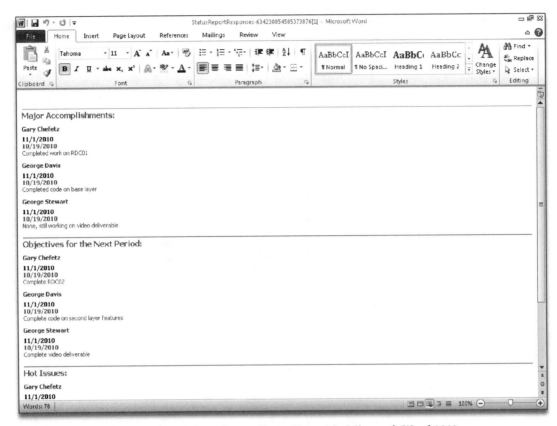

Figure 14 - 16: Merged team Status Report in Microsoft Word 2010

From the Microsoft Word application, you can edit the merged team status report document and then save it. After saving it, you can e-mail the document to your manager or upload the document to the Document Library of a related project for further sharing.

Viewing Unrequested Status Reports

Resources may occasionally send you an unrequested status report, or may include you as an additional recipient of a *Status Report* response to another manager. To view either of these types of status reports, navigate to the *Status Reports* page, click the *Go To* pick list button from the *Responses* section and click the *Status Reports: Miscellaneous* item on the pick list. Project Server 2010 displays the *Miscellaneous Status Reports* page as shown in Figure 14 - 17.

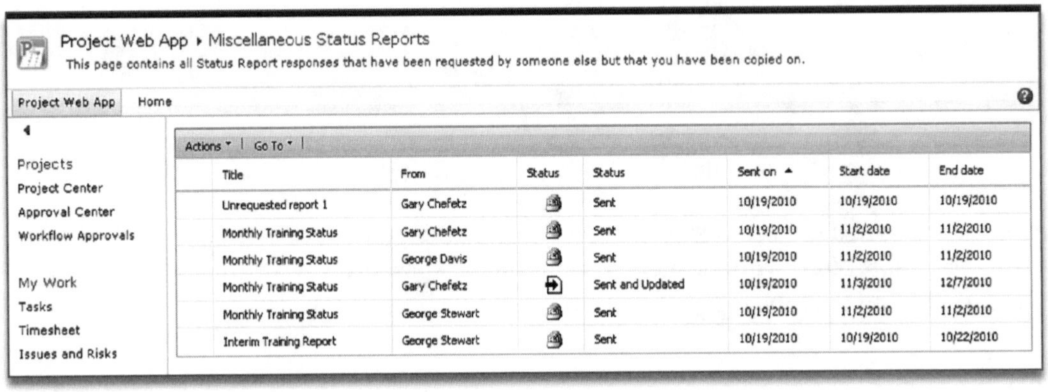

Figure 14 - 17: Miscellaneous Status Reports page

To view an *Unrequested* status report or the copy of a *Status Report* response, click the name of the status report you want to view. Project Server 2010 displays the *Status Report Responses* page for the selected status report. Figure 14 - 18 shows the *Status Report Responses* page for the Interim Training *Unrequested* status report from George Stewart.

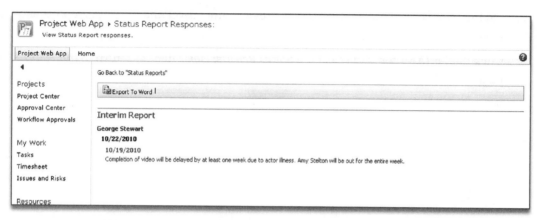

Figure 14 - 18: Unrequested Status Report from George Stewart

As with individual or merged team status reports, you can export the status report to Microsoft Word by clicking the *Export to Word* button. Click the *Go Back to "Status Reports"* link to return to the *Status Reports* page.

 Warning: When you click the *Go Back to "Status Reports"* link, the system returns you to the *Status Reports* page rather than the *Miscellaneous Status Reports* page. The only way to return directly to the *Miscellaneous Status Reports* page is to click the *Back* button in your Internet Explorer application.

 Hands On Exercise

Exercise 14-3

View status report responses.

1. Navigate to the *Status Reports* page and in the *Requests* section, click the name of your own *Status Report* request.

2. Select the cells of all of your resources and then click the *Open* button.

3. On the *Status Report Responses* page, click the *Export to Word* button and export the merged team status report to Microsoft Word.

4. After viewing the report, close the Microsoft Word application and do not save the document.

5. On the *Status Report Responses* page, click the *Go Back to "Status Reports"* link to return to the *Status Reports* page.

6. In the *Responses* section of the *Status Reports* page, click the *Go To* pick list button and select the *Status Reports: Miscellaneous* item on the pick list.

7. On the *Miscellaneous Status Reports* page, review any miscellaneous status reports shown on the page.

8. Click the *Go To* button and select the *Status Reports: Home* item to return to the *Status Reports* page.

Module 15

Working in the Resource Center

Learning Objectives

After completing this module, you will be able to:

- Apply Resource Center views
- View resource availability
- View resource assignment information
- Edit resource details for a group of resources
- Edit resource details individually for a group of resources
- Open a group of resources for editing in Project Professional 2010

Inside Module 15

Using the Resource Center

When you click the *Resource Center* link in the *Quick Launch* menu, Project Server 2010 displays the *Resource Center* page shown in Figure 15 - 1. The *Resource Center* page contains a data grid that displays all of the resources your security permissions allow you to see in the enterprise resource pool. By default, the system applies the *All Resources* view when you display the *Resource Center* page the first time. This view displays all resources, grouped by resource type (Work, Material, and Cost).

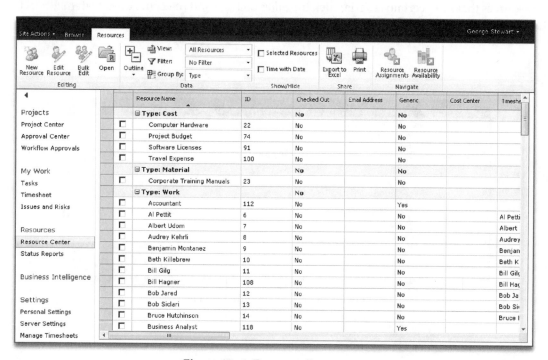

Figure 15 - 1: Resource Center page

The *Resource Center* page provides a central location from which you can manage all aspects of enterprise resources that you have permission to manage. From this page, you can do each of the following:

- View resource assignments across all enterprise projects.

- View resource availability across all enterprise projects.

- Edit resource information, if you have the necessary security permissions.

Before you begin working with resources in the *Resource Center* page notice the options available to you in the *Data* section of the *Resources* ribbon. Use the *Settings* buttons and selectors shown in Figure 15 - 2 to quickly filter, group, or search through the resources shown in the *Resource Center* page.

Figure 15 - 2: Data Section of the Resources ribbon

The *Resource Center* displays only enterprise resources. It does not display local resources.

To filter for resources that meet certain criteria, click the *Filter* pick list and select the *Custom* item. Project Server 2010 displays the *Custom Filter* dialog shown in Figure 15 - 3.

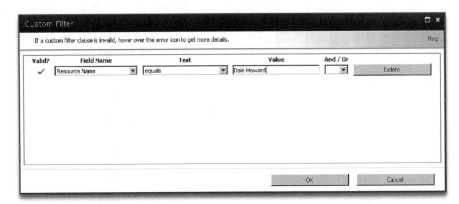

Figure 15 - 3: Custom Filter dialog

Using the *Grouping* selector, you can group by any field in the view. You can also sort on any field by hovering over any field heading, select the pick list and choose either *Ascending* or *Descending* from the menu. Use the *Outline* pick list to show any level in your grouping. For example, select the *Outline Level 1* option from this menu to show all grouping collapsed and expandable.

Applying Resource Center Views

To apply a view in the *Resource Center* page, click the *View* pick list in the *Data* section of the *Resources* ribbon. The pick list includes all standard and custom views that your permissions allow you to see. Project Server 2010 includes five default views, including *All Resources*, *Material Resources*, *Work Resources*, *Resources by Team*, and *Cost Resources*.

The *All Resources* view displays all resources, grouped by resource type. The *Material Resources* view displays only material resources, while the *Work Resources* view displays only work resources. The *Resources by Team* view displays team resources grouped by team. The *Cost Resources* view, shown in Figure 15-4, displays only budget cost and expense cost resources.

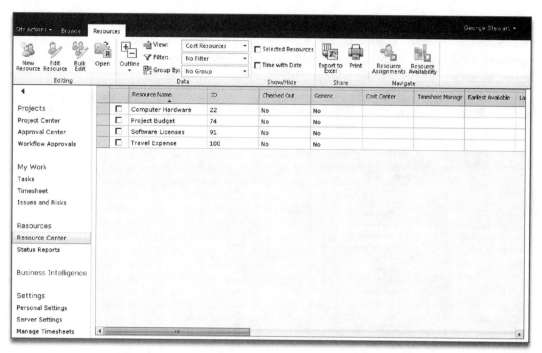

Figure 15 - 4: Cost Resources view in the Resource Center

 Your Project Server administrator controls the views available to you in the Resource Center. If you need a custom view, contact your Project Server administrator for assistance.

Selecting and Deselecting Resources

After applying a view, you must select one or more resources before activating other features available in the *Resource Center* page. To select a resource, click the option checkbox to the left of the resource's name. To quickly select all resources or to quickly clear your resource selections, float your mouse pointer over the checkbox header column to reveal the pick list menu arrow. Select the *Select All* or *Clear All* item on the menu as shown in Figure 15 - 5.

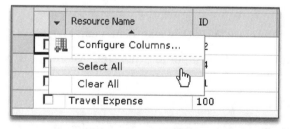

Figure 15 - 5: Select All or Clear All

After selecting resources, you can view availability or assignment information for the selected resources, or edit the details for the selected resources. To show the list of selected resources, select the *Selected Resources* checkbox in the *Show/Hide* section of the *Resources* ribbon. The system dynamically displays the list on the right side of the page as shown in Figure 15 - 6.

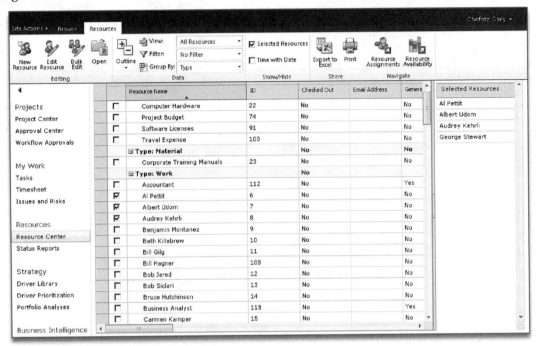

Figure 15 - 6: Resource Center with selected resources panel

Notice that the *Selected Resources* panel appears to the right of the grid. Deselect the *Selected Resources* option to hide the *Selected Resources* panel. Select the *Time with Date* option in the *Show/Hide* section of the ribbon to add the time-stamp to any date field displayed in the grid as shown in the *Last Modified* field in Figure 15 - 7.

Unique ID	Last Modified
db8f7967-5375-4	8/29/2010 9:31 PM
f2edda74-ab3c-4	8/29/2010 9:31 PM
50dd21ed-84b5-	8/29/2010 9:31 PM
ed5d46ac-8a5a-	8/29/2010 9:31 PM
	8/29/2010 9:31 PM
155b2b41-c142-	8/29/2010 9:31 PM

Figure 15 - 7: Date with Timestamp example

Project Web App also allows you to print the grid, or to export it to Microsoft Excel.

 MsProjectExperts recommends that you export to Excel before printing as the print functionality is limited in Project Web App.

Viewing Resource Availability

You can use the Resource Center to analyze availability for one or more resources across all projects in the Project Server database. Begin by selecting the resources in the data grid and then click the *Resource Availability* button from the *Navigate* section of the *Resources* ribbon. Project Server 2010 displays the *Resource Availability* page shown in Figure 15 - 8.

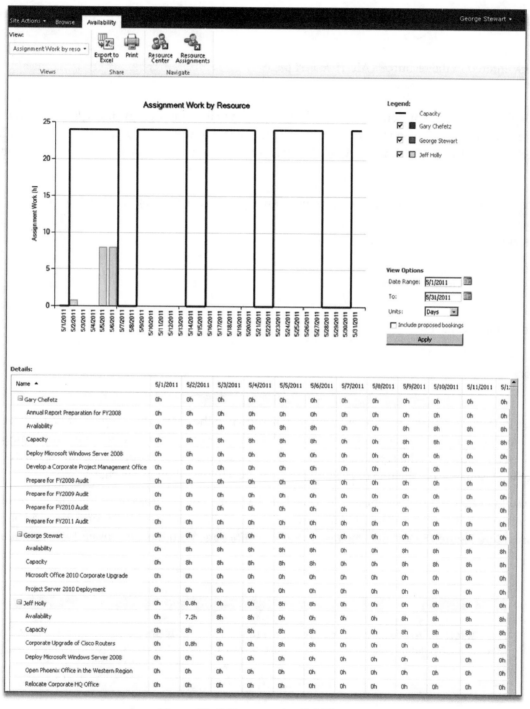

Figure 15 - 8: Resource Availability page

The *Resource Availability* page contains two sections: a chart at the top and a *Details* section with a timesheet grid at the bottom. For each selected resource, the timesheet grid displays the following information:

- Availability

- Capacity

- Assignment work for each project in which the resource is a team member

- Work entered in the resource's *My Timesheet* page

The chart displays a graphic representation of the data displayed in the timesheet grid. The *Resource Availability* page uses Project Server 2010 terminology that may be new to you. **Capacity** refers to what we formerly termed "Availability" in Project Server 2002 and 2003, while **Availability** is what we formerly termed "Remaining Availability".

In the upper left corner of the page, the *View* pick list allows you to select one of four available views:

- Assignment Work by Resource

- Assignment Work by Project

- Remaining Availability

- Work

Each of these four views controls the presentation of data shown in the chart. The *Assignment Work by Resource* view shows a stacked bar chart of the assignment work for each selected resource, along with a line chart of the total capacity for all selected resources. In the *Legend* area of the page, select or deselect the option checkboxes to the left of each resource name to dynamically include or exclude the resource's information in the chart.

The *Assignment Work by Project* view shows a stacked bar chart for all of the projects for the selected resources and a line chart for the total capacity for all selected resources, along with bars for timesheet information and optional availability information. Figure 15 - 9 shows the *Resource Availability* page with the *Assignment Work by Project* view applied.

 If you select the *Availability* check box option, Project Server 2010 shows you the total Availability (Remaining Availability) for all selected resources with a stacked bar chart.

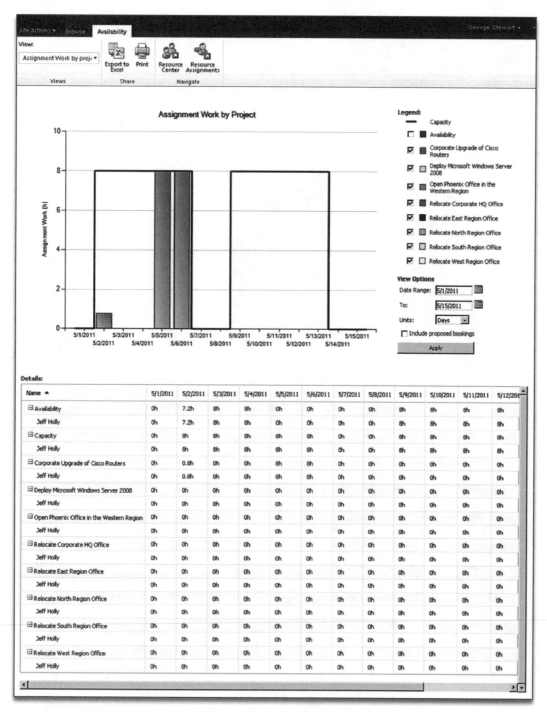

Figure 15 - 9: Resource Availability with the Assignment Work by Project view applied

The *Remaining Availability* view displays a bar chart showing the remaining availability for each selected resource. With multiple resources selected, this view is difficult to use; therefore, you should select resources individually to see their remaining availability. Figure 15 - 10 shows the *Resource Availability* page with the *Remaining Availability* view applied with one resource selected.

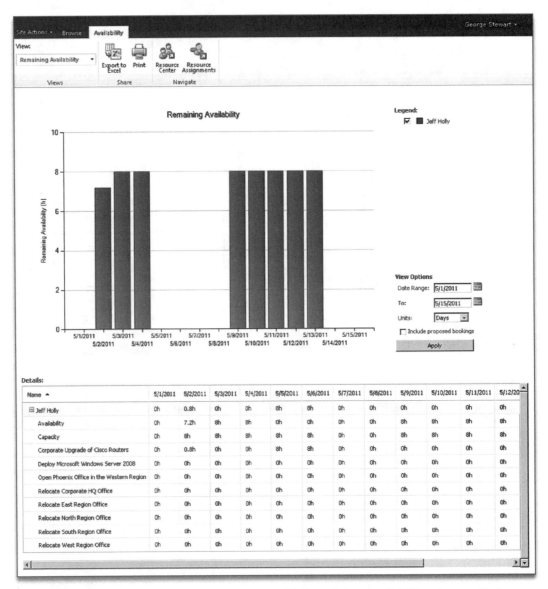

Figure 15 - 10: Resource Availability page with Remaining Availability view applied

The *Work* view displays a bar chart showing the total assigned work for each selected resource. With multiple resources selected, this view is difficult to use; therefore, you should select resources individually to see their assigned work. Figure 15 - 11 shows the *Resource Availability* page with the *Work* view applied with one resource selected.

Name	5/1/2011	5/2/2011	5/3/2011	5/4/2011	5/5/2011	5/6/2011	5/7/2011	5/8/2011	5/9/2011	5/10/2011	5/11/2011	5/12/20
Jeff Holly	0h	0.8h	0h	0h	8h	8h	0h	0h	0h	0h	0h	0h
Availability	0h	7.2h	8h	8h	0h	0h	0h	0h	8h	8h	8h	8h
Capacity	0h	8h	8h	8h	8h	8h	0h	0h	8h	8h	8h	8h
Corporate Upgrade of Cisco Routers	0h	0.8h	0h	0h	8h	8h	0h	0h	0h	0h	0h	0h
Deploy Microsoft Windows Server 2008	0h	0h	0h	0h	0h	0h	0h	0h	0h	0h	0h	0h
Open Phoenix Office in the Western Region	0h	0h	0h	0h	0h	0h	0h	0h	0h	0h	0h	0h
Relocate Corporate HQ Office	0h	0h	0h	0h	0h	0h	0h	0h	0h	0h	0h	0h
Relocate East Region Office	0h	0h	0h	0h	0h	0h	0h	0h	0h	0h	0h	0h
Relocate North Region Office	0h	0h	0h	0h	0h	0h	0h	0h	0h	0h	0h	0h
Relocate South Region Office	0h	0h	0h	0h	0h	0h	0h	0h	0h	0h	0h	0h
Relocate West Region Office	0h	0h	0h	0h	0h	0h	0h	0h	0h	0h	0h	0h

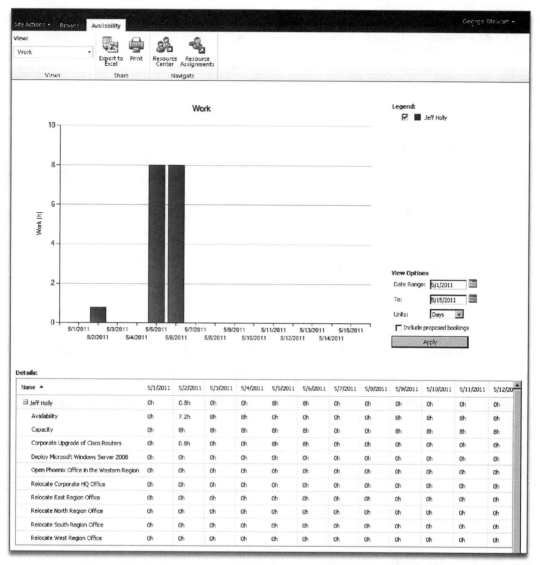

Figure 15 - 11: Resource Availability page with the Work view applied

By default, the chart and timesheet show a 2-week period beginning in the current week. To change the date range, select a start date in the *Date Range* field and a period end date in the *To* field in the *View Options* section in the middle of the page to the right of the chart as shown in Figure 15 - 12. Click the *Apply* button to apply your selection.

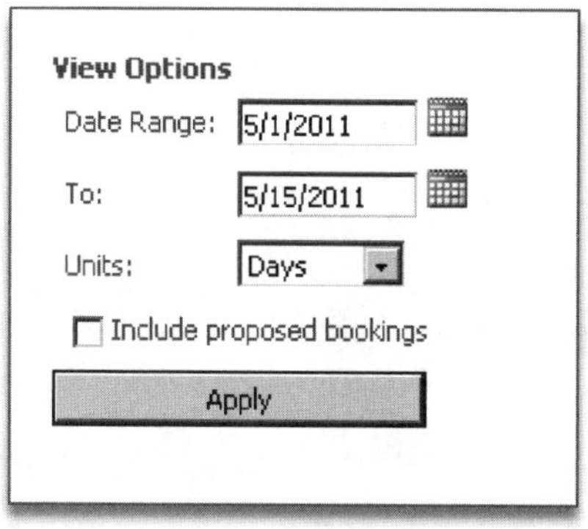

Figure 15 - 12: View Options

Project Server 2010 maintains your selected *Date Range* settings the next time you return to the *Resource Availability* page. To return to the *Resource Center* page, click the *Resource Center* button in the *Navigate* section of the *Resources* ribbon.

Hands On Exercise

Exercise 15-1

Explore the Resource Center and then determine current work levels and availability for a resource.

1. Click the *Resource Center* link in the Quick Launch menu.

2. Select one or more resources by clicking the checkbox to the left of their name(s).

3. In the *Navigate* section of the *Resources* ribbon, click the *Resource Availability* button.

4. In the *Views* section of the *Availability* ribbon click the *View* pick list and select different availability views.

5. Select and deselect projects or resources in the various detailed displays.

6. Select each of the available views and examine the information presented about each resource or project.

7. In the *Navigate* section of the *Availability* ribbon, click the *Resource Center* button to return to the *Resource Center* page.

Viewing Resource Assignments

After selecting one or more resources on the *Resource Center* page, click the *Resource Assignments* button in the *Navigate* section of the *Resources* ribbon to view all project work currently assigned to the selected resource(s). The system displays the *Resource Assignments* page shown in Figure 15 - 13. Using the *Resource Assignments* page, you can determine the total amount of task work assigned to each selected resource and determine the specific times during which each resource has scheduled work.

Warning: To access the *Resource Assignments* page, you must select no more than 100 resources..

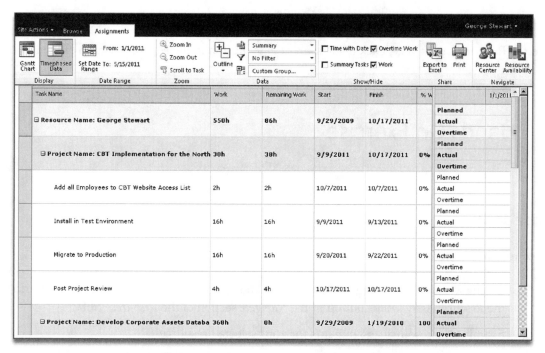

Figure 15 - 13: Resource Assignments page

The *Resource Assignments* page includes a table on the left that lists resource assignments, with either a Gantt chart on the right or a time-phased grid on the right that depicts the periods for each resource assignment. Use either the *Gantt Chart* button or the *Timephased Data* button in the *Display* section of the *Assignments* ribbon to switch between these two views. You can also set a date range for the timephased data using the *Set Date Range* button from the *Date Range* section of the *Assignments* ribbon. By default, Project Server 2010 groups the resource assignment information by resource name and then by project name.

You can choose whether you would like the system to include summary tasks in the display by selecting the *Summary Tasks* checkbox in the *Show/Hide* section of the ribbon. Use the *Time with Date* option to display dates with times, and deselect the *Overtime Work* option to hide the *Overtime* item in the timephased display or deselect the *Work* option to hide the *Planned* item in the time-phased grid.

Use the *Zoom In, Zoom Out,* and *Scroll to Task* buttons in the *Zoom* section of the ribbon to navigate in the Gantt chart. By default, the *Summary* view is the only available selection on the *View* pick list in the *Data* section of the ribbon unless your Project Server administrator creates additional views for your organization. The table in the *Summary* view includes the following fields:

- Task Name

- Work

- Remaining Work

- Start

- Finish

- % Work Complete

- Comments

- Resource Name

- Project Name

To return to the *Resource Center* page, click the *Resource Center* button in the *Navigate* section of the ribbon.

Hands On Exercise

Exercise 15-2

View resource assignments.

1. On the *Resource Center* page, select the checkboxes for Al Petit and George Stewart and then click the *Resource Assignments* button in the *Navigate* section of the *Resources* ribbon.

2. Examine the resource assignments for your selected resources.

3. In the *Display* section of the *Assignments* ribbon click the *Zoom In, Zoom Out,* and *Scroll to Task* buttons to navigate in the Gantt chart.

4. In the *Display* section of the *Assignments* ribbon, click the *Timephased Data* button.

5. In the *Data* section of the *Assignments* ribbon click the *View* pick list button and apply any custom views created by your Project Server administrator.

6. In the *Navigate* section of the *Assignments* ribbon, click the *Resource Center* button on the ribbon to return to the *Resource Center* page.

Editing Resource Details

If you are a member of the Administrators group or the Resource Managers group, and the Resource Managers group has the correct permissions, you can edit resource information from the *Resource Center* page. Begin by selecting the option checkbox for the resource(s) you want to edit. Project Server 2010 allows you to edit resource information several ways:

- Edit the details for a group of resources simultaneously in Project Web App (Bulk Edit).

- Edit the details for one or more resources individually in Project Web App (Single or Batch Edit).

- Edit additional resource information in Project Professional 2010.

To edit the details for a group of resources simultaneously, click the *Bulk Edit* button in the *Editing* section of the *Resources* ribbon. Project Server 2010 displays the *Bulk Edit* page for the selected resources as shown in Figure 15 - 14. Notice in Figure 15 - 14 that I selected four resources for bulk editing and that the system displays the resource names in the page header.

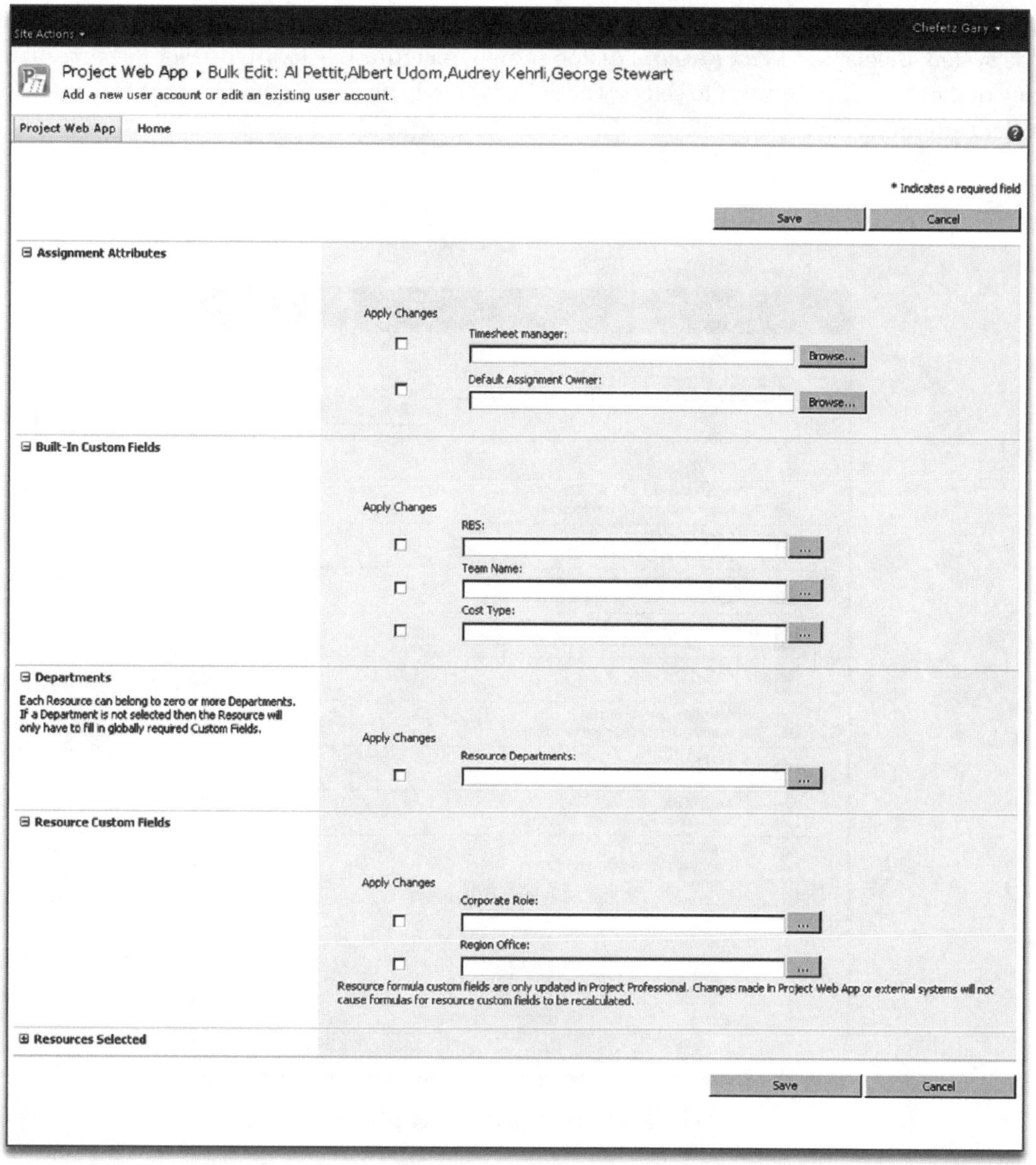

Figure 15 - 14: Bulk Edit page for four selected resources

The *Bulk Edit* page contains six sections in which you can edit resource details that apply to all selected resources. The *Assignment Attributes* section contains two important fields: the *Timesheet Manager* and *Default Assignment Owner* fields. The *Timesheet Manager* field must contain the name of the manager who approves timesheets for the selected resources. The system uses the *Default Assignment Owner* field value to determine on whose *Tasks* page to display task assignments when a manager publishes a project. If your organization uses team leaders who are responsible for re-porting progress on behalf of their team members, then enter the team leader's name in this field. If each selected re-source must see assigned tasks on his/her own *Tasks* page, then you cannot use the *Bulk Edit* page when editing values in this field. Instead, you must edit each resource individually.

To select a value in either the *Timesheet Manager* field or the *Default Assignment Owner* field, click the *Browse* button for that field. The system displays the *Pick Resource* dialog shown in Figure 15 - 15. In the *Pick Resource* dialog, double-click the name of the resource you want to select. The system closes the *Pick Resource* dialog and enters the selected name in the field automatically.

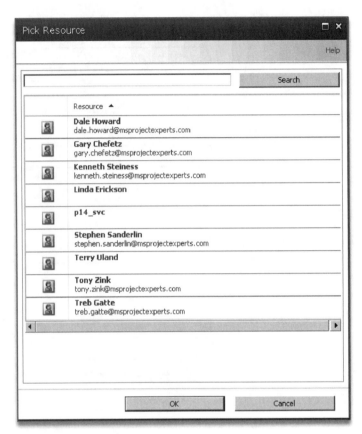

Figure 15 - 15: Pick Resource dialog

The *Built-In Custom Fields* section contains the three built-in custom enterprise resource fields that ship with Project Server 2010: *RBS, Team Name,* and *Cost Type* fields. The *Departments* section contains one field: the *Resource Departments* field. You use this field for resources that belong to more than one department. If you do not select a department, the resource will only have to fill in globally required custom fields. The *Resource Custom Fields* section contains any custom enterprise resource fields specifically created for your organization. Notice in Figure 15 - 14, shown previously, that the *Resource Custom Fields* section contains two custom enterprise fields, the *Corporate Role* and *Region Office* fields. The system collapses the *Resources Selected* section by default, as this section does not contain any editable fields.

To select a value for a field in either the *Built-In Custom Fields* section or the *Resource Custom Fields* section, click the *Select Value* button (...) to the right of the field and select a value from the pick list. For example, Figure 15 - 16 shows the pick list for the *Team Name* field.

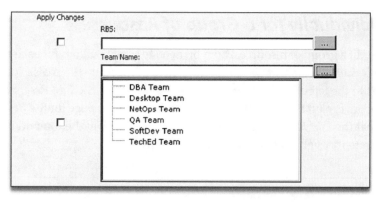

Figure 15 - 16: Team Name pick list items

If you edit any field on the *Bulk Edit* page, you must select the *Apply Changes* option checkbox to the left of the field name. Figure 15 - 17 shows the *Bulk Edit* page after I set the *Timesheet Manager* field value to *Stephen Sanderlin* and the *Team Name* field value to *Desktop Team* for the four selected resources. Notice that I selected the *Apply Changes* option checkbox for these two fields as well. Click the *Save* button. Project Server 2010 applies the field changes to each of the resources you selected.

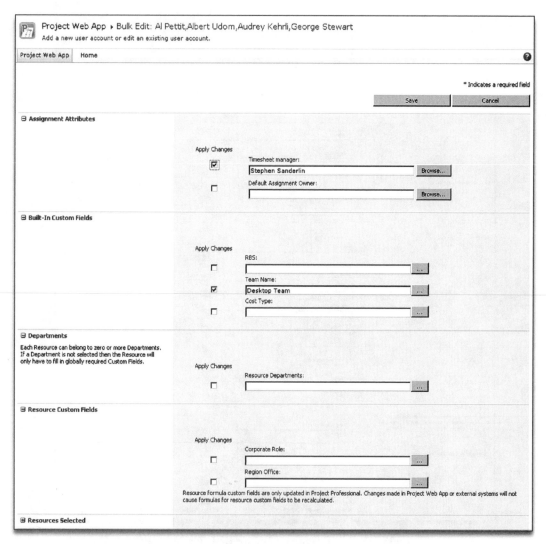

Figure 15 - 17: Bulk Edit page after editing two fields

Editing Details Individually for a Group of Resources

At times you may need to edit a group of resources, but you need to specify values for each resource individually. For example, I need to set the *Default Assignment Owner* field for each of the four resources I selected in the last example. Select the option checkbox to the left of each resource name and then click the *Edit Resource* button from the *Editing* section of the *Resources* ribbon. Project Server 2010 displays the *Edit Resource* page for the first selected resource shown in Figure 15 - 18. Notice that the *Edit Resource* page contains three buttons at the top and bottom (not shown) of the page that you use to navigate through each of the selected resources.

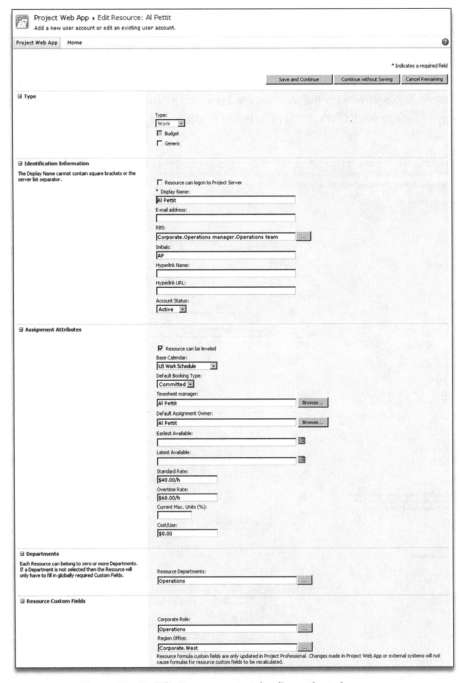

Figure 15 - 18: Edit Resource page for first selected resource

On the *Edit Resource* page for the first selected resource, change the values in any of the individual fields as needed. When you finish editing the first resource, click the *Save and Continue* button. The system displays the *Edit Resource* page for the next selected resource. Continue editing each selected resource, and click the *Save and Continue* button on each page. When you finish editing the last selected resource on the *Edit Resource* page, you only have two options: the *Save* and *Cancel* buttons. Click the *Save* button to save your changes or click the *Cancel* button to return to the *Resource Center* page. Should you decide to skip any of the selected resources during your editing, click the *Continue without Saving* button. To cancel at any time without continuing, click the *Cancel Remaining* button.

Editing Resource Information in Project Professional 2010

Project Server 2010 does not allow you to edit every resource field using either the *Bulk Edit* page or the *Edit Resource* page in Project Web App. If you need to edit resource fields not contained on either of these pages, you must edit the selected resources in Project Professional 2010. To edit resources using Project Professional 2010, navigate to the *Resource Center* page, select the option checkbox to the left of each resource name, and then click the *Open* button from the *Editing* section of the *Resources* ribbon. The system launches Project Professional 2010, checks out the selected resources, and opens them applying the *Resource Sheet* view shown in Figure 15 - 19.

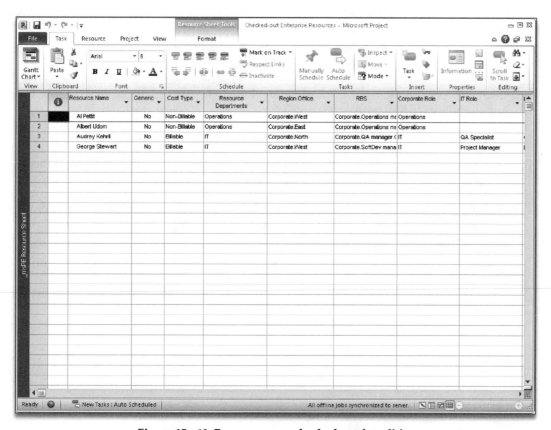

Figure 15 - 19: Four resources checked out for editing

With the resources checked out, you can edit any standard or custom enterprise resource field. When you complete your changes, save and close the resources and exit Project Professional 2010.

Hands On Exercise

Exercise 15-3

Edit resource details for multiple resources.

1. On the *Resource Center* page, select two or more resources and then click the *Bulk Edit* button in the *Editing* section of the *Resources* ribbon.

2. On the *Bulk Edit* page, change the details for the selected resources in one or more fields except for the *RBS* field, and then click the *Save* button to save your changes and return to the *Resource Center* page.

3. Click the *Edit Resource* button in the *Editing* section of the *Resources* ribbon.

4. On the *Edit Resource* page for each selected resource, enter appropriate information in one or more fields and then click the *Save and Continue* button to work through the list of resources. When you edit the last selected resource, click the *Save* button to save your changes and return to the *Resource Center* page.

5. Click the *Open* button in the *Editing* section of the *Resources* ribbon to open the selected resources in Project Professional 2010.

6. Notice the standard information shown in the *Resource Sheet* view.

7. Double-click the name of any resource and examine the custom resource information for the selected resource.

8. Click the *Cancel* button to close the *Resource Information* dialog, then close the checked out enterprise resources. Click the *File* tab to navigate to the *Backstage* and click the *Exit* button to exit Project Professional 2010.

Module 16

Working with the Project Center and Project Views

Learning Objectives

After completing this module, you will be able to:

- Work with features in the Project Center
- Work with Project Center views
- Work with detailed Project views
- Access Project Workspace features from the Project Center
- Open projects from the Project Center page
- Check in a project
- Close enterprise projects to update
- Edit project details and open a project in the Project Center

Inside Module 16

746

Using the Project Center

In Project Server 2010, the Project Center is the central location for project and portfolio information, a launching point for new projects and the gateway to editing projects on the web, a new feature in Project Server 2010. To navigate to the *Project Center* page, click the *Project Center* link in the *Quick Launch* menu. Figure 16 - 1 shows the *Project Center* page with a custom view applied and the *Quick Launch* menu collapsed. The *Project Center* page displays a data grid with a project list on the left and a Gantt chart on the right. The project list displays a single line of information about each project and proposed project, with multiple columns of information about each item.

The Gantt chart displays one or two Gantt bars representing the life span of the project. When the system displays two Gantt bars, one represents the baseline schedule while the other represents the current schedule of the project.

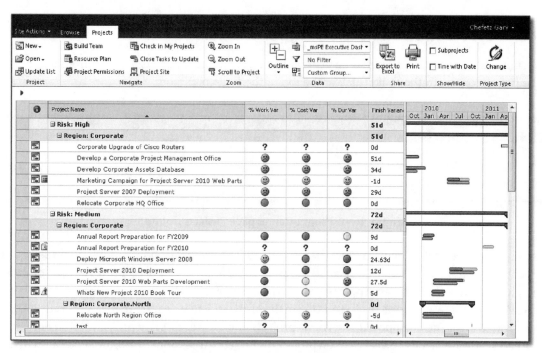

Figure 16 - 1: Project Center page with custom view applied

The *Project Center* page allows you to do each of the following:

- View the portfolio of active and proposed enterprise projects.

- View master projects and subprojects.

- Navigate to the Project Site for a project, or navigate directly to the *Risks, Issues, Documents,* or *Deliverables* page for the project.

- Create new enterprise projects and proposed projects.

- Edit the properties for an enterprise project or proposed project.

- Drill down to a detailed Project view to view or edit the project.

- Build a team or create a Resource Plan for any project.

- Open a single project or a group of projects in Project Professional 2010.

- Set individual permissions for a project.

- Close tasks to updates in a project.

- Check in a project stuck in a checked-out state.

In this module, I discuss all of the above topics except for how to create a new enterprise project plan or proposed enterprise project because I discussed these topics previously in Modules 03 and 04. Review these modules for specific instructions on these topics.

Using the Projects Ribbon in the Project Center

Figure 16 - 2 shows the *Project Center* page for a user with project manager permissions. Notice the *Projects* ribbon at the top of the page, along with the *Projects* tab at the top of the *Projects* ribbon.

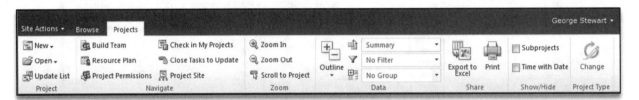

Figure 16 - 2: Project Center page Projects ribbon

The *Projects* ribbon has one context-sensitive tab, the *Projects* tab. The *Projects* ribbon contains menu selections in seven sections: *Project, Navigate, Zoom, Data, Share, Show/Hide* and *Project Type*. If you used prior versions of Project Server, you can see right away that Project Web App has a much richer set of available functionality than ever before. For example, Project Web App now supports project editing in the browser, a new feature in Project Server 2010. The *Project* section allows you to create new proposed enterprise projects and new enterprise projects. From here, you can drill down to projects for editing in the browser or open projects in Project Professional 2010, and you can synchronize data between projects and SharePoint lists.

The *Navigate* section provides familiar functions carried forward from previous versions including *Build Team, Resource Plan, Check in My Projects, Close Tasks to Update* and a button to navigate to the *Project Site* for a selected project, formerly known as the *Project Workspace* in Project Server 2007. You use tools in the *Zoom* section to zoom the timescale of the Gantt chart and scroll to projects in the Gantt chart. From the *Data* section you can collapse outline levels in views that contain multi-level grouping, select and apply views, and apply ad-hoc filters and grouping to your views. Use the *Share* section to export your view to Microsoft Excel or to send it to a printer. The *Show/Hide* section provides two toggle options, the first displays subprojects along with master projects and the second determines whether the system displays the time in date fields. Finally, the *Project Type* section contains one selection, *Change*. You use this to change the *Project Type* of a proposed or existing project.

Using Project Center Views

The *Project Center* page displays only the projects and proposed projects that you have permission to see, including projects and proposed projects that you own. Unless you have additional privileges in the system, these may be the only projects that you see. The first time you access the *Project Center* page, the system displays the default *Summary* view, unless your Project Server administrator removed that view. The system provides five standard views that you can select from the pick list in the *Data* section of the page:

- Summary

- Tracking

- Cost

- Earned Value

- Work

The *Summary* view, shown in Figure 16 - 3, displays the "vital statistics" for each project, with columns showing the project's *Start* date, *Finish* date, *% Complete*, *Work*, *Duration*, and *Owner*. The *Summary* view includes a Gantt chart with a single Gantt bar for each project and a black stripe indicating project progress. Notice in Figure 16 - 3 that several projects contain a black stripe within the blue Gantt bar, indicating the current progress for each project.

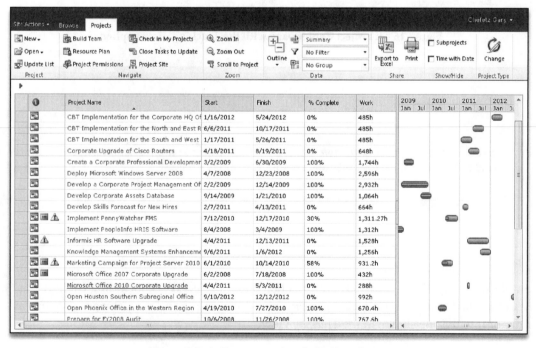

Figure 16 - 3: Summary view in Project Center

The *Tracking* view displays variance information about each project using the following fields: *% Complete, Actual Cost, Actual Duration, Actual Finish, Actual Start, Actual Work, Baseline Finish, Baseline Start, Duration, Remaining Duration, Finish,* and *Start.* The *Tracking* view, shown in Figure 16 - 4, displays a *Tracking* Gantt chart with two Gantt bars for each project. The top Gantt bar represents the current schedule for each project, while the bottom Gantt bar represents the baseline schedule for each project. The black stripe in the top Gantt bar indicates project progress.

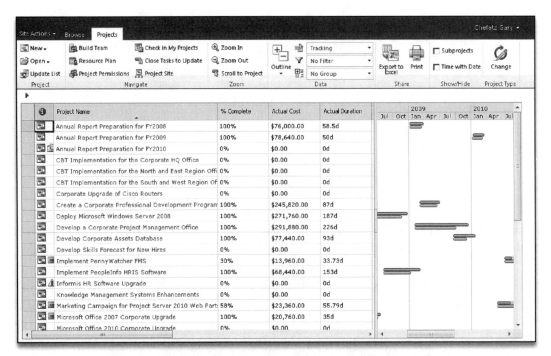

Figure 16 - 4: Project Center page with the Tracking view applied

 If you do not see the lower of the two Gantt bars for a project in the *Tracking* view, this indicates that you did not set a baseline for the project before you published it.

The *Cost* view shown in Figure 16 - 5 displays information about project costs, including columns for *Finish, Start, Cost, Baseline Cost, Actual Cost, Fixed Cost, Cost Variance,* and *Remaining Cost.* The *Cost* view also displays a *Tracking* Gantt chart identical to the one shown in the *Tracking* view.

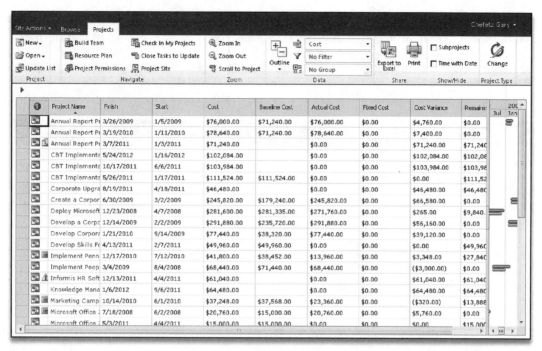

Figure 16 - 5: Project Center page with the Cost view applied

The *Earned Value* view displays the calculated earned value at the project level for each project. This view includes columns for *Finish, Start, Cost, Baseline Cost, BCWP, BCWS, SV, CV, ACWP,* and *VAC*. The *Earned Value* view shown in Figure 16 - 6 includes the same *Tracking* Gantt chart as the *Tracking* and *Cost* views.

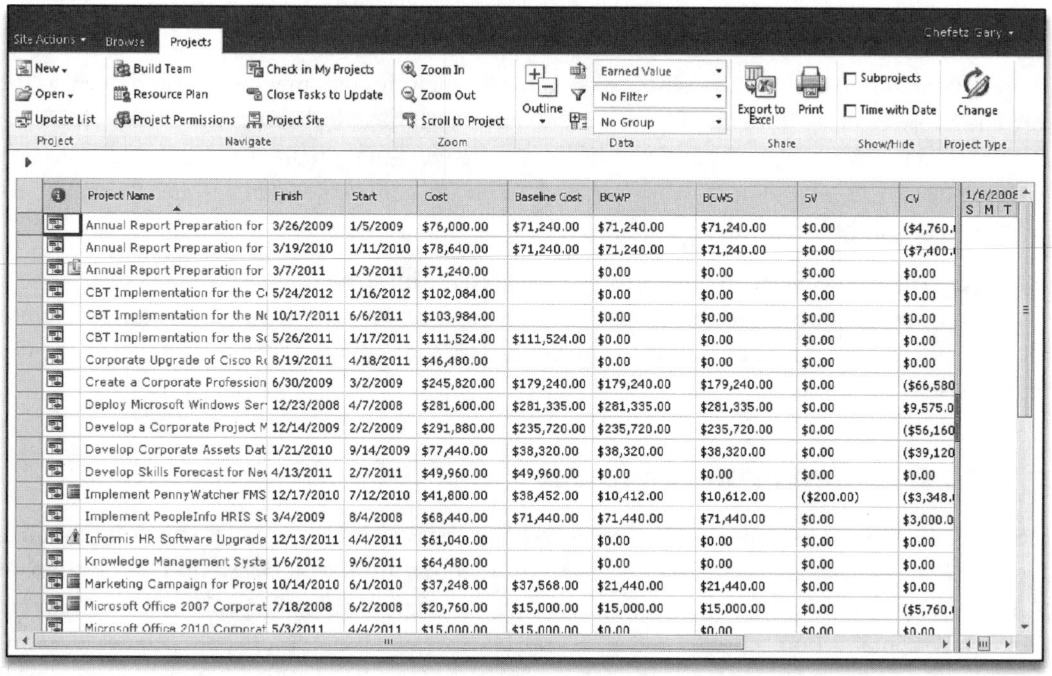

Figure 16 - 6: Project Center page with the Earned Value view applied

The *Work* view displays information about project work hours with columns for *% Work Complete, Finish, Remaining Work, Start, Work, Baseline Work, Actual Work,* and *Work Variance.* The *Work* view shown in Figure 16 - 7 displays the same *Tracking* Gantt chart found in all other *Project Center* views.

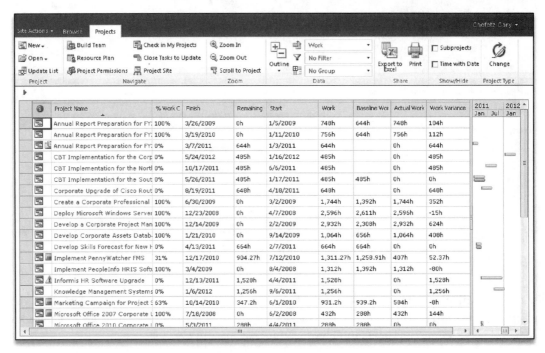

Figure 16 - 7: Project Center page with the Work view applied

In addition to the five standard views, the *View* pick list may also include custom views created by your Project Server administrator. The Project Center is a great forum for the use of graphical indicators in custom views. For example, Figure 16 - 1, displayed previously, shows an *Executive Summary* view that displays several columns containing custom graphical indicators. The *%Cost Var, % Work Var,* and *%Dur Var* columns reveal variance for each project using a red, yellow, or green stoplight indicator.

As with the *Resource Center* page, you can filter, group, or search the information presented in the *Project Center* page. Use the *Zoom In* and *Zoom Out* buttons to change the timescale of the Gantt chart. You can change the timescale to periods as small as 15-minute intervals or as large as half years. Use the *Scroll to Task* button to scroll the Gantt chart to the start date of the selected project.

Working with Detailed Project Views

Some pages contain more than one context-sensitive tab, such as the *Project Details* page. This page contains three such tabs, including the *Project, Task,* and *Options* tabs, grouped together under the *Schedule Tools* section, as shown in Figure 16 - 8. You navigate to the *Project Details* page by clicking on the name of a project in the *Project Center* page. The *Project Detail* page contains both a *Project* and a *Task* tab because you must access both project-level and task-level functions to use the features on this page. Notice the convenient *Status* bar notification just below the ribbon.

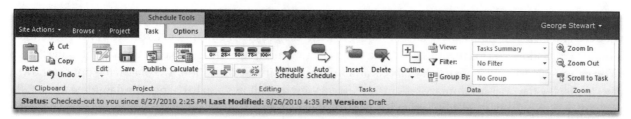

Figure 16 - 8: Project Details page with the Task ribbon selected

In the *Task* ribbon shown in Figure 16 - 8, notice the *Clipboard* section on the far left and the *Editing* and *Tasks* sections in the center. These three sections contain the new web-based project editing tools available in Project Server 2010 using familiar functionality similar to what you find in Project Professional 2010. This exciting new capability supports much stronger project management collaboration, allowing numerous users to participate in project schedule development, or even to manage simple projects from end to end, including project tracking, without using Project Professional 2010. Notice that the *Data* and *Zoom* sections provide you with tools to manipulate the data display and Gantt chart displays, respectively. Finally, the *Project* section makes the most common Project-level functions conveniently available without the need to switch to the *Project* tab.

In the preceding paragraph, I use the word "simple" to describe the project editing tools available using the Project Web App interface. These tools are a subset of the editing capabilities you find in Project Professional 2010, and are limited in their functionality. For example, you cannot specify a Units value when assigning one or more resources to tasks; the system uses the 100% units value automatically. When setting dependencies between tasks, the system limits you to only the Finish-To-Start (FS) dependency, and you cannot add *Lag* time or *Lead* time. Despite these limitations, this new capability represents a giant advance in Project Web App usability.

If you click the *Project* tab, the system displays the *Project* ribbon shown in Figure 16 - 9. This ribbon provides redundant *Edit* and *Save* buttons, and provides the only way to close and check in a project after editing on the web via the *Close* button in the *Project* section. The *Navigate* section provides navigation to the *Project Site* page using the *Project Site* button or to any of the four primary *Project Site* features using the *Documents*, *Issues*, *Risks* and *Deliverables* buttons. You also find *Build Team* and *Resource Plan* buttons to activate these two features and a new *Project Permissions* button that allows you to set project-level permissions specific to your selected project. Finally, the *Previous* and *Next* buttons allow you to switch between schedule pages and the *Project Fields* page where you can edit the *Project Name*, *Project Start Date* and *Project Owner* fields as well as any enterprise custom fields applicable to the specific project. Note in the figure that the system grays out the *Edit* button because the project is open for editing.

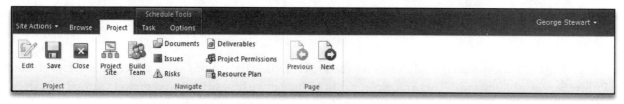

Figure 16 - 9: Project Details page with the Project ribbon selected

Click the *Options* tab and the system displays the *Options* contextual ribbon shown in Figure 16 - 10. In the *Share* section of the *Options* ribbon, notice that you can choose to print the project or export it to Excel. The *Link To* section contains buttons that allow you to create links from tasks to Documents, Issues and Risks contained in the Project's *Project Site*. You can even create any one of these objects and link them all in one operation. The *Show/Hide* option allows you to select to display the project summary task in the current view and allows you to change the date/time format. Finally, this ribbon also provides quick access to the *Close Tasks to Updates* feature also available in the Project Center.

Figure 16 - 10: Project Details page with the Options ribbon selected

In addition to viewing a single line of information about each project in the portfolio, the Project Center links you to detailed views of any project. Click the name of any project in the data grid of the *Project Center* page and the system displays the *Project Details* page, as shown for the Microsoft Office 2010 Corporate Upgrade project in Figure 16 - 11.

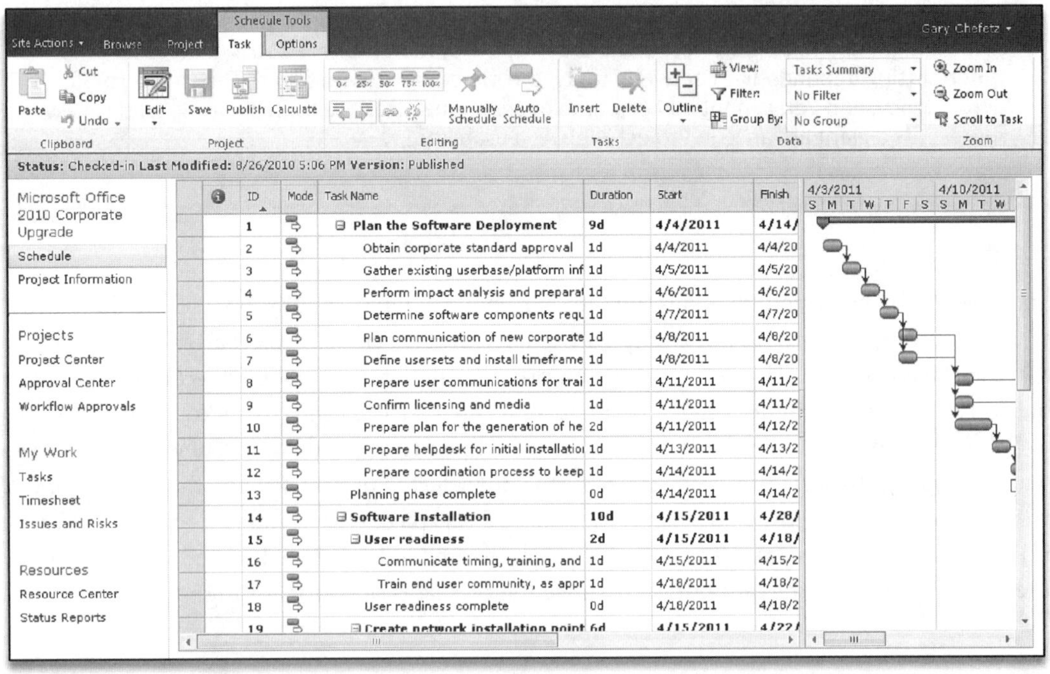

Figure 16 - 11: Project Details page of the selected project

The *View* pick list offers nineteen default views for the *Project Details* page along with any custom views created by your Project Server administrator. These nineteen views include three types of detailed project views: *Task* views, *Assignment* views, and *Resource* views. Table 16 - 1 lists the available views for each type.

The system remembers which detailed project view you select each time you display the *Project Details* page, and returns to that view when you select another project from the *Project Center* page.

Task Views	Assignment Views	Resource Views
Tasks Cost	Assignments Cost	Resources Cost
Tasks Detail	Assignments Detail	
Tasks Earned Value	Assignments Earned Value	Resources Earned Value
Tasks Leveling		
Tasks Schedule		
Tasks Summary	Assignments Summary	Resources Summary
Tasks Top-Level		
Tasks Tracking	Assignments Tracking	
Tasks Work	Assignments Work	Resources Work

Table 16 - 1: Available Views on the Project Details page

Like *Project Center* views, you can apply grouping and filtering to any detailed project view. Use the *Zoom In* and *Zoom Out* buttons to change the Gantt chart timescale from periods as small as 15-minute intervals to as large as years. Use the *Scroll to Task* button to scroll the Gantt chart to the start date of the selected task.

Hands On Exercise

Exercise 16-1

Explore Project Center views.

1. Click the *Project Center* link in the Quick Launch menu.

2. In the *Data* section of the *Projects* ribbon, click the *View* pick list and apply each of the five default *Project Center* views individually.

3. Explore the information shown in each *Project Center* view.

4. Reapply the *Summary* view.

5. In the *Data* section of the *Projects* ribbon, click the *Group by* pick list and select the *Owner* field.

6. Note that the display changes to the grouped view.

7. In the *Data* section of the *Projects* ribbon, select the *Filter* pick list to create your own custom filter and note the results.

Exercise 16-2

Explore detailed Project views from the Project Center.

1. Click the name of a project in the *Project Center* data grid.

2. In the *Data* section of the *Task* ribbon, select any *Assignments* view from the *View* pick list.

3. In the *Data* section of the *Task* ribbon, select any *Resources* view from the *View* pick list.

4. In the *Data* section of the *Task* ribbon, select any *Tasks* view from the *View* pick list.

5. Click the *Project Center* link in the Quick Launch menu to return to the *Project Center* page.

Editing Projects in Project Web App

Not only can you view information in project detail views, you can also edit projects using these views. You can open a project for editing within Project Web App or open a project for editing in Project Professional 2010 from the *Project Center* page in Project Web App.

Opening Projects in Project Professional 2010 from the Project Center

The filtering and grouping capabilities in the Project Center make it an ideal location from which to open one or more enterprise projects, particularly if you have many projects in your Project Server data store. While the *Open* dialog in Project Professional 2010 allows you to group projects on custom enterprise fields, you cannot use multiple views the way you can in the *Project Center*, and you cannot create ad-hoc filters the way you can in the *Project Center* page.

To open an individual project in Project Professional 2010 from the *Project Center* page, select the header row for a project in a *Project Center* view and click the *Edit* pick list. The system displays the pick list show in Figure 16 - 12.

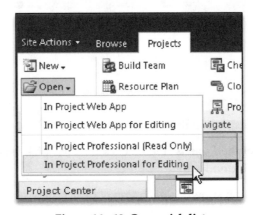

Figure 16 - 12: Open pick list

Notice that you have four selections, one for read/write and one for read-only for both Project Professional 2010 and Project Web App. When you select either *In Project Professional (Read Only)* or *In Project Professional for Editing,* the system launches Project Professional 2010 (if you have not already launched it), and then checks out and opens the selected project. You can edit and save your project once it is open.

Warning: Before attempting to open a project from the *Project Center* page, you must confirm that the URL you entered for your login account in Project Professional 2010 **precisely matches** the URL you use to access Project Web App. If these two URLs do not match precisely and you attempt to open a project from the *Project Center* page, Project Server 2010 displays an error message indicating that the required version of Project is not installed and the system fails to open the project.

Opening Multiple Projects to Create a Master Project

To open multiple projects simultaneously, use the **Ctrl** key to select two or more projects, and then click the *Edit* pick list. Instead of opening each selected project individually, the system creates a master project in Project Professional 2010 with each of the selected projects as subprojects of the master project. You can use a master project to set cross-project dependencies between tasks in the selected projects, or to analyze trends in the portfolio of selected projects. Figure 16 - 13 shows a master project consisting of four subprojects.

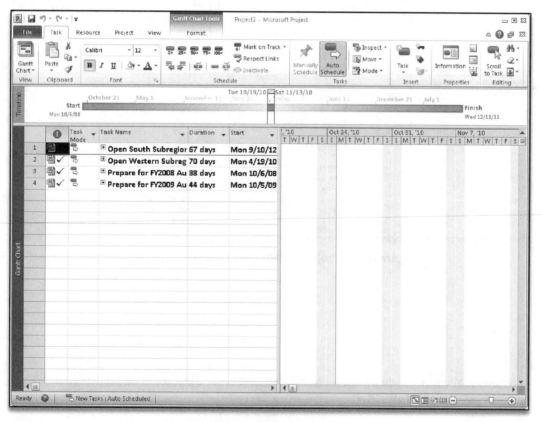

Figure 16 - 13: Master project includes four subprojects

After you create the master project, expand each of the subprojects by clicking the *Expand/Collapse* indicator (the + sign) to the left of each project name. To limit the amount of scrolling you must do to open each subproject, begin with the last subproject, and work your way toward the top. Edit each subproject as per your requirements, including setting cross-project dependencies between the various subprojects. If you save and publish a master project in Project Server 2010, the master project appears as a regular project in the *Project Center* page except that it has a unique icon indicating that it is a master project.

When you click the name of a master project in the *Project Center* page, the system displays a detailed master project view that allows you to expand the details in each subproject. Figure 16 - 14 shows the *Project Details* page for the master project with one of the subprojects expanded to show the project details.

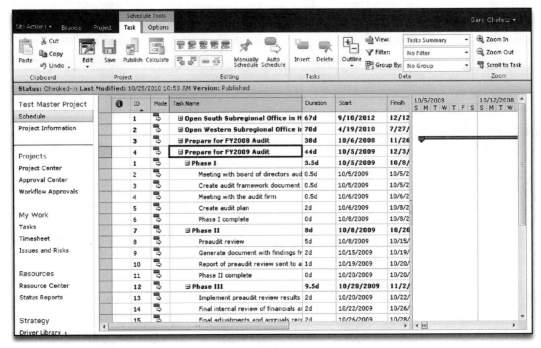

Figure 16 - 14: Project Details page for a master project

 Warning: You cannot edit a Master Project in Project Web App. Instead, you must use the Project Professional client application.

Hands On Exercise

Exercise 16-3

Create a master project from the Project Center page.

1. Select several projects in the *Project Center* page. In the *Project* section of the *Projects* ribbon, click the *Open* pick list and select the *In Project Professional for Editing* item.

2. Notice how the system creates a master project in Project Professional 2010.

3. Expand each subproject, beginning with the last project and working your way to the top.

4. Save and publish the master project.

5. Close and check in the master project and then exit Project Professional 2010.

6. Press the **F5** function key to refresh the *Project Center* page or navigate to the *Project Center* page by clicking the *Project Center* link in the Quick Launch menu.

7. Click the name of the master project to display the *Project Details* page. Note: you must select a *Task* view to see the master project.

8. Expand one of the subprojects in the *Project Details* page.

9. Click the *Project Center* link in the Quick Launch menu to return to the *Project Center* page.

Editing Individual Projects in Project Web App

Select the header row for a single project in the *Project Center* data grid and then click the *Open* pick list from the *Project* section of the *Projects* ribbon. Select the *In Project Web App* item from the list and the system displays the *Schedule* page for the project as shown in Figure 16 - 15. Notice that the only items active on the *Task* ribbon are the *Edit* button in the *Project* section, the *Copy* button in the *Clipboard* section, and various options to control the view in both the *Data* and *Zoom* sections. Notice also the status bar below the ribbon telling you that the project is checked-in and the last modified date. You cannot use the scheduling tools until you check out the project for editing.

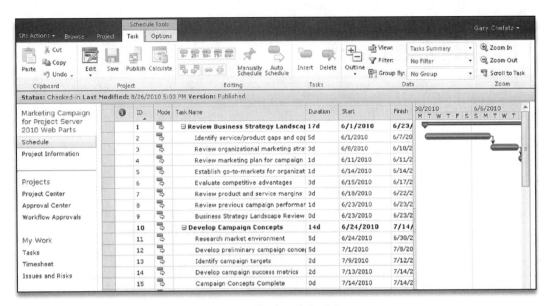

Figure 16 - 15: Project Schedule page

When you open a project that is in a stage of a workflow that occurs prior to allowing users to edit the schedule, you may not be able to access the *Schedule* page for the project. Instead, the system displays the set of *Project Detail Pages* that the creator of the workflow determined that you should see at the current stage.

To edit the project, click on the *Edit* pick list from the *Project* section of the *Task* ribbon and choose the *In Project Web App* item. The system opens the project for editing, refreshes the page, updates the *Status* bar below the ribbon to indicate the project is checked out, and makes all but the *Edit* button on the ribbon available for use as shown in Figure 16 - 16.

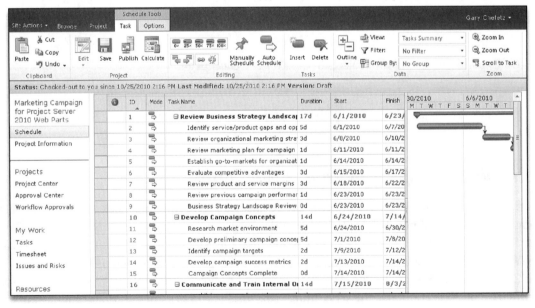

Figure 16 - 16: Project Open for Editing

When you open a project in Project Web App, you may see as few as one *Project Detail* page besides the *Schedule* page or you may see quite a few. If your project is not past a proposal stage, you might not see the *Schedule* page. Your Project Server implementer or administrator who manages your *Project Detail Pages* or workflow determines the pages that you encounter here as well as their contents. Because these can vary widely from system to system, I cannot predict everything that you might encounter. Some pages may contain data that you can edit while other pages may present data that you cannot edit. You should see the *Schedule* page once a project is beyond an approval stage that allows you to manage it, and you should see at least one *Project Detail* page that allows you to edit basic project information, such as the *Project Name*, and other general information as well as local and enterprise custom fields. In the example above, I select the *Project Information* page from the *Quick Launch* menu and the system displays the *Project Information* page shown in Figure 16 - 17. Note that similar pages in your system might not have the same name.

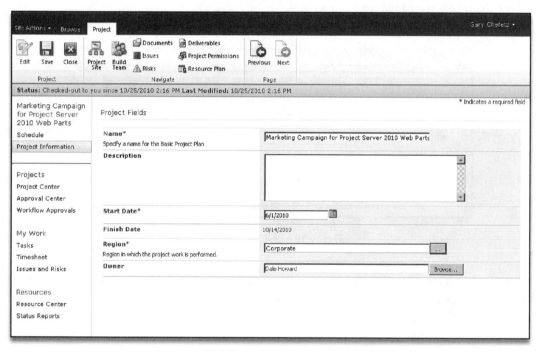

Figure 16 - 17: Project Information page

Renaming a Project using Project Web App

To rename the project, edit the name shown in the *Name* field. When you edit the name of the project, this action renames the project in the Project Server 2010 database. Changing the name in the *Owner* field allows the new owner to see and open the project in Project Professional 2010, if they do not otherwise have permission to access the project. In addition to editing the *Project Name* and *Owner* fields, you can also edit the values in any custom enterprise Project fields.

After you make your changes on the *Project Details* page, click the *Save* button in the *Project* section of the *Project* ribbon to save the changes in the *Draft* database. While the system saves the changes, it displays progress information in the upper right corner of the page.

Warning: To rename the project, you must both save and publish the project. When you save the project, the system changes the project name in the *Draft* database. When you publish the project, the system changes the project name in the *Published* database and in the Project Site associated with the project.

If you want to publish the changes to the *Published* database, click the *Schedule* link or the *Project Name* link from the *Quick Launch* menu. The system displays the *Schedule* page. On the *Tasks* ribbon, click the *Publish* button in the *Projects* section. While the system publishes the changes, it displays progress information in the upper right corner of the page. When finished, click on the *Project* tab to expose the *Project* ribbon and then click the *Close* button. The system displays the *Close* dialog shown in Figure 16 - 18.

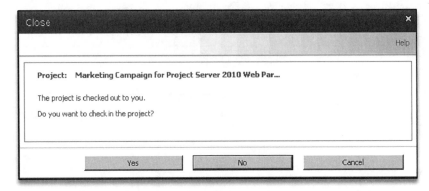

Figure 16 - 18: Close dialog

The *Close* dialog gives you the option to check in your project by clicking the *Yes* button or the option to check out your project by clicking the *No* button. Click the *Cancel* button if you want to cancel your action. Clicking the *Yes* button closes and checks in the project so that others can edit it.

Rename a Project Using Project Professional 2010

You can also rename a project using Project Professional 2010 by completing the following steps:

1. Click the *File* tab and then click the *Open* item in the *Backstage* menu.

2. In the *Open* dialog, double-click the *Retrieve the list of all projects from Project Server* item.

3. Right-click on the name of a project and click *Rename* on the shortcut menu.

4. Enter the new name for the enterprise project and then press the **Enter** key on your computer keyboard.

5. In the confirmation dialog, click the *OK* button.

6. Open the project from the *Open* dialog.

7. Publish the project again.

Hands On Exercise

Exercise 16-4

Edit the Project details for an enterprise project.

1. Select the **Microsoft Office 2010 Corporate Upgrade** project by clicking on the row header in the *Project Center* data grid. In the *Project* section of the *Projects* ribbon, click the *Open* pick list and select the *In Project Web App for Editing* item.

2. Click the *Project Information* link in the *Quick Launch* menu to display the *Project Details* page.

3. Change the value in the *Region* custom enterprise project field.

4. In the *Project* section of the *Project* ribbon, click the *Save* button.

5. Click the *Schedule* link or the *Microsoft Office 2010 Corporate Upgrade* link from the *Quick Launch* menu.

6. Click on the *Project* tab to display the *Project* ribbon. In the *Project* section of the *Project* ribbon, click the *Save* button to save your project, then close and check in your project.

Editing the Project Schedule in Project Web App

With your project open for editing and the *Schedule* page displayed in Project Web App, you can edit your project schedule in a variety of ways. You can create, edit, and delete tasks and you can link tasks using Project Web App. You can add resources to tasks using Project Web App, but this feature is limited to assigning resources at 100% units only. For the most part, the system limits you to editing only what you can see. For instance, you can create complex dependency relationships such as finish-to-finish, start-to-start and add lead or lag time to dependencies; however, neither the predecessor nor the successor columns appear in any of the default detail views that ship with Project Server. Therefore, you should ask your Project Server administrator to create one or more detail views suited to perform the type of editing you want to do. Figure 16 - 19 shows the *Predecessors* column added to the *Tasks Detail* view in Project Web App allowing me to create a complex dependency relationship. Using the *Link* button on the *Editing* section of the *Tasks* ribbon allows you to create finish-to-start dependencies only.

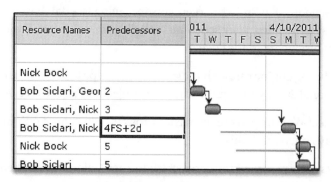

Figure 16 - 19: Predecessors added to Tasks Detail view

MSProjectExperts recommends that your Project Server administrator or implementer create views specifically for editing projects as the product team designed all of the default views for viewing and not editing. By creating views specifically for this purpose, you can expose the information you need to edit and not information that you do not want edited in Project Web App.

When you float your mouse pointer over a cell in the *Resource Names* column, the system reveals a pick list menu with the resource names shown in Figure 16 - 20.

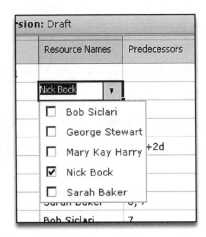

Figure 16 - 20: Resource Names column

Notice that the pick list allows you to select resources only, but it does not allow you to specify or edit the assignment units value. You also cannot specify the task type. Project Web App uses the default task type specified for the project. If you use *Fixed Work* as a task type in any of your projects, it renders them read-only in Project Web App.

Limitations when Editing Projects in Project Web App

There are a number of features not supported when you edit projects in Project Web App. The most important limitations are those that cause your project to be ineligible for editing as follows:

- Blank task lines or blank rows in a project schedule cause a project to open read-only and the system will not allow you to edit the schedule. Project in a stand-alone environment can handle blank lines, but realize that when you save your schedules to Project Server, you are saving to a database. Databases do not handle blank records very well. Besides making your schedule ineligible for editing in Project Web App, these can cause unexpected problems elsewhere in the system.

- The server-side scheduling engine cannot handle *Fixed Work* type tasks. If you include these in your schedule using Project Professional 2010, you cannot edit your project in Project Web App.

- Other than using Project Web App to create master projects, you cannot edit master projects in Project Web App. These will always open read-only.

- Project Web App does not support editing projects with Task Calendars applied. If you include these in your project schedules, they will open read-only in Project Web App.

Beyond those items that render your project read-only in Project Web App, you should be aware of functional limitations you face when editing a project on the web as follows:

- You cannot set a baseline from Project Web App. Before releasing your project to production, you must open it using Project Professional 2010 to save a baseline.

- You cannot edit assignment details in Project Web App. Actions like changing resource units or contouring work are beyond Project Web App's capabilities as is resource leveling. Just about everything you can think of doing to an assignment besides creating one at 100% units, is out of Project Web App's reach.

- You cannot make a task inactive using Project Web App.

- Cross-project links require that you use Project Professional 2010.

- You cannot make an assignment on summary tasks using Project Web App. Although there are some advanced scheduling techniques where assignments on summary tasks is useful, these are generally a bad idea and can cause unexpected results if you do not understand the ramifications.

- Cost and Material resource assignments are out of reach in Project Web App. You must use the Project Professional 2010 client to support these.

- Not surprisingly, you cannot set a *Task* type in Project Web App. Keep in mind the limitation of using *Fixed Work* tasks.

- You cannot edit a subproject, or create or edit master projects using Project Web App, except for the technique I showed you earlier in this module.

- You must set deadlines for tasks using Project Professional 2010, as nothing in Project Web App that allows you to do this.

- You must edit WBS fields using Project Professional 2010 as Project Web App does not support setting or editing these.

- The web-scheduling engine does not support *effort-driven* scheduling; therefore, you must address effort-driven tasks using Project Professional 2010. Notice that the system deselects the *effort-driven* option by default in Project 2010.

Tips for Editing Projects in Project Web App

Perhaps the most significant experience difference between editing in the client application versus editing in Project Web App is that Project Web App does not recalculate the schedule for you with every entry the way Project Professional 2010 does when you have the *Calculation* option set to *Automatic*. Opening and closing the file does invoke the scheduling engine similar to Project Professional 2010. Because there is no automatic calculation setting for Project Web App, you must use the *Calculate* button from the *Project* section of the *Task* ribbon to see the effect your edits have on the schedule when you edit details that cause the schedule to change.

When you edit projects in Project Web App, it is very easy to forget to save and check in your projects. Unlike the Project client, which will continue to remain open on your desktop until you close it, it is very easy to wander off to other tasks without saving your changes or checking in your project. You must be constantly mindful of this or you are likely to cause frustration for yourself and others by forgetting these important steps. If you are trying to edit a project in Project Web App and you cannot, ask yourself whether you remembered to open it for editing. Remember that the status bar that appears just below the ribbon when you open a project for editing contains important information regarding the current state of your project.

Checking In a Project from Project Web App

Occasionally you will leave a project in a checked-out state caused by a network problem or a workstation crash. Fortunately, the system allows you to check in your own projects without seeking administrative help. To check in a project, navigate to the *Project Center* page and click the *Check in my projects* item in the *Navigate* section of the *Projects* ribbon. Project Server 2010 displays the *Force Check-in My Projects* page shown in Figure 16 - 21.

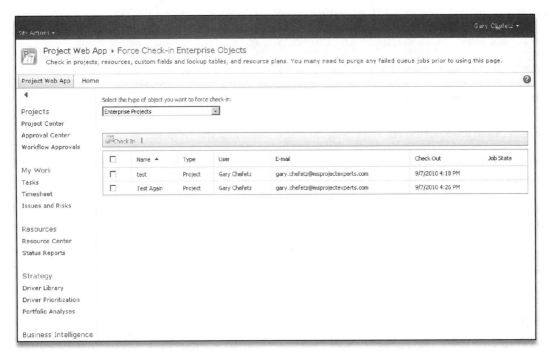

Figure 16 - 21: Force Check-in My Projects page

The *Force Check-in My Projects* page lists all projects currently checked out to you, including projects that are stuck in a checked-out state and projects that you currently have open in Project Professional 2010. Notice that Figure 16 - 21 displays only two projects.

To check in a project, select the option checkbox to the left of one or more projects to check in and click the *Check-In* button on the toolbar. The system displays the confirmation dialog shown in Figure 16 - 22. When you click the *OK* button, the system redisplays the *Force Check-in My Projects* page with the projects that you selected removed from the view.

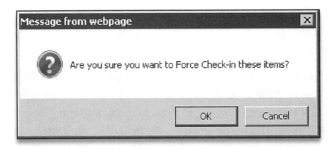

Figure 16 - 22: Confirmation dialog for Force Check-in

If you have administrative rights to force check-in projects in the system, you see more than your own projects in the *Force Check-in My Projects* page.

Closing Tasks to Updates

When you complete an enterprise project, or when you complete part of a project, you can close tasks in the project to prevent team members from entering additional progress on completed tasks. To close tasks to further updates, select the row header for a project in the *Project Center* page and click the *Close Tasks to Updates* item from the *Navigate* section of the *Projects* ribbon. Project Server 2010 displays the *Close Tasks to Update* page shown in Figure 16 - 23.

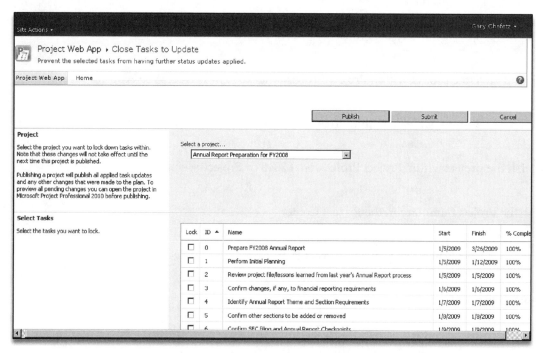

Figure 16 - 23: Close Tasks to Update page

 I previously discussed the *Close Tasks to Updates* page in Module 09, "Approving Time and Task Progress." As a part of updating task progress, you should close recently-completed tasks and cancelled tasks to update.

Notice that in the *Select a project* pick list, Project Server 2010 automatically chooses the project you selected in the *Project Center* page. The *Select Tasks* section of the page contains all tasks in the selected project. Select the option checkboxes in the *Lock* column to the left of all tasks that you have not previously closed and then click the *Submit* button to submit your changes and publish them later, or click the *Publish* button to finalize the action immediately. After publishing your project, the system locks the selected tasks to prevent team members from entering and submitting progress against them.

Warning: By default, Project Server 2010 applies sorting on the *ID* column, displaying the tasks in natural sequence order. Click any column header to re-sort the tasks by values in that column.

Setting Project Permissions

A new feature in Project Server 2010 allows project owners to set special permissions for users on the project. Without administrator rights a project manager can grant permissions so that Project Web App users, who cannot otherwise access the project, can perform specific actions on the project. Project Managers/Owners can grant the following permissions using this new feature:

- Open the project within Project Professional 2010 or Project Web App

- Edit and Save the project within Project Professional 2010 or Project Web App

- Edit Project Summary Fields within Project Professional 2010 or Project Web App

- Publish the project within Project Professional 2010 or Project Web App

- View the Project Summary in the Project Center

- View the Project Schedule Details in Project Web App

- View the Project Site

 In order for a project manager to use this feature, the project manager must have the *Manage Basic Project Security* category permission enabled.

To access the *Project Permissions* feature, select a project in the *Project Center* by clicking on its row header and then click on the *Project Permissions* item from the *Navigate* section of the *Projects* ribbon. If you already have your project open in Project Web App, select the *Project* ribbon if necessary, and click on *Project Permissions.* The system displays the *Project Permissions* page shown in Figure 16 - 24.

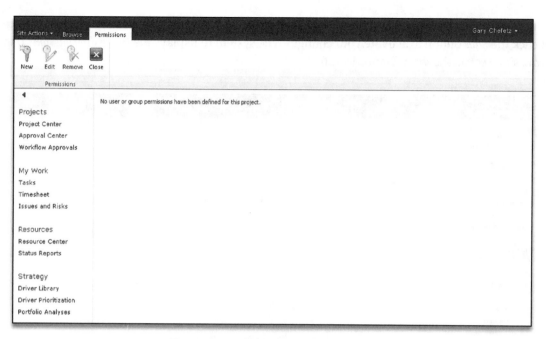

Figure 16 - 24: Project Permissions page

To create new permissions, click the *New* button from the *Permissions* section of the *Permissions* menu. The system displays the *Edit Project Permissions* page shown in Figure 16 - 25.

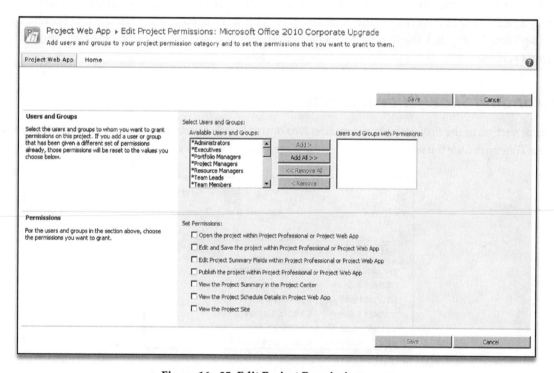

Figure 16 - 25: Edit Project Permissions page

Notice in the *Users and Groups* section of the page that you can specify permissions for entire security groups in Project Server as well as for individual users. Select a user or group from the *Available Users and Groups* list on the left and use the *Add* button to move them to the *Users and Groups with Permissions* box on the right. To select multiple users or groups, hold the **Ctrl** key to multi-select. Next, select the permissions that you want to grant to the selected user or users, and click the *Save* button to activate your changes. The system redisplays the *Project Permissions* page with the added permissions set as shown in Figure 16 - 26.

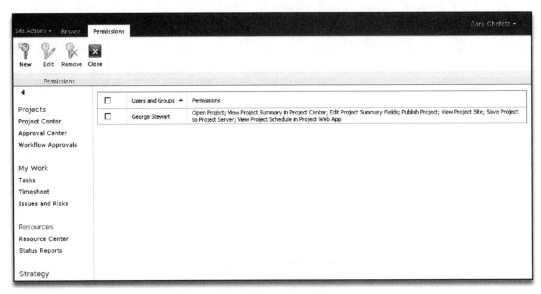

Figure 16 - 26: Project Permissions page with a Permission set displayed

Notice that I gave George Stewart all permissions available for this project. To edit the permission set once after creating it, simply select the checkbox next to the permission set you want to edit, and click the *Edit* button. To remove a permission set completely, click the *Remove* button after selecting it from the grid. Click the *Close* button to return to your previous screen.

Understanding Show/Hide Options

The *Show/Hide* section of the *Projects* ribbon contains two options: *Subprojects* and *Time with Date*. When you select the checkbox for *Time with Date* the system redisplays the page with a time in every date field as shown in Figure 16 - 27.

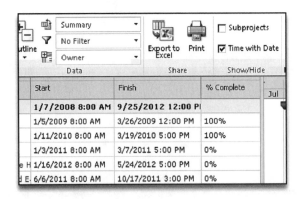

Figure 16 - 27: Showing Time with Date

Selecting the *Subprojects* checkbox produces a more subtle change to the page. When you deselect this in your view, and there are master projects in the system, you do not see the individual plans that are part of the master projects in the individual rows for projects. Instead, the system hides these from view and you must select the master project to drill down into the subprojects. When you select the *Subprojects* check box, the system displays the subprojects as individual project records and it displays the master project. Select the options that best fit your needs for any work session.

Navigating to the Project Site

You use the *Project Center* page to access the Project Sites for projects or to navigate directly to the *Risks, Issues, Documents,* or *Deliverables* page for a project. To navigate to the Project Site for any project, select the project row header and click the *Project Site* button from the *Navigate* section of the *Projects* ribbon. Project Server 2010 opens a new Internet Explorer window and displays the Project Site for your selected project as shown in Figure 16 - 28. The Project Center is your primary starting point for navigating to Project Sites as Microsoft eliminated a web part that displayed the sites in a list on the PWA home page. The eliminated web part was unpopular because it lacked display controls to make it useful for large project portfolios. Because I discussed Project Sites extensively in Modules 12 and 13, I do not discuss this topic again in this module.

Figure 16 - 28: Project Site home page

From the Project Site home page, you can drilldown into any of the functional lists for the project such as Risks, Issues or Documents associated with the project. You can also access these directly from the *Project Center* page if any of these items exist for a project. Notice the *Indicators* column identified with the icon ⓘ in the *Project Center* page shown in Figure 16 - 29.

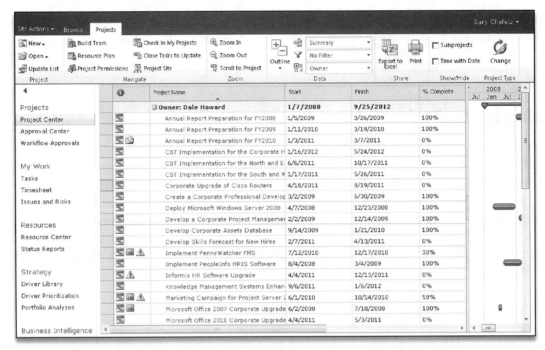

Figure 16 - 29: Project Center page shows indicators in the Indicators column

You can quickly see the meaning of the indicators by floating your mouse over any icon in the *Indicators* column for any project. The resulting tooltip displays the type of project and the number of Risks, Issues, and Documents associated with the project. Table 16 - 2 displays the indicators you may see in the *Indicators* column.

Indicator	Meaning
	Enterprise project
	Master Project
	Risks
	Issues
	Documents

Table 16 - 2: Indicators shown in the Project Center page

To access the *Risks, Issues, Documents,* or *Deliverables* page for any project, do one of the following:

- Click the *Risks, Issues,* or *Documents* indicator in the *Indicators* column to the left of the project.

- Select the row header for a project, click the *Project Site* button, and then select the *Risks, Issues, Documents,* or *Deliverables* in the Project Site home page.

Project Server 2010 opens a new Internet Explorer window and displays the Project Site for the selected project.

Project Center Summary

Since you created your first proposal in Module 03, you continuously return to the Project Center to launch most of the day-to-day tasks that you perform in Project Web App. The Project Center is the hub of most activity and the source for the latest information about your entire project portfolio.

Module 17

Working with Business Intelligence

Learning Objectives

After completing this module, you will be able to:

- Understand three common Business Intelligence uses for Project Managers
- Understand and be capable of using the Project Server 2010 Business Intelligence features
- Understand which data source is most applicable for a given need
- Create dashboard ready reports
- Create a basic dashboard

This module also assumes some basic knowledge of Excel operations, such as sorting and filtering.

Inside Module 17

Understanding Project Server 2010 Business Intelligence

What is Business Intelligence?

Business Intelligence (BI) is a set of processes, tools, and techniques for gathering, organizing, and analyzing large volumes of complex data in an effort to develop an accurate understanding of business dynamics, and you use it to improve strategic and tactical business decision-making. In other words, the purpose of BI is to capture large amounts of data, make some sense out of it, and use it to make sound business decisions. The ultimate goal is to develop the ability to spot problems and trends, and to make informed decisions to mitigate risks, improve efficiencies, and identify opportunities.

The data visualization aspects of the BI process are commonly referred to as reporting, a term with which you may be more familiar.

Project Server 2010 Business Intelligence differs from the Project Client Business Intelligence capabilities in that you are able to do analysis and reporting across multiple projects and resources across the organization. This enhanced scope enables you to see beyond your project plan and understand other impacts to your plan.

Levels of Business Intelligence

Business Intelligence needs are broken down into three major groups as shown in Figure 17 - 1. For Managers, the emphasis of this module will be on Personal and Collaborative BI.

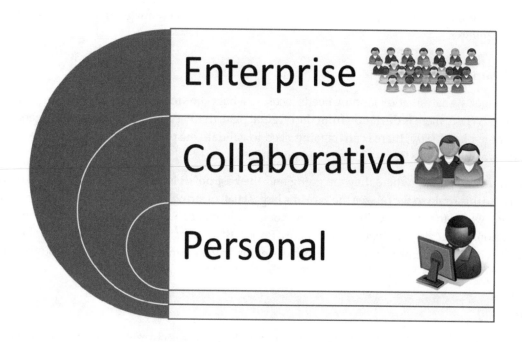

Figure 17 - 1: Levels of Business Intelligence

Personal Business Intelligence

Personal BI enables better decision-making for the person consuming the information in order to accomplish their work in a more effective manner. This type of BI can include personal ad hoc and single use reports, which you use to address short-term situations or specific questions, respectively. Personal BI also tends to be tactical in nature. An example of Personal BI is a Project Last Status Update report used by the Project Manager to ensure timely status updates from each Project Team member.

Collaborative Business Intelligence

Collaborative BI enables better information sharing and decision-making within an interested group of people where other methods of collaboration (email, face to face, etc.) can no longer meet the group's information needs effectively. Commonly, this BI addresses information needs of the Project Team, Project Stakeholders, Work Team or Department. This type of BI addresses both short term and long-term information needs of the group. An example of Collaborative BI is a Project Status Dashboard, which allows stakeholders to see current status, issues, risks and milestones.

Enterprise Business Intelligence

Enterprise BI enables better information sharing and decision-making where the system collects and uses requisite information across the Enterprise. Enterprise Business Intelligence typically focuses on long term needs. An example of Enterprise Business Intelligence is a Project Portfolio Cash Flow Projection report across all ongoing projects. Finance would use such a report as an input to their Enterprise Cash Flow Projection. Project Managers normally do not address Enterprise Business Intelligence needs.

Common Business Intelligence Needs

A project effort is similar to managing a car trip in many ways. The Project Manager's BI needs, as the driver, can be broken down as follows:

Analysis and Planning

The Project Manager's Analysis and Planning needs focus on what needs to occur to accomplish planned project goals and assumptions. Where there is deviation from the original plan, this need also encompasses the generation of alternatives to meet the plan. Lastly, there is an ongoing need to validate the plan against changing business conditions and project risks as to alert the Project Manager to potential issues.

Similarly, a driver determines where they are going and the best possible route to get there based on trip requirements. (We'll take this route so we can see the World's largest ball of string!). The driver also plans out where they are going (outcome), where they will possibly stop (milestones), and makes adjustments to achieve progress as weather and road conditions affect the plan (risk management). Project BI systems make it easier to accomplish this need just as GPS-based navigation systems have made it much easier for drivers to meet similar needs through automatic route generation.

Status Reporting

The Project Manager's Status Reporting needs focus on communicating the current state of the effort and health of the plan to the Project Team and to other interested parties. The current state need ensures that all interested parties receive consistent information for decision-making and planning.

Similarly, the current position of a driver can be the most valuable information delivered by a navigation system. By knowing where you are, you can plan a path to a specific destination.

Progress Monitoring

Project Managers monitor progress so that they can clearly communicate short-term plans and ensure that the team is expending the effort required to meet the plan objectives. Variations of effort at this level can translate to larger progress issues over time. Similarly, a navigation system calculates the average speed of the driver and time to goal. If the driver decides to make a large number of stops, gets caught in traffic or decides to take a scenic detour, the navigation system shows the impact accordingly.

Understanding the Project Server 2010 Business Intelligence Features

It is important for the Project Manager to understand what tools and data the system provides to meet their information needs. The Project Manager toolbox has three components: data, reporting tools and built-in content.

Understanding Available Data

Project Server 2010 generates a great deal of data about the current state of projects, resources, timesheets and the interactions between them. All Business Intelligence data for Project Server 2010 is contained within two data stores. The first is the relational data store, commonly referred to as either the *Reporting* database or RDB. This data store is always available, assuming your Project Server Administrator provided you with the appropriate security access. The other data store contains one or more optional OLAP analytical databases. The Project Server Administrator determines the number and content of these OLAP databases. I cover these two data stores in detail in subsequent sections. All OLAP analytical data derives from the Reporting Database.

Which Data Should I Use?

You should base your decision as to which data source to use on two primary factors, the timeliness of the data you need and the type of intelligence you require. Table 17 – 1 shows examples of needs and the appropriate data for such need. The data in the Reporting Database is most appropriate for factual intelligence needs that require near real time accuracy. The system places the data in the Reporting Database at nearly the same time that Project publishes and other save operations occur. Therefore, the RDB best serves any short term or near term information need. You can best use this data for situations where lists of information are necessary.

OLAP data, on the other hand, is best suited for analytical intelligence needs. The construction of the OLAP data structures the data in such a fashion as to optimize it for doing aggregation and summation of data. However, the freshness of the data is only as good as the last time you refreshed the OLAP data. In some cases, this data can be several days old. Therefore, OLAP data may be better suited to longer-term data analysis.

Example Question	OLAP Data	Relational Data
What are the differences in average Project Risk exposure between organizational regions?	X	
What projects will complete this month?		X
Have all timesheets been processed for the prior period?		X
How does the level of administrative time this quarter compare to that of past quarters?	X	

Table 17 - 1: Examples of Needs and Appropriate Data for Need

Relational Data

The primary data elements contained within the RDB are as follows:

- Project Decisions
- Projects
- Tasks
- Assignments
- Resources
- Issues
- Risks
- Deliverables
- Workflows
- Tasks by Day
- Assignments by Day
- Resources by Day
- Timesheet and Administrative Time
- Other Supporting entities such as Time reporting periods, etc.

You can visualize these elements as related elements using the diagram in Figure 17 - 2. You should use the diagram to decide what data entities are required to support a particular Business Intelligence need. For example, you create a report of timesheet entries which you group by Project Manager and Resource Type. You include Projects, Timesheet Lines, Resources and Resource Types in your query. You must also include the Resource entity because you make the relationship between Resource Type and Timesheet Lines through the Resource entity.

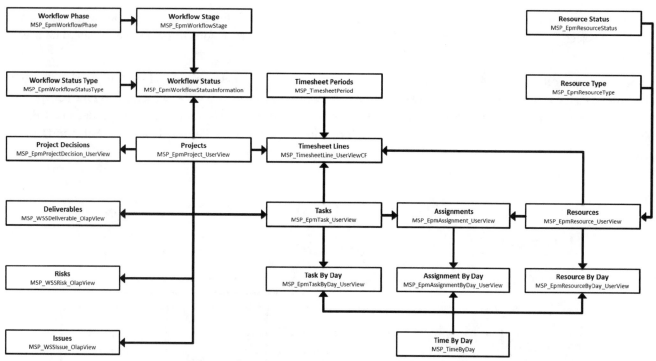

Figure 17 - 2: Reporting Database Item Relationships

Analytical Data

The OLAP data entities are similar to that present in the Relational data. You will see Projects, Tasks, Resources, Assignments, Timesheet, and Time itself. However, the system optimizes the organization of this data for analysis and exploration without the need for complex queries or knowledge of Structured Query Language (SQL).

Understanding how OLAP data is organized and the terms used helps you navigate your way to solving your information needs as well as making it easier for you to find additional information. A database contains each instance of OLAP data. Project Server supports multiple OLAP databases, so your particular OLAP instance may contain all Project Server data or just data related to your Project and/or Resource department.

There are fourteen OLAP cubes within each Project Server OLAP database. Each cube organizes the data to support a particular information need. An Excel report template for each cube within a particular OLAP database provides easy access to the data. In order to get the most from OLAP, you should understand four terms and what they mean. These terms relate to Excel functionality, which you learn about when you author reports. You structure OLAP data by:

- Measures
- Dimensions
  - Attributes
    - ⊙ Attribute properties

Measures are the aggregated factual data upon which you base your analysis. In Project Server, measures are *Cost*, *Duration*, or *Number* fields as the system can aggregate these values via summing, averaging, etc. Examples of measures are *Capacity* and *Work*.

Dimensions categorize and provide context to the underlying *Measure* data. For example, to breakdown *Capacity* and *Work* by Project, Resource, you use the Project List and Resource List Dimensions to provide requisite data breakdown.

Dimensions are collections of *Attribute* values where each attribute represents a unique value. You can also structure attributes as a hierarchy. The Resource Breakdown Structure dimension illustrates how each RBS value (Corporate, Corporate.Sales, Corporate.Sales and Corporate.IT) represents an attribute as shown in Figure 17 - 3. Because RBS is a hierarchical dimension, the *Corporate at Level 1* RBS value results in a rollup of data from Corporate.Sales and Corporate.IT at Level 2.

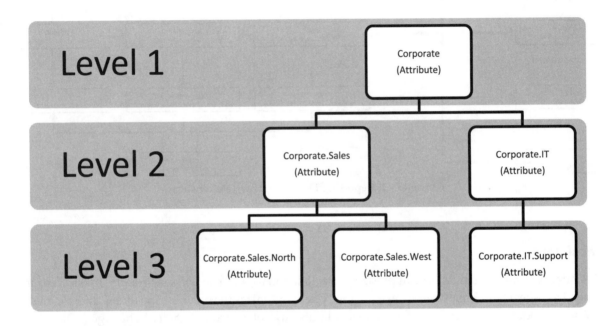

Figure 17 - 3: Example of the RBS Dimension with Hierarchy Levels and Attributes

Attributes can also have Properties, which extended information related to the attribute. For example, a project called *Implement PennyWatcher FMS*, which is an attribute in the Project List dimension, has properties such as a Project Start Date of 2/11/2011 and a Percent Complete of 0%.

Understanding the Toolset

Project Server 2010 has several Business Intelligence tools you can use to meet your needs. The primary tools covered here will be those that Project Managers most commonly use.

Excel

The cornerstone of Project Reporting depends on Excel 2007 or later versions and their PivotTable/Pivot Chart functionality shown in Figure 17 - 4. Pivot functionality is the only way to create Excel reports that can pull the latest data on demand from the Project Server. You use Excel to author new reports, change existing reports to meet current need and to view reports on the desktop. You use the Excel client exclusively to meet your Personal Business Intelligence needs.

Excel connects to the Project Server Data Stores via a file known as an Office Data Connection (ODC). The ODC file contains the details of how to connect to the data source. The Project Server Business Intelligence Center contains a library of ODCs that you can re-use to create new reports. I cover this topic in more detail in a later Hands On Exercise.

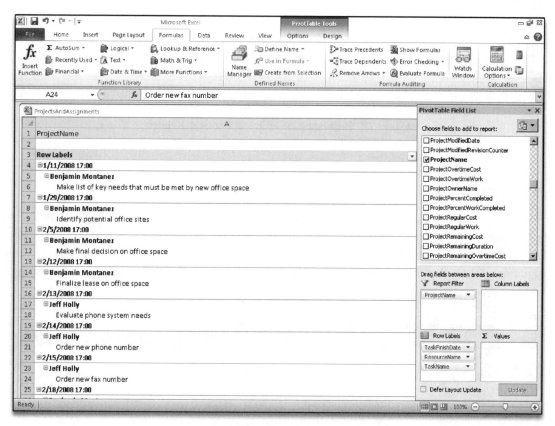

Figure 17 - 4: Example of Excel PivotTable

Excel Services

Excel Services is SharePoint functionality that enables you to publish and share Excel Reports via a SharePoint site as shown in Figure 17 - 5. When you create a report in Excel client, it publishes the report through Excel Services. Once published, anyone with the appropriate security rights can use the interactive report. Once enabled on a SharePoint farm, a report author can host and render reports on any site within the farm. This flexibility provides Project Managers with the ability to customize reporting specific to the needs of each project that they manage.

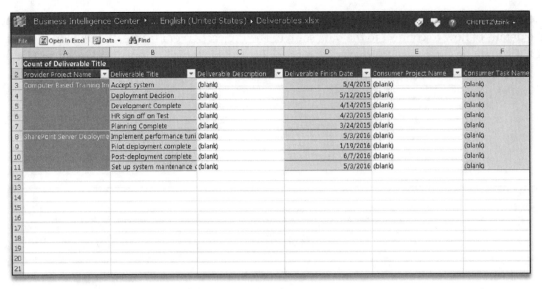

Figure 17 - 5: Example of an Excel Services Report

SharePoint Web Part Pages

SharePoint Web Part Pages, as shown in Figure 17 - 6, are pages that host web parts, and enable you to create customized BI dashboards as. Web parts are modular containers that enable you to create a customized experience without coding or IT involvement. Web parts can host specific content, like reports, RSS feeds, or text you type. You can also link them together so that all web parts act in unison to show different information related to the same project, resource and so on.

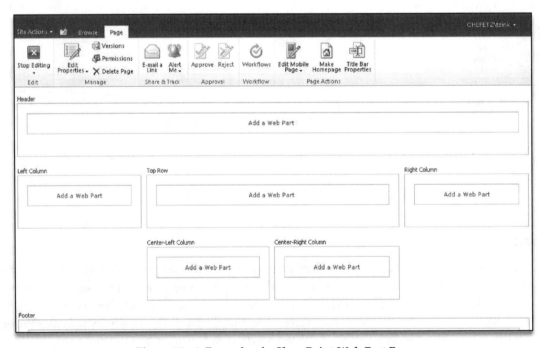

Figure 17 - 6: Example of a SharePoint Web Part Page

The Business Intelligence Center

The Business Intelligence Center, a sub-site of your PWA site in the SharePoint hierarchy, organizes and provides immediate access to all of these report delivery tools in a single location. This site, evolved from the Microsoft Office SharePoint Server 2007 Reporting Center, ties all of the BI tools together and provides a starting point for a Project Server BI portal.

The intent of the Business Intelligence Center is to provide a starting point for authors and to house BI content for Enterprise and Collaborative BI needs. In this module's Hands On Exercises, I show you how to use your Project Team Site as a Collaborative and Personal BI portal. The Business Intelligence Center also contains the central authorized library of all Office Data Connections used in the system.

To visit the Business Intelligence Center, click the *Business Intelligence* link in the *Quick Launch* menu. The system displays the *Business Intelligence Center* home page shown in Figure 17 - 7. To navigate back to the PWA site, click the *Project Web App* tab located above the *Quick Launch* menu in the upper left corner of the page.

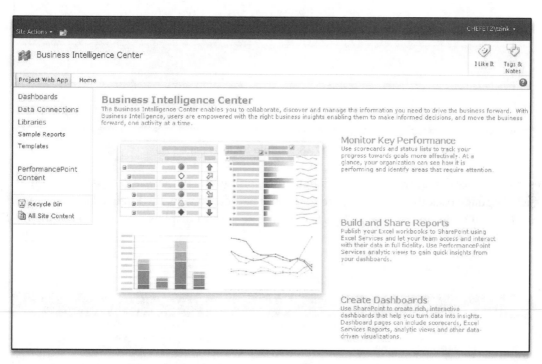

Figure 17 - 7: Business Intelligence Center home page

Understanding Sample Content

Project Server provides a number of content types that give your report development a significant boost. From Sample reports to report templates, and pre-provisioned Office Data Connections files for both the Reporting database and OLAP cubes, getting started with building reports in Project Server has never been easier. Using these basic parts as building blocks, you can quickly take advantage of the rich SharePoint and Office reporting tools at your disposal.

Built-In Sample Reports

Project Server 2010 provides sample Microsoft Excel reports that the system pre-connects to the Project Server Reporting Database through ODC files saved in the Project Server BI Data Store. Microsoft intended that these reports provide the report author with a starting point for creating new reports. The system targets some of these reports to PMO use and you can repurpose many of them for use on a specific project. To view these reports, visit the *Business Intelligence Center* site and click the *Sample Reports* link in the *Quick Launch* menu. The system displays the *Sample Reports* page shown in Figure 17 - 8.

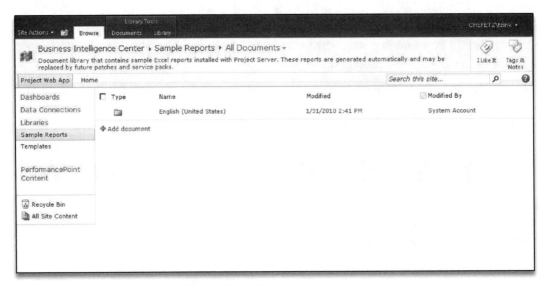

Figure 17 - 8: Sample Reports page

The Business Intelligence Center supports multi-language reporting, and the *Sample Reports* library contains a separate folder for each language pack that you configure for Project Server. To view the English language reports, click the *English (United States)* folder in the *Sample Reports* library. The system displays the contents of the *English (United States)* folder as shown in Figure 17 - 9.

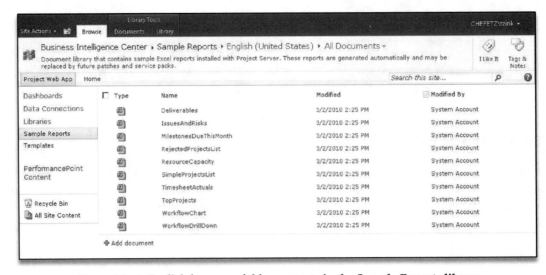

Figure 17 - 9: English language folder contents in the Sample Reports library

The *Sample Reports* library contains the following sample reports:

- Deliverables (Deliverables.xlsx)

- Issues and Risks (IssuesAndRisks.xlsx)

- Milestones Due This Month (MilestonesDueThisMonth.xlsx)

- Rejected Projects (RejectedProjectsLists.xlsx)

- Resource Capacity (ResourceCapacity.xlsx)

- Simple Projects List (SimpleProjectsList.xlsx)

- Timesheet Actuals (TimesheetActuals.xlsx)

- Top Projects (TopProjects.xlsx)

- Workflow Chart (WorkflowChart.xlsx)

- Workflow Drilldown (WorkflowDrillDown.xlsx)

Deliverables Report

The *Deliverables* report extracts a listing of all Project Server 2010 deliverables from the Project Server *Reporting* database and displays the data in Excel PivotTable format in your web browser, as shown in Figure 17 - 10.

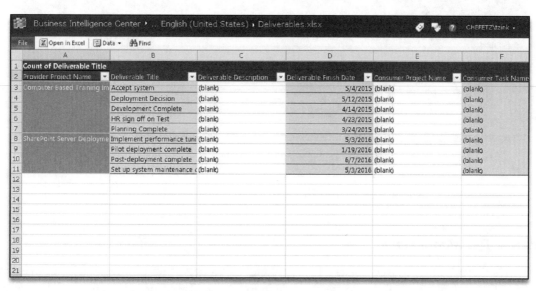

Figure 17 - 10: Deliverables report

Issues and Risks Report

The *Issues and Risks* report extracts a listing of all Project Server issues and risks from the Project Server RDB and displays the data in Excel PivotTable format in your web browser, as shown in Figure 17 - 11 and Figure 17 - 12.

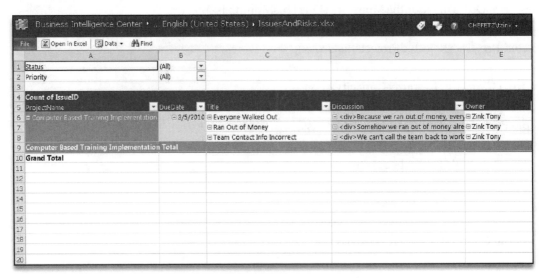

Figure 17 - 11: Issues and Risks report, Issues tab

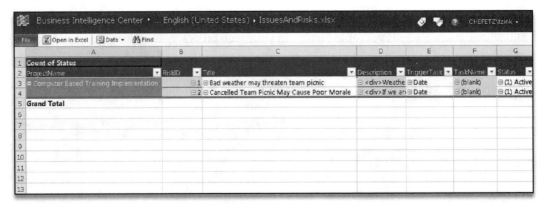

Figure 17 - 12: Issues and Risks report, Risks tab

Milestones Due This Month Report

The *Milestones Due This Month* report extracts a listing of all Project Server milestones that you have scheduled to complete during the current month and displays the data in Excel PivotTable format in your web browser, as shown in Figure 17 - 13.

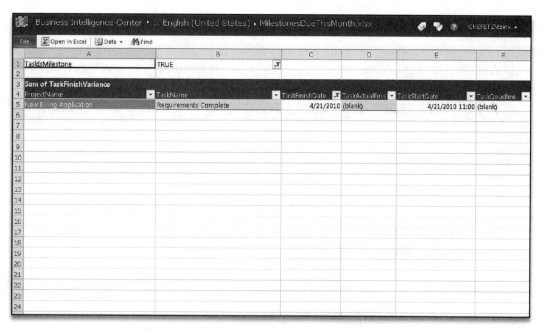

Figure 17 - 13: Milestones Due This Month report

Rejected Projects Report

The *Rejected Projects* report extracts a listing of all rejected Project Server projects and displays the data in Excel Pivot-Table format in your web browser, as shown in Figure 17 - 14.

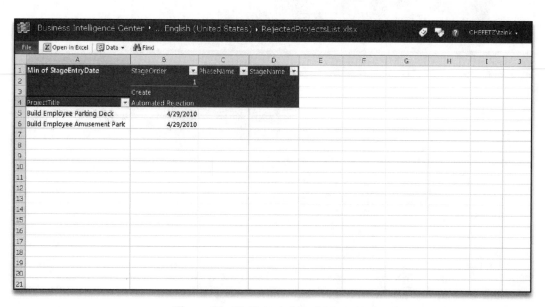

Figure 17 - 14: Rejected Projects report

Resource Capacity Report

The *Resource Capacity* report extracts a listing of all Project Server resource capacities and displays the data in Excel PivotTable and PïvotChart format in your web browser, as shown in Figure 17 - 15 and Figure 17 - 16.

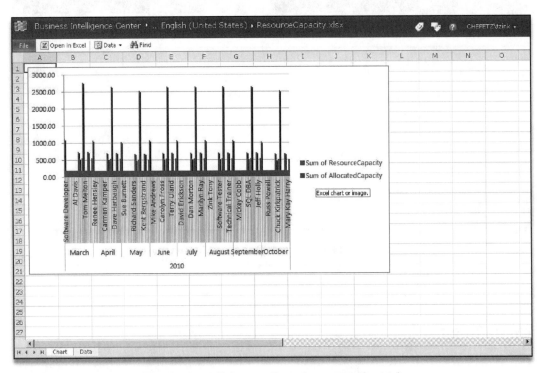

Figure 17 - 15: Resource Capacity report, chart tab

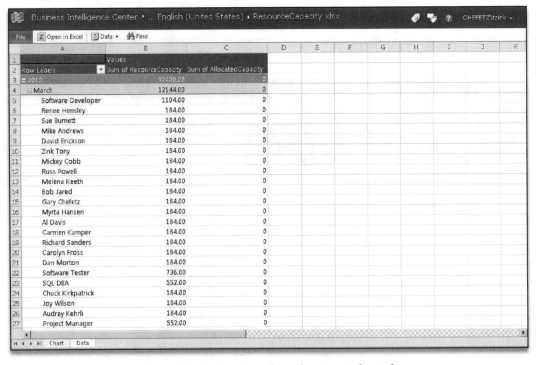

Figure 17 - 16: Resource Capacity report, data tab

Simple Projects List Report

The *Simple Projects List* report extracts a listing of all Project Server projects from the Project Server RDB and displays the data in Excel PivotTable format in your web browser, as shown in Figure 17 - 17.

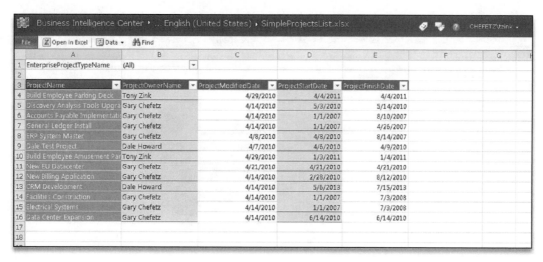

Figure 17 - 17: Simple Projects List report

Timesheet Actuals Report

The *Timesheet Actuals* report extracts a listing of all Project Server timesheet work hours from the Project Server RDB and displays the data in an approval process step grouping, in Excel PivotTable format in your web browser, as shown in Figure 17 - 18.

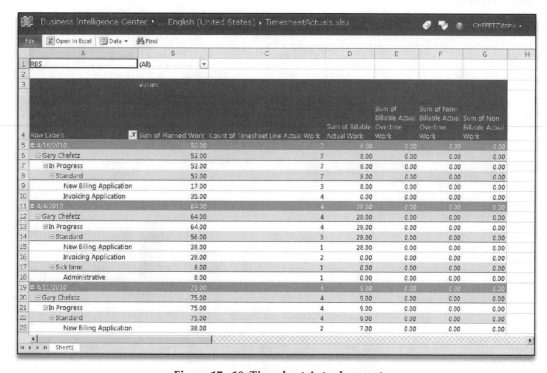

Figure 17 - 18: Timesheet Actuals report

Top Projects Report

The *Top Projects* report extracts a listing of top proposals and costs from the Project Server Reporting Database and displays the data in Excel PivotTable and PivotChart format in your web browser, as shown in Figure 17 - 19.

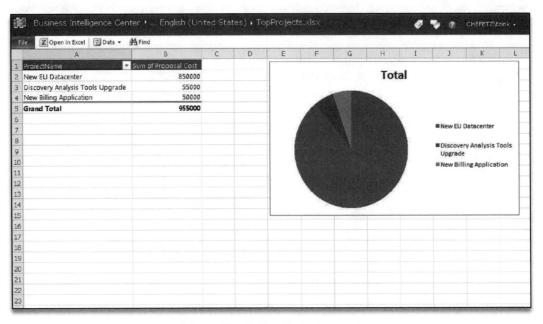

Figure 17 - 19: Top Projects report

Workflow Chart Report

The *Workflow Chart* report displays a count of all projects by system workflow stage from the Project Server RDB and displays the data in Excel PivotTable and PivotChart format in your web browser, as shown in Figure 17 - 20.

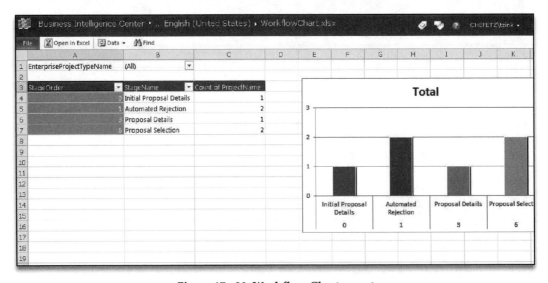

Figure 17 - 20: Workflow Chart report

Workflow Drilldown Report

The *Workflow Drilldown* report extracts a listing of detailed workflow stage status information from the Project Server RDB and displays the data in Excel PivotTable format in your web browser, as shown in Figure 17 - 21.

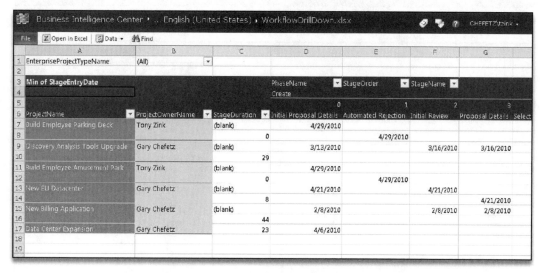

Figure 17 - 21: Workflow Drilldown report

Report Templates

Project Server provides you with Microsoft Excel report templates that use the pre-connected ODC files to get you quickly connected to your data. To view these report templates, from the Business Intelligence Center click the *Templates* link in the *Quick Launch* menu. The system displays the *Templates* page shown in Figure 17 - 22.

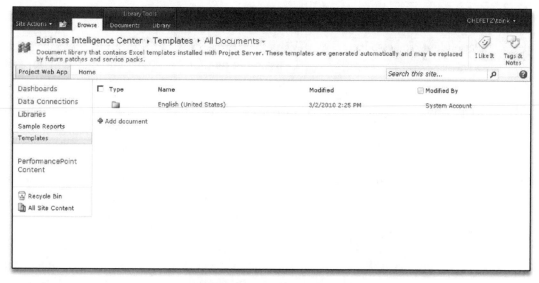

Figure 17 - 22: Templates page

The Business Intelligence Center supports multi-language reporting, and the *Templates* library contains a separate folder for each language pack that you provision for your Project Server. To view the English language reports, click the *English (United States)* folder in the *Templates* library. The system displays the contents of the *English (United States)* folder as shown in Figure 17 - 23.

Figure 17 - 23: English language folder contents in the Templates library

The Excel report templates help you build new reports quickly. You can use these as starting points to develop your own custom reports. The system provides templates for each language available on the server.

The English language folder contains seven report templates that arrive pre-connected to the Project Server Reporting Database as shown in Table 17 - 2.

Report Name	File	Description	Example Use
Dependent Projects	DependentProjects.xltx	Visualizes Project to Deliverable relationships.	Report of projects which have a dependency on your published deliverables.
Issues	Issues.xltx	Visualizes Issues data with related Projects and Tasks data.	Report of active issues by assigned resource across your projects.
Projects and Assignments	ProjectsAndAssignments.xltx	Visualizes Project, Task, Assignment, Resource relationship data.	Report of projects and tasks by assigned resource in a given RBS node.
Projects and Tasks	ProjectsAndTasks.xltx	Visualizes Project and Task relationship data.	Task analysis comparing planned start dates to actual start dates.

Report Name	File	Description	Example Use
Resources	Resources.xltx	Visualizes Resource information.	Breakdown of Resource Standard Rates organized by Resource Breakdown Structure value.
Risks	Risks.xltx	Visualizes Risks data with related Project and Tasks data.	Average risk exposure by project.
Timesheet	Timesheet.xltx	Visualizes Timesheet data with related Project and Resource data.	Audit report comparing timesheet entered hours to planned hours.

Table 17 - 2: Built-In Report Descriptions

Every time you create a new OLAP database, the system automatically creates another folder in the *Templates* library containing an additional 14 report templates for that new OLAP database. Each folder contains 14 templates preconnected to each of the 14 OLAP cubes in each OLAP database as shown in Table 17 - 3.

Report Name	File	Description	Example Use
OLAP Assignment Non-Timephased	OlapAssignmentNonTimephased.xltx	Visualizes point in time Assignment data with related Project, Task and Resource data.	Current Actual Cost total by Project.
OLAP Assignment Timephased	OlapAssignmentTimephased.xltx	Visualizes Assignment data over time with related Project, Task and Resource data.	Current Actual Cost total by Project by Month
OLAP Deliverables	OlapDeliverables.xltx	Visualize Deliverable data.	Count of projects consuming my project's deliverables.
OLAP EPM Timesheet	OlapEpmTimesheet.xltx	Visualize Timesheet data with related Task, Project and Resource data.	Timesheet entries by Project by Month.
OLAP Issues	OlapIssues.xltx	Visualize Issue data.	Active Issues for a particular Vendor across Projects.

Report Name	File	Description	Example Use
OLAP Portfolio Analyzer	OlapPortfolioAnalyzer.xltx	Visualize Assignment and Resource data over time with related Project, Task and Resource Plan data.	Resources by Project which have Resource Plan allocations.
OLAP Project Non-Timephased	OlapProjectNonTimephased.xltx	Visualize point in time Project data.	Projects and Remaining Work grouped by Region custom field.
OLAP Project SharePoint	OlapProjectSharePoint.xltx	Visualize point in time Project data with related Risk, Issue and Deliverable data.	Project Summary with Issue, Risk, Deliverable counts and Overall Risk Exposure
OLAP Project Timesheet	OlapProjectTimesheet.xltx	Visualize Project data over time with related Resource, Timesheet, and Task measures.	Analyze Capacity against Timesheet entries and Actual Work on Tasks against Capacity over time
OLAP Resource Non-Timephased	OlapResourceNonTimephased.xltx	Visualize point in time Resource cost data	Standard rate and Overtime rate of all resources grouped by RBS
OLAP Resource Timephased	OlapResourceTimephased.xltx	Visualize Resource capacity data over time.	Resource Capacity for Quarter 4 2011 by Skill resource custom field.
OLAP Risks	OlapRisks.xltx	Visualize Risk data.	List of risks across all projects which have an exposure of 5 days or more.
OLAP Task Non-Timephased	OlapTaskNonTimephased.xltx	Visualize point in time Task data.	Overallocated non-summary, active tasks across all Projects.
OLAP Timesheet	OlapTimesheet.xltx	Visualize Timesheet data.	Planned and actual administrative time by Month.

Table 17 - 3: Built-In OLAP Template Descriptions

Note that the file extension for the Excel report templates is *.xltx*, rather than *.xlsx*, indicating that they are Excel template files.

Warning: When saving a report created from an Excel report template, verify that you have changed the file extension to *.xlsx*. Otherwise, it will not render in Excel Services.

Office Data Connections

The system pre-connects the sample Excel reports and report templates in the Business Intelligence Center to their respective data sources in the Project Server BI Data Store via an Office Data Connection (ODC) file. The Business Intelligence Center manages these data connections centrally in the *Data Connections* library so that you can share these connections between report authors.

The key benefit for external ODC files is that different reports can use one connection. Therefore, if you are writing a new report, you can use an existing ODC to get to your data. This eliminates the need for you to know things like database server names and SQL queries.

The ODC library contains 13 shared Office Data Connection (ODC) files for connecting to the Project Server Reporting Database, and it contains 14 shared Office Data Connection (ODC) files for connecting reports to each OLAP Database that is available on the server. I show the relationship between Excel Reports, ODCs and your data in Figure 17 - 24.

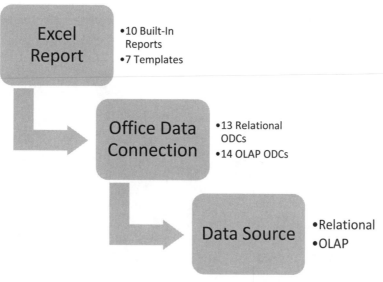

Figure 17 - 24: Excel - ODC - Data Source Relationship

To view these data connection files, navigate to the Business Intelligence Center and click the *Data Connections* link in the *Quick Launch* menu. The system displays the *Data Connections* page shown in Figure 17 - 25.

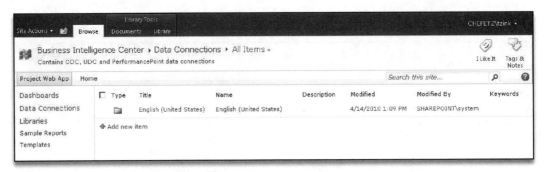

Figure 17 - 25: Data Connections page

To view the English language data connection files, click the *English (United States)* folder in the *Data Connections* library. The system displays the *English (United States)* folder partially shown in Figure 17 - 26.

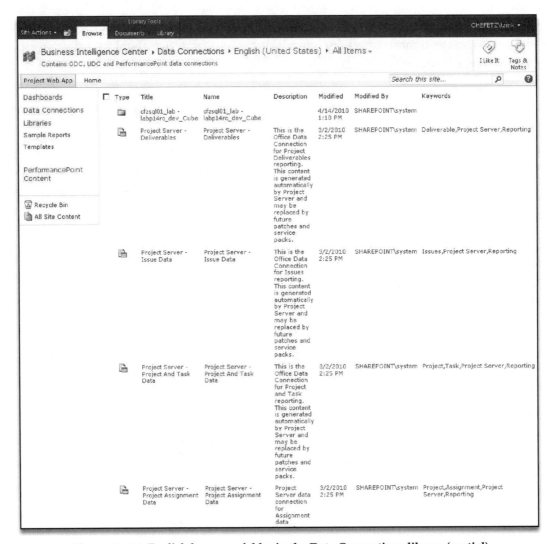

Figure 17 - 26: English language folder in the Data Connections library (partial)

The English language folder contains 13 data connection files for connecting reports to the Project Server Reporting database:

- Project Server - Deliverables (Project Server - Deliverables.odc)

- Project Server - Issue Data (Project Server - Issue Data.odc)

- Project Server - Project And Task Data (Project Server - Project And Task Data.odc)

- Project Server - Project Assignment Data (Project Server - Project Assignment Data.odc)

- Project Server - Rejected Projects List (Project Server - Rejected Projects List.odc)

- Project Server - Resource Capacity (Project Server - Resource Capacity.odc)

- Project Server - Resource Data (Project Server - Resource Data.odc)

- Project Server - Risk Data (Project Server - Risk Data.odc)

- Project Server - Simple Projects List (Project Server - Simple Projects List.odc)

- Project Server - Timesheet Data (Project Server - Timesheet Data.odc)

- Project Server - Top Projects Data (Project Server - Top Projects Data.odc)

- Project Server - Workflow Chart Data (Project Server - Workflow Chart Data.odc)

- Project Server - Workflow Drilldown Data (Project Server - Workflow Drilldown Data.odc)

I illustrate the ODC utilization in the Built-In Reports and Report Templates in Table 17 - 4 and Table 17 - 5.

ODC	Template Name	Description
Project Server - Deliverables.odc	Dependent Projects	Visualizes Project to Deliverable relationships.
Project Server - Issue Data.odc	Issues	Visualizes Issues data with related Projects and Tasks data.
Project Server - Project Assignment Data.odc	Projects and Assignments	Visualizes Project, Task, Assignment, Resource relationship data.
Project Server - Project And Task Data.odc	Projects and Tasks	Visualizes Project and Task relationship data.
Project Server - Resource Data.odc	Resources	Visualizes Resource information.
Project Server - Risk Data.odc	Risks	Visualizes Risks data with related Project and Tasks data.
Project Server - Timesheet Data.odc	Timesheet	Visualizes Timesheet data with related Project and Resource data.

Table 17 - 4: ODC to Template Cross-reference

ODC	Report Name	Description
Project Server - Deliverables.odc	Deliverables	Visualizes Deliverable data
Project Server - Issue Data.odc Project Server - Risk Data.odc	Issues and Risks	Visualizes Issues and Risks data
Project Server - Project And Task Data.odc	Milestones Due This Month	Visualizes all milestones across all projects due this month
Project Server - Rejected Projects List.odc	Rejected Projects	Visualizes projects that were rejected from Portfolio process
Project Server - Resource Capacity.odc	Resource Capacity	Visualizes timephased resource capacity for all resources
Project Server - Simple Projects List.odc	Simple Projects List	Visualizes a simple list of Projects
Project Server - Timesheet Data.odc	Timesheet Actuals	Visualizes all timesheet entries and their current process state by time reporting period

ODC	Report Name	Description
Project Server - Top Projects Data.odc	Top Projects	Visualize the top projects in terms of proposal cost
Project Server - Workflow Chart Data.odc	Workflow Chart	Visualize what projects are in which process stage
Project Server - Workflow Drilldown Data.odc	Workflow Drilldown	Visualize process status across processes.

Table 17 - 5: ODC to Report Cross-reference

The *English language* folder also contains a sub-folder for each OLAP database, each containing 14 data connection files for connecting reports to each of the 14 OLAP cubes in the OLAP database:

- OLAP Assignment Non Timephased (OlapAssignmentNonTimephased.odc)

- OLAP Assignment Timephased (OlapAssignmentTimephased.odc)

- OLAP Deliverables (OlapDeliverables.odc)

- OLAP EPM Timesheet (OlapEpmTimesheet.odc)

- OLAP Issues (OlapIssues.odc)

- OLAP Portfolio Analyzer (OlapPortfolioAnalyzer.odc)

- OLAP Project Non Timephased (OlapProjectNonTimephased.odc)

- OLAP Project SharePoint (OlapMSProjectSharePoint.odc)

- OLAP Project Timesheet (OlapProjectTimesheet.odc)

- OLAP Resource Non Timephased (OlapResourceNonTimephased.odc)

- OLAP Resource Timephased (OlapResourceTimephased.odc)

- OLAP Risks (OlapRisks.odc)

- OLAP Task Non Timephased (OlapTaskNonTimephased.odc)

- OLAP Timesheet (OlapTimesheet.odc)

Using the Project Server 2010 Business Intelligence Features

Viewing a report starts with accessing a report in SharePoint as shown in Figure 17 - 27. For discussion purposes, you will use the Sample Reports that you find in the Business Intelligence Center.

Figure 17 - 27: High Level View Report Process

Viewing Reports

To visit the Business Intelligence Center, click the *Business Intelligence* link in the PWA *Quick Launch* menu. The system displays the *Business Intelligence Center* home page shown in Figure 17 - 28. Notice in the figure that I am hovering my mouse pointer over the *Sample Reports* link. To navigate to the *Sample Reports* library, click on the link. To navigate back to the PWA site, click the *Project Web App* tab located above the *Quick Launch* menu in the upper left corner of the page.

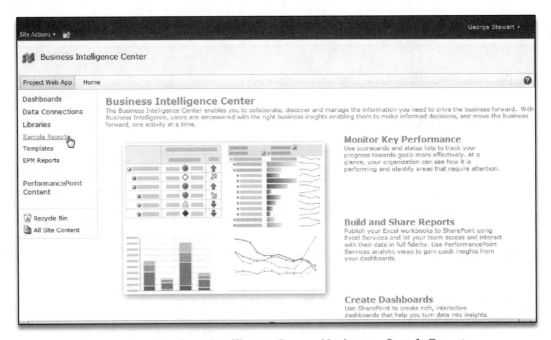

Figure 17 - 28: Business Intelligence Center - Navigate to Sample Reports

The Business Intelligence Center supports multi-language reporting, and the *Sample Reports* library contains a separate folder for each language pack that you configure for Project Server. To view the English language reports, click the *English (United States)* folder in the *Sample Reports* library as I am doing in Figure 17 - 29.

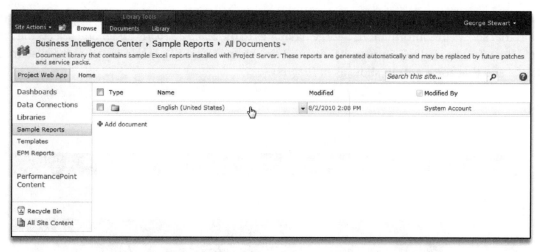

Figure 17 - 29: Select Sample Reports Folder by Language

The system displays the *Sample Reports* library shown in Figure 17 - 30. To view a report, you click on the link to select the name of the report.

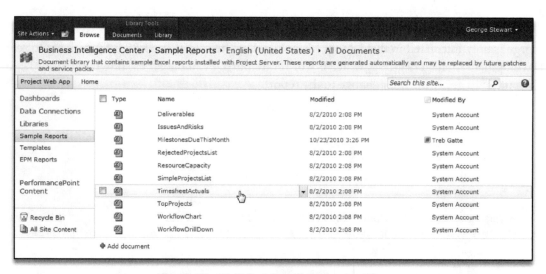

Figure 17 - 30: Select Sample Report to View

For example, George Stewart needs to see where timesheet entries are in the overall process. Aware that there is a *Built-In* report that shows this information, George navigates to the *Sample Reports* folder and selects the *Timesheet Actuals* report. After a few seconds, George sees the report shown in Figure 17 - 31. He sees that the system has not approved all time and that some entries show as *In Progress*.

	Business Intelligence Center ▸ ... English (United States) ▸ TimesheetActuals.xlsx						George Stewart ▾
File ☒ Open in Excel ⊞ Data ▾ 🔍 Find							

	A	B	C	D	E	F	G
1	RBS	(All)	▾				
2							
3		Values					
4	Row Labels	Sum of Planned Work	Count of Timesheet Line Actual Work	Sum of Billable Actual Work	Sum of Billable Actual Overtime Work	Sum of Non-Billable Actual Overtime Work	Sum of Non-Billable Actual Work
5	⊟ 10/17/2010	24.00	10	48.00	0.00	0.00	0.00
6	⊟ Treb Gatte	0.00	2	8.00	0.00	0.00	0.00
7	⊟ In Progress	0.00	2	8.00	0.00	0.00	0.00
8	⊟ Training	0.00	1	4.00	0.00	0.00	0.00
9	Administrative	0.00	1	4.00	0.00	0.00	0.00
10	⊟ Administrative	0.00	1	4.00	0.00	0.00	0.00
11	Administrative	0.00	1	4.00	0.00	0.00	0.00
12	⊟ George Stewart	24.00	8	40.00	0.00	0.00	0.00
13	⊟ Approved	24.00	8	40.00	0.00	0.00	0.00
14	⊟ Standard	24.00	4	7.00	0.00	0.00	0.00
15	Project Server 2010 Deployment	24.00	4	7.00	0.00	0.00	0.00
16	⊟ Training	0.00	1	6.00	0.00	0.00	0.00
17	Administrative	0.00	1	6.00	0.00	0.00	0.00
18	⊟ Sick time	0.00	1	8.00	0.00	0.00	0.00
19	Administrative	0.00	1	8.00	0.00	0.00	0.00
20	⊟ Administrative	0.00	1	16.00	0.00	0.00	0.00
21	Administrative	0.00	1	16.00	0.00	0.00	0.00
22	⊟ Meetings	0.00	1	3.00	0.00	0.00	0.00

Sheet1

Figure 17 - 31: Web View of Sample Report

Because George is only interested in the data for his own group, he selects the *RBS* filter pick list to select only his Software Development Managers group, which is **Corporate.SoftDev.manager** as shown in Figure 17 - 32. He then clicks the *OK* button to apply his filter change to the report.

A quick way to select only one value in a long filter list is to first deselect the *Select All* value. This removes every selection from the filter. Then select just the values you wish to see in the report.

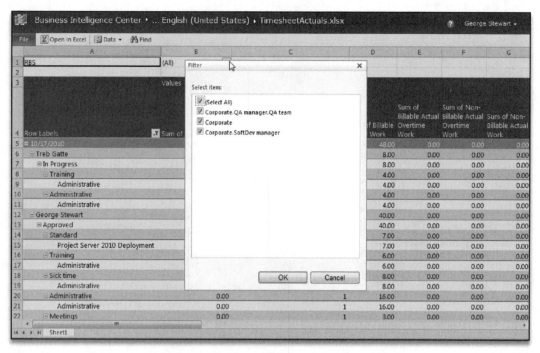

Figure 17 - 32: Example of Web Interactivity

Creating a Report

Creating a new report in Excel involves the four key steps shown in Figure 17 - 33. I cover each of these steps in detail in this topical section. At the end of this section, the Hands On Exercise will take you through the basic process.

Open the Excel Template

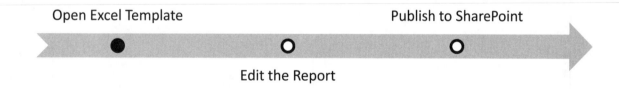

Figure 17 - 33: High Level Edit Process

Creating a new report starts with an Excel Template which can be found in the Business Intelligence Center. To visit the Business Intelligence Center, click the *Business Intelligence* link in the PWA *Quick Launch* menu. The system displays the *Business Intelligence Center* home page shown in Figure 17 - 34. To navigate back to the PWA site, click the *Project Web App* tab located above the *Quick Launch* menu in the upper left corner of the page.

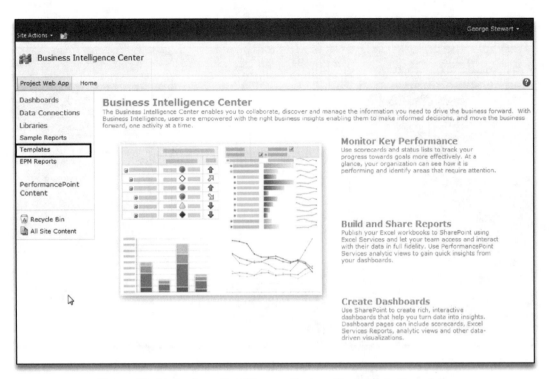

Figure 17 - 34: Business Intelligence Center - Navigate to Templates

The Business Intelligence Center supports multi-language reporting, and the *Templates* library contains a separate folder for each language pack that you configure for Project Server. To view the English language reports, click the *English (United States)* folder in the *Templates* library as shown in Figure 17 - 35.

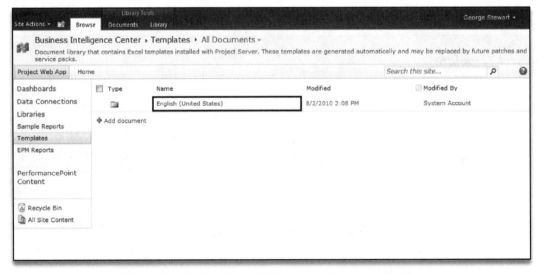

Figure 17 - 35: Templates Folder - Open Language Folder

Once you select the appropriate template for creating your report, hover over the template name to get the context menu as shown in Figure 17 - 36 and select the *Edit in Microsoft Excel* item.

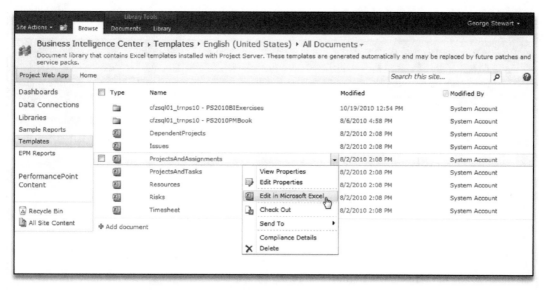

Figure 17 - 36: Edit Template in Microsoft Excel

The Business Intelligence Center will prompt you with a security warning as shown in Figure 17 - 37. This prompt allows you to cancel the template open process in case you opened this file accidentally. Click the *OK* button to continue the template open process and the Excel client opens.

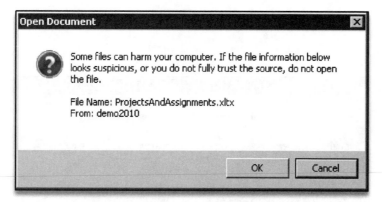

Figure 17 - 37: Open Document Confirmation

Depending on your system security configuration, Excel may disable data connections as a security precaution. This prevents you from accidentally opening a malicious file from the Internet. However, you will need to enable data connections for the template if you wish to create a report. If you are using Excel 2007, you will only see the prompt shown in Figure 17 - 38. You should click the *Enable Content* button to begin writing a report.

If you are using Excel 2010, you will see both prompts as shown in Figure 17 - 38 and Figure 17 - 39. You should click the *Enable Content* button. The system then presents you with the third security warning to make this a trusted document. As you are likely to use this template again, click the *Yes* button to make this template trusted and to begin writing your report.

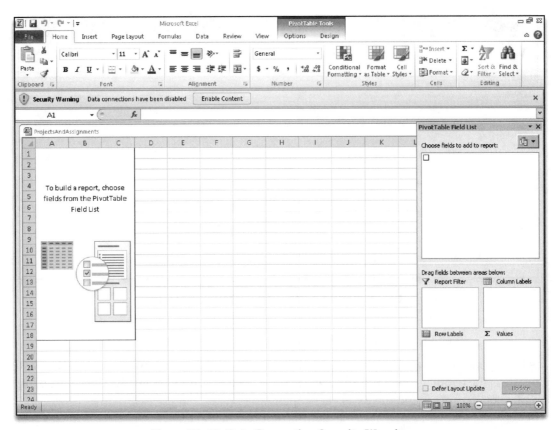

Figure 17 - 38: Data Connection Security Warning

Figure 17 - 39: Make Template a Trusted Document

As the template continues to open, a series of messages will appear in the Excel status bar, indicating that Excel is connecting to the data source. After a few seconds, you see the empty PivotTable shown in Figure 17 - 40, where you will begin creating your report.

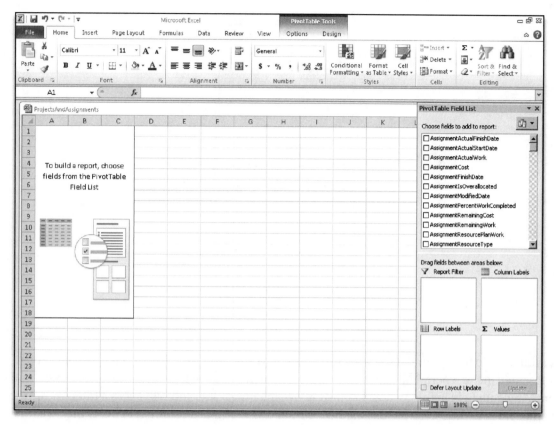

Figure 17 - 40: Template prior to making modifications

Edit the Report

I now move to the second step of the Edit Process as shown in Figure 17 - 41.

Figure 17 - 41: High Level Edit Process

The PivotTable Field List is on the right side of the Excel template. This list is composed of 6 components which you should understand to write a report.

Figure 17 - 42 shows the list of available data fields for your report. The list is in alphabetical order to make it easier to find the data field you need. Product-generated data field names begin with the name of the data entity to which it belongs. For example, all project-related data fields have a name starting with Project. Therefore, Project Name is ProjectName in the list.

Figure 17 - 42: PivotTable Field List

Typically, you need to filter your data to what is relevant to your report user. Report Filters enable you to customize the data presented in the report. The *Report Filter* area, as shown in Figure 17 - 43, is where you designate fields as Report Filters. Any data field in this area will appear above the PivotTable and will act as a filter for the report. While there are other ways to filter a report, this method is a good way to make common Report Filters very visible to the report user. To specify a data field as a Report Filter, drag the data fields from the *Field* list into this area as shown in Figure 17 - 43.

Figure 17 - 43: PivotTable Report Filter Fields

It is likely you want to display rows of data in your report. To designate which data fields will appear in the row, you should drag them into the *Row Labels* area as shown in Figure 17 - 44. The order of the data fields in this area will determine where the field appears in the row. For example, if the topmost field is ProjectOwnerName, then ProjectOwnerName will be the left most field in the report row. If you need to reorder the fields, you can drag them around in the *Row Label* area.

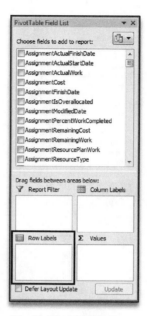

Figure 17 - 44: PivotTable Report Rows

In some cases, you may need to create a *Cross-tabulation* or *Cross-tab* report. A *Cross-tab* report has both rows and columns where the intersection of the two values has meaning. A common column use is a time series where you need to show totals by month or by quarter. To designate a data field as a column, you drag it into the column label area shown in Figure 17 - 45.

Figure 17 - 45: PivotTable Report Columns

If your report requires totals or averages of a particular data field, you should place that data field in the ∑ *Values* area as shown in Figure 17 - 46. Fields in this area should be numeric or date type fields since you can only aggregate those field types.

Figure 17 - 46: PivotTable Calculated Values

Each time you make a change in these four areas, the report re-queries the database. If the report is over a large dataset, this behavior may not be desirable. At the very bottom of the PivotTable Field List is a checkbox and button, as shown in Figure 17 - 47. Selecting the *Defer Layout Update* item will defer the data refresh process until you tell Excel to do so. This is very handy if you are making many changes or are creating a new report. To update the data once you make your changes, click the *Update* button. Deselecting the *Defer Layout Update* item will return the report to its normal behavior.

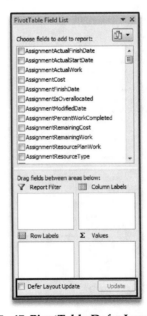

Figure 17 - 47: PivotTable Defer Layout Setting

Warning: You must be a member of the Active Directory group that your organization uses for report authors, in order to perform the exercises in this book.

Hands On Exercise

Exercise 17-1 for Excel 2007 and 2010 Users

Build a basic Tasks Due report from a report template.

1. In Project Web App, click on the *Business Intelligence* link on the *Quick Launch* menu to navigate to the Business Intelligence Center, click on the *Templates* link located in the *Libraries* section of the *Quick Launch* menu, then click on the *English* folder to display the available templates.

2. Open the *ProjectsAndAssignments* template by selecting it and in the *Open & Check out* section of the *Documents* ribbon, click the *Edit Document* button. If you see a Security Warning, click to allow the content. (Warning dialogs may vary).

3. Add the following fields into the *Row Labels* area:
    *   TaskName
    *   ResourceName
    *   ProjectName
    *   TaskFinishDate

4. Add the following fields to the *Report Filter* area:
    *   ResourceIsTeam
    *   ResourceType
    *   TaskIsActive
    *   TaskPercentCompleted
    *   TaskIsManuallyScheduled
    *   TaskIsMilestone

5. At the top of the report, change the values for the filter fields as follows:
    *   Click the *ResourceIsTeam* pick list and set the value to *False* to exclude tasks assigned to team resources.

- Click the *ResourceType* pick list and set the value to 2 to show only tasks assigned to work resources.

- Click the *TaskIsActive* pick list and set the value to *True* to show only active tasks.

- Click the *TaskPercentCompleted* pick list and in the filter dialog, select the *Select Multiple Items* checkbox. Then deselect the *100* value in the filter value list so that completed tasks do not display and click the *OK* button.

- Click the *TaskIsManuallyScheduled* pick list and set the value to *False* to exclude manually scheduled tasks.

- Click the *TaskIsMilestone* pick list and set the value to *False* to display only non-milestone tasks.

6. At the top of the report, change the labels for the *Filter* fields to make them more readable as follows:

- Select the *ResourceIsTeam* cell and type *Team Resource?* to rename it.

- Select the *ResourceType* cell and type *Resource Type*.

- Select the *TaskIsActive* cell and type *Active Task?*

- Select the *TaskPercentCompleted* cell and type *% Complete*.

- Select the *TaskIsManuallyScheduled* cell and type *Manually Scheduled?*

- Select the *TaskIsMilestone* cell and type *Milestone?*

7. Reorder the *Row Label* fields in this order:

- TaskFinishDate

- TaskName

- ProjectName

- ResourceName

8. Do not save this report yet as you use it for the next exercise.

Publish the Report

I now move to the last step of the edit process shown in Figure 17 - 48.

Figure 17 - 48: High Level Edit Process

In order to make a report accessible to others, you should publish the report to a SharePoint site as shown in Figure 17 - 49. *Publish* is different from *Save* or *Save As* since the *Publish* option makes it possible to designate the visibility of parts of the report to the report user. The *Save* command saves the report to SharePoint but does not give you any additional options.

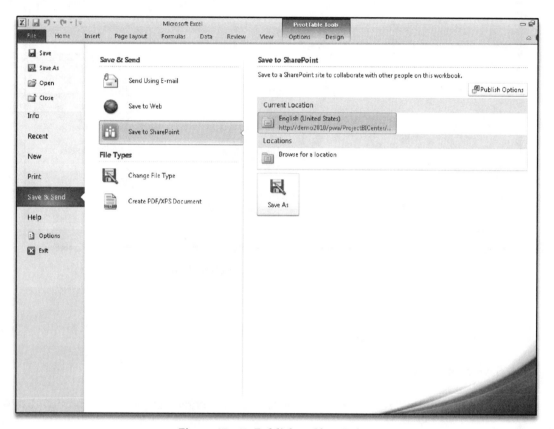

Figure 17 - 49: Publish to SharePoint

To publish a report, follow these steps:

1. Select the *File* menu

2. Select the *Save & Send* option

3. Select the *Save to SharePoint* item

4. Double click on the *Browse for a location* item

5. Because you opened a template from the *Templates* folder, Excel will attempt to publish your report there by default. You should not save reports in the *Templates* folder.

6. Select the *Save As* button and the *Save As* dialog appears as shown in Figure 17 - 50.

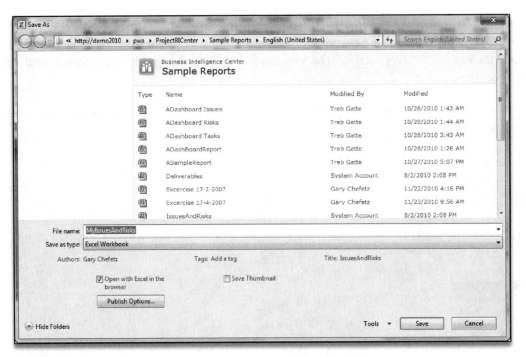

Figure 17 - 50: Browse to a Location dialog

- Before the final save, fill in the following values:

  - Save your file to the following directory

    - http://[*YourServerName*]/pwa/ProjectBICenter/Sample%20Reports/English%20(United%2 0States)/

  - Rename your report with a unique name

  - Select *Excel Workbook (*.xlsx)* in the *Save as type* field

  - Select the *Open with Excel in the Browser* checkbox

- Click the *Save* button

- After a few seconds, you see a screen similar to Figure 17 - 51.

Warning: Change your *Save As Type* to *Excel Workbook (*.xlsx)* prior to saving! Otherwise, you will be saving a template to the BI Center, which will not render in the browser.

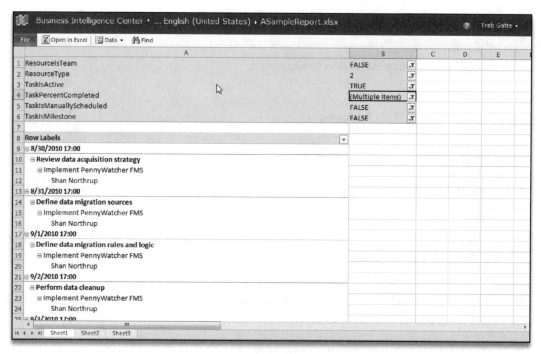

Figure 17 - 51: Web Rendered Report

Hands On Exercise

Exercise 17-2 for Excel 2010 Users

Publish the report from Exercise 17-1 to a SharePoint site.

1. Using the Excel client from the report in Exercise 17-1, select the *File* menu.

2. Select the *Save & Send* option in the Excel *Backstage*. Select the *Save to SharePoint* option.

3. Select the *Browse for a location* option.

4. Click the *Save As* button.

5. Update the directory location at the top of the dialog with your URL and press the **Enter** key on your computer keyboard to point the *Save As* dialog to that location.

    *   http://[*YourServerName*]/pwa/ProjectBICenter/Sample%20Reports/English%20(United%20States)/

6. Give your report a unique name that you can recognize.

7. Change the *Save As type* field to *Excel Workbook (*.xlsx)*, if necessary.

8. Select the *Open with Excel in the Browser* option.

9. Click the *Save* button.

You should see your report rendered in the browser.

Exercise 17-2 for Excel 2007 Users

Publish the report from Exercise 17-1 to a SharePoint site.

1. Using the Excel client from the report in Exercise 17-1, click the *Office* button.

2. Select the *Publish* item and select *Excel Services* in the fly-out menu.

3. Select the *Browse for a location* option in the *Save As* dialog. Update the directory location by entering the URL for your sample reports library (sample shown below) in the *File name* field, add a forward slash at the end, and type a unique name for your report.

   - http://[*YourServerName*]/pwa/ProjectBICenter/Sample%20Reports/English%20(United%20States)/

4. Change the *Save As type* field to *Excel Workbook (*.xlsx)*, if necessary.

5. Select the *Open in Excel Services* checkbox.

6. Click the *Save* button.

You should see your report rendered in the browser.

Applying Basic Formatting

If you have used Excel before, I assume you know how to format a cell. Formatting in a PivotTable is similar but has some oddities of which you should be aware. The method to format *Date* or *Number* values differs based on whether they are in the *Rows Labels* area, *Columns Labels* area or the ∑ *Values* area of the PivotTable.

Row Labels

To format a *Row Label* data field, float your mouse pointer over the top of the first data field instance to format. When the cursor changes to a downward pointing arrow, as shown in Figure 17 - 52, select the cell. The system highlights all instances of the data field. Use the *Format* pick list on the Excel *Home* tab to format the cells accordingly.

Figure 17 - 52: Selection cursor for Row Labels

Column Labels

In a *Cross-Tab* report, dates and numbers can appear as columns. To format those values, select the row selector and use the *Format* pick list on the Excel *Home* tab to format accordingly.

∑ Values

To format a ∑ *Values* data field, double-click the column header in the report to open the *Field Settings* dialog. Select the *Number Format* button at the bottom to open the *Format Cells* dialog. Set the desired numeric or date format and click the *OK* button twice to return.

Adding Fit and Finish Formatting

The report you created in the Hands On Exercises is usable but not ready for production use. You use that report as the basis for going through the *Advanced Editing* options you need to make your reports effective.

When you select a PivotTable, you see two new contextual tabs that appear in the *Excel* ribbon. These are the *Design* tab and *Options* tab shown in Figure 17 - 53 and Figure 17 - 54, respectively. The *Design* tab functionality focuses on the look of your report while the *Options* tab contains a number of functions that enable you to control the report experience. I cover the functionality of both tabs in greater detail in the next topical section.

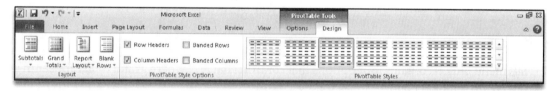

Figure 17 - 53: PivotTable Design tab

Figure 17 - 54: PivotTable Options tab

Using the Design Tab

The *PivotTable Tools Design* tab contains functionality that controls the visual look of your report. I cover the most common options for report writing in this topical section.

Subtotals Menu Button

The *Subtotals* pick list contains four options that control whether subtotals appear and where you would like them to appear in the report. This option is global for all fields in the report and requires a field in the $\sum$ *Values* area for you to see any impact. I list the options and what they do in Table 17 - 6.

In a later section, you learn how to control this setting on a data field basis, providing you with more control over totaling. Unless you have a need for totals on every field, I suggest that you select the *Do Not Show Subtotals* item and control this on a data field basis.

Option	Functionality
Do Not Show Subtotals	Removes all subtotals for all fields in the PivotTable.
Show all Subtotals at Bottom of Group	Inserts a totals row beneath each grouping data field in the report.
Show all Subtotals at Top of Group	Displays a total in line with the grouping data field without inserting lines into the report.
Include Filtered Items in Totals	This new for 2010 setting allows you to include items in the roll-up total, though you may have filtered them out of the report view.

Table 17 - 6: Subtotals Menu Button Options

Grand Totals Menu Button

The *Grand Totals* menu button contains four options that control what and where grand totals appear in your report. The options, which are self-explanatory, are as follows:

- *Off for Rows and Columns*

- *On for Rows and Columns*

- *On for Rows Only*

- *On for Columns Only*

Report Layout Menu Button

The *Report Layout* menu button contains five options, which control the presentation of the data fields in your report as shown in Table 17 - 7. This option controls one of the most important design decisions of your report. There is new functionality in Excel 2010, which enhances your ability to control the general layout of the report.

You can also control this setting at the field level, which I cover in a later section of this module, providing finer control over presentation.

Option	Functionality	Example	Uses
Show in **Compact** Form	Shows all data fields in a compact tree structure	XXX XXX XXX	Works best with when the number of data fields is greater than can be viewed horizontally and the report delivery is online. Enables the report user to open and close groups.
Show in Outline Form	Shows all data fields in a wide outline form, sometimes resembling a staircase	XXXXX XXXXX XXXXX	Works best with a small number of data fields and the report delivery is online. Enables the report user to open and close groups
Show in Tabular Form	Shows all data fields as a table but does not show repeating values by default	XXXX XXXX XXXXX XXXX XXXXX XXXXX	Works best for printed report delivery and a number of data fields that will fit across the medium. Can be used online with the open/close functionality
Repeat All Item Labels	Note: This function has no impact on the Compact Form. Repeats all item labels for each group of repeating values	Outline Form looks like: XXXX XXXX XXXXX XXXX XXXXX XXXXX Tabular Form looks like: XXXX XXXX XXXXX XXXX XXXX XXXXX XXXX XXXX XXXXX	Can be very useful for printed reports for place keeping or where there are a lot of lined under a particular group and group will span a page or screen. Use cautiously in online reports as repeating data can make reports hard to read.
Do Not Repeat All Item Labels	Default value that does not show all values for repeating values.	See defaults for Outline Form and Tabular Form above.	Useful for online report presentation where repeated same values can create visual clutter.

Table 17 - 7: Report Layout options

Blank Rows Menu Button

The *Blank Rows* menu button contains two options that control whether a blank line appears between data groups in your report. Blank lines provide additional visual breaks between data groups and are effective for printed reports. The options, which are self-explanatory, are as follows:

- *Insert Blank Line after Each Item*

- *Remove Blank Line after Each Item*

PivotTable Styles Gallery

The *PivotTable Styles* gallery is the quickest way to format the look and feel of your report as shown in Figure 17 - 55. Your report layout strongly influences how these gallery options appear to you. As you hover your mouse over each option, you can see the *Active Preview* of the selection's impact if chosen. You should choose a style that makes the data presented as easy to view and understand as possible.

Also note, that the system links colors for these gallery items to the *Page Layout* tab, *Colors* pick list. Any changes made there will have an immediate impact on your report colors. Unless you truly desire a pink report, I advise you use caution.

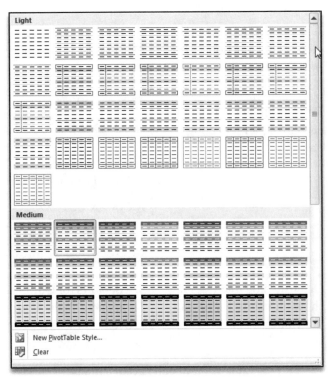

Figure 17 - 55: PivotTable Style gallery

Hands On Exercise

Exercise 17-3 for Excel 2007 and Excel 2010 Users

Modify a report to be a Tabular report with column totals.

1. Open the report you created in Exercise 17-1 in the Excel client, if necessary.

2. Add the *TaskRemainingWork* data field to the ∑ *Values* area.

3. Hover your mouse pointer over the first occurrence of the *TaskFinishDate* field, to expose the down arrow. When the down arrow appears, click to select all occurrences.

4. Click the *Home* tab and from the *Number* section use the pick list in the upper area to apply the *Short Date* format.

5. Click on the *Sum of TaskRemainingWork* header and change it to *Remaining Work*. In the *Number* section of the *Home* ribbon, use the *Number* pick list to format using the *Accounting with 2 decimal places* option and change the *Symbol* value to *None*.

6. Click the *Design* tab in the *PivotTable Tools* ribbon group and from the *PivotTable Styles* section use the gallery to change the *PivotTable Style* item to *Pivot Style Medium 9*.

    *   Hover your mouse pointer over a style to display its name.

7. From the *Layout* section of the *Design* ribbon, click the *Subtotals* pick list button and select the *Show all subtotals at top of group* item.

8. From the *Layout* section of the *Design* ribbon, click the *Grand Totals* pick list button and select the *On for Columns Only* item.

9. From the *Layout* section of the *Design* ribbon, click the *Report Layout* pick list and select the *Show in Tabular form* item.

10. Resize columns to show all data.

11. Excel 2010 users, click on the *File* tab, select the *Save & Send* tab in the *Backstage* and the double-click the *Current Location* item to publish the report to the server.

12. Excel 2007 users, click on the *Office* button, select the *Publish* item then the *Excel Services* selection. Click the *Save* button to save the updated report.

Working with the Options Tab

The PivotTable *Options* contextual tab contains several functions that impact how the PivotTable behaves and what core elements appear. In this section, I cover the common options for report writing.

PivotTable Options

The PivotTable *Options* pick list shown in Figure 17 - 56 is very important when creating a new report that you intend to use on a regular basis. You should review these settings during report creation as they control the basic visual properties and refresh data settings for the report. You typically set these only once during report creation.

Figure 17 - 56: PivotTable Options - Options pick list

Click the *Options* item and the system displays the *Pivot Table Options* dialog shown in Figure 17 - 57 and Figure 17 - 58. The first figures displays the *Layout & Format* tab while the second figure shows the *Data* tab.

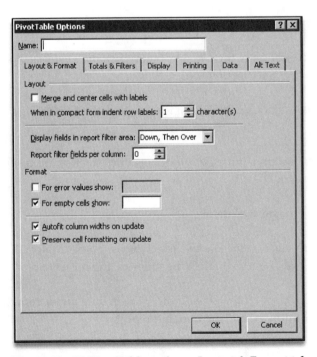

Figure 17 - 57: PivotTable options - Layout & Format tab

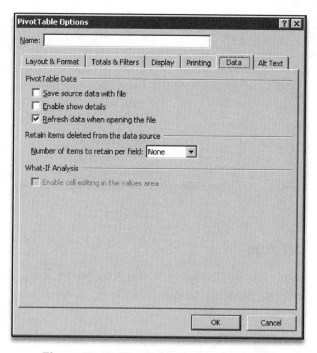

Figure 17 - 58: PivotTable options - Data tab

I list the most common four settings found in the aforementioned tabs in Table 17 - 8 along with explanations of their functionality and recommended settings.

Tab	Figure	Option	Function	Recommended Setting
Layout & Format	Figure 17 - 57	PivotTable Name	Enables you to designate a name for the PivotTable	**Recommend: Name your PivotTable** Give the PivotTable a name that you can easily identify. You will use this name later when conditional publishing is covered.
Layout & Format	Figure 17 - 57	Autofit column widths on Update	When selected, Excel autofits your columns automatically on data refresh.	**Recommend: Deselect** This functionality makes it hard to control the format of the report, which can lead to the report being wider than your screen resolution.
Layout & Format	Figure 17 - 57	Preserve cell formatting on update	When selected, prevents Excel from resetting the PivotTable formatting to the default settings on data refresh	**Recommend: Select** Otherwise, you lose any conditional formatting and other modifications on a data refresh

Tab	Figure	Option	Function	Recommended Setting
Data	Figure 17 - 58	Refresh data when opening the file	When selected, the Excel report auto-matically retrieves the latest data and gets rid of any cached data.	**Recommend: Select** Otherwise, user confusion occurs when the system uses out-of-date data to make a decision.

Table 17 - 8: List of Pertinent PivotTable Option Settings

Working with Field Settings

Use the *Active Field* field to change the name of the selected data field. For example, you decide that the *TaskWorkPer-centComplete* value is too long; select the field and change the value to *% Work Comp*. When you press the **Enter** key, the system reflects your change in the PivotTable.

Clicking on the *Field Setting* button, shown in Figure 17 - 59, provides options that enable you to control the display of data at the individual data field level rather than at the report level.

Figure 17 - 59: Field Settings Button on the PivotTable Options tab

You can find the key settings on the *Layout & Print* tab of the dialog shown in Figure 17 - 60.

Figure 17 - 60: PivotTable Data Field Settings dialog - Layout & Print tab

I list examples of how each setting impacts the PivotTable in Table 17 - 9.

Setting	Effect	Example

Show item labels in outline form	When selected, the data field appears in a wide outline form, sometimes resembling a staircase	XXXXX
		   XXXXX
		      XXXXX

Show item labels in tabular form	When selected, the data field appears as a table but does not show repeating values by default	XXXX XXXX XXXXX XXXX XXXXX XXXXX
Repeat item labels	When selected, the data field is repeated for each group of repeating values	Outline Form looks like: XXXX XXXX XXXXX XXXX XXXXX XXXXX Tabular Form looks like: XXXX XXXX XXXXX XXXX XXXX XXXXX XXXX XXXX XXXXX

Insert blank line after each item label	When selected, inserts a blank line between each group of like values for the data field.	XXXXX
		   XXXXX
		      XXXXX

Insert page break after each item	Whenever the value of the data field changes, the system inserts a page break. This is very useful in reports that are to be printed	XXXX XXXX ------------------------------ YYYYY

Table 17 - 9: Data Field Setting Examples

Applying Grouping

The *Group* group of the Excel PivotTable *Options* tab contains three buttons:

- The *Group Selection/Ungroup* buttons enable you to dynamically group contiguous rows or columns into a collapsible group. If you are analyzing large amounts of data, you use these buttons to create dynamic groups that fit your analytical needs.

- The *Group Field* button enables you to meet a common Project Management reporting need of reporting data by week, month, and quarter. The *Group Field* button enables dynamic grouping of date data fields or number data fields into groups you specify.

You select the date or number field to group in the PivotTable by clicking the *Group Field* button. If you selected a date field, you see Figure 17 - 61. Note that the date groupings are *Days, Months, Quarters,* and *Years.* What happens if you want to group by week? Figure 17 - 61 illustrates the configuration for week grouping where you select *Days* and designate the number of days as *seven.* This approach enables other possibilities for date grouping such as bi-weekly reporting needs.

For grouping data by week, MSProjectExperts recommends you use *Group by Days* and *number of days* set to 7.

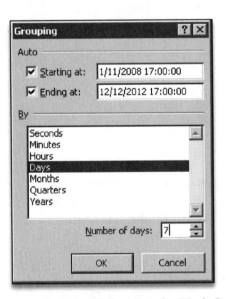

Figure 17 - 61: Grouping dialog, Date by Week Grouping

If you selected a numeric field, you see Figure 17 - 62. You define the groups by starting and ending values and define how wide to make each group.

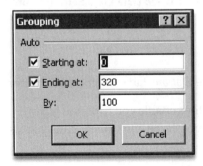

Figure 17 - 62: Grouping Dialog Example for Numeric Data

Summarizing Values

The *Summarize Values* menu button shown in Figure 17 - 63 enables the type of value aggregation performed on the selected field in the $\sum$ *Values* area of the PivotTable. You can also use this button to change the default calculation assigned by Excel to the numeric data field you placed in the $\sum$ *Values* area of the PivotTable in cases where it assigned an incorrect operation. Select the field in question in the PivotTable and use this button to correct the operation.

Figure 17 - 63: Calculations pick list of PivotTable Options Tab

The most used choices in the *Summarize Values* menu are:

- Sum

- Count

- Average

- Min

- Max

- Product

There is also a *More* options selection to provide five more aggregation alternatives.

Fields, Items and Sets Menu Button and Calculated Fields Menu Item

Use the *Fields, Items and Sets* button from the *Calculations* pick list to create your own calculated fields in the $\sum$ *Values* area of the PivotTable. Figure 17 - 64 shows an example of a custom calculation where the user is comparing Baseline Work to Work. This value is calculated automatically when the system refreshes the PivotTable data.

Most of the formula operators in Excel are available for use and Excel provides you with a list of data fields that you can use in a formula in the *Fields* list.

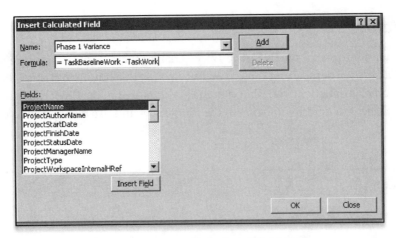

Figure 17 - 64: Insert Calculated Field dialog

+/- Buttons

Use the *+/- Buttons* button at the right side of the *Options* tab to hide or show the collapse/expand buttons next to each field in the PivotTable. If you intend to print a report, this option will help reduce visual clutter in the report.

Hands On Exercise

Exercise 17-4 for Excel 2007 and Excel 2010 Users

Update the report developed in Exercise 17-1 to make it printer friendly.

1. Open the report you created in Exercise 17-1 in the Excel client, if necessary.

2. From the *PivotTable* section of the *Options* ribbon, click the *Options* pick list and select the *Options* item. Give your pivot table a name in the *Name* field. In the *Layout & Format* tab of the *PivotTable Options* dialog, deselect the checkbox for the *Autofit column widths on update* option. Click the *OK* button.

3. Click on the *TaskFinishDate* item in the *Row Labels* section and select the *Field Settings* item from the popup menu. Click on the *Layout & Print* tab, select the *Show item labels in outline form* option, and then click the *OK* button to close the *Field Settings* dialog.

4. Hover your mouse pointer over the *TaskFinishDate* field header in the spreadsheet and click to select all when the downward arrow appears. In the *Group* section of the *Options* ribbon, click the *Group Selection* button and use the *Grouping* dialog to group the item by week, by selecting the *Days* option and entering a value of 7 in the *Number of days* field. Click the *OK* button in the dialog.

5. Add the *AssignmentWork* item to the ∑ *Values* area of the PivotTable.

6. In the ∑ *Values* area of the PivotTable, click on the *AssignmentWork* item and select the *Value Field Settings* item from the popup menu. Change the *Summarize Values By* setting from *Assignment-Work* to *Sum*. Click the *OK* button to close the *Value Field Settings* dialog.

7. Add the *Task Work* item to the ∑ *Values* area of the PivotTable and use the same technique you used in the previous step to verify that it is set to *Sum*.

For Excel 2010 Users

8. Click the *Calculations* button and click on the *Fields, Items, & Sets* pick list, then select the *Calculated Field* item to add a calculated field named *% of Task*. In the *Calculated Field* dialog, enter the name in the *Name* field. Enter "AssignmentWork/TaskWork" without the quotes in the *Formula* field. Click the *OK* button.

For Excel 2007 Users

8. In the *Tools* section of the *Options* ribbon, click the *Formulas* button and select the *Calculated Field* item to add a calculated field named *% of Task*. In the *Calculate Field* dialog, enter the name in the *Name* field. Enter "AssignmentWork/TaskWork" without the quotes in the *Formula* field. Click the *OK* button.

For Excel 2007 and Excel 2010 Users

9. Float your mouse pointer over the header for your new field until you see the downward pointing arrow and click to select all instances. Right-click on the header and select the *Format Cells* item. In the *Format Cells* dialog, format the *Sum of % of Task* item as a percentage with no decimals and click the *OK* button.

10. Resize columns in your spreadsheet to best display the data to your liking.

11. Update the field names as follows:

   - *TaskFinishDate* to *Finish Week*

   - *TaskName* to *Task*

   - *ProjectName* to *Project*

   - *Resource Name* to *Resource*

   - *RemainingWork* to *Remaining Work*

   - *Sum of TaskRemainingWork* to *Remaining*

   - *Sum of AssignmentWork* to *Assigned*

   - *Sum of TaskWork* to *Task Work*

   - *Sum of % of Task* to *% Task*

12. Right Justify the column headers that display numeric data.

13. Publish your report to SharePoint.

Advanced Formatting

In this section, I cover advanced aspects of Excel where there is relevance to Project Server Business Intelligence.

Data Field Level Filtering for Date Fields

PivotTables offer support for special *Date* field filtering for *Date* data fields as shown in Figure 17 - 65. This feature enables you restrict report data to the current month or quarter without user intervention. To specify a date filter:

- Select a *Date* data field in the PivotTable

- Select the *Filter* dropdown button in the data field heading

- Select the *Date Filters...* item

- Select the date filter to apply

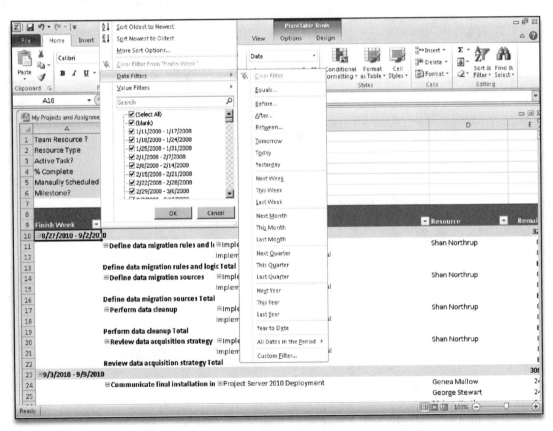

Figure 17 - 65: PivotTable Date filters for Date Data fields

Key Performance Indicators using Conditional Formatting

Your Business Intelligence need likely includes Key Performance Indicator (KPI) reporting. You can accomplish this type of reporting, in addition to other data visualizations, using an *Icon Set* conditional formatting as shown in Figure 17 - 66. KPIs, when used properly, provide visual indicators that draw the user's attention to significant data.

Figure 17 - 66: KPI Icon Sets for PivotTable Conditional Formatting

To apply *Icon Set* conditional formatting to a data field, do the following:

1. Select the top most cell of the data field to apply the formatting.

 Warning: Due to an Excel quirk, do not select the entire column, just the first value cell in the column.

2. On the *Home* tab, select the *Conditional Formatting* menu button.

3. Select the *Icon Sets...* item.

4. Select an Icon Set. The system will apply the Icon Set to that cell. A new menu appears next to that cell as shown in Figure 17 - 67. Select the *All cells showing 'Remaining' values for 'Resource'* option.

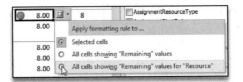

Figure 17 - 67: Icon Set Formatting menu

 This procedure is to avoid the Excel quirk that applies conditional formatting to Totals rows. If you have based your KPI on % of Total, including the Column Total in this calculation will give you incorrect results. If you follow this procedure, the system only applies conditional formatting to the detail rows.

5. The system will apply conditional formatting to all detail rows.

The default *Conditional Formatting* rules applied are probably not using the criteria you desire. To change this, you need to edit the *Conditional Formatting* rule by doing the following:

- In the *Home* tab, select the *Conditional Formatting* menu button.

- Select the *Manage Rules…* item. The system displays the *Conditional Formatting Rules Manager* dialog shown in Figure 17 - 68.

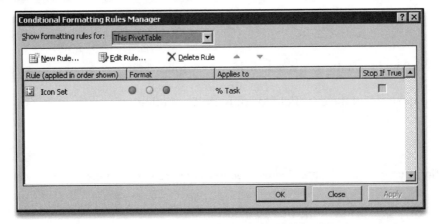

Figure 17 - 68: Conditional Formatting Rules Manger

- Select the rule to edit and click the *Edit Rule* button and the system displays the dialog shown in Figure 17 - 69. This dialog enables you to change the basis for displaying each icon, reversing the order of icons, and showing icons only.

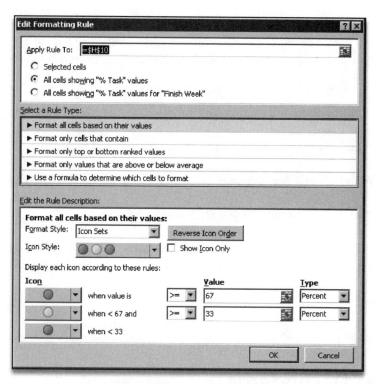

Figure 17 - 69: Edit Formatting Rule Dialog

Hands On Exercise

Exercise 17-5 for Excel 2007 and Excel 2010 Users

Apply date filtering and conditional formatting to a report.

1. Open the report you created in Exercise 17-1 in the Excel client, if necessary.

2. Select the *TaskFinishDate* item (now called **Finish Week**), apply the *Next Month* date filter to the field by clicking on the pick list button in the field header, and then select the *Date Filters* item from the popup menu. Next, select the *Next Month* filter from the fly-out menu.

3. Click on the first value in the *Remaining* data field and from the *Styles* section of the *Home* ribbon, click the *Conditional Formatting* button and select the *Icon Sets* item from the menu. Select the *Green Yellow Red* icon set.

4. Click the *Formatting* button next to the first value and select the *All cells showing "Remaining" values* item.

5. From the *Styles* section of the *Home* ribbon, click on the *Conditional Formatting* button and select the *Manage Rules* button. The system displays the *Conditional Formatting Rules Manager* dialog. Select the *Icon Set* item in the dialog and click the *Edit Rule* button. The system displays the *Edit Formatting Rule* dialog.

6. Apply KPI formatting to the *Remaining* data field as follows:

   - Numbers greater than or equal to 200 display red icons.

   - Numbers less than 200 or greater than or equal to 100 display yellow icons.

   - Numbers less than 100 display green icons.

7. Click the *OK* button in the *Edit Formatting Rule* dialog, then click the *Apply* button in the *Conditional Formatting Rules Manager* dialog, and then click the *OK* button to close the dialog.

8. Close your report.

Understanding Dashboards

Dashboards are a highly desired Business Intelligence capability but often people implement them badly. Dashboards are a way of bringing a small number of distinct data visualizations together to answer a specific need or tell a story. A dashboard **is not** a random set of 25 charts thrown together on a screen because they look good together. A dashboard also does not need to have fancy charts or other graphics. It simply needs to address the information need effectively.

The most effective dashboards have the minimum number of data visualizations needed to tell the story and no more. It is important that when you develop dashboards, you resist the temptation of "one more report". As a rule of thumb, keep the number to 3-6 components to prevent scrolling. You should endeavor to minimize scrolling and prioritize key data to appear on the initial screen.

The dashboard functionality covered here is SharePoint-based dashboards. You can emulate a dashboard within Excel, using slicers to link PivotTables. However, SharePoint dashboards allow you to aggregate content from other sources beyond Excel. Excel-based dashboards are very useful for meeting Collaborative Business Intelligence needs and you can easily modify them to meet changing business needs.

Dashboards are relatively easy to build once you understand the basics of how they work. In order to build a dashboard, I introduce you to a few more concepts before I delve into the construction process.

Dashboard Components

The dashboard you learn how to build next is a *SharePoint Web Part* page hosting Excel *Web Access* web parts and a *Page Filter* web part, which the system links together via *Parameter* connections. You can add other types of web parts but these are the core to Project Business Intelligence. I depict these relationships in Figure 17 - 70.

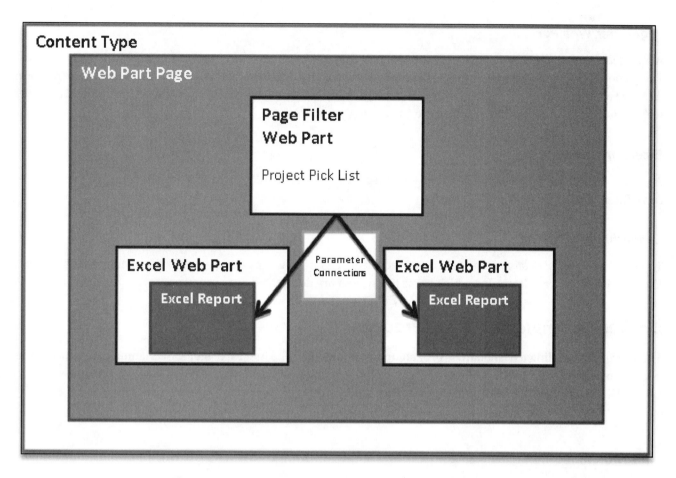

Figure 17 - 70: SharePoint Dashboard Component Relationships

Content Types

A content type is a SharePoint template for a specific type of reusable data. A content type can contain information items such as specific column information, attached workflows, document templates, and other settings. *Web Part* pages are a content type and thus, will have a different behavior from a regular document even though you can store both types of items in a Document Library.

Web Part page

The *Web Part* page is a SharePoint document that hosts the dashboard components. The primary decisions you make when you create a *Web Part* page is to determine the name of the page and the layout to use.

Web Parts

These are the individual containers for your reports on the *Web Part* page. The primary functions of the web parts are:

- To control what actions users can take with your report

- To manage the visual layout of the report on the page

- To enable filter connectivity with other web parts so that they act in concert

Page Filter Web Part

A *Page Filter* web part is a special SharePoint web part that uses parameters to connect multiple web parts together. These connections enable the web parts to function in unison. There are several types of *Page Filters* and these perform different actions. Some require the person configuring the web part to enter a list of allowable values. Other *Page Filter* web parts retrieve information based on the current logged-in user.

Excel Parameter

A parameter is a special Excel range, usually defined for a PivotTable filter field that enables the Excel report to receive filter values from a *Page Filter* web part.

Conditional Publishing

The Excel *Conditional Publishing* function enables control of which specific parts of your Excel report are visible within Excel Services and can determine which items the system are designated as parameters.

Dashboard Implementation Process

The process of building a dashboard is broken up into four steps. The first three steps are planning steps as it is important to define what you are building and why before delving into the mechanics. Following this process, shown in Figure 17 - 71, ensures that you create your dashboard in an efficient manner.

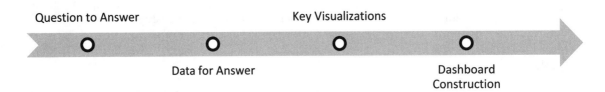

Question to Answer | Key Visualizations
Data for Answer | Dashboard Construction

Figure 17 - 71: Dashboard Development Process

Question to Answer

Before building a dashboard, you should be clear on the question you want your dashboard to address. This information helps you determine what elements to present and how best to structure these elements. Questions do not need to be complex but should be straightforward and easy to describe.

You should also understand what type of action you want to result from this information. If your intent is to spur action, then you should structure the data presentation to support that goal. For example, if you want individual accountability, then the responsible individual's name should be prominent in the presentation.

For example, you your team to have easy access to the data answering the question "What activities are due on the project next week?" You also need your team to act upon these items in a timely manner, especially those due next week. You want to build this for a 3-month project so you do not want to invest a lot of building it.

Data for Answer

To answer the question "What activities are due on the project next week?" you want data for project tasks, issues, and risks. For this dashboard, you decide that the complete data set you need is as follows:

- Tasks

    - Task Name

    - Task Finish Date

    - The name of the person assigned to the task

    - Project Name

- Issues

    - Title

    - Assigned to

    - Due Date

    - Project Name

- Risks

    - Title

    - Assigned to

    - Due date

    - Project Name

Key Visualizations

To keep it simple, you create three separate data lists with conditional formatting. You use *Yellow* to highlight dates occurring next week. You use *Red* to highlight items with missing data. It is prudent to document everything that you need to do to build your reports. The report specification tables that follow provide you with one example of such documentation. First, select the appropriate template for each list as shown in Table 17 - 10.

Report	Template	Rationale
Upcoming Tasks	ProjectAndAssignments	Need resource name, which requires assignment data
Upcoming Issues	Issues	Has the data needed
Upcoming Risks	Risks	Has the data needed

Table 17 - 10: Match Reports to Templates

I outline the requirements for the Upcoming Tasks report display in Table 17 - 11.

Item	Details
Row Labels	TaskFinishDate ResourceName TaskName
Setup PivotTable filter	Use ProjectName
Set up field filter as a Report parameter	Assign range name ProjectName to field
PivotTable formatting	Show in Tabular Form No Subtotals No Grand Totals PivotTable Name: PVTasks Use default theme +/- buttons on Dates formatted as Short Date
Conditional formatting	Use date filters to show only this week.

Table 17 - 11: Upcoming Tasks Specifications

I outline the Upcoming Issues report specification in Table 17 - 12.

Item	Details
Row Fields	Status Due Date Assigned To Title
Setup PivotTable filter	Use ProjectName
Set up field filter as a Report parameter	Assign range name ProjectName to field

Item	Details
PivotTable formatting	Show in Tabular Form
	No Subtotals
	No Grand Totals
	PivotTable Name: PVIssues
	Use default theme
	+/- buttons on
	Dates formatted as Short Date
Conditional formatting	Highlight dates due next week

Table 17 - 12: Upcoming Issues Specification

I outline the Upcoming Risks report specification in Table 17 - 13.

Item	Details
Row Fields	Status
	Due Date
	AssignedToResource
	Title
Setup PivotTable filter	Use ProjectName
Set up field filter as a Report parameter	Assign range name ProjectName to field
PivotTable formatting	Show in Tabular Form
	No Subtotals
	No Grand Totals
	PivotTable Name: PVRisks
	Use default theme
	+/- buttons on
	Dates formatted as Short Date
Conditional formatting	Highlight dates due next week

Table 17 - 13: Upcoming Risks Specification

Dashboard Construction

For discussion purposes, you have already built the reports as specified above. Now, it is time to bring the pieces together to begin creating your dashboard.

Creating a Parameter

In each of the reports above, you use *ProjectName* as a *Report* filter. In order for this filter to be usable in the Dashboard, you define the filter as a parameter so that the filter can receive its setting from the *Page Filter* web part on the *Dashboard* page.

There are three steps to create and use a parameter:

- Define the *Filter* field as a one cell Named Range

- Add it as a *Published* parameter

- Connect it to the *Page Filter* web part

Define the Filter Field as a One Cell Named Range

In order for a field to be visible external to the Excel Report, it has to be defined as a *Named Range* as shown in Figure 17 - 72. To define the *Filter* field as such, do the following:

1. Select the *Filter* field value.

2. Click the *Formulas* tab.

3. Select the *Define Names* pick list.

4. Enter the Range Name in the *Name* field.

5. Click the *OK* button.

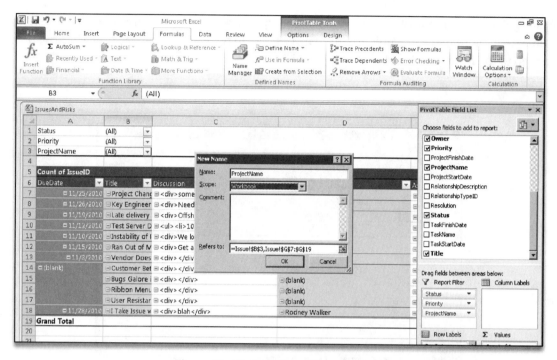

Figure 17 - 72: Defining a Named Range

Conditional Publishing

In the *Backstage,* there is a *Publish Options* button that I did not include as part of the regular publishing steps. To publish a parameter, select the *Publish Options* button **before publishing** your Excel Report. The *Publish Options* dialog displays as shown in Figure 17 - 73.

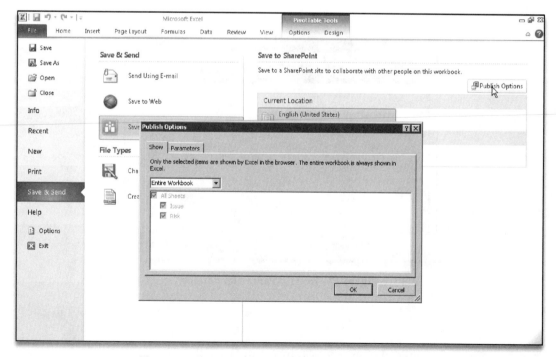

Figure 17 - 73: Backstage with Publish Options dialog

The *Show* tab enables you to control which aspects of the report are visible in Excel Services. This can be especially handy if you have a report that you would like to share but you do not want to share all of the information. To define a parameter, go to the *Parameters* tab shown in Figure 17 - 74.

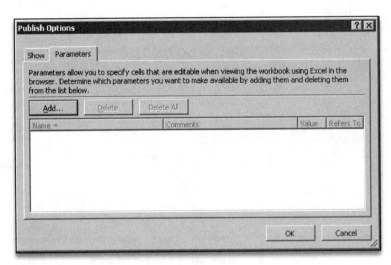

Figure 17 - 74: Publish Options - Add Parameter

Click the *Add* button and the system opens the *Add Parameters* dialog shown in Figure 17 - 75.

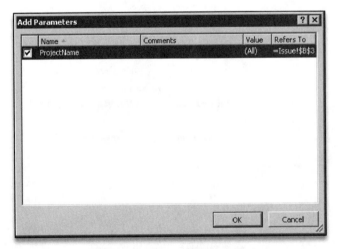

Figure 17 - 75: Add Parameters dialog

Select the checkbox next to the name of your new parameter and click the *OK* button.

Hands On Exercise

Exercise 17-6 for Excel 2007 and Excel 2010 Users

Build the Upcoming Tasks report.

1. Navigate to the Business Intelligence Center and click the *Templates* link in the *Quick Launch* menu. Click on the *English (United States)* link to open the English language folder. Click on the *ProjectsAndTasks* template name to launch the template. In the *Open* dialog, select the *Read Only* option and click the *OK* button. The system launches the template in Excel.

2. Click the *Enable Content* button if prompted by a security warning. Make the file trusted if prompted.

3. Add *TaskFinishDate, ResourceName,* and the *TaskName* fields to the *Row Labels* area.

4. Add the *ProjectName* field to the *Report Filter* area.

5. In the *Layout* section of the *Design* ribbon, click the *Subtotals* button and select the *Do Not Show Subtotals* item. Click the *Grand Totals* button and select the *Off for Rows and Columns* item. Click the *Report Layout* button and select the *Show in Tabular Form* item.

6. Select the *ProjectName* field and from the *Defined Names* section of the *Formulas* ribbon, click the *Define Name* button. Enter the name "ProjectNM" without the quotes in the *Name* field and click the *OK* button.

7. Format the *TaskFinishDate* column as a short date.

8. Click the filter pick list on the *TaskFinishDate* column header and float your mouse pointer over the *Date Filters* item, and select the *Next Week* item.

9. Arrange the column sizes to best view the data, give your column headers friendly names.

10. On the *Options* ribbon, enter the name "PVTasks" without the quotes in the *PivotTable Name* field.

For Excel 2010 Users

11. Click on the *File* menu and select the *Save & Send* tab. Select the *Save to SharePoint* option.

12. Click the *Publish Options* button in the upper right corner of the page and select the *Parameters* tab in the *Publish Options* dialog. Click the *Add* button and select the named item you created in step 6. Click the *OK* button to close the *Add Parameters* dialog and then click the *OK* button to close the *Publish Options* dialog.

13. Locate and select the URL for your sample reports library under the *Recent Locations* section and click the *Save As* button. In the *Save As* dialog, enter "Upcoming Tasks" without the quotes in the *File Name* field and select the *Excel Workbook* item in the *Save as Type* pick list. Click the *Save* button to save your new report.

14. Close your report

For Excel 2007 Users

11. Select the *Publish* item and select the *Excel Services* item in the fly-out menu.

12. Select the *Browse for a location* option in the *Save As* dialog. Update the directory location by entering the URL for your sample reports library (sample shown below) in the *File name* field and add a forward slash at the end and type "Upcoming Tasks" without the quotes as the name for your report.

    • http://[*YourServerName*]/pwa/ProjectBICenter/Sample%20Reports/English%20(United%20States)/

13. Change the *Save As type* field to Excel Workbook (*.xlsx), if necessary. Select the *Open in Excel Services* checkbox. Click the *Save* button

14. Close your report.

Exercise 17-7 for Excel 2007 and Excel 2010 Users

Build the Upcoming Risks report.

1. Navigate to the Business Intelligence Center and click the *Templates* link in the *Quick Launch* menu. Click on the *English (United States)* link to open the English language folder. Click on the *Risks* template name to launch the template. In the *Open* dialog, select *Read Only* and click the *OK* button. The system launches the template in Excel.

2. Click the *Enable Content* button if prompted by a security warning. Make the file trusted, if prompted.

3. Add *Status, DueDate, AssignedToResource,* and the *Title* fields to the *Row Labels* area.

4. Add the *ProjectName* field to the *Report Filter* area.

5. In the *Layout* section of the *Design* ribbon, click the *Subtotals* button and select the *Do Not Show Subtotals* item. Click the *Grand Totals* button and select the *Off for Rows and Columns* item. Click the *Report Layout* button and select the *Show in Tabular Form* item.

6. Select the *ProjectName* field and from the *Defined Names* section of the *Formulas* ribbon, click the *Define Name* button. Enter the name "ProjectNM" without the quotes in the *Name* field and click the *OK* button.

7. Format the *TaskFinishDate* column as a short date.

8. Click the filter pick list on the *DueDate* column header and float your mouse pointer over the *Date Filters* item, and select the *Next Week* item.

9. Arrange the column sizes to best view the data, give your column headers friendly names.

10. On the *Options* ribbon, enter the name "PVIssues" without the quotes in the *PivotTable Name* field.

For Excel 2010 Users

11. Click on the *File* menu and select the *Save & Send* tab. Select the *Save to SharePoint* option.

12. Click the *Publish Options* button in the upper right corner of the page and select the *Parameters* tab in the *Publish Options* dialog. Click the *Add* button and select the named item you created in step 6. Click the *OK* button to close the *Add Parameters* dialog and then click the *OK* button to close the *Publish Options* dialog.

13. Locate and select the URL for your sample reports library under the *Recent Locations* section and click the *Save As* button. In the *Save As* dialog, enter "Upcoming Risks" without the quotes in the *File Name* field and select the *Excel Workbook* item in the *Save as Type* pick list. Click the *Save* button to save your new report.

14. Close your report.

For Excel 2007 Users

11. Select the *Publish* item and select the *Excel Services* item in the fly-out menu.

12. Select the *Browse for a location* option in the *Save As* dialog. Update the directory location by entering the URL for your sample reports library (sample shown below) in the *File name* field and add a forward slash at the end and type "Upcoming Risks" without the quotes as the name for your report.

    - http://[*YourServerName*]/pwa/ProjectBICenter/Sample%20Reports/English%20(United%20States)/

13. Change the *Save As type* field to Excel Workbook (*.xlsx), if necessary. Select the *Open in Excel Services* checkbox. Click the *Save* button.

14. Close your report.

Exercise 17-8 for Excel 2007 and Excel 2010 Users

Build the Upcoming Issues report.

1. Navigate to the Business Intelligence Center and click the *Templates* link in the *Quick Launch* menu. Click on the *English (United States)* link to open the English language folder. Click on the *Issues* template name to launch the template. In the *Open* dialog, select the *Read Only* item and click the *OK* button. The system launches the template in Excel.

2. Click the *Enable Content* button if prompted by a security warning. Make the file trusted, if prompted.

3. Add *Status, DueDate, AssignedToResource,* and the *Title* fields to the *Row Labels* area.

4. Add the *ProjectName* field to the *Report Filter* area.

5. In the *Layout* section of the *Design* ribbon, click the *Subtotals* button and select the *Do Not Show Subtotals* item. Click the *Grand Totals* button and select the *Off for Rows and Columns* item. Click the *Report Layout* button and select the *Show in Tabular Form* item.

6. Select the *ProjectName* field and from the *Defined Names* section of the *Formulas* ribbon, click the *Define Name* button. Enter the name "ProjectNM" without the quotes in the *Name* field and click the *OK* button.

7. Format the *TaskFinishDate* column as a short date.

8. Click the filter pick list on the *DueDate* column header and float your mouse pointer over the *Date Filters* item, and select the *Next Week* item.

9. Arrange the column sizes to best view the data and give your column headers friendly names.

10. On the *Options* ribbon, enter the name "PVIssues" without the quotes in the *PivotTable Name* field.

For Excel 2010 Users

11. Click on the *File* menu and select the *Save & Send* tab. Select the *Save to SharePoint* option.

12. Click the *Publish Options* button in the upper right corner of the page and click the *Parameters* tab in the *Publish Options* dialog. Click the *Add* button and select the named item you created in step 6. Click the *OK* button to close the *Add Parameters* dialog and then click the *OK* button to close the *Publish Options* dialog.

13. Locate and select the URL for your sample reports library under the *Recent Locations* section and click the *Save As* button. In the *Save As* dialog, enter "Upcoming Issues" without the quotes in the *File Name* field and select the *Excel Workbook* item in the *Save as Type* pick list. Click the *Save* button to save your new report.

14. Close your report.

For Excel 2007 Users

11. Select the *Publish* item and select the *Excel Services* item in the fly-out menu.

12. Select the *Browse for a location* option in the *Save As* dialog. Update the directory location by entering the URL for your sample reports library (sample shown below) in the *File name* field and add a forward slash at the end and type "Upcoming Issues" without the quotes as the name for your report.

    • http://[*YourServerName*]/pwa/ProjectBICenter/Sample%20Reports/English%20(United%20States)/

13. Change the *Save As type* field to Excel Workbook (*.xlsx), if necessary. Select the *Open in Excel Services* checkbox. Click the *Save* button.

14. Close your report.

Adding the Content Type to the Document Library

The *Dashboard* page can live in any SharePoint site to which you have the rights to add content. For this example, I am building a dashboard intended for the Project Team site, which allows me to take advantage of the site's security access so that the dashboard is only available to Project Team members.

Web Part pages are documents and must be stored in a document library. You can choose to use the *Project Documents* folder in your Project Team site or you can create another folder for this purpose. I use the *Project Documents* folder for this example. *Web Part* pages are not normally a default content type for document libraries. Therefore, you must execute a **one-time** procedure on this document library to add this content type so that you can create *Web Part* pages.

Hands On Exercise

Exercise 17-9

Add the Web Part page content type to your Deploy Training Advisor Software project site.

1. Navigate to your Deploy Training Advisor Software project site.

2. Click the *Project Documents* link from the *Quick Launch* menu.

3. Click the *Settings* button on the *Library* tab.

4. In the *General Settings* section, select the *Advanced Setting* item.

5. In the *Content* section, set the *Allow management of content types* value to *Yes* and click the *OK* button.

6. Scroll to the *Content Types* section of the *Document Library Setting* page and click the *Add from existing site content types* link.

7. In the *Available Site Content Types* list, scroll to, and select the *Web Part Page* item and click the *Add* button.

8. Click the *OK* button. Verify that you now see the *Web Part* page content type listed as shown in Figure 17 - 76. You can now create *Web Part* pages in this document library.

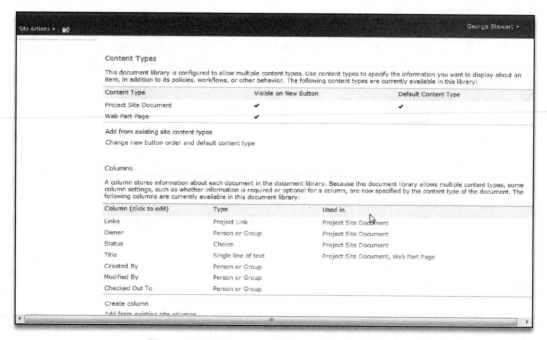

Figure 17 - 76: Document Library Content Types

Create a Web Part Page

Return to your document library and click the *Documents* tab to display the *Documents* ribbon. Select the *New Document* menu button and select the *Web Part Page* item as shown in Figure 17 - 77.

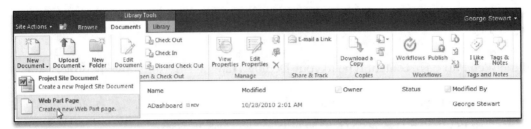

Figure 17 - 77: Create Web Part page button

On the *New Web Part Page* page shown in Figure 17 - 78, specify the name of your *Web Part* page and the layout of the page.

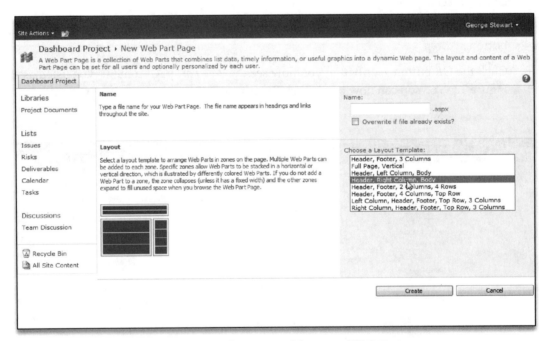

Figure 17 - 78: Specify Name and Layout of Web Part page

Adding Reports to the Dashboard

You now see the *Edit Web Part* page shown in Figure 17 - 79. *Zones* are the boxes on the page, where the name of the zone is in the upper left corner of the box.

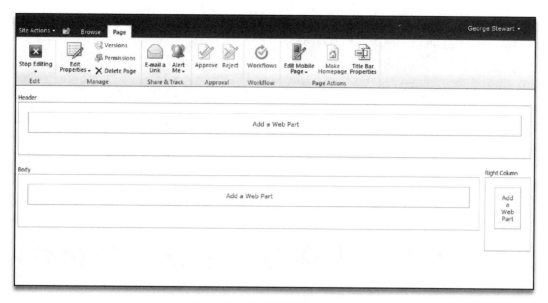

Figure 17 - 79: Edit Web Part page

Click the *Add a Web Part* link in the *Body* zone to add an *Excel Web Access* web part. When you click this link, you will see the *Web Part* gallery shown in Figure 17 - 80.

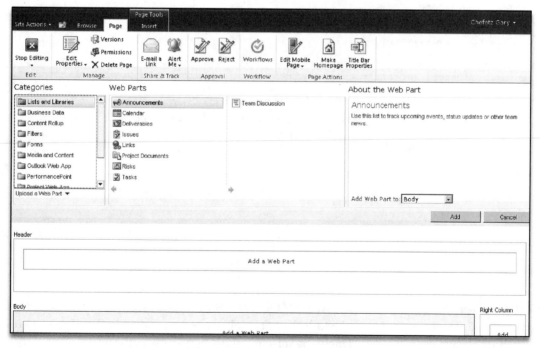

Figure 17 - 80: Web Part gallery

In the *Categories* section, select the *Business Data* item; in the *Web Parts* section, select the *Excel Web Access* item and click the *Add* button. The system redisplays the Dashboard page as shown in Figure 17 - 81.

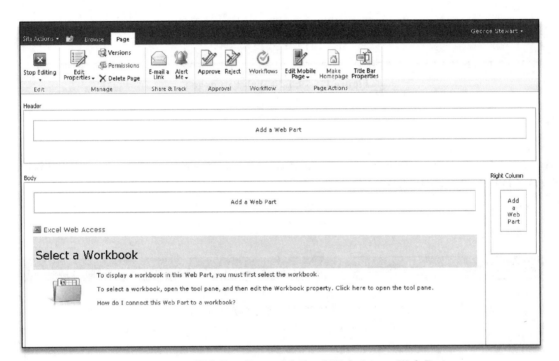

Figure 17 - 81: Web Part Page with Excel Web Access Web Part

Select the *Click here to open the tool pane* link. The *Web Part* tool pane allows you to set the properties for the web part as shown in Figure 17 - 82. These properties can include the title, toolbar options, and which Excel report to display. You can also access the tool pane via the *Web Part* menu by selecting the down arrow in the upper right corner of the web part and selecting the *Edit Web Part* item.

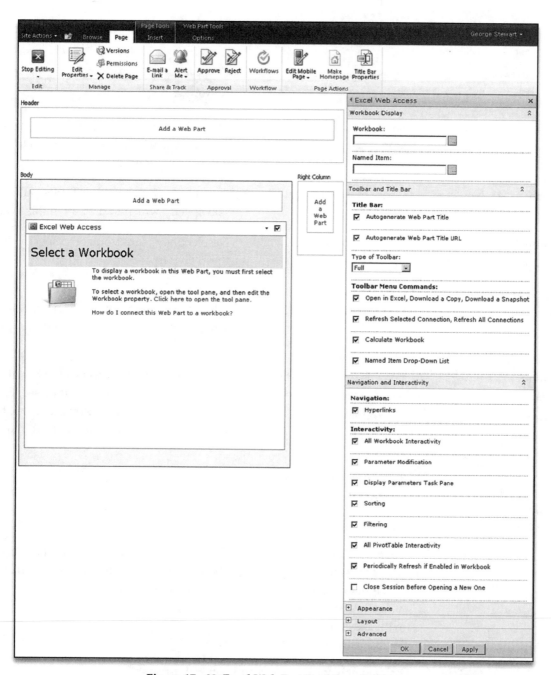

Figure 17 - 82: Excel Web Part Tool Pane Settings

Table 17 - 14 presents a list of commonly used settings for the tool pane.

Setting	Required?	Value	Rationale
Workbook	Yes	Full URL to your Excel report	The Excel Report to display in this Web Part. You can use the ellipsis button […] to browse to your Excel Report in the SharePoint farm.
Named Item	No	Name of the PivotTable	If you have multiple PivotTables published, you specify which to display in this Web Part.
Autogenerate the Web Part Title	No	Suggest deselecting	Deselecting means you get to specify the title of the Web Part.
Type of Toolbar	No	For this dashboard exercise, select None	This value really depends on the level of capability you wish to give to the user. None provides them with no way to open the Spreadsheet in the client.
Toolbar Menu Commands	No	For this dashboard, deselect Named Item Drop-Down List	If you choose to give users a toolbar, this section controls which options they see. For this dashboard, since there is only one tab, the system turns off the drop-down list to reduce clutter.
Title (Expand Appearance Section)	No	Put in the name of the Report displayed in the Web Part	
Height	No	*Note:* This function has a bug so you have to specify a height or it defaults the value to 400 pixels. Start with 200 and modify after trying with your data.	Controls the amount of visual space taken by the Web Part. The proper setting can keep space usage to a minimum.

Table 17 - 14: Commonly Used Settings for Excel Web Access Web Parts

You repeat this process for each Excel Report web part you add to the page. Note: You can rearrange web parts by dragging them around on the page.

Hands On Exercise

Exercise 17-10

Create a web part page and add your Excel reports.

1. Navigate to the home page of your Deploy Training Advisor Software project site and click the *Project Documents* link in the *Quick Launch* menu.

2. From the *New* section of the *Documents* ribbon, click the *New Document* pick list and select the *Web Part Page* item from the list.

3. In the *New Web Part Page* page, enter "Next Week" without the quotes in the *Name* field, and select the *Header, Right Column, Body* item in the *Choose a Layout* selector and click the *Create* button.

4. In the *Body* section of the new web part page, click the *Add a Web Part* link. After the system opens the *Web Part Gallery* at the top of the page, in the *Category* section select the *Business Data* item. In the web part list, select the *Excel Web Access* web part and click the *Add* button.

5. In the *Select a Workbook* area, click on the *Click here to open the tool pane* link. In the tool pane, click the *Ellipsis* button for the *Workbook* field to open the *Select an Asset* dialog. Use the navigation tool on the left of the dialog to expand the Business Intelligence Center, and locate and expand the English folder of the *Sample Reports* folder.

6. Select the *Upcoming Tasks* workbook and click the *OK* button. In the *Named Item* field, type "PVTasks" without the quotes, which is the name you gave your pivot table. In the *Type of Toolbar* pick list select the *None* option. Deselect all of the options in the *Toolbar Menu Commands* section. Expand the *Appearance* section, in the Title field remove the "Excel Web Access" text, and in the *Height* section set the *Height* value to *200*. Click the *OK* button at the bottom of the tool pane.

7. In the *Body* section of the page, click the *Add a Web Part* link, select the *Excel Web Access* web part from the gallery, and click the *Add* button.

8. In the *Select a Workbook* area, click on the *Click here to open the tool pane* link. In the tool pane, click the *Ellipsis* button for the *Workbook* field to open the *Select an Asset* dialog. Use the navigation tool on the left of the dialog to expand the Business Intelligence Center, and locate and expand the English folder of the *Sample Reports* folder.

9. Select the *Upcoming Issues* workbook and click the *OK* button. In the *Named Item* field, type "PVIssues" without the quotes, which is the name you gave your pivot table. In the *Type of Toolbar* pick list, select the *None* option. Deselect all of the options in the *Toolbar Menu Commands* section. Expand the *Appearance* section, in the *Title* field remove the "Excel Web Access" text, and in the *Height* section set the *Height* value to *200*. Click the *OK* button at the bottom of the tool pane.

10. Repeat steps 7 – 9 to add the *Upcoming Risks* report to your new dashboard. For the *Name* item, type "PVRisks" without the quotes.

Add the Choice Filter Web Part

For this discussion, I limit the reporting range to one project. Therefore, the built-in *Choice Filter* web part easily meets the requirement.

 If you use this technique in a production environment, any changes to the Project name will require a change to this filter.

Click the *Add a Web Part* link in the *Right Column* zone to add a *Choice Page Filter* web part. When you click this link, you will see the *Web Part* gallery as shown previously in Figure 17 - 80. Select the *Filters* category on the left, and then select the *Choice Filters* item under the *Web Parts* section.

Select the *Open the tool pane* link to open the *Web Part* tool pane. Change the *Web Part* settings as set forth in Table 17 - 15.

Setting	Required?	Value	Rationale
Filter Name	Yes	For this discussion, change this to Project	This is the name used in the Connections.
List of Choices	Yes	Enter or copy/paste the name of the project for this dashboard	
Title	No	For this discussion, change this to Project	This name displays next to the filter.
Default Value (Expand the Advanced Filter Options)	No	For this discussion, enter or copy/paste the name of the project for this dashboard	This setting eliminates the need for the user to select any value to see the reports.

Table 17 - 15: Choice Filter Settings

Connect the Page Filter to the Excel Web Access Web Parts

The final step of constructing the dashboard is to connect the *Choice Page Filter* item to each Excel Web Access web part.

1. Select the *Web Part menu arrow* item in the upper right corner of the *Choice Page Filter* web part.

2. Select the *Connections, Send Filter Values To* item to the name of the Excel Report as shown in Figure 17 - 83.

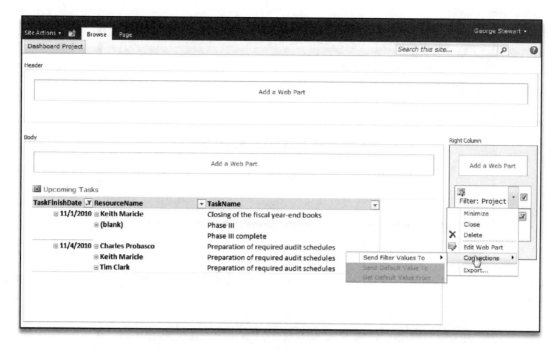

Figure 17 - 83: Edit Connections between Web Parts

3.   Select the *Send Filter Values To…* item from the pick list and chose a web part from the fly out menu as shown in Figure 17 - 84.

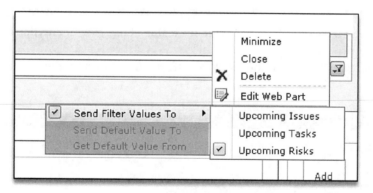

Figure 17 - 84: Select Web Part Connection Type

4.   The system displays the *Choose Connection* dialog shown in Figure 17 - 85.

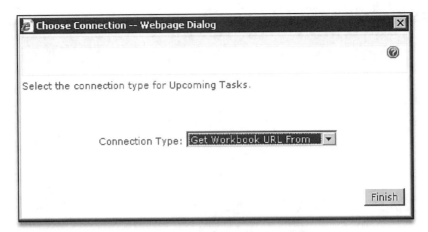

Figure 17 - 85: Choose Connection dialog

5. In the *Connection Type* pick list, select the *Get Filter Values From* item. The dialog display changes as shown in Figure 17 - 86.

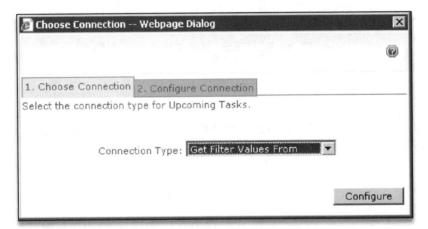

Figure 17 - 86: Choose Connections dialog - Configure Connections

6. Click on the *Configure* button or the *Configure Connection* tab and the display changes as shown in Figure 17 - 87.

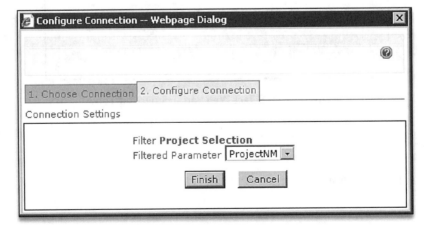

Figure 17 - 87: Configure Connection Settings

7. Verify that you selected ProjectNM for the *Filtered Parameter*. Repeat for each Excel Web Access web part on the page.

8. When complete, select the *Page* tab in the Ribbon.

9. Click the *Stop Editing* button.

You now have a complete functional dashboard.

Hands On Exercise

Exercise 17-11

Add the Choice Filter web part to your dashboard page and configure the connections to your reports.

1. Return to your new dashboard page and click the *Add a Web Part* link in the *Right Column* zone to open the Web Part gallery. Select the *Filters* category on the left, and then select the *Choice Filter* item in the gallery and click the *Add* button.

2. Select the Web Part menu arrow item in the upper right corner of the *Choice Filter* web part and select the *Connections, Send Filter Values To* item and select the name of one of your Excel Reports.

3. In the *Connection Type* pick list in the dialog, select the *Get Filter Values From* item. In the dialog, click on the *Configure* button or the *Configure Connection* tab. Select ProjectNM in the *Filtered Parameter* pick list and click the *Finish* button.

4. Repeat steps 2 - 4 for the other two Excel reports.

5. Select the Web Part menu arrow item in the upper right corner of the *Choice Filter* web part and select the *Edit Web Part* item.

6. In the web part tool pane, rename the filter to "Project" without the quotes in the *Filter Name* field.

7. In the *Type each choice on a separate line...* section, enter the exact name for your Deploy Training Advisor Software project. Expand the *Advanced Filter Options* section and enter the same value into the *Default Value* field.

8. Expand the *Appearance* section and set the *Title* field to "Project" without the quotes, and select the *None* option in the *Chrome Type* pick list. Scroll to the bottom and click the *OK* button.

9. In the *Edit* section of the *Page* ribbon, click the *Stop Editing* button. Your new dashboard page should look something like the one shown in Figure 17 - 88.

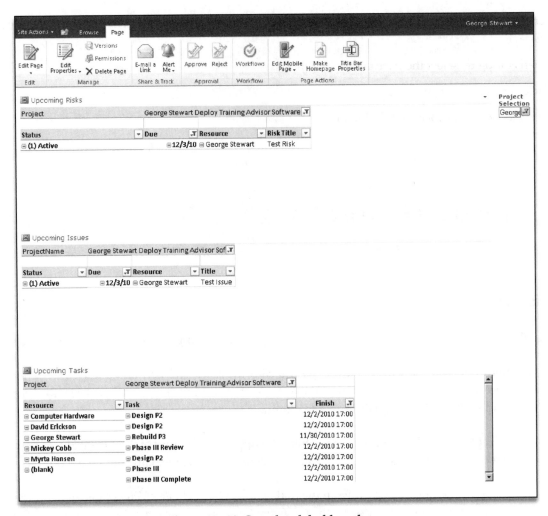

Figure 17 - 88: Completed dashboard page

Business Intelligence Summary

In this module, you learned the basic skills you need to start building useful reports and dashboards. This is only the beginning. To take this to the next level, you might add the dashboard page you just created to the *Project Site* template for your system making this a permanent fixture for all project sites. You can add styling to the page to make it more interesting and you might use conditional formatting techniques you learned about earlier in the module to render the data more visibly pleasing.

Index

T

You may also need these books!

Buy direct from our website or your favorite bookseller

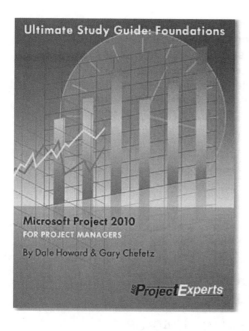

Ultimate Study Guide: Foundations Microsoft Project 2010

ISBN 978-1-934240-13-7

A comprehensive learning system for Microsoft Project 2010. The latest from the authoring team of Gary L. Chefetz and Dale A. Howard, is based on MSProjectExperts successful courseware series. Ultimate Study Guide combines a field-tested learning approach with in-depth reference to deliver the most comprehensive combined leaning/reference manual ever published for Microsoft Project.

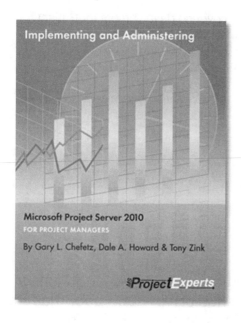

Implementing and Administering Microsoft Project Server 2010

ISBN 978-1-934240-09-0

Implementing and Administering Microsoft Project Sever 2010 is your essential reference guide for installing, configuring and deploying Project Server to your enterprise. This book begins with the organizational strategies you need to succeed with an EPM deployment and follows through with an implementation plan and step-by-step instructions for installing, configuring and deploying the Project Server 2010 platform to your organization. Loaded with best practices, warnings and tips from Project Sever gurus Gary Chefetz and Dale Howard, Implementing and Administering Microsoft Project Server sets the gold standard for Project Server implementation.

What's New Study Guide
Microsoft Project 2010

ISBN 978-1-934240-16-8

A learning guide to get you up to speed with the revolutionary new features in Microsoft Office Project 2010. Learn how to use manually scheduled tasks, the team planner, and the new user interface. The content of this book derives from the Ultimate Study Guide: Foundations, Microsoft Project 2010.

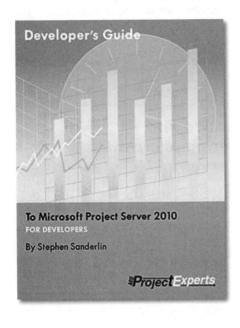

Developer's Guide To Microsoft
Project Server 2010

ISBN 978-1-934240-08-3

The first book covering development for Project Server. A complete guide to the PSI, including sample code that you can use to build your own solutions.

CONSULTING

TRAINING

BOOKS AND COURSEWARE

SUPPORT

You deserve the best, do not settle for less! MSProjectExperts is a Microsoft Gold Certified Partner specializing in Microsoft Office Project Server since its first release. This is not something we "also do," it's all we do. Microsoft recognizes our consultants as being among the world's top experts with three Microsoft Project MVPs on staff.

MSProjectExperts

90 John Street, Suite 404

New York, NY 10038

(646) 736-1688

To learn more about MSProjectExperts:

http://www.msprojectexperts.com

For the best Project and Project Server training available:

http://www.projectservertraining.com

To learn more about our books:

http://www.projectserverbooks.com

For FAQs and other free support:

http://www.projectserverexperts.com